KU-410-531

Discovering Statistics Using SPSS for Windows

ISM   Introducing Statistical Methods

Series editor: Daniel B. Wright, *University of Sussex*

This series provides accessible but in-depth introductions to statistical methods that are not covered in any detail in standard introductory courses. The books are aimed both at the beginning researcher who needs to know how to use a particular technique and the established researcher who wishes to keep up to date with recent developments in statistical data analysis.

Editorial board

Glynis Breakwell, *University of Surrey*

Jan de Leeuw, *University of California, Los Angeles*

Colm O'Muircheartaigh, *London School of Economics*

Willem Saris, *Universiteit van Amsterdam*

Howard Schuman, *University of Michigan*

Karl van Meter, *Centre National de la Recherche Scientifique, Paris*

Other titles in this series

Introducing Multilevel Modeling
Ita Kreft and Jan de Leeuw

Introducing Social Networks
Alain Degenne and Michel Forsé

Introducing ANOVA and ANCOVA
Andrew Rutherford

Introducing LISREL: A Guide for the Uninitiated
Adamantios Diamantopoulos and Judy Siguaw

Chris Pattison

Discovering Statistics Using SPSS for Windows

Advanced Techniques for the Beginner

Andy Field

SAGE Publications

London • Thousand Oaks • New Delhi

For my brother Paul and my cat Beana

© Andy Field 2000
First Published 2000. Reprinted 2000, 2001, 2002.

All rights reserved. No part of this publication may be reproduced,
stored in a retrieval system, transmitted or utilized in any form or by
any means, electronic, mechanical, photocopying, recording or
otherwise, without permission in writing from the Publishers.

SAGE Publications Ltd
6 Bonhill Street
London EC2A 4PU

SAGE Publications Inc
2455 Teller Road
Thousand Oaks, California 91320

SAGE Publications India Pvt Ltd
32, M-Block Market
Greater Kailash - I
New Delhi 110 048

British Library Cataloguing in Publication data

A catalogue record for this book is available from the British Library

ISBN 0 7619 5754 5
ISBN 0 7619 5755 3 (pbk)

Library of Congress catalog card number available

Typeset by Andy Field
Printed in Great Britain by The Cromwell Press Ltd., Trowbridge,
Wiltshire

Contents

Preface

'Karma Police, arrest this man, he talks in maths he buzzes like a fridge, he's like a detuned radio'

Radiohead (1997)

Since time immemorial, social science students have despised statistics. For one thing, most have non-mathematical backgrounds, which makes understanding complex statistical equations very difficult. The major advantage in being taught statistics in the early 1990s (as I was) compared to the 1960s was the development of computer software to do all of the hard work. The advantage of learning statistics now rather than 5 years ago is that these packages are now considerably easier to use thanks to Windows™. SPSS is, in my opinion, the best of the commercially available statistical packages and is commonly used in most universities. So what possessed me to write a book about it?

Many good textbooks already exist that describe statistical theory. Howell (1997), Stevens (1992) and Wright (1997) have all written wonderful and clear books but use computer examples only as addenda to the theory. Likewise, several excellent books on SPSS already exist (Kinnear and Gray, 1997 and Foster, 1998), but these concentrate on 'doing the test'. Using SPSS without any statistical knowledge can be a dangerous thing (it is only a tool, not a divine source of wisdom). As such, I want to use SPSS as a tool for teaching statistical concepts. In doing so I hope that the reader will gain a better understanding of both theory and practice.

Primarily, I want to answer the kinds of questions that I found myself asking while using SPSS as an undergraduate (things like 'What does that button do?', 'What the hell does this output mean?'). SPSS has a complex set of options for each test, many of which are overlooked by books and tutors alike. I hope to be able to explain what these options actually do and why you might use them. Related to this point I want to be non-prescriptive. Too many books tell the reader what to do ('click on this button', 'do this', 'do that' etc.) and this can create the impression that statistics and SPSS are inflexible. SPSS has many options designed to allow you to tailor a given test to your particular needs. Therefore, although I make recommendations, I hope to encourage the reader to make their own decisions about which options are appropriate for the analysis they want to do.

A second aim was to have a book that could be read at a number of levels. There are chapters for first-year undergraduates (1, 2 and 6), chapters for second-year undergraduates (4, 7, 8 and 9) and chapters on more advanced topics that postgraduates might use (5, 10 and 11). All of these chapters should be accessible to everyone, and where difficult material is presented you'll find that it is accompanied by a character called *Smart Alex*. Alex is a pretty scary looking guy (see left) and so if you see him you know that something scary is about to be explained. When the hard stuff is over he reappears to let you know that it's safe to continue. If you're a bit of a smart aleck yourself, then read these sections, otherwise steer clear of Alex!

My final aim is, for me, the most important. I used to be awful at maths. At 13 I almost came bottom of my class, yet 12 years later I have just finished writing a statistics textbook. How did that happen? The difference between the 13 year old who failed his exam and the 15 year old who did quite well was a good teacher: my brother, Paul. He was good because he made the subject interesting and relevant to me. This rings true with what my students at both Sussex University and Royal Holloway (University of London) have told me—they appreciate the 'human touch'. So, some examples are light-hearted and there is a large dose of my humour thrown in—which might be a bad thing because I am a lecturer and, therefore, have no sense of humour! This flippancy might not be to everyone's liking, but I have honestly tried my hardest to make this book both as interesting and as entertaining as possible.

An accompanying set of SPSS data files on CD-ROM is included with example datasets for each chapter. You will need to open these files from SPSS - please refer to section 1.2.6 Retrieving a file.

This book is the result of 2 years (give or take a few weeks to write up my Ph.D.) of trying to fulfil these aims. It isn't perfect and so I'd love to have feedback (good or bad) from the people who really matter: you, the readers.

Andy Field

Email: andyf@cogs.susx.ac.uk
Web: http://www.cogs.susx.ac.uk/users/andyf/index.html

Acknowledgements

Thanks to Simon Dunkley and SPSS Inc. for allowing me use of their screen images. SPSS can be contacted at 444 North Michigan Avenue, Chicago, Illinois 60611 (USA) or First Floor, St. Andrew's House, West Street, Woking, GU21 1EB (UK). Also check out their web pages (http://www.spss.com) for support and information.

I am grateful to Dan Wright and several anonymous reviewers who read all or parts of this book. Their patience and wisdom led to vast improvements. Many thanks to Victoria Bourne who provided an invaluable undergraduate perspective on several chapters.

I am grateful to Simon Ross for being a *very* patient editor! Also, many thanks to Richard Fidczuk for his efforts at the final stage of production.

Writing this book was a very long and solitary process. I owe my sanity to the following for providing great sounds to which to write: Fugazi, Beck, Busta Rhymes, Abba, The Cardiacs, Mercury Rev, Ben & Jason, Plug, Roni Size, Supergrass, Massive Attack, Elvis Costello, The Smashing Pumpkins, Radiohead, Placebo, Money Mark, Love, Hefner, Nick Cave, DJ Shadow, Elliott Smith, Muse, Arvo Pärt, AC/DC and Quasi.

I produced the final version of this book using Word97, which I found very frustrating!

Finally, very special thanks to Dan Wright for having such unfaltering faith in my ability to write this book. Despite giving you no evidence that I was capable of anything let alone writing a book, you encouraged me from the very beginning—I hope your expectations are met.

1 Some Preliminaries

There are several things that I need to talk about before the main body of this book. Although it seems obvious that I would like you to read Chapter 1 first (otherwise I wouldn't have placed it at the beginning) I am aware that many students derive little pleasure from reading statistics books in their entirety and prefer to dip into relevant chapters. With this in mind, I urge you to read Chapter 1 before any other because the contents are important in understanding what follows. The two things I need to talk about are: (1) model building and linear models; and (2) the SPSS environment itself. Bear with me, it won't take long.

1.1. Statistical Models

1.1.1. Model Building

In the social sciences we are usually interested in discovering something about a phenomenon that we assume actually exists (something I refer to as a real-world phenomenon). These real-world phenomena can be anything from the behaviour of interest rates in the economic market to the behaviour of undergraduates at the end-of-exam party. Whatever the phenomenon we desire to explain, we seek to explain it by collecting data from the real world, and then using these data to draw conclusions about what is being studied. As statisticians our job is to take the available data and to use them in a meaningful way and this often involves building statistical models of the phenomenon of interest.

The reason for building statistical models of real-world data is best explained by analogy. Imagine an engineer wishes to build a bridge across a river. That engineer would be pretty daft if she just built any old bridge, because the chances are that it would fall down. Instead, an engineer collects data from the real world: she looks at bridges in the real world and sees what materials they are made from, what structures they use and so on (she might even collect data about whether these bridges are damaged!). She then uses this information to construct a model. She builds a scaled-down version of the real-world bridge because it is impractical, not to mention expensive, to build the actual bridge itself. The model may differ from reality in a number of ways—it will be smaller for a start—but the engineer will try to build a model that best fits the situation of interest based on the data available. Once the model has been built, it can be used to predict things about the real world: for example, the engineer might test whether the bridge can withstand strong winds by placing the model in a wind tunnel. It seems obvious that it is important that the model is an accurate representation of the real world. Social scientists do much the same thing as engineers: we build models of real-world processes in an attempt to predict how these processes operate under certain conditions. We don't have direct access to the processes, so we collect data that represent the processes and then use these data to build statistical models (we reduce the process to a statistical model). We then use this statistical model to make predictions about the real-world phenomenon. Just like the engineer, we want our models to be as accurate as possible so that we can be confident that the predictions we make are also accurate. However, unlike engineers we don't have access to the real-world situation and so we can only ever *infer* things about psychological, societal or economic processes based upon the models we build. If we want our inferences to be accurate then the statistical model we build must represent the data collected (the *observed data*) as closely as possible. The degree to which a statistical model represents the data collected is known as the *fit* of the model and this is a term you will frequently come across.

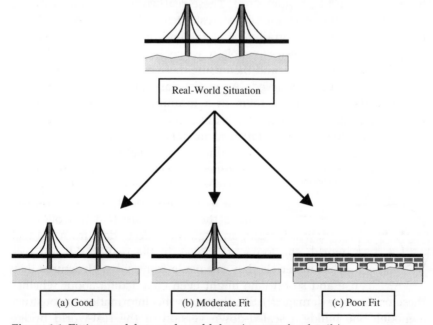

Figure 1.1: Fitting models to real-world data (see text for details)

Figure 1.1 illustrates the kinds of models that an engineer might build to represent the real-world bridge that she wants to create. The first model (a) is an excellent representation of the real-world situation and is said to be a *good fit* (i.e. there are a few small differences but the model is basically a very good replica of reality). If this model is used to make predictions about the real world, then the engineer can be confident that these predictions will be very accurate, because the model so closely resembles reality. So, if the model collapses in a strong wind, then there is a good chance that the real bridge would collapse also. The second model (b) has some similarities to the real world: the model includes some of the basic structural features, but there are some big differences from the real-world bridge (namely the absence of one of the supporting towers). This is what we might term a *moderate fit* (i.e. there are some differences between the model and the data but there are also some great similarities). If the engineer uses this model to make predictions about the real world then these predictions may be inaccurate and possibly catastrophic (for example, if the bridge collapses in strong winds this could be due to the absence of a second supporting tower). So, using this model results in predictions that we can have some confidence in but not complete confidence. The final model (c) is completely different to the real-world situation. This model bears no structural similarities to the real bridge and so could be termed a poor fit (in fact, it might more accurately be described as an abysmal fit!). As such, any predictions based on this model are likely to be completely inaccurate. Extending this analogy to the social sciences we can say that it is important when we fit a statistical model to a set of data that this model fits the data well. If our model is a poor fit of the observed data then the predictions we make from it will be equally poor.

1.1.2.   Populations and Samples

As researchers, we are interested in finding results that apply to an entire population of people or things. For example, psychologists want to discover processes that occur in all humans, biologists might be interested in processes that occur in all cells, economists want to build models that apply to all salaries and so on. A population can be very general (all human beings) or very narrow (all male ginger cats called Bob), but in either case scientists rarely, if ever, have access to every member of a population. Psychologists cannot collect data from every human being and ecologists cannot observe every male ginger cat called Bob. Therefore, we collect data from a small subset of the population (known as a *sample*) and use these data to infer things about the population as a whole. The bridge-building engineer cannot make a full-size model of the bridge she wants to build and so she builds a small-scale model and tests this model under various conditions. From the results obtained from the small-scale model the engineer infers things about how the full-sized bridge will respond. The small-scale model may respond differently to a full-sized version of the bridge, but the larger the model, the more likely it is to behave in the same way as the full-size bridge. This metaphor can be extended to social scientists. We never have access to the entire population (the real-size bridge) and so we collect smaller samples (the scaled-down bridge) and use the behaviour within the sample to infer things about the behaviour in the population. The bigger the sample, the more likely it is to reflect the whole population. If we take several random samples from the population, each of these samples will give us slightly different results. However, on average, large samples should be fairly similar.

1.1.3.   Simple Statistical Models

1.1.3.1.   The Mean, Sums of Squares, Variance and Standard Deviations

One of the simplest models used in statistics is the mean. Some of you may have trouble thinking of the mean as a model, but in fact it is because it represents a summary of data. The mean is a hypothetical value that can be calculated for any data set, it doesn't have to be a value that is actually observed in the data set. For example, if we took five statistics lecturers and measured the number of friends that they had, we might find the following data: 1, 2, 3, 3 and 4. If we take the mean number of friends, this can be calculated by adding the values we obtained, and dividing by the number of values measured: $(1 + 2 + 3 + 3 + 4)/5 = 2.6$. Now, we know that it is impossible to have 2.6 friends (unless you chop someone up with a chainsaw and befriend their arm) so the mean value is a *hypothetical* value. As such, the mean is a model created to summarize our data. Now, we can determine whether this is an accurate model by looking at how different our real data are from the model that we have created. One way to do this is to look at the difference between the data we observed and the model fitted. Figure 1.2 shows the number of friends that each statistics lecturer had, and also the mean number that we calculated earlier on. The line representing the mean can be thought of as our model, and the circles are the observed data. The diagram also has a series of vertical lines that connect each observed value to the mean value. These lines represent the differences between the observed data and our model and can be thought of as the error in the model. We can calculate the magnitude of these differences by simply subtracting the mean value ($\bar{x}$) from each of the observed values (x_i).[1] For example, lecturer 1 had only 1 friend and so the difference is $x_1 - \bar{x} = 1 - 2.6 = -1.6$. You might notice that the difference is a minus number, and this represents the fact that our model *overestimates* this lecturer's popularity: it predicts that he will have 2.6 friends yet in reality he has only 1 friend (bless him!). Now, how can we use these differences to estimate the accuracy of the model? One possibility is to add up the differences (this would give us an estimate of the total error). If we were to do this we would find that:

total error = sum of differences

$$= \sum (x_i - \bar{x}) = (-1.6) + (-0.6) + (0.4) + (0.4) + (1.4) = 0$$

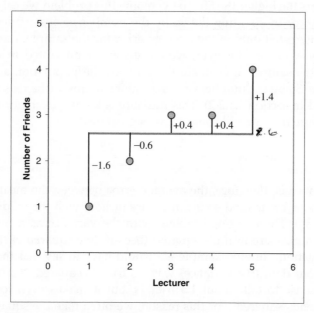

Figure 1.2: Graph showing the difference between the observed number of friends that each statistics lecturer had, and the mean number of friends

So, in effect the result tells us that there is no total error between our model and the observed data, so, the mean is a perfect representation of the data. Now, this clearly isn't true: there were errors but some of them were positive, some were negative and they have simply cancelled each other out. It is clear that we need to avoid the problem of which direction the error is in and one mathematical way to do this is to square each error,[2] that is multiply each error by itself. So, rather than

---

[1] The x_i simply refers to the observed score for the *i*th person (so, the *i* can be replaced with a number that represents a particular individual). For these data: for lecturer 1, $x_i = x_1 = 1$; for lecturer 3, $x_i = x_3 = 3$; for lecturer 5, $x_i = x_5 = 4$.

[2] When you multiply a negative number by itself it becomes positive.

calculating the sum of errors, we calculate the sum of squared errors. In this example:

$$\text{sum of squared errors (SS)} = \sum (x_i - \bar{x})(x_i - \bar{x})$$
$$= (-1.6)^2 + (-0.6)^2 + (0.4)^2 + (0.4)^2 + (1.4)^2$$
$$= 2.56 + 0.36 + 0.16 + 0.16 + 1.96$$
$$= 5.20$$

The sum of squared errors (SS) is a good measure of the accuracy of our model. However, it is fairly obvious that the <u>sum of squared errors</u> is dependent upon the amount of data that has been collected—the more data points the higher the SS. <u>To overcome this problem we calculate the average error by dividing the SS by the number of observations (N).</u> If we are interested only in the average error for the sample, then we can divide by N alone. However, we are generally interested in using the error in the sample to estimate the error in the population and so we divide the SS by the number of observations minus 1 (the reason why is explained in section 7.1.3.2). This measure is known as the *variance* and is a measure that we will come across a great deal:

$$\text{variance } (s^2) = \frac{\text{SS}}{N-1} = \frac{\sum (x_i - \bar{x})^2}{N-1} = \frac{5.20}{4} = 1.3$$

<u>The variance is, therefore, the average error between the mean and the observations made (and so is a measure of how well the model fits the actual data).</u> There is one problem with the variance as a measure: it gives us a measure in units squared (because we squared each error in the calculation). In our example we would have to say that the average error in our data (the variance) was 1.3 friends squared. It makes little enough sense to talk about 1.3 friends, but it makes even less to talk about friends-squared! For this reason, we often take the square root of the variance (which ensures that the measure of average error is in the same units as the original measure). This measure is known as the standard deviation and is simply the square root of the variance. In this example the standard deviation is:

$$s = \sqrt{1.3} = 1.14$$

The standard deviation is, therefore, a measure of how well the mean represents the data. Small standard deviations (relative to the value of the mean itself) indicate that data points are close to the mean. A large standard deviation (relative to the mean) indicates that the data points are distant from the mean (i.e. the mean is not an accurate representation of the data). Figure 1.3 shows the overall ratings (on a five-point scale) of two lecturers after each of five different lectures. Both lecturers had an average rating of 2.6 out of 5 across the lectures.

However, the first lecturer had a standard deviation of 0.55 (relatively small compared to the mean). It should be clear from the graph that ratings for this lecturer were consistently close to the mean rating. There was a small fluctuation, but generally his lectures did not vary in popularity. As such, the mean is an accurate representation of his ratings. The mean is a good fit of the data. The second lecturer, however, had a standard deviation of 1.82 (relatively high compared to the mean). The ratings for this lecturer are clearly more spread from the mean, that is, for some lectures he received very high ratings, and for others his ratings were appalling. Therefore, the mean is not such an accurate representation of his performance because there was a lot of variability in the popularity of his lectures. The mean is a poor fit of the data. This illustration should hopefully make clear why the standard deviation is a measure of how well the mean represents the data.

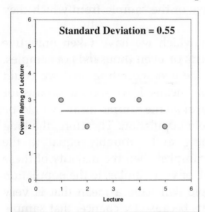 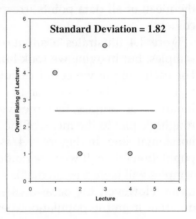

Figure 1.3: Graphs illustrating data that have the same mean but different standard deviations

The discussion of means, sums of squares and variance may seem a side-track from the initial point, but in fact the mean is probably one of the simplest statistical models that can be fitted to data. As such, the mean illustrates the concept of a statistical model and the variance and standard deviation illustrate how the goodness-of-fit of a model can be measured.

1.1.3.2. The Standard Error

Many students get confused about the difference between the standard deviation and the standard error (usually because the difference is never explained clearly). However, the standard error is an important concept to grasp, so I'll do my best to explain it to you. We have already learnt that social scientists use samples as a way of estimating the behaviour in a population. I also mentioned that if you take several samples from a population, then these samples would differ slightly. Imagine that we were interested in the ratings of all lecturers (so, lecturers in general were the population). We could take five samples from this population with each sample containing five different lecturers.

Figure 1.4 illustrates this scenario. The ellipses represent the five samples, and contain the overall ratings of five lecturers (the grey dots). For each sample we can calculate the average, or *sample mean* (represented by a horizontal line). As you can see in the diagram, each sample has a slightly different mean: the lecturers in sample 1 had a mean rating of 1, whereas the lecturers in sample 4 had a mean rating of 3. If you calculated the average rating of all samples, then the value would be the mean of the sample means. The long dark horizontal line represents this overall mean (this value is the same as if you calculate the mean of all data points irrespective of the sample from which they come).

Figure 1.4 illustrates a situation in which we have taken only five samples, but imagine we took hundreds or even thousands of samples. For each sample we could calculate the average rating, and we could then calculate the average of all sample means. If we were to do this for hundreds of samples, then the average of all the sample means would be roughly equal to the mean of the whole population. Therefore, the long horizontal line in Figure 1.4 is going to be roughly equal to the population mean. If we take random samples, then the majority of these samples will have a mean that is equal, or very similar, to the population mean. However, the occasional sample will have a mean that is very different from the population (perhaps because by chance, that sample contained a lot of very good lecturers). This is also illustrated in Figure 1.4: the majority of samples have average values close to the population average (as shown by the short arrows between the population mean and the sample means), but the first and last samples have means that are distant from the population mean. If you think about this logically, if we want to infer things about a population, by using a sample, it is important that we know how well that sample represents the population. In this example, if we used samples 2, 3 or 4 we could be confident about any conclusions we make, because the sample means are representative of the population mean. However, if we happened to use either sample 1 or sample 5, then our conclusions would be inaccurate (because these two samples are not characteristic of the population as a whole). So, how can we gauge whether a sample is representative?

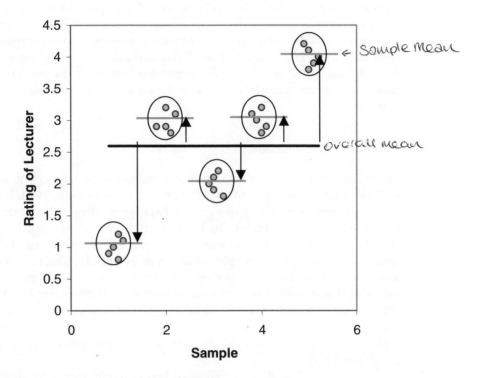

Figure 1.4: Graph illustrating the standard error (see text for details)

Think back to the discussion of the standard deviation. We used the standard deviation as a measure of how representative the mean was of the observed data. Small standard deviations represented a scenario in which most data points were close to the mean, a large standard deviation represented a situation in which data points were widely spread from the mean. If you were to calculate the standard deviation between *sample means* then this too would give you a measure of how much variability there was between the means of different samples. The standard deviation of sample means is known as the *standard error*. Therefore, the standard error could be calculated by taking the difference between each sample mean and the overall mean (the arrows in Figure 1.4), squaring these differences, adding them up, and then dividing by the number of samples. To clarify this point, look at the similarity between Figure 1.4 and Figure 1.2. Of course, in reality we cannot collect hundreds of samples and so we rely on approximations of the standard error (luckily for us lots of clever statisticians have calculated ways in which the standard error can be worked out from the sample standard deviation). So, in short, the standard error is the standard deviation of sample means. As such, it is a measure of how representative a sample is likely to be of the population. A large standard error (relative to the sample mean) means that there is a lot of variability between the means of different samples and so the sample we have might not be representative of the population. A small standard error indicates that most sample means are similar to the population mean and so our sample is likely to be an accurate reflection of the population.

1.1.4.   *Linear Models*

The mean is an example of what we call a statistical model, but you may well ask what other kinds of statistical models can be built. Well, if the truth is known there is only one model that is generally used, and this is known as the linear model. To some social scientists it may not be entirely obvious that my previous statement is correct, yet a statistician would acknowledge my sentiment much more readily. The reason for this is that there are a variety of different names given to statistical procedures that are based on the linear model. A classic example is that analysis of variance (ANOVA) and regression are identical systems (Cohen, 1968), yet they have different names and are used largely in different contexts (due to a divide in methodological philosophies—see Cronbach, 1957).

The word *linear* literally means 'relating to a line' but in statistical terms the line to which it refers is a straight one. A linear model is, therefore, a model that is based upon a straight line. Simplistically, this means that we are usually trying to summarize our observed data in terms of a straight line. For example, in the chapter describing regression, it will become clear that two variables can be negatively related (this just means that as values of one variable increase, values of the other variable decrease). In such circumstances, the relationship may be summarized by a straight line. Suppose we measured how many chapters of this book a person had read, and then measured their spiritual enrichment, we could represent these hypothetical data in the form of a scatterplot in which each dot represents an individual's score on both variables. Figure 1.5 shows such a graph, and also shows the same graph but with a line that summarizes the pattern of these data. A third version of the scatterplot is also included but has a curved line to summarize the general pattern of the data. As such, Figure 1.5 illustrates how we can fit different types of models to the same data. In this case we can use a straight line to represent our data and it shows that the more chapters a person reads, the less their spiritual enrichment. However, we can also use a curved line to summarize the data and this shows that when most, or all, of the chapters have been read, spiritual enrichment seems to increase slightly (presumably because once the book is read everything suddenly makes sense—yeah, as if!). Neither of the two types of model is necessarily correct, but it will be the case that one model fits the data better than another and this is why when we use statistical models it is important for us to assess how well a given model fits the data.

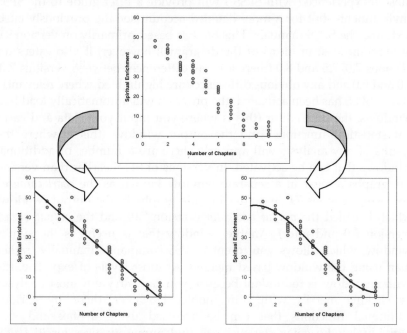

Figure 1.5: Shows a scatterplot of some data with no model fitted to the data, with a linear model fitted, and with a non-linear model fitted

Most of the statistics used in the social sciences are based on linear models, which means that we try to fit straight line models to the data collected. This is interesting because most published scientific studies are ones with statistically significant results. Given that most social scientists are only ever taught how to use techniques based on the linear model, published results will be those that have successfully used linear models. Data that fit a non-linear pattern are likely to be wrongly ignored (because the wrong model will have been applied to the data, leading to non-significant results). It is possible, therefore, that some areas of science are progressing in a biased way, so, if you collect data that look non-linear, why not try redressing the balance and investigating different statistical techniques!

1.2. The SPSS Environment

There are several excellent texts that give introductions to the general environment within which SPSS operates. The best ones include Kinnear and Gray (1997) and Foster (1998). These texts are well worth reading if you are unfamiliar with Windows and SPSS generally because I am assuming at least some knowledge of the system. However, I appreciate the limited funds of most students and so to make this text usable for those inexperienced with SPSS I will provide a brief guide to the SPSS environment—but for a more detailed account see the previously cited texts and the SPSS manuals. This book is based primarily on version 9.0 of SPSS (at least in terms of the diagrams); however, it also caters for versions 7.0, 7.5 and 8.0 (there are few differences between versions 7.0, 8.0 and 9.0 and any obvious differences are highlighted where relevant).

Once SPSS has been activated, the program will automatically load two windows: the data editor (this is where you input your data and carry out statistical functions) and the output window (this is where the results of any analysis will appear). There are a number of additional windows that can be activated. In versions of SPSS earlier than version 7.0, graphs appear in a separate window known as the *chart carousel*; however, versions 7.0 and after include graphs in the output window, which is called the *output navigator* (version 7.0) and the *output viewer* (version 8.0 and after). Another window that is useful is the syntax window, which allows you to enter SPSS commands manually (rather than using the window-based menus). At most levels of expertise, the syntax window is redundant because you can carry out most analyses by clicking merrily with your mouse. However, there are various additional functions that can be accessed using syntax and sick individuals who enjoy statistics can find numerous uses for it! I will pretty much ignore syntax windows because those of you who want to know about them will learn by playing around and the rest of you will be put off by their inclusion (interested readers should refer to Foster, 1998, Chapter 8).

1.2.1. The Data Editor

The main SPSS window includes a data editor for entering data. This window is where most of the action happens. At the top of this screen is a menu bar similar to the ones you might have seen in other programs (such as Microsoft Word). Figure 1.6 shows this menu bar and the data editor. There are several menus at the top of the screen (e.g. *File*, *Edit* etc.) that can be activated by using the computer mouse to move the on-screen arrow onto the desired menu and then pressing the left mouse button once (pressing this button is usually known as *clicking*). When you have clicked on a menu, a menu box will appear that displays a list of options that can be activated by moving the on-screen arrow so that it is pointing at the desired option and then clicking with the mouse. Often, selecting an option from a menu makes a window appear; these windows are referred to as *dialog boxes*. When referring to selecting options in a menu I will notate the action using bold type with arrows indicating the path of the mouse (so, each arrow represents placing the on-screen arrow over a word and clicking the mouse's left button). So, for example, if I were to say that you should select the *Save As ...* option in the *File* menu, I would write this as select **File⇒Save As ....**

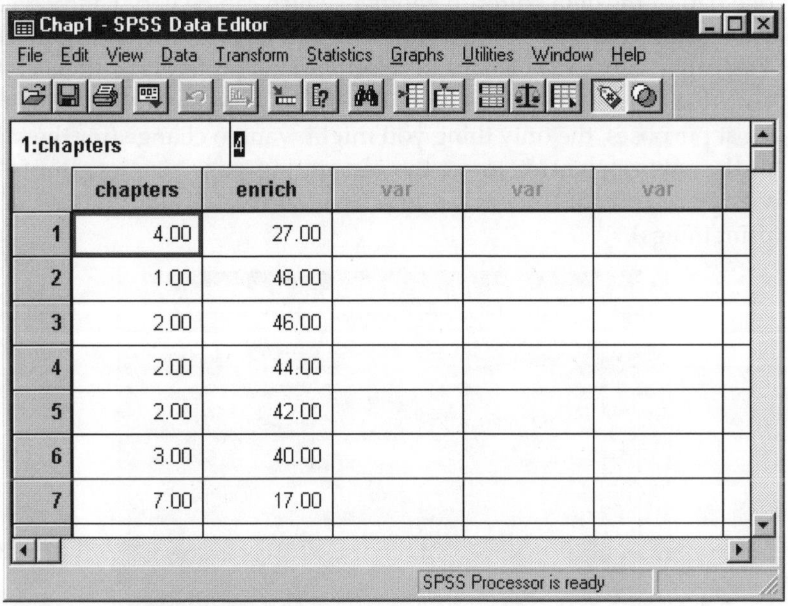

Figure 1.6: The SPSS data editor

Within these menus you will notice that some letters are underlined: these underlined letters represent the *keyboard shortcut* for accessing that function. It is possible to select many functions without using the mouse, and the experienced keyboard user may find these shortcuts faster than manoeuvring the mouse arrow to the appropriate place on the screen. The letters underlined in the menus indicate that the option can be obtained by simultaneously pressing ALT on the keyboard and the underlined letter. So, to access the *Save As...* option, using only the keyboard, you should press ALT and F on the keyboard simultaneously (which activates the *File* menu) then, keeping your finger on the ALT key, press A (which is the underlined letter).

Below is a brief reference guide to each of the menus and some of the options that they contain. This is merely a summary and we will discover the wonders of each menu as we progress through the book.

- **File**: This menu allows you to do general things such as saving data, graphs, or output. Likewise, you can open previously saved files and print graphs, data or output. In essence, it contains all of the options that are customarily found in *File* menus.
- **Edit**: This menu contains edit functions for the data editor. In SPSS for Windows it is possible to *cut* and *paste* blocks of numbers from one part of the data editor to another (which can be very handy when you realize that you've entered lots of numbers in the wrong place). You can also use the *Options* to select various preferences such as the font that is used for the output. The default preferences are fine for most purposes, the only thing you might want to change (for the sake of the environment) is to set the text output page size length of the viewer to infinite (this saves hundreds of trees when you come to print things).

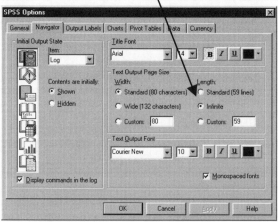

- **Data**: This menu allows you to make changes to the data editor. The important features are *insert variable*, which is used to insert a new variable into the data editor (i.e. add a column); *insert case*, which is used to add a new row of data between two existing rows of data; *split file*, which is used to split the file by a grouping variable (see section 2.4.1); and *select cases*, which is used to run analyses on only a selected sample of cases.
- **Transform**: You should use this menu if you want to manipulate one of your variables in some way. For example, you can use *recode* to change the values of certain variables (e.g. if you wanted to adopt a slightly different coding scheme for some reason). The *compute* function is also useful for transforming data (e.g. you can create a

new variable that is the average of two existing variables). This function allows you to carry out any number of calculations on your variables (see section 6.2.2.1).

- **Analyze:** This menu is called **Statistics** in version 8.0 and earlier. The fun begins here, because the statistical procedures lurk in this menu. Below is a brief guide to the options in the statistics menu that will be used during the course of this book (this is only a small portion of what is available):

  (a) **Descriptive Statistics:** This menu is called **Summarize** in version 8.0 and earlier. This menu is for conducting descriptive statistics (mean, mode, median etc.), frequencies and general data exploration. There is also a command called *crosstabs* that is useful for exploring frequency data and performing tests such as chi-square, Fisher's exact test and Cohen's kappa.

  (b) **Compare Means:** This is where you can find *t*-tests (related and unrelated—Chapter 6) and one-way independent ANOVA (Chapter 7).

  (c) **General Linear Model:** This is called *ANOVA Models* in version 6 of SPSS. This menu is for complex ANOVA such as two-way (unrelated, related or mixed), one-way ANOVA with repeated measures and multivariate analysis of variance (MANOVA).

  (d) **Correlate:** It doesn't take a genius to work out that this is where the correlation techniques are kept! You can do bivariate correlations such as Pearson's R, Spearman's rho (ρ) and Kendall's tau (τ) as well as partial correlations (see Chapter 3).

  (e) **Regression:** There are a variety of regression techniques available in SPSS. You can do simple linear regression, multiple linear regression (Chapter 4) and more advanced techniques such as logistic regression (Chapter 5).

  (f) **Data Reduction:** You find factor analysis here (Chapter 11).

  (g) **Nonparametric:** There are a variety of non-parametric statistics available such the chi-square goodness-of-fit statistic, the binomial test, the Mann-Whitney test, the Kruskal-Wallis test, Wilcoxon's test and Friedman's ANOVA (Chapter 2).

- **Graphs:** SPSS comes with its own, fairly versatile, graphing package. The types of graphs you can do include: bar charts, histograms, scatterplots, box-whisker plots, pie charts and error bar graphs to name but a few. There is also the facility to edit any graphs to make them look snazzy—which is pretty smart if you ask me.

- **View:** This menu deals with system specifications such as whether you have grid lines on the data editor, or whether you display value labels (exactly what value labels are will become clear later).

- **Window:** This allows you to switch from window to window. So, if you're looking at the output and you wish to switch back to your data sheet, you can do so using this menu. There are icons to shortcut most of the options in this menu so it isn't particularly useful.

- **Help**: This is an invaluable menu because it offers you on-line help on both the system itself and the statistical tests. Although the statistics help files are fairly useless at times (after all, the program is not supposed to teach you statistics) and certainly no substitute for acquiring a good knowledge of your own, they can sometimes get you out of a sticky situation.

As well as the menus there are also a set of *icons* at the top of the data editor window (see Figure 1.6) that are shortcuts to specific, frequently used, facilities. All of these facilities can be accessed via the menu system but using the icons will save you time. Below is a brief list of these icons and their function:

This icon gives you the option to open a previously saved file (if you are in the data editor SPSS assumes you want to open a data file, if you are in the output viewer, it will offer to open a viewer file).

This icon allows you to save files. It will save the file you are currently working on (be it data or output). If the file hasn't already been saved it will produce the *save data as* dialog box.

This icon activates a dialog box for printing whatever you are currently working on (either the data editor or the output). The exact print options will depend on the printer you use. One useful tip when printing from the output window is to highlight the text that you want to print (by holding the mouse button down and dragging the arrow over the text of interest). In version 7.0 onwards, you can also select parts of the output by clicking on branches in the viewer window (see section 1.2.4). When the *print* dialog box appears remember to click on the option to print only the selected text. Selecting parts of the output will save a lot of trees because by default SPSS will print everything in the output window.

Clicking this icon will activate a list of the last 12 dialog boxes that were used. From this list you can select any box from the list and it will appear on the screen. This icon makes it easy for you to repeat parts of an analysis.

This icon allows you to go directly to a case (i.e. a subject). This is useful if you are working on large data files. For example, if you were analysing a survey with 3000 respondents it would get pretty tedious scrolling down the data sheet to find a particular subject's responses. This icon can be used to skip directly to a case (e.g. case 2407). Clicking on this icon activates a dialog box that requires you to type in the case number required.

Clicking on this icon will give you information about a specified variable in the data editor (a dialog box allows you to choose which variable you want summary information about).

This icon allows you to search for words or numbers in your data file and output window.

Clicking on this icon inserts a new case in the data editor (so, it creates a blank row at the point that is currently highlighted in the data editor). This function is very useful if you need to add new data or if you forget to put a particular subject's data in the data editor.

Clicking this icon creates a new variable to the left of the variable that is currently active (to activate a variable simply click once on the name at the top of the column).

Clicking on this icon is a shortcut to the **Data⇒Split File ...** function (see section 2.4.1). Social scientists often conduct experiments on different groups of people. In SPSS we differentiate groups of people by using a coding variable (see section 1.2.3.1), and this function lets us divide our output by such a variable. For example, we might test males and females on their statistical ability. We can code each subject with a number that represents their gender (e.g. 1 = female, 0 = male). If we then want to know the mean statistical ability of each gender we simply ask the computer to split the file by the variable **gender**. Any subsequent analyses will be performed on the men and women separately.

This icon shortcuts to the **Data⇒Weight Cases ...** function. This function is necessary when we come to input frequency data (see section 2.8.2) and is useful for some advanced issues in survey sampling.

This icon is a shortcut to the **Data⇒Select Cases ...** function. If you want to analyze only a portion of your data, this is the option for you! This function allows you to specify what cases you want to include in the analysis.

Clicking this icon will either display, or hide, the value labels of any coding variables. We often group people together and use a coding variable to let the computer know that a certain subject belongs to a certain group. For example, if we coded gender as 1 = female, 0 = male then the computer knows that every time it comes across the value 1 in the **gender** column, that subject is a female. If you press this icon, the coding will appear on the data editor rather than the numerical values; so, you will see the words *male* and *female* in the **gender** column rather than a series of numbers. This idea will become clear in section 1.2.3.1.

1.2.2.   Inputting Data

When you first load SPSS it will provide a blank data editor with the title *New Data*. When inputting a new set of data, you must input your data in a logical way. The SPSS data editor is arranged such that *each row represents data from one subject while each column represents a variable*. There is no discrimination between independent and dependent variables: both types should be placed in a separate column. The key point is that each row represents one participant's data. Therefore, any information about that case should be entered across the data editor. For example, imagine you were interested in sex differences in perceptions of pain created by hot and cold stimuli. You could place some people's hands in a bucket of very cold water for a minute and ask them to rate how painful they thought the experience was on a scale of 1 to 10. You could then ask them to hold a hot potato and again measure their perception of pain. Imagine I was a subject. You would have a single row representing my data, so there would be a different column for my name, my age, my gender, my pain perception for cold water, and my pain perception for a hot potato: Andy, 25, male, 7, 10. The column with the information about my gender is a grouping variable: I can belong to either the group of males or the group of females, but not both. As such, this variable is a between-group variable (different people belong to different groups). Therefore, between-group variables are represented by a single column in which the group to which the person belonged is defined using a number (see section 1.2.3.1). Variables that specify to which of several groups a person belongs can be used to split up data files (so, in the pain example you could run an analysis on the male and female subjects separately—see section 2.4.1). The two measures of pain are a repeated measure (all subjects were subjected to hot and cold stimuli). Therefore, levels of this variable can be entered in separate columns (one for pain to a hot stimulus and one for pain to a cold stimulus).

In summary, any variable measured with the same subjects (a repeated measure) should be represented by several columns (each column representing one level of the repeated measures variable). However, when a between-group design was used (e.g. different subjects were assigned to each level of the independent variable) the data will be represented by two columns: one that has the values of the dependent variable and one that is a coding variable indicating to which group the subject belonged. This idea will become clearer as you learn about how to carry out specific procedures.

The data editor is made up of lots of *cells*, which are just boxes in which data values can be placed. When a cell is active it becomes highlighted with a black surrounding box (as in Figure 1.7). You can move around the data editor, from cell to cell, using the arrow keys ← ↑ ↓ → (found on the right of the keyboard) or by clicking the mouse on the cell that you wish to activate. To enter a number into the data editor simply move to the cell in which you want to place the data value, type the value, then press the appropriate arrow button for the direction in which you wish to move. So, to enter a row of data, move to the far left of the row, type the value and then press → (this process inputs the value and then moves you into the next cell on the left).

1.2.3.   Creating a Variable

There are several steps to creating a variable in the SPSS data editor (see Figure 1.7):

- Move the on-screen arrow (using the mouse) to the grey area at the top of the first column (the area labelled *var*.
- Double-click (i.e. click two times in quick succession) with the left button of the mouse.
- A dialog box should appear that is labelled *define variable* (see Figure 1.7).
- In this dialog box there will be a default variable name (something like **var00001**) that you should delete. You can then give the variable a more descriptive name. There are some general rules about variable names, such as that they must be 8 characters or less and you cannot use a blank space. If you violate any of these rules the computer will tell you that the variable name is invalid when you click on OK. Finally, the SPSS data editor is not case sensitive, so if you use capital letters in this dialog box it ignores them. However, SPSS is case sensitive to labels typed into the _Variable Label_ part of the *define labels* dialog box (see section 1.2.3.1); these labels are used in the output.
- If you click on OK at this stage then a variable will be created in the data editor for you. However, there are some additional options that you might find useful.

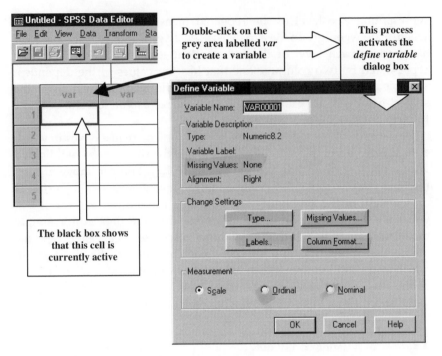

Figure 1.7: Creating a variable

In versions 8 and 9 of SPSS, the *define variable* dialog box contains three options for selecting the level of measurement at which the variable was measured (earlier versions do not have these options). If you are using the variable as a coding variable (next section) then the data are categorical (also called *nominal*) and so you should click on the <u>N</u>ominal option. For example, if we asked people whether reading this chapter bores them they will answer *yes* or *no*. Therefore, people fall into two categories: bored and not bored. There is no indication as to exactly how bored the bored people are and therefore the data are merely labels, or categories into which people can be placed. Interval data are scores that are measured on a scale along the whole of which intervals are equal. For example, rather than asking people if they are bored we could measure boredom along a 10-point scale (0 being very interested and 10 being very bored). For data to be interval it should be true that the increase in boredom represented by a change from 3 to 4 along the scale should be the same as the change in boredom represented by a change from 9 to 10. Ratio data have this property, but in addition we should be able to say that someone who had a score of 8 was twice as bored as someone who scored only 4. These two types of data are represented by the *Scale* option. It should be obvious that in some social sciences (notably psychology) it is extremely difficult to establish whether data are interval (can we really tell whether a change on the boredom scale represents a genuine change in the experience of boredom?). A lower level of measurement is ordinal data, which does not quite have the property of interval data, but we can be confident that higher scores represent higher levels of a construct. We might not be sure that an increase in boredom of 1 on the scale represents the same change in experience between 1 and 2 as it does between 9 and 10. However, we can be confident that someone who scores 9 was, in reality, more bored than someone who scored only 8. These data would be ordinal and so you should select <u>O</u>rdinal. The *define variable* dialog box also has four buttons that you can click on to access other dialog boxes and these functions will be described in turn.

1.2.3.1. Creating Coding Variables

In the previous sections I have mentioned coding variables and this section is dedicated to a fuller description of this kind of variable (it is a type of variable that you will use a lot). A coding variable (also known as a grouping variable) is a variable consisting of a series of numbers that represent levels of a treatment variable. In experiments, coding variables are used to represent independent variables that have been measured between groups (i.e. different subjects were assigned to different groups). So, if you were to run an experiment with one group of subjects in an experimental condition and a different group of subjects in a control group, you might assign the experimental group a code of 1, and the control group a code of 0. When you come to put the data into the data editor, then you would create a variable (which you might call **group**) and type in the value 1 for any subjects in the experimental group, and 0 for any subject in the control group. These codes tell the computer that all of the cases that have been assigned the value 1 should be treated as belonging to the same group, and likewise for the subjects assigned the value 0.

There is a simple rule for how variables should be placed in the SPSS data editor: levels of the between-group variables go down the data editor whereas levels of within-subject (repeated measures) variables go across the data editor. We shall see exactly how we put this rule into operation in chapter 6.

To create a coding variable we create a variable in the usual way, but we have to tell the computer which numeric codes we are assigning to which groups. This can be done by using the Labels... button in the *define variable* dialog box (see Figure 1.7) to open the *define labels* dialog box (see Figure 1.8). In the *define labels* dialog box there is room to give your variable a more descriptive title. For the purposes of the data editor itself, I have already mentioned that variable labels have to be 8 characters or less and that they have to be lower case. However, for the purposes of the output, it is possible to give our variable a more meaningful title (and this label can also have capital letters and space characters too—great!). If you want to give a variable a more descriptive title then simply click with the mouse in the white space next to where it says *Variable Label* in the dialog box. This will place the cursor in that space, and you can type a title: in Figure 1.8 I have chosen the title *Experimental Condition*. The more important use of this dialog box is to specify group codings. This can be done in three easy steps. First, click with the mouse in the white space next to where it says *Value* (or press ALT and U at the same time) and type in a code (e.g. 1). These codes are completely arbitrary: for the sake of convention people usually use 1, 2 and 3 etc., but in practice you could have a code of 495 if you were feeling particularly arbitrary. The second step is to click the mouse in the white space below, next to where it says *Value Label* (or press ALT and E at the same time) and type in an appropriate label for that group. In Figure 1.8 I have typed in 0 as my code and given this a label of *Control*. The third step is to add this coding to the list by clicking on ⌐Add⌐. In Figure 1.8 I have already defined my code for the experimental group, to add the coding for the control group I must click on ⌐Add⌐. When you have defined all of your coding values simply click on ⌐OK⌐; if you click on ⌐OK⌐ and have forgotten to add your final coding to the list, SPSS will display a message warning you that any pending changes will be lost. In plain English this simply tells you to go back and click on ⌐Add⌐.

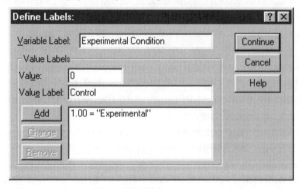

Figure 1.8: Defining coding values in SPSS

Having defined your codings, you can then go to the data editor and type these numerical values into the appropriate column. What is really groovy is that you can get the computer to display the codings themselves, or the value labels that you gave them by clicking on 🔳 (see Figure 1.9). Figure 1.9 shows how the data should be arranged for a coding variable. Now remember that each row of the data editor represents one subject's data and so in this example it is clear that the first five subjects were in the experimental condition whereas subjects 6–

10 were in the control group. This example also demonstrates why grouping variables are used for variables that have been measured between subjects: because by using a coding variable it is impossible for a subject to belong to more than one group. This situation should occur in a between-group design (i.e. a subject should not be tested in both the experimental and the control group). However, in repeated measures designs (within subjects) each subject is tested in every condition and so we would not use this sort of coding variable (because each subject does take part in every experimental condition).

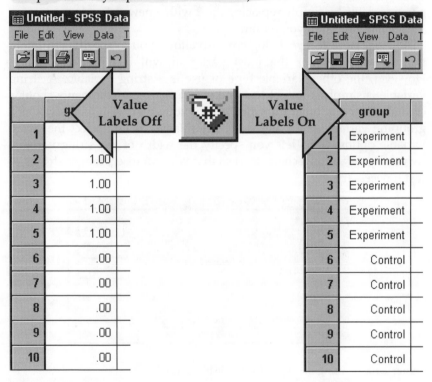

Figure 1.9: Coding values in the data editor with the value labels switched off and on

1.2.3.2. Types of Variables

There are different types of variables that can be used in SPSS. In the majority of cases you will find yourself using numeric variables. These variables are ones that contain numbers and include the type of coding variables that have just been described. However, one of the other options when you create a variable is to specify the type of variable and this is done by clicking on ⬚Type... in the *define variable* dialog box. Clicking this button will activate the dialog box in Figure 1.10, which shows the default settings. By default, a variable is set up to store 8 digits, but you can change this value by typing a new number in the space labelled _Width_ in the dialog box. Under normal circumstances you wouldn't require SPSS to retain any more than 8 characters unless you were doing calculations that need to be particularly precise. Another default setting is to have 2 decimal places displayed (in fact, you'll notice by default that when you type in whole numbers SPSS will add a decimal place with two zeros after it—this can be disconcerting initially!). It is easy enough to change the number of decimal places for a given variable by simply replacing the 2 with a new value depending on the level of precision you require.

The *define variable type* dialog box also allows you to specify a different type of variable. For the most part you will use numeric values. However, the other variable type of use is a string variable. A string variable is simply a line of text and could represent comments about a certain subject, or other information that you don't wish to analyze as a grouping variable (such as the subject's name). If you select the string variable option, SPSS lets you specify the width of the string variable (which by default is 8 characters) so that you can insert longer strings of text if necessary.

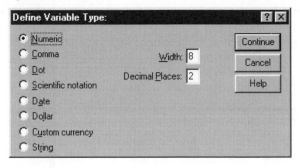

Figure 1.10: Defining the type of variable being used

1.2.3.3. *Missing Values*

Although as researchers we strive to collect complete sets of data, it is often the case that we have missing data. Missing data can occur for a variety of reasons: in long questionnaires participants accidentally miss out questions; in experimental procedures mechanical faults can lead to a datum not being recorded; and in research on delicate topics (e.g. sexual behaviour) subjects may exert their right not to answer a question. However, just because we have missed out on some data for a subject doesn't mean that we have to ignore the data we do have (although it sometimes creates statistical difficulties). However, we do need to tell the computer that a value is missing for a particular subject. The principle behind missing values is quite similar to that of coding variables in that we choose a numeric value to represent the missing data point. This value simply tells the computer that there is no recorded value for a participant for a certain variable. The computer then ignores that cell of the data editor (it does not use the value you select in the analysis). You need to be careful that the chosen code doesn't correspond with any naturally occurring data value. For example, if we tell the computer to regard the value 9 as a missing value and several subjects genuinely scored 9, then the computer will treat their data as missing when, in reality, it is not.

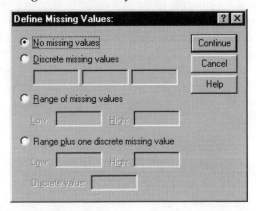

Figure 1.11: Defining missing values

To specify missing values you simply click on ⟨Missing Values...⟩ in the *define variable* dialog box to activate the *define missing values* dialog box (see Figure 1.11). By default SPSS assumes that no missing values exist but if you do have data with missing values you can choose to define them in one of three ways. The first is to select discrete values (by clicking on the circle next to where it says *Discrete missing values*) which are single values that represent missing data. SPSS allows you to specify up to three discrete values to represent missing data. The reason why you might choose to have several numbers to represent missing values is that you can assign a different meaning to each discrete value. For example, you could have the number 8 representing a response of 'not applicable', a code of 9 representing a 'don't know' response, and a code of 99 meaning that the subject failed to give any response. As far as the computer is concerned it will ignore any data cell containing these values; however, using different codes may be a useful way to remind you of why a particular score is missing. Usually, one discrete value is enough and in an experiment in which attitudes are measured on a 100-point scale (so scores vary from 1 to 100) you might choose 999 to represent missing values because this value cannot occur in the data that have been collected. The second option is to select a range of values to represent missing data and this is useful in situations in which it is necessary to exclude data falling between two points. So, we could exclude all scores between 5 and 10. The final option is to have a range of values and one discrete value.

1.2.3.4. Changing the Column Format

The final option available to us when we define a variable is to adjust the formatting of the column within the data editor. Click on Column Format... in the *define variable* dialog box and the dialog box in Figure 1.12 will appear. The default option is to have a column that is 8 characters wide with all numbers and text aligned to the right-hand side of the column. Both of these defaults can be changed: the column width by simply deleting the value of 8 and replacing it with a value suited to your needs, and the alignment by clicking on one of the deactivated circles (next to either *Left* or *Center*). It is very useful to adjust the column width when you have a coding variable with value labels that exceed 8 characters in length.

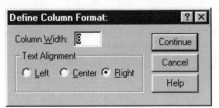

Figure 1.12: Defining the format of the column

1.2.4.   The Output Viewer

Alongside the main SPSS window, there is a second window known as the output viewer (or *output navigator* in versions 7.0 and 7.5). In earlier versions of SPSS this is simply called the output window and its function is, in essence, the same. However, whereas the output window of old displayed only statistical results (in a very bland font I might add), the new, improved and generally amazing output viewer will happily display graphs, tables and statistical results and all in a much nicer font. Rumour has it that future versions of SPSS will even include a tea-making facility in the output viewer (I live in hope!).

Figure 1.13 shows the basic layout of the output viewer. On the right-hand side there is a large space in which the output is displayed. SPSS displays both graphs and the results of statistical analyses in this part of the viewer. It is also possible to edit graphs and to do this you simply double-click on the graph you wish to edit (this creates a new window in which the graph can be edited). On the left-hand side of the output viewer there is a tree diagram illustrating the structure of the output. This tree diagram is useful when you have conducted several analyses because it provides an easy way of accessing specific parts of the output. The tree structure is fairly self-explanatory in that every time you conduct a procedure (such as drawing a graph or running a statistical procedure), SPSS lists this procedure as a main heading.

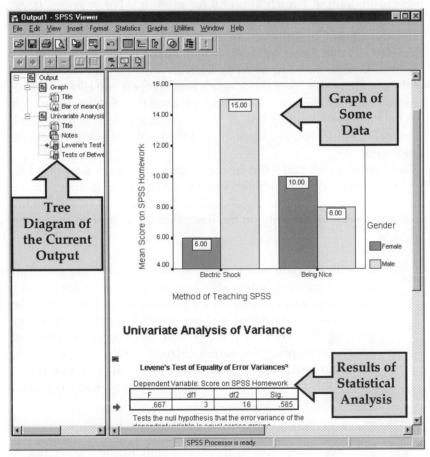

Figure 1.13 The output viewer

In Figure 1.13 I conducted a graphing procedure and then conducted a univariate analysis of variance (ANOVA) and so these names appear as main headings. For each procedure there are a series of sub-procedures, and these are listed as branches under the main headings. For example, in the ANOVA procedure there are a number of sections to the output such as a Levene's test (which tests the assumption of homogeneity of variance) and the between-group effects (i.e. the *F*-test of whether the means are significantly different). You can skip to any one of these sub-components of the ANOVA output by clicking on the appropriate branch of the tree diagram. So, if you wanted to skip straight to the between-group effects you should move the on-screen arrow to the left-hand portion of the window and click where it says *Tests of Between-Subjects Effects*. This action will highlight this part of the output in the main part of the viewer. You can also use this tree diagram to select parts of the output (which is useful for printing). For example, if you decided that you wanted to print out a graph but you didn't want to print the whole output, you can click on the word *Graph* in the tree structure and that graph will become highlighted in the output. It is then possible through the print menu to select to print only the selected part of the output. In this context it is worth noting that if you click on a main heading (such as *Univariate Analysis of Variance*) then SPSS will highlight not only that main heading but all of the sub-components as well. This is extremely useful when you want to print the results of a single statistical procedure.

There are a number of icons in the output viewer window that help you to do things quickly without using the drop-down menus. Some of these icons are the same as those described for the data editor window so I will concentrate mainly on the icons that are unique to the viewer window.

 As with the data editor window, this icon activates the print menu. However, when this icon is pressed in the viewer window it activates a menu for printing the output. When the print menu is activated you are given the default option of printing the whole output, or you can choose to select an option for printing the output currently visible on the screen, or most useful is an option to print a selection of the output. To choose this last option you must have already selected part of the output (see above).

 This icon returns you to the data editor in a flash!

 This icon takes you to the last output in the viewer (so, it returns you to the last procedure you conducted).

 This icon *promotes* the currently active part of the tree structure to a higher branch of the tree. For example, in Figure 1.13 the *Tests of Between-Subjects Effects* are a sub-component under the heading of *Univariate Analysis of Variance*. If we wanted to promote this part of the output to a higher level (i.e. to make it a main heading) then this is done using this icon.

This icon is the opposite of the above in that it *demotes* parts of the tree structure. For example, in Figure 1.13 if we didn't want the *Univariate Analysis of Variance* to be a unique section we could select this heading and demote it so that it becomes part of the previous heading (the *Graph* heading). This button is useful for combining parts of the output relating to a specific research question.

This icon collapses parts of the tree structure, which simply means that it hides the sub-components under a particular heading. For example, in Figure 1.13 if we selected the heading *Univariate Analysis of Variance* and pressed this icon, all of the sub-headings would disappear. The sections that disappear from the tree structure don't disappear from the output itself; the tree structure is merely condensed. This can be useful when you have been conducting lots of analyses and the tree diagram is becoming very complex.

This icon expands any collapsed sections. By default all of the main headings are displayed in the tree diagram in their expanded form. If, however, you have opted to collapse part of the tree diagram (using the icon above) then you can use this icon to undo your dirty work.

This icon and the following one allow you to show and hide parts of the output itself. So, you can select part of the output in the tree diagram and click on this icon and that part of the output will disappear. It isn't erased, but it is hidden from view. So, this icon is similar to the collapse icon listed above except that it affects the output rather than the tree structure. This is useful for hiding less relevant parts of the output.

This icon undoes the previous one, so if you have hidden a selected part of the output from view and you click on this icon, that part of the output will reappear. By default, all parts of the output are shown and so this icon is not active: it will become active only once you have hidden part of the output.

Although this icon looks rather like a paint roller, it unfortunately does not paint the house for you. What it does do is to insert a new heading into the tree diagram. For example, if you had several statistical tests that related to one of many research questions you could insert a main heading and then demote the headings of the relevant analyses so that they all fall under this new heading.

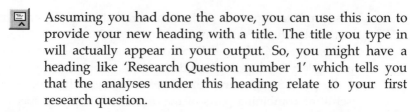 Assuming you had done the above, you can use this icon to provide your new heading with a title. The title you type in will actually appear in your output. So, you might have a heading like 'Research Question number 1' which tells you that the analyses under this heading relate to your first research question.

This final icon is used to place a text box in the output window. You can type anything into this box. In the context of the previous two icons, you might use a text box to explain what your first research question is (e.g. 'My first research question is whether or not boredom has set in by the end of the first chapter of my book. The following analyses test the hypothesis that boredom levels will be significantly higher at the end of the first chapter than at the beginning').

1.2.5.   Saving Files

Although most of you should be familiar with how to save files in Windows it is a vital thing to know and so I will briefly describe what to do. To save files simply use the ▣ icon (or use the menus: **File**⇒**Save** or **File**⇒**Save As...**). If the file is a new file, then clicking this icon will activate the *Save As* ... dialog box (see Figure 1.14). If you are in the data editor when you select *Save As* ... then SPSS will save the data file you are currently working on, but if you are in the viewer window then it will save the current output.

There are a number of features of the dialog box in Figure 1.14. First, you need to select a location at which to store the file. Typically, there are two types of locations where you can save data: the hard drive (or drives) and the floppy drive (and with the advent of rewritable CD-ROM drives, zip drives, jaz drives and the like you may have many other choices of location on your particular computer). The first thing to do is select either the floppy drive, by double clicking on ▣, or the hard drive, by double clicking on ▣. Once you have chosen a main location the dialog box will display all of the available folders on that particular device (you may not have any folders on your floppy disk in which case you can create a folder by clicking on ▣). Once you have selected a folder in which to save your file, you need to give your file a name. If you click in the space next to where it says *File name*, a cursor will appear and you can type a name of up to ten letters. By default, the file will be saved in an SPSS format, so if it is a data file it will have the file extension *.sav*, and if it is a viewer document it will have the file extension *.spo*. However, you can save data in different formats such as

Microsoft Excel files and tab-delimited text. To do this just click on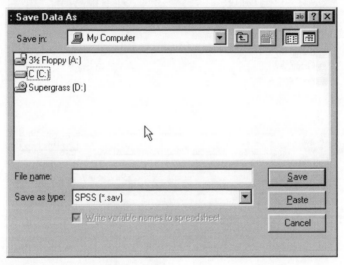
where it says *Save as type* and a list of possible file formats will be
displayed. Click on the file type you require. Once a file has previously
been saved, it can be saved again (updated) by clicking ▣. This icon
appears in both the data editor and the viewer, and the file saved
depends on the window that is currently active. The file will be saved in
the location at which it is currently stored.

Figure 1.14: The s*ave data as* dialog box

1.2.6.   Retrieving a File

Throughout this book you will work with data files that have been
provided on a floppy disk. It is, therefore, important that you know how
to load these data files into SPSS. The procedure is very simple. To open
a file, simply use the 🖾 icon (or use the menus: **File⇒Open**) to activate
the dialog box in Figure 1.15. First, you need to find the location at
which the file is stored. If you are loading a file from the floppy disk
then access the floppy drive by clicking on ▼ where it says *Look in* and a
list of possible location drives will be displayed. Once the floppy drive
has been accessed you should see a list of files and folders that can be
opened. As with saving a file, if you are currently in the data editor then
SPSS will display only SPSS data files to be opened (if you are in the
viewer window then only output files will be displayed). You can open
a folder by double-clicking on the folder icon. Once you have tracked
down the required file you can open it either by selecting it with the
mouse and then clicking on ⌷ <u>Open</u> ⌷, or by double-clicking on the icon
next to the file you want (e.g. double-clicking on 🖾). The data/output

will then appear in the appropriate window. If you are in the data editor and you want to open a viewer file, then click on 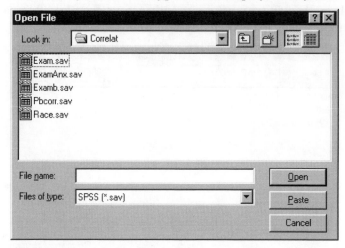 where it says *Files of type* and a list of alternative file formats will be displayed. Click on the appropriate file type (viewer document (*.spo*), Excel file (*.xls*), text file (*.dat*, *.txt*)) and any files of that type will be displayed for you to open.

Figure 1.15: Dialog box to open a file

1.3.   Further Reading

Einspruch, E. L. (1998). *An introductory guide to SPSS for Windows.* Thousand Oaks, CA: Sage.

Foster, J. J. (1998). *Data analysis using SPSS for Windows: a beginner's guide.* London: Sage.

2 Exploring Data

The first stage in any data analysis is to explore the data collected to get some idea of any patterns within it. Usually we look at descriptive statistics such as means, modes, medians, frequencies and so on. However, it is also important to see whether our data meet the criteria necessary for the statistical procedures we intend to use. With the exception of the tests described in this chapter and Chapter 5, all of the statistical procedures in this book are *parametric tests*. A parametric test is one that requires parametric data and for data to be parametric certain assumptions must be true. If you use a parametric test when your data are not parametric then the results are likely to be inaccurate. Therefore, it is very important that you check the assumptions before deciding which statistical test is appropriate. This chapter describes some simple ways in which data can be described, explains the assumptions of parametric data and how they can be tested, and looks at what can be done when the assumptions are violated.

2.1.   A Quick Guide to Simple Graphs

The easiest way to see the trend of your data is by plotting a graph. SPSS has the facilities to plot numerous different types of graph. If you click on the *Graphs* menu, a menu bar should drop down showing you the variety of graphs on offer. You may be familiar with some of these graphs (e.g. pie charts, bar charts etc.):

- **Bar:** Usually used to plot means of different groups of people (*Summaries for groups of cases*), or means of different variables (*Summaries of separate variables*).
- **Line:** Also used for plotting means.
- **Pie:** Used for plotting frequencies and percentages.
- **Boxplot:** Box-whisker diagram used for showing the median, spread and inter-quartile range of scores.
- **Error Bar:** Shows the mean and the 95% confidence interval for that mean (see Chapter 6).
- **Scatter:** Shows relationships between two variables (see Chapter 3).
- **Histogram:** Shows the frequency of different scores (useful for checking the distribution of scores).

Imagine we were interested in looking at the differences between lecturers and students. We took a random sample of five lecturers and five psychology students from Royal Holloway and then measured several variables: how many friends they had, their weekly alcohol consumption (in units), their yearly income (in pounds) and how neurotic they were (higher score is more neurotic). These data are in Table 2.1 and you should enter them into the SPSS data editor using what you learnt in Chapter 1. To create a variable you need to (1) move the on-screen arrow (using the mouse) to the grey area at the top of a column; (2) double-click with the left button of the mouse to make the *define variable* dialog box appear; (3) replace the default variable name (**var00001**) with something meaningful; and (4) click on ⬛ OK ⬛. You can now enter the data for that variable by making sure that you are in the appropriate column, typing the number and then moving to a new cell using the arrow keys. For the grouping variable (the one describing whether a person was a lecturer or student) you can create the variable in the same way but you must tell the computer which numeric codes represent the two groups. In the *define variable* dialog box click on ⬛ Labels.. ⬛ to open the *define labels* dialog box. In this dialog box specify a code and label for each of the two groups (I used a code of 1 to represent lecturers and a code of 2 to represent students). Having defined your codes, you can then go to the data editor and type these numerical values into the appropriate column (so if a person was a lecturer type a value of 1, if they were a student type the value 2).

Table 2.1: Data for differences between students and lecturers

Type of Person	No. of Friends	Alcohol Consumption	Income (p.a.)	Neuroticism
Lecturer	5	10	20000	10
Lecturer	2	15	40000	17
Lecturer	0	20	35000	14
Lecturer	4	5	22000	13
Lecturer	1	30	50000	21
Student	10	25	5000	7
Student	12	20	100	13
Student	15	16	3000	9
Student	12	17	10000	14
Student	17	18	10	13

Having entered these data we can look at trends by using graphs. To draw a graph, simply click on the word describing the graph that you want to plot. In most cases you will be presented with a provisional dialog box asking you whether you'd like to plot a *simple chart* or a *clustered* one (see Figure 2.1). A simple chart is one in which you plot one graph element per group or variable. For example we might want to plot the average number of friends for lecturers and students. As such, we want one bar representing the average number of friends that lecturers had and one representing the average number that students had. We could also plot a single line (connecting the lecturers' average to the students' average) or a boxplot (one representing the lecturers' data and one representing the students). If you want to plot one bar for different groups (this is used when you have a between-group design), then you should select *Summaries for groups of cases*. If you have only one group and you want to plot a graph of several dependent variables (a repeated measures design) then select *Summaries of separate variables*. An example of this would be if we ignored whether the person was a lecturer or student and just wanted to plot the average number of friends and the average neuroticism score on the same graph.

What is the difference between a simple graph and a clustered graph?

A clustered chart is one in which each group or category of people has several chart elements. These graphs can be useful if you want to plot two independent variables. For example, if we had noted the gender of each student and lecturer we would have two independent variables (gender and job) and one dependent variable (number of friends). Therefore, we could use a clustered plot to display the average number of friends for lecturers and students and have separate bars (or lines) representing males and females. In this latter case, in which both variables were measured using a between-group design, the *Summaries for groups of cases* option should be used. Alternatively, you can plot values of several groups along several variables. Imagine we wanted to plot the average number of friends and the average neuroticism score and split these scores according to whether the person was a lecturer or student. We want to plot two bars for the lecturers (one representing the number of friends and one representing neuroticism) and two for the students. To plot this graph we should choose a clustered chart but ask for *Summaries of separate variables*.

When a type of graph has been selected (simple or clustered) you need to click on ⬚Define⬚ to move to the next dialog box. On many occasions you will see the term *Category axis*, and this refers to the X-axis (horizontal). This axis usually requires a grouping variable (in these examples I have used *type of person*). Variables can be selected by clicking on them in the variable list (left-hand side of dialog box) and moving them to the appropriate space by using the ⬚▸⬚ button. In the case of bar charts, you can make the bars represent many things (number of cases etc.), but on the vast majority of occasions you will want them to represent the mean value and so you should select *Other summary function* and then enter a variable. The default function is the mean, but clicking on Change Summary... enables this default to be changed. Once the graphs options have been selected click on OK and the graph will appear in the output viewer. These charts can then be edited by double-clicking on them in the viewer. This action produces a new window (called the *chart editor*) in which you can change just about any property of the graph by double-clicking with the mouse (have a play around with some of the functions!).

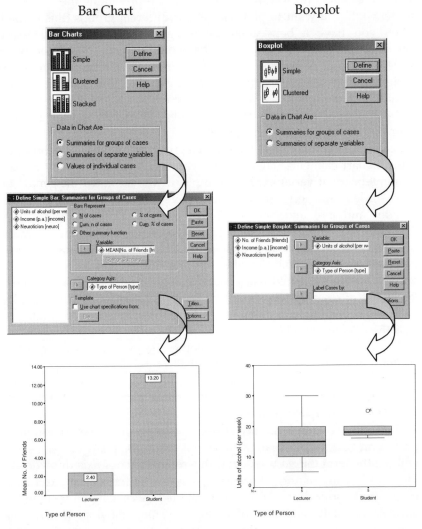

Figure 2.1: Plotting graphs on SPSS

Try putting some of these principles into practice using our lecturer-student data. Figure 2.1 shows how to create a bar chart and boxplot of two of the variables measured for the lecturers. Follow these options and see whether you can re-create these graphs (remember that you can edit them to add bar labels and change the colours). A bar chart of the means is a useful way to see the pattern of results (i.e. which group got the highest scores). In Figure 2.1 the graph shows us at a glance that students, on average, have more friends than their lecturers. Boxplots tell us a little bit more. For one thing the whiskers on the plot (the lines that stick out of the top and bottom) give an indicator of the spread of scores. More important, unusual cases can be identified (outliers) because they are displayed as a dot outside of the main range of scores. In Figure 2.1, the boxplot displayed has a single outlier who is represented by the dot above the graph. This person is a student who drank rather more than the other students. The dark line also shows the median score, so we can tell that the median amount of units drunk was higher for students than lecturers. Try plotting graphs of some of the other variables.

2.2. Assumptions of Parametric Data

Throughout this book you will become aware of my obsession with assumptions and checking them. All parametric tests have four basic assumptions that must be met for the test to be accurate. Many students find checking assumptions a pretty tedious affair, and often get confused about how to tell whether or not an assumption has been met. Therefore, this chapter is designed to take you on a step-by-step tour of the world of parametric assumptions (wow, how exciting!). Now, you may think that assumptions are not very exciting, but they can have great benefits: for one thing you can impress your supervisor/lecturer by spotting all of the test assumptions that they have violated throughout their career. You can then rubbish, on statistical grounds, the theories they have spent their lifetime developing—and they can't argue with you. Well, as I always say, 'if you're going to go through the agony of doing statistics, you may as well do them properly'. The assumptions of parametric tests are as follows:

1. **Normally distributed data**: It is assumed that the data are from a normally distributed population. The rationale behind hypothesis testing relies on having normally distributed populations and so if

this assumption is not met then the logic behind hypothesis testing is flawed (Chapter 6 briefly describes the principles of hypothesis testing). Most researchers eyeball their sample data (using a histogram) and if the sample data look roughly normal, then researchers assume that the populations are also. We shall see in this chapter that you can go a step beyond this approach and test whether your sample data are normal.

2. **Homogeneity of variance**: This assumption means that the variances should not change systematically throughout the data. In designs in which you test several groups of subjects this assumption means that each of these groups should have the same variance. In correlational designs, this assumption means that the variance of one variable should be stable at all levels of the other variable.

3. **Interval data**: Data should be measured at least at the interval level. This means that the distance between points of your scale should be equal at all parts along the scale. For example, if you had a 10-point anxiety scale, then the difference in anxiety represented by a change in score from 2 to 3 should be the same as that represented by a change in score from 9 to 10.

4. **Independence**: This assumption is that data from different subjects are independent, which means that the behaviour of one participant does not influence the behaviour of another. In repeated measures designs (in which subjects are measured in more than one experimental condition), we expect scores in the experimental conditions to be non-independent for a given subject, but behaviour between different participants should be independent.

The assumptions of interval data and independent measurements are, unfortunately, tested only by common sense. The assumption of homogeneity of variance is tested in different ways for different procedures and so we will discuss these tests as the need arises. This leaves us with only the assumption of normality to check. The easiest way to check this assumption is to look at the distribution of the sample data. If the sample data are normally distributed then we tend to assume that they came from a normally distributed population. Likewise if our sample is not normally distributed then we assume that it came from a non-normal population. So, to test this assumption we need to obtain summary statistics of our data that relate to the distribution of scores. Over the next three sections I'll show you how to obtain these summary statistics, and how to apply a statistical procedure to test whether data are normal. Throughout these sections we will use the data in the file **SPSSExam.sav**. This file contains data regarding students' performance on an SPSS exam. Four variables were measured: **exam** (first-year SPSS exam scores as a percentage), **computer** (measure of computer literacy in percent), **lecture** (percentage of SPSS lectures attended), and **numeracy** (a measure of numerical ability out of 15).

2.3. Obtaining Summary Statistics for One Group

2.3.1. Frequencies: Running the Analysis

To begin with open the file **SPSSExam.sav** (see section 1.2.6 for a reminder of how to open a file). To see the distribution of the variables, we can use the *frequencies* command, which is accessed using the file path **Analyze**⇒**Descriptive Statistics**⇒**Frequencies** ...[1]. The main dialog box is shown in Figure 2.2. The variables in the data editor should be listed on the left-hand side, and they can be transferred to the box labelled *Variable(s)* by clicking on a variable (or highlighting several with the mouse) and then clicking on ▶. Any analyses you choose to do will be done on every variable listed in the *Variable(s)* box. If a variable listed in the *Variable(s)* box is selected using the mouse, it can be transferred back to the variable list by clicking on the arrow button (which should now be pointing in the opposite direction). By default, SPSS produces a frequency distribution of all scores in table form. However, there are two other dialog boxes that can be selected that provide other options. The *statistics* dialog box is accessed by clicking on Statistics..., and the *charts* dialog box is accessed by clicking on Charts....

The *statistics* dialog box allows you to select several options of ways in which a distribution of scores can be described, such as measures of central tendency (mean, mode, median), measures of variability (range, standard deviation, variance, quartile splits), measures of shape (kurtosis and skewness). To describe the characteristics of the data we should select the mean, mode, median, standard deviation, variance and range. To check that a distribution of scores is normal, we need to look at the values of kurtosis and skewness. The *charts* option provides a simple way to plot the frequency distribution of scores (as a bar chart, a pie chart or a histogram). The most useful chart is the histogram, and for the purpose of checking normality, we should select the option of displaying a normal curve on the histogram. When you have selected the appropriate options, return to the main dialog box by clicking on Continue. Once in the main dialog box, click OK to run the analysis.

---

[1] Remember that this menu path would be **Statistics**⇒**Summarize**⇒**Frequencies** ... in version 8.0 and earlier.

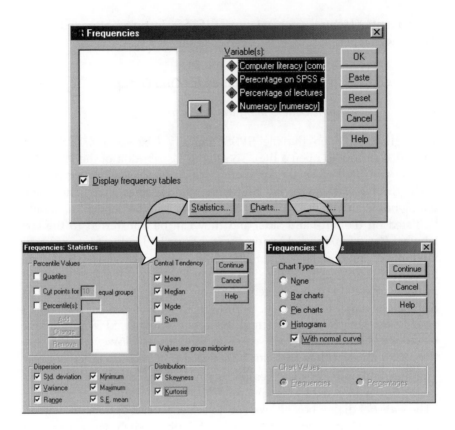

Figure 2.2: Dialog boxes for the *frequencies* command

2.3.2.   SPSS Output

SPSS Output 2.1 shows the table of descriptive statistics for the four variables in this example. From this table, we can see that, on average, students attended nearly 60% of lectures, obtained 58% in their SPSS exam, scored only 51% on the computer literacy test, and only 5 out of 15 on the numeracy test. In addition, the standard deviation for computer literacy was relatively small compared to that of the percentage of lectures attended and exam scores. These latter two variables had several modes (*multimodal*). The other important measures are the skewness and the kurtosis, both of which have an associated standard error. The values of skewness and kurtosis should be zero in a normal distribution. Positive values of skewness indicate a pile-up of scores on the left of the distribution, whereas negative values indicate a pile-up on the right. Positive values of kurtosis indicate a pointy distribution whereas negative values indicate a flat distribution. The further the value is from zero, the more likely it is that the data are not normally distributed. However, the actual values of skewness and kurtosis are not, in themselves, informative. Instead, we need to take the value and convert it to a z-score. A z-score is simply a score from a distribution that has a mean of zero and a standard deviation of 1. The reason for converting scores to a z-score is because it is a way of standardizing them. So, we can take any variable measured in any units and convert it to a z-score. By converting to a z-score we can compare any scores even if they were originally measured in different units. To transform any score to a z-score you simply subtract the mean of the distribution and then divide by the standard deviation of the distribution. Skewness is converted to a z-score in exactly this way, but for kurtosis we need to square root this value.

$$z_{skewness} = \frac{S-0}{SE_{skewness}} \qquad z_{kurtosis} = \sqrt{\frac{K-0}{SE_{kurtosis}}}$$

In the above equations, the values of S (skewness) and K (kurtosis) and their respective standard errors are produced by SPSS. These z-scores can be compared against values that you would expect to get by chance alone and, as a rule of thumb, a value above 2 (well, 1.96 to be precise) is considered significantly different from chance to be problematic. However, in small samples this criterion should be increased to 2.5 (2.58 to be exact) and in very large samples no criterion should be applied! For the SPSS exam scores, the z-score of skewness is −0.174/0.241 = −0.72. For numeracy, the z-score of skewness is 0.961/0.241 = 3.99. It is pretty clear then that the numeracy scores are positively skewed, indicating a pile-up of scores on the left of the distribution (so, most students got low scores). Try calculating the z-scores for the other variables.

The output provides tabulated frequency distributions of each variable (not reproduced here). These tables list each score and the number of times that it is found within the data set. In addition, each frequency value is expressed as a percentage of the sample (in this case the frequencies and percentages are the same because the sample size was 100). Also, the cumulative percentage is given, which tells us how many cases (as a percentage) fell below a certain score. So, for example, we can see that 66% of numeracy scores were 5 or less, 74% were 6 or less, and so on. Looking in the other direction, we can work out that only 8% (100–92%) got scores greater than 8.

Statistics

		Computer literacy	Percentage on SPSS exam	Percentage of lectures attended	Numeracy
N	Valid	100	100	100	100
	Missing	0	0	0	0
Mean		50.7100	58.1000	59.7650	4.8500
Std. Error of Mean		.8260	2.1316	2.1685	.2706
Median		51.5000	60.0000	62.0000	4.0000
Mode		54.00	72.00[a]	48.50[a]	4.00
Std. Deviation		8.2600	21.3156	21.6848	2.7057
Variance		68.2282	454.3535	470.2296	7.3207
Skewness		-.174	-.107	-.422	.961
Std. Error of Skewness		.241	.241	.241	.241
Kurtosis		.364	-1.105	-.179	.946
Std. Error of Kurtosis		.478	.478	.478	.478
Range		46.00	84.00	92.00	13.00
Minimum		27.00	15.00	8.00	1.00
Maximum		73.00	99.00	100.00	14.00

a. Multiple modes exist. The smallest value is shown

SPSS Output 2.1

Finally, we are given histograms of each variable with the normal distribution overlaid. These graphs are displayed in Figure 2.3 and show us several things. First, it looks as though computer literacy is fairly normally distributed (a few people are very good with computers and a few are very bad, but the majority of people have a similar degree of knowledge). The exam scores are very interesting because this distribution is quite clearly not normal, in fact, it looks suspiciously bimodal (there are two peaks indicative of two modes). This observation corresponds with the earlier information from the table of descriptive statistics. Lecture attendance is generally quite normal, but the tails of the distribution are quite heavy (i.e. although most people attend the majority of lectures, there are a reasonable number of dedicated souls who attend them all and a larger than 'normal' proportion who attend very few). This is why there are high frequencies at the two ends of the distribution. Finally, the numeracy test has produced very positively skewed data (i.e. the majority of people did very badly on this test and only a few did well). This corresponds with what the skewness statistic indicated.

Descriptive statistics and histograms are a good way of getting an instant picture of the distribution of your data. This snapshot can be very useful: for example, the bimodal distribution of SPSS exam scores instantly indicates a trend that students are typically either very good at statistics or struggle with it (there are relatively few who fall in between these extremes). Intuitively, this finding fits with the nature of the subject: statistics is very easy once everything falls into place, but before that enlightenment occurs it all seems hopelessly difficult! Although there is a lot of information that we can obtain from histograms and descriptive information about a distribution, there are more objective ways in which we can assess the degree of normality in a set of data (see section 2.5).

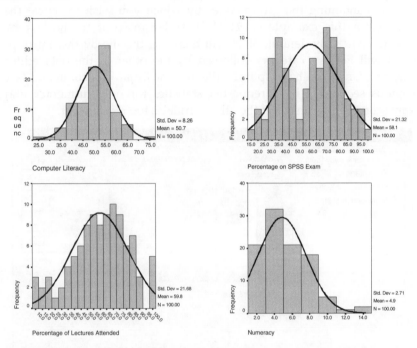

Figure 2.3: Histograms of the SPSS exam data

2.4.   Obtaining Summary Information for Several Groups

2.4.1.   Running the Analysis: The Split File Command

There are several ways to produce basic descriptive statistics for separate groups of people (and we will come across some of these methods in the next section). However, I intend to use this opportunity to introduce you to a function called *split file*, which allows you to repeat any analysis on several groups of cases. The *split file* function allows you to specify a grouping variable (remember these variables are used to specify categories of people). Any subsequent procedure in SPSS will then be carried out, in turn, on each category specified by that grouping variable. For the SPSS exam data, there is a variable called **uni** indicating whether the student attended Sussex University or Duncetown University. If we wanted to obtain separate descriptive statistics for each of these samples, we could split the file, and then proceed using the *frequencies* command described in the previous section. To split the file, simply use the menu path **Data⇒Split File ...** or click on ▦. In the resulting dialog box select the option *Organize output by groups*. Once this option is selected, the *Groups Based on* box will activate. Select the variable containing the group codes by which you wish to repeat the analysis (in this example select **Uni**), and transfer it to the box by clicking on ▣. By default, SPSS will then sort the file by these groups (i.e. it will list one category followed by the other in the data editor window). Once you have split the file, use the *frequencies* command (see previous section). I have requested statistics for only **numeracy** and **exam** scores), you can select the other variables too if you want.

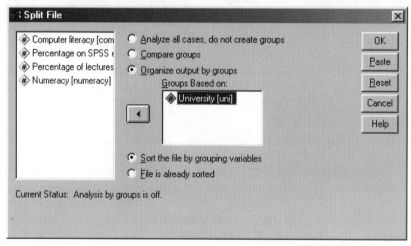

Figure 2.4: Dialog box for the *split file* command.

2.4.2.   Output

The SPSS output is split into two sections: first the results for students at Duncetown University, then the results for those attending Sussex University. SPSS Output 2.2 shows the two main summary tables. From these tables it is clear that Sussex students scored higher on both their SPSS exam and the numeracy test than their Duncetown counterparts. In fact, looking at the means reveals that, on average, Sussex students scored 6% more on the SPSS exam than Duncetown students, and had numeracy scores twice as high. The standard deviations for both variables are slightly higher for Sussex, but not greatly so.

Duncetown University

Statistics[a]

		Percentage on SPSS exam	Numeracy
N	Valid	50	50
	Missing	0	0
Mean		54.4400	3.1800
Std. Error of Mean		2.7779	.2094
Median		53.0000	3.0000
Mode		47.00	2.00
Std. Deviation		19.6429	1.4803
Variance		385.8433	2.1914
Skewness		.259	.621
Std. Error of Skewness		.337	.337
Kurtosis		-.893	-.100
Std. Error of Kurtosis		.662	.662
Range		77.00	6.00
Minimum		22.00	1.00
Maximum		99.00	7.00

a. University = Duncetown University

Sussex University

		Percentage on SPSS exam	Numeracy
N	Valid		
	Missing	0	0
Mean		61.7600	6.5200
Std. Error of Mean		3.1774	.3717
Median		67.5000	6.5000
Mode		77.00	5.00
Std. Deviation		22.4677	2.6283
Variance		504.7984	6.9078
Skewness		-.482	.697
Std. Error of Skewness		.337	.337
Kurtosis		-.931	.648
Std. Error of Kurtosis		.662	.662
Range		82.00	12.00
Minimum		15.00	2.00
Maximum		97.00	14.00
a.			

SPSS Output 2.2

SPSS Exam Mark

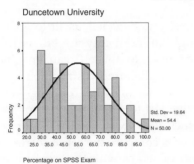

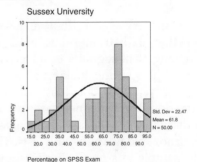

Numeracy

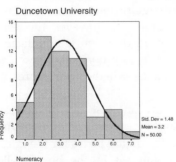

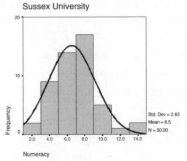

Figure 2.5: Distributions of exam and numeracy scores for Duncetown University and Sussex University students

Figure 2.5 shows the histograms of these variables split according to the university attended. For exam marks, the distributions are both bimodal. So, it seems that regardless of the university, there is always a split between students: they either do really well (one mode around 70%) or really badly (second mode at 35%). However, at Sussex, there is a greater concentration of students around the higher mode (the peak is taller). For numeracy scores, the distribution is slightly positively skewed in the Duncetown group (there is a larger concentration at the lower end of scores) whereas Sussex students are fairly normally distributed around a mean of 7. Therefore, the overall positive skew observed before is due to the mixture of universities (the Duncetown students contaminate Sussex's normally distributed scores!). When you have finished with the *split file* command, remember to *switch it off* (otherwise SPSS will carry on doing every analysis on each group separately). To switch this function off, return to the *split file* dialog box and select *Analyze all cases, do not create groups*.

2.5.   Testing whether a Distribution is Normal

2.5.1.   *Running the Analysis*

It is all very well to look at histograms, but they tell us little about whether a distribution is close enough to normality to be useful. Looking at histograms is subjective and open to abuse (I can imagine researchers sitting looking at a completely distorted distribution and saying 'yep, well Bob, that looks normal to me', and Bob replying 'yep, sure does'). What is needed is an objective test to decide whether or not a distribution is normal. Fortunately, such tests exist: the Kolmogorov-Smirnov and Shapiro-Wilk tests. These tests compare the set of scores in the sample to a normally distributed set of scores with the same mean and standard deviation. If the test is non-significant ($p > 0.05$) it tells us that the distribution of the sample is not significantly different from a normal distribution (i.e. it is probably normal). If, however, the test is significant ($p < 0.05$) then the distribution in question is significantly different from a normal distribution (i.e. it is non-normal). These tests are great: in one easy procedure they tell us whether our scores are normally distributed (nice!).

The Kolmogorov-Smirnov (K-S from now on) test can be accessed through the *explore* command (**Analyze**⇒**Descriptive Statistics**⇒**Explore...**).[2] Figure 2.6 shows the dialog boxes for the *explore* command. First, enter any variables of interest in the box labelled *Dependent List* by highlighting them on the left-hand side and transferring them by clicking on ▶. For this example, just select the exam scores and numeracy scores. It is also possible to select a factor (or grouping variable) by which to split the output (so, if you select **uni** and transfer it to the box labelled *Factor List*, SPSS will produce exploratory

---

[2] This menu path would be **Statistics**⇒**Summarize**⇒**Explore...** in version 8.0 and earlier.

analysis for each group—a bit like the *split file* command). If you click on Statistics... a dialog box appears, but the default option is fine (it will produce means, standard deviations and so on). The more interesting option for our purposes is accessed by clicking on Plots... . In this dialog box select the option ☑ Normality plots with tests, and this will produce both the K-S test and normal Q-Q plots for all of the variables selected. By default, SPSS will produce boxplots (split according to group if a factor has been specified) and stem and leaf diagrams as well. Click on Continue to return to the main dialog box and then click OK to run the analysis.

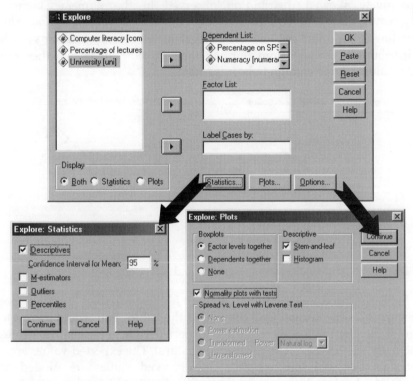

Figure 2.6: Dialog boxes for the *explore* command

2.5.2. Output

The first table produced by SPSS contains descriptive statistics (mean etc.) and should have the same values as the tables obtained using the frequencies procedure. The important table is that of the Kolmogorov-Smirnov test. This table includes the test statistic itself, the degrees of freedom (which should equal the sample size) and the significance value of this test. Remember that a significant value (*Sig.* less than 0.05)

Tests of Normality

	Kolmogorov-Smirnov[a]		
	Statistic	df	Sig.
Percentage on SPSS exam	.102	100	.012
Numeracy	.153	100	.000

a. Lilliefors Significance Correction

indicates a deviation from normality. For both numeracy and SPSS exam, the K-S test is highly significant, indicating that both distributions are not normal. This result is likely to reflect the bimodal distribution found for exam scores, and the positively skewed distribution observed in the numeracy scores. However, these tests confirm that these deviations were *significant*. This finding is important because the histograms tell us only that our sample distributions deviate from normal; they do not tell us whether this deviation is large enough to be important.

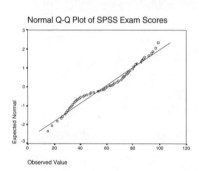 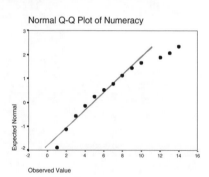

Figure 2.7: Normal Q-Q plots of numeracy and SPSS exam scores

SPSS also produces a normal Q-Q plot for any variables specified (see Figure 2.7). The normal Q-Q chart plots the values you would expect to get if the distribution were normal (expected values) against the values actually seen in the data set (observed values). The expected values are a straight diagonal line, whereas the observed values are plotted as individual points. If the data are normally distributed, then the observed values (the dots on the chart) should fall exactly along the straight line (meaning that the observed values are the same as you would expect to get from a normally distributed data set). Any deviation of the dots from the line represents a deviation from normality. So, if the Q-Q plot looks like a straight line with a wiggly snake wrapped around it then you have some deviation from normality! In both of the variables analysed we already know that the data are not normal, and these plots confirm this observation because the dots deviate substantially from the line. It is noteworthy that the deviation is greater for the numeracy scores, and this is consistent with the higher significance value of this variable on the Kolmogorov-Smirnov test. A deviation from normality such as this tells us that we cannot use a parametric test, because the assumption of normality is not tenable. In these circumstances we can sometimes turn to non-parametric tests as a means of testing the hypothesis of interest. In the next section we shall look at some of the non-parametric procedures available on SPSS.

2.6. What to Do if You Have Non-Normal Data: Non-Parametric Tests

Non-parametric tests are sometimes known as assumption-free tests because they make no assumptions about the type of data on which they can be used. Most of these tests work on the principle of ranking the data, that is, finding the lowest score and giving it a rank of 1, then finding the next highest score and giving it a rank of 2, and so on. This process results in high scores being represented by large ranks, and low scores being represented by small ranks. The analysis is then carried out on the ranks rather than the actual data. This process is an ingenious way around the problem of using data that breaks the parametric assumptions. However, this ingenuity comes at a price: by ranking the data we lose some information about the magnitude of difference between scores and because of this non-parametric tests are less powerful than the parametric counterparts. The notion of statistical power is fairly simple: it refers to the ability of a test to find an effect that genuinely exists. So, by saying that non-parametric tests are less powerful, we are saying that if there is a genuine effect in our data, then a parametric test is more likely to detect it than a non-parametric one. Therefore, there is an increased chance of a type II error (i.e. more chance of accepting that there is no difference between groups when, in reality, a difference exists). In real terms, you are more likely to miss a significant effect if you use a non-parametric test.

2.6.1. Mann-Whitney Test

The Mann-Whitney test is used for testing differences between means when there are two conditions and different subjects have been used in each condition. For example, a neurologist might carry out an experiment to investigate the depressant effects of certain recreational drugs. She tested 20 clubbers in all: 10 were given an ecstasy tablet to take on a Saturday night and 10 were allowed only to drink alcohol. Levels of depression were measured using the Beck Depression Inventory (BDI) the day after and midweek. When the data are collected using different subjects in each group, we need to input the data using a coding variable. So, the data editor will have three columns of data. The first column is a coding variable (called something like **drug**) which, in this case, will have only two codes (for convenience I suggest 1 = ecstasy group, and 2 = alcohol group). The second column will have values for the dependent variable (BDI) measured the day after (call this variable **sunbdi**) and the third will have the midweek scores on the same questionnaire (call this variable **wedbdi**). The data are in Table 2.2 in which the group codes are shown (rather than the group names).

Table 2.2: Data for drug experiment

Subject	Drug	BDI (Sunday)	BDI (Wednesday)
1	1	15	28
2	1	14	35
3	1	23	35
4	1	26	24
5	1	24	39
6	1	22	32
7	1	16	27
8	1	18	29
9	1	30	36
10	1	17	35
11	2	16	5
12	2	15	24
13	2	20	6
14	2	15	14
15	2	16	9
16	2	13	7
17	2	14	17
18	2	19	6
19	2	18	3
20	2	18	10

When you enter the data into SPSS remember to tell the computer that a code of 1 represents the group that were given ecstasy, and that a code of 2 represents the group that were restricted to alcohol

Tests of Normality

	Kolmogorov-Smirnov[a]			Shapiro-Wilk		
	Statistic	df	Sig.	Statistic	df	Sig.
Beck Depression Inventory (Sunday)	.190	20	.057	.896	20	.037
Beck Depression Inventory (Wednesday)	.161	20	.185	.893	20	.033

a. Lilliefors Significance Correction

(see section 1.2.3.1). There were no specific predictions about which drug would have the most effect so the analysis should be two-tailed. First, we would run some exploratory analysis on the data (see section 2.5). If you do these analyses you should find that the data are not normally distributed for either variable according to the Shapiro-Wilk statistic. This finding would alert us to the fact that a non-parametric test should be used. You should note that by using the K-S test one of the variables appears to be normal—it is just about non-significant. This finding highlights an important difference between the K-S test and the Shapiro-Wilk test: in general the Shapiro-Wilk test is more accurate.

2.6.1.1. Running the Analysis

First, access the main dialog box by using the **Analyze⇒Nonparametric Tests⇒2 Independent Samples ...** menu pathway (see Figure 2.8). Once the dialog box is activated, select both dependent variables from the list (click on **sunbdi** then, holding the mouse button down, drag over **wedbdi**) and transfer them to the box labelled *Test Variable List* by clicking on ▶. Next, select the independent variable (the grouping variable), in this case **drug**, and transfer it to the box labelled *Grouping Variable*. When the grouping variable has been selected the Define Groups... button becomes active and you should click on it to activate the *define groups* dialog box. SPSS needs to know what numeric codes you assigned to your two groups, and there is a space for you to type the codes. In this example we coded our ecstasy group as 1 and our alcohol group as 2, and so you should type these two values in the appropriate space. When you have defined the groups, click on Continue to return to the main dialog box. If you click on Options... then another dialog box appears that gives you options for the analysis. These options are not particularly useful because, for example, the option that provides descriptive statistics does so for the entire data set (so doesn't break down values according to group membership). For this reason, I recommend obtaining descriptive statistics using the methods we learnt about in sections 2.4 and 2.5. To run the analyses return to the main dialog box and click on OK.

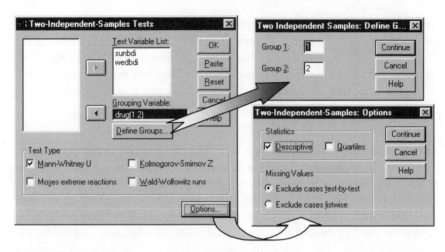

Figure 2.8: Dialog boxes for the Mann-Whitney test

2.6.1.2. Output from the Mann-Whitney Test

The Mann-Whitney test works by looking at differences in the ranked positions of scores in different groups. Therefore, the first part of the output summarizes the data after it has been ranked. Specifically, SPSS tells us the average and total ranks in each condition (see SPSS Output 2.3). Now, the Mann-Whitney test relies on scores being ranked from lowest to highest: therefore, the group with the lowest mean rank is the group with the greatest number of lower scores in it. Similarly, the group that has the highest mean rank should have a greater number of high scores within it. Therefore, this initial table can be used to ascertain which group had the highest scores, which is useful in case we need to interpret a significant result.

Ranks

	Type of Drug	N	Mean Rank	Sum of Ranks
Beck Depression Inventory (Sunday)	Ecstasy	10	12.75	127.50
	Alcohol	10	8.25	82.50
	Total	20		
Beck Depression Inventory (Wednesday)	Ecstasy	10	15.45	154.50
	Alcohol	10	5.55	55.50
	Total	20		

SPSS Output 2.3

The second table (SPSS Output 2.4) provides the actual test statistics for the Mann-Whitney test. There are many variations on the Mann-Whitney test; in fact, Mann, Whitney and Wilcoxon all came up with statistically comparable techniques for analysing ranked data. The form of the test commonly taught is that of the Mann-Whitney test. However,

Wilcoxon developed a different procedure, which can be converted into a *z*-score and, therefore, can be compared against critical values of the normal distribution. SPSS provides both statistics and the *z*-score for the Wilcoxon statistic.

Test Statistics[b]

	Beck Depression Inventory (Sunday)	Beck Depression Inventory (Wednesday)
Mann-Whitney U	27.500	.500
Wilcoxon W	82.500	55.500
Z	-1.709	-3.750
Asymp. Sig. (2-tailed)	.087	.000
Exact Sig. [2*(1-tailed Sig.)]	.089[a]	.000[a]

a. Not corrected for ties.

b. Grouping Variable: Type of Drug

SPSS Output 2.4

SPSS Output 2.4 has a column for each variable (one for **sunbdi** and one for **wedbdi**) and in each column there is the value of Mann-Whitney's *U* statistic[3], the value of Wilcoxon's statistic and the associated *z* approximation. The important part of the table is the significance value of the test, which gives the two-tailed probability that the magnitude of the test statistic is a chance result. This significance value can be used as it is when no prediction has been made about which group will differ from which. However, if a prediction has been made (for example, if we said that ecstasy users would be more depressed than alcohol users the day after taking the drug) then we need to calculate the one-tailed probability. This value can be obtained by taking the two-tailed value and dividing it by two. For these data, the Mann-Whitney test is non-significant (two-tailed) for the depression scores taken on the Sunday. This finding indicates that ecstasy is no more of a depressant, the day after taking it, than alcohol: both groups report comparable levels of depression. However, for the midweek measures the results are highly significant ($p < 0.001$). The value of the mean rankings indicates that the ecstasy group had significantly higher levels of depression midweek than the alcohol group. This conclusion is

---

[3] *U* is calculated using an equation in which N_1 and N_2 are the sample sizes of groups 1 and 2 respectively, and R_1 is the sum of ranks for group 1:

$$U = N_1 N_2 + \frac{N_1(N_1 + 1)}{2} - R_1$$

$$U_{Sun} = (10 \times 10) + \frac{10(11)}{2} - 127.50 = 27.50$$

$$U_{Wed} = (10 \times 10) + \frac{10(11)}{2} - 154.50 = 0.50$$

reached by noting that for the Wednesday scores, the average rank is higher in the ecstasy users (15.45) than in the alcohol users (5.55).

2.6.2.   The Wilcoxon Signed-Rank Test

2.6.2.1.   Running the Analysis

The Wilcoxon test is used in situations in which there are two sets of scores to compare, but these scores come from the same subjects. As such, you can think of it as a Mann-Whitney test for repeated measures data. Imagine the experimenter was now interested in the change in depression levels, within subjects, for each of the two drugs. We now want to compare the BDI scores on Sunday to those on Wednesday. We can use the same data as before, but because we want to look at the change for each drug separately, we need to use the *split file* command and ask SPSS to split the file by the variable **drug**. This process ensures that any subsequent analysis is done for the ecstasy group and the alcohol group separately. Once the file has been split, select the Wilcoxon test dialog box by using the file path **Analyze⇒Nonparametric Tests⇒2 Related Samples ...** (Figure 2.9).

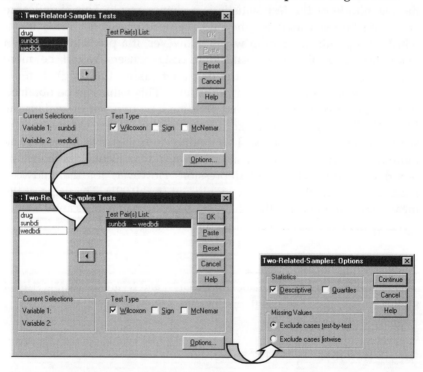

Figure 2.9: Dialog boxes for the Wilcoxon test

Once the dialog box is activated, select two variables from the list (click on the first variable with the mouse and then the second). The first variable you select (**sunbdi**) will be named as *Variable 1* in the box labelled *Current Selections*, and the second variable you select (**wedbdi**) appears as *Variable 2*. When you have selected two variables, transfer them to the box labelled *Test Pair(s) List* by clicking on ▶. If you want to carry out several Wilcoxon tests then you can select another pair of variables, transfer them to the variables list, and then select another pair and so on. In this case, we want only one test. If you click on Options... then another dialog box appears that gives you the chance to select descriptive statistics. Unlike the Mann-Whitney test, the descriptive statistics here are worth having, because it is the change across variables (columns in the data editor) that is relevant. To run the analysis, return to the main dialog box and click on OK .

2.6.3. Output from SPSS

2.6.3.1. Ecstasy Group

If you have split the file, then the first set of results obtained will be for the ecstasy group (SPSS Output 2.5). The first table provides information about the ranked scores. It tells us the number of negative ranks (these are people for whom the Sunday score was greater than the Wednesday score) and the number of positive ranks (subjects for whom the Wednesday score was greater than the Sunday score). The table shows that for 9 of the 10 subjects, their score on Wednesday was greater than on Sunday, indicating greater depression midweek compared to the morning after. There were no tied ranks (i.e. subjects who scored the same on both days). The table also shows the average number of negative and positive ranks and the sum of positive and negative ranks. Below the table are footnotes, which tell us to what the positive and negative ranks relate (so provide the same kind of explanation as I've just made—see, I'm not clever, I just read the footnotes!). If we were to look up the significance of Wilcoxon's test by hand, we would take the lowest value of the two types of ranks, so our test value here would be the sum of negative ranks (e.g. 1). However, this value can be converted to a z-score and this is what SPSS does. The advantage of this approach is that it allows exact significance values to be calculated based on the normal distribution. The second table in SPSS Output 2.5 tells us that the test statistic is based on the negative ranks, that the z-score is -2.703 and that this value is significant at $p = 0.007$. Therefore, because this value is based on the *negative* ranks, we should conclude that when taking ecstasy there was a significant increase in depression (as measured by the BDI) from the morning after to midweek. If the test statistic had been based on the positive ranks then this would have told us that the results were in the opposite direction (namely BDI scores were greater the morning after compared to midweek). Therefore, we can conclude that for ecstasy users there was a significant increase in depression from the next day to midweek ($z = -2.70, p < 0.01$).

Ranks[d]

		N	Mean Rank	Sum of Ranks
Beck Depression Inventory (Wednesday) - Beck Depression Inventory (Sunday)	Negative Ranks	1[a]	1.00	1.00
	Positive Ranks	9[b]	6.00	54.00
	Ties	0[c]		
	Total	10		

a. Beck Depression Inventory (Wednesday) < Beck Depression Inventory (Sunday)

b. Beck Depression Inventory (Wednesday) > Beck Depression Inventory (Sunday)

c. Beck Depression Inventory (Sunday) = Beck Depression Inventory (Wednesday)

d. Type of Drug = Ecstasy

Test Statistics[b,c]

	Beck Depression Inventory (Wednesday) - Beck Depression Inventory (Sunday)
Z	-2.703[a]
Asymp. Sig. (2-tailed)	.007

a. Based on negative ranks.

b. Wilcoxon Signed Ranks Test

c. Type of Drug = Ecstasy

SPSS Output 2.5

2.6.3.2. *Alcohol Group*

The remainder of the output should contain the same two tables but for the alcohol group (if it does not, then you probably forgot to split the file). As before, the first table in SPSS Output 2.6 provides information about the ranked scores. It tells us the number of negative ranks (these are people who were more depressed on Sunday than on Wednesday) and the number of positive ranks (subjects who were more depressed on Wednesday than on Sunday). The table shows that for 8 of the 10 subjects, their score on Sunday was greater than on Wednesday, indicating greater depression the morning after compared to midweek. As with the ecstasy takers there were no tied ranks. The table also shows the average number of negative and positive ranks and the sum of positive and negative ranks. Below the table are footnotes that tell us to what the positive and negative ranks relate. As before, the lowest value of ranked scores is converted to a z-score. The second table tells us that the test statistic is based on the positive ranks, that the z-score is -1.988 and that this value is significant at $p = 0.047$. Therefore, we should conclude (based on the fact that *positive* ranks were used) that when taking alcohol there was a significant decline in depression (as measured by the BDI) from the morning after to midweek ($z = -1.99$, $p < 0.05$).

Ranks[d]

		N	Mean Rank	Sum of Ranks
Beck Depression Inventory (Wednesday) - Beck Depression Inventory (Sunday)	Negative Ranks	8[a]	5.88	47.00
	Positive Ranks	2[b]	4.00	8.00
	Ties	0[c]		
	Total	10		

a. Beck Depression Inventory (Wednesday) < Beck Depression Inventory (Sunday)
b. Beck Depression Inventory (Wednesday) > Beck Depression Inventory (Sunday)
c. Beck Depression Inventory (Sunday) = Beck Depression Inventory (Wednesday)
d. Type of Drug = Alcohol

Test Statistics[b,c]

	Beck Depression Inventory (Wednesday) - Beck Depression Inventory (Sunday)
Z	-1.988[a]
Asymp. Sig. (2-tailed)	.047

a. Based on positive ranks.
b. Wilcoxon Signed Ranks Test
c. Type of Drug = Alcohol

SPSS Output 2.6

From the results of the two different groups, we can see that there is an opposite effect when alcohol is taken, to when ecstasy is taken. Alcohol makes you slightly depressed the morning after but this depression has dropped by midweek. Ecstasy also causes some depression the morning after consumption; however, this depression increases towards the middle of the week. Of course, to see the true effect of the morning after we would have had to take measures of depression before the drugs were administered! This opposite effect between groups of people is known as an interaction (i.e. you get one effect under certain circumstances, and a different effect under other circumstances) and you'll be learning about interactions later in this book (so remember this chapter well!) .

2.7. A Quick Look at Clustered Charts

In the previous example, we had one variable measured using different subjects (the type of drug taken), but each subject was also given measures on two separate days (so, this variable was repeated measures). A situation in which there are two variables and one has been measured between groups and the other is a repeated measure is called a mixed design (see Chapter 9). This scenario is a useful way to illustrate how to plot clustered graphs. To graph the data from the previous example, you must first remember to switch off the *split file* command so that we are analysing all cases (see section 2.4). Then select the main bar chart dialog box by using the **Graphs**⇒ **Bar...** menu path. In this dialog box, click on the picture labelled *Clustered* (this option allows us to plot the between-groups variable) and then select *Summaries of separate variables* (this option allows us to plot the repeated measure). When these options have been selected, click on Define . The next dialog box has two spaces. The first asks what variables you want the bars to represent. You should select the variables representing different levels of the repeated measures variable (in this case **sunbdi** and **wedbdi**), and transfer them to the box labelled *Bars Represent*. A second space is labelled *Category Axis*, and you should transfer the between-groups variable (**drug**) into this space. By default, SPSS will display mean values of the selected variables; however, you can display other values by clicking on Change Summary... . When all of the options have been selected click on OK to draw the graph. The resulting graph is shown in Figure 2.10. It is pretty clear that the clusters of bars represent the two groups (the between-groups variable) while the bars within each cluster represent the different days (the repeated measures variable). If you double-click on the graph you can edit it in a separate window and make it pretty (like I have!).

You can see how this graph clearly shows the pattern of results found with the Wilcoxon tests. For the ecstasy takers, depression scores increased from the morning after to midweek. This is shown by the bar representing depression measured on Wednesday (light bar) being much taller than the bar representing the depression scores measured on Sunday (dark bar). The opposite pattern is observed for the alcohol group, that is, the bar representing depression measured on Wednesday (light bar) is shorter than the bar representing the depression scores measured on Sunday (dark bar). Another interesting thing to note is that both bars are taller in the ecstasy group. The dark bar is slightly higher than the dark bar for the alcohol group. This indicates that depression scores on Sunday were higher in the ecstasy group than in the alcohol group. This difference is what was tested by the first Mann-Whitney test (which was non-significant at the 0.05 level). The light bar in the ecstasy group is considerably taller than the light bar in the alcohol group. This indicates that depression scores measured midweek were much higher after taking ecstasy than after taking alcohol. This difference was tested using the second Mann-Whitney test and this was found to be a highly significant difference (see section 2.6.1.2). These more complex graphs can be an invaluable way to picture your data to help you understand what on earth is going on.

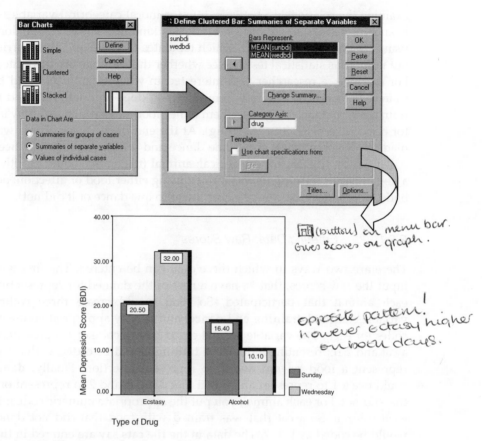

Figure 2.10: Plotting graphs of mixed designs

2.8.   Categorical Data: Chi-Square and Crosstabulation

Sometimes, we are interested not in test scores, or continuous measures, but in categorical variables. Categorical variables are what we have so far termed grouping variables, so, they are variables that describe categories of people. There are different types of categorical variable (see section 3.2.3.6), but in theory a person, or case, should fall into only one category. Good examples of categorical variables are gender (with few exceptions people can be only biologically male or biologically female[4]), pregnancy (a woman can be only pregnant or not pregnant), and voting in an election (you are allowed to vote for only one candidate). When we

---

[4] Before anyone completely slates me, I am aware that numerous chromosomal and hormonal conditions exist that complicate the matter. Also, people can have a different gender identity to their biological gender.

examine the relationship between two (or more) categorical variables it is known as crosstabulation. On SPSS, this kind of analysis can be done using the *crosstabs* command, which tabulates the data and then carries out numerous statistical tests to see whether the variables are associated. For example, a researcher was interested in whether animals could be trained to line dance. He took some cats and dogs (**animal**) and tried to train them to dance by giving them either food or affection as a reward for dance-like behaviour (**training**). At the end of the week a note was made of which animals could line dance and which could not (**dance**). All of these variables are categorical: **animal** (the animal could be either a dog or a cat), **training** (it was trained using either food or affection, not both), and **dance** (the animal either learnt to line dance or it did not).

2.8.1.   Entering Data: Raw Scores

There are two ways in which these data can be entered. The first is to input the raw scores, that is, have a row of the data editor representing each animal that participated. So, you would create three coding variables (**animal, training** and **dance**) and specify appropriate numeric codes for each. The variable **animal** could have a code of 1 representing a cat and 2 representing a dog. The **training** could be coded with a 1 to represent a food reward and 2 to represent affection. Finally, **dance** could use a 1 to represent an animal that danced and 2 to represent one that did not. For each animal, you put the appropriate numeric code into each column. So a cat that was trained with food that did not dance would be coded as 1, 1, 2. The data in the file **cats.sav** are entered in this way and you should be able to identify the three variables described. There were 134 animals in all and so there are 134 rows of data.

2.8.2.   Entering Data: Weight Cases

An alternative method of data entry is to create the same coding variables as before, but to have a fourth variable that represents the number of animals that fell into each combination of categories. In other words we input frequency data (the number of cases that fall into a particular category). We could call this variable **frequent**. Figure 2.11 shows the data editor with the fourth variable added. Now, instead of having 134 rows, each one representing a different animal, we have one row representing each combination of categories and a variable telling us how many animals fell into this category combination. So, the first row represents cats who had food as a reward and who then danced. The variable **frequent** tells us that there were 26 cats that had food as a reward and then danced. This information is represented by 26 different rows in the file **cats.sav**. Extending this principle, we can see that when affection was used as a reward only 6 cats danced compared to 24 dogs.

	animal	training	dance	frequent	var
1	Cat	Food as Re	Yes	26.00	
2	Cat	Food as Re	No	6.00	
3	Cat	Affection as	Yes	6.00	
4	Cat	Affection as	No	30.00	
5	Dog	Food as Re	Yes	23.00	
6	Dog	Food as Re	No	9.00	
7	Dog	Affection as	Yes	24.00	
8	Dog	Affection as	No	10.00	

Figure 2.11: Data entry using weighted cases

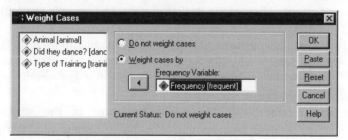

Figure 2.12: The dialog box for the *weight cases* command

Entering data using a variable representing the number of cases that fall into a combination of categories can be quite labour saving. However, to analyze data entered in this way we must tell the computer that the variable **frequent** represents the number of cases that fell into a particular combination of categories. Access the *weight cases* function by using the menu path **Data**⇒**Weight Cases ...** to access the dialog box in Figure 2.12. Select the *Weight cases by* option and then select the variable in which the number of cases is specified (in this case **frequent**) and transfer it to the box labelled *Frequency variable* by clicking on ▶. This process tells the computer that it should weight each category combination by the number in the column labelled **frequent**. Therefore, the computer will pretend, for example, that there are 26 rows of data that have the category combination 1, 1, 1 (representing cats trained with food who danced).

2.8.3.   Running the Analysis

Summarizing data that fall into categories is done using the *crosstabs* command (which also produces the chi-square test). *Crosstabs* is in the *Descriptive Statistics* menu (**Analyze⇒Descriptive Statistics⇒Crosstabs…**). To begin with, we are not interested in whether there is a distinction between dogs and cats on the task, we merely want to see whether animals can be trained using the two methods. Figure 2.13 shows the dialog boxes for the *crosstabs* command. First, enter one of the variables of interest in the box labelled *Row(s)* by highlighting it on the left-hand side and transferring it by clicking on ⬛. For this example, I selected **dance** to be the rows of the table. Next, select the other variable of interest (**training**) and transfer it to the box labelled *Column(s)* by clicking on ⬛. In addition, it is possible to select a layer variable (i.e. you can split the rows of the table into further categories). In this case, it would make sense to place **animal** in this box because SPSS would then split the crosstabulation table into a section for dogs and a section for cats. If you click on ⬛ Statistics… a dialog box appears in which you can specify various statistical tests. The options available are:

- **Chi-square:** This performs the basic Pearson chi-square test. The chi-square test detects whether there is a significant association between two categorical variables. However, it does not say anything about how strong that association might be.
- **Phi and Cramer's *V*:** These are measures of the strength of association between two categorical variables. Phi is used with 2×2 contingency tables (tables in which you have two categorical variables and each variable has only two categories). Phi is calculated by taking the chi-square value and dividing it by the sample size and then taking the square root of this value. If one of the two categorical variables contains more than two categories then Cramer's *V* is preferred to phi because phi fails to reach its maximum value of zero (indicating no association) in these circumstances.
- **Lambda:** Goodman and Kruskal's λ measures the proportional reduction in error that is achieved when membership of a category of one variable is used to predict category membership on the other variable. A value of 1 means that one variable perfectly predicts the other whereas a value of 0 indicates that one variable in no way predicts the other.
- **Kendall's statistic:** This statistic is discussed in section 3.2.3.5.

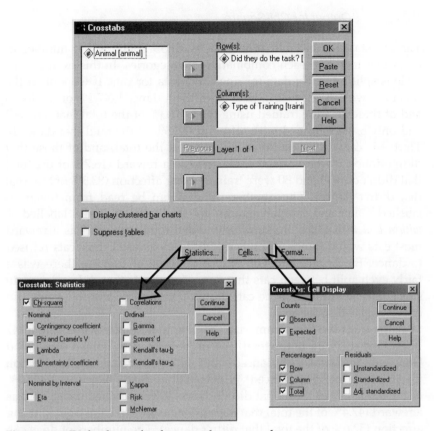

Figure 2.13: Dialog boxes for the *crosstabs* command

These are the most important options under the statistics menu for categorical data. Select the chi-square test, the continuity correction, phi and lambda and then click on Continue. If you click on Cells... a dialog box appears in which you can specify the type of data displayed in the crosstabulation table. It is important that you ask for expected counts because for chi-square to be accurate these expected counts must exceed certain values. The basic rule of thumb is that with 2 × 2 contingency tables no expected values should be below 5. In larger tables the rule is that all expected counts should be greater than 1 and no more than 20% of expected counts should be less than 5. It is also useful to have a look at the row, column and total percentages because these values are usually more easily interpreted than the actual frequencies and provide some idea of the origin of any significant effects. Once these options have been selected click on Continue to return to the main dialog box and then click OK to run the analysis.

2.8.4.   Output for Chi-Square

The crosstabulation table produced by SPSS contains the number of cases that falls into each combination of categories. In this example the table is split into two: data for dogs and data for cats. If we look at the cats first, we can see that in total 32 of them danced (47.1% of the total) and of these 26 were trained using food (81.3% of the total that danced) and only 6 were trained with affection (18.8% of the total that danced). Thirty-six cats didn't dance at all (52.9% of the total) and of those that didn't dance, 6 were trained using food as a reward (16.7% of the total that didn't dance) and 30 were trained using affection (83.3% of the total that didn't dance). The numbers of cats can be read from the rows labelled *Count* and the percentages are read from the rows labelled *% within Did they dance?* In summary, when food was used as a reward most cats would dance, but when affection was used most cats refused to dance. Furthermore, if you ignore the type of training there was a fairly even split between cats that danced and cats that didn't dance. In short, only about half of the cats would dance at all and those that did dance only did so for food.

For the dogs we can summarize the data in a similar way. In total 47 dogs danced (71.2% of the total) and of these 23 were trained using food (48.9% of the total that danced) and 24 were trained with affection (51.1% of the total that danced). Nineteen dogs didn't dance at all (28.8% of the total) and of those that didn't dance, 9 were trained using food as a reward (47.4% of the total that didn't dance) and 10 were trained using affection (52.6% of the total that didn't dance). The numbers of dogs can be read from the rows labelled *Count* and the percentages are read from the rows labelled *% within Did they dance?* In summary, a lot more dogs danced (71.2%) than didn't (28.8%). In both categories about half were trained with affection and half with food as a reward. In short, dogs seem more willing to dance, and they don't mind what training method is used.

Before moving on to look at the test statistics it is vital that we check that the assumption for chi-square has been met. The assumption is that in 2 × 2 tables (which is what we have here), all expected counts should be greater than 5. If you look at the expected counts in the crosstabulation table, it should be clear that the smallest expected count is 9.2 (for dogs who were trained with food but didn't dance). This value still exceeds 5 and so the assumption has been met. If you found an expected count lower than 5 the only remedy is to collect more data to try to boost the proportion of cases falling into each category.

Did they dance? * Type of Training * Animal Crosstabulation

Animal					Type of Training		Total
					Food as Reward	Affection as Reward	
Cat	Did they dance?	Yes	Count		26	6	32
			Expected Count		15.1	16.9	32.0
			% within Did they dance?		81.3%	18.8%	100.0%
			% within Type of Training		81.3%	16.7%	47.1%
			% of Total		38.2%	8.8%	47.1%
		No	Count		6	30	36
			Expected Count		16.9	19.1	36.0
			% within Did they dance?		16.7%	83.3%	100.0%
			% within Type of Training		18.8%	83.3%	52.9%
			% of Total		8.8%	44.1%	52.9%
	Total		Count		32	36	68
			Expected Count		32.0	36.0	68.0
			% within Did they dance?		47.1%	52.9%	100.0%
			% within Type of Training		100.0%	100.0%	100.0%
			% of Total		47.1%	52.9%	100.0%
Dog	Did they dance?	Yes	Count		23	24	47
			Expected Count		22.8	24.2	47.0
			% within Did they dance?		48.9%	51.1%	100.0%
			% within Type of Training		71.9%	70.6%	71.2%
			% of Total		34.8%	36.4%	71.2%
		No	Count		9	10	19
			Expected Count		9.2	9.8	19.0
			% within Did they dance?		47.4%	52.6%	100.0%
			% within Type of Training		28.1%	29.4%	28.8%
			% of Total		13.6%	15.2%	28.8%
	Total		Count		32	34	66
			Expected Count		32.0	34.0	66.0
			% within Did they dance?		48.5%	51.5%	100.0%
			% within Type of Training		100.0%	100.0%	100.0%
			% of Total		48.5%	51.5%	100.0%

SPSS Output 2.7

We can test these patterns in the data by using a chi-square test. This test examines whether there is an association between two categorical variables (in this case the type of training and whether the animal danced or not). As part of the *crosstabs* procedure SPSS produces a table that includes the chi-square statistic and its significance value. The Pearson chi-square statistic tests whether the two variables are independent. If the significance value is small enough (conventionally *Sig.* must be less than 0.05) then we reject the hypothesis that the variables are independent and accept the hypothesis that they are in some way related. The value of the chi-square statistic is given in the table (and the degrees of freedom) as is the significance value for both the cat and dog data. For the cats, the chi-square is highly significant ($p < 0.001$), indicating that the type of training used had a significant effect on whether an animal would dance. A series of other statistics are also included in the table (many of which have to be specifically requested using the options in the dialog box in Figure 2.13).

- **Continuity correction**: Yates' continuity corrected chi-square is designed for situations in which you have two categorical variables, both containing two categories (as is the situation here). There is still some debate as to whether or not this correction is even accurate, let alone necessary, and so I recommend you ignore it (Howell, 1997 provides an excellent discussion of the problem with Yates' correction for continuity).
- **Likelihood ratio**: For large samples this statistic will be the same as Pearson's chi-square. Although this statistic tells us much the same as Pearson's chi-square its calculation is based on maximum-likelihood theory. The general idea behind this theory is that you collect some data and create a model for which the probability of obtaining the observed set of data is maximized, then compare this model to the probability of obtaining those data under the null hypothesis. This statistic should be used when there are small samples.

Underneath this table there are several footnotes relating to the assumption that expected counts should be greater than 5. If you forgot to check this assumption yourself, SPSS kindly gives a summary of the number of expected counts below 5. In this case, there were no expected frequencies less than 5 for either dogs or cats and so we know that the chi-square statistic should be accurate.

For the cats, the highly significant result indicates that there is an association between the type of training and whether the cat danced or not. What we mean by an association is that the pattern of responses (i.e. the proportion of cats that danced to the proportion that did not) in the two training conditions is significantly different. This significant finding reflects the fact that when food is used as a reward, about 80% of cats learn to dance and 20% do not, whereas when affection is used, the opposite is true (about 80% refuse to dance and 20% do dance). For the dogs, there is no such significant result (in fact, this finding is so non-significant that the probability of the chi-square statistic being a chance result is almost 1). This finding reflects the fact that the pattern of responses for the dogs was identical in the two training conditions. Figure 2.14 highlights these differences: the pattern of dancing behaviour in the two training conditions is opposite for cats, but identical in dogs. Therefore, we can conclude that the type of training offered to them significantly influences the cats: they will dance for food but not for love! The type of training, on the other hand, does not influence dogs: they will dance for food and affection. Having lived with a lovely cat for a few years now, this supports my cynical view that they will do nothing unless there is a bowl of cat-food waiting for them at the end of it!

Chi-Square Tests

Animal		Value	df	Asymp. Sig. (2-sided)	Exact Sig. (2-sided)	Exact Sig. (1-sided)
Cat	Pearson Chi-Square	28.363[b]	1	.000		
	Continuity Correction[a]	25.830	1	.000		
	Likelihood Ratio	30.707	1	.000		
	Fisher's Exact Test				.000	.000
	Linear-by-Linear Association	27.946	1	.000		
	N of Valid Cases	68				
Dog	Pearson Chi-Square	.013[c]	1	.908		
	Continuity Correction[a]	.000	1	1.000		
	Likelihood Ratio	.013	1	.908		
	Fisher's Exact Test				1.000	.563
	Linear-by-Linear Association	.013	1	.909		
	N of Valid Cases	66				

a. Computed only for a 2x2 table

b. 0 cells (.0%) have expected count less than 5. The minimum expected count is 15.06.

c. 0 cells (.0%) have expected count less than 5. The minimum expected count is 9.21.

SPSS Output 2.8

If requested, SPSS will produce another table of output containing some additional statistical tests. Most of these tests are measures of the strength of association. These measures are based on modifying the chi-square statistic to take account of sample size and degrees of freedom and they try to restrict the range of the test statistic from 0 to 1 (to make them similar to the correlation coefficient described in Chapter 3).

- **Phi**: This statistic is accurate for 2×2 contingency tables. However, for tables with greater than two dimensions the value of phi may not lie between 0 and 1 because the chi-square value can exceed the sample size. Therefore, Pearson suggested the use of the coefficient of contingency.
- **Contingency coefficient**: This coefficient ensures a value between 0 and 1 but, unfortunately, it seldom reaches its upper limit of 1 and for this reason Cramer devised Cramer's *V*.
- **Cramer's *V***: When both variables have only two categories, phi and Cramer's *V* are identical. However, when variables have more than two categories Cramer's statistic can attain its maximum of one— unlike the other two— and so it is the most useful.

For the cats, Cramer's statistic is 0.646 out of a possible maximum value of 1. This represents quite a strong association between the type of training and whether the cats danced or not. This value is highly significant ($p < 0.001$) indicating that a value of the test statistic that is this big is unlikely to have happened by chance, and therefore the strength of the relationship is significant. For the dogs, Cramer's statistic is 0.014, which is very close to the lower limit of 0. This indicates that the association between these variables is extremely weak for dogs. The probability that this value is a chance result is 0.908 (which is very close to 1, which would represent complete certainty that the value occurred by chance). These results confirm what the chi-square test already told us: the type of training used is significantly related to whether an animal will line dance or not for cats, but this is not true for dogs.

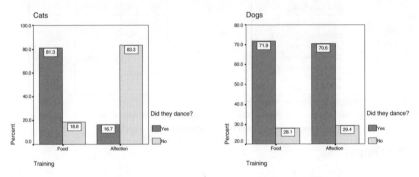

Figure 2.14

Symmetric Measures

Animal			Value	Approx. Sig.
Cat	Nominal by Nominal	Phi	.646	.000
		Cramer's V	.646	.000
		Contingency Coefficient	.543	.000
	N of Valid Cases		68	
Dog	Nominal by Nominal	Phi	.014	.908
		Cramer's V	.014	.908
		Contingency Coefficient	.014	.908
	N of Valid Cases		66	

a. Not assuming the null hypothesis.

b. Using the asymptotic standard error assuming the null hypothesis.

SPSS Output 2.9

2.8.5.   *Words of Warning*

Just to recap some important points about the chi-square test. The chi-square test is a non-parametric test; however, it is not an assumption-free test. For the test to be meaningful it is imperative that each person or case contributes to only one cell of the contingency table. Therefore, you cannot use a chi-square test on a repeated measures design (for example if we had trained some cats with food to see if they would dance and then trained the same cats with affection to see if they would dance). A second important point is that the expected frequencies should be greater than 5. Although it is acceptable in larger contingency tables to have up to 20% of expected frequencies below 5, the result is a loss of statistical power (so, the test may fail to detect a genuine effect). Even in larger contingency tables no expected frequencies should be below 1. Finally, proportionately small differences in cell frequencies can result in statistically significant associations between variables. Therefore, we must look at row and column percentages to interpret any effects we get. These percentages will reflect the patterns of data far better than the frequencies themselves (because these frequencies will be dependent on the sample sizes in different categories).

2.9.   Further Reading

For SPSS:

Foster, J. J. (1998). *Data analysis using SPSS for Windows: a beginner's guide*. London: Sage.

Kinnear, P. R. & Gray, C. D. (1997). *SPSS for Windows made simple* (2nd edition). Hove: Psychology Press.

For Theory:

Siegel, S. & Castellan, N. J. (1988). *Nonparametric statistics for the behavioral sciences* (2nd edition). New York: McGraw-Hill. This text is the most comprehensive but is not for the faint-hearted.

Wright, D. B. (1997). *Understanding statistics: an introduction for the social sciences*. London: Sage.

Relationships

3 Correlation

3.1.   Introduction

It is often interesting for researchers to know what relationship exists, if any, between two or more variables. A correlation is a measure of the linear relationship between variables. For example, I might be interested in whether there is a relationship between the amount of time spent reading this book, and the reader's understanding of SPSS. There are a number of ways in which these two variables could be related: (1) they could be *positively related*, which would mean that the more time the reader spent reading this book, the better their understanding of SPSS; (2) they could be not related at all, which would mean that a reader's understanding of SPSS remained the same regardless of how much time they spend reading this book; or (3) they could be *negatively related*, which would mean that the more a person reads this book, the worse their understanding of SPSS gets. How can we tell if two variables are related?

3.1.1.   *A Detour into the World of Covariance*

The simplest way to look at whether two variables are associated is to look at whether they *covary*. To understand what covariance is, we first need to think back to the concept of variance that we met in Chapter 1. Remember that the variance of a single variable represents the average amount that the data vary from the mean. Numerically, it is described by equation (3.1).

$$\text{Variance}(s^2) = \frac{\sum(x_i - \bar{x})^2}{N-1} = \frac{\sum(x_i - \bar{x})(x_i - \bar{x})}{N-1} \tag{3.1}$$

The mean of the sample is represented by $\bar{x}$, x_i is the data point in question and N is the number of observations (see section 1.1.3.1). If we are interested in whether two variables are related, then we are interested in whether changes in one variable are met with similar changes in the other variable. Therefore, when one variable deviates from its mean we would expect the other variable to deviate from its mean in a similar way. To illustrate what I mean, imagine we took five people and subjected them to a certain number of advertisements promoting toffee sweets, and then measured how many packets of those sweets each person bought during the next week. The data are in Table 3.1.

Table 3.1

Subject:	1	2	3	4	5	**Mean**
Adverts Watched	5	4	4	6	8	**5.4**
Packets Bought	8	9	10	13	15	**11.0**

If there were a relationship between these two variables, then as one variable deviates from its mean, the other variable should deviate from its mean in the same or the directly opposite way. Figure 3.1 shows the data for each subject (squares represent the number of packets bought and circles represent the number of adverts watched); the dotted line is the average number of packets bought and the dark horizontal line is the average number of adverts watched. The vertical lines represent the differences between the observed values and the mean of the relevant variable. The first thing to notice about Figure 3.1 is that there is a very similar pattern of differences for both variables. For the first three subjects the observed values are below the mean for both variables, for the last two people the observed values are above the mean for both variables. This pattern is indicative of a potential relationship between the two variables (because it seems that if a person's score is below the mean for one variable then their score for the other will also be below the mean).

So, how do we calculate the exact similarity between the pattern of differences of the two variables displayed in Figure 3.1? One possibility is to calculate the total amount of difference but we would have the same problem as in the single variable case (see section 1.1.3.1). Also, by simply adding the differences, we would gain little insight into the *relationship* between the variables. Now, in the single variable case, we squared the differences to eliminate the problem of positive and negative differences cancelling out each other. When there are two variables, rather than squaring each difference, we can multiply the difference for one variable by the corresponding difference for the second variable. If both errors are positive or negative then this will give us a positive value (indicative of the errors being in the same direction), but if one error is positive and one negative then the resulting product will be negative (indicative of the errors being opposite in direction). When we multiply the differences of one variable by the corresponding differences of the second variable, we get what is known as the *cross-product deviations*. As with the variance, if we want an average value of the combined differences for the two variables, we must divide by the number of observations (we actually divide by $N-1$). This averaged sum of combined differences is known as the *covariance*. We can write the covariance in equation form as in equation (3.2)—you will notice that the equation is the same as the equation for variance, except that instead of squaring the differences, we multiply them by the corresponding difference of the second variable. ↗ 2 different variables

$$\text{cov}(x,y) = \frac{\Sigma(x_i - \bar{x})(y_i - \bar{y})}{N-1} \qquad (3.2)$$

For the data in Figure 3.1 we reach the following value:

$$
\begin{aligned}
\text{cov}(x,y) &= \frac{\Sigma(x_i - \bar{x})(y_i - \bar{y})}{N-1} \\
&= \frac{(-0.4)(-3) + (-1.4)(-2) + (-1.4)(-1) + (0.6)(2) + (2.6)(4)}{4} \\
&= \frac{1.2 + 2.8 + 1.4 + 1.2 + 10.4}{4} \\
&= \frac{17}{4} \\
&= 4.25
\end{aligned}
$$

Calculating the covariance is a good way to assess whether two variables are related to each other. A positive covariance indicates that as one variable deviates from the mean, the other variable deviates in the same direction. On the other hand, a negative covariance indicates that as one variable deviates from the mean (e.g. increases), the other deviates from the mean in the opposite direction (e.g. decreases).

There is, however, one problem with covariance as a measure of the relationship between variables and that is that it depends upon the scales of measurement used. So, covariance is not a standardized measure. For example, if we use the data above and assume that they represented two variables measured in miles then the covariance is 4.25 (as calculated above). If we then convert these data into kilometres (by multiplying all values by 1.609) and calculate the covariance again then you should find that it increases to 11. This dependence on the scale of measurement is a problem because it means that we cannot compare covariances in an objective way—so, we cannot say whether a covariance is particularly large or small relative to another data set unless both data sets were measured in the same units.

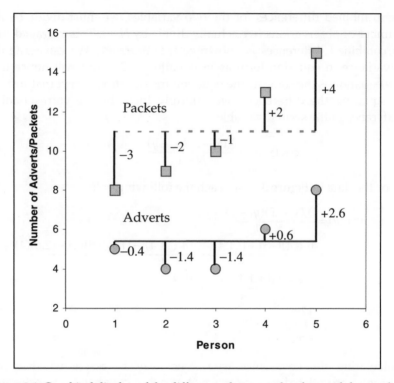

Figure 3.1: Graphical display of the differences between the observed data and the means of two variables

3.1.2.   *Standardization and the Correlation Coefficient*

To overcome the problem of dependence on the measurement scale, we need to convert the covariance into a standard set of units. This process is known as *standardization*. A very basic form of standardization would be to insist that all experiments use the same units of measurement, say, metres—that way, all results could be easily compared. However, what happens if you want to measure attitudes—you'd be hard pushed to measure them in metres! Therefore, we need a unit of measurement into which any scale of measurement can be converted. The unit of measurement we use is the *standard deviation*. We came across this measure in section 1.1.3.1 and saw that, like the variance, it is a measure of the average deviation from the mean. If we divide any distance from the mean by the standard deviation, it gives us that distance in standard deviation units. For example, for the data in Table 3.1, the standard deviation for the number of packets bought is approximately 3.0 (the exact value is 2.91). In Figure 3.1 we can see that the observed value for subject 1 was 3 packets less than the mean (so, there was an error of –3 packets of crisps). The standard deviation is approximately 3, so we can say that that the difference between subject 1's score and the mean was –1 standard deviation. So, we can express the deviation from the mean for a subject in standard units by dividing by the standard deviation.

It follows from this logic that if we want to express the covariance in a standard unit of measurement we can simply divide by the standard deviation. When we calculate the covariance we actually cross-multiply the deviations for two variables and so we must also multiply the standard deviations of the two variables before dividing by this product. The standardized covariance value is known as a correlation coefficient and is defined by equation (3.3) in which s_x is the standard deviation of the first variable and s_y is the standard deviation of the second variable (all other letters are the same as in the equation defining covariance).

$$r = \frac{\text{cov}_{xy}}{s_x s_y} = \frac{\sum(x_i - \bar{x})(y_i - \bar{y})}{(N-1)s_x s_y} \tag{3.3}$$

The coefficient in equation (3.3) is known as the *Pearson product-moment correlation coefficient* and was invented by Pearson (what a surprise!)[1]. By standardizing the covariance we end up with a value that has to lie between –1 and +1 (if you find a correlation coefficient less than –1 or more than +1 you can be sure that something has gone hideously wrong!). A coefficient of +1 indicates that the two variables are perfectly positively correlated, so as one variable increases, the other increases by a proportionate amount. Conversely, a coefficient of –1 indicates a perfect negative relationship: if one variable increases the other decreases by a proportionate amount. A coefficient of zero indicates no linear relationship at all and so if one variable changes the other stays the same. This chapter is concerned with simple correlation techniques and acts as a precursor to the chapter on multiple regression.

3.2.   Conducting a Correlation Analysis on SPSS

3.2.1.   Data Entry

Data entry for correlation, regression and multiple regression is straightforward because each variable is entered in a separate column. So, for each variable you have measured, create a variable in the data editor with an appropriate name, and enter a subject's scores across one row of the data editor. There may be occasions on which you have one or more categorical variables (such as gender) and these variables can

---

[1] You will find Pearson's product-moment correlation coefficient denoted by both r and R. Typically, the upper-case form is used in the context of regression.

also be entered in a column (but remember to define appropriate value labels). As an example, if we wanted to calculate the correlation between the two variables in Table 3.1 we would enter these data as in Figure 3.2. Throughout this chapter we are going to analyze a data set based on undergraduate exam performance. The data for several examples are stored in a single file on the sample disk called **ExamAnx.sav**. If you open this data file you will see that these data are laid out in the data editor as separate columns and that **gender** has been coded appropriately. We will discover to what each of the variables refers as we progress through this chapter.

	adverts	packets	
1	5.00	8.00	
2	4.00	9.00	
3	4.00	10.00	
4	6.00	13.00	
5	8.00	15.00	
6			

Figure 3.2: Data entry for correlation. The data editor tells us that subject 1 was shown 5 adverts and subsequently purchased 8 packets of crisps

3.2.2.   Preliminary Analysis of the Data: the Scatterplot

Before conducting any correlational analysis it is *essential* to plot a scatterplot to look at the general trend of the data. A scatterplot is simply a graph that plots each subject's score on one variable against their score on another (and their score on a third variable can also be included on a 3-D scatterplot). A scatterplot tells us a number of things about the data such as whether there seems to be a relationship between the variables, what kind of relationship it is and whether any cases are markedly different from the others. A case that differs substantially from the general trend of the data is known as an *outlier* and such cases can severely bias the correlation coefficient (see section 4.2.4.1 for more detail). Therefore, we use a scatterplot to show us if any cases look like outliers.

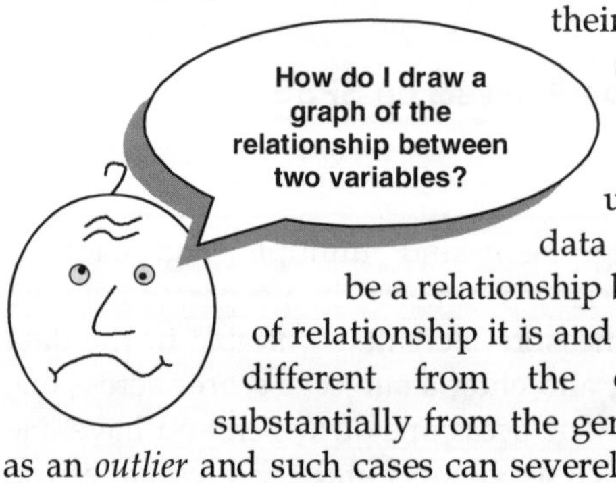

> How do I draw a graph of the relationship between two variables?

Drawing a scatterplot using SPSS is dead easy. Simply use the menus as follows: **Graphs**⇒**Scatter ....** This activates the dialog box in Figure 3.3, which in turn gives you four options for the different types of scatterplot available. By default a simple scatterplot is selected as is shown by the black rim around the picture. If you wish to draw a different scatterplot then move the on-screen arrow over one of the other pictures and click with the left button of the mouse. When you have selected a scatterplot click on Define .

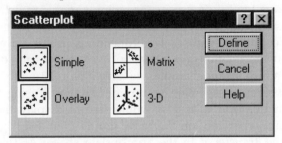

Figure 3.3: Main *scatterplot* dialog box

3.2.2.1. Simple Scatterplot

This type of scatterplot is for looking at just two variables. For example, a psychologist was interested in the effects of exam stress on exam performance. So, she devised and validated a questionnaire to assess state anxiety relating to exams (called the Exam Anxiety Questionnaire, or EAQ). This scale produced a measure of anxiety scored out of 100. Anxiety was measured before an exam, and the percentage mark of each student on the exam was used to assess the exam performance. Before seeing if these variables were correlated, the psychologist would draw a scatterplot of the two variables (her data are in the file **ExamAnx.sav** and you need to have this file loaded into SPSS). To plot these two variables you can leave the default setting of *Simple* in the main *scatterplot* dialog box and click on Define . This process brings up another dialog box, which is shown in Figure 3.4. In this dialog box all of the variables in the data editor are displayed on the left-hand side and there are several empty spaces on the right-hand side. You simply click on a variable from the list on the left and move it to the appropriate box by using one of the ▶ buttons.

- **Y Axis**: Specify the variable that you wish to be plotted on the *Y*-axis (ordinate or vertical axis) of the graph. This variable should be the dependent variable[2], which in this case is **exam** performance. Use the mouse to select **exam** from the list (which will become highlighted) and then click on ▶ to transfer it to the space under the label *Y Axis*.

- **X Axis**: Specify the variable you wish to be plotted on the *X*-axis (abscissa or horizontal axis) of the scatterplot. This variable should be the independent variable, which in this case is **anxiety**. You can highlight this variable and transfer it to the space under the label *X Axis*.

- **Set Markers by**: You can use a grouping variable to define different categories on the scatterplot (it will display each category using a different colour or symbol). This function is useful, for example, for looking at the relationship between two variables for different age groups. In the current example, we have data relating to whether the student was male or female, so it might be worth using the variable **gender** in this option. If you would like to display the male and female data separately on the same graph, then select **gender** from the list and transfer it to the appropriate space. At this stage, the dialog box should look like Figure 3.4.

- **Label Cases by**: If you have a variable that distinguishes each case, then you can use this function to display that label on the scatterplot. So, you could have the subject's name, in which case each point on the scatterplot will be labelled with the name of the subject who contributed that data point. In situations where there are lots of data points this function has limited use.

When you have completed these options you can click on Titles..., which displays a dialog box that gives you space to type in a title for the scatterplot. You can also click on Options..., which allows you decide whether you want to ignore missing values.

---

[2] In experimental research it is customary to plot the independent variable on the horizontal axis and the dependent variable on the vertical axis. In this form of controlled research, the implication is that changes in the independent variable (the variable that the experimenter has manipulated) cause changes in the dependent variable. In correlational research, variables are measured simultaneously and so no cause-and-effect relationship can be established. As such, these terms are used loosely!

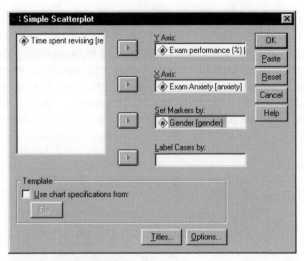

Figure 3.4: Dialog box for a simple scatterplot

The resulting scatterplot is shown in Figure 3.5. The scatterplot on your screen will look slightly different in that the male and female data will be displayed in different colours. Unfortunately this book isn't printed in colour and so I have replaced the male and female markers with different symbols (this also provided the opportunity for me to show off by using gender-appropriate symbols!). The scatterplot shows that the majority of students suffered from high levels of anxiety (there are very few cases that had anxiety levels below 60). Also, there are no obvious outliers in that most points seem to fall within the vicinity of other points. There also seems to be some general trend in the data such that higher levels of anxiety are associated with lower exam scores and low levels of anxiety are almost always associated with high examination marks. The gender markers show that anxiety seems to affect males and females in the same way (because the different symbols are fairly evenly interspersed). Another noticeable trend in these data is that there were no cases having low anxiety and low exam performance—in fact, most of the data are clustered in the upper region of the anxiety scale.

Had there been any data points which obviously didn't fit the general trend of the data then it would be necessary to try to establish if there was a good reason why these subjects responded so differently. Sometimes outliers are just errors of data entry (i.e. you mistyped a value) and so it is wise to double-check the data in the editor window for any case that looks unusual. If an outlier can't be explained by incorrect data entry, then it is important to try to establish whether there might be a third variable affecting this person's score. For example, a student could be experiencing anxiety about something other than the exam and their score on the anxiety questionnaire might have picked up on this anxiety, but it may be specific anxiety about the exam that interferes with performance. Hence, this subject's unrelated anxiety did not affect their performance, but resulted in a high anxiety score. If there is a good reason for a subject responding differently to everyone else then you can consider eliminating that subject from the analysis in the interest of building an accurate model. However, subjects' data should not be eliminated because they don't fit with your hypotheses—only if there is a good explanation of why they behaved so oddly.

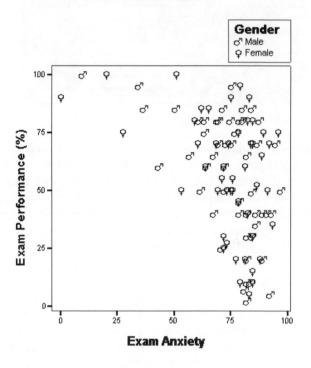

Figure 3.5: Scatterplot of exam performance against exam anxiety

3.2.2.2. Overlay Scatterplot

An overlay scatterplot is one in which several pairs of variables are plotted on the same axes. As an example, imagine our researcher decided that exam anxiety might not be the only factor contributing to exam performance. So, she also asked subjects to keep a revision diary from which she calculated the number of hours spent revising for the exam. She wanted to look at the role of both exam anxiety and revision time on exam performance and, as such, it became useful to plot the relationships between revision time and exam performance and between exam anxiety and performance simultaneously. To get the best use out of this type of scatterplot keep one variable constant and plot it against several others. In the examination example, in which the effect of both anxiety and revision time on exam performance is of interest, you should plot **anxiety** (*X*) against **exam** (*Y*), and then overlay **revise** (*X*) against **exam** performance (*Y*). To plot these combinations, click on *Overlay* in the main *scatterplot* dialog box (see Figure 3.3) and the dialog box in Figure 3.6 appears. To select a pair of variables, click on one variable from the list (this will appear as *Variable 1* in the section labelled *Current Selections*) and then select a second variable (this will be listed as *Variable 2*). Transfer the variable pair by clicking ▶. The pair will appear in the space labelled *Y-X Pairs*. The order of variables relates to the axis on which they will be plotted, so in Figure 3.6 **exam** will appear on the *Y*-axis and **anxiety** on the *X*-axis. The second pairing of **exam** and **revise** should also be transferred to the *Y-X* pair list such that **exam** is listed first (and so is plotted on the *Y*-axis) and **revise** second (so will be plotted on the *X*-axis). If, when you transfer two variables, they appear the wrong way round to how you want to plot them, you can swap the order of variables (and hence the axis on which they will be plotted) by clicking on Swap Pair.

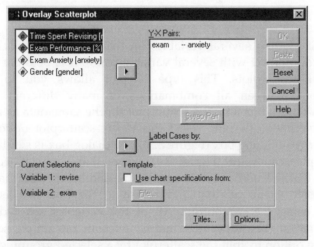

Figure 3.6: Dialog box for creating an overlay scatterplot. The first pair of variables has already been specified and the second pair has been selected but not transferred to the pair list

From Figure 3.7 it is clear that although anxiety is negatively related to exam performance, it looks as though exam performance is positively related to revision time. So, as revision time increases, exam performance increases also, but as anxiety increases, exam performance decreases. The overlay scatterplot clearly shows these different relationships.

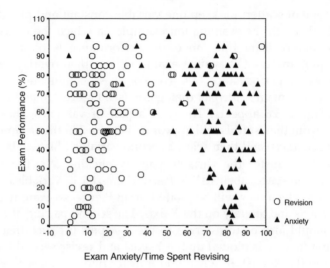

Figure 3.7: Scatterplot of exam scores against both exam anxiety and time spent revising

3.2.2.3. *Matrix Scatterplot*

Instead of plotting several variables on the same axes (which can be difficult to interpret with several variable pairs), it is possible to plot a matrix of scatterplots. This type of plot allows you to see the relationship between all combinations of many different pairs of variables. To conduct a matrix scatterplot for the same data as was used for the overlay scatterplot, select the *Matrix* scatterplot option in the main *scatterplot* dialog box (Figure 3.3). The dialog box is similar to that of a simple scatterplot (Figure 3.4) except that you can list several variables that will all be plotted against one another. For our data, select and transfer **exam**, **anxiety** and **revise** to the box labelled *Matrix Variables* using the ▶ button. All of the variables selected will be plotted against each other in a matrix. As with the simple scatterplot there is an option to split the scatterplot by a selected grouping variable (*Set Markers by* ...) but there is no need to use this option for these data. The resulting scatterplot of exam performance against exam anxiety and revision time is shown in Figure 3.8.

The six scatterplots in Figure 3.8 represent the various combinations of each variable plotted against each other variable. So, the grid references represent the following plots:

- **B1**: exam performance (*Y*) vs. anxiety (*X*)
- **C1**: exam performance (*Y*) vs. revision time (*X*)

- **A2**: anxiety (*Y*) vs. exam performance (*X*)
- **C2**: anxiety (*Y*) vs. revision time (*X*)
- **A3**: revision time (*Y*) vs. exam performance (*X*)
- **B3**: revision time (*Y*) vs. anxiety (*X*)

Thus, the three scatterplots below the diagonal of the matrix are the same plots as the ones above the diagonal but with the axes reversed. From this matrix we can see that revision time and anxiety are inversely related (so, the more time spent revising the less anxiety the subject had about the exam). Also, in the scatterplot of revision time against anxiety (grid C2 and B3) there looks as though there is one possible outlier— there is a single subject who spent very little time revising yet suffered very little anxiety about the exam. As all subjects who had low anxiety scored highly on the exam we can deduce that this person also did well on the exam (wow, don't you just hate a smart aleck!). We could choose to examine this case more closely if we believed that their behaviour was caused by some external factor (such as taking brain-pills!). Matrix scatterplots are very convenient for examining pairs of relationships between variables. However, I don't recommend plotting them for more than three or four variables because they become very confusing indeed!

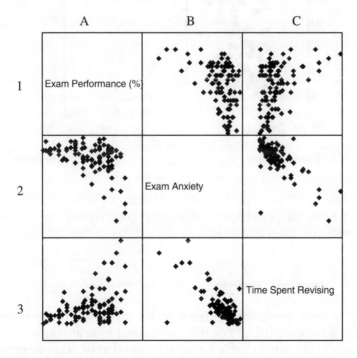

Figure 3.8: Matrix scatterplot of exam performance, exam anxiety and revision time. Grid references have been added for clarity

3.2.2.4. 3-D Scatterplot

A 3-D scatterplot is used to display the relationship between three variables. To create a 3-D scatterplot, select the *3-D* option from the main *scatterplot* dialog box (Figure 3.3). The resulting dialog box is basically the same as that used for a simple scatterplot except that there is room to specify a variable to be plotted on the Z-axis. Using Figure 3.4 as a guide, select **exam** to go on the Y-axis, **anxiety** as the X-axis and **revise** as the Z-axis. The resulting scatterplot is shown in Figure 3.9. 3-D scatterplots can be quite difficult to interpret and so their usefulness in exploring data can be limited; however, they are great for displaying data in a concise way.

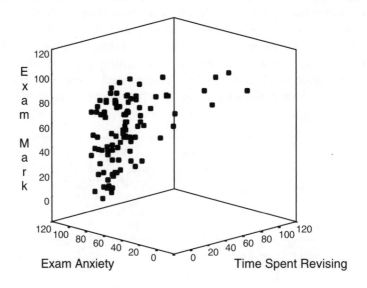

Figure 3.9: 3-D Scatterplot of exam performance plotted against exam anxiety and the amount of time spent revising.

3.2.3.   Bivariate Correlation

Having taken a preliminary glance at the data, we can proceed to conducting the correlation. For this provisional look at correlations we will return to the data in Table 3.1, which looked at whether there was a relationship between the number of adverts watched and the number of packets of toffees subsequently purchased. Create two columns in the data editor and input these data (the lazy among you can access the file **Advert.sav** on the disk).

There are two types of correlation: *bivariate* and *partial*. A bivariate correlation is a correlation between two variables (as described at the beginning of this chapter) whereas a partial correlation looks at the relationship between two variables while 'controlling' the effect of one or more additional variables. Pearson's product-moment correlation coefficient and Spearman's rho should be familiar to most students and are examples of bivariate correlation coefficients. To conduct a bivariate correlation you need to find the *Correlate* option of the *Analyze* menu. The main dialog box is accessed by the menu path **Analyze⇒Correlate⇒Bivariate ...** and is shown in Figure 3.10. Using the dialog box it is possible to select which of three correlation statistics you wish to perform. The default setting is Pearson's product-moment correlation, but you can also calculate Spearman's correlation and Kendall's correlation—we shall see the differences between these correlation coefficients in due course. In addition, it is possible to specify whether or not the test is one- or two-tailed. A one-tailed test should be selected when you have a directional hypothesis (e.g. 'the more adverts a person watches, the more packets of sweets they will have bought'). A two-tailed test (the default) should be used when you cannot predict the nature of the relationship (i.e. 'I'm not sure whether watching more adverts will be associated with an increase or a decrease in the number of packets of sweets a person buys').

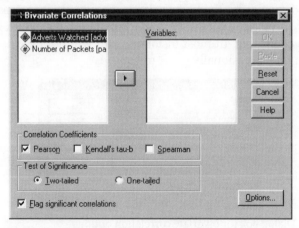

Figure 3.10: Dialog box for conducting a bivariate correlation

Having accessed the main dialog box, you should find that the variables in the data editor are listed on the left-hand side of the dialog box (Figure 3.10). There is an empty box labelled *Variables* on the right-hand side. You can select any variables from the list using the mouse

and transfer them to the *Variables* box by clicking on 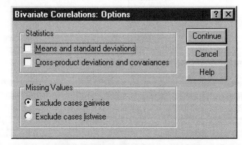. SPSS will create
a table of correlation coefficients for all of the combinations of variables.
This table is called a correlation matrix. For our current example, select
the variables **adverts** and **packets** and transfer them to the variables list.
Having selected the variables of interest you can choose between three
correlation coefficients: Pearson's product-moment correlation
coefficient, Spearman's rho, and Kendall's tau. Any of these can be
selected by clicking on the appropriate tick-box with a mouse.

If you click on 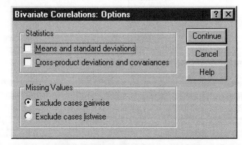 then another dialog box appears with two
Statistics options and two options for missing values (Figure 3.11). The
Statistics options are enabled only when Pearson's correlation is selected;
if Pearson's correlation is not selected then these options are disabled
(they appear in a light grey rather than black and you can't activate
them). This deactivation occurs because these two options are
meaningful only for parametric data and the Pearson correlation is used
with those kinds of data. If you select the tick-box labelled *Means and
standard deviations* then SPSS will produce the mean and standard
deviation of all of the variables selected for correlation. If you activate
the tick-box labelled *Cross-product deviations and covariances* then SPSS
will give you the values of these statistics for each of the variables being
correlated. The cross-product deviations tell us the sum of the products
of mean corrected variables, which is simply the numerator (top half) of
equation (3.2). The covariances option gives us values of the covariance
between variables, which could be calculated manually using equation
(3.2). In other words, these covariance values are the cross-product
deviations divided by (N–1) and represent the unstandardized
correlation coefficient. In most instances, you will not need to use these
options but they occasionally come in handy!

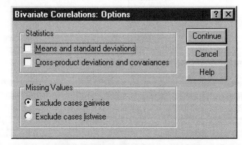

Figure 3.11: Dialog box for bivariate correlation options

To illustrate what these options do, select them for the advert data.
Leave the default options in the main dialog box as they are. The
resulting output from SPSS is shown in SPSS Output 3.1. The section
labelled *Sum of Squares and Cross-products* shows us the cross-product (17
in this example) that we calculated from equation (3.2), and the sums of

squares for each variable. The sums of squares are calculated from the top half of equation (3.1). The value of the covariance between the two variables is 4.25, which is the same value as was calculated from equation (3.2). The covariance within each variable is the same as the variance for each variable (so, the variance for the number of adverts seen is 2.8, and the variance for the number of packets bought is 8.5). These variances can be calculated manually from equation (3.1).

Correlations

		Adverts Watched	Number of Packets
Adverts Watched	Pearson Correlation	1.000	.871
	Sig. (2-tailed)	.	.054
	Sum of Squares and Cross-products	11.200	17.000
	Covariance	2.800	4.250
	N	5	5
Number of Packets	Pearson Correlation	.871	1.000
	Sig. (2-tailed)	.054	.
	Sum of Squares and Cross-products	17.000	34.000
	Covariance	4.250	8.500
	N	5	5

SPSS Output 3.1: Output from the SPSS correlation procedure

3.2.3.1. Pearson's Correlation Coefficient

Pearson's correlation coefficient was described in full at the beginning of this chapter. For those of you unfamiliar with basic statistics, it is not meaningful to talk about means unless we have data measured at an interval or ratio level (for revision see section 2.2 or Wright, 1997). As such, Pearson's coefficient requires parametric data because it is based upon the average deviation from the mean. However, in reality it is an extremely robust statistic. This is perhaps why the default option in SPSS is to use Pearson's method. However, if your data are non-parametric then you should deselect the Pearson tick-box.

Reload the data from the file **ExamAnx.sav** so that we can calculate the correlation between exam performance, revision time and exam anxiety. The data from the exam performance study are parametric and so a Pearson's correlation can be applied. Access the main *bivariate correlations* dialog box (**Analyze⇒Correlate⇒Bivariate ...**) and transfer **exam, anxiety** and **revise** to the box labelled *Variables* (Figure 3.12). The dialog box also allows you to specify whether the test should be one- or two-tailed. One-tailed tests should be used when there is a specific direction to the hypothesis being tested, and two-tailed tests should be used when a relationship is expected, but the direction of the relationship is not predicted. Our researcher predicted that at higher levels of anxiety, exam performance would be poor. Therefore, the test for these variables should be one-tailed because before the data were collected the researcher predicted a specific kind of relationship. What's more, a positive correlation between revision time and exam performance was predicted so this test too should be one-tailed. To ensure that the output displays the one-tailed significance values select ⊙ One-tailed and then click OK .

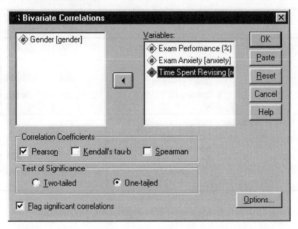

Figure 3.12: Completed dialog box for the exam performance data

SPSS Output 3.2 provides a matrix of the correlation coefficients for the three variables. Underneath each correlation coefficient both the significance value of the correlation and the sample size (N) on which it is based are displayed. Each variable is perfectly correlated with itself (obviously) and so $r = 1$ along the diagonal of the table. Exam performance is negatively related to exam anxiety with a Pearson correlation coefficient of $r = -0.441$ and there is a less than 0.001 probability that a correlation coefficient this big would have occurred by chance in a sample of 103 people (as indicated by the ** after the coefficient). This significance value tells us that the probability of this correlation being a 'fluke' is very low (close to zero in fact). Hence, we can have confidence that the relationship between exam performance and anxiety is genuine. Usually, social scientists accept any probability value below 0.05 as being statistically meaningful and so any probability value below 0.05 is regarded as indicative of genuine effect (and SPSS will mark any correlation coefficient significant at this level with a *). The output also shows that exam performance is positively related to the amount of time spent revising, with a coefficient of $r = 0.397$, which is also significant at $p < 0.001$. Finally, exam anxiety appears to be negatively related to the time spent revising ($r = -0.709, p < 0.001$).

In psychological terms, this all means that as anxiety about an exam increases, the percentage mark obtained in that exam decreases. Conversely, as the amount of time revising increases, the percentage obtained in the exam increases. Finally, as revision time increases the student's anxiety about the exam decreases. So there is a complex interrelationship between the three variables.

Correlations

		Exam performance (%)	Exam Anxiety	Time spent revising
Exam performance (%)	Pearson Correlation	1.000	-.441**	.397**
	Sig. (1-tailed)	.	.000	.000
	N	103	103	103
Exam Anxiety	Pearson Correlation	-.441**	1.000	-.709**
	Sig. (1-tailed)	.000	.	.000
	N	103	103	103
Time spent revising	Pearson Correlation	.397**	-.709**	1.000
	Sig. (1-tailed)	.000	.000	.
	N	103	103	103

**. Correlation is significant at the 0.01 level (1-tailed).

SPSS Output 3.2: Output from SPSS 9.0 for a Pearson's correlation

3.2.3.2. A Word of Warning about Interpretation: Causality

A considerable amount of caution must be taken when interpreting correlation coefficients because they give no indication of the direction of *causality*. So, in our example, although we can conclude that exam performance goes down as anxiety about that exam goes up, we cannot say that high exam anxiety *causes* bad exam performance. This caution is for two reasons:

• **The third variable problem**: In any bivariate correlation causality between two variables cannot be assumed because there may be other measured or unmeasured variables affecting the results. This is known as the *third variable* problem or the *tertium quid*. In our example you can see that revision time does relate significantly to both exam performance and exam anxiety and there is no way of telling which of the two independent variables, if either, are causing exam performance to change. So, if we had measured only exam anxiety and exam performance we might have assumed that high exam anxiety caused poor exam performance. However, it is clear that poor exam performance could be explained equally well by a lack of revision. There may be several additional variables that influence the correlated variables and these variables may not have been measured by the researcher. So, there could be another, unmeasured, variable that affects both revision time and exam anxiety.

- **Direction of causality**: Correlation coefficients say nothing about which variable causes the other to change. Even if we could ignore the third variable problem described above, and we could assume that the two correlated variables were the only important ones, the correlation coefficient doesn't indicate in which direction causality operates. So, although it is intuitively appealing to conclude that exam anxiety causes exam performance to change, there is no *statistical* reason why exam performance cannot cause exam anxiety to change. Although the latter conclusion makes no human sense (because anxiety was measured before exam performance), the correlation does not tell us that it isn't true.

3.2.3.3.   Using R^2 for Interpretation

Although we cannot make direct conclusions about causality, we can take the correlation coefficient a step further by squaring it. The correlation coefficient squared (R^2) is a measure of the amount of variability in one variable that is explained by the other. For example, we may look at the relationship between exam anxiety and exam performance. Exam performances vary from subject to subject because of any number of factors (different ability, different levels of preparation and so on). If we add up all of this variability (rather like when we calculated the sum of squares in section 1.1.3.1) then we would have an estimate of how much variability exists in exam performances. We can then use R^2 to tell us how much of this variability is accounted for by exam anxiety. These two variables had a correlation of -0.4410 and so the value of R^2 will be $(-0.4410)^2 = 0.194$. This value tells us how much of the variability in exam performance can be explained by exam anxiety. If we convert this value into a percentage (multiply by 100) we can say that exam anxiety accounts for 19.4% of the variability in exam performance. So, although exam anxiety was highly correlated to exam performance, it can account for only 19.4% of variation in exam scores. To put this value into perspective, this leaves 80.6% of the variability still to be accounted for by other variables. I should note at this point that although R^2 is an extremely useful measure of the substantive importance of an effect, it cannot be used to infer causal relationships. Although we usually talk in terms of 'the variance in y accounted for by x' or even the variation in one variable explained by the other, this still says nothing of which way causality runs. So, although exam anxiety can account for 19.4% of the variation in exam scores, it does not necessarily cause this variation.

3.2.3.4. *Spearman's Rho*

Spearman's correlation coefficient is a non-parametric statistic and so can be used when the data have violated parametric assumptions and/or the distributional assumptions (see section 2.2). Spearman's tests works by first ranking the data, and then applying Pearson's equation (equation (3.3)) to those ranks. As a statistics lecturer I am always interested in the factors that determine whether a student will do well on a statistics course. One potentially important factor is their previous expertise with mathematics (at the very least past experience will determine whether an equation makes sense!). Imagine I took 25 students and looked at their degree grades for the statistics course at the end of their first year at university. In the UK, a student can get a first class mark, an upper second class mark, a lower second, a third, a pass or a fail. These grades are categories, but they have an order to them (an upper second is better than a lower second). I could also ask these students what grade they got in their GCSE maths exams. In the UK GCSEs are school exams taken at age 16 that are graded A, B, C, D, E or F. Again, these grades are categories that have an order of importance (an A grade is better than all of the lower grades). When you have categories like these that can be ordered in a meaningful way, the data are said to be *ordinal*. The data are not interval, because the difference between a pass mark and a third is very different from the difference between an upper second and a first. When data have been measured at only the ordinal level they are said to be non-parametric and Pearson's correlation is not appropriate. Therefore, the Spearman correlation coefficient is used. The data for this study are in the file **grades.sav**. The data are in two columns: one labelled **stats** and one labelled **gcse**. Each of the categories described above has been coded with a numeric value. In both cases, the highest grade (first class or A grade) has been coded with the value 1, with subsequent categories being labelled 2, 3 and so on. Note that for each numeric code I have provided a value label (just like we did for coding variables).

The procedure for doing the Spearman correlation is the same as for the Pearson's correlation except that in the *bivariate correlations* dialog box (Figure 3.12), we need to select ☑ Spearman and deselect the option for a Pearson correlation. At this stage, you should also specify whether you require a one- or two-tailed test. For the example above, I predicted that better grades in GCSE maths would correlate with better degree grades for my statistics course. This hypothesis is directional and so a one-tailed test should be selected.

SPSS Output 3.3 shows the output for a Spearman correlation on the variables **stats** and **gcse**. The output is very similar to that of the Pearson correlation: a matrix is displayed giving the correlation coefficient between the two variables (0.455), underneath is the significance value of this coefficient (0.011) and finally the sample size (25). The significance value for this correlation coefficient is less than 0.05; therefore, it can be concluded that there is a significant relationship between a student's grade in GCSE maths and their degree grade for their statistics course. The correlation itself is positive: therefore, we can conclude that as GCSE grades improve, there is a corresponding improvement in degree grades for statistics. As such, the hypothesis was supported. Finally, it is good to check that the value of N corresponds to the number of observations that were made. If it doesn't then data may have been excluded for some reason.

Correlations

			Statistics Grade	GCSE Maths Grade
Spearman's rho	Statistics Grade	Correlation Coefficient	1.000	.455*
		Sig. (1-tailed)	.	.011
		N	25	25
	GCSE Maths Grade	Correlation Coefficient	.455*	1.000
		Sig. (1-tailed)	.011	.
		N	25	25

*. Correlation is significant at the .05 level (1-tailed).

SPSS Output 3.3: Output from SPSS 9.0 for a Spearman correlation

3.2.3.5.   *Kendall's Tau (Non-Parametric)*

Kendall's tau is another non-parametric correlation and it should be used rather than Spearman's coefficient when you have a small data set with a large number of tied ranks. This means that if you rank all of the scores and many scores have the same rank, the Kendall's tau should be used. Although Spearman's statistic is the more popular of the two coefficients, there is much to suggest that Kendall's statistic is actually a better estimate of the correlation in the population (see Howell, 1997, p. 293). As such, we can draw more accurate generalizations from Kendall's statistic than from Spearman's. To carry out Kendall's correlation on the statistics degree grades data simply follow the same steps as for the Pearson and Spearman correlation but select ☑ Kendall's tau-b and deselect the Pearson option. The output is much the same as for Spearman's correlation.

You'll notice from SPSS Output 3.4 that the actual value of the correlation coefficient is less than the Spearman correlation (it has decreased from 0.455 to 0.354). Despite the difference in the correlation coefficients we can still interpret this result as being a highly significant positive relationship (because the significance value of 0.015 is less than 0.05). However, Kendall's value is a more accurate gauge of what the correlation in the population would be. As with the Pearson correlation we cannot assume that the GCSE grades caused the degree students to do better in their statistics course.

Correlations

			Statistics Grade	GCSE Maths Grade
Kendall's tau_b	Statistics Grade	Correlation Coefficient	1.000	.354*
		Sig. (1-tailed)	.	.015
		N	25	25
	GCSE Maths Grade	Correlation Coefficient	.354*	1.000
		Sig. (1-tailed)	.015	.
		N	25	25

*. Correlation is significant at the .05 level (1-tailed).

SPSS Output 3.4: Output from SPSS 9.0 for Kendall's tau

3.2.3.6. Biserial and Point-Biserial Correlations

The biserial and point-biserial correlation coefficients are distinguished by only a conceptual difference yet their statistical calculation is quite different. These correlation coefficients are used when one of the two variables is dichotomous (that is, it is categorical with only two categories). An example of a dichotomous variable is being pregnant because a woman can be either pregnant or not (they cannot be 'a bit pregnant'). Often it is necessary to investigate relationships between two variables when one of the variables is dichotomous. The difference between the use of biserial and point-biserial correlations depends on whether the dichotomous variable is discrete or continuous. This difference is very subtle. A discrete, or true, dichotomy is one for which there is no underlying continuum between the categories. An example of this is whether someone is dead or alive: a person can be only dead or alive, they can't be 'a bit dead'. Although you might describe a person as being 'half-dead'— especially after a heavy drinking session—they are clearly still alive if they are still breathing! Therefore, there is no continuum between the two categories. However, it is possible to have a dichotomy for which a continuum does exist. An example is passing or failing a statistics test: some people will only just fail whilst others will fail by a large margin, likewise some people will scrape a pass whilst others clearly excel. So although subjects fall into only two categories there is clearly an underlying continuum along which people lie. Hopefully, it is clear that in this case there is some kind of continuum underlying the dichotomy, because some people passed or failed more dramatically than others. *The point-biserial correlation coefficient (r_{pb}) is used when one variable is a discrete dichotomy, whereas the biserial correlation coefficient (r_b) is used when one variable is a continuous dichotomy.* The biserial correlation coefficient cannot be calculated directly in SPSS: first you must calculate the point-biserial correlation coefficient and then use an equation to adjust that figure.

Imagine that I was interested in the relationship between the gender of a cat, and how much time they spent away from home (what can I say, I love cats so these things interest me). I had heard that male cats disappeared for substantial amounts of time on long distance roams around the neighbourhood (something about hormones driving them to find mates) whereas female cats tended to be more homebound. So, I used this as a purr-fect (sorry!) excuse to go and visit lots of my friends and their cats. I took a note of the gender of the cat and then asked the owners to note down the number of hours that their cat was absent from home over a week. Clearly one variable is parametric (the time spent away from home), whilst the other is dichotomous (gender of the cat: male or female). A point-biserial correlation has to be calculated and this is simply a Pearson correlation when the dichotomous variable is coded with different values. So, to conduct these correlations in SPSS assign the **gender** variable a coding scheme as described in section 1.2.3.1 (in the saved data the coding is 1 for a male and 0 for a female). The **time** variable simply has time in hours recorded as normal. These data are in the file **pbcorr.sav**. Carry out a Pearson's correlation (as in 3.2.3.1).

Correlations

		Time away from home (hours)	Gender of cat
Time Away from Home (Hours)	Pearson Correlation	1.000	.378*
	Sig. (1-tailed)	.	.001
	N	60	60
Gender of Cat	Pearson Correlation	.378**	1.000
	Sig. (1-tailed)	.001	.
	N	60	60

** . Correlation is significant at the 0.01 level (1-tailed).

SPSS Output 3.5: Output from SPSS 9.0 for the point-biserial correlation

SPSS Output 3.5 shows the correlation matrix of **time** and **gender**. The point-biserial correlation coefficient is $r_{pb} = 0.378$, which has a one-tailed significance value of 0.001. The significance test for this correlation is actually the same as performing an independent samples *t*-test on the data (see Chapter 6). The sign of the correlation (i.e. whether the relationship was positive or negative) will depend entirely on which way round the coding of the dichotomous variable was made. To prove that this is the case, the data file **pbcorr.sav** has an extra variable called **recode** which is the same as the variable **gender** except that the coding is reversed (1 = female, 0 = male). If you repeat the Pearson correlation using **recode** instead of **gender** you will find that the correlation coefficient becomes –0.378. The sign of the coefficient is completely dependent on which category you assign to which code and so we must ignore all information about the direction of the relationship. However, we can still interpret R^2 as before. So in this example, $R^2 = (0.378)^2 = 0.143$. Hence, we can conclude that gender accounts for 14.3% of the variability in time spent away from home.

Imagine now that we wanted to convert the point-biserial correlation into the biserial correlation coefficient (r_b) (because some of the male cats were neutered and so there might be a continuum of maleness that underlies the gender variable). We must use equation (3.4) in which P_1 is the proportion of cases that fell into category 1 (the number of male cats) and P_2 is the proportion of cases that fell into category 2 (the number of female cats). In this equation y is the ordinate of the normal distribution at the point where there is $P_1\%$ of the area on one side and $P_2\%$ on the other (this will become clearer as we do an example).

$$r_b = \frac{r_{pb}\sqrt{(P_1 P_2)}}{y} \tag{3.4}$$

To calculate P_1 and P_2 simply use the menus: **Analyze**⇒**Descriptive Statistics**⇒**Frequencies** and select the variable **gender**. There is no need to click on any further options as the defaults will give you what you need to know (namely the percentage of male and female cats). It turns out that 53.3% (0.533 as a proportion) of the sample were female (this is P_2) whilst the remaining 46.7% (0.467 as a proportion) were male (this is P_1). To calculate y, we use these values and the values of the normal distribution displayed in appendix 12.1. Find the ordinate when the normal curve is split with 0.467 as the smaller portion and 0.533 as the larger portion (in actual fact we will have to use the nearest values to those, which are 0.4681 and 0.5319 respectively). The ordinate value is 0.3977. If we replace these values into equation (3.4) we get 0.475 (see below), which is quite a lot higher than the value of the point-biserial correlation (0.378). Therefore, the choice of correlation coefficient can make a substantial difference to the result. You should, therefore, be careful to decide whether your dichotomous variable has an underlying continuum, or whether it is a truly discrete variable.

$$r_b = \frac{r_{pb}\sqrt{(p_1 p_2)}}{y}$$

$$= \frac{(0.378)\sqrt{(0.533 \times 0.467)}}{0.3977}$$

$$= 0.475$$

3.2.4.   Partial Correlation

3.2.4.1.   The Theory behind Part and Partial Correlation

I mentioned earlier that there is a type of correlation that can be done that allows you to look at the relationship between two variables when the effects of a third variable are held constant. For example, analyses of the exam anxiety data (in the file **ExamAnx.sav**) showed that exam performance was negatively related to exam anxiety, but positively related to revision time, and revision time itself was negatively related to exam anxiety. This scenario is complex, but given that we know that revision time is related to both exam anxiety and exam performance, then if we want a pure measure of the relationship between exam anxiety and exam performance we need to take account of the influence of revision time. Using the values of R^2 for these relationships, we know that exam anxiety accounts for 19.4% of the variance in exam performance, that revision time accounts for 15.7% of the variance in exam performance, and that revision time accounts for 50.2% of the variance in exam anxiety. If revision time accounts for half of the variance in exam anxiety, then it seems feasible that at least some of the 19.4% of variance in exam performance that is accounted for by anxiety is the same variance that is accounted for by revision time. As such, some of the variance in exam performance explained by exam anxiety is not *unique* and can be accounted for by revision time. A correlation between two variables in which the effects of other variables are held constant is known as a partial correlation.

Figure 3.13 illustrates the principle behind partial correlation. In part 1 of the diagram there is a box labelled exam performance that represents the total variation in exam scores (this value would be the variance of exam performance). There is also a box that represents the variation in exam anxiety (again, this is the variance of that variable). We know already that exam anxiety and exam performance share 19.4% of their variation (this value is the correlation coefficient squared). Therefore, the variations of these two variables overlap (because they share variance) creating a third box (the one with diagonal lines). The overlap of the boxes representing exam performance and exam anxiety is the common variance. Likewise, in part 2 of the diagram the shared variation between exam performance and revision time is illustrated. Revision time shares 15.7% of the variation in exam scores. This shared variation is represented by the area of overlap (filled with diagonal lines). We know that revision time and exam anxiety also share 50% of their variation: therefore, it is very probable that some of the variation in exam performance shared by exam anxiety is the same as the variance shared by revision time.

Part 3 of the diagram shows the complete picture. The first thing to note is that the boxes representing exam anxiety and revision time have a large overlap (this is because they share 50% of their variation). More important, when we look at how revision time and anxiety contribute to exam performance we see that there is a portion of exam performance that is shared by both anxiety and revision time (the dotted area). However, there are still small chunks of the variance in exam performance that are unique to the other two variables. So, although in part 1 exam anxiety shared a large chunk of variation in exam performance, some of this overlap is also shared by revision time. If we remove the portion of variation that is also shared by revision time, we get a measure of the unique relationship between exam performance and exam anxiety. We use partial correlations to find out the size of the unique portion of variance. Therefore, we could conduct a partial correlation between exam anxiety and exam performance while 'controlling' the effect of revision time. Likewise, we could carry out a partial correlation between revision time and exam performance 'controlling' for the effects of exam anxiety.

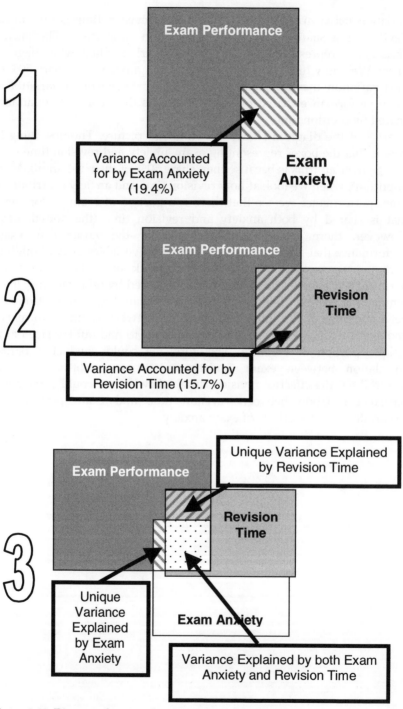

Figure 3.13: Diagram showing the principle of partial correlation

3.2.4.2. Partial Correlation Using SPSS

To conduct a partial correlation on the exam performance data select the *Correlate* option from the *Analyze* menu and then select *Partial* (**Analyze⇒Correlate⇒Partial**) and the dialog box in Figure 3.14 will be activated. This dialog box lists all of the variables in the data editor on the left-hand side and there are two empty spaces on the right-hand side. The first space is for listing the variables that you want to correlate and the second is for declaring any variables the effects of which you want to control. In the example I have described, we want to look at the unique effect of exam anxiety on exam performance and so we want to correlate the variables **exam** and **anxiety**, while controlling for **revise**. Figure 3.14 shows the completed dialog box. If you click on <u>Options...</u> then another dialog box appears as shown in Figure 3.15.

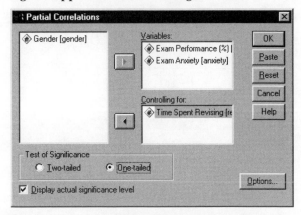

Figure 3.14: Main dialog box for conducting a partial correlation

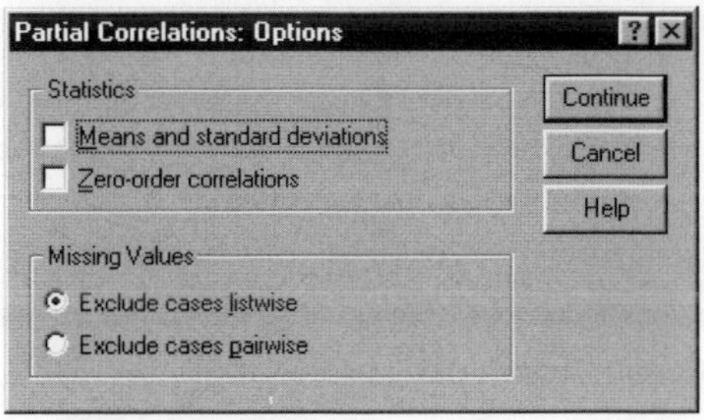

Figure 3.15: Options for partial correlation

These further options are similar to those in bivariate correlation except that you can choose to display zero-order correlations. Zero-order correlations are the bivariate correlation coefficients without controlling for any other variables. So, in our example, if we select the tick-box for zero-order correlations SPSS will produce a correlation matrix of

anxiety, **exam** and **revise**. If you haven't conducted bivariate correlations before the partial correlation then this is a useful way to compare the correlations that haven't been controlled against those that have. This comparison gives you some insight into the contribution of different variables. Tick the box for zero-order correlations but leave the rest of the options as they are.

```
PARTIAL CORRELATION COEFFICIENTS

Zero Order Partials

                  EXAM       ANXIETY       REVISE

EXAM             1.0000      -.4410         .3967
                (     0)    (   101)      (   101)
                 P= .        P= .000      P= .000


ANXIETY          -.4410      1.0000        -.7092
                (   101)    (     0)      (   101)
                 P= .000     P= .          P= .000


REVISE            .3967      -.7092        1.0000
                (   101)    (   101)      (     0)
                 P= .000     P= .000       P= .


(Coefficient / (D.F.) / 1-tailed Significance)

PARTIAL CORRELATION COEFFICIENTS

Controlling for..    REVISE

                  EXAM       ANXIETY

EXAM             1.0000      -.2467
                (     0)    (   100)
                 P= .        P= .006


ANXIETY          -.2467      1.0000
                (   100)    (     0)
                 P= .006     P= .


(Coefficient / (D.F.) / 1-tailed Significance)

 " . " is printed if a coefficient cannot be computed
```

SPSS Output 3.6: Output from a partial correlation

SPSS Output 3.6 shows the output for the partial correlation of exam anxiety and exam performance controlling for revision time. The first thing to notice is the matrix of zero-order correlations, which we asked for using the *options* dialog box. The correlations displayed here are identical to those obtained from the Pearson correlation procedure (compare this matrix with the one in SPSS Output 3.2). Underneath the zero-order correlations is a matrix of correlations for the variables

anxiety and **exam** but controlling for the effect of revision. In this instance we have controlled for one variable and so this is known as a first-order partial correlation. It is possible to control for the effects of two variables at the same time (a second-order partial correlation) or control three variables (a third-order partial correlation) and so on. First, notice that the partial correlation between exam performance and exam anxiety is –0.2467, which is considerably less than the correlation when the effect of revision time is not controlled for ($r = -0.4410$). In fact, the correlation coefficient is nearly half what it was before. Although this correlation is still statistically significant (its p value is still below 0.05), the relationship is diminished. In terms of variance, the value of R^2 for the partial correlation is 0.06, which means that exam anxiety can now account for only 6% of the variance in exam performance. When the effects of revision time were not controlled for, exam anxiety shared 19.4% of the variation in exam scores and so the inclusion of revision time has severely diminished the amount of variation in exam scores shared by anxiety. As such, a truer measure of the role of exam anxiety has been obtained. Running this analysis has shown us that exam anxiety alone does explain much of the variation in exam scores, and we have discovered a complex relationship between anxiety and revision that might otherwise have been ignored. Although causality is still not certain, because relevant variables are being included, the third variable problem is, at least, being addressed in some form.

3.2.4.3. Semi-Partial (or Part) Correlations

In the next chapter, we come across another form of correlation known as a semi-partial correlation (also referred to as a part correlation). While I'm babbling on about partial correlations it is worth me explaining the difference between this type of correlation and a semi-partial correlation. When we do a partial correlation between two variables, we control for the effects of a third variable. Specifically, the effect that the third variable has on *both* variables in the correlation is controlled. In a semi-partial correlation we control for the effect that the third variable has on only one of the variables in the correlation. Figure 3.16 illustrates this principle for the exam performance data. The partial correlation that we calculated took account not only of the effect of revision on exam performance, but also of the effect of revision on anxiety. If we were to calculate the semi-partial correlation for the same data, then this would control for only the effect of revision on exam performance (the effect of revision on exam anxiety is ignored). Partial correlations are most useful for looking at the unique relationship between two variables when other variables are ruled out. Semi-partial correlations are, therefore, useful when trying to explain the variance in one particular variable (an outcome) from a set of predictor variables. This idea leads us nicely toward Chapter 4 …

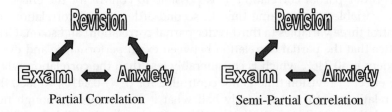

Partial Correlation   Semi-Partial Correlation

Figure 3.16: The difference between a partial and a semi-partial correlation

3.3.   Further Reading

Wright, D. B. (1997). *Understanding statistics: an introduction for the social sciences*. London: Sage. This book has a very clear introduction to the concept of correlation and regression (Chapter 5).

Howell, D. C. (1997). *Statistical methods for psychology* (4th edition). Belmont, CA: Duxbury. Chapter 9 provides more detailed coverage of correlation and regression than Wright but is less reader-friendly. Chapter 10 is great for biserial and point-biserial correlation.

4 Regression

4.1. An Introduction to Regression

Correlations can be a very useful research tool but they tell us nothing about the predictive power of variables. In regression analysis we fit a predictive model to our data and use that model to predict values of the dependent variable (DV) from one or more independent variables (IVs).[1] Simple regression seeks to predict an outcome from a single predictor whereas multiple regression seeks to predict an outcome from several predictors. This is an incredibly useful tool because it allows us to go a step beyond the data that we actually possess. The model that we fit to our data is a linear one and can be imagined by trying to summarize a data set with a straight line (think back to Figure 1.5).

With any data set there are a number of lines that could be used to summarize the general trend and so we need a way to decide which of many possible lines to chose. For the sake of drawing accurate conclusions we want to fit a model that *best* describes the data. There are several ways to fit a straight line to the data you have collected. The simplest way would be to use your eye to gauge a line that looks as though it summarizes the data well. However, the 'eyeball' method is very subjective and so offers no assurance that the model is the best one that could have been chosen. Instead, we use a mathematical technique to establish the line that best describes the data collected. This method is called the *method of least squares*.

How do I fit a straight line to my data?

---

[1] Unfortunately, you will come across people (and SPSS for that matter) referring to regression variables as dependent and independent variables (as in controlled experiments). However, correlational research by its nature seldom controls the independent variables to measure the effect on a dependent variable. Instead, variables are measured simultaneously and without strict control. It is, therefore, inaccurate to label regression variables in this way. For this reason I label 'independent variables' as *predictors*, and the 'dependent variable' as the *outcome*.

4.1.1. *Some Important Information about Straight Lines*

To use linear regression it is important that you know a few algebraic details of straight lines. Any straight line can be drawn if you know two things: (1) the slope (or gradient) of the line, and (2) the point at which the line crosses the vertical axis of the graph (known as the *intercept* of the line). The equation of a straight line is defined in equation (4.1), in which Y is the outcome variable that we want to predict and X_i is the ith subject's score on the predictor variable. β_1 is the gradient of the straight line fitted to the data and β_0 is the intercept of that line. There is a residual term, ε_i, which represents the difference between the score predicted by the line for subject i and the score that subject i actually obtained. The equation is often conceptualized without this residual term (so, ignore it if it's upsetting you); however, it is worth knowing that this term represents the fact our model will not fit perfectly the data collected.

$$Y = \beta_0 + \beta_1 X_i + \varepsilon_i \qquad (4.1)$$

A particular line has a specific intercept and gradient. Figure 4.1 shows a set of lines that have the same intercept but different gradients, and a set of lines that have the same gradient but different intercepts. Figure 4.1 also illustrates another useful point: that the gradient of the line tells us something about the nature of the relationship being described. In Chapter 3 we saw how relationships can be either positive or negative (and I don't mean the difference between getting on well with your girlfriend and arguing all the time!). A line that has a gradient with a positive value describes a positive relationship, whereas a line with a negative gradient describes a negative relationship. So, if you look at the graph in Figure 4.1 in which the gradients differ but the intercepts are the same, then the thicker line describes a positive relationship whereas the thinner line describes a negative relationship.

If it is possible to describe a line knowing only the gradient and the intercept of that line, then we can use these values to describe our model (because in linear regression the model we use is a straight line). So, the model that we fit to our data in linear regression can be conceptualized as a straight line that can be described mathematically by equation (4.1). With regression we strive to find the line that best describes the data collected, then estimate the gradient and intercept of that line. Having defined these values, we can insert different values of our predictor variable into the model to estimate the value of the outcome variable.

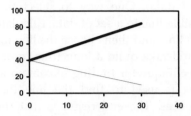 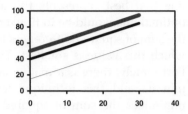

Same intercept, different slopes　　Same slope, different intercepts

Figure 4.1: Shows lines with the same gradients but different intercepts, and lines that share the same intercept but have different gradients

4.1.2.　The Method of Least Squares

I have already mentioned that the method of least squares is a way of finding the line that best fits the data (i.e. finding a line that goes through, or as close to, as many of the data points as possible). This 'line of best fit' is found by ascertaining which line, of all of the possible lines that could be drawn, results in the least amount of difference between the observed data points and the line. Figure 4.2 shows that when any line is fitted to a set of data, there will be small differences between the values predicted by the line, and the data that were actually observed. We are interested in the vertical differences between the line and the actual data because we are using the line to predict values of Y from values of the X variable. Although some data points fall exactly on the line, others lie above and below the line, indicating that there is a difference between the model fitted to these data and the data collected. Some of these differences are positive (they are above the line, indicating that the model underestimates their value) and some are negative (they are below the line, indicating that the model overestimates their value). These differences are usually called *residuals*. In the discussion of variance in section 1.1.3.1 I explained that if we sum positive and negative differences then they tend to cancel each other out. To avoid this problem we square the differences before adding them up. These squared differences provide a gauge of how well a particular line fits the data: if the squared differences are large, the line is not representative of the data; if the squared differences are small then the line is representative. The sum of squared differences (or sum of squares for short) can be calculated for any line that is fitted to some data; the 'goodness-of-fit' of each line can then be compared by looking at the sum of squares for each. The method of least squares works by selecting the line that has the lowest sum of squared differences (so it chooses the line that best represents the observed data). One way to select this optimal line would be to fit every possible line to a set of data, calculate the sum of squared differences for each line, and then choose the line for which this value is smallest. This would take quite a long time to do! Fortunately, there is a mathematical technique for finding maxima and minima and this technique (calculus) is used to find the line that minimizes the sum of squared differences. The end result is that the value of the slope and intercept of the 'line of best fit' can be estimated. Social scientists generally refer to this line of best fit as a regression line.

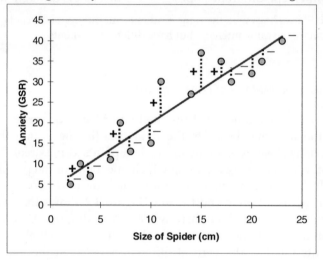

Figure 4.2: This graph shows a scatterplot of some data with a line representing the general trend. The vertical lines (dotted) represent the differences (or residuals) between the line and the actual data

4.1.3.   *Assessing the Goodness-of-Fit: Sums of Squares, R and R^2*

Once we have found the line of best fit it is important that we assess how well this line fits the actual data (we assess the *goodness-of-fit* of the model). In section 1.1.3.1 we saw that one measure of the adequacy of a model is the sum of squared differences. Sticking with this theme, there are several sums of squares that can be calculated to help us gauge the contribution of our model to predicting the outcome. Imagine that I was interested in predicting record sales (Y) from the amount of money spent advertising that record (X). One day my boss came in to my office and said 'Andy, how many records will we sell if we spend £100,000 on advertising?' If I didn't have an accurate model of the relationship between record sales and advertising, what would my best guess be?

Well, probably the best answer I could give would be the mean number of record sales (say, 200,000) because on average that's how many records we expect to sell. This response might well satisfy a brainless record company executive. However, what if he had asked 'How many records will we sell if we spend £1 on advertising?' Again, in the absence of any accurate information, my best guess would be to give the average number of sales (200,000). There is a problem: whatever amount of money is spent on advertising I always predict the same levels of sales. It should be pretty clear then that the mean is fairly useless as a model of a relationship between two variables—but it is the simplest model available.

So, as a basic strategy for predicting the outcome, we might choose to use the mean, because on average (*sic*) it will be a fairly good guess of an outcome. Using the mean as a model, we can calculate the difference between the observed values, and the values predicted by the mean. We saw in section 1.1.3.1 that we square all of these differences to give us the sum of squared differences. This sum of squared differences is known as the *total sum of squares* (denoted SS_T) because it is the total amount of differences present when the most basic model is applied to the data. This value represents how good the mean is as a model of the observed data. Now, if we fit the more sophisticated model to the data, such as a line of best fit, we can again work out the differences between this new model and the observed data. In the previous section we saw that the method of least squares finds the best possible line to describe a set of data by minimizing the difference between the model fitted to the data and the data themselves. However, even with this optimal model there is still some inaccuracy, which is represented by the differences between each observed data point and the value predicted by the regression line. As before, these differences are squared before they are added up so that the directions of the differences do not cancel out. The result is known as the *sum of squared residuals* (SS_R). This value represents the degree of inaccuracy when the best model is fitted to the data. We can use these two values to calculate how much better the regression line (the line of best fit) is than just using the mean as a model (i.e. how much better is the best possible model than the worst model?). The improvement in prediction resulting from using the regression model rather than the mean is calculated by calculating the difference between SS_T and SS_R. This difference shows us the reduction in the inaccuracy of the model resulting from fitting the regression model to the data. This improvement is the *model sum of squares* (SS_M). Figure 4.3 shows each sum of squares graphically.

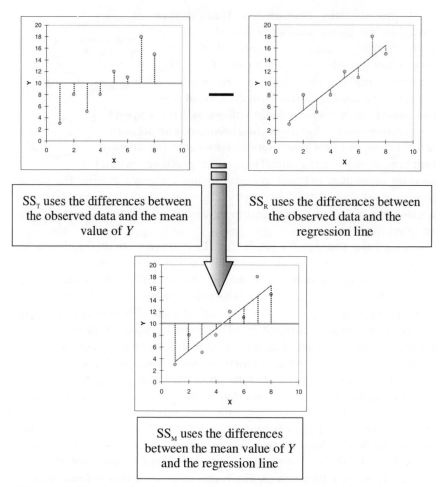

Figure 4.3: Diagram showing from where the regression sums of squares derive

If the value of SS_M is large then the regression model is very different from using the mean to predict the outcome variable. This implies that the regression model has made a big improvement to how well the outcome variable can be predicted. However, if SS_M is small then using the regression model is little better than using the mean (i.e. the regression model is no better than taking our 'best guess'). A useful measure arising from these sums of squares is the proportion of improvement due to the model. This is easily calculated by dividing the sum of squares for the model by the total sum of squares. The resulting value is called R^2 and to express this value as a percentage you should multiply it by 100. So, R^2 represents the amount of variance in the outcome explained by the model (SS_M) relative to how much variation there was to explain in the first place (SS_T). Therefore, as a percentage, it represents the percentage of the variation in the outcome that can be explained by the model.

$$R^2 = \frac{SS_M}{SS_T} \qquad (4.2)$$

Interestingly, this value is the same as the R^2 we met in Chapter 3 (section 3.2.3.3) and you'll notice that it is interpreted in the same way. Therefore, in simple regression we can take the square root of this value to obtain the Pearson correlation coefficient. As such, the correlation coefficient provides us with a good estimate of the overall fit of the regression model, and R^2 provides us with a good gauge of the substantive size of the relationship.

A second use of the sums of squares in assessing the model is through the F-test. The F-test is something we will cover in greater depth in Chapter 7, but briefly this test is based upon the ratio of the improvement due to the model (SS_M) and the difference between the model and the observed data (SS_R). In fact, rather than using the sums of squares themselves, we take the mean sums of squares (referred to as the *mean squares* or MS). To work out the mean sums of squares it is necessary to divide by the degrees of freedom (this is comparable to calculating the variance from the sums of squares—see section 1.1.3.1). For SS_M the degrees of freedom are simply the number of variables in the model, and for SS_R they are the number of observations minus the number of parameters being estimated (i.e. the number of beta coefficients including the constant). The result is the mean squares for the model (MS_M) and the residual mean squares (MS_R). At this stage it isn't essential that you understand how the mean squares are derived (it is explained in Chapter 7). However, it is important that you understand that the F-ratio (equation (4.3)) is a measure of how much the model has improved the prediction of the outcome compared to the level of inaccuracy of the model.

$$F = \frac{MS_M}{MS_R} \qquad (4.3)$$

If a model is good, then we expect the improvement in prediction due to the model to be large (so, MS_M will be large) and the difference between the model and the observed data to be small (so, MS_R will be small). In short, a good model should have a large F-ratio (greater than one at least) because the top half of equation (4.3) will be bigger than the bottom. The exact magnitude of this F-ratio can be assessed using critical values for the corresponding degrees of freedom.

4.1.4.   *Simple Regression on SPSS*

So far, we have seen a little of the theory behind regression, albeit restricted to the situation in which there is only one predictor. To help clarify what we have learnt so far, we will go through an example of a simple regression on SPSS. Earlier on I asked you to imagine that I worked for a record company and that my boss was interested in predicting record sales from advertising. There are some data for this example in the file **Record1.sav**. This data file has 200 rows, each one representing a different record. There are also two columns, one representing the sales of each record in the week after release and the other representing the amount (in pounds) spent promoting the record before release. This is the format for entering regression data: the outcome variable and any predictors should be entered in different columns, and each row should represent independent values of those variables. The pattern of the data is shown in Figure 4.4 and it should be clear that a positive relationship exists: so, the more money spent advertising the record, the more it is likely to sell. Of course there are some records that sell well regardless of advertising (top left of scatterplot), but there are none that sell badly when advertising levels are high (bottom right of scatterplot). The scatterplot also shows the line of best fit for these data: bearing in mind that the mean would be represented by a flat line at around the 200,000 sales mark, the regression line is noticeable different.

Figure 4.4: Scatterplot showing the relationship between record sales and the amount spent promoting the record

To find out the parameters that describe the regression line, and to see whether this line is a useful model, we need to run a regression analysis.

To do the analysis you need to access the main dialog box by using the **Analyze**⇒**Regression**⇒**Linear…** menu path. Figure 4.5 shows the resulting dialog box. There is a space labelled *Dependent* in which you should place the outcome variable (in this example **sales**). So, select **sales** from the list on the left-hand side, and transfer it by clicking on ◻. There is another space labelled *Independent(s)* in which any predictor variable should be placed. In simple regression we use only one predictor (in this example **adverts**) and so you should select **adverts** from the list and click on ◻ to transfer it to the list of predictors. There are a variety of options available, but these will be explored within the context of multiple regression (see section 4.2). For the time being just click on ◻ᴏᴋ to run the basic analysis.

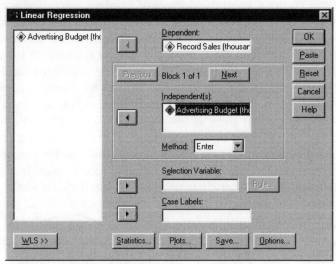

Figure 4.5: Main dialog box for regression

4.1.5.   Output from SPSS

4.1.5.1. Overall Fit of the Model

The first table provided by SPSS is a summary of the model. This summary table provides the value of R and R^2 for the model that has been derived. For these data, R has a value of 0.578 and because there is only one predictor, this value represents the simple

Model Summary

Model	R	R Square	Adjusted R Square	Std. Error of the Estimate
1	.578[a]	.335	.331	65.9914

a. Predictors: (Constant), Advertising Budget (thousands of pounds)

SPSS Output 4.1

correlation between advertising and record sales (you can confirm this by running a correlation using what you were taught in Chapter 3). The value of R^2 is 0.335, which tells us that advertising expenditure can account for 33.5% of the variation in record sales. In other words, if we are trying to explain why some records sell more than others, we can look at the variation in sales of different records. There might be many factors that can explain this variation, but our model, which includes only advertising expenditure, can explain 33% of it. This means that 66% of the variation in record sales cannot be explained by advertising alone. Therefore, there must be other variables that have an influence also.

The next part of the output reports an analysis of variance (ANOVA— see Chapter 7). The summary table shows the various sums of squares described in Figure 4.3 and the degrees of freedom associated with each. From these two values, the average sums of squares (the mean squares) can be calculated by dividing the sums of squares by the associated degrees of freedom. The most important part of the table is the F-ratio, which is calculated using equation (4.3), and the associated significance value of that F-ratio. For these data, F is 99.59, which is significant at $p <$ 0.001 (because the value in the column labelled *Sig.* is less than 0.001). This result tells us that there is less than a 0.1% chance that an F-ratio this large would happen by chance alone. Therefore, we can conclude that our regression model results in significantly better prediction of record sales than if we used the mean value of record sales. In short, the regression model overall predicts record sales significantly well.

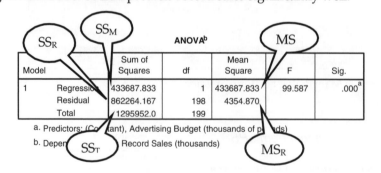

SPSS Output 4.2

4.1.5.2. *Model Parameters*

The ANOVA tells us whether the model, overall, results in a significantly good degree of prediction of the outcome variable. However, the ANOVA doesn't tell us about the individual contribution of variables in the model (although in this simple case there is only one variable in the model and so we can infer that this variable is a good predictor). The table in SPSS Output 4.3 provides details of the model parameters (the beta values) and the significance of these values. We saw in equation (4.1) that β_0 was the Y intercept and this value is the value B for the constant. So, from the table, we can say that β_0 is 134.14, and this can be interpreted as meaning that when no money is spent on advertising (when $X = 0$), the model predicts that 134,140 records will be sold (remember that our unit of measurement was thousands of records). We can also read off the value of β_1 from the table and this value represents the gradient of the regression line. It is 9.612 E–02, which in unabbreviated form is 0.09612.[2] Although this value is the slope of the regression line, it is more useful to think of this value as representing *the change in the outcome associated with a unit change in the predictor*. Therefore, if our predictor variable is increased by 1 unit (if the advertising budget is increased by 1), then our model predicts that 0.096 extra records will be sold. Our units of measurement were thousands of pounds and thousands of records sold, so we can say that for an increase in advertising of £1000 the model predicts 96 (0.096 × 1000 = 96) extra record sales. As you might imagine, this investment is pretty bad for the record company: they invest £1000 and get only 96 extra sales! Fortunately, as we already know, advertising accounts for only one-third of record sales!

Coefficients[a]

Model		Unstandardized Coefficients		Standardized Coefficients	t	Sig.
		B	Std. Error	Beta		
1	(Constant)	134.140	7.537		17.799	.000
	Advertising Budget (thousands of pounds)	9.612E-02	.010	.578	9.979	.000

a. Dependent Variable: Record Sales (thousands)

SPSS Output 4.3

---

[2] You might have noticed that this value is reported by SPSS as 9.612 E–02 and many students find this notation confusing. Well, this notation simply means 9.61×10^{-2} (which might be a more familiar notation). OK, some of you are still confused. Well think of E–02 as meaning 'move the decimal place 2 steps to the left', so 9.612 E–02 becomes 0.09612. If the notation read 9.612 E–01, then that would be 0.9612, and if it read 9.612 E–03, that would be 0.009612. Likewise, think of E+02 (notice the minus sign has changed) as meaning 'move the decimal place 2 places to the right'. So 9.612 E+02 becomes 961.

The values of β represent the change in the outcome resulting from a unit change in the predictor. If the model was useless at predicting the outcome, then if the value of the predictor changes, what might we expect the change in the outcome to be? Well, if the model is very bad then we would expect the change in the outcome to be zero. Think back to Figure 4.3 (see the panel representing SS_T) in which we saw that using the mean was a very bad way of predicting the outcome. In fact, the line representing the mean is flat, which means that as the predictor variable changes, the value of the outcome does *not* change (because for each level of the predictor variable, we predict that the outcome will equal the mean value). The important point here is that a bad model (such as the mean) will have regression coefficients of zero for the predictors. A regression coefficient of zero means: (a) a unit change in the predictor variable results in no change in the predicted value of the outcome (the predicted value of the outcome does not change at all), and (b) the gradient of the regression line is zero, meaning that the regression line is flat. Hopefully, what should be clear at this stage is that if a variable significantly predicts an outcome, then it should have a β value significantly different from zero. This hypothesis is tested using a *t*-test (see Chapter 6). The *t*-statistic tests the null hypothesis that the value of β is zero: therefore, if it is significant we accept the hypothesis that the β value is significantly different from zero and that the predictor variable contributes significantly to our ability to estimate values of the outcome.

One problem with testing whether the β values are different from zero is that their magnitude depends on the units of measurement (for example advertising budget has a very small β value, yet it seems to have a strong relationship to record sales). Therefore, the *t*-test is calculated by taking account of the standard error. The standard error tells us something about how different β values would be if we took lots and lots of samples of data regarding record sales and advertising budgets and calculated the β values for each sample. We could plot a frequency distribution of these samples to discover whether the β values from all samples would be relatively similar, or whether they would be very different. We can use the standard deviation of this distribution (known as the *standard error*) as a measure of the similarity of β values across samples. If the standard error is very small, then it means that most samples are likely have a β value similar to the one in the sample collected (because there is little variation across samples). The *t*-test tells us whether the β value is different from zero relative to the variation in β values for similar samples. When the standard error is small even a small deviation from zero can reflect a meaningful difference because β is representative of the majority of possible samples.

Equation (4.4) shows how the *t*-test is calculated and you'll find a general version of this equation in Chapter 6 (equation (6.1)). The β_{expected} is simply the value of β that we would expect to obtain if the null hypothesis were true. I mentioned earlier that the null hypothesis is that β is zero and so this value can be replaced by zero. The equation simplifies to become the observed value of β divided by the standard error with which it is associated.[3]

$$t = \frac{\beta_{\text{observed}} - \beta_{\text{expected}}}{SE_\beta}$$

$$= \frac{\beta}{SE_\beta}$$

(4.4)

The values of *t* can then be compared to the values that we would expect to find by chance alone: if *t* is <u>very large</u> then it is unlikely to have occurred by chance. SPSS provides the exact probability that the observed value of *t* is a chance result, and as a general rule, if this observed significance is less than 0.05, then social scientists agree that the result reflects a genuine effect. For these two values, the probabilities are 0.000 (zero to 3 decimal places) and so we can say that the probability of these *t* values occurring by chance is less than 0.001. Therefore, they reflect genuine effects. We can, therefore, conclude that advertising budget makes a significant contribution ($p < 0.001$) to predicting record sales.

4.1.5.3. Using the Model

So far, we have discovered that we have a useful model, one that significantly improves our ability to predict record sales. However, the next stage is often to use that model to make some predictions. The first stage is to define the model by replacing the β values in equation (4.1) with the values from SPSS Output 4.3. In addition, we can replace the X and Y with the variable names so that the model becomes:

$$\begin{aligned} \text{Record Sales} &= \beta_0 + \beta_1 \text{Advertising Budget}_i \\ &= 134.14 + (0.09612 \times \text{Advertising Budget}_i) \end{aligned}$$

(4.5)

It is now possible to make a prediction about record sales, by replacing the advertising budget with a value of interest. For example, imagine a

---

[3] To see that this is true you can use the values from SPSS Output 4.3 to calculate *t* for the constant. For advertising budget, the standard error has been rounded to 3 decimal places, so to verify how *t* is calculated you should use the un-rounded value. This value is obtained by double-clicking the table in the SPSS output and then double-clicking the value that you wish to see in full. You should find that $t = 0.096124/0.009632 = 9.979$.

Coefficient – a value that expresses the degree to which some relationship between factors is to be found

...ecord.
...we can
...er that

(4.6)

To summarize what we have learnt so far, in simple linear regression the outcome variable Y is predicted using the equation of a straight line (equation (4.1)). Given that we have collected several values of Y and X, the unknown parameters in the equation can be calculated. They are calculated by fitting a model to the data (in this case a straight line) for which the sum of the squared differences between the line and the actual data points is minimized. This method is called the method of least squares. Multiple regression is a logical extension of these principles to situations in which there are several predictors. A similar equation can be derived in which each predictor variable has its own coefficient, and the outcome variable is predicted from a combination of all the variables multiplied by their respective coefficients plus a residual term (see equation (4.7)).

> **What is the difference between simple and multiple regression?**

$$Y = \beta_0 + \beta_1 X_1 + \beta_2 X_2 + \ldots + \beta_n X_n + \varepsilon_i \qquad (4.7)$$

Y is the outcome variable, β_1 is the coefficient of the first predictor (X_1), β_2 is the coefficient of the second predictor (X_2), β_n is the coefficient of the nth predictor (X_n), and ε_i is the difference between the predicted and the observed value of Y for the ith subject. In this case, the model fitted is more complicated, but the basic principle is the same as simple regression. That is, we seek to find the linear combination of predictors that correlate maximally with the outcome variable. Therefore, when we refer to the regression model in multiple regression, we are talking about a model in the form of equation (4.7).

record executive wanted to spend £100,000 on advertising a new record. Remembering that our units are already in thousands of pounds, we can simply replace the advertising budget with 100. He would discover that record sales should be around 144,000 for the first week of sales.

$$\text{Record Sales} = 134.14 + (0.09612 \times \text{Advertising Budget}_i)$$
$$= 134.14 + (0.09612 \times 100) \tag{4.6}$$
$$= 143.75$$

4.2.   Multiple Regression

To summarize what we have learnt so far, in simple linear regression the outcome variable Y is predicted using the equation of a straight line (equation (4.1)). Given that we have collected several values of Y and X, the unknown parameters in the equation can be calculated. They are calculated by fitting a model to the data (in this case a straight line) for which the sum of the squared differences between the line and the actual data points is minimized. This method is called the method of least squares. Multiple regression is a logical extension of these principles to situations in which there are several predictors. A similar equation can be derived in which each predictor variable has its own coefficient, and the outcome variable is predicted from a combination of all the variables multiplied by their respective coefficients plus a residual term (see equation (4.7)).

> **What is the difference between simple and multiple regression?**

$$Y = \beta_0 + \beta_1 X_1 + \beta_2 X_2 + \ldots + \beta_n X_n + \varepsilon_i \tag{4.7}$$

Y is the outcome variable, β_1 is the coefficient of the first predictor (X_1), β_2 is the coefficient of the second predictor (X_2), β_n is the coefficient of the nth predictor (X_n), and ε_i is the difference between the predicted and the observed value of Y for the ith subject. In this case, the model fitted is more complicated, but the basic principle is the same as simple regression. That is, we seek to find the linear combination of predictors that correlate maximally with the outcome variable. Therefore, when we refer to the regression model in multiple regression, we are talking about a model in the form of equation (4.7).

Equation (4.4) shows how the *t*-test is calculated and you'll find a general version of this equation in Chapter 6 (equation (6.1)). The β_{expected} is simply the value of β that we would expect to obtain if the null hypothesis were true. I mentioned earlier that the null hypothesis is that β is zero and so this value can be replaced by zero. The equation simplifies to become the observed value of β divided by the standard error with which it is associated.[3]

$$t = \frac{\beta_{\text{observed}} - \beta_{\text{expected}}}{SE_\beta}$$

$$= \frac{\beta}{SE_\beta}$$

(4.4)

The values of *t* can then be compared to the values that we would expect to find by chance alone: if *t* is very large then it is unlikely to have occurred by chance. SPSS provides the exact probability that the observed value of *t* is a chance result, and as a general rule, if this observed significance is less than 0.05, then social scientists agree that the result reflects a genuine effect. For these two values, the probabilities are 0.000 (zero to 3 decimal places) and so we can say that the probability of these *t* values occurring by chance is less than 0.001. Therefore, they reflect genuine effects. We can, therefore, conclude that advertising budget makes a significant contribution ($p < 0.001$) to predicting record sales.

4.1.5.3. Using the Model

So far, we have discovered that we have a useful model, one that significantly improves our ability to predict record sales. However, the next stage is often to use that model to make some predictions. The first stage is to define the model by replacing the β values in equation (4.1) with the values from SPSS Output 4.3. In addition, we can replace the X and Y with the variable names so that the model becomes:

$$\text{Record Sales} = \beta_0 + \beta_1 \text{Advertising Budget}_i$$

$$= 134.14 + (0.09612 \times \text{Advertising Budget}_i)$$

(4.5)

It is now possible to make a prediction about record sales, by replacing the advertising budget with a value of interest. For example, imagine a

---

[3] To see that this is true you can use the values from SPSS Output 4.3 to calculate *t* for the constant. For advertising budget, the standard error has been rounded to 3 decimal places, so to verify how *t* is calculated you should use the un-rounded value. This value is obtained by double-clicking the table in the SPSS output and then double-clicking the value that you wish to see in full. You should find that $t = 0.096124/0.009632 = 9.979$.

4.2.1. An Example of a Multiple Regression Model

Imagine that our record company executive was interested in extending his model of record sales to incorporate another variable. We know already that advertising accounts for 33% of variation in record sales, but a much larger 67% remains unexplained. The record executive could measure a new predictor to the model in an attempt to explain some of the unexplained variation in record sales. He decides to measure the number of times the record is played on Radio 1 (Britain's national radio station) during the week prior to release. The existing model that we derived using SPSS (see equation (4.5)) can now be extended to include this new variable (**airplay**).

$$\text{Record Sales} = \beta_0 + \beta_1 \text{Advertising Budget}_i + \beta_2 \text{Airplay} \qquad (4.8)$$

predictors + constant

The new model is based on equation (4.7) and includes a β value for both predictors (and, of course, the constant). If we calculate the β values, we could make predictions about record sales based not only on the amount spent on advertising but also in terms of radio play. There are only two predictors in this model and so we could display this model graphically in three dimensions (Figure 4.6).

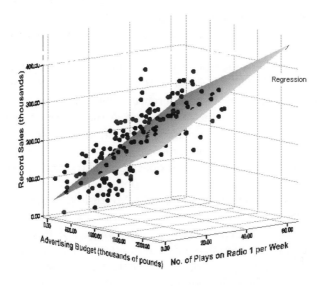

Figure 4.6: Scatterplot of the relationship between record sales, advertising budget and radio play

Equation (4.7) describes the shaded trapezium in the diagram (this is known as the regression *plane*) and the black dots represent the observed data points. Like simple regression, the plane fitted to the data aims to best predict the observed data. However, there are invariably some differences between the model and the real-life data (this fact is evident because some of the dots do not lie exactly on the shaded area of the graph). The β value for advertising describes the slope of the top and bottom of the regression plane whereas the β value for airplay describes the slope of the left and right sides of the regression plane. Knowledge of these two slopes allows us to place the regression plane in space.

It is fairly easy to visualise a regression model with two predictors, because it is possible to plot the regression plane using a 3-D scatterplot. However, multiple regression can be used with three, four or even ten predictors. Although you can't immediately visualize what such complex models look like, or know what the β values represent, you should be able to apply the principles of these basic models to more complex scenarios.

4.2.2.   Sums of Squares, R and R^2

When we have several predictors, the partitioning of sums of squares is the same as in the single variable case except that the model we refer to takes the form of equation (4.7) rather than simply being a two-dimensional straight line. Therefore, an SS_T can be calculated that represents the difference between the observed values and the mean value. SS_R still represents the difference between the values of Y predicted by the model and the observed values. Finally, SS_M can still be calculated and represents the difference between the values of Y predicted by the model and the mean value. Although the computation of these values is much more complex than in simple regression, conceptually these values are the same.

When there are several predictors it does not make sense to look at the simple correlation coefficient and instead SPSS produces a multiple correlation coefficient (labelled *Multiple R*). Multiple R is the correlation between the observed values of Y and the values of Y predicted by the multiple regression model. Therefore, large values of the multiple R represent a large correlation between the predicted and observed values of the outcome. A multiple R of 1 represents a situation in which the model perfectly predicts the observed data. As such, multiple R is a gauge of how well the model predicts the observed data. It follows that the resulting R^2 can be interpreted in the same way as simple regression: it is the amount of variation in the outcome variable that is accounted for by the model.

4.2.3.   Methods of Regression

If we are interested in constructing a complex model with several predictors, then how do we decide which predictors to use? A great deal of care should be taken in selecting predictors for a model because the values of the regression coefficients depend upon the variables in the model. Therefore, the predictors included and the way in which they are entered into the model can have a great impact. In an ideal world, predictors should be selected based on past research.[4] If new predictors are being added to existing models then select these new variables based on the substantive *theoretical* importance of these variables. One thing *not* to do is select hundreds of random predictors, bung them all into a regression analysis and hope for the best. In addition to the problem of selecting predictors, there are a number of ways in which variables can be entered into a model. When predictors are all completely uncorrelated the order of variable entry has very little effect on the parameters calculated; however, in social science research we rarely have uncorrelated predictors and so the method of predictor selection is crucial.

4.2.3.1.   Hierarchical (Blockwise Entry)

In hierarchical regression predictors are selected based on past work and the experimenter decides in which order to enter predictors into the model. As a general rule, known predictors (from other research) should be entered into the model first in order of their importance in predicting the outcome. After known predictors have been entered, the experimenter can add any new predictors into the model. New predictors can either be entered all in one go, in a stepwise manner, or hierarchically (such that the new predictor suspected to be the most important is entered first).

4.2.3.2.   Forced Entry

Forced entry (or *Enter* as it is known in SPSS) is a method in which all predictors are forced into the model simultaneously. Like hierarchical, this method relies on good theoretical reasons for including the chosen predictors, but unlike hierarchical the experimenter makes no decision about the order in which variables are entered.

---

[4] I, rather cynically, qualify this suggestion by proposing that predictors be chosen based on past research that has utilized good methodology. If basing such decisions on regression analyses, select predictors based only on past research that has used regression appropriately and yielded reliable, generalizable models!

4.2.3.3. Stepwise Methods

In stepwise methods decisions about the order in which predictors are entered into the model are based on a purely mathematical criterion. In the *forward* method, an initial model is defined that contains only the constant (β_0). The computer then searches for the predictor (out of the ones available) that best predicts the outcome variable—it does this by selecting the predictor that has the highest simple correlation with the outcome. If this predictor significantly improves the ability of the model to predict the outcome, then this predictor is retained in the model and the computer searches for a second predictor. The criterion used for selecting this second predictor is that it is the variable that has the largest semi-partial correlation with the outcome. Let me explain this in plain English. Imagine that the first predictor can explain 40% of the variation in the outcome variable, then there is still 60% left unexplained. The computer searches for the predictor that can explain the biggest part of the remaining 60% (so, it is not interested in the 40% that is already explained). In statistical terms you can think of this like a partial correlation in that the computer correlates each of the predictors with the outcome while controlling for the effect of the first predictor. The reason that it is called a *semi*-partial correlation is because the effects of the first predictor are partialled out of only the remaining predictors, and are not controlled for in the outcome itself. This semi-partial correlation gives a measure of how much 'new variance' in the outcome can be explained by each remaining predictor (see section 3.2.4). The predictor that accounts for the most new variance is added to the model and, if it makes a significant contribution to the predictive power of the model, it is retained and another predictor is considered.

The *stepwise* method in SPSS is the same as the forward method, except that each time a predictor is added to the equation, a removal test is made of the least useful predictor. As such the regression equation is constantly being reassessed to see whether any redundant predictors can be removed. The *backward* method is the opposite of the forward method in that the computer begins by placing all predictors in the model and then calculating the contribution of each one. Looking at the significance value of the *t*-test for that predictor assesses the contribution of each predictor. This significance value is compared against a removal criterion (which can be either an absolute value of the test statistic or a probability value for that test statistic). If a predictor meets the removal criterion (i.e. if it is not making a statistically significant contribution to how well the model predicts the outcome variable) it is removed from the model and the model is re-estimated for the remaining predictors. The contribution of the remaining predictors is then reassessed.

4.2.3.4. *Choosing a Method*

SPSS allows you to opt for any one of these methods and it is important to select an appropriate one. The forward, backward and stepwise methods all come under the general heading of *stepwise methods* because they all rely on the computer selecting variables based upon mathematical criteria. Many writers argue that this takes many important methodological decisions out of the hands of the researcher. What's more, the models derived by computer often take advantage of random sampling variation and so decisions about which variables should be included will be based upon slight differences in their semi-partial correlation. However, these slight statistical differences may contrast dramatically with the theoretical importance of a predictor to the model. For this reason stepwise methods are best avoided except for exploratory model building (see Wright, 1997, p. 181). When there is a sound theoretical literature available, then base your model upon what past research tells you. Include any meaningful variables in the model in their order of importance. After this initial analysis, repeat the regression but this time exclude any variables that were statistically redundant the first time around. There are important considerations in deciding which predictors should be included. First, it is important not to include too many predictors. As a general rule, the fewer predictors the better, and certainly include only predictors for which you have a good theoretical grounding (it is meaningless to measure hundreds of variables and then put them all into a regression model). So, be selective and remember you should have at least 15 subjects per predictor.

Which method of regression should I use?

4.2.4. *Assessing the Regression Model I: Diagnostics*

When we have produced a model based on a sample of data there are two important questions to ask: (a) does the model fit the observed data well, or is it influenced by a small number of cases, and (b) can my model generalize to other samples? These questions are vital to ask because they affect how we use the model that has been constructed. These questions are also, in some sense, hierarchical because we wouldn't want to generalize a bad model. However, it is a mistake to think that because a model fits the observed data well we can

How do I tell if my model is accurate?

draw conclusions beyond our sample. Generalization is a critical additional step and if we find that our model is not generalizable, then we must restrict any conclusions based on the model to the sample used. First, we will look at how we establish whether a model is an accurate representation of the actual data, and in section 4.2.5 we move on to look at how we assess whether a model can be used to make inferences beyond the sample of data that has been collected.

4.2.4.1.   Outliers and Residuals

An outlier is a case that differs substantially from the main trend of the data. Figure 4.7 shows an example of such a case. Outliers can cause your model to be biased because they affect the values of the estimated regression coefficients. For example, Figure 4.7 uses the same data as Figure 4.2 except that the score of one subject has been changed to be an outlier (in this case a person who was very calm in the presence of a very big spider). The change in this one point has had a dramatic effect on the regression model chosen to fit the data. With the outlier present, the regression model changes: its gradient is reduced (the line become flatter) and the intercept increases (the new line will cross the Y-axis at a higher point). It should be clear from this diagram that it is important to try to detect outliers to see whether the model is biased in this way.

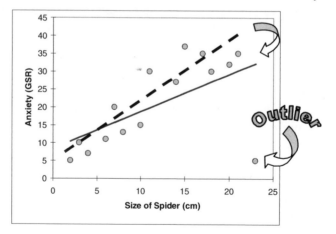

Figure 4.7: Graph demonstrating the effect of an outlier. The dashed line represents the original regression line for these data (see Figure 4.2), whereas the complete line represents the regression line when an outlier is present

If you think about how you might detect an outlier, how do you think you might do it? Well, we know that an outlier, by its nature, is very different from all of the other scores. This being true, do you think that the model will predict that person's score very accurately? The answer is clearly *no*: looking at Figure 4.7 it is evident that even though the outlier has biased the model, the model still predicts that one value very badly (the regression line is long way from the outlier). Therefore, if we were to work out the differences between the data values that were collected, and the values predicted by the model, we could detect an outlier by looking for large differences. This process is the same as looking for cases that the model predicts inaccurately. The differences between the values of the outcome predicted by the model and the values of the outcome observed in the sample are known as *residuals*. These residuals effectively represent the error present in the model. If a model fits the sample data well then all residuals will be small (if the model was a perfect fit of the sample data—all data points fall on the regression line—then all residuals would be zero). If a model is a poor fit of the sample data then the residuals will be large. Also, if any cases stand out as having a large residual, then they could be outliers.

The normal (or *unstandardized*) residuals described above are measured in the same units as the outcome variable and so are difficult to interpret across different models. What we can do is to look for residuals that stand out as being particularly large. However, we cannot define a universal cut-off point for what constitutes a large residual. To overcome this problem, we use *standardized residuals*, which are the residuals divided by an estimate of their standard deviation. We came across standardization in section 1.1.3.1 as a means of converting variables into a standard unit of measurement (the standard deviation). By converting residuals into standardized residuals we can compare residuals from different models and devise universal guidelines for what constitutes an acceptable (or unacceptable) value. Standardized residuals have some useful characteristics: in an average, normally distributed sample, 95% should lie between −2 and +2, and 99% should lie between −2.5 and +2.5. Therefore, standardized residuals with an absolute value greater than 3 are cause for concern (because in an average sample a value this high is unlikely to happen by chance). What's more, if more than 1% of our sample have standardized residuals with an absolute value greater than 2.5 there is evidence that the level of error within our model is unacceptable (i.e. the model is a fairly poor fit of the sample data). Furthermore, if more than 5% of cases have standardized residuals with an absolute value greater than 2 then there is also evidence that the model is a poor representation of the actual data.

A third form of residual is the *Studentized residual*, which is the unstandardized residual divided by an estimate of its standard deviation that varies point-by-point. These residuals have the same properties as the standardized residuals but usually provide a more precise estimate of the error variance of a specific case.

4.2.4.2. *Influential Cases*

As well as testing for outliers by looking at the error in the model, it is also possible to look at whether certain cases exert undue influence over the parameters of the model. So, if we were to delete a certain case, would we obtain different regression coefficients? This type of analysis can help to determine whether the regression model is stable across the sample, or whether it is biased by a few influential cases. Again, this process will unveil outliers.

 There are several residual statistics that can be used to assess the influence of a particular case. One statistic is the *adjusted predicted value* for a case when that case is excluded from the analysis. In effect, the computer calculates a new model without a particular case and then uses this new model to predict the value of the outcome variable for the case that was excluded. If a case does not exert a large influence over the model then we would expect the adjusted predicted value to be very similar to the predicted value when the case is included. Put simply, if the model is stable then the predicted value of a case should be the same regardless of whether that case was used to calculate the model. The difference between the adjusted predicted value and the original predicted value is known as the *deleted residual*. If a case is not influential then its deleted residual should be zero—hence, we expect non-influential cases to have small deleted residuals. However, as with residuals, we have the problem that this statistic depends on the units of measurement of the outcome and so a deleted residual of 0.5 will be very small if the outcome ranges from 1 to 100, but very large if the outcome varies from 0 to 1. Therefore, the deleted residual can be divided by the standard error to give a standardized value known as the *Studentized deleted residual*. This residual can be compared across different regression analyses because it is measured in standard units.

The deleted residuals are very useful to assess the influence of a case on the ability of the model to predict that case. However, they do not provide any information about how a case influences the model as a whole (i.e. the impact that a case has on the model's ability to predict *all* cases). One statistic that does consider the effect of a single case on the model as a whole is *Cook's distance*. Cook's distance is a measure of the overall influence of a case on the model and Cook and Weisberg (1982) have suggested that values greater than 1 may be cause for concern.

A second measure of influence is *leverage* (sometimes called *hat values*), which gauges the influence of the observed value of the outcome variable over the predicted values. The average leverage value is defined as $(k+1)/n$ in which k is the number of predictors in the model and n is the number of subjects.[5] Leverage values can lie between 0 (indicating that the case has no influence whatsoever) and 1 (indicating that the case has complete influence over prediction). If no cases exert undue influence over the model then we would expect all of the leverage value to be close to the average value $((k + 1)/n)$. Hoaglin and Welsch (1978) recommend investigating cases with values greater than twice the average $(2(k + 1)/n)$ and Stevens (1992) recommends using three times the average $(3(k + 1)/n)$ as a cut-off point for identifying cases having undue influence. We shall see how to use these cut-off points in section 4.4.1.6. However, cases with large leverage values will not necessarily have a large influence on the regression coefficients because they are measured on the outcome variables rather than the predictors.

Related to the leverage values are the *Mahalanobis distances*, which measure the distance of cases from the mean(s) of the predictor variable(s). You need to look for the cases with the highest values. It is not easy to establish a cut-off point at which to worry, although Barnett and Lewis (1978) have produced a table of critical values dependent on the number of predictors and the sample size. From their work it is clear that even with large samples ($N = 500$) and 5 predictors, values above 25 are cause for concern. In smaller samples ($N = 100$) and with fewer predictors (namely 3) values greater than 15 are problematic, and in very small samples ($N = 30$) with only 2 predictors values greater than 11 should be examined. However, for more specific advice, refer to Barnett and Lewis's (1978) table.

It is possible to run the regression analysis with a case included and then rerun the analysis with that same case excluded. If we did this, undoubtedly there would be some difference between the β coefficients in the two regression equations. This difference would tell us how much influence a particular case has on the parameters of the regression model. To take a hypothetical example, imagine two variables that had a perfect negative relationship except for a single case (case 30). If a regression analysis was done on the 29 cases that were perfectly linearly related then we would get a model in which the predictor variable X perfectly predicts the outcome variable Y, and there are no errors. If we then ran the analysis but this time include the case that didn't conform (case 30), then the resulting model has different parameters. Some data are stored in the file **dfbeta.sav** which illustrate such a situation. Try running a simple regression first with all the cases included and then

---

[5] You may come across the average leverage denoted as p/n in which p is the number of parameters being estimated. In multiple regression, we estimate parameters for each predictor and also for a constant and so p is equivalent to the number of predictors plus one ($k + 1$).

with case 30 deleted. The results are summarized in Table 4.1, which shows (1) the parameters for the regression model when the extreme case is included or excluded; (2) the resulting regression equations, and (3) the value of Y predicted from subject 30's score on the X variable (which is obtained by replacing the X in the regression equation with subject 30's score for X, which was 1).

When case 30 is excluded, these data have a perfect negative relationship: hence the coefficient for the predictor (β_1) is –1 (remember that in simple regression this term is the same as the Pearson correlation coefficient), and the coefficient for the constant (the intercept, β_0) is 31. However, when case 30 is included, both parameters are reduced[6] and the difference between the parameters is also displayed. The difference between a parameter estimated using all cases and estimated when one case is excluded is known as the *DFBeta* in SPSS. DFBeta is calculated for every case and for each of the parameters in the model. So, in our hypothetical example, the DFBeta for the constant is –2, and the DFBeta for the predictor variable is 0.1. By looking at the values of the DFBetas, it is possible to identify cases that have a large influence on the parameters of the regression model. Again, the units of measurement used will affect these values and so SPSS produces a *standardized DFBeta*. These standardized values are easier to use because universal cut-off points can be applied. In this case absolute values above 1 indicate cases that substantially influence the model parameters (although Stevens, 1992, suggests looking at cases with absolute values greater than 2).

Table 4.1: Shows the difference in the parameters of the regression model when one case is excluded

Parameter (β)	Case 30 Included	Case 30 Excluded	Difference
Constant (intercept)	29.00	31.00	–2.00
Predictor (gradient)	–0.90	–1.00	0.10
Model (regression line):	$Y = (-0.9)X + 29$	$Y = (-1)X + 31$	
Predicted Y	28.10	30.00	–1.09

A related statistic is the *DFFit*, which is the difference between the predicted value for a case when the model is calculated including that case and when the model is calculated excluding that case: in this example the value is –1.09 (see Table 4.1). SPSS also produces standardized versions of the DFFit values. A final measure is that of the *covariance ratio* (CVR), which is a measure of whether a case influences the variance of the regression parameters. A description of the computation of this statistic would leave most readers dazed and

---

[6] The value of β_1 is reduced because the data no longer have a perfect linear relationship and so there is now variance that the model cannot explain.

confused, so suffice to say that when this ratio is close to 1 the case is having very little influence on the variances of the model parameters. Belsey et al. (1980) recommend the following:

- If $CVR_i > 1 + [3(k + 1)/n]$ then deleting the ith case will damage the precision of some of the model's parameters.
- If $CVR_i < 1 - [3(k + 1)/n]$ then deleting the ith case will improve the precision of some of the model's parameters.

In both equations, k is the number of predictors, CVR_i is the covariance ratio for the ith subject, and n is the sample size.

4.2.4.3. Summary

There are a lot of diagnostic statistics that should be examined after a regression analysis, and it is difficult to summarize this wealth of material into a concise conclusion. However, one thing I would like to stress is a point made by Belsey et al. (1980) who noted the dangers inherent in these procedures. The point is that diagnostics are tools that enable you to see how good or bad your model is in terms of fitting the sampled data. They are a way of assessing your model. They are *not*, however, a way of justifying the removal of data points to effect some desirable change in the regression parameters (for example, deleting a case that changes a non-significant β value into a significant one). Stevens (1992), as ever, offers excellent advice:

> If a point is a significant outlier on Y, but its Cook's distance is < 1, there is no real need to delete that point since it does not have a large effect on the regression analysis. However, one should still be interested in studying such points further to understand why they did not fit the model. (p. 118)

4.2.5. Assessing the Regression Model II: Generalization

When a regression analysis is done, an equation can be produced that is correct for the sample of observed values. However, in the social sciences we are usually interested in generalizing our findings outside of the sample. So, although it can be useful to draw conclusions about a particular sample of people, it is usually more interesting if we can then assume that our conclusions are true for a wider population. For a regression model to generalize we must be sure that underlying assumptions have been met, and to test whether the model does generalize we can look at cross-validating it.

4.2.5.1. Checking Assumptions

To draw conclusions about a population based on a regression analysis done on a sample, several assumptions must be true (see Berry, 1993).

- **Variable types**: All predictor variables must be quantitative or categorical, and the outcome variable must be quantitative, continuous and unbounded. By quantitative I mean that they should be measured at the interval level and by unbounded I mean that there should be no constraints on the variability of the outcome. If the outcome is a measure ranging from 1 to 10 yet the data collected vary between 3 and 7, then these data are constrained.
- **Non-Zero variance**: The predictors should have some variation in value (i.e. they do not have variances of zero).
- **No perfect multicollinearity**: There should be no perfect linear relationship between two or more of the predictors. So, the predictor variables should not correlate highly.
- **Predictors are uncorrelated with 'external variables'**: *External variables* are variables that haven't been included in the regression model which influence the outcome variable.[7] These variables can be thought of as similar to the 'third variable' that was discussed with reference to correlation. This assumption means that there should be no external variables that correlate with any of the variables included in the regression model. Obviously, if external variables do correlate with the predictors, then the conclusions we draw from the model become unreliable (because other variables exist that can predict the outcome just as well).
- **Homoscedasticity**: At each level of the predictor variable(s), the variance of the residual terms should be constant. This just means that the residuals at each level of the predictor(s) should have the same variance (homoscedasticity); when the variances are very unequal there is said to be *heteroscedasticity*.
- **Independent errors**: For any two observations the residual terms should be uncorrelated (or independent). This eventuality is sometimes described as a lack of *autocorrelation*.
- **Normally distributed errors**: It is assumed that the residuals in the model are random, normally distributed, variables with a mean of zero. This assumption simply means that the differences between the

---

[7] Some authors choose to refer to these external variables as part of an error term that includes any random factor in the way in which the outcome varies. However, to avoid confusion with the residual terms in the regression equations I have chosen the label 'external variables'. Although this term implicitly washes over any random factors, I acknowledge their presence here!

model and the observed data are most frequently zero or very close to zero, and that differences much greater than zero happen only occasionally.

- **Independence**: It is assumed that all of the values of the outcome variable are independent (in other words each value of the outcome variable comes from a separate subject).
- **Linearity**: The mean values of the outcome variable for each increment of the predictor(s) lie along a straight line. In plain English this means that it is assumed that the relationship we are modelling is a linear one. If we model a non-linear relationship using a linear model then this obviously limits the generalizability of the findings.

This list of assumptions probably seems pretty daunting and in fact most undergraduates (and some academics for that matter) tend to regard assumptions as rather tedious things about which no-one really need worry. In fact, when I mention statistical assumptions to most psychologists they tend to give me that 'you really are a bit of a pedant' look and then ignore me. However, regardless of my status as a pedant, there are good reasons for taking assumptions seriously. Imagine that I go over to a friend's house, the lights are on and it's obvious that someone is at home. I ring the doorbell and no-one answers. From that experience, I conclude that my friend hates me and that I am a terrible, unlikeable, person. How tenable is this conclusion? Well, there is a reality that I am trying to tap (namely whether my friend likes or hates me), and I have collected data about that reality (I've gone to his house, seen that he's at home, rang the doorbell and got no response). Imagine that in reality my friend likes me (he never was a good judge of character!); in this scenario, my conclusion is false. Why have my data led me to the wrong conclusion? The answer is simple: I had assumed that my friend's doorbell was working and under this assumption the conclusion that I made from my data was accurate (my friend heard the bell but chose to ignore it because he hates me). However, this assumption was not true—his doorbell was not working, which is why he didn't answer the door—and as a consequence the conclusion I drew about reality was completely false.

Enough about doorbells, friends and my social life: the point to remember is that when assumptions are broken we stop being able to draw accurate conclusions about reality. In terms of regression, when the assumptions are met, the model that we get for a sample can be accurately applied to the population of interest (the coefficients and parameters of the regression equation are said to be *unbiased*). Some people assume that this means that when the assumptions are met the regression model from a sample is always identical to the model that would have been obtained had we been able to test the entire population. Unfortunately, this belief isn't true. What an unbiased model does tell us is that *on average* the regression model from the sample is the same as the population model. However, you should be clear that even when the assumptions are met, it is possible that a model obtained from a sample may not be the same as the population model— but the likelihood of them being the same is increased.

4.2.5.2. Cross-Validation of the Model

Even if we can't be confident that the model derived from our sample accurately represents the entire population, there are ways in which we can assess how well our model can predict the outcome in a different sample. Assessing the accuracy of a model across different samples is known as cross-validation. If a model can be generalized, then it must be capable of accurately predicting the same outcome variable from the same set of predictors in a different group of people. If the model is applied to a different sample and there is a severe drop in its predictive power, then the model clearly does *not* generalize. As a first rule of thumb, for social scientists, we should aim to *have at least 15 subjects per predictor* to obtain a reliable regression model. Once we have a regression model there are two main methods of cross-validation.

- **Adjusted R^2**: In SPSS, not only are the values of R and R^2 calculated, but also an adjusted R^2. This adjusted value indicates the loss of predictive power or *shrinkage*. Whereas R^2 tells us how much of the variance in Y is accounted for by the regression model from our sample, the adjusted value tells us how much variance in Y would be accounted for if the model had been derived from the population from which the sample was taken. SPSS derives the adjusted R^2 using Wherry's equation. However, this equation has been criticized because it tells us nothing about how well the regression model would predict an entirely different set of data (how well can the model predict scores of a different sample of data from the same population?). One version of R^2 that does tell us how well the model cross-validates uses Stein's formula which is shown in equation (4.9) (see Stevens, 1992).

$$\text{adjusted } R^2 = 1 - \left[\left(\frac{n-1}{n-k-1} \right) \left(\frac{n-2}{n-k-2} \right) \left(\frac{n+1}{n} \right) \right] (1 - R^2) \tag{4.9}$$

In Stein's equation, R^2 is the unadjusted value, n is the number of subjects and k is the number of predictors in the model. For the more mathematically minded of you, it is worth using this equation to cross-validate a regression model.

- **Data splitting**: This approach involves randomly splitting your data set in half, computing a regression equation on both halves of the data and then comparing the resulting models. However, researchers rarely have large enough data sets to perform this kind of analysis.

4.2.5.3. Multicollinearity

Multicollinearity exists when there is a strong correlation between two or more predictors in a regression model. Multicollinearity poses a problem only for multiple regression because (without wishing to state the obvious) simple regression requires only one predictor. *Perfect collinearity* exists when at least one predictor is a perfect linear combination of the others (the simplest example being two predictors that are perfectly correlated—they have a correlation coefficient of 1). If there is perfect collinearity between predictors it becomes impossible to obtain unique estimates of the regression coefficients because there are an infinite number of combinations of coefficients that would work equally well. Put simply, if we have two predictors that are perfectly correlated, then the values of β for each variable are interchangeable. The good news is that perfect collinearity is rare in real-life data. The bad news is that less than perfect collinearity is virtually unavoidable. Low levels of collinearity pose little threat to the models generated by SPSS, but as collinearity increases so do the standard errors of the β coefficients, which in turn affects whether these coefficients are found to be statistically significant. In short, high levels of collinearity increase the probability that a good predictor of the outcome will be found non-significant and rejected from the model (a type II error). There are three other reasons why the presence of multicollinearity poses a threat to the validity of multiple regression analysis.

- **It limits the size of R**: Remember that R is a measure of the multiple correlation between the predictors and the outcome and that R^2 indicates the variance in the outcome for which the predictors account. Imagine a situation in which a single variable predicts the outcome variable fairly successfully (e.g. $R = 0.80$) and a second predictor variable is then added to the model. This second variable might account for a lot of the variance in the outcome (which is why it is included in the model), but the variance it accounts for is the same variance accounted for by the first variable. In other words, once the variance accounted for by the first predictor has been removed, the second predictor accounts for very little of the remaining variance (the second variable accounts for very little *unique variance*). Hence, the overall variance in the outcome accounted for by the two predictors is little more than when only one predictor is used (so R might increase from 0.80 to 0.82). This idea is connected to the notion of partial correlation that was explained in Chapter 3. If, however, the two predictors are completely uncorrelated, then the second predictor is likely to account for different variance in the outcome to that accounted for by the first predictor. So, although in itself the second predictor might account for only a little of the variance in the outcome, the variance it does account for is different to that of the other predictor (and so when both predictors are included, R is substantially larger, say 0.95). Therefore, having uncorrelated predictors is beneficial.

- **Importance of predictors**: Multicollinearity between predictors makes it difficult to assess the individual importance of a predictor. If the predictors are highly correlated, and each accounts for similar variance in the outcome, then how can we know which of the two variables is important? Quite simply we can't tell which variable is important—the model could include either one, interchangeably.

- **Unstable predictor equations**: I have described how multicollinearity increases the variances of the regression coefficients, resulting in unstable predictor equations. This means that the estimated values of the regression coefficients (the β values) will be unstable from sample to sample.

One way of identifying multicollinearity is to scan a correlation matrix of all of the predictor variables and see if any correlate very highly (by very highly I mean correlations of above 0.80 or 0.90). This is a good 'ball park' method but misses more subtle forms of multicollinearity. Luckily, SPSS produces various collinearity diagnostics, one of which is the *variance inflation factor* (VIF). The VIF indicates whether a predictor has a strong linear relationship with the other predictor(s). Although there are no hard and fast rules about what value of the VIF should be cause for concern, Myers (1990) suggests that a value of 10 is a good value at which to worry. What's more, Bowerman and O'Connell (1990) suggest that if the average VIF is greater than 1, then multicollinearity may be biasing the regression model. Related to the VIF is the *tolerance* statistic, which is its reciprocal (1/VIF). As such, values below 0.1 indicate serious problems although Menard (1995) suggests that values below 0.2 are worthy of concern.

Other measures that are useful in discovering whether predictors are dependent are the *eigenvalues of the scaled, uncentred cross-products matrix,* the *condition indexes* and the *variance proportions*. These statistics are extremely complex and will be covered as part of the interpretation of SPSS output (see section 4.4.1.5).

4.3.   How to Do Multiple Regression Using SPSS

4.3.1.   Main Options

Imagine that the record company executive was now interested in
extending the model of record sales to incorporate other variables. He
decides to measure two new variables: (1) the number of times the
record is played on Radio 1 (England's largest national radio station)
during the week prior to release (**airplay**), and (2) the attractiveness of
the band (**attract**). Before a record is released, the executive notes the
amount spent on advertising, the number of times the record is played
on radio the week before release, and the attractiveness of the band. He
does this for 200 different records (each made by a different band).
Attractiveness was measured by asking a random sample of the target
audience to rate the attractiveness of each band on a scale from 0
(hideous potato-heads) to 10 (gorgeous sex objects). The mode
attractiveness given by the sample was used in the regression (because
he was interested in what the majority of people thought, rather than the
average of people's opinions).

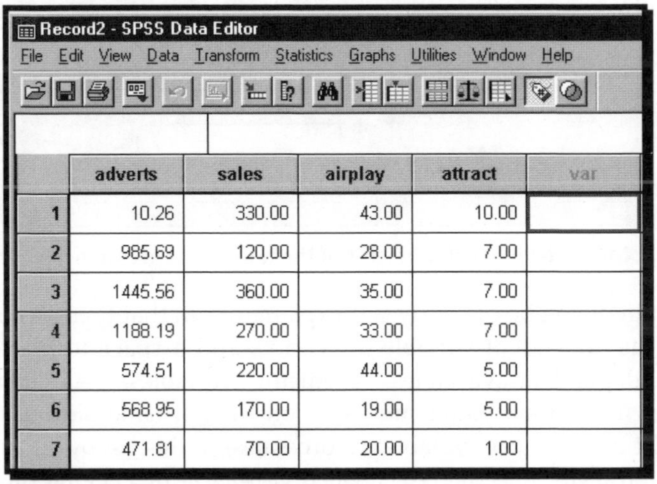

	adverts	sales	airplay	attract	var
1	10.26	330.00	43.00	10.00	
2	985.69	120.00	28.00	7.00	
3	1445.56	360.00	35.00	7.00	
4	1188.19	270.00	33.00	7.00	
5	574.51	220.00	44.00	5.00	
6	568.95	170.00	19.00	5.00	
7	471.81	70.00	20.00	1.00	

Figure 4.8: Data layout for multiple regression

These data are in the file **Record2.sav** and you should note that each
variable has its own column (the same layout as for correlation), and
each row represents a different record. So, the first record had £10,260
spent advertising it, it sold 330,000 copies, it received 43 plays on Radio
1 the week before release and it was made by a band that the majority of
people rated as gorgeous sex objects (Figure 4.8).

The executive has past research indicating that advertising budget is a
significant predictor of record sales, and so he should include this

variable in the model first. His new variables (**airplay** and **attract**) should, therefore, be entered into the model *after* advertising budget. This method is hierarchical (the researcher decides in which order to enter variables into the model based on past research). To do a hierarchical regression in SPSS we have to enter the variables in blocks (each block representing one step in the hierarchy). To get to the main *regression* dialog box you must go to the *Analyze* menu and select *Regression* and then *Linear* (**Analyze⇒Regression⇒Linear**). The main dialog box is shown in Figure 4.9 and is the same as when we encountered it for simple regression.

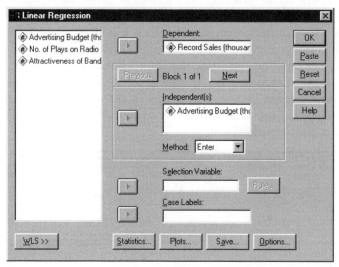

Figure 4.9: Main dialog box for block 1 of the multiple regression

The main dialog box is fairly self-explanatory in that there is a space to specify the dependent variable (outcome), and a space to place one or more independent variables (predictor variables). As usual, the variables in the data editor are listed on the left-hand side of the box. Highlight the outcome variable (record sales) in this list by clicking on it and then transfer it to the box labelled *Dependent* by clicking on ▶. We also need to specify the predictor variable for the first block. We decided that advertising budget should be entered into the model first (because past research indicates that it is an important predictor), so, highlight this variable in the list and transfer it to the box labelled *Independent(s)* by clicking on ▶. Underneath the *Independent(s)* box, there is a drop-down menu for specifying the *Method* of regression (see section 4.2.3). You can select a different method of variable entry for each block by clicking on ▼, next to where it says *Method*. The default option is forced entry, and this is the option we want, but if you were carrying out more exploratory work, you might decide to use one of the stepwise methods (forward, backward, stepwise or remove).

Having specified the first block in the hierarchy, we need to move onto to the second. To tell the computer that you want to specify a new block of predictors you must click on Next. This process clears the *Independent(s)* box so that you can enter the new predictors (you should also note that above this box it now reads *Block 2 of 2* indicating that you are in the second block of the two that you have so far specified). We decided that the second block would contain both of the new predictors and so you should click on **airplay** and **attract** in the variables list and transfer them, one by one, to the *Independent(s)* box by clicking on ▶. The dialog box should now look like Figure 4.10. To move between blocks use the Previous and Next buttons (so, for example, to move back to block 1, click on Previous).

It is possible to select different methods of variable entry for different blocks in a hierarchy. So, although we specified forced entry for the first block, we could now specify a stepwise method for the second. Given that we have no previous research regarding the effects of attractiveness and airplay on record sales, we might be justified in requesting a stepwise method for this block. However, because of the problems with stepwise methods, I am going to stick with forced entry for both blocks in this example.

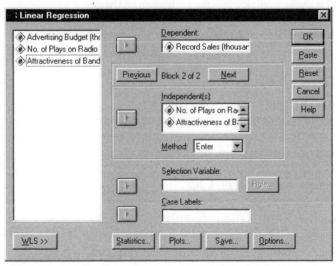

Figure 4.10: Main dialog box for block 2 of the multiple regression

4.3.2.   Statistics

In the main *regression* dialog box click on 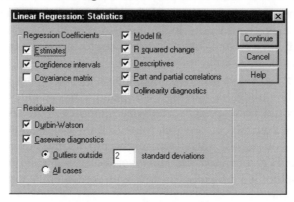 Statistics... to open a dialog box for selecting various important options relating to the model (Figure 4.11). Most of these options relate to the parameters of the model; however, there are procedures available for checking the assumptions of no multicollinearity (collinearity diagnostics) and independence of errors (Durbin-Watson). When you have selected the statistics you require (I recommend all but the covariance matrix as a general rule) click on Continue to return to the main dialog box.

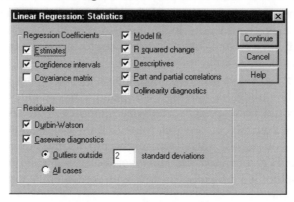

Figure 4.11: *Statistics* dialog box for regression analysis

- **Estimates**: This option is selected by default because it gives us the estimated coefficients of the regression model (i.e. the estimated β values). Test statistics and their significance are produced for each regression coefficient: a t-test is used to see whether each β differs significantly from zero (see section 4.1.5.2).[8]
- **Confidence intervals**: This option, if selected, produces confidence intervals for each of the unstandardized regression coefficients. Confidence intervals can be a very useful tool in assessing the likely value of the regression coefficients in the population—I shall describe their exact interpretation later.
- **Covariance matrix**: If selected, this option will display a matrix of the covariances, correlation coefficients and variances between the regression coefficients of each variable in the model. A variance-covariance matrix is produced with variances displayed along the

---

[8] Remember that for simple regression, the value of β is the same as the correlation coefficient. When we test the significance of the Pearson correlation coefficient, we test the hypothesis that the coefficient is different from zero; it is, therefore, sensible to extend this logic to the regression coefficients. For those interested in why a t-test is used I recommend reading Howell (1997), Chapter 9, section 10 (p. 257).

diagonal and covariances displayed as off-diagonal elements. The correlations are produced in a separate matrix.

- **Model fit**: This option is vital and so is selected by default. It provides not only a statistical test of the model's ability to predict the outcome variable (the *F*-test–see section 4.1.3), but also the value of R (or multiple R), the corresponding R^2, and the adjusted R^2.
- **R squared change**: This option displays the change in R^2 resulting from the inclusion of a new predictor (or block of predictors). This measure is a useful way to assess the contribution of new predictors (or blocks) to explaining variance in the outcome.
- **Descriptives**: If selected, this option displays a table of the mean, standard deviation and number of observations of all of the variables included in the analysis. A correlation matrix is also displayed showing the correlation between all of the variables and the one-tailed probability for each correlation coefficient. This option is extremely useful because the correlation matrix can be used to assess whether predictors are interrelated (which can be used to establish whether there is multicollinearity).
- **Part and partial correlations**: This option produces the zero-order correlation (the Pearson correlation) between each predictor and the outcome variable. It also produces the partial correlation between each predictor and the outcome, controlling for all other predictors in the model. Finally, it produces the part correlation (or semi-partial correlation) between each predictor and the outcome. This correlation represents the relationship between each predictor and the part of the outcome that is not explained by the other predictors in the model. As such, it measures the unique relationship between a predictor and the outcome (see section 3.2.4).
- **Collinearity diagnostics**: This option is for obtaining collinearity statistics such as the VIF, tolerance, eigenvalues of the scaled, uncentred cross-products matrix, condition indexes and variance proportions (see section 4.2.5.3).
- **Durbin-Watson**: This option produces the Durbin-Watson test statistic, which tests for correlations between errors. Specifically, it tests whether adjacent residuals are correlated (remember one of our assumptions of regression was that the residuals are independent). In short, this option is important for testing whether the assumption of independent errors is tenable. The test statistic can vary between 0 and 4 with a value of 2 meaning that the residuals are uncorrelated. A value greater than 2 indicates a negative correlation between adjacent residuals whereas a value below 2 indicates a positive correlation. Unfortunately, SPSS does not provide the significance value of this test, so you must decide for yourself whether the value is different enough from 2 to be cause for concern. The size of the

Durbin-Watson statistic depends upon the number of predictors in the model, and the number of observations. For accuracy, you should look up the exact acceptable values in Durbin and Watson's (1951) original paper. As a very conservative rule of thumb, values less than 1 or greater than 3 are definitely cause for concern; however, values closer to 2 may still be problematic depending on your sample and model.

- **Casewise diagnostics**: This option, if selected, lists the observed value of the outcome, the predicted value of the outcome, the difference between these values (the residual) and this difference standardized. Furthermore, it will list these values either for all cases, or just for cases for which the standardized residual is greater than 3 (when the ± sign is ignored). This criterion value of 3 can be changed, and I recommend changing it to 2 for reasons that will become apparent. A summary table of residual statistics indicating the minimum, maximum, mean and standard deviation of both the values predicted by the model and the residuals (see section 4.3.4) is also produced.

4.3.3.   Regression Plots

Once you are back in the main dialog box, click on [Plots...] to activate the regression *plots* dialog box shown in Figure 4.12. This dialog box provides the means to specify a number of graphs, which can help to establish the validity of some regression assumptions. Most of these plots involve various *residual* values, which will be described in more detail in section 4.3.4.

On the left-hand side of the dialog box is a list of several variables.

- **DEPENDNT** (*the outcome variable*).
- ***ZPRED** (*the standardized predicted values* of the dependent variable based on the model). These values are standardized forms of the values predicted by the model.
- ***ZRESID** (*the standardized residuals, or errors*). These values are the standardized differences between the observed data and the values that the model predicts).
- ***DRESID** (*the deleted residuals*). See section 4.2.4.1 for details.
- ***ADJPRED** (the *adjusted predicted values*). See section 4.2.4.1 for details.
- ***SRESID** (*the Studentized residual*).
- ***SDRESID** (the *Studentized deleted residual*). This value is the deleted residual divided by its standard error.

The variables listed in this dialog box all come under the general heading of residuals, and were discussed in detail in section 4.2.4.1. For a basic analysis it is worth plotting *ZRESID (Y-axis) against *ZPRED (X-axis), because this plot is useful to determine whether the assumptions of random errors and homoscedasticity have been met. A plot of *SRESID (y-axis) against *ZPRED (x-axis) will show up any heteroscedasticity also. Although often these two plots are virtually identical, the latter is more sensitive on a case-by-case basis. To create these plots simply select a variable from the list, and transfer it to the space labelled either X or Y (which refer to the axes) by clicking ▶. When you have selected two variables for the first plot (as is the case in Figure 4.12) you can specify a new plot by clicking on Next . This process clears the spaces in which variables are specified. If you click on Next and would like to return to the plot that you last specified, then simply click on Previous . You can specify up to nine plots.

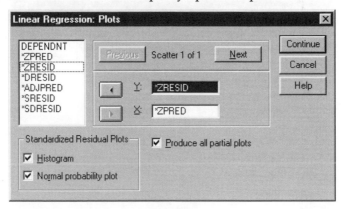

Figure 4.12: Linear regression: *plots* dialog box

You can also select the tick-box labelled *Produce all partial plots* which will produce scatterplots of the residuals of the outcome variable and each of the predictors when both variables are regressed separately on the remaining predictors. Regardless of whether the previous sentence made any sense to you, these plots have several important characteristics that make them worth inspecting. First, the gradient of the regression line between the two residual variables is equivalent to the coefficient of the predictor in the regression equation. As such, any obvious outliers on a partial plot represent cases that might have undue influence on a predictor's regression coefficient. Second, non-linear relationships between a predictor and the outcome variable are much more detectable using these plots. Finally, they are a useful way of detecting collinearity. For these reasons, I recommend requesting them.

There are several options for plots of the standardized residuals. First, you can select a histogram of the standardized residuals (this is extremely useful for checking the assumption of normality of errors). Second, you can ask for a normal probability plot, which also provides information about whether the residuals in the model are normally distributed. When you have selected the options you require, click on Continue to take you back to the main *regression* dialog box.

4.3.4.   *Saving Regression Diagnostics*

In section 4.2.4 we met two types of regression diagnostics: those that help us assess how well our model fits our sample and those that help us detect cases that have a large influence on the model generated. In SPSS we can choose to save these diagnostic variables in the data editor (so, SPSS will calculate them and then create new columns in the data editor in which the values are placed).

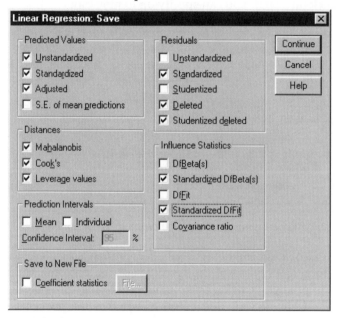

Figure 4.13: Dialog box for regression diagnostics

To save regression diagnostics you need to click on Save... in the main *regression* dialog box. This process activates the *save* new variables dialog box (see Figure 4.13). Once this dialog box is active, it is a simple matter to tick the boxes next to the required statistics. Most of the available options were explained in section 4.2.4 and Figure 4.13 shows, what I consider to be, a fairly basic set of diagnostic statistics. Standardized (and Studentized) versions of these diagnostics are generally easier to interpret and so I suggest selecting them in preference to the unstandardized versions. Once the regression has been run, SPSS creates a column in your data editor for each statistic requested and it has a standard set of variable names to describe each one. After the name, there will be a number that refers to the analysis that has been run. So, for the first regression run on a data set the variable names will be followed by a 1, if you carry out a second regression it will create a new set of variables with names followed by a 2 and so on. The names of the variables in the data editor are displayed below. When you have selected the diagnostics you require (by clicking in the appropriate boxes), click on [Continue] to return to the main *regression* dialog box.

- **pre_1**: unstandardized predicted value.
- **zpr_1**: standardized predicted value.
- **adj_1**: adjusted predicted value.
- **sep_1**: standard error of predicted value.
- **res_1**: unstandardized residual.
- **zre_1**: standardized residual.
- **sre_1**: Studentized residual.
- **dre_1**: deleted residual.
- **sdr_1**: Studentized deleted residual.
- **mah_1**: Mahalanobis distance.
- **coo_1**: Cook's distance.
- **lev_1**: centred leverage value.
- **sdb0_1**: standardized DFBETA (intercept).
- **sdb1_1**: standardized DFBETA (predictor 1).
- **sdb2_1**: standardized DFBETA (predictor 2).
- **sdf_1**: standardized DFFIT.
- **cov_1**: covariance ratio.

4.3.4.1. Further Options

As a final step in the analysis, you can click on [Options...] to take you to the *options* dialog box (Figure 4.14). The first set of options allows you to change the criteria used for entering variables in a stepwise regression. If you insist on doing stepwise regression, then it's probably best that you leave the default criterion of 0.05 probability for entry alone. However, you can make this criterion more stringent (0.01). There is also the option to build a model that doesn't include a constant (i.e. has no Y intercept). This option should also be left alone! Finally, you can select a method for dealing with missing data points. By default, SPSS excludes cases listwise, which means that if a person has a missing value for any variable, then they are excluded from the whole analysis. So, for example, if our record company boss didn't have an attractiveness score for one of his bands, their data would not be used in the regression model. Often a better option is to excluded cases on a pairwise basis, which means that if a subject has a score missing for a particular variable, then their data are excluded only from calculations involving the variable for which they have no score. So, data for the band for which there was no attractiveness rating would still be used to calculate the relationships between advertising budget, airplay and record sales. A final option is to replace the missing score with the average score for this variable and then include that case in the analysis (so, our example band would be given an attractiveness rating equal to the average attractiveness of all bands). The problem with this final choice is that it is likely to suppress the true value of the standard deviation (and more importantly the standard error). The standard deviation will be suppressed because for that case there will be no difference between the mean and the score, whereas if data had been collected for that case there would, almost certainly, have been some difference between the score and the mean. Obviously, if the sample is large and the number of missing values small then this is not a serious consideration. However, if there are many missing values this choice is potentially dangerous because smaller standard errors are more likely to lead to significant results that are a product of the data replacement rather than a genuine effect.

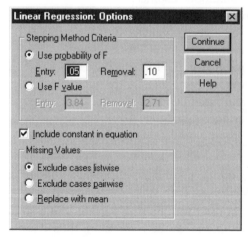

Figure 4.14: Options for linear regression

4.4.   Running the Analysis and Interpreting the Output

A good strategy to adopt with regression is to measure predictor variables for which there are sound theoretical reasons for expecting them to predict the outcome. Run a regression analysis in which all predictors are entered into the model and examine the output to see which predictors contribute substantially to the model's ability to predict the outcome. Once you have established which variables are important, rerun the analysis including only the important predictors and use the resulting parameter estimates to define your regression model. If the initial analysis reveals that there are two or more significant predictors then you could consider ‘running a forward stepwise analysis (rather than forced entry) to find out the individual contribution of each predictor.

I have spent a lot of time explaining the theory behind regression and some of the diagnostic tools necessary to gauge the accuracy of a regression model. It is important to remember that SPSS may appear to be very clever, but in fact it is not. Admittedly, it can do lots of complex calculations in a matter of seconds, but what it can't do is control the quality of the model that is generated—to do this requires a human brain (and preferably a trained one). SPSS will happily generate output based on any garbage you decide to feed into the data editor and SPSS will not judge the results or give any indication of whether the model can be generalized or if it is valid. However, SPSS provides the statistics necessary to judge these things, and at this point our brains must take over the job—which is slightly worrying!

Having selected all of the relevant options and returned to the main dialog box, we need to click on [OK] to run the analysis. SPSS will spew out copious amounts of output in the viewer window, and we now turn to look at how to make sense of this information.

4.4.1.   Model Statistics

4.4.1.1.   Descriptives

The output described in this section is produced using the options in the linear regression *statistics* dialog box (see Figure 4.11). To begin with, if you selected the *Descriptives* option, SPSS will produce the table seen in SPSS Output 4.4. This table tells us the mean and standard deviation of each variable in our data set, so, we now know that the average number of record sales was 193,000. This table isn't necessary for interpreting the regression model, but it is a useful summary of the data. In addition to the descriptive statistics, selecting this option produces a correlation matrix too. This table shows three things. First, the table shows the value of the Pearson correlation coefficient between every pair of variables (for example, we can see that the advertising budget had a large positive correlation with record sales, $R = 0.578$). Second, the 1-tailed significance of each correlation is displayed (for example, the correlation above is significant, $p < 0.001$). Finally, the number of cases contributing to each correlation ($N = 200$) is shown.

You might notice that along the diagonal of the matrix the values for the correlation coefficients are all 1.00 (i.e. a perfect positive correlation). The reason for this is that these values represent the correlation of each variable with itself, so obviously the resulting values are 1. The correlation matrix is extremely useful for getting a rough idea of the relationships between predictors and the outcome, and for a preliminary look for multicollinearity. If there is no multicollinearity in the data then there should be no substantial correlations ($R > 0.9$) between predictors.

If we look only at the predictors (ignore record sales) then the highest correlation is between the attractiveness of the band and the amount of airplay which is significant at a 0.01 level ($R = 0.182$, $p = 0.005$). Despite the significance of this correlation, the coefficient is small and so it looks as though our predictors are measuring different things (there is no collinearity). We can see also that of all of the predictors the number of plays on Radio 1 correlates best with the outcome ($R = 0.599$, $p < 0.001$) and so it is likely that this variable will best predict record sales.

Descriptive Statistics

	Mean	Std. Deviation	N
Record Sales (thousands)	193.2000	80.6990	200
Advertising Budget (thousands of pounds)	614.4123	485.6552	200
No. of plays on Radio 1 per week	27.5000	12.2696	200
Attractiveness of Band	6.7700	1.3953	200

Correlations

		Record Sales (thousands)	Advertising Budget (thousands of pounds)	No. of plays on Radio 1 per week	Attractiveness of Band
Pearson Correlation	Record Sales (thousands)	1.000	.578	.599	.326
	Advertising Budget (thousands of pounds)	.578	1.000	.102	.081
	No. of plays on Radio 1 per week	.599	.102	1.000	.182
	Attractiveness of Band	.326	.081	.182	1.000
Sig. (1-tailed)	Record Sales (thousands)	.	.000	.000	.000
	Advertising Budget (thousands of pounds)	.000	.	.076	.128
	No. of plays on Radio 1 per week	.000	.076	.	.005
	Attractiveness of Band	.000	.128	.005	.
N	Record Sales (thousands)	200	200	200	200
	Advertising Budget (thousands of pounds)	200	200	200	200
	No. of plays on Radio 1 per week	200	200	200	200
	Attractiveness of Band	200	200	200	200

SPSS Output 4.4: Descriptive statistics for regression analysis

4.4.1.2. Summary of Model

The next section of output describes the overall model (so, it tells us whether the model is successful in predicting record sales). Remember that we chose a hierarchical method and so each set of summary statistics is repeated for each stage in the hierarchy. In SPSS Output 4.5 you should note that there are two models. Model 1 refers to the first stage in the hierarchy when only advertising budget is used as a predictor. Model 2 refers to when all three predictors are used. SPSS Output 4.5 is the *model summary* and this table was produced using the *Model fit* option. This option is selected by default in SPSS because it provides us with some very important information about the model: the values of R, R^2 and the adjusted R^2. If the R *squared change* and *Durbin-Watson* options were selected, then these values are included also (if they weren't selected you'll find that you have a smaller table).

The model summary table is shown in SPSS Output 4.5 and you should notice that under this table SPSS tells us what the dependent variable (outcome) was and what the predictors were in each of the two models. In the column labelled R are the values of the multiple correlation coefficient between the predictors and the outcome. When only advertising budget is used as a predictor, this is the simple correlation between advertising and record sales (0.578). In fact all of the statistics for model 1 are the same as the simple regression model earlier (see section 4.1.5). The next column gives us a value of R^2, which we already know is a measure of how much of the variability in the outcome is accounted for by the predictors. For the first model its value is 0.335, which means that advertising budget accounts for 33.5% of the variation in record sales. However, when the other two predictors are included as well (model 2), this value increases to 0.665 or 66.5% of the variance in record sales. Therefore, if advertising accounts for 33.5%, we can tell that attractiveness and radio play account for an additional 33%.[9] So, the inclusion of the two new predictors has explained quite a large amount of the variation in record sales.

Model Summary[c]

Model	R	R Square	Adjusted R Square	Std. Error of the Estimate	R Square Change	F Change	df1	df2	Sig. F Change	Durbin-Watson
1	.578[a]	.335	.331	65.9914	.335	99.587	1	198	.000	
2	.815[b]	.665	.660	47.0873	.330	96.447	2	196	.000	1.950

a. Predictors: (Constant), Advertising Budget (thousands of pounds)
b. Predictors: (Constant), Advertising Budget (thousands of pounds), Attractiveness of Band, No. of plays on Radio 1 per week
c. Dependent Variable: Record Sales (thousands) *(outcome)* Predicting record sales. (No)

— Closer to 2 the better < 1 or > 3 problem

SPSS Output 4.5: Regression model summary

---

[9] 33% = 66.5% − 33.5% (this value is the R *Square Change* in the table).

The adjusted R^2 gives us some idea of how well our model generalizes and ideally we would like its value to be the same, or very close to, the value of R^2. In this example the difference for the final model is small (in fact the difference between the values is $0.665 - 0.660 = 0.005$ (about 0.5%). This shrinkage means that if the model were derived from the population rather than a sample it would account for approximately 0.5% less variance in the outcome. Advanced students might like to apply Stein's formula to the R^2 to get some idea of the likely value of it in different samples. Stein's formula was given in equation (4.9) and can be applied by replacing n with the sample size (200) and k with the number of predictors (3).

$$\text{adjusted } R^2 = 1 - \left[\left(\frac{200-1}{200-3-1} \right) \left(\frac{200-2}{200-3-2} \right) \left(\frac{200+1}{200} \right) \right] (1 - 0.665)$$
$$= 1 - [(1.015)(1.015)(1.005)](0.335)$$
$$= 1 - 0.347$$
$$= 0.653$$

This value is very similar to the observed value of R^2 (0.665) indicating that the cross-validity of this model is very good.

The change statistics are provided only if requested and these tell us the change in the F-ratio resulting from each block of the hierarchy. So, model 1 causes R^2 to change from zero to 0.335, and this change in the amount of variance explained gives rise to an F-ratio of 99.587, which is significant with a probability less than 0.001. The addition of the new predictors (model 2) causes R^2 to increase by 0.330 (see above) and this change in the amount of variance that can be explained gives rise to an *increase* in the F-ratio of 99.467, which is again significant ($p < 0.001$). The change statistics therefore tell us about the difference made by adding new predictors to the model.

Finally, if you requested the Durbin-Watson statistic it will be found in the last column of the table. This statistic informs us about whether the assumption of independent errors is tenable (see section 4.3.2). As a conservative rule I suggested that values less than 1 or greater than 3 should definitely raise alarm bells (although I urge you to look up precise values for the situation of interest). The closer to 2 that the value is, the better, and for these data the value is 1.950, which is so close to 2 that the assumption has almost certainly been met.

The next part of the output contains an analysis of variance (ANOVA) that tests whether the model is significantly better at predicting the outcome than using the mean as a 'best guess' (SPSS Output 4.6). Specifically, the F-ratio represents the ratio of the improvement in prediction as a result of fitting the model relative to the inaccuracy that still exists in the model (see section 4.1.3). This table is again split into two sections: one for each model. We are told the value of the sum of squares for the model (this value is SS_M in section 4.1.3 and represents the improvement in prediction resulting from fitting a regression line to the data rather than using the mean as an estimate of the outcome). We are also told the residual sum of squares (this value is SS_R in section 4.1.3 and represents the total difference between the model and the observed data). We are also told the degrees of freedom (*df*) for each term. In the case of the improvement due to the model, this value is equal to the number of predictors (1 for the first model and 3 for the second), and for SS_R it is the number of observations (200) minus the number of coefficients in the regression model. The first model has two coefficients (one for the predictor and one for the constant) whereas the second has four (one for each of the three predictors and one for the constant). Therefore, model 1 has 198 degrees of freedom whereas model 2 has 196. The average sum of squares (MS) is then calculated for each term by dividing the SS by the *df*. The *F*-ratio is calculated by dividing the average improvement in prediction by the model (MS_M) by the average difference between the model and the observed data (MS_R). If the improvement due to fitting the regression model is much greater than the inaccuracy within the model then the value of *F* will be greater than 1 and SPSS calculates the exact probability of obtaining the value of *F* by chance. For the initial model the *F*-ratio is 99.587, which is very unlikely to have happened by chance ($p < 0.001$). For the second model the value of *F* is even higher (129.498), which is also highly significant ($p < 0.001$). We can interpret these results as meaning that the initial model significantly improved our ability to predict the outcome variable, but that the new model (with the extra predictors) was even better (because the *F*-ratio is more significant).

ANOVA[c]

Model		Sum of Squares	df	Mean Square	F	Sig.
1	Regression	433687.833	1	433687.833	99.587	.000[a]
	Residual	862264.167	198	4354.870		
	Total	1295952.0	199			
2	Regression	861377.418	3	287125.806	129.498	.000[b]
	Residual	434574.582	196	2217.217		
	Total	1295952.0	199			

a. Predictors: (Constant), Advertising Budget (thousands of pounds)

b. Predictors: (Constant), Advertising Budget (thousands of pounds), Attractiveness of Band, No. of Plays on Radio 1 per Week

c. Dependent Variable: Record Sales (thousands)

SPSS Output 4.6

4.4.1.3. Model Parameters

So far we have looked at several summary statistics telling us whether or not the model has improved our ability to predict the outcome variable. The next part of the output is concerned with the parameters of the model. SPSS Output 4.7 shows the model parameters for both steps in the hierarchy. Now, the first step in our hierarchy was to include advertising budget (as we did for the simple regression earlier in this chapter) and so the parameters for the first model are identical to the parameters obtained in SPSS Output 4.3. Therefore, we will be concerned only with the parameters for the final model (in which all predictors were included). The format of the table of coefficients will depend on the options selected. The confidence interval for the β values, collinearity diagnostics and the part and partial correlations will be present only if selected in the dialog box in Figure 4.11.

[handwritten: Standardised Beta values]

Coefficients[a]

Model		Unstandardized Coefficients		Standardized Coefficients	t	Sig.	95% Confidence Interval for B	
		B	Std. Error	Beta			Lower Bound	Upper Bound
1	(Constant)	134.140	7.537		17.799	.000	119.278	149.002
	Advertising Budget (thousands of pounds)	9.612E-02	.010	.578	9.979	.000	.077	.115
2	(Constant)	-26.613	17.350		-1.534	.127	-60.830	7.604
	Advertising Budget (thousands of pounds)	8.488E-02	.007	.511	12.261	.000	.071	.099
	No. of plays on Radio 1 per week	3.367	.278	.512	12.123	.000	2.820	3.915
	Attractiveness of Band	11.086	2.438	.192	4.548	.000	6.279	15.894

a. Dependent Variable: Record Sales (thousands)

[handwritten: +ve Predictors as advertising ↑ so do record sales so they do with airplay + band attractiveness]

[handwritten: Attractiveness has less of an impact]

Coefficients[a]

Model		Correlations			Collinearity Statistics	
		Zero-order	Partial	Part	Tolerance	VIF
1	Advertising Budget (thousands of pounds)	.578	.578	.578	1.000	1.000
2	Advertising Budget (thousands of pounds)	.578	.659	.507	.986	1.015
	No. of plays on Radio 1 per week	.599	.655	.501	.959	1.043
	Attractiveness of Band	.326	.309	.188	.963	1.038

a. Dependent Variable: Record Sales (thousands)

[handwritten: largest zero order correlation]

[handwritten: add together to get ave VIF]

[handwritten: values do not cross zero.]

SPSS Output 4.7: Coefficients of the regression model[10]

Remember that in multiple regression the model takes the form of equation (4.7) and in that equation there are several unknown quantities (the β values). The first part of the table gives us estimates for these β values and these values indicate the individual contribution of each predictor to the model. If we replace the β values into equation (4.7) we find that we can define the model as in equation (4.10).

---

[10] To spare your eyesight I have split this part of the output into two tables; however, it should appear as one long table in the SPSS viewer.

$$\text{Sales} = \beta_0 + \beta_1\text{Advertising}_i + \beta_2\text{Airplay}_i + \beta_3\text{Attractiveness}_i$$
$$= -26.61 + (0.08\text{Advertising}_i) + (3.37\text{Airplay}_i) \quad\quad (4.10)$$
$$+ (11.09\text{Attractiveness}_i)$$

The β values tell us about the relationship between record sales and each predictor. If the value is positive we can tell that there is a positive relationship between the predictor and the outcome whereas a negative coefficient represents a negative relationship. For these data all three predictors have positive β values indicating positive relationships. So, as advertising budget increases, record sales increase; as plays on the radio increase so do record sales; and finally more attractive bands will sell more records. The β values tell us more than this though. They tell us to what degree each predictor effects the outcome *if the effects of all other predictors are held constant.*

- **Advertising budget** (β = 0.085): This value indicates that as advertising budget increases by one unit, record sales increase by 0.085 units. Both variables were measured in thousands, therefore, for every £1000 more spent on advertising, an extra 0.085 thousand records (85 records) are sold. This interpretation is true only if the effects of attractiveness of the band and airplay are held constant.
- **Airplay** (β = 3.367): This value indicates that as the number of plays on radio in the week before release increases by one, record sales increase by 3.367 units. Therefore, every additional play of a song on radio (in the week before release) is associated with an extra 3.367 thousand records (3367 records) being sold. This interpretation is true only if the effects of attractiveness of the band and advertising are held constant.
- **Attractiveness** (β = 11.086): This value indicates that a band rated one higher on the attractiveness scale can expect additional record sales of 11.086 units. Therefore, every unit increase in the attractiveness of the band is associated with an extra 11.086 thousand records (11,086 records) being sold. This interpretation is true only if the effects of radio airplay and advertising are held constant.

Each of these beta values has an associated standard error indicating to what extent these values would vary across different samples, and these standard errors are used to determine whether or not the β value differs significantly from zero. As we saw in section 4.1.5.2, a t-statistic can be derived that tests whether a β value is significantly different from zero. In simple regression, a significant value of t indicates that the slope of the regression line is significantly different from horizontal, but in multiple regression, it is not so easy to visualize what the value tells us.

Well, it is easiest to conceptualize the *t*-tests as measures of whether the predictor is making a significant contribution to the model. Therefore, if the *t*-test associated with a β value is significant (if the value in the column labelled *Sig.* is less than 0.05) then the predictor is making a significant contribution to the model. The smaller the value of *Sig.* (and the larger the value of *t*) the greater the contribution of that predictor. For this model, the advertising budget ($t(196) = 12.26$, $p < 0.001$), the amount of radio play prior to release ($t(196) = 12.12$, $p < 0.001$) and attractiveness of the band ($t(196) = 4.55$, $p < 0.001$) are all significant predictors of record sales. From the magnitude of the *t*-statistics we can see that the advertising budget and radio play had a similar impact whereas the attractiveness of the band had less impact.

The β values and their significance are important statistics to look at; however, the standardized versions of the β values are in many ways easier to interpret (because they are not dependent on the units of measurement of the variables). The standardized beta values are provided by SPSS and they tell us the number of standard deviations that the outcome will change as a result of one standard deviation change in the predictor. All of the standardized beta values are measured in standard deviation units and so are directly comparable: therefore, they provide a better insight into the 'importance' of a predictor in the model. The standardized beta values for airplay and advertising budget are virtually identical (0.512 and 0.511 respectively) indicating that both variables have a comparable degree of importance in the model (this concurs with what the magnitude of the *t*-statistics told us[11]). To interpret these values literally, we need to know the standard deviations of all of the variables and these values can be found in SPSS Output 4.4.

- **Advertising budget** (*standardized* $\beta = 0.511$): This value indicates that as advertising budget increases by one standard deviation (£485,655), record sales increase by 0.511 standard deviations. The standard deviation for record sales is 80,699 and so this constitutes a change of 41,240 sales (0.511 × 80,699). Therefore, for every £485,655 more spent on advertising, an extra 41,240 records are sold. This interpretation is

---

[11] The reason why the relative magnitude of the *t*-statistics are comparable to the standardized beta values is because they are derived by dividing by the standard error and so they represent a *Studentized* version of the beta values. The standardized beta values are calculated by dividing by the standard deviation. In Chapter 1 we saw that the standard deviation and standard error are closely related: therefore, standardized and Studentized statistics are, in some sense, comparable.

[handwritten: A Constant Something That does not vary]

true only if the effects of attractiveness of the band and airplay are held constant.

- **Airplay** (*standardized* β = 0.512): This value indicates that as the number of plays on radio in the week before release increases by one standard deviation (12.27), record sales increase by 0.512 standard deviations. The standard deviation for record sales is 80,699 and so this constitutes a change of 41,320 sales (0.512 × 80,699). Therefore, if Radio 1 plays the song an extra 12.27 times in the week before release, 41,320 extra record sales can be expected. This interpretation is true only if the effects of attractiveness of the band and advertising are held constant.
- **Attractiveness** (*standardized* β = 0.192): This value indicates that a band rated one standard deviation (1.40 units) higher on the attractiveness scale can expect additional record sales of 0.192 standard deviations units. This constitutes a change of 15,490 sales (0.192 × 80,699). Therefore, a band with an attractiveness rating 1.40 higher than another band can expect 15,490 additional sales. This interpretation is true only if the effects of radio airplay and advertising are held constant.

[handwritten left margin: etc values tell us about relationship record sales + predictor. Standardised unit beta values. × SD]

These standardized coefficients give a better insight into the relative contribution of each variable. Imagine that we collected 100 samples of data measuring the same variables as our current model. For each sample we could create a regression model to represent the data. If the model is reliable then we hope to find very similar parameters in both. Therefore, each sample should produce approximately the same β values. The confidence interval of the unstandardized beta values tells us the boundaries within which the β values of 95% of samples would fall. Therefore, if we'd collected 100 samples, we are saying that 95% of these samples would give rise to β values within the boundaries of the confidence interval. In a good model the confidence intervals should be small indicating that 95% of samples would produce parameters very similar to the ones obtained. The sign (positive or negative) of the β values tells us about the direction of the relationship between the predictor and the outcome. Therefore, we would expect a very bad model to have confidence intervals that cross zero, indicating that in some samples the predictor has a negative relationship to the outcome whereas in others it has a positive relationship. In this model, the two best predictors (advertising and airplay) have very tight confidence intervals indicating that the estimates for the current model are likely to be representative of 95% of other samples. The interval for attractiveness is wider (but still does not cross zero) indicating that the parameter for this variable is less representative, but nevertheless significant.

[handwritten right margin: An unspecified Constant. a probability distribution, population scores summary]

If you asked for part and partial correlations, then they will appear in the output in separate columns of the table. The zero-order correlations are the simple Pearson's correlation coefficients (and so correspond to the values in SPSS Output 4.4). The partial correlations represent the relationships between each predictor and the outcome variable, controlling for the effects of the other two predictors. The part correlations represent the relationship between each predictor and the outcome, controlling for the effect that the other two variables have on the outcome. In effect, these part correlations represent the unique relationship that each predictor has with the outcome. If you opt to do a stepwise regression, you would find that variable entry is based initially on the variable with the largest zero-order correlation and then on the part correlations of the remaining variables. Therefore, airplay would be entered first (because it has the largest zero-order correlation), then advertising budget (because its part correlation is bigger than attractiveness) and then finally attractiveness. Try running a forward stepwise regression on these data to see if I'm right! Finally, we are given details of the collinearity statistics, but these will be discussed in section 4.4.1.5.

4.4.1.4. Excluded Variables

At each stage of a regression analysis SPSS provides a summary of any variables that have not yet been entered into the model. In a hierarchical model, this summary has details of the variables that have been specified to be entered in subsequent steps, and in stepwise regression this table contains summaries of the variables that SPSS is considering entering into the model. For this example, there is a summary of the excluded variables for the first stage of the hierarchy (there is no summary for the second stage because all predictors are in the model). The summary gives an estimate of each predictor's β value if it was entered into the equation at this point and calculates a t-test for this value. In a stepwise regression, SPSS should enter the predictor with the highest t-statistic and will continue entering predictors until there are none left with t-statistics that have significance values less than 0.05. The partial correlation also provides some indication as to what contribution (if any) an excluded predictor would make if it were entered into the model.

Excluded Variables[b]

Model		Beta In	t	Sig.	Partial Correlation	Collinearity Statistics		
						Tolerance	VIF	Minimum Tolerance
1	No. of plays on Radio 1 per week	.546[a]	12.513	.000	.665	.990	1.010	.990
	Attractiveness of Band	.281[a]	5.136	.000	.344	.993	1.007	.993

a. Predictors in the Model: (Constant), Advertising Budget (thousands of pounds)

b. Dependent Variable: Record Sales (thousands)

(handwritten margin notes:) tolerance < 0.1 indicates a serious problem. < 0.2 potential problem

No so strong correlation <7 2 or more predictors

SPSS Output 4.8

4.4.1.5. Assessing the Assumption of No Multicollinearity

SPSS Output 4.7 provided some measures of whether there is collinearity in the data. Specifically, it provides the VIF and tolerance statistics (with tolerance being 1 divided by the VIF). There are a few guidelines from section 4.2.5.3 that can be applied here.

- If the largest VIF is greater than 10 then there is cause for concern (Myers, 1990; Bowerman and O'Connell, 1990).
- If the average VIF is substantially greater than 1 then the regression may be biased (Bowerman and O'Connell, 1990).
- Tolerance below 0.1 indicates a serious problem.
- Tolerance below 0.2 indicates a potential problem (Menard, 1995).

For our current model the VIF values are all well below 10 and the tolerance statistics all well above 0.2; therefore, we can safely conclude that there is no collinearity within our data. To calculate the average VIF we simply add the VIF values for each predictor and divide by the number of predictors (*k*):

$$\overline{\text{VIF}} = \frac{\sum_{i=1}^{k} \text{VIF}_i}{k} = \frac{1.015 + 1.043 + 1.038}{3} = 1.032$$

The average VIF is very close to 1 and this confirms that collinearity is not a problem for this model. SPSS also produces a table of eigenvalues of the scaled, uncentred cross-products matrix, condition indexes and variance proportions. There is a lengthy discussion, and example, of collinearity in section 5.4.2.1 and how to detect it using variance proportions and so I will limit myself now to saying that we are looking for large variance proportions on the same *small* eigenvalues. Therefore, in SPSS Output 4.9 we look at the bottom few rows of the table (these are the small eigenvalues) and look for any variables that both have high variance proportions for that eigenvalue. The variance proportions vary between 0 and 1, and for each predictor should be distributed across different dimensions (or eigenvalues). For this model, you can see that each predictor has most of its variance loading onto a different dimension (advertising has 96% of variance on dimension 2, airplay has 93% of variance on dimension 3 and attractiveness has 92% of variance on dimension 4). These data represent a classic example of no multicollinearity. For an example of when collinearity exists in the data and some suggestions about what can be done, see Chapters 5 and 11 (section 5.4.2.1).

Collinearity Diagnostics

Model	Dimension	Eigenvalue	Condition Index	(Constant)	Advertising Budget (thousands of pounds)	No. of plays on Radio 1 per week	Attractiveness of Band
					Variance Proportions		
1	1	1.785	1.000	.11	.11		
	2	.215	2.883	.89	.89		
2	1	3.562	1.000	.00	.02	.01	.00
	2	.308	3.401	.01	.96	.05	.01
	3	.109	5.704	.05	.02	.93	.07
	4	2.039E-02	13.219	.94	.00	.00	.92

a. Dependent Variable: Record Sales (thousands)

SPSS Output 4.9

no multicollinearity below 0.1 0.2.

4.4.1.6. Casewise Diagnostics

SPSS produces a summary table of the residual statistics and these should be examined for extreme cases. SPSS Output 4.10 shows any cases that have a standardized residual less than −2 or greater than 2 (remember that we changed the default criterion from 3 to 2 in Figure 4.11). I mentioned in section 4.2.4.1 that in an ordinary sample we would expect 95% of cases to have standardized residuals within ±2. We have a sample of 200, therefore it is reasonable to expect about 10 cases (5%) to have standardized residuals outside of these limits. From SPSS Output 4.10 we can see that we have 12 cases (6%) that are outside of the limits: therefore, our sample is within 1% of what we would expect. In addition, 99% of cases should lie within ± 3 and so we would expect only 1% of cases to lie outside of these limits. From the cases listed here, it is clear that two cases (1%) lie outside of the limits (cases 164 and 169). Therefore, our sample appears to conform to what we would expect for a fairly accurate model. These diagnostics give us no real cause for concern except that case 169 has a standardized residual greater than 3, which is probably large enough for us to investigate this case further.

You may remember that in section 4.3.4 we asked SPSS to save various diagnostic statistics. You should find that the data editor now contains columns for these variables. It is perfectly acceptable to check these values in the data editor, but you can also get SPSS to list the values in your viewer window too. To list variables you need to use the *Case Summaries* command, which can be found by using the **Analyze⇒Reports⇒Case Summaries** ... menu path[12]. Figure 4.15 shows the dialog box for this function. Simply select the variables that you want to list and transfer them to the box labelled *Variables* by clicking on ▶. By default, SPSS will limit the output to the first 100 cases, but if you want to list all of your cases then simply deselect this option. It is also very important to select the *Show case numbers* option because otherwise you might not be able to identify a problem case.

Casewise Diagnostics

Case Number	Std. Residual	Record Sales (thousands)	Predicted Value	Residual
1	2.125	330.00	229.9203	100.0797
2	-2.314	120.00	228.9490	-108.9490
10	2.114	300.00	200.4662	99.5338
47	-2.442	40.00	154.9698	-114.9698
52	2.069	190.00	92.5973	97.4027
55	-2.424	190.00	304.1231	-114.1231
61	2.098	300.00	201.1897	98.8103
68	-2.345	70.00	180.4156	-110.4156
100	2.066	250.00	152.7133	97.2867
164	-2.577	120.00	241.3240	-121.3240
169	3.061	360.00	215.8675	144.1325
200	-2.064	110.00	207.2061	-97.2061

a. Dependent Variable: Record Sales (thousands)

[handwritten annotations: shows no of cases of standardised residuals outside units above 5% in above dodgy; Y Outcome]

SPSS Output 4.10

One useful strategy is to use the casewise diagnostics to identify cases that you want to investigate further. So, to save space, I created a coding variable (1= include, 0 = exclude) so that I could specify the 12 cases listed in SPSS Output 4.10 in one group, and all other cases in the other. By using this coding variable and specifying it as a grouping variable in the *summarize cases* dialog box, I could look at those 12 cases together and discard all others.

SPSS Output 4.11 shows the influence statistics for the 12 cases that I selected. None of them have a Cook's distance greater than 1 (even case 169 is well below this criterion) and so none of the cases is having an undue influence on the model. The average leverage can be calculated as 0.02 ($k + 1/n = 4/200$) and so we are looking for values either twice as large as this (0.04) or three times as large (0.06) depending on which statistician you trust most (see section 4.2.4.2)! All cases are within the boundary of three times the average and only case 1 is close to two times the average. Finally, from our guidelines for the Mahalanobis distance we saw that with a sample of 100 and three predictors, values greater

[handwritten annotation: to check cases influence]

---

[12] **Statistics⇒Summarize⇒Case Summaries** ... in version 8.0 and earlier.

than 15 were problematic. We have three predictors and a larger sample
size, so this value will be a conservative cut-off, yet none of our cases
come close to exceeding this criterion. The evidence suggests that there
are no influential cases within our data (although all cases would need
to be examined to confirm this fact).

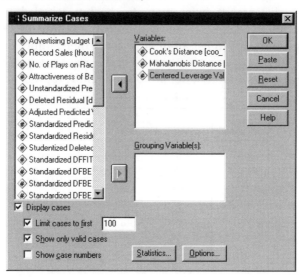

Figure 4.15

We can look also at the DFBeta statistics to see whether any case would
have a large influence on the regression parameters. An absolute value
greater than 1 is a problem and in all cases the values lie within ±1,
which shows that these cases have no undue influence over the
regression parameters. There is also a column for the covariance ratio.
We saw in section 4.2.4.2 that we need to use the following criteria:

- $\text{CVR}_i > 1 + [3(k + 1)/n] = 1 + [3(3 + 1)/200] = 1.06$
- $\text{CVR}_i < 1 - [3(k + 1)/n] = 1 - [3(3 + 1)/200] = 0.94.$

Therefore, we are looking for any cases that deviate substantially from
these boundaries. Most of our 12 potential outliers have CVR values
within or just outside these boundaries. The only case that causes
concern is case 169 (again!) whose CVR is some way below the bottom
limit. However, given the Cook's distance for this case, there is probably
little cause for alarm.

You would have requested other diagnostic statistics and from what
you know from the earlier discussion of them you are well-advised to
glance over them in case of any unusual cases in the data. However,

from this minimal set of diagnostics we appear to have a fairly reliable model that has not been unduly influenced by any subset of cases.

Case Summaries

	Case Number	Standardized DFBETA Intercept	Standardized DFBETA ADVERTS	Standardized DFBETA AIRPLAY	Standardized DFBETA ATTRACT	Standardized DFFIT	COVRATIO
1	1	-.31554	-.24235	.15774	.35329	.48929	.97127
2	2	.01259	-.12637	.00942	-.01868	-.21110	.92018
3	10	-.01256	-.15612	.16772	.00672	.26896	.94392
4	47	.06645	.19602	.04829	-.17857	-.31469	.91458
5	52	.35291	-.02881	-.13667	-.26965	.36742	.95995
6	55	.17427	-.32649	-.02307	-.12435	-.40736	.92486
7	61	.00082	-.01539	.02793	.02054	.15562	.93654
8	68	-.00281	.21146	-.14766	-.01760	-.30216	.92370
9	100	.06113	.14523	-.29984	.06766	.35732	.95888
10	164	.17983	.28988	-.40088	-.11706	-.54029	.92037
11	169	-.16819	-.25765	.25739	.16968	.46132	.85325
12	200	.16633	-.04639	.14213	-.25907	-.31985	.95435
Total N		12	12	12	12	12	12

[handwritten: further away]
[handwritten: less than 1]

SPSS Output 4.11

Case Summaries

	Case Number	Cook's Distance	Mahalanobis Distance	Centered Leverage Value
1	1	.05870	8.39591	.04219
2	2	.01089	.59830	.00301
3	10	.01776	2.07154	.01041
4	47	.02412	2.12475	.01068
5	52	.03316	4.81841	.02421
6	55	.04042	4.19960	.02110
7	61	.00595	.06880	.00035
8	68	.02229	2.13106	.01071
9	100	.03136	4.53310	.02278
10	164	.07077	6.83538	.03435
11	169	.05087	3.14841	.01582
12	200	.02513	3.49043	.01754
Total N		12	12	12

SPSS Output 4.12

4.4.1.7. *Checking Assumptions*

As a final stage in the analysis, you should check the assumptions of the model. We have already looked for collinearity within the data and used Durbin-Watson to check whether the residuals in the model are independent. In section 4.3.3 we asked for a plot of *ZRESID against *ZPRED and for a histogram and normal probability plot of the residuals. The graph of *ZRESID and *ZPRED should look like a random array of dots evenly dispersed around zero. If this graph funnels out, then the chances are that there is heteroscedasticity in the data. If there is any sort of curve in this graph then the chances are that the data has broken the assumption of linearity. Figure 4.16 shows several examples of the plot of standardized residuals against standardized predicted values. Panel (a) shows the graph for the data in our record sales example. Note how the points are randomly and evenly dispersed throughout the plot. This pattern is indicative of a situation in which the assumptions of linearity and homoscedasticity have been met. Panel (b) shows a similar plot for a data set that violates the assumption of homoscedasticity. Note that the points form the shape of a funnel so they become more spread out across the graph. This funnel shape is typical of heteroscedasticity and indicates increasing variance across the residuals. Panel (c) shows a plot of some data in which there is a non-linear relationship between the outcome and the predictor. This pattern is shown up by the residuals. A line illustrating the curvilinear relationship has been drawn over the top of the graph to illustrate the trend in the data. Finally, panel (d) represents a situation in which the data not only represent a non-linear relationship but also show heteroscedasticity. Note first the curved trend in the data, and then also note that at one end of the plot the points are very close together whereas at the other end they are widely dispersed. When these assumptions have been broken you will not see these exact patterns, but hopefully these plots will help you to understand the types of anomalies you should look out for.

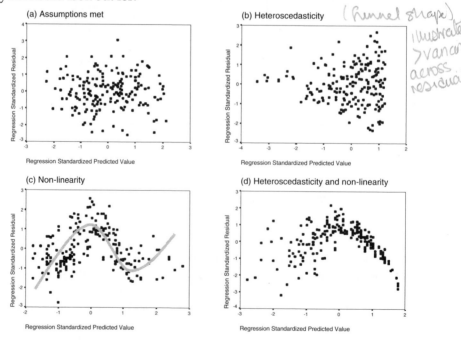

Figure 4.16: Plots of *ZRESID against *ZPRED

Normality of Residuals

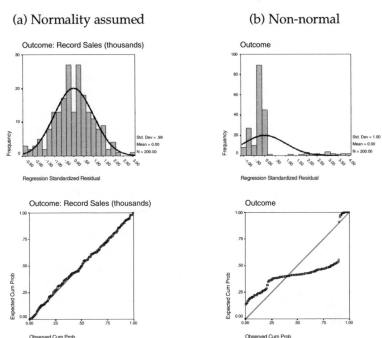

(a) Normality assumed

(b) Non-normal

Figure 4.17: Histograms and normal P-P plots of normally distributed residuals (left-hand side) and non-normally distributed residuals (right-hand side)

To test the normality of residuals, we must look at the histogram and normal probability plot selected in Figure 4.12. Figure 4.17 shows the histogram and normal probability plot of the data for the current example (left-hand side). The histogram should look like a normal distribution (a bell-shaped curve). SPSS draws a curve on the histogram to show the shape of the distribution. For the record company data, the distribution is roughly normal (although there is a slight deficiency of residuals exactly on zero). Compare this histogram with the extremely non-normal histogram next to it and it should be clear that the non-normal distribution is extremely skewed (unsymmetrical). So, you should look for a curve that has the same shape as the one for the record sales data: any deviation from this curve is a sign of non-normality and the greater the deviation the more non-normally distributed the residuals. The normal probability plot also shows up deviations from normality (see Chapter 2). The straight line in this plot represents a normal distribution, and the points represent the observed residuals. Therefore, in a perfectly normally distributed data set, all points will lie on the line. This is pretty much what we see for the record sales data. However, next to the normal probability plot of the record sales data is an example of an extreme deviation from normality. In this plot, the dots are very distant from the line, which indicates a large deviation from normality. For both plots, the non-normal data are extreme cases and you should be aware that the deviations from normality are likely to be subtler. Of course, you can use what you learnt in Chapter 2 to do a K-S test on the standardized residuals to see whether they deviate significantly from normality.

A final set of plots specified in Figure 4.12 was the partial plots. These plots are scatterplots of the residuals of the outcome variable and each of the predictors when both variables are regressed separately on the remaining predictors. I mentioned earlier that obvious outliers on a partial plot represent cases that might have undue influence on a predictor's regression coefficient and that non-linear relationships and heteroscedasticity can be detected using these plots as well.

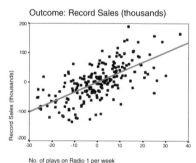

Outcome: Record Sales (thousands)

Advertising Budget (thousands of pounds)

For advertising budget the partial plot shows the strong positive relationship to record sales. The gradient of the line is β for advertising in the model (this line does not appear by default). There are no obvious outliers on this plot, and the cloud of dots is evenly spaced out around the line, indicating homoscedasticity.

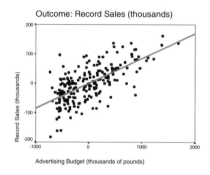

Outcome: Record Sales (thousands)

No. of plays on Radio 1 per week

For airplay the partial plot shows a strong positive relationship to record sales. The gradient and pattern of the data are similar to advertising (which would be expected given the similarity of the standardized betas of these predictors). There are no obvious outliers on this plot, and the cloud of dots is evenly spaced around the line, indicating homoscedasticity.

The residuals
at each level of
the predictor(s)
should have the
same level.

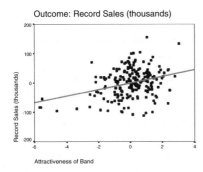

Outcome: Record Sales (thousands)

Attractiveness of Band

For attractiveness the partial plot shows a positive relationship to record sales. The relationship looks less linear than the other predictors do and the dots seem to funnel out indicating greater variance at high levels of attractiveness. There are no obvious outliers on this plot, but the funnel-shaped cloud of dots might indicate a violation of the assumption of homoscedasticity. We would be well advised to collect some more data for unattractive bands to verify the current model.

4.4.2. *Summary*

This chapter has looked very thoroughly at how a regression analysis should be carried out and how to check the assumptions of the model. The example used gave rise to a model that appears, in most senses, to be both accurate for the sample and generalizable to the population. The only slight glitch is some concern over whether attractiveness ratings had violated the assumption of homoscedasticity. Therefore, we could conclude that in our sample advertising budget and airplay are fairly equally important in predicting record sales. Attractiveness of the band is a significant predictor of record sales but is less important than the other two predictors (and probably needs verification because of possible heteroscedasticity). The assumptions seem to have been met and so we can probably assume that this model would generalize to any record being released.

In general, multiple regression is a long process and should be done with care and attention to detail. There are a lot of important things to consider and you should approach the analysis in a systematic fashion. I hope this chapter helps you to do that!

4.5.   Further Reading

Bowerman, B. L. & O'Connell, R. T. (1990). *Linear statistical models: an applied approach* (2nd edition). Belmont, CA: Duxbury. This text is only for the mathematically minded or postgraduate students but provides an extremely thorough exposition of regression analysis.

Howell, D. C. (1997). *Statistical methods for psychology* (4th edition). Belmont, CA: Duxbury. Chapters 9 and 15 are excellent introductions to the mathematics behind regression analysis.

Stevens, J. (1992). *Applied multivariate statistics for the social sciences* (2nd edition). Hillsdale, NJ: Erlbaum. Chapter 3.

5 Logistic Regression

5.1. Introduction: Background to Logistic Regression

We have seen already how an outcome can be predicted from a number of predictor variables using multiple regression. Well, in a nutshell, logistic regression is multiple regression but with an outcome variable that is a categorical dichotomy and predictor variables that are continuous or categorical. In plain English, this simply means that we can predict which of two categories a person is likely to belong to given certain other information. A trivial example is to look at which variables predict whether a person is male or female. We might measure the following variables: laziness, pig-headedness, alcohol consumption and number of burps that a person does in a day. Using logistic regression, we might find that all of these variables predict the gender of the person, but the technique will also allow us to predict whether a certain person is likely to be male or female. So, if we picked a random person and discovered they scored highly on laziness, pig-headedness, alcohol consumption and the number of burps, then the regression model might tell us that, based on this information, this person is likely to be male. Admittedly, it is unlikely that a researcher would ever be interested in the relationship between flatulence and gender (it is probably too well established by experience to warrant research!), but logistic regression can have life-saving applications. In the biomedical literature (that is medical research) logistic regression has applications such as formulating models about the sorts of factors that might determine whether a tumour is cancerous or benign (for example). A database of patients can be used to establish which variables are influential in predicting the malignancy of a tumour. These variables can then be measured for a new patient and their values placed in a logistic regression model, from that a probability of malignancy could be estimated. If the probability value of the tumour being malignant is suitably low then the doctor may decide not to carry out expensive and painful surgery that in all likelihood is unnecessary.

In the social sciences we rarely face such life-threatening decisions yet logistic regression is still a very useful tool. For this reason, it is tragic that many textbooks often overlook it. In this chapter I hope to redress the balance by explaining the principles behind logistic regression and how to carry out the procedure on SPSS.

5.2. What Are the Principles behind Logistic Regression?

I don't wish to dwell on the underlying principles of logistic regression because they aren't necessary to understand the test (I am living proof of this fact). However, I do wish to just draw a few parallels to normal regression in an attempt to couch logistic regression in a framework that will be familiar to everyone who has got this far in the book (what do you mean you haven't read the regression chapter yet—naughty, naughty!). Now would be a good time for the equation-phobes to look away. In simple linear regression, we saw that the outcome variable Y is predicted from the equation of a straight line:

$$Y = \beta_0 + \beta_1 X_1 + \varepsilon_i \qquad (5.1)$$

in which β_0 is the Y intercept, β_1 is the gradient of the straight line, X_1 is the value of the predictor variable and ε is a residual term. Given the values of Y and X_1, the unknown parameters in the equation can be estimated by finding a solution for which the squared distance between the observed and predicted values of the dependent variable is minimized (the method of least squares).

This stuff should all be pretty familiar. In multiple regression, in which there are several predictors, a similar equation is derived in which each predictor has its own coefficient. As such, Y is predicted from a combination of each predictor variable multiplied by its respective regression coefficient.

$$Y = \beta_0 + \beta_1 X_1 + \beta_2 X_2 + ... + \beta_n X_n + \varepsilon_i \qquad (5.2)$$

in which β_n is the regression coefficient of the corresponding variable X_n. In logistic regression, instead of predicting the value of a variable Y from a predictor variable X_1 or several predictor variables (Xs), we predict the *probability* of Y occurring given known values of X_1 (or Xs). The logistic regression equation bears many similarities to the regression equations just described. In its simplest form, when there is only one predictor variable X_1, the logistic regression equation from which the probability of Y is predicted is given by equation (5.3).

$$P(Y) = \frac{1}{1 + e^{-(\beta_0 + \beta_1 X_1 + \varepsilon_i)}} \qquad (5.3)$$

in which $P(Y)$ is the probability of Y occurring, e is the base of natural logarithms, and the other coefficients form a linear combination much the same as in simple regression. In fact, you might notice that the bracketed portion of the equation is identical to the linear regression equation in that there is a constant (β_0), a predictor variable (X_1) and a coefficient (or weight) attached to that predictor (β_1). Just like linear regression, it is possible to extend this equation so as to include several predictors. When there are several predictors the equation becomes:

$$P(Y) = \frac{1}{1 + e^{-Z}}$$

(5.4)

$$Z = \beta_0 + \beta_1 X_1 + \beta_2 X_2 + ... + \beta_n X_n + \varepsilon_i$$

Equation (5.4) is the same as the equation used when there is only one predictor except that the linear combination has been extended to include any number of predictors. So, whereas the one-predictor version of the logistic regression equation contained the simple linear regression equation within it, the multiple-predictor version contains the multiple regression equation.

Despite the similarities between linear regression and logistic regression, there is a good reason why we cannot apply linear regression directly to a situation in which the outcome variable is dichotomous. The reason is that one of the assumptions of linear regression is that the relationship between variables is linear (see section 4.2.5.1). In that section we saw how important it is that the assumptions of a model are met for that model to be accurate. Therefore, for linear regression to be a valid model, the observed data should contain a linear relationship. When the outcome variable is dichotomous, this assumption is usually violated (see Berry, 1993). One way around this problem is to transform the data using the logarithmic transformation (see Berry and Feldman, 1985). This has the effect of making the *form* of the relationship linear whilst leaving the relationship itself as non-nolinear (so, it is a way of expressing a non-linear relationship in a linear way). The logistic regression equation described above is based on this principle: it expresses the multiple linear regression equation in logarithmic terms and thus overcomes the problem of violating the assumption of linearity.

The exact form of the equation can be arranged in a number of ways but the version I have chosen expresses the equation in terms of the probability of Y occurring (i.e. the probability that a case belongs in a certain category). As such, the resulting value from the equation is a probability value that varies between 0 and 1. A value close to zero means that Y is very unlikely to have occurred, and a value close to 1 means that Y is very likely to have occurred. Also, just like linear regression, each predictor variable in the logistic regression equation has its own coefficient. When we run the analysis we need to estimate the value of these coefficients so that we can solve the equation. These parameters are estimated by fitting models, based on the available predictors, to the observed data. The chosen model will be the one that, when values of the predictor variables are placed in it, results in values of Y closest to the observed values. Specifically, the values of the parameters are estimated using the *maximum-likelihood method*, which selects coefficients that make the observed values most likely to have occurred. So, as with multiple regression, we try to fit a model to our data that allows us to estimate values of the outcome variable from known values of the predictor variable or variables.

5.3.   A Research Example

As my first research example I am going to look at a simple example from developmental psychology. A good example of a dichotomy is the passing or failing of a test, which in developmental psychology terms often relates to the possession (or not) of a cognitive ability. This example looks at children's understanding of display rules based on the child's age, and whether the child possesses a theory of mind. Put simplistically, a display rule is a convention of displaying an appropriate emotion in a given situation. For example, if you receive a Christmas present that you don't like, the appropriate emotional display is to smile politely and say 'thank you Auntie Kate, I've always wanted a rotting cabbage'. The inappropriate emotional display is to start crying and scream 'why did you buy me a rotting cabbage you selfish old bag?' There is some evidence that young children lack an understanding of appropriate display rules and this has been linked to the acquisition of a theory of mind (which is simply the ability to understand what another person might be thinking).

For this example, our researchers are interested in whether the understanding of emotional display rules was linked to having a theory of mind. The rationale is that it might be necessary for a child to understand how another person thinks to realize how their emotional displays will affect that person: if you can't put yourself in Aunt Kate's mind, then you won't realize that she might be upset by you calling her an old bag. To test this theory, a number of children were given a standard false belief task (a task used to measure whether someone has a theory of mind) that they could either pass or fail and their age in months was also measured. In addition, each child was given a display rule task, which they could either pass or fail. So, the following variables were measured:

- **Outcome (dependent variable)**: Possession of display rule understanding (Did the child pass the test: Yes/No?).

- **Predictor (independent variable)**: Possession of a theory of mind (Did the child pass the false belief task: Yes/No?).
- **Predictor (independent variable)**: Age in months.

In this experiment, there is a dichotomous outcome variable, a categorical predictor and a continuous predictor. This scenario is ideal for logistic regression.

5.3.1. Running the Analysis

To carry out logistic regression, the data must be entered as for normal regression: they are arranged in the data editor in three columns (one representing each variable). The data can be found in the file **display.sav** in the Chapter 5 file of the data disk. Looking at the data editor you should notice that both of the categorical variables have been entered as coding variables (see section 1.2.3.1), that is, numbers have been specified to represent categories. For ease of interpretation, the outcome variable should be coded 1 (event occurred) and 0 (event did not occur); in this case, 1 represents having display rule understanding, and 0 represents an absence of display rule understanding. For the false belief task a similar coding has been used (1 = passed the false belief task, 2 = failed the false belief task). Logistic regression is located in the *Regression* menu accessed via the *Analyze* menu: **Analyze⇒Regression⇒Binary Logistic**. Following this menu path activates the main *logistic regression* dialog box shown in Figure 5.1.

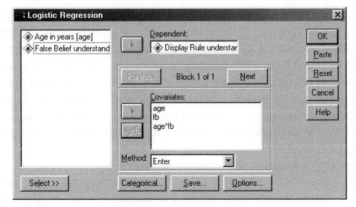

Figure 5.1: *Logistic regression* main dialog box

The main dialog box is very similar to the standard *regression* option box. There is a space to place a dependent variable (or outcome variable). In this example, the outcome was the display rule task, so we can simply click on **display** and transfer it to the *Dependent* box by clicking on 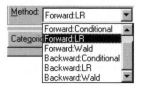. There is also a box for specifying the covariates (the predictor variables). It is possible to specify both main effects and interactions in logistic regression. To specify a main effect, simply select one predictor (for example **age**) and then transfer this variable to the *Covariates* box by clicking ⊡. To input an interaction, click on more than one variable on the left-hand side of the dialog box (i.e. highlight two or more variables) and then click on >a*b> to move them to the *Covariates* box. In this example there are only two predictors and therefore there is only one possible interaction (the **age** × **fb** interaction), but if you have three predictors then you can select several two-way interactions and the three-way interaction as well.

5.3.1.1. Method of Regression

As with multiple regression, there are a number of different methods that can be used in logistic regression. You can select a particular method of regression by clicking on the down arrow next to the box labelled *Method*. Figure 5.2 shows part of the logistic regression menu when the methods of regression are activated.

Figure 5.2: Method of regression

The Forced Entry Method: The default method of conducting the regression is 'enter'. This is the same as forced entry in multiple regression in that all of the covariates are placed into the regression model in one block, and parameter estimates are calculated for each block. Some researchers believe that this method is the only appropriate method for theory testing (Studenmund and Cassidy, 1987) because stepwise techniques are influenced by random variation in the data and so seldom give replicable results if the model is retested within the same sample.

Stepwise Methods: If you are undeterred by the criticisms of stepwise methods, then you can select either a forward or a backward stepwise method. When the forward method is employed the computer begins with a model that includes only a constant and then adds single predictors into the model based on a specific criterion. This criterion is the value of the *score* statistic: the variable with the most significant score statistic is added to the model. The computer proceeds until none of the remaining predictors have a significant score statistic (the cut-off point for significance being 0.05). At each step, the computer also examines the variables in the model to see whether any should be removed. It does this in one of three ways. The first way is to use the likelihood ratio statistic (the *Forward:LR* method) in which case the current model is compared to the model when that predictor is removed. If the removal of that predictor makes a significant difference to how well the model fits the observed data, then the computer retains that predictor (because the model is better if the predictor is included). If, however, the removal of the predictor makes little difference to the model then the computer rejects that predictor. Rather than using the likelihood ratio statistic, which estimates how well the model fits the observed data, the computer could use the conditional statistic as a removal criterion (*Forward:Conditional*). This statistic is an arithmetically less intense version of the likelihood ratio statistic and so there is little to recommend it over the likelihood ratio method. The final criterion is the Wald statistic, in which case any predictors in the model that have significance values of the Wald statistic (above the default removal criterion of 0.1) will be removed. Of these methods the likelihood ratio method is the best removal criterion because the Wald statistic can, at times, be unreliable (see Section 5.3.2.1).

The opposite of the forward method is the backward method. This method uses the same three removal criteria, but instead of starting the model with only a constant, it begins the model with all predictors included. The computer then tests whether any of these predictors can be removed from the model without having a substantial effect on how well the model fits the observed data. The first predictor to be removed will be the one that has the least impact on how the model fits the data.

The method of regression chosen will depend on a number of things. The main consideration is whether you are testing a theory or merely carrying our exploratory work. As noted earlier, some people believe that stepwise methods have no value for theory testing. However, stepwise methods are defensible when used in situations in which no previous research exists on which to base hypotheses for testing, and in situations where causality is not of interest and you merely wish to find a model to fit your data (Menard, 1995; Agresti and Finlay, 1986). If you do decide to use a stepwise method then the backward method is preferable to the forward method. This is because of *suppressor* effects, which occur when a predictor has a significant effect but only when another variable is held constant. Forward selection is more likely than backward elimination to exclude predictors involved in suppressor effects. As such, the forward method runs a higher risk of making a type

II error. In terms of the test statistic used in stepwise methods, the Wald statistic has a tendency to be inaccurate in certain circumstances (something I will talk more about in due course) and so the likelihood ratio method is best.

5.3.1.2.   *Categorical Predictors*

In this example there is one categorical predictor variable. One of the great things about logistic regression is that it is quite happy to accept categorical predictors. However, it is necessary to 'tell' SPSS which variables, if any, are categorical by clicking on Categorical... in the main *logistic regression* dialog box to activate the dialog box in Figure 5.3. In this dialog box, the covariates are listed on the left-hand side, and there is a space on the right-hand side in which categorical covariates can be placed. Simply highlight any categorical variables you have (in this example click on **fb**) and transfer them to the *Categorical Covariates* box by clicking ▶. In Figure 5.3, **fb** has already been selected and transferred.

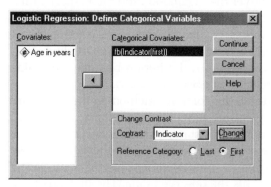

Figure 5.3: Defining categorical variables in logistic regression

There are many ways in which you can treat categorical predictors: by default, SPSS will use deviation contrasts on all categorical variables. We shall see in Chapter 7 that deviation contrasts compare the effect of each category (except the reference category, which can be the first or last) with the overall effect of all of the categories. There are a number of other contrasts that can be used depending on what you need to test. Clicking on the down arrow in the *Change Contrast* box accesses these contrasts. Figure 5.4 shows that it is possible to select simple contrasts, difference contrasts, Helmert contrasts, repeated contrasts and polynomial contrasts just as in ANOVA (see Table 7.6). These techniques will be discussed in detail in Chapter 7 and so there is no need to explain what these contrasts actually do. However, one form of contrast that we won't encounter elsewhere is the indicator contrast and you'll notice in Figure 5.3 that this is the contrast I have selected. When an indicator contrast is used, levels of the categorical variable are recoded using standard dummy variable coding (see section 6.4.4).

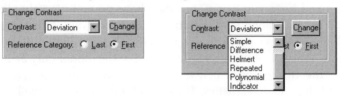

Figure 5.4: Selecting contrasts for categorical predictors

5.3.1.3. Obtaining Residuals

As with linear regression it is possible to ask SPSS to save a set of residuals as new variables in the data editor. These residual variables can then be examined to see how well the model fits the observed data. To save residuals click on ⬚*Save...* in the main *logistic regression* dialog box (Figure 5.1). SPSS saves each of the selected variables into the data editor but they can be listed in the output viewer by using the *Case Summaries* command (see section 4.4.1.6) and selecting the residual variables of interest. The residuals dialog box in Figure 5.5 gives us a number of options and most of these are the same as those in multiple regression (refer to section 4.3.4). Two residuals that are unique to logistic regression are the *predicted probabilities* and the *predicted group memberships*. The predicted probabilities are the probabilities of Y occurring given the values of each predictor for a given subject. As such, they are derived from equation (5.4) for a given case. The predicted group membership is self-explanatory in that it predicts to which of the two categories of Y a subject is most likely to belong based on the model. The group memberships are based on the predicted probabilities and I will explain these values in more detail when we consider how to interpret the residuals. It is worth selecting all of the available options, or as a bare minimum select the same options as in Figure 5.5.

I cannot stress enough the importance of examining residuals after any analysis. One of the many benefits of computer packages over analysing data by hand is that it is very easy to obtain residual diagnostics, which would otherwise be incredibly time consuming to obtain and would require a fairly substantial understanding of algebra. Nevertheless, the advancement of computing facilities has probably not been met with a proportionate advancement in the consideration of residuals. Sadly, social scientists, who have spent far too long being trained only to hunt out probability values below 0.05, often ignore the examination of residuals! I have stressed the importance of building accurate models, and that running a regression without checking how well the model fits

the data is like buying a new pair of trousers without trying them on—
they might look fine on the hanger but get them home and you find
you're Johnny-tight-pants. The trousers might do their job (they cover
your legs and keep you warm) but they have no real-life value (because
they cut off the blood circulation to your legs and other important
appendages). Likewise, regression does its job regardless of the data—it
will create a model—but the real-life value of the model may be limited.

Testing the degree to which a model fits the data collected is the
essence of diagnostic statistics. If the model fits the data well, then we
can have more confidence that the coefficients of the model are accurate
and are not being influenced by a few stray data points. At best, failure
to examine residuals can lead to ignorance of inaccurate coefficients in a
model. At worst this inaccurate model could then be used to accept a
theoretical hypothesis that is, in fact, not true.

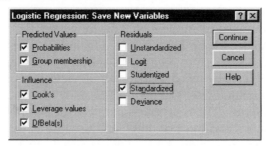

Figure 5.5: Dialog box for obtaining residuals for logistic regression

5.3.1.4. Further Options

There is a final dialog box that offers further options. This box is shown
in Figure 5.6 and is accessed by clicking on ⌐Options...⌐ in the main *logistic
regression* dialog box. For the most part, the default settings in this dialog
box are fine. I mentioned in section 5.3.1.1 that when a stepwise method
is used there are default criteria for selecting and removing predictors
from the model. These default settings are displayed in the *options*
dialog box under *Probability for Stepwise*. The probability thresholds can
be changed, but there is really no need unless you have a good reason
for wanting harsher criteria for variable selection. Another default is to
arrive at a model after a maximum of 20 iterations. When we fit a model
to our data we try to fit the best model possible and the maximum
iterations can be conceived of as the maximum number of attempts that
the computer will make to find the best model. Unless you have a very
complex model, 20 iterations will be more than adequate. We saw in
Chapter 4 that regression equations contain a constant that represents
the Y intercept (i.e. the value of Y when the value of the predictors is
zero). By default SPSS includes this constant in the model, but it is

possible to run the analysis without this constant and this has the effect of making the model pass through the origin (i.e. Y is zero when X is zero). Given that we are usually interested in producing a model that best fits the data we have collected, there is little point in running the analysis without the constant included.

One option that is very useful is a classification plot, which is a histogram of the actual and predicted values of the outcome variable. This plot is useful for assessing the fit of the model to the observed data. It is also possible to do a *Casewise listing of residuals* either for any cases for which the standardized residual is greater than 2 standard deviations (this value can be changed but the default is sensible), or for all cases. I recommend a more thorough examination of residuals but this option can be useful for a quick inspection. You can ask SPSS to display a confidence interval for the exp β statistic (see section 5.3.2.3) and by default SPSS displays a 90% confidence interval; this should really be changed to a 95% interval, and it is a useful statistic to have. More important, in versions 8.0 and 9.0 of SPSS you can request the *Hosmer-Lemeshow goodness-of-fit* statistic, which can be used to assess how well the chosen model fits the data. The remaining options are fairly unimportant: you can choose to display all statistics and graphs at each stage of an analysis (the default), or only after the final model has been fitted. Finally, you can display a correlation matrix of parameter estimates for the terms in the model, and you can display coefficients and log-likelihood values at each iteration of the parameter estimation process—the practical function of doing this is lost on most of us mere mortals!

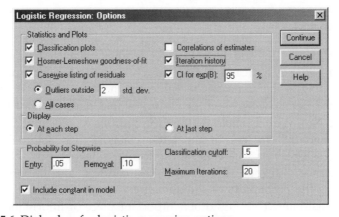

Figure 5.6: Dialog box for logistic regression options

5.3.2. Output

Select a *Forward:LR* method of regression and choose the options mentioned in the previous sections. Having spent a vast amount of time telling you never to do stepwise analyses, it's probably a bit strange to hear me suggest doing forward regression here. Well, for one thing this study is the first in the field and so we have no past research to tell us which variables to expect to be reliable predictors. Second, I didn't show you a stepwise example in the regression chapter and so this will be a useful way to demonstrate how a stepwise procedure operates! When you have selected a *Forward:LR* method in the *logistic regression* dialog box (Figure 5.1) you can click on OK and watch the output spew out in the viewer window. I shall explain each part of the analysis in turn.

```
Dependent Variable Encoding:

Original          Internal
Value             Value
      .00         0
     1.00         1

                                     Parameter
                       Value   Freq  Coding
                                      (1)
FB
  No                     .00   29    .000
  Yes                   1.00   41   1.000

      Interactions:

INT_1    AGE by FB(1)
```

SPSS Output 5.1

SPSS Output 5.1 tells us the parameter codings given to the categorical predictor variable. Indicator coding was chosen with two categories, and so the coding is the same as the values in the data editor. If *deviation* coding had been chosen then the coding would have been −1 (**fb** Yes) and 1 (**fb** No). With a *simple* contrast the codings would have been −0.5 (**fb** No) and 0.5 (**fb** Yes) if the latter category was selected as the reference category or vice versa if the former category was selected as the reference category. The parameter codings are important for calculating the probability of the outcome variable ($P(Y)$), but we shall come to that later. The only other important piece of information from this portion of the output is that we are told that we have requested one interaction in the model and we are given a code, INT_1, to represent this parameter. It might seem pointless to assign the interaction a code; however, in situations in which several interactions exist it can be a great space-saving device.

```
Dependent Variable..   DISPLAY     Display Rule understanding

Beginning Block Number  0.   Initial Log Likelihood Function

-2 Log Likelihood   96.124319

* Constant is included in the model.

Estimation terminated at iteration number 2 because
Log Likelihood decreased by less than .01 percent.

              Iteration History:

Iteration   Log Likelihood    Constant
        1        -48.062168    .22857143
        2        -48.062159    .22957438

Classification Table for DISPLAY
                    Predicted
                  No      Yes      Percent Correct
                  N   I   Y
Observed          I-------I-------I
   No      N   I    0  I   31  I        .00%
                  I-------I-------I
   Yes     Y   I    0  I   39  I     100.00%
                  I-------I-------I
                        Overall   55.71%



-------------- Variables in the Equation ---------------

Variable      B      S.E.    Wald    df   Sig    R    Exp(B)

Constant    .2296   .2406   .9103    1  .3400


Beginning Block Number  1.   Method: Forward Stepwise (LR)

-------------- Variables not in the Equation -------------
Residual Chi Square      26.257 with   3 df   Sig = .0000

Variable               Score    df     Sig       R

AGE                   15.9559    1    .0001    .3810
FB(1)                 24.6167    1    .0000    .4851
AGE by FB(1)          23.9868    1    .0000    .4783
```

SPSS Output 5.2

For this first analysis we requested a forward stepwise method and so the initial model is derived using only the constant in the regression equation. SPSS Output 5.2 tells us about the model when only the constant is included (i.e. all predictor variables are omitted). When including only the constant, the computer bases the model on assigning every subject to a single category of the outcome variable. In this example, SPSS can decide either to predict that every subject has display rule understanding, or to predict that all subjects do not have display rule understanding. It could make this decision arbitrarily, but because it is crucial to try to maximize how well the model predicts the observed data SPSS will predict that every subject belongs to the category in which most observed cases fell. In this example there were 39 children who had display rule understanding and only 31 who did not. Therefore, if SPSS predicts that every child has display rule understanding then this prediction will be correct 39 times out of 70 (i.e. 56% approx.). However, if SPSS predicted that every child did not have display rule understanding, then this prediction would be correct only 31 times out of 70 (44% approx.). As such, of the two available options it is better to predict that all children had display rule understanding because this results in a greater number of correct predictions. The output shows a contingency table for the model in this basic state. You can see that SPSS has predicted that all children have display rule understanding, which results in 0% accuracy for the children who were observed to have no display rule understanding, and 100% accuracy for those children observed to have passed the display rule task. Overall, the model correctly classifies 55.71% of children. The next part of the output summarizes the model, and at this stage this entails quoting the value of the constant (β_0), which is equal to 0.2296.

The final part of this section of the output is the part labelled *Variables not in the Equation*. The top line in this section reports the residual chi-square as 26.257 (which is significant at $p < 0.0001$). This statistic tells us that the coefficients for the variables not in the model are significantly different from zero—in other words that the addition of one or more of these variables to the model will significantly affect its predictive power. If the probability for the residual chi-square had been greater than 0.05 it would have meant that none of the variables excluded from the model could make a significant contribution to the predictive power of the model. As such, the analysis would have terminated at this stage.

The next part of the output lists each of the predictors in turn with a value of Roa's efficient score statistic for each one. In large samples when the null hypothesis is true, the score statistic is identical to the Wald statistic and the likelihood ratio statistic. It is used at this stage of the analysis because it is computationally less intensive than the Wald statistic and so can still be calculated in situations when the Wald statistic would prove prohibitive. Like any test statistic Roa's score statistic has a specific distribution from which statistical significance can be obtained. In this example, all excluded variables have significant score statistics at $p < 0.001$ and so all three could potentially make a contribution to the model. However, as mentioned in section 5.3.1.1, the stepwise calculations are relative and so the variable that will be selected for inclusion is the one with the highest value for the score statistic that is significant at a 0.05 level of significance. In this example, that variable will be **fb** because it has the highest value of the score statistic. The next part of the output deals with the model after this predictor has been added.

Table 5.1: Crosstabulation of display rule understanding with false belief understanding

		False Belief Understanding (fb)	
		No	Yes
Display Rule Understanding (display)	No	23	8
	Yes	6	33

The model now includes false belief understanding (**fb**) as a predictor and so it classifies whether a child has display rule understanding based on whether they passed or failed the false belief task. Now, this can be easily explained if we look at the crosstabulation for the variables **fb** and **display**.[1] The model will use false belief understanding to predict whether a child has display rule understanding by applying the crosstabulation table shown in Table 5.1. So, the model predicts that all of the children who showed false belief understanding will have display rule understanding. There were 41 children with false belief understanding, so the model predicts that these 41 children had display rule understanding (as such it is correct 33 times out of 41, and incorrect 8 times out of 41). In addition, this new model predicts that all of the 29 children who didn't show false belief understanding did not show display rule understanding (as such it is correct 23 times out of 29 and incorrect 6 times out of 29).

SPSS Output 5.3 shows the results from this new model. First, the output tells us about the variable(s) entered at stage 1 of the procedure. In this example only one variable has been entered, that is **fb**. The output then provides some summary statistics about the model as a whole. There are two summary statistics used: the log-likelihood statistic and the goodness-of-fit statistic. The log-likelihood statistic is analogous to the error sum of squares in multiple regression and as such is an indicator of how much unexplained information there is after the model has been fitted. It, therefore, follows that large values of the log-likelihood statistic indicate poorly fitting statistical models, because the larger the value of the log-likelihood, the more unexplained observations there are. In SPSS, rather than reporting the log-likelihood itself, the value is multiplied by –2 (and sometimes referred to as –2LL):

---

[1] The dialog box to produce this table can be obtained through the menus by **Analyze⇒Descriptive Statistics⇒Crosstabs**.

this multiplication is done because –2LL has an approximately chi-square distribution and so makes it possible to compare values against those that we might expect to get by chance alone. The goodness-of-fit statistic is a test of the statistical significance of the combined effects of the independent variables within the model.

```
Variable(s) Entered on Step Number
1..        FB          False Belief understanding

Estimation terminated at iteration number 3 because
Log Likelihood decreased by less than .01 percent.

   -2 Log Likelihood          70.042
   Goodness of Fit            69.999
   Cox & Snell - R^2            .311
   Nagelkerke - R^2             .417

                     Chi-Square      df Significance

   Model                26.083        1        .0000
   Block                26.083        1        .0000
   Step                 26.083        1        .0000

-------------------------------------------------------
Classification Table for DISPLAY
The Cut Value is .50
                     Predicted
                 No      Yes      Percent Correct
                 N  I    Y
Observed       +-------+-------+
   No     N   I   23  I   8  I    74.19%
               +-------+-------+
   Yes    Y   I    6  I  33  I    84.62%
               +-------+-------+
                     Overall   80.00%
```

SPSS Output 5.3

At this stage of the analysis the value of –2 log-likelihood should be less than the value when only the constant was included in the model (because lower values of –2LL indicate that the model is predicting the outcome variable more accurately). When only the constant was included, –2LL = 96.1243, but now **fb** has been included this value has been reduced to 70.042. This reduction tells us that the model is better at predicting display rule understanding than it was before **fb** was added. The question of how much better the model predicts the outcome variable can be assessed using the *model chi-square statistic*, which measures the difference between the model as it currently stands and the model when only the constant was included. The value of the model chi-square statistic is, therefore, equal to –2LL with **fb** included minus the value of –2LL when only the constant was in the model (96.1243 –

70.0420 = 26.083). This value has a chi-square distribution and so its statistical significance can be easily calculated. In this example, the value is significant at a 0.05 level and so we can say that overall the model is predicting display rule understanding significantly better than it was with only the constant included. The model chi-square is an analogue of the *F*-test for the linear regression sum of squares (see Chapter 4). In an ideal world we would like to see a non-significant –2LL (indicating that the amount of unexplained data is minimal) and a highly significant model chi-square statistic (indicating that the model including the predictors is significantly better than without those predictors). However, in reality it is possible for both statistics to be highly significant.

There is a second statistic called the *step* statistic that indicates the improvement in the predictive power of the model since the last stage. At this stage there has been only one step in the analysis and so the value of the improvement statistic is the same as the model chi-square. However, in more complex models in which there are three or four stages, this statistic gives you a measure of the improvement of the predictive power of the model since the last step. Its value is equal to –2LL at the current step minus –2LL at the previous step. If the improvement statistic is significant then it indicates that the model now predicts the outcome significantly better than it did at the last step, and in a forward regression this can be taken as an indication of the contribution of a predictor to the predictive power of the model. Similarly, the *block* statistic provides the change in –2LL since the last block (for use in hierarchical or blockwise analyses).

Finally, the classification table at the end of this section of the output indicates how well the model predicts group membership. Because the model is using false belief understanding to predict the outcome variable, this classification table is the same as Table 5.1. The current model correctly classifies 23 children who don't have display rule understanding but misclassifies 8 others (i.e. it correctly classifies 74.19% of cases). For children who do have display rule understanding, the model correctly classifies 33 and misclassifies 6 cases (i.e. correctly classifies 84.62% of cases). The overall accuracy of classification is, therefore, the weighted average of these two values (80%). So, when only the constant was included, the model correctly classified 56% of children, but now, with the inclusion of **fb** as a predictor, this has risen to 80%.

The next part of the output (SPSS Output 5.4) is crucial because it tells us the estimates for the coefficients for the predictors included in the model. This section of the output gives us the coefficients and statistics for the variables that have been included in the model at this point (namely **fb** and the constant). The β value is the same as the β value in linear regression: they are the values that we need to replace in equation (5.4) to establish the probability that a case falls into a certain category. We saw in linear regression that the value of β represents the change in the outcome resulting from a unit change in the predictor variable. The interpretation of this coefficient in logistic regression is very similar in that it represents the change in the *logit* of the outcome variable associated with a one-unit change in the predictor variable. The logit of the outcome is simply the natural logarithm of the odds of Y occurring.

```
----------------- Variables in the Equation -----------------

  Variable            B       S.E.     Wald     df     Sig      R

  FB(1)            2.7607    .6045   20.8562     1    .0000   .4429
  Constant        -1.3437    .4584    8.5921     1    .0034


                              95% CI for Exp(B)
  Variable         Exp(B)      Lower      Upper

  FB(1)           15.8117    4.8352    51.7065
```

SPSS Output 5.4

5.3.2.1. The Wald Statistic

The crucial statistic is the Wald statistic,[2] which has a chi-square distribution and tells us whether the β coefficient for that predictor is significantly different from zero. If the coefficient is significantly different from zero then we can assume that the predictor is making a significant contribution to the prediction of the outcome (Y). In this sense it is analogous to the *t*-tests found in multiple regression. Equation (5.5) shows how the Wald statistic is calculated (and includes the values from this example). The Wald statistic is usually used to ascertain whether a variable is a significant predictor of the outcome: however, it is probably more accurate to examine the likelihood ratio statistics. The reason why the Wald statistic should be used cautiously is because when the regression coefficient (β) is large, the standard error tends to become inflated, resulting in the Wald statistic being underestimated (see Menard, 1995). The inflation of the standard error increases the probability of rejecting a predictor as being significant when in reality it is making a significant contribution to the model (i.e. you are more likely to make a type II error).

---

[2] SPSS actually quotes the Wald statistic squared.

$$\text{Wald}^2 = \left(\frac{\beta}{\text{SE}}\right)^2$$

$$= \left(\frac{2.7607}{0.6045}\right)^2 \tag{5.5}$$

$$= 20.8562$$

5.3.2.2. *R* and R^2

When we talked about linear regression, one measure of the usefulness of the model was the multiple correlation coefficient *R* and the corresponding R^2 value. SPSS calculates a version of this multiple correlation in logistic regression known as the *R*-statistic. This *R*-statistic is the partial correlation between the outcome variable and each of the predictor variables and it can vary between –1 and 1. A positive value indicates that as the predictor variable increases so does the likelihood of the event occurring. A negative value implies that as the predictor variable increases the likelihood of the outcome occurring decreases. If a variable has a small value of *R* then it contributes only a small amount to the model.

The equation for *R* is given in equation (5.6). The –2LL is the –2 log-likelihood for the original model (96.12 in this case), the Wald statistic is calculated as described before, and the degrees of freedom can be read from the summary table for the variables in the equation. However, because this value of *R* is dependent upon the Wald statistic it is by no means an accurate measure (I mentioned before how the Wald statistic can be inaccurate under certain circumstances). For this reason the value of *R* should be treated with some caution, and it is invalid to square this value and interpret it as you would in linear regression.

> Is there a logistic regression equivalent of R^2?

$$R = \pm \sqrt{\left(\frac{\text{Wald} - (2 \times df)}{-2\text{LL(Original)}}\right)} \tag{5.6}$$

There is some controversy over what would make a good analogue to the R^2 value in linear regression, but one measure described by Hosmer and Lemeshow (1989) can be easily calculated. In SPSS terminology, Hosmer and Lemeshow's measure (R_L^2) is calculated by dividing the model chi-square by the *original* –2LL. In this example the model chi-square after all variables have been entered into the model is 26.083, and the original –2LL (before any variables were entered) was 96.12. So, R_L^2 = 26.083/96.12 = 0.271, which is different to the value we would get by squaring the value of R given in the output ($R^2 = 0.4429^2 = 0.196$). R_L^2 is the proportional reduction in the absolute value of the log-likelihood measure and as such it is a measure of how much the badness-of-fit improves as a result of the inclusion of the predictor variables. It can vary between 0 (indicating that the predictors are useless at predicting the outcome variable) and 1 (indicating that the model predicts the outcome variable perfectly). So, in terms of interpretation it can be seen as similar to the R^2 in linear regression in that it provides a gauge of the substantive significance of the model.

5.3.2.3.   Exp β

More crucial to the *interpretation* of logistic regression is the value of exp β (*exp(B)* in the SPSS output), which is an indicator of the change in odds resulting from a unit change in the predictor. As such, it is similar to the β coefficient in logistic regression but easier to understand (because it doesn't require a logarithmic transformation). In this example, the predictor variable is categorical which makes exp β easier to explain. The odds of an event occurring are defined as the probability of an event occurring divided by the probability of that event not occurring (see equation (5.7)) and should not be confused with the more colloquial usage of the word to refer to probability.

$$\text{odds} = \frac{P(\text{event})}{P(\text{no event})} \qquad (5.7)$$

To calculate the change in odds that results from a unit change in the predictor for this example, we must first calculate the odds of a child having display rule understanding given that they *don't* have second-order false belief task understanding. We then calculate the odds of a child having display rule understanding given that they *do* have false belief understanding. Finally, we calculate the proportionate change in these two odds.

To calculate the first set of odds, we need to use equation (5.3) to calculate the probability of a child having display rule understanding given that they failed the false belief task. If we had more than one predictor we would use equation (5.4). There are three unknown quantities in this equation: the coefficient of the constant (β_0), the coefficient for the predictor (β_1) and the value of the predictor itself (X). The parameter coding at the beginning of the output told us that children who failed the false belief task were coded with a 0, so we can use this value in place of X. The value of β_1 has been estimated for us as 2.7607 (see *Variables in the Equation* in SPSS Output 5.4), and the coefficient for the constant can be taken from the same table and is −1.3437. We can calculate the odds as in equation (5.8).

$$P(\text{event } Y) = \frac{1}{1 + e^{-(\beta_0 + \beta_1 X_1)}}$$

$$P(\text{event } Y) = \frac{1}{1 + e^{-[-1.3437 + (2.7607 \times 0)]}}$$

$$= 0.2069$$

$$P(\text{no event } Y) = 1 - P(\text{event } Y)$$

$$= 0.7931$$

(5.8)

$$\text{odds} = \frac{0.2069}{0.7931}$$

$$= 0.2609$$

Now, we calculate the same thing after the predictor variable has changed by one unit. In this case, because the predictor variable is dichotomous, we need to calculate the odds of a child passing the display rule task, given that they have *passed* the false belief task. So, the value of the false belief variable is now 1 (rather than 0). The resulting calculations are shown in equation (5.9).

$$P(\text{event } Y) = \frac{1}{1 + e^{-(\beta_0 + \beta_1 X_1)}}$$

$$P(\text{event } Y) = \frac{1}{1 + e^{-[-1.3437 + (2.7607 \times 1)]}}$$

$$= 0.8049$$

(5.9)

$$P(\text{no event } Y) = 1 - P(\text{event } Y)$$

$$= 0.1951$$

$$\text{odds} = \frac{0.8049}{0.1951}$$

$$= 4.1256$$

We now know the odds before and after a unit change in the predictor variable. It is now a simple matter to calculate the proportionate change in odds by dividing the odds after a unit change in the predictor by the odds before that change.

$$\begin{aligned} \text{proportionate} \\ \text{change in odds} \end{aligned} = \frac{\text{odds after a unit change in the predictor}}{\text{original odds}}$$

$$= \frac{4.1256}{0.2609}$$

$$= 15.8129$$

(5.10)

You should notice that the value of the proportionate change in odds is the same as the value that SPSS reports for exp β (allowing for differences in rounding). Therefore, we can interpret exp β in terms of the change in odds. If the value is greater than 1 then it indicates that as the predictor increases, the odds of the outcome occurring increase. Conversely, a value less than 1 indicates that as the predictor increases, the odds of the outcome occurring decrease. In this example, we can say that the odds of a child who has false belief understanding also having display rule understanding are 15 times higher than those of a child who does not have false belief understanding.

  In the options (see section 5.3.1.4), we requested a confidence interval for exp β and it can also be found in the output. The way to interpret this confidence interval is to say that if we ran 100 experiments and calculated confidence intervals for the value of exp β, then these intervals would encompass the actual value of exp β in the population (rather than the sample) on 95 occasions. So, in this case, we can be fairly confident that the population value of exp β lies between 4.84 and 51.71. However, there is a chance that a sample could give a confidence interval that 'misses' the true value.

5.3.2.4. The Classification Plot

The next part of the output displays the classification plot that we requested in the *options* dialog box. This plot is a histogram of the predicted probabilities of a child passing the display rule task. If the model perfectly fits the data, then this histogram should show all of the cases for which the event has occurred on the right-hand side, and all the cases for which the event hasn't occurred on the left-hand side. In other words, all the children who passed the display rule task should appear on the right and all those who failed should appear on the left. In this example, the only significant predictor is dichotomous and so there are only two columns of cases on the plot. If the predictor is a continuous variable, the cases are spread out across many columns. As a rule of thumb, the more that the cases cluster at each end of the graph, the better. This statement is true because such a plot would show that when the outcome did actually occur (i.e. the child did pass the display rule task) the predicted probability of the event occurring is also high (i.e. close to 1). Likewise, at the other end of the plot it would show that when the event didn't occur (i.e. when the child failed the display rule task) the predicted probability of the event occurring is also low (i.e. close to zero). This situation represents a model that is correctly predicting the observed outcome data. If, however, there are a lot of points clustered in the centre of the plot then it shows that for many cases the model is predicting a probability of 0.5 that the event will occur. In other words, for these cases there is little more than a 50:50 chance that the data are correctly predicted—as such the model could predict these cases just as accurately by simply tossing a coin! Also, a good model will ensure that few cases are misclassified, in this example there are two Ns on the right of the model and one Y on the left of the model. These are misclassified cases, and the fewer of these there are, the better the model.

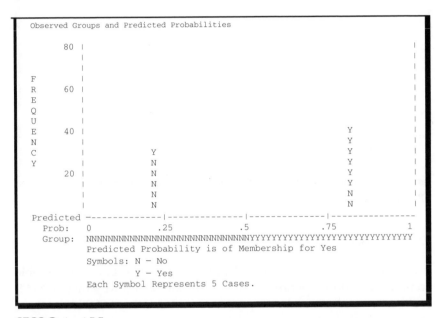

SPSS Output 5.5

Below the classification graph are the test statistics for **fb** if it were removed from the model (SPSS Output 5.6). Now, remember earlier on I said how the regression would place variables into the equation and then test whether they then met a removal criterion. Well, the *Model if Term Removed* part of the output tells us the effects of removal. The important thing to note is the significance value of the log-likelihood ratio (log LR). The log LR for this model is highly significant ($p < 0.0001$) which tells us that removing **fb** from the model would have a significant effect on the predictive ability of the model—in other words, it would be a very bad move to remove it!

Finally, we are told about the variables currently not in the model. First of all, the residual chi-square, which is non-significant, tells us that none of the remaining variables have coefficients significantly different from zero. Furthermore, each variable is listed with its score statistic and significance value, and for both variables their coefficients are not significantly different from zero (as can be seen from the significance values of 0.1283 for age and 0.2615 for the interaction of age and false belief understanding). Therefore, no further variables will be added to the equation.

```
---------------- Model if Term Removed ------------------

 Term          Log                                Significance
 Removed       Likelihood      -2 Log LR    df    of Log LR

 FB            -48.062         26.083        1         .0000


-------------- Variables not in the Equation ----------------

 Residual Chi Square        2.521 with        2 df     Sig = .2835

 Variable              Score     df      Sig       R

 AGE                  2.3134     1      .1283    .0571
 AGE by FB(1)         1.2610     1      .2615    .0000

No more variables can be deleted or added.
```

SPSS Output 5.6

5.3.2.5. *Listing Predicted Probabilities*

It is possible to list the expected probability of the outcome variable occurring based on the final model. In section 5.3.1.3 we saw that SPSS could save residuals and also predicted probabilities. SPSS saves these predicted probabilities and predicted group memberships as variables in the data editor and names them PRE_1 and PGR_1 respectively. These probabilities can be listed using the **Analyze⇒Reports⇒Case Summaries…** dialog box (see section 4.4.1.6). SPSS Output 5.7 shows a selection of the predicted probabilities (because the only significant predictor was a dichotomous variable, there will be only two different probability values). It is also worth listing the predictor variables as well to clarify from where the predicted probabilities come.

We found from the model that the only significant predictor of display rule understanding was false belief understanding. This could have a value of either 1 (pass the false belief task) or 0 (fail the false belief task). If these two values are placed into equation (5.4) with the respective regression coefficients, then the two probability values are derived. In fact, we calculated these values as part of equation (5.8) and equation (5.9) and you should note that the calculated probabilities correspond to the values in PRE_1. These values tells us that when a child doesn't possess second-order false belief understanding (**fb** = 0), there is a probability of 0.2069 that they will pass the display rule task—

approximately a 21% chance (1 out of 5 children). However, if the child does pass the false belief task (**fb** = 1), there is a probability of 0.8049 that they will pass the display rule task—an 80.5% chance (4 out of 5 children). Consider that a probability of 0 indicates no chance of the child passing the display rule task, and a probability of 1 indicates that the child will definitely pass the display rule task. Therefore, the values obtained provide strong evidence for the role of false belief understanding as a prerequisite for display rule understanding.

	AGE	FB	DISPLAY	PRE_1	PGR_1
1	24.00	.00	.00	.20690	.00
6	29.00	.00	1.00	.20690	.00
11	32.00	.00	.00	.20690	.00
16	36.00	.00	.00	.20690	.00
21	29.00	.00	.00	.20690	.00
26	30.00	.00	.00	.20690	.00
31	41.00	.00	1.00	.20690	.00
36	40.00	1.00	1.00	.80487	1.00
41	49.00	1.00	1.00	.80487	1.00
46	52.00	1.00	.00	.80487	1.00
51	63.00	1.00	1.00	.80487	1.00
56	70.00	1.00	1.00	.80487	1.00
61	73.00	1.00	1.00	.80487	1.00
66	79.00	1.00	1.00	.80487	1.00

Number of cases read: 70   Number of cases listed: 14

SPSS Output 5.7

Assuming we are content that the model is accurate and that false belief understanding has some substantive significance, then we could conclude that false belief understanding is the single best predictor of display rule understanding. Furthermore age and the interaction of age and false belief understanding in no way predict display rule understanding. As a homework task, why not rerun this analysis using the forced entry method of analysis —how do your conclusions differ?

This conclusion is fine in itself, but to be sure that the model is a good one, it is important to examine the residuals. In section 5.3.1.3 we saw how to get SPSS to save various residuals in the data editor. We can now list these residuals using the **Analyze⇒Reports⇒Case Summaries** dialog box and interpret them.

5.3.2.6. Interpreting Residuals

The main purpose of examining residuals in logistic regression is to (1) isolate points for which the model fits poorly, and (2) isolate points that exert an undue influence on the model. To assess the former we examine the residuals, especially the Studentized residual, standard residual and deviance statistics. All of these statistics have the common property that 95% of cases in an average, normally distributed sample should have values which lie within ± 2, and 99% of cases should have values that lie within ± 2.5. Therefore, any values outside of ± 3 are cause for concern and any outside of ± 2.5 should be examined more closely. To assess the influence of individual cases we use influence statistics such as Cook's distance (which is interpreted in the same way as for linear regression: as a measure of the change in the regression coefficient if a case is deleted from the model). Also, the value of DFBeta, which is a standardized version of Cook's statistic, tells us something of the influence of certain cases— any values greater than 1 indicate possible influential cases. Additionally, leverage statistics or hat values, which should lie between 0 (the case has no influence whatsoever) and 1 (the case exerts complete influence over the model), tell us about whether certain cases are wielding undue influence over the model. The expected value of leverage is defined as for linear regression. These statistics were explained in more detail in Chapter 4. The top of SPSS Output 5.8 lists each of the variable names and what they represent. There are additional comments to summarize the expected values of some of the statistics and the output has been edited so not all cases are reported.

```
  11 new variables have been created.
    Name            Contents

    PRE_1           Predicted Value
    PGR_1           Predicted Group
    COO_1           Cook's Distance
    LEV_1           Leverage    (lies between 0 = no influence, 1 = total
influence)
    RES_1           Residual
    LRE_1           Logit Residual
    SRE_1           Studentized Residual    (should lie between +/- 2 or 3)
    ZRE_1           Standardized Residual   (should lie between +/- 2)
    DEV_1           Deviance                (should lie between +/- 2)
    DFB0_1          Dfbeta for the constant  (should be less than 1)
    DFB1_1          Dfbeta for FB(1)         (should be less than 1)


  With ZRE_1, SRE_1, and DEV_1 we would expect 5% of any sample to lie above
  +/- 2, and 1% to lie above +/- 2.5.
  Expected value of leverage = k+1/N (where k = no. of predictors, N = sample
  size).
  For these data average leverage = 2/70 = 0.03
```

SPSS Output 5.8

	COO_1	LEV_1	DFB0_1	DFB1_1
1	.00932	.03448	−.04503	.04503
6	.13690	.03448	.17262	−.17262
7	.00932	.03448	−.04503	.04503
8	.00932	.03448	−.04503	.04503
9	.13690	.03448	.17262	−.17262
10	.00932	.03448	−.04503	.04503
11	.00932	.03448	−.04503	.04503
12	.00606	.02439	.00000	.03106
13	.00932	.03448	−.04503	.04503
14	.10312	.02439	.00000	−.12812
15	.00932	.03448	−.04503	.04503
16	.00932	.03448	−.04503	.04503
17	.13690	.03448	.17262	−.17262
18	.00932	.03448	−.04503	.04503
19	.00606	.02439	.00000	.03106
20	.00932	.03448	−.04503	.04503
21	.00932	.03448	−.04503	.04503
22	.00606	.02439	.00000	.03106
23	.00606	.02439	.00000	.03106
24	.10312	.02439	.00000	−.12812
25	.00932	.03448	−.04503	.04503
26	.00932	.03448	−.04503	.04503
28	.00932	.03448	−.04503	.04503
29	.00606	.02439	.00000	.03106
30	.00932	.03448	−.04503	.04503
31	.13690	.03448	.17262	−.17262
32	.00932	.03448	−.04503	.04503
33	.00606	.02439	.00000	.03106
37	.10312	.02439	.00000	−.12812
38	.00606	.02439	.00000	.03106
39	.13690	.03448	.17262	−.17262
40	.10312	.02439	.00000	−.12812
41	.00606	.02439	.00000	.0310
42	.00606	.02439	.00000	.03106
46	.10312	.02439	.00000	−.12812
47	.00606	.02439	.00000	.03106
48	.00932	.03448	−.04503	.04503
49	.00932	.03448	−.04503	.04503
50	.10312	.02439	.00000	−.12812
51	.00606	.02439	.00000	.03106
57	.10312	.02439	.00000	−.12812
58	.00606	.02439	.00000	.03106
59	.00606	.02439	.00000	.03106
60	.13690	.03448	.17262	−.17262
61	.00606	.02439	.00000	.03106
68	.10312	.02439	.00000	−.12812
69	.00606	.02439	.00000	.03106
70	.00606	.02439	.00000	.03106

Number of cases read: 70   Number of cases listed: 70

SPSS Output 5.8 (cont.)

All cases have DFBetas less than 1, and leverage statistics (LEV_1) close to the calculated expected value of 0.03. There are also no unusually high values of Cook's distance (COO_1) which, all in all, means that there are no influential cases having an effect on the model. Cook's distance is an unstandardized measure and so there is no absolute value at which you can say that a case is having an influence, Instead, you should look for values of Cook's distance which are particularly high compared to the other cases in the sample. However, Stevens (1992) suggests that a value greater than 1 is problematic. About half of the leverage values are a little high but given that the other statistics are fine, this is probably no cause for concern.

	RES_1	SRE_1	ZRE_1	DEV_1
1	-.20690	-.69294	-.51076	-.68089
2	-.20690	-.69294	-.51076	-.68089
3	-.20690	-.69294	-.51076	-.68089
4	-.20690	-.69294	-.51076	-.68089
5	-.20690	-.69294	-.51076	-.68089
6	.79310	1.80654	1.95787	1.77512
7	-.20690	-.69294	-.51076	-.68089
8	-.20690	-.69294	-.51076	-.68089
9	.79310	1.80654	1.95787	1.77512
10	-.20690	-.69294	-.51076	-.68089
11	-.20690	-.69294	-.51076	-.68089
12	.19513	.66708	.49237	.65889
13	-.20690	-.69294	-.51076	-.68089
14	-.80487	-1.83028	-2.03097	-1.80782
15	-.20690	-.69294	-.51076	-.68089
16	-.20690	-.69294	-.51076	-.68089
17	.79310	1.80654	1.95787	1.77512
18	-.20690	-.69294	-.51076	-.68089
19	.19513	.66708	.49237	.65889
20	-.20690	-.69294	-.51076	-.68089
21	-.20690	-.69294	-.51076	-.68089
22	.19513	.66708	.49237	.65889
23	.19513	.66708	.49237	.65889
24	-.80487	-1.83028	-2.03097	-1.80782
25	-.20690	-.69294	-.51076	-.68089
26	-.20690	-.69294	-.51076	-.68089
27	-.20690	-.69294	-.51076	-.68089
28	-.20690	-.69294	-.51076	-.68089
29	.19513	.66708	.49237	.65889
30	-.20690	-.69294	-.51076	-.68089
31	.79310	1.80654	1.95787	1.77512
32	-.20690	-.69294	-.51076	-.68089
33	.19513	.66708	.49237	.65889
34	.19513	.66708	.49237	.65889
35	.19513	.66708	.49237	.65889

SPSS Output 5.9

36	.19513	.66708	.49237	.65889
37	−.80487	−1.83028	−2.03097	−1.80782
38	.19513	.66708	.49237	.65889
39	.79310	1.80654	1.95787	1.77512
40	−.80487	−1.83028	−2.03097	−1.80782
41	.19513	.66708	.49237	.65889
42	.19513	.66708	.49237	.65889
43	.19513	.66708	.49237	.65889
44	.19513	.66708	.49237	.65889
45	.19513	.66708	.49237	.65889
46	−.80487	−1.83028	−2.03097	−1.80782
47	.19513	.66708	.49237	.65889
48	−.20690	−.69294	−.51076	−.68089
49	−.20690	−.69294	−.51076	−.68089
50	−.80487	−1.83028	−2.03097	−1.80782
51	.19513	.66708	.49237	.65889
52	.19513	.66708	.49237	.65889
53	.19513	.66708	.49237	.65889
54	.19513	.66708	.49237	.65889
55	.19513	.66708	.49237	.65889
56	.19513	.66708	.49237	.65889
57	−.80487	−1.83028	−2.03097	−1.80782
58	.19513	.66708	.49237	.65889
59	.19513	.66708	.49237	.65889
60	.79310	1.80654	1.95787	1.77512
61	.19513	.66708	.49237	.65889
62	.19513	.66708	.49237	.65889
63	.19513	.66708	.49237	.65889
64	.19513	.66708	.49237	.65889
65	.19513	.66708	.49237	.65889
66	.19513	.66708	.49237	.65889
67	.19513	.66708	.49237	.65889
68	−.80487	−1.83028	−2.03097	−1.80782
69	.19513	.66708	.49237	.65889
70	.19513	.66708	.49237	.65889

SPSS Output 5.9 (cont.)

Although there seem to be no influential cases in the data, there still might be an outlying case that could affect the coefficient values of the model. Examining the residuals can check this possibility. SPSS Output 5.9 shows a listing of the residuals for the display rule data. The residual (RES_1) is an unstandardized value and so outliers have to be isolated by looking for values substantially greater than the rest of the sample. The standardized (ZRE_1), Studentized (SRE_1) and deviance (DEV_1) statistics all have values of less than ± 2.5 and predominantly have values less than ± 2 and so there seems to be very little here to concern us. If substantial outliers or influential cases had been isolated, you are not justified in eliminating these cases to make the model fit better. Instead these cases should be inspected closely to try to isolate a good reason why they were unusual. It might simply be an error in inputting data, or it could be that the case was one which had a special reason for being unusual: for example the child had found it hard to pay attention to the false belief task and you had noted this at the time of the experiment. In such a case, you may have good reason to exclude the case and duly note the reasons why.

5.4.   Another Example

This example is inspired by events in the soccer World Cup finals of 1998. Unfortunately for me (being an Englishman), I was subjected to watching England get knocked out of the championships by losing a penalty shootout. Now, if I were the England coach, I might be interested in finding out what factors predict whether or not a player will score a penalty. Those of you who hate football can read this example as being factors that predict success in a free-throw in basketball or netball, a penalty in hockey or a penalty kick in rugby or American football. Now, this research question is perfect for logistic regression because our outcome variable is a dichotomy: a penalty can be either scored or missed. Imagine that past research (Hoddle et al. 1998!!) had shown that there are two factors that reliably predict whether a penalty kick will be saved or scored. The first factor is whether the player taking the kick is a worrier (this factor can be measured using a measure such as the Penn State Worry Questionnaire, PSWQ). The second factor is the player's past success rate at scoring (so, whether the player has a good track record of scoring penalty kicks). It is fairly well accepted that anxiety has detrimental effects on performance of a variety of tasks and so it was also predicted that state anxiety might be able to account for some of the unexplained variance in penalty success.

This example is a classic case of building on a well-established model, because two predictors are already known and we want to test the effect of a new one. So, 75 football players were selected at random and before taking a penalty kick in competition they were given a state anxiety questionnaire to complete (to assess anxiety before the kick was taken). These players were also asked to complete the PSWQ to give a measure of how much they worried about things generally, and their past success rate was obtained from a database. Finally, a note was made of whether the penalty was scored or missed. The data can be found in the file **penalty.sav**, which contains four variables—each in a separate column.

- **Scored**: This variable is our outcome and it is coded such that 0 = penalty missed, and 1 = penalty scored.
- **Pswq**: This variable is the first predictor variable and it gives us a measure of the degree to which a player worries.

- **Previous**: This variable is the percentage of penalties scored by a particular player in their career. As such, it represents previous success at scoring penalties.
- **Anxious**: This variable is our third predictor and it is a variable that has not previously been used to predict penalty success. **Anxious** is a measure of state anxiety before taking the penalty.

5.4.1.   Running the Analysis: Block Entry Regression

To run the analysis, we must first select the main *logistic regression* dialog box, and using the mouse to specify **Analyze⇒Regression⇒Binary Logistic** can do this. In this example, we know of two previously established predictors and so it is a good idea to enter these predictors into the model in a single block. Then we can add the new predictor in a second block (by doing this we effectively examine an old model and then add a new variable to this model to see whether the model is improved). This method is known as block entry and Figure 5.7 shows how it is specified.

It is easy to do block entry regression. First you should use the mouse to select the variable **scored** from the variables list and then transfer it to the box labelled *Dependent* by clicking on ▣. Second, you should select the two previously established predictors. So, select **pswq** and **previous** from the variables list and transfer them to the box labelled *Covariates* by clicking on ▣. Our first block of variables is now specified. To specify the second block, click on ⬜Next⬜ to clear the *Covariates* box, which should now be labelled *Block 2 of 2*. Now select **anxious** from the variables list and transfer it to the box labelled *Covariates* by clicking on ▣. We could at this stage select some interactions to be included in the model, but unless there is a sound theoretical reason for believing that the predictors should interact there is no need. Make sure that *Enter* is selected as the method of regression (this method is the default and so should be selected already).

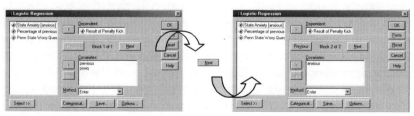

Figure 5.7: Block entry method of regression

Once the variables have been specified, you should select the options described in sections 5.3.1.3 and 5.3.1.4, but because none of the predictors are categorical there is no need to use the *Categorical...* option. When you have selected the options and residuals that you want you can return to the main *logistic regression* dialog box and click on [OK].

5.4.2.   Interpreting Output

The output of the logistic regression will be arranged in terms of the blocks that were specified. In other words, SPSS will produce a regression model for the variables specified in block 1, and then produce a second model that contains the variables from both blocks 1 and 2. The results from block 1 are shown in SPSS Output 5.10 and in this analysis we forced SPSS to enter **previous** and **pswq** into the regression model. First, the output tells us that 75 cases have been accepted, that the dependent variable has been coded 0 and 1 (because this variable was coded as 0 and 1 in the data editor, these codings correspond exactly to the data in SPSS). Crucially, we are then told that at block number 0 (i.e. when no variables have been entered into the model) the –2LL is 103.64. This value is a gauge of how much information cannot be explained by the model (i.e. it is the total amount of information that needs to be explained by the model).

The next part of the output tells us about block 1: as such it provides information about the model after the variables **previous** and **pswq** have been added. The first thing to note is that the –2LL has dropped to 48.66, which is a change of 54.98 (which is the value given by the *model chi-square*). This value tells us about the model as a whole whereas the *block* tells us how the model has improved since the last block. The change in the amount of information explained by the model is significant ($p < 0.0001$) and so using previous experience and worry as predictors significantly improves our ability to predict penalty success. Finally, the classification table shows us that 84% of cases can be correctly classified using **pswq** and **previous**.

In the display rule example, SPSS did not produce Hosmer and Lemeshow's goodness-of-fit test. The reason is that this test can't be calculated when there is only one predictor and that predictor is a categorical dichotomy! However, for this example the test can be calculated. The important part of this test is the test statistic itself (7.93) and the significance value (0.3388). This statistic tests the hypothesis that the observed data are significantly different from the predicted values from the model. So, in effect, we want a non-significant value for this test (because this would indicate that the model does not differ significantly from the observed data). We have a non-significant value here, which is indicative of a model that is predicting the real-world data fairly well.

The part of SPSS Output 5.10 labelled *Variables in the Equation* then tells us the parameters of the model when **previous** and **pswq** are used as predictors. The significance values of the Wald statistics for each predictor indicate that both **pswq** and **previous** significantly predict penalty success ($p < 0.01$). The values of exp β for **previous** indicates that if the percentage of previous penalties scored goes up by one, then the odds of scoring a penalty also increase (because exp β is greater than 1). The confidence interval for this value ranges from 1.02 to 1.11 so we can be very confident that the value of exp β in the population lies somewhere between these two values. What's more, because both values are greater than 1 we can also be confident that the relationship between **previous** and penalty success found in this sample is true of the whole population of footballers. The values of exp β for **pswq** indicate that if the level of worry increases by one point along the Penn State worry scale, then the odds of scoring a penalty decrease (because exp β is less than 1). The confidence interval for this value ranges from 0.68 to 0.93 so we can be very confident that the value of exp β in the population lies somewhere between these two values. In addition, because both values are less than 1 we can be confident that the relationship between **pswq** and penalty success found in this sample is true of the whole population of footballers. If we had found that the confidence interval ranged from less than 1 to more than 1, then this would limit the generalizability of our findings because the value exp β in the population could indicate either a positive ($exp(B) > 1$) or negative ($exp(B) < 1$) relationship.

A glance at the classification plot also brings us good news because most cases are clustered at the ends of the plots and few cases lie in the middle of the plot. This reiterates what we know already: that the model is correctly classifying most cases. We can, at this point, also calculate R^2 (see section 5.3.2.2) by dividing the model chi-square by the original value of –2LL. The result is shown in equation (5.11) and we can interpret the result as meaning that the model can account for 53% of the variance in penalty success (so, roughly half of what makes a penalty kick successful is still unknown).

$$R^2 = \frac{\text{model chi} - \text{square}}{\text{original} - 2\text{LL}}$$
$$= \frac{54.977}{103.6385}$$
$$= 0.53$$

(5.11)

```
Dependent Variable Encoding:

Original       Internal
Value          Value
    .00        0
   1.00        1

Dependent Variable..   SCORED      Result of Penalty Kick

Beginning Block Number  0.  Initial Log Likelihood Function

-2 Log Likelihood    103.6385

* Constant is included in the model.
Beginning Block Number  1.  Method: Enter

Variable(s) Entered on Step Number
1..        PSWQ        Penn State Worry Questionnaire
           PREVIOUS    Percentage of previous penalties scored

Estimation terminated at iteration number 5 because
Log Likelihood decreased by less than .01 percent.

    -2 Log Likelihood       48.662
    Goodness of Fit         50.670
    Cox & Snell - R^2         .520
    Nagelkerke - R^2          .694


                      Chi-Square    df Significance

    Model               54.977      2       .0000
    Block               54.977      2       .0000
    Step                54.977      2       .0000

---------- Hosmer and Lemeshow Goodness-of-Fit Test-----------

       SCORED   = Missed Penalty   SCORED   = Scored Penalty

  Group   Observed    Expected    Observed    Expected    Total

    1      8.000       7.904        .000        .096       8.000
    2      8.000       7.779        .000        .221       8.000
    3      8.000       6.705        .000       1.295       8.000
    4      4.000       5.438       4.000       2.562       8.000
    5      2.000       3.945       6.000       4.055       8.000
    6      2.000       1.820       6.000       6.180       8.000
    7      2.000       1.004       6.000       6.996       8.000
    8      1.000        .298       7.000       7.702       8.000
    9       .000        .108      11.000      10.892      11.000


                      Chi-Square    df Significance

  Goodness-of-fit test    7.9302     7      .3388
-----------------------------------------------------------------
```

SPSS Output 5.10

```
Classification Table for SCORED
The Cut Value is .50
                                    Predicted
                    Missed Penalty  Scored Penalty    Percent
Correct
                         M        I        S
Observed               +---------------+---------------+
   Missed Penalty   M  I    30     I     5      I    85.71%
                       +---------------+---------------+
   Scored Penalty   S  I     7     I    33      I    82.50%
                       +---------------+---------------+
                                            Overall   84.00%



----------------- Variables in the Equation -----------------

Variable             B        S.E.      Wald     df      Sig        R

PSWQ             -.2301      .0798    8.3086      1    .0039    -.2467
PREVIOUS          .0648      .0221    8.6086      1    .0033     .2525
Constant         1.2802     1.6701     .5876      1    .4434


                          95% CI for Exp(B)
Variable         Exp(B)    Lower      Upper

PSWQ              .7945     .6794      .9290
PREVIOUS        1.0669    1.0217     1.1141



                Observed Groups and Predicted Probabilities

       16 +                                                        +
          I                                                        I
          I                                                        I
    F     I                                                        I
    R   12 +                                                       +
    E     I                                                       SI
    Q     I                                                       SI
    U     I                                                       SI
    E    8 +                                                      S+
    N       IMM                                                   SI
    C       IMM                                                   SI
    Y       IMM                                                   SI
         4 +MM                  .                                SS+
            IMM        M          SS              S       S      SSI
            IMMM     M  M  S    SM   S       S   SS    SM SSS   SSSI
            IMMMM MM  M  M MMS M   MM   S    S   S   SM MSM SSM SSSSI
Predicted --------------+---------------+---------------+---------------
    Prob:  0          .25             .5             .75            1
    Group:   MMMMMMMMMMMMMMMMMMMMMMMMMMMMMMMSSSSSSSSSSSSSSSSSSSSSSSSSSSSSSS

          Predicted Probability is of Membership for Scored Penalty
          The Cut Value is .50
          Symbols: M - Missed Penalty
                   S - Scored Penalty
          Each Symbol Represents 1 Case.
```

SPSS Output 5.10 (cont.)

SPSS Output 5.11 shows what happens to the model when our new predictor is added (**anxious**). This part of the output describes block 2, which is just the model described in block 1 but with a new predictor added. So, we begin with the model that we had in block 1 and we then add **anxious** to it. The effect of adding anxious to the model is to reduce the –2 log-likelihood to 47.416 (a reduction of 1.246 from the model in block 1 as shown in the *model chi-square* and *block* statistics). This improvement is non-significant which tells us that including **anxious** in the model has not significantly improved our ability to predict whether a penalty will be scored or missed. The classification table tells us that the model is now correctly classifying 85.33% of cases. Remember that in block 1 there were 84% correctly classified and so an extra 1.33% of cases are now classified (not a great deal more—in fact, examining the table shows us that only one extra case has now been correctly classified).

The section labelled *Variables in the Equation* now contains all three predictors and something very interesting has happened: **pswq** is still a significant predictor of penalty success, however, **previous** experience no longer significantly predicts penalty success. In addition, state anxiety appears not to make a significant contribution to the prediction of penalty success. How can it be that previous experience no longer predicts penalty success, and neither does anxiety, yet the ability of the model to predict penalty success has improved slightly?

```
Beginning Block Number   2.   Method: Enter

Variable(s) Entered on Step Number
1..        ANXIOUS    State Anxiety

Estimation terminated at iteration number 5 because
Log Likelihood decreased by less than .01 percent.

   -2 Log Likelihood        47.416
   Goodness of Fit          50.389
   Cox & Snell - R^2          .527
   Nagelkerke - R^2           .704


                    Chi-Square      df Significance

   Model              56.223        3        .0000
   Block               1.246        1        .2643
   Step                1.246        1        .2643
```

SPSS Output 5.11

```
---------- Hosmer and Lemeshow Goodness-of-Fit Test-----------

     SCORED   = Missed Penalty   SCORED   = Scored Penalty

  Group   Observed     Expected     Observed     Expected     Total
    1       8.000        7.926        .000          .074       8.000
    2       8.000        7.769        .000          .231       8.000
    3       9.000        7.649        .000         1.351       9.000
    4       4.000        5.425       4.000         2.575       8.000
    5       1.000        3.210       7.000         4.790       8.000
    6       4.000        1.685       4.000         6.315       8.000
    7       1.000        1.049       7.000         6.951       8.000
    8        .000         .222       8.000         7.778       8.000
    9        .000         .067      10.000         9.933      10.000

                     Chi-Square    df Significance

  Goodness-of-fit test     9.9367     7         .1922


-------------------------------------------------------------


Classification Table for SCORED
The Cut Value is .50
                              Predicted
                     Missed Penalty  Scored Penalty    Percent
Correct
                          M      I      S
Observed               +---------------+---------------+
   Missed Penalty   M  I    30    I      5    I  85.71%
                       +---------------+---------------+
   Scored Penalty   S  I     6    I     34    I  85.00%
                       +---------------+---------------+
                                      Overall  85.33%




----------------- Variables in the Equation ------------------

Variable            B        S.E.      Wald      df      Sig        R

PSWQ             -.2514     .0840     8.9534      1     .0028    -.3780
PREVIOUS          .2026     .1293     2.4544      1     .1172     .0966
ANXIOUS           .2758     .2526     1.1926      1     .2748     .0000
Constant       -11.4922   11.8016      .9483      1     .3302


                        95% CI for Exp(B)
Variable        Exp(B)     Lower      Upper

PSWQ             .7777     .6597      .9169
PREVIOUS        1.2246     .9504     1.5779
ANXIOUS         1.3176     .8031     2.1617
```

SPSS Output 5.11 (cont.)

```
                      Observed Groups and Predicted Probabilities

          16 +                                                              +
             I                                                              I
             I                                                              I
    F        I                                                              I
    R        12 +                                                           +
    E        I                                                              SI
    Q        I                                                              SI
    U        I                                                              SI
    E        8 +M                                                           S+
    N        IM                                                             SI
    C        IM                                                             SI
    Y        IMM                                                            SSI
          4 +MM            M                                S              SS+
             IMM           M   S                            SS              SSI
             IMMMM         M   S              S           S MS   SS        SSSI
             IMMMMMM MM  M M   S   S   MM MMS     S        S SSMSMM SSSS M SSSI
    Predicted --------------+---------------+---------------+----------------
      Prob:  0           .25             .5             .75               1
      Group: MMMMMMMMMMMMMMMMMMMMMMMMMMMMMMMMMMMMMMMSSSSSSSSSSSSSSSSSSSSSSSSSSSSSSSSSSSS

             Predicted Probability is of Membership for Scored Penalty
             The Cut Value is .50
             Symbols: M - Missed Penalty
                      S - Scored Penalty
             Each Symbol Represents 1 Case.


    CASE  Observed
          SCORED           Pred    PGroup    Resid    ZResid
      58 S M **            .9312      S      -.9312   -3.6790

          S=Selected U=Unselected cases
          ** = Misclassified cases

      * Cases with Studentized residuals greater than 2 are listed.
        The Cut Value is .50
```

SPSS Output 5.11 (cont.)

The classification plot is similar to before and the contribution of **pswq** to predicting penalty success is relatively unchanged. What has changed is the contribution of previous experience. If we examine the values of exp β for both **previous** and **anxious** it is clear that they both potentially have a positive relationship to penalty success (i.e. as they increase by a unit, the odds of scoring improve). However, the confidence intervals for these values cross 1, which indicates that the direction of this relationship may be unstable in the population as a whole (i.e. the value of exp β in our sample may be quite different to the value if we had data from the entire population).

You may be tempted to use this final model to say that although worry is a significant predictor of penalty success, the previous finding that experience plays a role is incorrect. This would be a dangerous conclusion to make and we shall see why.

5.4.2.1. Testing for Multicollinearity

In section 4.2.5.3 we saw how multicollinearity can affect the parameters of a regression model. Logistic regression is equally as prone to the biasing effect of collinearity and it is essential to test for collinearity following a logistic regression analysis. Unfortunately, SPSS does not have an option for producing collinearity diagnostics in logistic regression (which can create the illusion that it is unnecessary to test for it!). However, you can obtain statistics such as the tolerance and VIF by simply running a linear regression analysis using the same outcome and predictors. So, for the current example, access the *linear regression* dialog box by using the mouse to specify **Analyze⇒Regression⇒Linear**. The completed dialog box is shown in Figure 5.8. It is unnecessary to specify lots of options (we are using this technique only to obtain tests of collinearity) but it is essential that you click on Statistics... and then select *Collinearity diagnostics* in the dialog box. Once you have selected ☑ Collinearity diagnostics , switch off all of the default options, click on Continue to return you to the *linear regression* dialog box, and then click on OK to run the analysis.

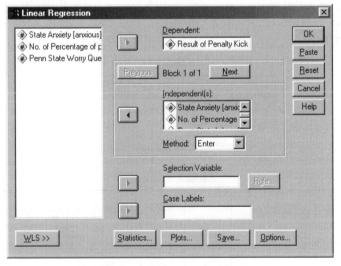

Figure 5.8: *Linear regression* dialog box for penalty data

The results of the linear regression analysis are shown in SPSS Output 5.12. From the first table we can see that the tolerance values are 0.014 for **previous** and **anxious** and 0.575 for **pswq**. In Chapter 4 we saw various criteria for assessing collinearity. Menard (1995) suggests that a tolerance value less than 0.1 almost certainly indicates a serious collinearity problem. Myers (1990) also suggests that a VIF value greater than 10 is cause for concern and in these data the values are over 70 for both **anxious** and **previous**. It seems from these values that there is an issue of collinearity between the predictor variables. We can investigate this issue further by examining the collinearity diagnostics.

SPSS Output 5.12 also shows a table labelled *Collinearity Diagnostics*. In this table, we are given the eigenvalues of the scaled, uncentred cross-products matrix, the condition index and the variance proportions for each predictor. If any of the eigenvalues in this table are much larger than others then the uncentred cross-products matrix is said to be ill-conditioned, which means that the solutions of the regression parameters can be greatly affected by small changes in the predictors or outcome. In plain English, these values give us some idea as to how accurate our regression model is: if the eigenvalues are fairly similar then the derived model is likely to be unchanged by small changes in the measured variables. The *condition indexes* are another way of expressing these eigenvalues and represent the square root of the ratio of the largest eigenvalue to the eigenvalue of interest (so, for the dimension with the largest eigenvalue, the condition index will always be 1). For these data the final dimension has a condition index of 81.3, which is massive compared to the other dimensions. Although there are no hard and fast rules about how much larger a condition index needs to be to indicate collinearity problems, this case clearly shows that a problem exists.

Coefficients[a]

Model		Collinearity Statistics	
		Tolerance	VIF
1	State Anxiety	.014	71.764
	Percentage of previous penalties scored	.014	70.479
	Penn State Worry Questionnaire	.575	1.741

a. Dependent Variable: Result of Penalty Kick

Collinearity Diagnostics[a]

Model	Dimension	Eigenvalue	Condition Index	Variance Proportions			
				(Constant)	State Anxiety	Percentage of previous penalties scored	Penn State Worry Questionnaire
1	1	3.434	1.000	.00	.00	.00	.01
	2	.492	2.641	.00	.00	.00	.04
	3	7.274E-02	6.871	.00	.01	.00	.95
	4	5.195E-04	81.303	1.00	.99	.99	.00

a. Dependent Variable: Result of Penalty Kick

SPSS Output 5.12: Collinearity diagnostics for penalty data

The final step in analysing this table is to look at the variance proportions. The variance of each regression coefficient can be broken down across the eigenvalues and the variance proportions tell us the proportion of the variance of each predictor's regression coefficient that is attributed to each eigenvalue. These proportions can be converted to percentages by multiplying them by 100 (to make them more easily understood). So, for example, for **pswq** 95% of the variance of the regression coefficient is associated with eigenvalue number 3, 4% is associated with eigenvalue number 2, and 1% is associated with eigenvalue number 1. In terms of collinearity, we are looking for predictors that have high proportions on the same *small* eigenvalue, because this would indicate that the variances of their regression coefficients are dependent. So we are interested mainly in the bottom few rows of the table (which represent small eigenvalues). In this example, 99% of the variance in the regression coefficients of both **anxiety** and **previous** is associated with eigenvalue number 4 (the smallest eigenvalue), which clearly indicates dependency between these variables.

The result of this analysis is pretty clear cut: there is collinearity between state anxiety and previous experience of taking penalties and this dependency results in the model becoming biased. To illustrate from where this collinearity stems, SPSS Output 5.13 shows the result of a Pearson correlation between all of the variables in this regression analysis (you can run such an analysis yourself). From this output we can see that **anxious** and **previous** are highly negatively correlated ($r = -0.99$), in fact they are nearly perfectly correlated. Both **previous** and **anxious** correlate with penalty success[3] but because they are correlated so highly with each other, it is unclear which of the two variables predicts penalty success in the regression.

This discussion begs the question of what to do when you have identified collinearity. Well, put simply, there's not much you can do. One obvious solution is to omit one of the variables (so, for example, we might stick with the model from block 1 that ignored state anxiety). The problem with this should be obvious: there is no way of knowing which variable to omit. The resulting theoretical conclusions are, therefore, meaningless because, statistically speaking, any of the variables involved in collinearity could be omitted. In short, there are no statistical grounds for omitting one variable over another. Even if a predictor is removed, Bowerman and O'Connell (1990) recommend that another equally important predictor that does not have such strong multicollinearity replace it. They go on to suggest collecting more data to see whether the multicollinearity can be lessened. Another possibility when there are several predictors involved in the multicollinearity is to

---

[3] As a point of interest, some may question whether it is legitimate to do a Pearson correlation on a dichotomous variable such as penalty success; however, this is simply doing a point-biserial correlation as described in Chapter 3.

run a factor analysis on these predictors and to use the resulting factor scores as a predictor (see Chapter 11). The safest (although unsatisfactory) remedy is to acknowledge the unreliability of the model. So, if we were to report the analysis of which factors predict penalty success, we might acknowledge that previous experience significantly predicted penalty success in the first model, but propose that this experience might affect penalty taking by increasing state anxiety. This statement would be highly speculative because the correlation between **anxious** and **previous** tells us nothing of the direction of causality, but it would acknowledge the inexplicable link between the two predictors. I'm sure that many of you may find the lack of remedy for collinearity grossly unsatisfying—unfortunately statistics is frustrating sometimes!

Correlations

		Result of Penalty Kick	State Anxiety	Percentage of previous penalties scored	Penn State Worry Questionnaire
Result of Penalty Kick	Pearson Correlation	1.000	-.668**	.674**	-.675**
	Sig. (2-tailed)	.	.000	.000	.000
	N	75	75	75	75
State Anxiety	Pearson Correlation	-.668**	1.000	-.993**	.652**
	Sig. (2-tailed)	.000	.	.000	.000
	N	75	75	75	75
Percentage of previous penalties scored	Pearson Correlation	.674**	-.993**	1.000	-.644**
	Sig. (2-tailed)	.000	.000	.	.000
	N	75	75	75	75
Penn State Worry Questionnaire	Pearson Correlation	-.675**	.652**	-.644**	1.000
	Sig. (2-tailed)	.000	.000	.000	.
	N	75	75	75	75

** Correlation is significant at the 0.01 level (2-tailed).

SPSS Output 5.13

5.5.   Further Reading

Hutcheson, G. & Sofroniou, N. (1999). *The multivariate social scientist.* London: Sage. Chapter 4.

Menard, S. (1995). *Applied logistic regression analysis.* Sage university paper series on quantitative applications in the social sciences, 07-106. Thousand Oaks, CA: Sage. This is a fairly advanced text, but great nevertheless. Unfortunately, few basic-level texts include logistic regression so you'll have to rely on what I've written!

Differences

6 Comparing Two Means

6.1. Revision of Experimental Research

Often in the social sciences we are not just interested in looking at which variables covary, or predict an outcome. Instead, we might want to look at the effect of one variable on another by systematically changing some aspect of that variable. So, rather than collecting naturally occurring data as in correlation and regression, we manipulate one variable to observe its effect on another. As a simple case, we might want to see what the effect of positive encouragement has on learning about statistics. I might, therefore, randomly split some students into two different groups:

- **Group 1 (positive reinforcement)**: During seminars I congratulate all students in this group on their hard work and success. Even when people get things wrong, I am supportive and say things like 'that was very nearly the right answer, you're coming along really well' and then give the student a nice piece of chocolate.
- **Group 2 (negative reinforcement)**: This group receives a normal university style seminar, so during seminars I give relentless verbal abuse to all of the students even when they give the correct answer. I demean their contributions and am patronizing and dismissive of everything they say. I tell students that they are stupid, worthless and shouldn't be doing the course at all.

The thing that I have manipulated is the teaching method (positive reinforcement versus negative reinforcement). This variable is known as the *independent variable* (IV) and in this situation it is said to have two levels, because it has been manipulated in two ways (i.e. reinforcement has been split into two types: positive and negative). Once I have carried out this manipulation I must have some kind of outcome that I am interested in measuring. In this case it is statistical ability, and I could measure this variable using the end of year statistics exam results. This outcome variable is known as the *dependent variable*, or DV, because we assume that these scores will depend upon the type of teaching method used (the independent variable).

6.1.1. Methods of Collecting Data

When we collect data, we can choose between two methods of data collection. The first is to manipulate the independent variable using different subjects. This method is the one described above, in which different groups of people take part in each experimental condition (a *between-group* or *between-subjects* design). The second method is to manipulate the independent variable using the same subjects. Simplistically, this method means that we give a group of students positive reinforcement for a few weeks and test their statistical abilities and then begin to give this same group negative reinforcement for a few weeks before testing them again (a *within-subject* or *repeated measures* design). The way in which the data are collected determines the type of test that is used to analyze the data.

6.1.2. Two Types of t-Test

The experiment that I described is the simplest form of experiment that can be done: only one independent variable is manipulated in only two ways and only one dependent variable is measured. This experiment is the simplest because there are only two experimental conditions that are compared. The *t*-test was designed to analyze this scenario. Of course, there are more complex experimental designs and we will look at these in subsequent chapters. There are, in fact, two different *t*-tests and the one you use depends on whether the independent variable was manipulated using the same subjects or different:

- **Independent means *t*-test**: This test is used when there are two experimental conditions and different subjects were assigned to each condition (this is sometimes called the *independent measures* or *independent samples* *t*-test).
- **Dependent means *t*-test**: This test is used when there are two experimental conditions and the same subjects took part in both conditions of the experiment (this test is sometimes referred to as the *matched-pairs* or *paired-samples* *t*-test).

6.1.3.   Rationale for the t-Test

Both *t*-tests have a similar rationale:

- Two samples of data are collected and the sample means calculated. These means might differ by either a little or a lot.
- If the samples come from the same population, then we expect their means to be roughly equal (see section 1.1.3.2). Although it is possible for their means to differ by chance alone, we would expect large differences between sample means to occur very infrequently. Under what's known as *the null hypothesis* we assume that the experimental manipulation has no effect on the subjects: therefore, we expect the sample means to be identical, or very similar.
- We compare the difference between the sample means that we collected to the difference between the sample means that we would expect to obtain by chance. We use the standard error (see section 1.1.3.2) as a gauge of the variability between sample means. If the standard error is small, then we expect most samples to have very similar means. When the standard error is large we expect to obtain large differences in sample means by chance alone. If the difference between the samples we have collected is larger than what we would expect based on the standard error then we can assume one of two things:
  - (a) That sample means in our population fluctuate a lot by chance alone and we have, by chance, collected two samples that are atypical of the population from which they came).
  - (b) The two samples come from different populations but are typical of their respective parent population. In this scenario, the difference between samples represents a genuine difference between the samples (and so the null hypothesis is incorrect).
- As the observed difference between the sample means gets larger, the more confident we become that the second explanation is correct (i.e. that the null hypothesis should be rejected). If the null hypothesis is incorrect, then we accept what is known as *the experimental hypothesis*, that is that the two sample means differ because of the different experimental manipulation imposed on each sample.

In essence, we calculate the *t*-test using equation (6.1), but the exact form that this equation takes will depend on how the data were collected (i.e. whether the same or different subjects were used in each experimental condition).

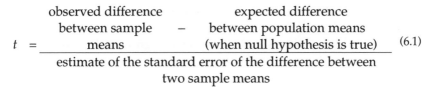

$$t = \frac{\text{observed difference between sample means} - \text{expected difference between population means (when null hypothesis is true)}}{\text{estimate of the standard error of the difference between two sample means}} \quad (6.1)$$

Related *t*-Test: In a repeated measures experiment that has two conditions, the same subjects participate in both conditions. So, we measure subject's behaviour in condition 1 *and* in condition 2. If there is no experimental manipulation then we expect a person's behaviour to be the same in both conditions. We expect this because external factors such as age, gender, IQ, motivation and arousal will be the same for both conditions (a person's gender etc. will not change from when they are tested in condition 1 to when they are tested in condition 2). If the performance measure is reliable, and the variable or characteristic that we are measuring remains stable over time, then it is probable that a subject's performance in condition 1 will be very highly related to their performance in condition 2. So, subjects who score highly in condition 1 will also score highly in condition 2, and those who have low scores for condition 1 will have low scores in condition 2.

If we introduce an experimental manipulation, then we do something different to subjects in condition 1, to what we do to them in condition 2. So, the only difference between conditions 1 and 2 is the manipulation that the experimenter has made. Therefore, any differences between the means of the two conditions is probably due to the experimental manipulation.

Independent *t*-Test: In this design we still have two conditions, but this time different subjects participate in each condition. One group of people participates in one experimental condition, while a second group of people participates in the other. If we did nothing to the groups, then we would still find some variation between behaviour between the two conditions because the people in the different conditions will vary in their ability, motivation, IQ and other factors. In short, the type of factors that were held constant in the repeated measures design are free to vary in the independent measures design.

In a repeated measures design, differences between two conditions can be caused by only two things: (1) the manipulation that was carried out on the subjects, or (2) any other factor that might affect the way in which a person performs from one time to the next. The latter factor is likely to be fairly minor compared to the influence of the experimental manipulation. In an independent design, differences between the two conditions can also be caused by one of two things: (1) the manipulation that was carried out on the subjects, or (2) differences between the characteristics of the people allocated to each of the groups. The latter factor in this instance is likely to create considerable random variation both within each condition, and between them.

As such, in both the repeated measures design and the independent measures design there are always two sources of variation:

- **Systematic variation**: This variation is due to the experimenter doing something to all of the subjects in one condition but not in the other condition.
- **Unsystematic variation**: This variation results from random factors that exist between the experimental conditions (such as natural differences in ability).

The effect of our experimental manipulation is likely to be more apparent in a repeated measures design than in a between-group design because in the former unsystematic variation can be caused only by differences in the way in which someone behaves at different times. In between-group designs we have differences in innate ability contributing to the unsystematic variation. Therefore, this error variation will almost always be much larger than if the same subjects had been used. When we look at the effect of our experimental manipulation, it is always against a background of 'noise' caused by random, uncontrollable differences between our conditions. In a repeated measures design this 'noise' is kept to a minimum and so the effect of the experiment is more likely to show up. This means that repeated measures designs have more power to detect effects that genuinely exist than independent designs.

6.1.3.1. Randomization

In both repeated measures and independent measures designs it is important to try to keep the unsystematic variation to a minimum. By keeping the unsystematic variation as small as possible we get a more sensitive measure of the experimental manipulation. Generally, scientists use the randomization of subjects to achieve this goal. The *t*-test works by identifying the systematic and unsystematic sources of variation and then comparing them. This comparison allows us to see whether the experiment has generated considerably more variation than we would have got had we just tested subjects without the experimental manipulation. Randomization is important because it eliminates most other sources of systematic variation, which allows us to be sure that any systematic variation between experimental conditions is due to the manipulation of the independent variable.

Repeated Measures: If the same people participate in more than one experimental condition, although they are naive during the first experimental condition they come to the second experimental condition with prior experience of what is expected of them. At the very least they will be familiar with the dependent measure. The two most important sources of systematic variation in this type of design are:

- **Practice effects**: Subjects may perform differently in the second condition because of familiarity with the experimental situation and/or the measures being used.
- **Boredom**: Subjects may perform differently in the second condition because they are tired or bored from having completed the first condition.

Although these effects are impossible to eliminate completely, we can ensure that they produce no systematic variation between our conditions. We can do this by *counterbalancing* the order in which a person participates in a condition. We can randomly decide that a subject either has condition 1 before condition 2, or that they have condition 2 before condition 1. If we look back at the teaching method example at the beginning of this chapter, if the same subjects were used in both conditions, then we might find that statistical ability was higher after the negative reinforcement condition. However, every student experienced the negative reinforcement after the positive reinforcement and so went into the negative reinforcement condition already having a better knowledge of statistics than when they began the positive reinforcement condition. So, the apparent improvement after negative reinforcement is not due to the experimental manipulation (i.e. it's not because negative reinforcement works), it is because subjects had attended statistics seminars by the time they had finished the negative reinforcement condition. We can ensure that the number of statistics seminars does not introduce a systematic bias by randomizing the order of conditions, so we could randomly take half of the students and give them negative reinforcement first while the remainder have positive reinforcement first.

Independent Measures: A similar argument can be applied to between-group designs. We know that different subjects participate in different experimental conditions and that these subjects will differ in many respects (their IQ, attention span etc.). Although we know that these factors (known as *confounding variables*) contribute to the variation between conditions, we need to make sure that these variables contribute to the unsystematic variation (and *not* the systematic variation). The way to ensure that confounding variables are unlikely to contribute systematically to the variation between experimental conditions is to randomly allocate subjects to a particular condition. This should ensure that these confounding variables are evenly distributed across conditions.

A good example is the effects of alcohol on personality. You might give one group of people 5 pints, and keep a second group sober, and then count how many fights each person gets into. The effect that alcohol has on people can be very variable because of different tolerance levels: teetotal people can become very drunk on a small amount, whilst alcoholics need to consume vast quantities before the alcohol affects them. Now, if you allocated a bunch of teetotal subjects to the condition that consumed alcohol, then you might find no difference between them and the sober group (because the teetotal subjects are all unconscious after the first glass and so can't become involved in any fights). As such, the person's prior experiences with alcohol will create systematic variation that cannot be dissociated from the effect of the experimental manipulation. The best way to reduce this eventuality is to randomly allocate subjects to conditions.

6.2.   Inputting Data and Displaying Means with Error Bar Charts

Both the independent and dependent *t*-test procedures in SPSS produce means and standard deviations for each experimental condition. However, to better understand our data it is a good idea to plot graphs before we begin. These graphs help us to understand what is going on within the data and what kinds of results we might expect to obtain. Most of you should be familiar with bar charts (see Chapter 2) and these charts are often reported in academic papers. A bar chart is a nice way to summarize data but it gives a very narrow view of the data (for example it gives no indication of the number of scores that contributed to each mean, nor does it tell us how much variation there was in scores). A better way to examine data is with an error bar chart. An error bar chart displays the 95% confidence interval of the mean of each experimental condition. Therefore, it displays the mean of each group, but also displays a bar that represents the confidence interval for that mean. Now, we have come across the concept of a confidence interval before (Chapters 4 and 5). I explained previously that if we were to take 100 samples from a population and calculate the mean of each, then the confidence interval represents the limits within which 95 of those 100 means would fall. So, if a confidence interval has a lower limit of –10 and an upper limit of +10, then if we took 100 samples from the same population and calculated the mean, 95 of these means would lie within ±10 (the remaining 5 means would lie outside of these limits). Therefore, an error bar graph displays the limits within which the majority of sample means (from the same population) lie.

The *t*-test works on the principle that if two samples are taken from the same population then they should have fairly similar means. We know already that it is possible that any two samples could have slightly different means (and the standard error will tell us a little about how different we can expect sample means to be). Now, the confidence interval tells us the limits within which most samples will fall (in fact, the size of the confidence interval will depend on the size of the standard error). In the example above we know that 95% of sample means will be between –10 and +10, but that still means that we could take two samples and find that one had a sample mean of –10, whereas the other had a sample mean of 10. Therefore, by chance alone, it is possible to have two samples from the same population that differ by 20. If we took two samples and found that their means differed by 25, what do you think this would tell us? Well, put simply, we know that in 95% of pairs of samples we would expect a maximum difference between sample means of 20, and so if we obtain a difference greater than this value it suggests that our samples must come from different populations. OK, I can hear you all thinking 'so what if the samples come from a different population'? Well, if we have taken two random samples of people, and we have tested them on some measure (e.g. fear of statistics textbooks), then we expect these people to belong to the same population. If their sample means are so different as to suggest that, in fact, they come from different populations, why might this be? The answer is that our experimental manipulation has induced a difference between the samples.

To reiterate, when an experimental manipulation is successful, we expect to find that our samples have come from different populations. If the manipulation is unsuccessful, then we expect to find that the samples came from the same population (e.g. the sample means should be fairly similar). Now, the 95% confidence interval tells us something about the range of means that samples from a population can have. If we take samples from two populations, then we expect the confidence intervals to be different (in fact, to be sure that the samples were from different populations we would not expect the two confidence intervals to overlap). If we take two samples from the same population, then we would expect, if our measure is reliable, the confidence intervals to be very similar (i.e. they should overlap completely with each other). You may well ask where this diversion into the theory of hypothesis testing is leading us; well it follows from what I have just said that if our experimental manipulation is successful, then the confidence intervals of the experimental groups should not overlap. If the manipulation is unsuccessful then the confidence intervals will overlap. In terms of the error bar graph, we should find that if the bars on our error bar graph do not overlap this is indicative of a significant difference between groups.

6.2.1.   *Error Bar Graphs for Between-Group Designs*

When data are collected using different subjects in each group, we need to input the data using a coding variable (see section 1.2.3.1). So, the data editor will have two columns of data. The first column is a coding variable (called something like **group**) which, in the case of the *t*-test, will have two codes (for convenience I suggest 0 = group 1, and 1 = group 2). The second will have values for the dependent variable.

Table 6.1: Data from **spiderBG.sav**

Subject	Group	Anxiety
1	0	30
2	0	35
3	0	45
4	0	40
5	0	50
6	0	35
7	0	55
8	0	25
9	0	30
10	0	45
11	0	40
12	0	50
13	1	40
14	1	35
15	1	50
16	1	55
17	1	65
18	1	55
19	1	50
20	1	35
21	1	30
22	1	50
23	1	60
24	1	39

Throughout this chapter I use the same data set, not because I am too lazy to think up different data sets, but because it allows me to illustrate various things. The example relates to whether arachnophobia (fear of spiders) is specific to real spiders or whether pictures of spiders can evoke similar levels of anxiety. Twenty-four arachnophobes were used in all. Twelve were asked to play with a big hairy tarantula spider with big fangs and an evil look in its eight eyes. Their subsequent anxiety was measured. The remaining twelve were shown only pictures of the same big hairy tarantula and again their anxiety was measured. The data are in the file **spiderBG.sav**, but for those who want some practice in inputting data, they are also presented in Table 6.1. Remember that each row in the data editor represents a different subject's data. Therefore, you need a column representing the group to which they belonged and a second column representing their anxiety. The data in Table 6.1 show only the group codes and not the corresponding label. When you enter the data into SPSS remember to tell the computer that a code of 0 represents the group that were shown the picture, and that a code of 1 represents the group that saw the real spider (see section 1.2.3.1).

When you have entered the data (or accessed the file **spiderBG.sav**) you should access the *error bar* dialog box by using the mouse to click on **Graphs⇒Error Bar ….**. The initial dialog box is shown in Figure 6.1. There are two choices of error bar graph. The first is a simple error bar chart (for plotting levels of a single independent variable) and the second is a clustered error bar graph. The clustered graph can be used when a second between-group independent variable has been measured (such as gender—see section 2.7). We will stick to a simple error bar graph. The next choice is whether the data in the chart summarize groups of cases or separate variables. There is a simple rule here: select *Summaries for groups of cases* when the data were collected using different subjects (as is the case here) and select *Summaries of separate variables* when the data were collected using the same subjects (see section 2.1). When you have selected the appropriate options, click on Define.

Figure 6.1: Initial dialog box for error bar graphs

When you click on Define a new dialog box appears that allows you to specify which variables you want to plot. In this example we have only two variables: **group** and **anxiety**. So, using the mouse, select **anxiety** from the variables list and insert it into the space labelled *Variable* by clicking on 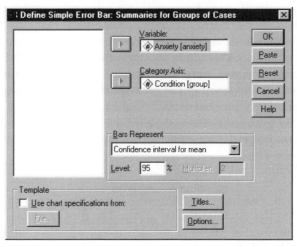. Then, highlight **group** in the variables list and transfer it to the space labelled *Category Axis* by clicking on ▶. You can plot numerous things using this type of graph and the default option is to plot the 95% confidence interval. This is the most useful type of graph and so the default options can be left as they are.

Figure 6.2: Main *error bar* dialog box for summaries for groups of cases

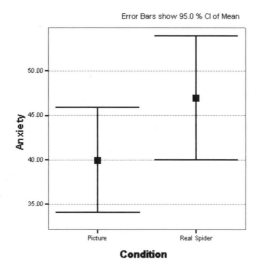

Figure 6.3: (Nicely edited!) error bar graph of **spiderBG.sav**

The resulting error bar graph is shown in Figure 6.3 and, as you can see, it looks like two Is. In the middle of each of the two bars is a square that represents the mean of each group. The vertical bar shows the confidence interval around that mean. So, from the graph of these data we can see that when a picture of a spider was used, the average level of anxiety was 40 and that 95 out of 100 samples from the same population would have means between about 34 and 46. However, when a real spider was used, the average level of anxiety was 47, and 95 out of 100 samples from the same population would have means between about 40 and 54. More important, the error bars overlap considerably, indicating that these samples are unlikely to be from different populations (so the experimental manipulation was unsuccessful). To see whether this last statement is true, you'll have to wait until section 6.4.3.

6.2.2. *Error Bar Graphs for Repeated Measures Designs*

If we repeated the study just described but using the same subjects in each condition, we could produce an error bar graph identical to that shown in Figure 6.3. The problem with creating an error bar graph of repeated measures data is that SPSS treats the data as though different groups of subjects were used. To prove that I'm not talking rubbish, the data for this study are included in a file called **spiderRM.sav**. In this file, the values of **anxiety** are identical to the between-group data. However, the data are arranged as if the same subjects were used in each condition (so, each subject was exposed to a picture of a spider and their anxiety was measured, and at some other time the same subjects were exposed to the real spider and their anxiety was measured again). The data are arranged differently now because the same subjects were used. In SPSS, each row of the data editor represents a single subject, and so with this design the data are arranged in two columns (one representing the **picture** condition and one representing the **real** condition). The data are displayed in Table 6.2 and I recommend that you try inputting these data into a new data editor file rather than accessing the file on disk.

To plot an error bar graph of these data simply select the *error bar* dialog box by using the mouse to select **Graphs**⇒**Error Bar ...** and then in the dialog box (see Figure 6.1) click on ⦿ Summaries of separate variables and then Define . This process will bring up the main dialog box. Once the dialog box is activated you simply select the two variables of interest (**picture** and **real**) and then click on OK . The resulting graph should be identical to the one that you plotted for the between-subject data. Now, this is a problem because I spent an awful lot of time telling you how repeated measures designs eliminated a lot of the unsystematic variance from the data, and by plotting repeated measures data in this way we ignore the repeated measures component of the data. Loftus and Masson (1994) suggest that one way to overcome this problem is to eliminate the between-subject variability by normalizing subject means (this just means ensuring that all subjects have the same mean across conditions). To normalize the means, we need to use the *compute* function of SPSS and carry out a number of steps (all of this was just a sneaky ploy to get you to use the *compute* function).

Table 6.2: Data from **spiderRM.sav**

Subject	Picture (Anxiety score)	Real (Anxiety Score)
1	30	40
2	35	35
3	45	50
4	40	55
5	50	65
6	35	55
7	55	50
8	25	35
9	30	30
10	45	50
11	40	60
12	50	39

6.2.2.1. The Compute Function

The *compute* command allows us to carry out various functions on columns of data. Some typical functions might be adding scores across several columns, taking the square root of the scores in a column, or calculating the mean of several variables. To access the *compute* dialog box, use the mouse to specify **Transform**⇒**Compute**.... The resulting dialog box is shown in Figure 6.4. In this dialog box there is a list of functions on the right-hand side, and a calculator-like keyboard in the centre. Most of the functions on the calculator are obvious but the most common are listed below.

Addition: This button places a plus sign in the command area. For example, 'picture + real' creates a column in which each row contains the score from the column labelled *picture* added to the score from the column labelled *real* (e.g. for subject 1: 30 + 40 = 70).

Subtraction: This button places a minus sign in the command area. E.g. 'picture – real' creates a column in which each row contains the score from the column labelled *real* subtracted from the score from the column labelled *picture* (e.g. for subject 1: 30 – 40 = –10).

Multiply: This button places a multiplication sign in the command area. For example, 'picture * real' creates a column that contains the score from the column labelled *picture* multiplied by the score from the column labelled *real* (e.g. for subject 1: 30 × 40 = 1200).

Divide: This button places a division sign in the command area. For example, 'picture/real' creates a column that contains the score from the column labelled *picture* divided by the score from the column labelled *real* (e.g. for subject 1: 30/40 = 0.75).

Exponentiation: This button is used to raise the preceding term by the power of the succeeding term. So, 'picture **2' creates a column that contains the scores in the *picture* column raised to the power of 2 (i.e. the square of each number in the *picture* column: for subject 1, $(30)^2 = 900$). Likewise, 'picture**3' creates a column with values of **picture** cubed.

Less than: This operation is usually used for 'include case' functions. If you click on the [if...] button, a dialog box appears that allows you to select certain cases on which to carry out the operation. So, if you typed 'picture < 30', then SPSS would carry out the *compute* function only for those subjects whose **anxiety** in the **picture** condition was less than 30 (i.e. if **anxiety** was 29 or less).

Less than or equal to: This operation is the same as above except that cases that are exactly 30 are included as well.

More than: This operation is generally used to include cases above a certain value. So, if you clicked on [if...] and then typed 'picture > 30' then SPSS will carry out any analysis only on cases for which **anxiety** in the **picture** condition was greater than 30 (i.e. 31 and above).

More than or equal to: This operation is the same as above but will include cases that are exactly 30 as well.

Equal to: You can use this operation to include cases for which subjects have a specific value. For example, 'picture = 30' typed in the *if* dialog box ensures that only cases that have a value of 30 for the **picture** condition are included.

Not equal to: This operation will include all cases except those will a specific value. So, 'picture ~= 30' will include all cases except those that had an **anxiety** score of 30 in the **picture** condition.

Variable type: This button opens a dialog box that allows you to give the new variable a full name, and to specify what type of variable it is (e.g. numeric).

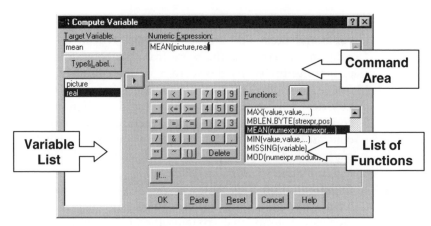

Figure 6.4: Dialog box for the compute function

The results of any *compute* function will be produced in a new column in the data editor and so the first thing to do is to type in a label for this new variable (in the box labelled *Target Variable*). If you type in a variable name that already exists in the data editor then SPSS will tell you and ask you whether you want to replace this existing variable. If you respond with *Yes* then SPSS will replace the data in the existing column with the result of the *compute* function. If you respond with *No* then nothing will happen and you will need to rename the target variable. The box labelled *Numeric Expression* is the space in which arithmetic commands are typed (I've called this space the command area). You can enter variable names into the command area by selecting the variable required from the variables list and then clicking on ▶. Likewise, you can select certain functions from the list of available functions and enter them into the command area by clicking on ▲.

Some of the most useful functions are listed in Table 6.3, which shows the standard form of the function, the name of the function, an example of how the function can be used and what SPSS would output if that example were used. There are several basic functions for calculating means, standard deviations and sums of columns. There are also functions such as the square root and logarithm functions that are useful for transforming data that are skewed (see Howell, 1997, Chapter 11 for a discussion of data transformation). For the interested reader, the SPSS base systems user's guide has details of all of the functions available through the *compute* dialog box (Norušis, 1997; see also SPSS Inc., 1997).

Table 6.3: Some useful *compute* functions

Function	Name	Example Input	Output
Mean(?,?, ..)	Mean	Mean(picture, real)	For each row, SPSS calculates the average of the variables **picture** and **real**
SD(?,?, ..)	Standard Deviation	SD(picture, real)	Across each row, SPSS calculates the standard deviation of the values in the columns labelled *picture* and *real*
SUM(?,?, ..)	Sum	SUM(picture, real)	For each row, SPSS adds the values in the columns labelled *picture* and *real*
SQRT(?)	Square Root	SQRT(picture)	Produces a column that contains the square root of each value in the column labelled *picture*. Useful for transforming skewed data or data with heterogeneous variances
ABS(?)	Absolute Value	ABS(picture)	Produces a variable that contains the absolute value of the values in the column labelled *picture* (absolute values are ones where the signs are ignored: so –5 becomes +5 and +5 stays as +5)
LG10(?)	Base 10 Logarithm	LG10(picture)	Produces a variable that contains the logarithmic (to base 10) values of **picture**. This is useful for transforming positively skewed data
Normal(stddev)	Normal Random Numbers	Normal(5)	Produces a variable containing pseudo-random numbers from a normal distribution with a mean of 0 and a standard deviation of 5

6.2.2.2. Step 1: Calculate the Mean for each Subject

Now we know something about the *compute* function, we can use this function to produce more accurate within-subject error bar charts. To begin with, we need to calculate the average anxiety for each subject and so we use the *mean* function. Access the main *compute* dialog box by using the **Transform**⇒**Compute…** menu path. Enter the name **mean** into the box labelled *Target Variable* and then scroll down the list of functions until you find the one called *MEAN(numexpr, numexpr,..)*. Highlight this function and transfer it to the command area by clicking on ◼. When the command is transferred, it appears in the command area as 'MEAN(?,?)' and the question marks should be replaced with variable names (which can be typed manually or transferred from the variables list). So replace the first question mark with the variable **picture**, and the second one with the variable **real**. The completed dialog box should look like the one in Figure 6.4.

6.2.2.3.   *Step 2: Calculate the Grand Mean*

The grand mean is the mean of all scores (regardless of which condition the score comes from) and so for the current data this value will be the mean of all 24 scores. One way to calculate this is by hand (i.e. add up all of the scores and divide by 24); however, an easier way is to use the means that we have just calculated. The means we have just calculated represent the average score for each subject and so if we take the average of those mean scores, we will have the mean of all subjects (i.e. the grand mean)—phew, there were a lot of means in that sentence! OK, to do this we can use a useful little gadget called the *descriptives* command. Access this function using the **Analyze⇒Descriptive Statistics⇒Descriptives...** menu path. The dialog box in Figure 6.5 should appear. The *descriptives* command is used to get basic descriptive statistics for variables and by clicking on ⬛Options... a second dialog box is activated. Select the variable **mean** from the list and transfer it to the box labelled *Variable(s)* by clicking on ▸. Then, use the *options* dialog box to specify only the mean (you can leave the default settings as they are, but it is only the mean in which we are interested). If you run this analysis the output should provide you with some self-explanatory descriptive statistics and from this summary table you should find that the mean is 43.50. This value is the grand mean, and we shall use this value in the following calculations.

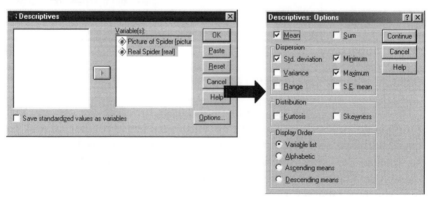

Figure 6.5: Dialog box for descriptive statistics

6.2.2.4. Step 3: Calculate the Adjustment Factor

If you look at the variable labelled **mean**, you should notice that the values for each subject are different, which tells us that some people had greater anxiety than others did across the conditions. The fact that subjects' mean anxiety scores differ represents individual difference between different people (so, it represents the fact that some of the subjects are generally more scared of spiders than others). These differences in natural anxiety to spiders contaminate the error bar graphs, which is why if we don't adjust the values that we plot, we will get the same graph as if a between-subjects design had been used. Loftus and Masson (1994) argue that to eliminate this contamination we should equalize the means between subjects (i.e. adjust the scores in each condition such that when we take the mean score across conditions, it is the same for all subjects). So, we need to calculate an adjustment factor by subtracting each subject's mean score from the grand mean. We can use the *compute* function to do this calculation for us. Activate the *compute* dialog box, give the target variable a name (I suggest **adjust**) and then using the command '43.5 – mean'. This command will take the grand mean (43.5) and subtract from it each subject's average anxiety level (see Figure 6.6).

This process creates a new variable in the data editor called **adjust**. The scores in the column **adjust** represent the difference between each subject's mean anxiety and the mean anxiety level across all subjects. You'll notice that some of the values are positive and these subjects are one's who were less anxious than average. Other subjects were more anxious than average and they have negative adjustment scores. We can now use these adjustment values to eliminate the between-subject differences in anxiety.

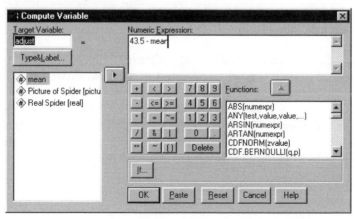

Figure 6.6: Calculating the adjustment factor

6.2.2.5. Step 4: Create Adjusted Values for each Variable

So far, we have calculated the difference between each subject's mean score and the mean score of all subjects (the grand mean). This difference can be used to adjust the existing scores for each subject. First we need to adjust the scores in the **picture** condition. Once again, we can use the *compute* command to make the adjustment. Activate the *compute* dialog box in the same way as before, and then title our new variable **picture2** (you can then click on ⌗Type&Label... and give this variable a label such as 'adjusted values for the picture condition'). All we are going to do is to add each subject's score in the **picture** condition to their adjustment value. Select the variable **picture** and transfer it to the command area by clicking on ▶, then click on ⊞ and select the variable **adjust** and transfer it to the command area by clicking on ▶. The completed dialog box is shown in Figure 6.7. Now do the same thing for the variable **real**: create a variable called **real2** that contains the values of **real** added to the value in the **adjust** column.

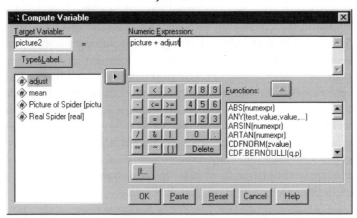

Figure 6.7: Adjusting the values of **picture**

Now, the variables **real2** and **picture2** represent the anxiety experienced in each condition, adjusted so as to eliminate any between-subject differences. If you don't believe me, then use the *compute* command to create a variable **mean2**, that is the average of **picture2** and **real2** (just like we did in section 6.2.2.2). You should find that the value in this column is the same for every subject, thus proving that the between-subject variability in means is gone: the value will be 43.50— the grand mean.

6.2.2.6. Drawing the Error Bar Graph

Drawing the graph itself is similar to the between-group scenario. First, access the main dialog box through the **Graphs⇒Error Bar …** menus. Then in this dialog box (see Figure 6.1) click on ⊙ Summaries of separate variables and then Define. This process will bring up the main dialog box. Once the dialog box is activated you simply select the two variables of interest (we want the adjusted values and so we need to select **picture2** and **real2**) and then click on OK (see Figure 6.8).

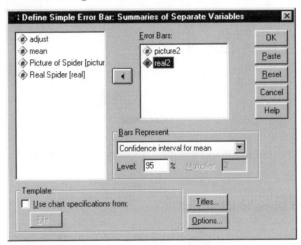

Figure 6.8: Dialog box for drawing an error bar graph of a repeated measures variable

The resulting error bar graph is shown in Figure 6.9. You'll notice that the error bar graph of the adjusted values is somewhat different to the error bar graph of the unadjusted values (look back to Figure 6.3). The first thing to notice is that the error bars do not overlap. Earlier I said that when error bars do not overlap we can be confident that our samples have not come from the same population (and so our experimental manipulation has been successful). Therefore, the graph of the repeated measures version of these data indicates that real spiders may have evoked significantly greater (because the mean is higher) degrees of anxiety than just a picture. This example illustrates how different conclusions can be reached depending upon whether data were collected using the same or different subjects (I expand upon this point in section 6.5).

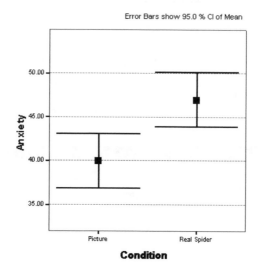

Figure 6.9: Error bar graph of the adjusted values of **spiderRM.sav**

6.3.   The Dependent *t*-Test

Now we know how to graph means, we can move onto analysing whether differences between group means are statistically meaningful. If we stay with our repeated measures data for the time being we can look at the dependent *t*-test, or paired-samples *t*-test. The paired *t*-test is easy to calculate. In effect we use a numeric version of equation (6.1).

$$t = \frac{\overline{D} - \mu_D}{s_D / \sqrt{N}}$$

(6.2)

Equation (6.2) compares the mean difference between our samples ($\overline{D}$) with the difference that we would expect to find between population means (μ_D), and then takes into account the standard error of the differences ($s_D / \sqrt{N}$). If the null hypothesis is true, then we expect there to be no difference between the population means (hence $\mu_D = 0$).

6.3.1.   *Sampling Distributions and the Standard Error*

In equation (6.1) I referred to the lower half of the fraction as the standard error of differences. The standard error was introduced in section 1.1.3.2 and is simply the standard deviation of what's known as a *sampling distribution*. If we took lots of samples from a population and

then calculated their means, we could plot
these means as a frequency distribution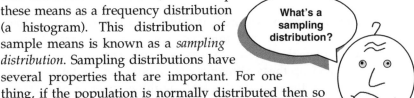
(a histogram). This distribution of
sample means is known as a *sampling
distribution*. Sampling distributions have
several properties that are important. For one
thing, if the population is normally distributed then so
is the sampling distribution (in fact, as long as the
samples contain more than 50 scores the sampling
distribution will always be normally distributed). The mean of the
sampling distribution is equal to the mean of the population—so, if you
calculated the average of all of the sample means then the value you
obtain should be the same as the population mean. This property makes
sense because if a sample is representative of the population then you
would expect its mean to be equal to that of the population. However,
sometimes samples are unrepresentative and their mean differs from the
population mean. On average though a sample mean will be very close
to the population mean and only rarely will the sample mean be
substantially different from the population. A final property of a
sampling distribution is that its standard deviation is equal to the
standard deviation of the population divided by the square root of the
number of observations in the sample. As I mentioned before, this
standard deviation is known as the standard error.

  We can extend this idea to look at the differences between sample
means. If you were to take several pairs of samples from a population
and calculate their means, then you could calculate the difference
between their means. I mentioned earlier that *on average* sample means
will be very similar to the population mean: therefore, most samples will
have very similar means. Therefore, most of the time the difference
between sample means from the same population will be zero, or close
to zero. However, sometimes one or both of the samples could have a
mean very deviant from the population mean and so it is possible to
obtain large differences between sample means by chance alone. If you
plotted these differences between sample means as a histogram, you
would again have a sampling distribution with all of the properties
previously described. The standard deviation of this sampling
distribution is called the standard error of differences. A small standard
error tells us that most pairs of samples from a population will have
very similar means (that is, the difference between sample means should
normally be very small). A large standard error tells us that sample
means can deviate quite a lot from the population mean and so
differences between pairs of samples can be quite large by chance alone.

6.3.2. *The Dependent t-Test Equation Explained*

In an experiment, a person's score in condition 1 will be different to their score in condition 2, and this difference could be very large or very small. If we calculate the differences between each person's score in each condition and add up these differences we would get the total amount of difference. If we then divide this total by the number of participants we get the average difference (so, how much, on average, a person's score differed in condition 1 compared to condition 2). This average difference is $\overline{D}$ in equation (6.2) and it is an indicator of the systematic variation in the data (i.e. it represents the experimental effect). We know that if we had taken two random samples from a population (and not done anything to these samples) then the means could be different just by chance. The degree to which two sample means are likely to differ is determined by the size of the standard error of differences. We need to be sure that the observed difference between our samples is due to our experimental manipulation (and not a chance result). Knowing the mean difference alone is not useful because it depends upon the scale of measurement and so we standardize the value. One way to standardize the sum of group differences would be to divide by the sample standard deviation of those differences (see section 1.1.3.1). If you think about what the standard deviation represents, it is a measure of the average deviation from the mean, and so the standard deviation of the differences between conditions represents the average deviation from the mean difference. As such, the standard deviation is a measure of how much variation there is between subjects' difference scores. As such, the standard deviation of differences represents the *unsystematic* variation in the experiment. To clarify, imagine that an alien came down and cloned me (because I am petrified of spiders) 12 times (heaven forbid that there should ever be 12 of me running around the planet!). All of my clones would be the same as me, and would behave in an identical way to me. Therefore, we would all be quite scared of the picture of the spider and might all have an anxiety score of 40. What's more, we would all be more scared of real spiders and so would have anxiety scores of 50. Remember that we are clones so we have behaved identically. If you calculated the difference between our anxiety scores for the picture and the real spider, the difference would be 10 for each of us. If we then calculate the standard deviation of these difference scores it will be zero (because we all got the same scores and so there is no variation at all between scores). Therefore, if all of our subjects were the same, the

How does the t-test actually work?

standard deviation would be zero, that is, there would be no unsystematic variation.

Although dividing by the standard deviation would be useful as a means of standardizing the average difference between conditions, we are interested in knowing how the difference between sample means compares to what we would expect to find had we not imposed an experimental manipulation. We can use the properties of the sampling distribution: instead of dividing the average difference between conditions by the standard deviation of differences, we could divide it by the standard error of differences. Dividing by the standard error not only standardizes the average difference between conditions, but also indicates how the difference between the two sample means compares in magnitude to what would be expected by chance alone. If the standard error is large, then large differences between samples are more common (because the distribution of differences is more spread out). Conversely, if the standard error is small, then large differences between sample means are uncommon (because the distribution is very narrow and centred around zero). Therefore, if the average difference between our samples is large, and the standard error of differences is small, then we can be confident that the difference we observed in our sample is not a chance result. If the difference is not a chance result then it must have been caused by the experimental manipulation.

In a perfect world, we could calculate the standard error by taking all possible pairs of samples from a population, calculating the differences between their means, and then working out the standard deviation of these differences. However, in reality this is impossible. Therefore, we estimate the standard error from the standard deviation of differences obtained within the sample (S_D) and the sample size (N).

If the standard error of differences is a measure of the unsystematic variation within the data, and the sum of difference scores represents the systematic variation, then it should be clear that the t-statistic is simply the ratio of the systematic variation in the experiment to the unsystematic variation. If the experimental manipulation creates any kind of effect, then we would expect the systematic variation to be much greater than the unsystematic variation (so at the very least, t should be greater than 1). If the experimental manipulation is unsuccessful then we might expect the variation caused by individual differences to be much greater than that caused by the experiment (and so t will be less than 1).

6.3.3. *Dependent t-Tests Using SPSS*

Using our spider data (**spiderRM.sav**), we have twelve spider-phobes who were exposed to a picture of a spider (**picture**) and on a separate occasion a real live tarantula (**real**). Their anxiety was measured in each condition (half of the subjects were exposed to the picture before the real spider while the other half were exposed to the real spider first). I have already described how the data are arranged, and so we can move straight onto doing the test itself. First, we need to access the main dialog box by using the **A̲nalyze⇒Compare M̲eans⇒P̲aired-Samples T Test ...** menu pathway (Figure 6.10). Once the dialog box is activated, select two variables from the list (click on the first variable with the mouse and then the second) and transfer them to the box labelled *Paired V̲ariables* by clicking on [▶]. If you want to carry out several *t*-tests then you can select another pair of variables, transfer them to the variables list, and then select another pair and so on. In this case, we want only one test. If you click on [Options...] then another dialog box appears that gives you the chance to change the width of the confidence interval that is calculated. The default setting is for a 95% confidence interval and this is fine; however, if you want to be stricter about your analysis you could choose a 99% confidence interval but you run a higher risk of failing to detect a genuine effect (a type II error). To run the analysis click on [OK].

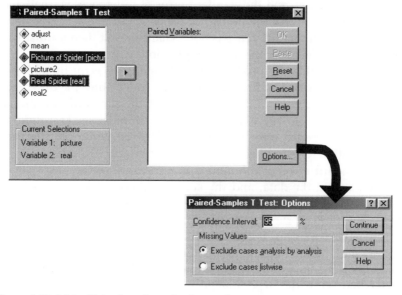

Figure 6.10: Main dialog box for paired-samples *t*-test

6.3.4.   Output from the Dependent t-Test

The resulting output produces three tables. SPSS Output 6.1 shows a table of summary statistics for the two experimental conditions. For each condition we are told the mean, the number of subjects (*N*) and the standard deviation of the sample. In the final column we are told the standard error (see section 6.3.1), which is the sample standard deviation divided by the square root of the sample size (SEM = $s/\sqrt{N}$), so for the picture condition SEM = $9.2932/\sqrt{12} = 9.2932/3.4641 = 2.68$.

SPSS Output 6.1 also shows the Pearson correlation between the two conditions. When repeated measures are used it is possible that the experimental conditions will correlate (because the data in each condition come from the same people and so there could be some constancy in their responses). SPSS provides the value of Pearson's r and the two-tailed significance value. For these data the experimental conditions yield a fairly large correlation coefficient ($r = 0.545$) but are not significantly correlated because $p > 0.05$.

Paired Samples Statistics

		Mean	N	Std. Deviation	Std. Error Mean
Pair 1	Picture of Spider	40.0000	12	9.2932	2.6827
	Real Spider	47.0000	12	11.0289	3.1838

Paired Samples Correlations

		N	Correlation	Sig.
Pair 1	Picture of Spider & Real Spider	12	.545	.067

SPSS Output 6.1

SPSS Output 6.2 shows the most important of the tables: the one that tells us whether the difference between the means of the two conditions was large enough to *not* be a chance result. First, the table tells us the mean difference between scores (this value—$\bar{D}$ in equation (6.2)—is the difference between the mean scores of each condition: $40 - 47 = -7$). The table also reports the standard deviation of the differences between the means and more importantly the standard error of the differences between subjects' scores in each condition (see section 6.2.1). The test statistic, t, is calculated by dividing the mean of differences by the standard error of differences (see equation (6.2): $t = -7/2.8311 = -2.47$). The size of t is compared against known values based on the degrees of freedom. When the same subjects have been used, the degrees of freedom are simply the sample size minus 1 ($df = N - 1 = 11$). SPSS uses the degrees of freedom to calculate the exact probability that a value of t as big as the one obtained could occur by chance. This probability value is in the column labelled *Sig.* By default, SPSS provides only the two-tailed probability, which is the probability when no prediction was made about the direction of group differences. If a specific prediction was made (for example, we might predict that anxiety will be higher when a real spider is used) then the one-tailed probability should be reported and this value is obtained by dividing the two-tailed probability by 2 (more on this later). The two-tailed probability for the spider data is very low ($p = 0.031$) and in fact it tells us that there is only a 3.1% chance that a value of t this big could happen by chance alone. As social scientists we are prepared to accept as statistically meaningful anything that has less than a 5% chance of occurring by chance. The fact that the *t* value is a minus number tells us that condition 1 (the **picture** condition) had a smaller mean than the second (the **real** condition) and so the real spider led to greater anxiety than the picture. When we report a *t*-test we always include the degrees of freedom (in this case 11), the value of the *t*-statistic, and the level at which this value is significant. Therefore, we can conclude that exposure to a real spider caused significantly more reported anxiety in spider-phobes than exposure to a picture ($t(11) = -2.47, p < 0.05$). This result was predicted by the error bar chart in Figure 6.9.

Paired Samples Test

		Paired Differences							
					95% Confidence Interval of the Difference				
		Mean	Std. Deviation	Std. Error Mean	Lower	Upper	t	df	Sig. (2-tailed)
Pair 1	Picture of Spider - Real Spider	-7.0000	9.8072	2.8311	-13.2312	-.7688	-2.473	11	.031

SPSS Output 6.2

The final thing that this output provides is a 95% confidence interval for the mean difference. Imagine we took 100 samples from a population and compared the differences between scores in pairs of samples, then calculated the mean of these differences ($\overline{D}$). We would end up with 100 mean differences between samples. The confidence interval tells us the boundaries within which 95 of these 100 means would lie.[1] So, 95% of mean differences will lie between −13.23 and −0.77. The importance of this interval is that it does not contain zero (i.e. both limits are negative) because this tells us that in 95% of samples the mean difference will not be zero. Crucially, if we were to compare pairs of random samples from a population we expect most of the differences between sample means to be zero. This interval tells us that, based on our two samples, 95% of differences between sample means will not be zero. Therefore, we can be confident that our two samples do not represent random samples from the same population. Instead they represent samples from different populations induced by the experimental manipulation.

---

[1] For those of you well up on the properties of the normal distribution, you should appreciate these limits represent the value of two standard deviations either side of the mean of the sampling distribution. For these data, in which the mean difference was −7 and the standard error was 2.8311, these limits will be −7 ± (2 × 2.8311). Those of you not familiar with the properties of the normal distribution may read Rowntree (1981, Chapters 4 and 5).

6.4. The Independent *t*-Test

6.4.1. *The Independent t-Test Equation Explained*

The independent *t*-test is used in situations in which there are two experimental conditions and different subjects have been used in each condition. There are two different equations that can be used to calculate the *t*-statistic depending on whether the samples contain an equal number of people. As with the related *t*-test we can calculate the *t*-statistic by using a numerical version of equation (6.1). With the dependent *t*-test we could look at differences between pairs of scores, because the scores came from the same subjects and so individual differences between conditions were eliminated. Hence, the difference in scores should reflect only the effect of the experimental manipulation. Now, when different subjects participate in different conditions then pairs of scores will differ not just because of the experimental manipulation, but also because of other sources of variance (such as individual differences between subjects' motivation and IQ etc.). If we cannot investigate differences between conditions on a *per subject* basis (by comparing pairs of scores as we did for the dependent *t*-test) then we must make comparisons on a *per condition* basis (by looking at the overall effect in a condition—see equation (6.3)).

$$t = \frac{\left(\overline{X}_1 - \overline{X}_2\right) - \left(\mu_1 - \mu_2\right)}{\text{estimate of the standard error}} \tag{6.3}$$

Instead of looking at differences between pairs of scores, we now look at differences between the overall means of the two samples and compare them to the differences we would expect to get between the means of the two populations from which the samples come. If the null hypothesis is true then the samples have been drawn from the same population. Therefore, under the null hypothesis $\mu_1 = \mu_2$ and $\mu_1 - \mu_2 = 0$. Therefore, under the null hypothesis the equation becomes

$$t = \frac{\overline{X}_1 - \overline{X}_2}{\text{estimate of the standard error}} \tag{6.4}$$

In the dependent *t*-test we divided the mean difference between pairs of scores by the standard error of these differences. For the independent *t*-test we are looking at differences between groups and so we need to divide by the standard deviation of differences between groups. We can still apply the logic of sampling distributions to this situation. Now, imagine we took several pairs of samples—each pair containing one sample from the two different populations—and compared the means of these samples. From what we have learnt about sampling distributions, we know that the majority of samples from a population will have fairly similar means. Therefore, if we took several pairs of samples (from different populations), the differences between the sample means will be similar across pairs. However, often the difference between a pair of sample means will deviate by a small amount and very occasionally it will deviate by a large amount. If we could plot a sampling distribution of the differences between every pair of sample means that could be taken from two populations, then we would find that it had a normal distribution with a mean equal to the difference between population means ($\mu_1 - \mu_2$). The sampling distribution would tell us by how much we can expect the means of two (or more) samples to differ. As before, the standard deviation of the sampling distribution (the standard error) tells us how variable the differences between sample means are by chance alone. If the standard deviation is high then large differences between sample means can occur by chance; if it is small then only small differences between sample means are expected. It, therefore, makes sense that we use the standard error of the sampling distribution to assess whether the difference between two sample means is statistically meaningful or simply a chance result. Specifically, we divide the difference between sample means by the standard deviation of the sampling distribution.

So, how do we obtain the standard deviation of the sampling distribution of differences between sample means? Well, we use the *variance sum law*, which states that the variance of a difference between two independent variables is equal to the sum of their variances (see Howell, 1997, Chapter 7). This statement means that the variance of the sampling distribution is equal to the sum of the variances of the two populations from which the samples were taken. We saw earlier that the standard error is the standard deviation of the sampling distribution of a population. We can use the sample standard deviations to calculate the standard error of each population's sampling distribution:

$$\text{SE of sampling distribution of population 1} = \frac{s_1}{\sqrt{N_1}}$$

$$\text{SE of sampling distribution of population 2} = \frac{s_2}{\sqrt{N_2}}$$

Therefore, remembering that the variance is simply the standard deviation squared, we can calculate the variance of each sampling distribution:

$$\text{variance of sampling distribution of population 1} = \left(\frac{s_1}{\sqrt{N_1}}\right)^2 = \frac{s_1^2}{N_1}$$

variance of sampling distribution of population 2 $= \left(\dfrac{s_2}{\sqrt{N_2}}\right)^2 = \dfrac{s_2^2}{N_2}$

The variance sum law means that to find the variance of the sampling distribution of differences we merely add together the variances of the sampling distributions of the two populations:

variance of the sampling distribution of differences $= \dfrac{s_1^2}{N_1} + \dfrac{s_2^2}{N_2}$

To find out the standard error of the sampling distribution of differences we merely take the square root of the variance (because variance is the standard deviation squared):

SE of the sampling distribution of differences $= \sqrt{\left(\dfrac{s_1^2}{N_1} + \dfrac{s_2^2}{N_2}\right)}$

Therefore, equation (6.4) becomes equation (6.5).

$$t = \dfrac{\overline{X}_1 - \overline{X}_2}{\sqrt{\left(\dfrac{s_1^2}{N_1} + \dfrac{s_2^2}{N_2}\right)}} \qquad (6.5)$$

Equation (6.5) is true only when the sample sizes are equal. Often in the social sciences it is not possible to collect samples of equal size (because, for example, people may not complete an experiment). When we want to compare two groups that contain different numbers of subjects then equation (6.5) is not appropriate. Instead the pooled variance estimate *t*-test is used which takes account of the difference in sample size by *weighting* the variance of each sample. The derivation of the *t*-statistic is merely to provide a conceptual grasp of what we are doing when we carry out a *t*-test on SPSS. Therefore, it isn't necessary to babble on about how the pooled variance *t*-test is calculated; suffice to say that SPSS knows how to do it and that's all that matters.

6.4.2. The Independent t-Test Using SPSS

I have probably bored most of you to the point of wanting to eat your own legs by now. Equations are boring and that is why SPSS was invented to help us minimize our contact with them. Using our spider data again (**spiderBG.sav**), we have twelve spider-phobes who were exposed to a picture of a spider and twelve different spider-phobes who were exposed to a real-life tarantula (the groups are coded using the variable **group**). Their anxiety was measured in each condition (**anxiety**). I have already described how the data are arranged (see section 6.2.1), and so we can move straight onto doing the test itself. First, we need to access the main dialog box by using the **Analyze⇒Compare Means⇒Independent-Samples T Test ...** menu pathway (see Figure 6.11). Once the dialog box is activated, select the dependent variable from the list (click on **anxiety**) and transfer it to the box labelled *Test Variable(s)* by clicking on ▣. If you want to carry out *t*-tests on several dependent variables then you can select other dependent variables and transfer them to the variables list. However, there are good reasons why it is not a good idea to carry out lots of tests (see Chapter 7).

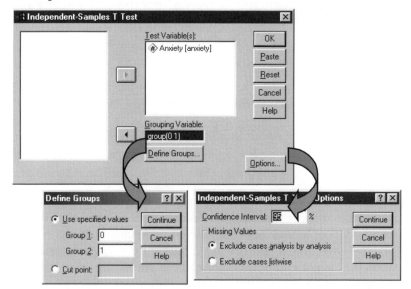

Figure 6.11: Dialog boxes for the independent means *t*-test

Next, we need to select an independent variable (the grouping variable). In this case, we need to select **group** and then transfer it to the box labelled *Grouping Variable*. When your grouping variable has been selected the Define Groups button will become active and you should click on it to activate the *define groups* dialog box. SPSS needs to know what numeric codes you assigned to your two groups, and there is a space for you to type the codes. In this example, we coded our picture group as 0 and our real group as 1, and so these are the codes that we type. Alternatively you can specify a *Cut point* in which case SPSS will assign all cases greater than or equal to that value to one group and all the values below the cut point to the second group. This facility is useful if you are testing different groups of subjects based on something like a median split. So, you might want to classify people as spider-phobes or non-spider-phobes, and so you measure their score on a spider phobia questionnaire and calculate the median. You then classify anyone with a score above the median as a phobic, and those below the median as non-phobes. Rather than recoding all of your subjects and creating a coding variable, you would simply type the median value in the box labelled *cut point*. When you have defined the groups, click on [Continue] to return to the main dialog box. If you click on [Options...] then another dialog box appears that gives you the same options as for the dependent *t*-test. To run the analysis click on [OK].

6.4.3.   Output from the Independent t-Test

The output from the independent *t*-test contains only two tables. The first table (SPSS Output 6.3) provides summary statistics for the two experimental conditions. From this table, we can see that both groups had 12 subjects (column labelled N). The group who saw the picture of the spider had a mean anxiety of 40, with a standard deviation of 9.29. What's more, the standard error of that group (the standard deviation of the sampling distribution) is 2.68 (SE = $9.2932/\sqrt{12}$ = 9.2932/3.4641 = 2.68). In addition, the table tells us that the average anxiety level in participants who were shown a real spider was 47, with a standard deviation of 11.03, and a standard error of 3.18 (SE = $11.03/\sqrt{12}$ = 11.03/3.4641 = 3.18).

Group Statistics

		N	Mean	Std. Deviation	Std. Error Mean
Anxiety	Picture	12	40.0000	9.2932	2.6827
	Real Spider	12	47.0000	11.0289	3.1838

SPSS Output 6.3

The second table of output (SPSS Output 6.4) contains the main test statistics. The first thing to notice is that there are two rows containing values for the test statistics: one row is labelled *Equal variances assumed*, while the other is labelled *Equal variances not assumed*. In section 2.2, we saw that parametric tests assume that the variances in experimental groups are roughly equal. Well, in reality there are adjustments that can be made in situations in which the variances are not equal. The rows of the table relate to whether or not this assumption has been broken. How do we know whether this assumption has been broken?

Well, we could just look at the values of the variances and see whether they are similar (for example, we know that the standard deviations of the two groups are 9.29 and 11.03 and if we square these values then we get the variances). However, this measure would be very subjective and probably prone to academics thinking 'ooh look, the variance in group 1 is only 3000 times larger than the variance in group 2: that's roughly equal'. Fortunately, there is a test that can be performed to see whether the variances are different enough to cause concern. Levene's test (as it is known) is similar to a *t*-test in that it tests the hypothesis that the variances in the two groups are equal (i.e. the difference between the variances is zero). Therefore, if Levene's test is significant at $p \leq 0.05$ then we can conclude that the null hypothesis is incorrect and that the variances are significantly different—therefore, the assumption of homogeneity of variances has been violated). If, however, Levene's test is non-significant (i.e. $p > 0.05$) then we must accept the null hypothesis that the difference between the variances is zero—the variances are roughly equal and the assumption is tenable. For these data, Levene's test is non-significant (because $p = 0.386$, which is greater than 0.05) and so we should read the test statistics in the row labelled *Equal variances assumed*. Had Levene's test been significant, then we would have read the test statistics from the row labelled *Equal variances not assumed*.

Independent Samples Test

		Levene's Test for Equality of Variances		t-test for Equality of Means						
		F	Sig.	t	df	Sig. (2-tailed)	Mean Difference	Std. Error Difference	95% Confidence Interval of the Mean	
									Lower	Upper
Anxiety	Equal variances assumed	.782	.386	-1.681	22	.107	-7.0000	4.1633	-15.6342	1.6342
	Equal variances not assumed			-1.681	21.385	.107	-7.0000	4.1633	-15.6486	1.6486

SPSS Output 6.4

Having established that the assumption of homogeneity of variances is met, we can move on to look at the *t*-test itself. We are told the mean difference ($\overline{X}_1 - \overline{X}_2 = 47 - 40 = -7$) and the standard error of the sampling distribution of differences, which is calculated using the lower half of equation (6.5).

$$\sqrt{\left(\frac{s_1^2}{N_1} + \frac{s_2^2}{N_2}\right)} = \sqrt{\left(\frac{9.29^2}{12} + \frac{11.03^2}{12}\right)}$$

$$= \sqrt{(7.19 + 10.14)}$$

$$= \sqrt{17.33}$$

$$= 4.16$$

The *t*-statistic is calculated by dividing the mean difference by the standard error of the sampling distribution of differences ($t = -7/4.16 = -1.68$). The value of t is then assessed against the value of t you might expect to get by chance when you have certain degrees of freedom. For the *t*-test, degrees of freedom are calculated by adding the two sample sizes and then subtracting the number of samples ($df = N_1 + N_2 - 2 = 12 + 12 - 2 = 22$). SPSS produces the exact significance value of *t*, and we are interested in whether this value is less than or greater than 0.05. In this case the two-tailed value of *p* is 0.107, which is greater than 0.05, and so we would have to conclude that there was no significant difference between the means of these two samples. In terms of the experiment, we can infer that spider-phobes are made equally anxious by pictures of spiders as they are by the real thing.

Now, we use the two-tailed probability when we have made no specific prediction about the direction of our effect. For example, if we were unsure whether a real spider would induce more or less anxiety, then we would have to use a two-tailed test. However, often in research we can make specific predictions about which group has the highest mean. In this example, it is likely that we would have predicted that a real spider would induce greater anxiety than a picture and so we predict that the mean of the real group would be greater than the mean of the picture group. In this case, we can use a one-tailed test (for more discussion of this issue see Wright, 1997, Chapter 2, or Rowntree, 1981, Chapter 7). Some students get very upset by the fact that SPSS produces only the two-tailed significance and are confused by why there isn't an option that can be selected to produce the one-tailed significance. The answer is simple: there is no need for an option because the one-tailed probability can be ascertained by dividing the two-tailed significance value by 2. In this case, the two-tailed probability was 0.107, therefore the one-tailed probability is 0.054 (0.107/2). The one-tailed probability is still greater than 0.05 (albeit by a small margin) and so we would still have to conclude that spider-phobes were equally as anxious when presented with a real spider as spider-phobes who were presented with a picture of the same spider. This result was predicted by the error bar chart in Figure 6.3.

6.4.4. The Independent t-Test as a General Linear Model

In Chapter 4 we saw that the *t*-test was used to test whether the regression coefficient of a predictor was equal to zero. The experimental design for which the independent *t*-test is used can be conceptualized as a regression equation (after all, there is one independent variable (predictor) and one dependent variable (outcome). Equation (4.1) shows that the slope and intercept of a line can define it. Equation (6.6) shows a very similar equation in which A_i is the dependent variable, β_0 is the intercept, β_1 is the weighting of the predictor, and G_i is the independent variable. Now, I've also included the same equation but with some of the letters replaced with what they represent in the spider experiment (so, A = **anxiety**, G = **group**). When we run an experiment with two conditions, the independent variable has only two values (group 1 or group 2). There are a number of ways in which these groups can be coded (in the spider example we coded group 1 with the value 0 and group 2 with the value 1). This coding variable is known as a *dummy variable* and values of this variable represent groups of people.

$$A_i = \beta_0 + \beta_1 G_i + \varepsilon_i$$
$$\text{Anxiety} = \beta_0 + \beta_1 \text{Group} + \varepsilon_i \tag{6.6}$$

Using the spider example, we know that the mean **anxiety** of the picture group was 40, and that the **group** variable is equal to 0 for this condition. Hence, when we look at what happens when the **group** variable is equal to 0 (the picture condition) equation (6.6) becomes (if we ignore the residual term):

$$40 = \beta_0 + (\beta_1 \times 0)$$
$$\beta_0 = 40$$

Therefore, β_0 (the intercept) is equal to the mean of the picture group (i.e. it is the mean of the group coded as 0). Now let's look at what happens when we consider when the **group** variable is equal to 1. This condition is the one in which a real spider was used and the mean **anxiety** ($\overline{X}_{real}$) of this condition was 47. Remembering that we have just found out that β_0 is equal to the mean of the picture group ($\overline{X}_{picture}$), equation (6.6) becomes:

$$47 = \beta_0 + (\beta_1 \times 1)$$
$$47 = 40 + \beta_1$$
$$\beta_1 = 47 - 40$$
$$\beta_1 = \overline{X}_{real} - \overline{X}_{picture}$$

β_1, therefore, represents the difference between the group means. As such, we can represent a two-group experiment as a regression equation in which the coefficient of the independent variable (β_1) is equal to the difference between group means, and the intercept (β_0) is equal to the mean of the group coded as zero. In regression, the t-test is used to ascertain whether the regression coefficient (β_1) is equal to zero, and when we carry out a t-test on grouped data we therefore test whether the difference between group means is equal to zero.

To prove that I'm not making it up as I go along, use the data in **spiderBG.sav** and run a simple linear regression using **group** as the predictor and **anxiety** as the outcome. **Group** is coded using a 0 and 1 coding scheme and so represents the dummy variable described above. The resulting SPSS output should contain the regression summary table shown in SPSS Output 6.5. The first thing to notice is the value of the constant (β_0): its value is 40, the same as the mean of the base category (the picture group). The second thing to notice is that the value of the regression coefficient β_1 is 7, which is the difference between the two group means ($47 - 40 = 7$). Finally, the t-statistic, which tests whether β_1 is significantly different from zero, is the same as for the independent t-test (see SPSS Output 6.4) and so is the significance value.[2]

This section has demonstrated that experiments can be represented in terms of linear models and this concept is essential in understanding the following chapters on the general linear model.

Coefficients[a]

Model		Unstandardized Coefficients		Standardized Coefficients	t	Sig.
		B	Std. Error	Beta		
1	(Constant)	40.000	2.944		13.587	.000
	Condition	7.000	4.163	.337	1.681	.107

a. Dependent Variable: Anxiety

SPSS Output 6.5: Regression analysis of between-group spider data

6.5. A Final Point: Between Groups or Repeated Measures?

The two examples in this chapter are interesting (honestly!) because they illustrate the difference between data collected using the same subjects and data collected using different subjects. The two examples in this chapter use the same scores in each condition. When analysed as though the data came from the same subjects the result was a significant difference between means, but when analysed as though the data came from different subjects there was no significant difference between group means. This may seem like a puzzling finding—after all the numbers were identical in both examples. What this illustrates is the relative *power* of repeated measures designs. When the same subjects are used across conditions the unsystematic variance (often called the error variance) is reduced dramatically, making it easier to detect any

---

[2] In fact, the value of the t-statistic is the same but has a positive sign rather than negative. You'll remember from the discussion of the point-biserial correlation in Chapter 2 that when you correlate a dichotomous variable the direction of the correlation coefficient depends entirely upon which cases are assigned to which groups. Therefore, the direction of the t-statistic here is similarly influenced by which group we select to be the base category (the category coded as zero).

systematic variance. It is often assumed that the way in which you collect data is irrelevant, but I hope to have illustrated that it can make the difference between detecting a difference and not detecting one. In fact, researchers have carried out studies using the same subjects in experimental conditions, and then repeated the study using different subjects in experimental conditions, and then used the method of data collection as an independent variable in the analysis. Typically, they have found that the method of data collection interacts significantly with the results found (see Erlebacher, 1977).

6.6.   Further Reading

Rowntree, D. (1981). *Statistics without tears: a primer for non-mathematicians*. London: Penguin. Chapters 4, 5, 6 and 7 provide an excellent and understandable introduction to the ideas of sampling distributions, hypothesis testing and statistical inference.

Wright, D. B. (1997). *Understanding statistics: an introduction for the social sciences*. London: Sage. Two excellent and clear chapters on the *t*-test (Chapters 3 and 4).

7 Comparing Several Means: ANOVA (GLM 1)

7.1.   Rationale for ANOVA

7.1.1.   The Basic Idea

The *t*-test is a useful tool in social science research; however, it is limited to situations in which there are only two levels of the independent variable (i.e. two experimental groups). It is common to run experiments in which there are three, four or even five levels of the independent variable and in these cases the *t*-test is inappropriate. Instead, a technique called analysis of variance (or ANOVA to its friends) is used. In Chapter 6 we saw that *t*-tests can be used when only one independent variable has been measured. However, ANOVA has the advantage that it can be used to analyze situations in which there are several independent variables. In these situations, ANOVA tells us how these independent variables interact with each other and what effects these interactions have on the dependent variable.

Before explaining how ANOVA works, it is worth mentioning why we don't simply carry out several *t*-tests to compare all combinations of groups that have been tested. Imagine a situation in which there were three experimental conditions and we were interested in differences between these three groups. If we were to carry out *t*-tests on every pair of groups, then we would have to carry out three separate tests: one to compare groups 1 and 2, one to compare groups 1 and 3, and one to compare groups 2 and 3. If each of these *t*-tests uses a 0.05 level of significance then for each test the probability of falsely rejecting the null hypothesis (known as a type I error) is only 5%. Therefore, the probability of no type I errors is 0.95 (95%) for each test. If we assume that each test is independent (hence, we can multiply the probabilities) then the overall probability of no type I errors is $(0.95)^3 = 0.95 \times 0.95 \times 0.95 = 0.857$, because the probability of no type I errors is 0.95 for each test and there are three tests. Given that the probability of no type I errors is 0.857, then we can calculate the probability of making at least one type I error by subtracting this number from 1 (remember that the maximum probability of any event occurring is 1). So, the probability of at least one type I error is $1 - 0.857$ = 0.143, or 14.3%. Therefore, across this group of tests, the probability of making a type I error has increased from 5% to 14.3%, a value greater than the criterion accepted by social scientists. This error rate across statistical tests conducted on the same experimental data is known as the *familywise* or *experimentwise* error rate. An experiment with three conditions is a relatively simple design, and so the severity of the effect of carrying out several tests is not severe. If you imagine that we now increase the number of experimental conditions from three to five (which is only two more groups) then the number of *t*-tests that would need to done increases to 10.[1] The familywise error rate can be calculated using the general equation (7.1), in which *n* is the number of tests carried out on the data. With 10 tests carried out, the familywise error rate is 0.40 ($1 - 0.95^{10} = 0.40$), which means that there is a 40% chance of having made at least one type I error. For this reason we use ANOVA rather than conducting lots of *t*-tests.

> **What does an ANOVA tell me?**

$$\text{familywise error} = 1 - (0.95)^n \tag{7.1}$$

When we perform a *t*-test, we test the hypothesis that the two samples have the same mean. Similarly, ANOVA tells us whether three or more means are the same, so, it tests the hypothesis that all group means are equal. An ANOVA produces an *F-statistic* or *F-ratio*, which is similar to the *t*-statistic in that it compares the amount of systematic variance in the data to the amount of unsystematic variance. However, ANOVA is an *omnibus* test, which means that it tests for an overall experimental effect: so, there are things that an ANOVA cannot tell us. Although ANOVA tells us whether the experimental manipulation was generally successful, it does not provide specific information about which groups

---

[1] These comparisons are group 1 vs. 2, 1 vs. 3, 1 vs. 4, 1 vs. 5, 2 vs. 3, 2 vs. 4, 2 vs. 5, 3 vs. 4, 3 vs. 5, and 4 vs. 5. The number of tests required is calculated using this equation:

$$\text{Number of comparisons}, C = \frac{k!}{2(k-2)!}$$

in which *k* is the number of experimental conditions. The ! symbol stands for *factorial*, which means that you multiply the value preceding the symbol by all of the whole numbers between zero and that value (so $5! = 5 \times 4 \times 3 \times 2 \times 1 = 120$). So, with 5 conditions we find that:

$$C = \frac{5!}{2(5-2)!} = \frac{120}{2 \times 6} = 10$$

were affected. Assuming an experiment was conducted with three different groups, the F-ratio simply tells us that the means of these three samples are not equal (i.e. that $\overline{X}_1 = \overline{X}_2 = \overline{X}_3$ is *not* true). However, there are a number of ways in which the means can differ. The first possibility is that all three sample means are significantly different ($\overline{X}_1 \neq \overline{X}_2 \neq \overline{X}_3$). A second possibility is that the means of group 1 and 2 are the same but group 3 has a significantly different mean from both of the other groups ($\overline{X}_1 = \overline{X}_2 \neq \overline{X}_3$). Another possibility is that groups 2 and 3 have similar means but group 1 has a significantly different mean ($\overline{X}_1 \neq \overline{X}_2 = \overline{X}_3$). Finally, groups 1 and 3 could have similar means but group 2 has a significantly different mean from both ($\overline{X}_1 = \overline{X}_3 \neq \overline{X}_2$). So, the F-ratio tells us only that the experimental manipulation has had some effect, but it doesn't tell us specifically what the effect was.

7.1.2.   ANOVA as Regression

Many social scientists are unaware that ANOVA and regression are conceptually the same procedure. The reason is largely historical in that two distinct branches of methodology developed in the social sciences: correlational research and experimental research. Researchers interested in controlled experiments adopted ANOVA as their flagship statistic whereas those looking for real-world relationships adopted multiple regression. As we all know, scientists are intelligent, mature and rational people and so neither group was tempted to slag off the other and claim that their own choice of methodology was far superior to the other (yeah right!). With the divide in methodologies came a chasm between the statistical methods adopted by the two opposing camps (Cronbach, 1957 documents this divide in a lovely article). This divide has lasted many decades to the extent that now students are generally taught regression and ANOVA in very different contexts and most textbooks teach ANOVA in an entirely different way to regression.

Although many considerably more intelligent people than me have attempted to redress the balance (notably the great Jacob Cohen, 1968), I am passionate about making my own small, feeble-minded attempt to enlighten you. There are many good reasons why I think ANOVA should be taught within the context of regression. First, it provides a familiar context: I wasted many trees trying to explain regression, so why not use this base of knowledge to explain a new concept (it should make it easier to understand). Second, the traditional method of teaching ANOVA (known as the variance-ratio method) is fine for simple designs, but becomes impossibly cumbersome in more complex situations (such as analysis of covariance). The regression model extends very logically to these more complex designs without the student needing to get bogged down in mathematics. Finally, the variance-ratio method becomes extremely unmanageable in unusual circumstances such as when you have unequal sample sizes. The regression method makes these situations considerably more simple. Although these reasons are good enough, it is also the case that SPSS has moved away from the variance-ratio method of ANOVA and progressed towards solely using the regression model (known as the general linear model, or GLM). The end result of the two approaches to ANOVA are the same and most textbooks already detail the variance-ratio approach (I recommend Howell, 1997), so it makes sense for me to tackle the regression approach.

So far, we have discovered that ANOVA is a way of comparing the ratio of systematic variance to unsystematic variance in an experimental study. The ratio of these variances is known as the *F*-ratio. Any of you who have read Chapter 4 should recognize the *F*-ratio (see section 4.1.3) because it was used to assess how well a regression model can predict an outcome compared to the error within that model. If you haven't read Chapter 4 (surely not!) have a look before you carry on. The *F*-ratio in ANOVA is exactly the same as in regression, except that the regression model contains only categorical predictors (i.e. grouping variables). So, just as the *t*-test could be represented by the linear regression equation (see section 6.4.4), ANOVA can be represented by the multiple regression equation in which the number of predictors is one less than the number of categories of the independent variable.

Let's take an example. There is a lot of controversy at the moment surrounding the drug Viagra. Viagra is a sexual stimulant (used to treat impotence) that has recently broken into the black market under the belief that it will make someone a better lover (oddly enough there seems to be a glut of journalists taking the stuff in the name of 'investigative journalism'... hmmm!). Suppose we tested this belief by taking three groups of subjects and administering one group with a placebo (such as a sugar pill), one group with a low dose of Viagra and one with a high dose. The dependent variable was an objective measure of libido (I will tell you only that it was measured over the course of a week—the rest I shall leave to your own imagination). The data can be found in the file **Viagra.sav** (which is described in detail later in this chapter) and are in Table 7.1.

At the end of the previous chapter we used a linear regression equation with one dummy variable to describe two experimental groups. This dummy variable was a categorical variable with two numeric codes (a 0 for one group and a 1 for the other). With three groups we must use two dummy variables and as a general rule there will always be one less dummy variable than there are categories of the independent variable. In the two-group case, we assigned one category as a base category (remember we chose the picture condition to act as a base) and this category was coded with a zero. When there are three categories we also need a base category and you should choose the condition with which you intend to compare the other groups. Usually this category will be the control group. In most well-designed social science experiments there will be a group of subjects who act as a baseline for other categories. This baseline group should act as the reference or base category, although the group you choose will depend upon the particular hypotheses that you want to test. In unbalanced designs (in which the group sizes are unequal) it is important that the base category contains a fairly large number of cases to ensure that the estimates of the regression coefficients are reliable. In the Viagra example, we can take the placebo group as the base category because this group was a placebo control. We are interested in comparing both the high and low dose groups to the group who received no Viagra at all. If the placebo group is the base category then the two dummy variables that we have to create represent the other two conditions: so, we should have one dummy variable called High and the other one called Low). The resulting regression equation is described in equation (7.2).

$$\text{Libido}_i = \beta_0 + \beta_2 \text{High}_i + \beta_1 \text{Low}_i + \varepsilon_i \tag{7.2}$$

Table 7.1: Data in **Viagra.sav**

	Placebo	Low Dose	High Dose
	3	5	7
	2	2	4
	1	4	5
	1	2	3
	4	3	6
$\overline{X}$	2.20	3.20	5.00
s	1.30	1.30	1.58
s^2	1.70	1.70	2.50
	Grand Mean = 3.467 Grand SD = 1.767 Grand Variance = 3.124		

In equation (7.2), a person's libido can be predicted from knowing their group code (i.e. the code for the High and Low dose dummy variables) and the intercept (β_0) of the model. The dummy variables in equation (7.2) can be coded in a number of ways, but the simplest way is to use a similar technique to that of the *t*-test. The base category is always coded as 0. If a subject was given a high dose of Viagra then they are coded with a 1 for the High dummy variable, and 0 for all other variables. If a subject was given a low dose of Viagra then they are coded with the value 1 for the Low dummy variable, and coded with a 0 for all other variables. Using this coding scheme we can express each group by combining the codes of the two dummy variables (see Table 7.2).

Table 7.2: Dummy coding for the three-group experimental design

Group	Dummy Variable 1 (High)	Dummy Variable 2 (Low)
Placebo	0	0
Low Dose Viagra	0	1
High Dose Viagra	1	0

Placebo Group: Let's examine the model for the placebo group. In the placebo group both the High and Low dummy variables are coded as 0. Therefore, if we ignore the error term (ε_i), the regression equation becomes:

$$\text{Libido} = \beta_0 + (\beta_2 \times 0) + (\beta_1 \times 0)$$
$$\text{Libido} = \beta_0$$

This is a situation in which the high and low dose groups have both been excluded (because they are coded with a 0). We are looking at predicting the level of libido when both doses of Viagra are ignored, and so the predicted value will be the mean of the placebo group (because this group is the only one included in the model). Hence, the intercept of the regression model, β_0, is always the mean of the base category (in this case the mean of the placebo group).

High Dose Group: If we examine the high dose group, the dummy variable High will be coded as 1 and the dummy variable Low will be coded as 0. If we replace the values of these codes into equation (7.2) the model becomes:

$$\text{Libido} = \beta_0 + (\beta_2 \times 1)(\beta_1 \times 0)$$
$$\text{Libido} = \beta_0 + \beta_2$$

We know already that β_0 is the mean of the placebo group. If we are interested in only the high dose group then the model should predict that the value of Libido for a given subject equals the mean of the high dose group. Given this information, the equation becomes:

$$\text{Libido} = \beta_0 + \beta_2$$
$$\overline{X}_{\text{High}} = \overline{X}_{\text{Placebo}} + \beta_2$$
$$\beta_2 = \overline{X}_{\text{High}} - \overline{X}_{\text{Placebo}}$$

Hence, β_2 represents the difference between the means of the high dose group and the placebo group.

Low Dose Group: Finally, if we look at the model when a low dose of Viagra has been taken, the dummy variable Low is coded as 1 (and hence High is coded as 0). Therefore, the regression equation becomes:

$$\text{Libido} = \beta_0 + (\beta_2 \times 0)(\beta_1 \times 1)$$
$$\text{Libido} = \beta_0 + \beta_1$$

We know that the intercept is equal to the mean of the base category and that for the low dose group the predicted value should be the mean libido for a low dose. Therefore the model can be reduced down to:

$$\text{Libido} = \beta_0 + \beta_1$$
$$\overline{X}_{\text{Low}} = \overline{X}_{\text{Placebo}} + \beta_1$$
$$\beta_1 = \overline{X}_{\text{Low}} - \overline{X}_{\text{Placebo}}$$

Hence, β_1 represents the difference between the means of the low dose group and the placebo group. This form of dummy variable coding is the simplest form, but as we shall see later, there are other ways in which variables can be coded to test specific hypotheses. These alternative coding schemes are known as *contrasts* (see section 7.1.4.2). The idea behind contrasts is that you code the dummy variables in such a way that the β values represent differences between groups that you are interested in testing.

To illustrate exactly what is going on I have created a file called **dummy.sav** in the Chapter 7 folder of the floppy disk. This file contains the Viagra data but with two additional variables (**dummy1** and **dummy2**) that specify to which group a data point belongs (as in Table 7.2). Access this file and run multiple regression analysis using **libido** as the outcome and **dummy1** and **dummy2** as the predictors. If you're stuck on how to run the regression then I suggest you read Chapter 4 again (see, these chapters are ordered for a reason)! The resulting analysis is shown in SPSS Output 7.1. It might be a good idea to remind yourself of the group means from Table 7.1. The first thing to notice is that the constant is equal to the mean of the base category (the placebo group). The regression coefficient for the first dummy variable (β_2) is equal to the difference between the means of the high dose group and the placebo group (5.0 − 2.2 = 2.8). Finally, the regression coefficient for the second dummy variable (β_1) is equal to the difference between the means of the low dose group and the placebo group (3.2 – 2.2 = 1). This analysis demonstrates how the regression model represents the three-group situation. We can see from the significance values of the t-tests that the difference between the high dose group and the placebo group (β_2) is significant because $p < 0.05$. The difference between the low dose and high dose group is not, however, significant ($p = 0.282$).

Coefficients[a]

Model		Unstandardized Coefficients		Standardized Coefficients	t	Sig.
		B	Std. Error	Beta		
1	(Constant)	2.200	.627		3.508	.004
	Dummy Variable 1	2.800	.887	.773	3.157	.008
	Dummy Variable 2	1.000	.887	.276	1.127	.282

a. Dependent Variable: Libido

SPSS Output 7.1

A four-group experiment can be described by extending the three-group scenario. I mentioned earlier that you will always need one less dummy variable than the number of groups in the experiment: therefore, this model requires three dummy variables. As before, we need to specify one category that is a base category (a control group). This base category should have a code of zero for all three dummy variables. The remaining three conditions will have a code of one for the dummy variable that described that condition and a code of zero for the other two dummy variables. Table 7.3 illustrates how the coding scheme would work.

Rule
1 less dummy
variable than
N of gps

Table 7.3: Dummy Coding for the four-group experimental design.

	Dummy Variable 1	Dummy Variable 2	Dummy Variable 3
Group 1	1	0	0
Group 2	0	1	0
Group 3	0	0	1
✳ **Group 4 (base)**	0	0	0

Control
gp code of 0 for all 3 dummy variables

7.1.3.   Calculating the F-Ratio

In Chapter 4 we learnt a little about the F-ratio and its calculation. To recap, we learnt that the F-ratio is used to test the overall fit of a regression model to a set of observed data. I have just explained how ANOVA can be represented as a regression equation, and this should help you to understand what the F-ratio tells you about your data. Figure 7.1 shows the Viagra data in graphical form (including the group means, the overall mean and the difference between each case and the group mean). In this example, there were three groups; therefore, we want to test the hypothesis that the means of three groups are different (so, the null hypothesis is that the group means are the same). If the group means were all the same, then we would not expect the placebo group to differ from the low dose group or the high dose group, and we would not expect the low dose group to differ from the high dose group. Therefore, on the diagram, the three dashed lines would be in the same vertical position (the exact position would be the grand mean). We can see from the diagram that the group means are actually different because the dashed lines (the group means) are in different vertical positions. We have just found out that in the regression model, β_2 represents the difference between the means of the placebo and the high dose group, and β_1 represents the difference in means between the low dose and placebo groups. These two distances are represented in Figure 7.1 by the vertical arrows. If the null hypothesis is true and all the groups have the same means, then these β coefficients should be zero (because if the group means are equal then the difference between them will be zero).

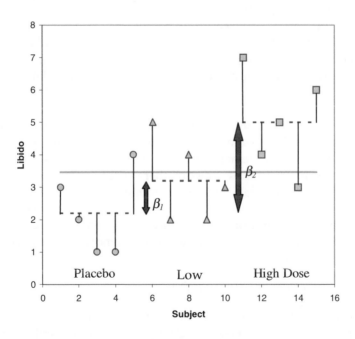

Figure 7.1: The Viagra data in graphical form. The dashed lines represent the mean libido of each group. The shapes represent the libido of individual subjects (different shapes indicate different experimental groups). The full horizontal line is the average libido of all subjects

The logic of ANOVA follows from what we understand about regression:

- The simplest model we can fit to a set of data is the grand mean (the mean of the outcome variable). When this basic model is fitted there will be a large amount of error between the model and the observed data.
- One of many straight lines can be chosen to model the data collected. If this model fits the data well then it must be better than using the grand mean.
- The intercept and one or more regression coefficients can describe the chosen line.
- The regression coefficients determine the slope of the line; therefore, the bigger the coefficients, the greater the deviation between the line and the grand mean.
- In ANOVA, the regression coefficients are defined by differences between group means.
- The bigger the differences between group means, the greater the difference between the regression line and the grand mean.
- If the differences between group means are large enough, then the resulting line will be a better fit of the data than the grand mean.
- Therefore, if the group means are significantly different, we would expect the regression model to be a better fit of the data than the grand mean.

We can see whether this last statement is true by comparing the improvement in fit due to using the model (rather than the grand mean) with the error that still remains. Another way of saying this is that when the grand mean is used as a model, there will be a certain amount of variation between the data and the grand mean. When a model is fitted it will explain some of this variation but some will be left unexplained. The *F*-ratio is the ratio of the explained to the unexplained variation. Look back at section 4.1.3 to refresh you memory on these concepts before reading on.

7.1.3.1. Total Sum of Squares (SS$_T$)

To find the total amount of variation within our data we calculate the difference between each observed data point and the grand mean. We then square these differences and add them together to give us the total sum of squares (SS$_T$).

$$SS_T = \sum \left(x_i - \overline{x}_{grand} \right)^2 \qquad (7.3)$$

We also saw in section 1.1.3.1 that the variance and the sums of squares are related such that variance, $s^2 = SS/(N-1)$, where N is the number of observations. Therefore, we can calculate the total sums of squares from the variance of all observations (the *grand variance*) by rearranging the relationship ($SS = s^2(N-1)$). The grand variance is the variation between all scores, regardless of the experimental condition from which the scores come. Therefore, in Figure 7.1 it would be the sum of the squared distances between each point and the horizontal line. The grand variance for the Viagra data is given in Table 7.1, and if we count the number of observations we find that there were 15 in all. Therefore, SS_T is calculated as follows:

$$SS_T = s_{grand}^2(n-1)$$
$$= 3.124(15-1)$$
$$= 3.124 \times 14$$
$$= 43.74$$

7.1.3.2. Degrees of Freedom

Before we move on, it is important to understand degrees of freedom. Degrees of freedom (*df*) is a very difficult concept to explain, and I have mentioned them several times throughout this book without defining the concept. Most textbooks are bad at explaining degrees of freedom (although Howell, 1997, pp. 53-54 does a good job) and I'm confident that this book will be no exception to this rule! I'll begin with an analogy. Imagine you're manager of a rugby team and you have a team sheet with 15 empty slots relating to the positions on the playing field. There is a standard formation in rugby and so each team has 15 specific positions that must be held constant for the game to be played. When the first player arrives, you have the choice of 15 positions in which to place this player. You place his name in one of the slots and allocate him to a position (e.g. scrum-half) and, therefore, one position on the pitch is now occupied. When the next player arrives, you have the choice of 14 positions but you still have the freedom to choose which position this player is allocated. However, as more players arrive, you will reach the point at which 14 positions have been filled and the final player arrives. With this player you have no freedom to choose where he or she plays— there is only one position left. Therefore there are 14 degrees of freedom, that is, for 14 players you have some degree of choice over where they play, but for 1 player you have no choice. The degrees of freedom is one less than the number of players.

In statistical terms the degrees of freedom relates to the number of observations that are free to vary. If we take a sample of four observations from a population, then these four scores are free to vary in any way (they can be any value). However, if we then use this sample of four observations to calculate the standard deviation of the population, we have to use the mean of the sample as an estimate of the population's mean. Thus we hold one parameter constant. Say that the mean of the sample was 10, then we assume that the population mean is 10 also and we keep this value constant. With this parameter fixed, can all four scores from our sample vary? The answer is no because to keep the mean constant only three values are free to vary. For example, if the values in the sample were 8, 9, 11, 12 (mean = 10) and we changed three of these values to 7, 15 and 8, then the final value *must* be 10 to keep the mean constant. Therefore, if we hold one parameter constant then the degrees of freedom must be one less than the sample size. This fact explains why when we use a sample to estimate the standard deviation of a population (as we did in section 1.1.3.1), we have to divide the sums of squares by $N - 1$ rather than N alone. For SS_T, we used the entire sample to calculate the sums of squares and so the total degrees of freedom (df_T) are one less than the total sample size $(N - 1)$. For the Viagra data, this value is 14.

7.1.3.3. Model Sum of Squares (SS_M)

So far, we know that the total amount of variation within the data is 43.74 units. We now need to know how much of this variation the regression model can explain. In the ANOVA scenario, the model is based upon differences between group means and so the model sums of squares tell us how much of the total variation can be explained by the fact that different data points come from different groups. In short, the model represents the effect of the experimental manipulation.

In section 4.1.3 we saw that the model sum of squares is calculated by taking the difference between the values predicted by the model, and the grand mean (see Figure 4.3). In ANOVA, the values predicted by the model are the group means (therefore, in Figure 7.1 the dashed lines represented the values of libido predicted by the model). For each subject the value predicted by the model is the mean for the group to which the subject belongs. In the Viagra example, the predicted value for the five subjects in the placebo group will be 2.2, for the five subjects in the low dose condition it will be 3.2, and the five subjects in the high dose condition it will be 5. The model sum of squares requires us to calculate the differences between each subject's predicted value and the grand mean. These differences are then squared and added together (for reasons that should be clear in your mind by now). We know that the predicted value for subjects in a particular group is the mean of that group. Therefore, the easiest way to calculate SS_M is to:

1. Calculate the difference between the mean of each group and the grand mean.
2. Square each of these differences.
3. Multiply each result by the number of subjects within that group (n_i).
4. Add the values for each group together.

The mathematical expression of this process is shown in equation (7.4).

$$SS_M = \sum n_i (\bar{x}_i - \bar{x}_{grand})^2 \qquad (7.4)$$

Using the means from the Viagra data, we can calculate SS_M as follows:

$$
\begin{aligned}
SS_M &= 5(2.200 - 3.467)^2 + 5(3.200 - 3.467)^2 + 5(5.000 - 3.467)^2 \\
&= 5(-1.267)^2 + 5(-0.267)^2 + 5(1.533)^2 \\
&= 8.025 + 0.355 + 11.755 \\
&= 20.135
\end{aligned}
$$

For SS_M, the degrees of freedom (df_M) will always be one less than the number of parameters estimated. In short, this value will be the number of groups minus 1. So, in the three-group case the degrees of freedom will always be 2 (because the calculation of the sums of squares is based on the group means—two of which will be free to vary in the population if the third is held constant).

7.1.3.4. Residual Sum of Squares (SS_R)

We now know that there are 43.74 units of variation to be explained in our data, and that our model can explain 20.14 of these units (nearly half). The final sum of squares is the residual sum of squares (SS_R), which tells us how much of the variation cannot be explained by the model. This value is the amount of variation caused by extraneous factors such as individual differences in weight, testosterone or whatever. Knowing SS_T and SS_M already, the simplest way to calculate SS_R is to subtract SS_M from SS_T ($SS_R = SS_T - SS_M$); however, telling you to do this provides little insight into what is being calculated. We saw in section 4.1.3 that the residual sum of squares is the difference between what the model predicts and what was actually observed. We already know that for a given subject, the model predicts the mean of the group to which that subject belongs. Therefore, SS_R is calculated by looking at the difference between the score obtained by a subject and the mean of the group to which the subject belongs. In graphical terms the vertical lines in Figure 7.1 represent this sum of squares. These distances between each data point and the group mean are squared and then added together to give the residual sum of squares, SS_R (see equation (7.5)).

$$SS_R = \sum (x_i - \bar{x}_i)^2 \qquad (7.5)$$

Now, the sum of squares for each group represents the sum of squared differences between each subject's score in that group and the group mean. Therefore, we can express SS_R as $SS_R = SS_{group1} + SS_{group2} + SS_{group3}$ ... and so on. Given that we know the relationship between the variance and the sums of squares, we can use the variances for each group of the Viagra data to create an equation like we did for the total sum of squares. As such, SS_R can be expressed as:

$$
\begin{aligned}
SS_R &= s_{group1}^2 (n_1 - 1) + s_{group2}^2 (n_2 - 1) + s_{group3}^2 (n_3 - 1) \\
&= (1.70)(5-1) + (1.70)(5-1) + (2.50)(5-1) \\
&= (1.70 \times 4) + (1.70 \times 4) + (2.50 \times 4) \\
&= 6.8 + 6.8 + 10 \\
&= 23.60
\end{aligned}
$$

The degrees of freedom for SS_R (df_R) is the total degrees of freedom minus the degrees of freedom for the model ($df_R = df_T - df_M = 14 - 2 = 12$).

7.1.3.5. Mean Squares

SS_M tells us how much variation the regression model (e.g. the experimental manipulation) explains and SS_R tells us how much variation is due to extraneous factors. However, because both of these values are summed values they will be influenced by the number of scores that were summed (for example, SS_M used the sum of only 3 different values (the group means) compared to SS_R and SS_T, which used the sum of 14 different values). To eliminate this bias we can calculate the average sum of squares (known as the *mean squares*, MS), which is simply the sum of squares divided by the degrees of freedom. The reason why we divide by the degrees of freedom rather than the number of parameters used to calculate the SS is because we are trying to extrapolate to a population and so some parameters within that populations will be held constant. So, for the Viagra data we find the following mean squares:

$$MS_M = \frac{SS_M}{df_M} = \frac{20.135}{2} = 10.067$$

$$MS_R = \frac{SS_R}{df_R} = \frac{23.60}{12} = 1.967$$

MS_M represents the average amount of variation explained by the model (e.g. the systematic variation), whereas MS_R is a gauge of the average amount of variation explained by extraneous variables (the unsystematic variation).

7.1.3.6. The F-Ratio

The *F*-ratio is a measure of the ratio of the variation explained by the model and the variation explained by unsystematic factors. It can be calculated by dividing the model mean squares by the residual mean squares.

$$F = \frac{MS_M}{MS_R} \qquad (7.6)$$

As with the independent *t*-test, the *F*-ratio is, therefore, a measure of the ratio of systematic variation to unsystematic variation. As such, it is the ratio of the experimental effect to the individual differences in performance. An interesting point about the *F*-ratio is that because it is the ratio of systematic variance to unsystematic variance, if its value is less than 1 then it must, by definition, represent a non-significant effect. The reason why this statement is true is because if the *F*-ratio is less than 1 it means that MS_R is greater than MS_M which in real terms means that there is more unsystematic than systematic variance. You can think of this in terms of the effect of natural differences in ability being greater than differences bought about by the experiment. In this scenario, we can, therefore, be sure that our experimental manipulation has been unsuccessful (because it has bought about less change than if we left our subjects alone!). For the Viagra data, the *F*-ratio is:

$$F = \frac{MS_M}{MS_R} = \frac{10.067}{1.967} = 5.12$$

This value is greater than 1, which indicates that the experimental manipulation had some effect above and beyond the effect of individual differences in performance. However, it doesn't yet tell us whether the *F*-ratio is large enough to not be a chance result.

7.1.3.7. Assumptions of ANOVA

The assumptions under which ANOVA is reliable are the same as for all parametric tests (see section 2.2). Namely, data should be from a normally distributed population, the variances in each experimental condition are fairly similar, observations should be independent and the dependent variable should be measured on at least an interval scale. Now, although I am always banging on about how important assumptions are, they are not completely inflexible. For example, Lunney (1970) investigated the use of ANOVA when the dependent variable was dichotomous (it could have values of only 0 or 1). The results showed that when the group sizes were equal ANOVA was accurate when there was at least 20 degrees of freedom and the smallest response category contained at least 20% of all responses. If the smaller response category contained less than 20% of all responses then ANOVA performed accurately only when there were 40 or more degrees of freedom. This study shows that ANOVA can be quite a robust procedure. However, in contrast Scariano and Davenport (1987) showed that when the assumption of independence is broken (i.e. observations across groups are correlated) then the type I error rate is substantially inflated. For example, using the conventional 0.05 type I error rate when observations are independent, if these observations are made to correlate moderately (say, with a Pearson coefficient of 0.5) when comparing three groups with 10 observations per group the actual type I error rate is 0.74 (a substantial inflation!). Therefore, if observations are correlated you might think that you are working with the accepted 0.05 error rate when in fact your error rate is closer to 0.75!

7.1.4.   Planned Contrasts

The F-ratio tells us only whether the model fitted to the data accounts for more variation than extraneous factors, but it doesn't tell us where the differences between groups lie. So, if the F-ratio is large enough to be statistically significant, then we know only that one or more of the differences between means is statistically significant (e.g. either β_2 or β_1 is statistically significant). It is, therefore, necessary after conducting an ANOVA to carry out further analysis to find out which groups differ. In multiple regression, each β coefficient is tested individually using a t-test and we could do the same for ANOVA. However, we would need to carry out two t-tests, which would inflate the familywise error rate (see section 7.1.1). Therefore, we need a way to contrast the different groups without inflating the type I error rate. There are two ways in which to achieve this goal. The first is to break down the variance accounted for by the model into component parts, the second is to compare every group (as if conducting several t-tests) but to use a stricter acceptance criterion such that the familywise error rate does not rise above 0.05. The first option can be done using planned comparisons (also known as *planned contrasts*[2]) whereas the latter option is done using *post hoc* comparisons (see next section). The difference between planned comparisons and *post hoc* tests can be likened to the difference between one- and two-tailed tests in that planned comparisons are done when you have specific hypotheses that you want to test, whereas *post hoc* tests are done when you have no specific hypotheses. Let's first look at planned contrasts.

7.1.4.1. Choosing which Contrasts to Do

In the Viagra example we could have had very specific hypotheses. For one thing, we would expect any dose of Viagra to change libido compared to the placebo group. As a second hypothesis we might believe that a high dose should increase libido more than a low dose. To do planned comparisons, these hypotheses must be derived *before* the data are collected. It is fairly standard in social sciences to want to compare experimental conditions to the control conditions as the first contrast, and then to see where the differences lie between the experimental groups. The ANOVA is based upon splitting the total variation into two component parts: the variation due to the experimental manipulation (SS_M) and the variation due to unsystematic factors (SS_R) (see Figure 7.2). Planned comparisons take this logic a step further by breaking down the variation due to the experiment into component parts (see Figure 7.3). The exact comparisons that are carried out depend upon the hypotheses you want to test. Figure 7.3 shows a situation in which the experimental variance is broken down to look at how much variation is created by the two drug conditions compared to the placebo condition (*contrast 1*). Then the variation explained by taking Viagra is broken down to see how much is explained by taking a high dose relative to a low dose (*contrast 2*).

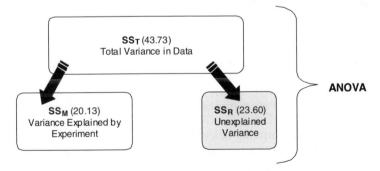

Figure 7.2: Partitioning variance for ANOVA

---

[2] The terms 'comparison' and 'contrast' are used interchangeably.

Typically, students struggle with the notion of planned comparisons, but there are several rules that can help you to work out what to do. The important thing to remember is that we are breaking down one chunk of variation into smaller independent chunks. This means several things. First, if a group is singled out in one comparison, then it should not reappear in another comparison. So, in Figure 7.3 contrast 1 involved comparing the placebo group to the experimental groups; because the placebo group is singled out, it should not be incorporated into any other contrasts. You can think of partitioning variance as being similar to slicing up a cake. You begin with a cake (the total sum of squares) and you then cut this cake into two pieces (SS_M and SS_R). You then take the piece of cake that represents SS_M and divide this up into smaller pieces. Once you have cut off a piece of cake you cannot stick that piece back onto the original slice, and you cannot stick it onto other pieces of cake, but you can divide it into smaller pieces of cake. Likewise, once a slice of variance has been split from a larger chunk, it cannot be attached to any other pieces of variance, it can only be subdivided into smaller chunks of variance. Now, all of this talk of cake is making me hungry, but hopefully it illustrates a point.

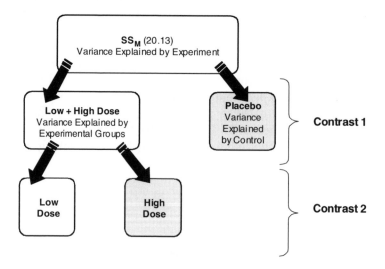

Figure 7.3: Partitioning of experimental variance into component comparisons

Now, as a second hint to selecting contrasts, the independence of contrasts rule that I've just explained (the cake slicing!) means that you should always have one less contrast than the number of groups (so, there will be $k-1$ contrasts (where k is the number of experimental conditions). Finally, each contrast must compare only two chunks of variance. This final rule is so that we can draw firm conclusions about what the contrast tells us. The F-ratio tells us that some of our means differ, but not which ones, and if we were to perform a contrast on more than two chunks of variance we would have the same problem. By comparing only two chunks of variance we can be sure that a significant result represents a difference between these two portions of experimental variation.

In most social science research we use at least one control condition, and in the vast majority of experimental designs we predict that the experimental conditions will differ from the control condition (or conditions). As such, *one big hint when planning comparisons is to compare all of the experimental groups with the control group or groups as your first comparison.* Once you have done this first comparison, any remaining comparisons will depend upon which of the experimental groups you predict will differ.

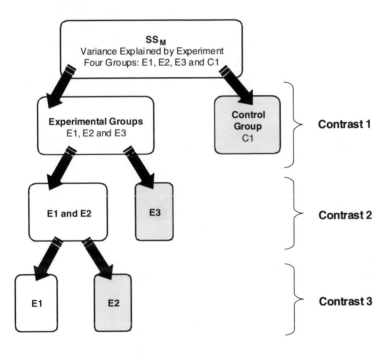

Figure 7.4: Partitioning variance for planned comparisons in a four-group experiment using one control group

To illustrate these principles, Figure 7.4 and Figure 7.5 show the contrasts that might be done in a four-group experiment. The first thing to notice is that in both scenarios there are three possible comparisons (one less than the number of groups). Also, every contrast compares only two chunks of variance. What's more, in both scenarios the first contrast is the same: the experimental groups are compared against the control group or groups. In Figure 7.4 there was only one control condition and so this portion of variance is used only in the first contrast (because it cannot be broken down any further). In Figure 7.5 there were two control groups, and so the portion of variance due to the control conditions (contrast 1) can be broken down again so as to see whether or not the scores in the control groups differ from each other (contrast 3).

In Figure 7.4, the first contrast contains a chunk of variance that is due to the three experimental groups and this chunk of variance is broken down by first looking at whether groups E1 and E2 differ from E3 (contrast 2). It is equally valid to use contrast 2 to compare groups E1 and E3 with E2, or to compare groups E2 and E3 with E1. The exact comparison that you choose depends upon your hypotheses. For contrast 2 in Figure 7.4 to be valid we need to have a good reason to expect group E3 to be different from the other two groups. The third comparison in Figure 7.4 depends on the comparison chosen for contrast 2. Contrast 2 necessarily had to involve comparing two experimental groups against a third, and the experimental groups chosen to be combined must be separated in the final comparison. As a final point, you'll notice that in Figure 7.4 and Figure 7.5, once a group has been singled out in a comparison, it is never used in any subsequent contrasts.

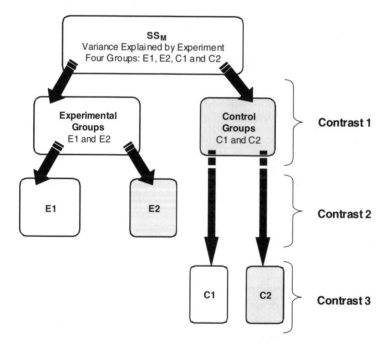

Figure 7.5: Partitioning variance for planned comparisons in a four-group experiment using two control groups

What does a planned contrast tell me?

When we carry out a planned contrast, we compare 'chunks' of variance and these chunks often consist of several groups. It is perhaps confusing to understand exactly what these contrasts tell us. Well, when you design a contrast that compares several groups to one other group, you are comparing the means of the groups in one chunk with the mean of the group in the other chunk. As an example, for the Viagra data I suggested that an appropriate first contrast would be to compare the two dose groups with the placebo group. The means of the groups are 2.20 (placebo), 3.20 (low dose) and 5.00 (high dose) and so the first comparison, which compared the two experimental groups to the placebo, is comparing 2.20 (the mean of the placebo group) to the average of the other two groups ((3.2 + 5.0)/2 = 4.10). If this first contrast turns out significant, then we can conclude that 4.10 is significantly greater than 2.20, which in terms of the experiment tells us that the average of the experimental groups is significantly different to the average of the controls. You can probably see that logically this means that, if the standard errors are the same, the experimental group with the highest mean (the high dose group) will be significantly different from the mean of the placebo group. However, the experimental group with the lower mean (the low dose group) might not necessarily differ from the placebo group; we have to use the final comparison to make sense of the experimental conditions. For the Viagra data the final comparison looked at whether the two experimental groups differ (i.e. is the mean of the high dose group significantly different from the mean of the low dose group?). If this comparison turns out to be significant then we can conclude that having a high dose of Viagra significantly affected libido compared to having a low dose. If the comparison is non-significant then we have to conclude that the dosage of Viagra made no difference to libido. In this latter scenario it is likely that both doses affect libido more than placebo, whereas the former case implies that having a low dose may be no different to having a placebo. However, the word *implies* is important here: it is possible that the low dose group might not differ from the placebo. To be completely sure we must carry out *post hoc* tests.

7.1.4.2. Defining Contrasts Using Weights

Hopefully by now you have got some idea of how to plan which comparisons to do (that is if your brain hasn't exploded by now). Much as I'd love to tell you that all of the hard work is now over and SPSS will magically carry out the comparisons that you've selected, it won't. To get SPSS to carry out planned comparisons we need to tell it which groups we would like to compare and doing this can be quite complex. In fact, when we carry out contrasts we assign values to certain variables in the regression model (sorry, I'm afraid that I have to start talking about regression again)—just as we did when we used dummy coding for the main ANOVA. To carry out contrasts we simply assign certain values to the dummy variables in the regression model. Whereas before we defined the experimental groups by assigning the dummy variables values of 1 or 0, when we perform contrasts we use different values to specify which groups we would like to compare. The resulting coefficients in the regression model (β_2 and β_1) represent the comparisons in which we are interested. The values assigned to the dummy variables are known as *weights*.

This procedure is horribly confusing, but there are a few basic rules for assigning values to the dummy variables to obtain the comparisons you want. I will explain these simple rules before showing how the process actually works. Remember the previous section when you read through these rules, and remind yourself of what I mean by a 'chunk' of variation!

- **Rule 1**: Choose sensible comparisons. Remember that you want to compare only two chunks of variation and that if a group is singled out in one comparison, that group should be excluded from any subsequent contrasts.
- **Rule 2**: Groups coded with positive weights will be compared against groups coded with negative weights. So, assign one chunk of variation positive weights and the opposite chunk negative weights.
- **Rule 3**: The sum of weights for a comparison should be zero: if you add up the weights for a given contrast the result should be zero.
- **Rule 4**: If a group is not involved in a comparison, automatically assign it a weight of zero. If we give a group a weight of zero then this eliminates that group from all calculations
- **Rule 5**: For a given contrast, the weights assigned to the group(s) in one chunk of variation should be equal to the number of groups in the opposite chunk of variation.

OK, let's follow some of these rules to derive the weights for the Viagra data. The first comparison we chose was to compare the two experimental groups against the control.

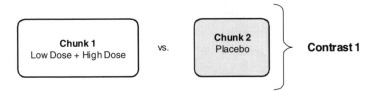

Therefore, the first chunk of variation contains the two experimental groups, and the second chunk contains only the placebo group. Rule 2 states that we should assign one chunk positive weights, and the other negative. It doesn't matter which way round we do this, but for convenience let's assign chunk 1 positive weights, and chunk 2 negative weights.

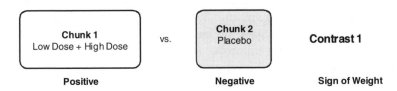

Using rule 5, the weight we assign to the groups in chunk 1 should be equivalent to the number of groups in chunk 2. There is only one group in chunk 2 and so we assign each group in chunk 1, a weight of 1. Likewise, we assign a weight to the group in chunk 2 that is equal to the number of groups in chunk 1. There are two groups in chunk 1 so we give the placebo group a weigh of 2. Then we combine the sign of the weights with the magnitude to give us weights of –2 (placebo), 1 (low dose) and 1 (high dose).

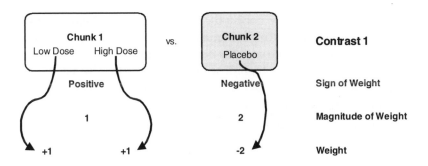

Rule 3 states that for a given contrast, the weights should add up to zero, and by following rules 2 and 5 this rule will always be followed (if you haven't followed these rules properly then this will become clear when you add the weights). So, let's check by adding the weights: sum of weights = $1 + 1 - 2 = 0$.

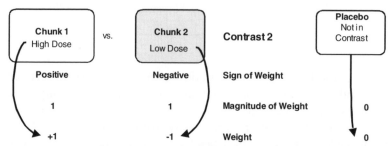

The second contrast was to compare the two experimental groups and so we want to ignore the placebo group. Rule 4 tells us that we should automatically assign this group a weight of zero (because this will eliminate this group from any calculations). We are left with two chunks of variation: chunk 1 contains the low dose group and chunk 2 contains the high dose group. By following rules 2 and 5 it should be obvious that one group is assigned a weight of +1 while the other is assigned a weight of –1. The control group is ignored (and so given a weight of zero). If we add the weights for contrast 2 we should find that they again add up to zero: sum of weights = $1 - 1 + 0 = 0$.

The weights for each contrast are codings for the two dummy variables in equation (7.2). Hence, these codings can be used in a multiple regression model in which β_2 represents contrast 1 (comparing the experimental groups to the control), β_1 represents contrast 2 (comparing the high dose group with the low dose group), and β_0 is the grand mean (equation (7.7)).

$$\text{Libido} = \beta_0 + \beta_2 \text{Contrast1} + \beta_1 \text{Contrast2} \qquad (7.7)$$

Each group is specified now not by the 0 and 1 coding scheme that we initially used, but by the coding scheme for the two contrasts. A code of –2 for contrast 1 and a code of 0 for contrast 2 identify subjects in the placebo group. Likewise, the high dose group is identified by a code of 1 for both variables, and the low dose group has a code of 1 for one contrast and a code of –1 for the other (see Table 7.4).

Table 7.4: Orthogonal contrasts for the Viagra data

Group	Dummy Variable 1 (Contrast1)	Dummy Variable 2 (Contrast2)	Product Contrast1 × Contrast2
Placebo	–2	0	0
Low Dose	1	–1	–1
High Dose	1	1	1
Total	0	0	0

It is important that the weights for a comparison sum to zero because it ensures that you are comparing two unique chunks of variation. Therefore, SPSS can perform a *t*-test. A more important consideration is that when you multiply the weights for a particular group, these products should also add up to zero (see final column of Table 7.4). If the products add to zero then we can be sure that the contrasts are *independent* or *orthogonal*. It is important for interpretation that contrasts are orthogonal.

What are orthogonal contrasts?

When we used dummy variable coding and ran a regression on the Viagra data, I commented that we couldn't look at the individual *t*-tests done on the regression coefficients because the familywise error rate is inflated (see section 7.1.4 and SPSS Output 7.1). However, if the contrasts are independent then the *t*-tests done on the β coefficients are independent also and so the resulting *p* values are uncorrelated. You might think that it is very difficult to ensure that the weights you choose for your contrasts conform to the requirements for independence but, provided you follow the rules I have laid out, you should always derive a set of *orthogonal* comparisons. You should double-check by looking at the sum of the multiplied weights and if this total is not zero then go back to the rules and see where you have gone wrong (see last column of Table 7.4).

Earlier on, I mentioned that when you used contrast codings in dummy variables in a regression model the β values represented the differences between the means that the contrasts were designed to test. Although it is reasonable for you to trust me on this issue, for the more advanced students I'd like to take the trouble to show you how the regression model works—this next part is not for the faint-hearted and so equation-phobes should move onto the next section! When we do planned contrasts, the intercept β_0 is equal to the grand mean (i.e. the value predicted by the model when group membership is not known):

$$\beta_0 = \text{grand mean} = \frac{\overline{X}_{\text{High}} + \overline{X}_{\text{Low}} + \overline{X}_{\text{Placebo}}}{3}$$

Placebo Group: If we use the contrast codings for the placebo group (see Table 7.4), the predicted value of libido equals the mean of the placebo group. The regression equation can, therefore, be expressed as:

$$\text{Libido} = \beta_2\text{Contrast1} + \beta_1\text{Contrast2} + \beta_0$$

$$\overline{X}_{Placebo} = (-2\beta_2) + (\beta_1 \times 0) + \left(\frac{\overline{X}_{High} + \overline{X}_{Low} + \overline{X}_{Placebo}}{3}\right)$$

Now, if we rearrange this equation and then multiply everything by 3 (to get rid of the fraction) we get:

$$2\beta_2 = \left(\frac{\overline{X}_{High} + \overline{X}_{Low} + \overline{X}_{Placebo}}{3}\right) - \overline{X}_{Placebo}$$

$$6\beta_2 = \overline{X}_{High} + \overline{X}_{Low} + \overline{X}_{Placebo} - 3\overline{X}_{Placebo}$$

$$6\beta_2 = \overline{X}_{High} + \overline{X}_{Low} - 2\overline{X}_{Placebo}$$

We can then divide everything by 2 to reduce the equation to its simplest form.

$$3\beta_2 = \left(\frac{\overline{X}_{High} + \overline{X}_{Low}}{2}\right) - \overline{X}_{Placebo}$$

$$\beta_2 = \tfrac{1}{3}\left[\left(\frac{\overline{X}_{High} + \overline{X}_{Low}}{2}\right) - \overline{X}_{Placebo}\right]$$

The equation above shows that β_2 represents the difference between the average of the two experimental groups and the control group:

$$3\beta_2 = \frac{\overline{X}_{High} + \overline{X}_{Low}}{2} - \overline{X}_{Placebo} = \frac{5 + 3.2}{2} - 2.2 = 1.9$$

We planned contrast 1 to look at the difference between the average of the experimental groups and the control and so it should now be clear how β_2 represents this difference. The observant among you will notice that rather than being the true value of the difference between experimental and control groups, β_2 is actually a third of this difference ($\beta_2 = 1.9/3 = 0.633$). The reason for this division is that the familywise error is controlled by making the regression coefficient equal to the actual difference divided by the number of groups in the contrast (in this case 3).

High Dose Group: For the situation in which the codings for the high dose group (see Table 7.4) are used the predicted value of libido is the mean for the high dose group, and so the regression equation becomes:

$$\text{Libido} = \beta_2 \text{Contrast1} + \beta_1 \text{Contrast2} + \beta_0$$
$$\overline{X}_{\text{High}} = (\beta_2 \times 1) + (\beta_1 \times 1) + \beta_0$$
$$\beta_1 = \overline{X}_{\text{High}} - \beta_2 - \beta_0$$

We know already what β_2 and β_0 represent so we place these values into the equation and then multiply by 3 to get rid of some of the fractions.

$$\beta_1 = \overline{X}_{\text{High}} - \beta_2 - \beta_0$$

$$\beta_1 = \overline{X}_{\text{High}} - \left\{ \frac{1}{3} \left[\left(\frac{\overline{X}_{\text{High}} + \overline{X}_{\text{Low}}}{2} \right) - \overline{X}_{\text{Placebo}} \right] \right\} - \left(\frac{\overline{X}_{\text{High}} + \overline{X}_{\text{Low}} + \overline{X}_{\text{Placebo}}}{3} \right)$$

$$3\beta_1 = 3\overline{X}_{\text{High}} - \left[\left(\frac{\overline{X}_{\text{High}} + \overline{X}_{\text{Low}}}{2} \right) - \overline{X}_{\text{Placebo}} \right] - \left(\overline{X}_{\text{High}} + \overline{X}_{\text{Low}} + \overline{X}_{\text{Placebo}} \right)$$

If we multiply everything by 2 to get rid of the other fraction, expand all of the brackets and then simplify the equation we get:

$$6\beta_1 = 6\overline{X}_{\text{High}} - \left(\overline{X}_{\text{High}} + \overline{X}_{\text{Low}} - 2\overline{X}_{\text{Placebo}} \right) - 2 \left(\overline{X}_{\text{High}} + \overline{X}_{\text{Low}} + \overline{X}_{\text{Placebo}} \right)$$

$$6\beta_1 = 6\overline{X}_{\text{High}} - \overline{X}_{\text{High}} - \overline{X}_{\text{Low}} + 2\overline{X}_{\text{Placebo}} - 2\overline{X}_{\text{High}} - 2\overline{X}_{\text{Low}} - 2\overline{X}_{\text{Placebo}}$$

$$6\beta_1 = 3\overline{X}_{\text{High}} - 3\overline{X}_{\text{Low}}$$

Finally, we can divide the equation by 6 to find out what β_1 represents (remember that $3/6 = 1/2$):

$$\beta_1 = \tfrac{1}{2} \left(\overline{X}_{\text{High}} - \overline{X}_{\text{Low}} \right)$$

We planned contrast 2 to look at the difference between the experimental groups:

$$\overline{X}_{\text{High}} - \overline{X}_{\text{Low}} = 5 - 3.2 = 1.8$$

It should now be clear how β_1 represents this difference. Again, rather than being the absolute value of the difference between the experimental groups, β_1 is actually half of this difference ($1.8/2 = 0.9$). The familywise error is again controlled, by making the regression coefficient equal to the actual difference divided by the number of groups in the contrast (in this case 2).

To illustrate these principles, I have created a file called **Contrast.sav** in which the Viagra data are coded using the contrast coding scheme used in this section. Run multiple regression analyses on these data using **libido** as the outcome and using **dummy1** and **dummy2** as the predictor variables (leave all default options). The main ANOVA for the model is the same as when dummy coding was used; however, the regression coefficients have now changed.

SPSS Output 7.2 shows the result of this regression. The first thing to notice is that the intercept is the grand mean, 3.467 (see, I wasn't telling lies). Second, the regression coefficient is one-third of the difference between the average of the experimental conditions and the control condition (see above). Finally, the regression coefficient for contrast 2 is half of the difference between the experimental groups (see above). So, when a planned comparison is done in ANOVA a *t*-test is conducted comparing the mean of one chunk of variation with the mean of a different chunk. From the significance values of the *t*-tests we can see that our experimental groups were significantly different from the control ($p < 0.05$) but that the experimental groups were not significantly different ($p > 0.05$).

Coefficients[a]

Model		Unstandardized Coefficients		Standardized Coefficients	t	Sig.
		B	Std. Error	Beta		
1	(Constant)	3.467	.362		9.574	.000
	Dummy Variable 1	.633	.256	.525	2.474	.029
	Dummy Variable 2	.900	.443	.430	2.029	.065

a. Dependent Variable: Libido

(*intercept*)

SPSS Output 7.2

7.1.4.3. Non-Orthogonal Comparisons

I have spent a lot of time labouring how to design appropriate orthogonal comparisons without mentioning the possibilities that non-orthogonal contrasts provide. Non-orthogonal contrasts are comparisons that are in some way related and the best way to get them is to disobey rule 1 in the previous section. Using my cake analogy again, non-orthogonal comparisons are where you slice up your cake and then try to stick slices of cake together again! So, for the Viagra data a set of non-orthogonal contrasts might be to have the same initial contrast (comparing experimental groups against the placebo), but then to compare the low dose group with the placebo. This disobeys rule 1 because the placebo group is singled out in the first contrast but used again in the second contrast. The coding for this set of contrasts is shown in Table 7.5 and by looking at the last column it is clear that when you multiply and add the codings from the two contrasts the sum is not zero. This tells us that the contrasts are not orthogonal.

Table 7.5: Non-orthogonal contrasts for the Viagra data

Group	Dummy Variable 1 (Contrast1)	Dummy Variable 2 (Contrast2)	Product Contrast1 × Contrast2
Placebo	−2	−1	2
Low Dose	1	0	0
High Dose	1	1	1
Total	0	0	3

Sum not 0

Are non-orthogonal contrasts legitimate? There is nothing intrinsically wrong with performing non-orthogonal contrasts. However, if you choose to perform this type of contrast you must be very careful in how you interpret the results. With non-orthogonal contrasts, the comparisons you do are related and so the resulting test statistics and p values will be correlated to some extent. For this reason you should use a more conservative probability level to accept that a given contrast is statistically meaningful (see section 7.1.5). For this reason I would advise conducting orthogonal planned comparisons whenever possible.

7.1.4.4. Standard Contrasts

Although under most circumstances you will design your own contrasts, there are special contrasts that have been designed to compare certain situations. Some of these contrasts are orthogonal whereas others are non-orthogonal. Many procedures in SPSS allow you to choose to carry out the contrasts mentioned in this section.

Table 7.6 shows the contrasts that are available in SPSS for procedures such as logistic regression (see section 5.3.1.2), factorial ANOVA and repeated measures ANOVA (see Chapters 8 and 9).Although the exact codings are not provided in Table 7.6, examples of the comparisons done in a three- and four-group situation are given (where the groups are labelled 1, 2, 3 and 1, 2, 3, 4 respectively). When you code variables in the data editor, SPSS will treat the lowest value code as group 1, the next highest code as group 2 and so on. Therefore, depending on which comparisons you want to make you should code your grouping variable appropriately (and then use Table 7.6 as a guide to which comparisons SPSS will carry out). One thing that clever readers might notice about the contrasts in Table 7.6 is that some are orthogonal (i.e. Helmert and difference contrasts) whilst the others are non-orthogonal (deviation, simple and repeated). You might also notice that the comparisons calculated using simple contrasts are the same as those given by using the dummy variable coding described in Table 7.2).

Table 7.6: Standard contrasts available in SPSS

Name	Definition	Contrast	3 Groups			4 Groups		
Deviation (first)	Compares the effect of each category (except first) to the overall experimental effect	1	2	vs.	(1,2,3)	2	vs.	(1,2,3,4)
		2	3	vs.	(1,2,3)	3	vs.	(1,2,3,4)
		3				4	vs.	(1,2,3,4)
Deviation (last)	Compares the effect of each category (except last) to the overall experimental effect	1	1	vs.	(1,2,3)	1	vs.	(1,2,3,4)
		2	2	vs.	(1,2,3)	2	vs.	(1,2,3,4)
		3				3	vs.	(1,2,3,4)
Simple (first)	Each category is compared to the first category	1	1	vs.	2	1	vs.	2
		2	1	vs.	3	1	vs.	3
		3				1	vs.	4
Simple (last)	Each category is compared to the last category	1	1	vs.	3	1	vs.	4
		2	2	vs.	3	2	vs.	4
		3				3	vs.	4
Repeated	Each category (except the first) is compared to the previous category	1	1	vs.	2	1	vs.	2
		2	2	vs.	3	2	vs.	3
		3				3	vs.	4
Helmert	Each category (except the last) is compared to the mean effect of all subsequent categories	1	1	vs.	(2, 3)	1	vs.	(2, 3, 4)
		2	2	vs.	3	2	vs.	(3, 4)
		3				3	vs.	4
Difference (reverse Helmert)	Each category (except the first) is compared to the mean effect of all previous categories	1	3	vs.	(2, 1)	4	vs.	(3, 2, 1)
		2	2	vs.	1	3	vs.	(2, 1)
		3				2	vs.	1

7.1.4.5. *Polynomial Contrasts: Trend Analysis*

One type of contrast deliberately omitted from Table 7.6 is the polynomial contrast. This contrast tests for trends in the data and in its most basic form it looks for a linear trend (i.e. that the group means increase proportionately). However, there are more complex trends such as quadratic, cubic and quartic trends that can be examined. Figure 7.6 shows diagrams of the types of trend that can exist in data sets. The linear trend should be familiar to you all by now and represents a simply proportionate change in the value of the dependent variable across ordered categories. A quadratic trend is where there is one change in the direction of the line (e.g. the line is curved in one place). An example of this might be a situation in which a drug enhances performance on a task at first but then as the dose increases the performance drops again. It should be fairly obvious that to find a quadratic trend you need at least three groups (because in the two-group situation there are not enough categories of the independent variable for the means of the dependent variable to change one way and then another). A cubic trend is where there are two changes in the direction of the trend. So, for example, the mean of the dependent variable at first goes up across the first couple of categories of the independent variable, then across the succeeding categories the means go down, but then across the last few categories the means rise again. To have two changes in the direction of the mean you must have at least four categories of the independent variable. The final trend that you are likely to come across is the quartic trend, and this trend has three changes of direction (and so you need at least five categories of the independent variable).

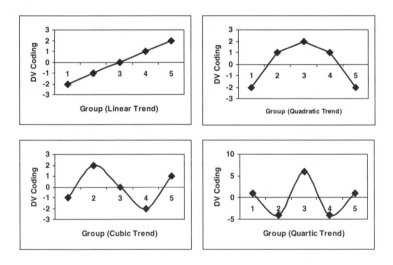

Figure 7.6: Linear, quadratic, cubic and quartic trends across five groups

Polynomial trends should be examined in data sets in which it makes sense to order the categories of the independent variable (so, for example, if you have administered five doses of a drug it makes sense to examine the five doses in order of magnitude). For the Viagra data there are only three groups and so we can expect to find only a linear or quadratic trend (and it would be pointless to test for any higher-order trends).

Each of these trends has a set of codes for the dummy variables in the regression model: so, we are doing the same thing that we did for planned contrasts except that the codings have already been devised to represent the type of trend of interest. In fact, the graphs in Figure 7.6 have been constructed by plotting the coding values for the five groups. In fact, if you add the codes for a given trend the sum will equal zero and if you multiply the codes you will find that the sum of the products also equals zero. Hence, these contrasts are orthogonal. The great thing about these contrasts is that you don't need to construct your own coding values to do them, because the codings already exist.

7.1.5.   Post Hoc Procedures

Often it is the case that you have no specific *a priori* predictions about the data you have collected and instead you are interested in exploring the data for any between-group differences that exist. This procedure is sometimes called *data mining* or *exploratory data analysis*. Now, personally I have always thought that these two terms have certain 'rigging the data' connotations to them and so I prefer to think of these procedures as 'finding the differences that I should have predicted if only I'd been clever enough'.

Post hoc tests consist of *pairwise comparisons* that are designed to compare all different combinations of the treatment groups. So, it is rather like taking every pair of groups and then performing a *t*-test on each pair of groups. Now, this might seem like a particularly stupid thing to say (but then again, I am particularly stupid) in the light of what I have already told you about the problems of inflated familywise error rates. However, pairwise comparisons control the familywise error by correcting the level of significance for each test such that the overall type I error rate (α) across all comparisons remains at 0.05. There are a number of ways in which the familywise error rate can be controlled. The most popular (and easiest) way is to divide α by the number of comparisons, thus ensuring that the cumulative type I error is below 0.05. Therefore, if we conduct 10 tests, we use 0.005 as our criterion for significance. This method is known as the *Bonferroni* method. There is a trade-off for controlling the familywise error rate and that is a loss of statistical power. This means that the probability of rejecting an effect that does actually exist is increased (this is called a type II error). By being more conservative in the type I error rate for each comparison, we increase the chance that we will miss a genuine difference in the data.

Therefore, when considering which *post hoc* procedure to use we need to consider three things: (1) does the test control the type I error rate, (2) does the test control the type II error rate (i.e. does the test have good statistical power) and (3) is the test reliable when the test assumptions of ANOVA have been violated?

Although I would love to go into tedious details about how all of the various *post hoc* tests work, there is really very little point. For one thing there are some excellent texts already available for those who wish to know (e.g. Toothaker, 1993 and Klockars and Sax, 1986), and for another SPSS provides no less than 18 *post hoc* procedures and so it would use up several square miles of rainforest to explain them. What is important is that you know which *post hoc* tests perform the best according to the three criteria mentioned above.

7.1.5.1. Type I (α) and Type II Error Rates

 The type I error rate and the statistical power of a test are linked. Therefore, there is always a trade-off: if a test is conservative (the probability of a type I error is small) then it is likely to lack statistical power (the probability of a type II error will be high). Therefore, it is important that multiple comparison procedures control the type I error rate but without a substantial loss in power. If a test is too conservative then we are likely to reject differences between means that are, in reality, meaningful.

The least-significant difference (*LSD*) pairwise comparison makes no attempt to control the type I error and is equivalent to performing multiple *t*-tests on the data. The only difference is that the LSD requires the overall ANOVA to be significant. The Studentized Newman-Keuls (*SNK*) procedure is also a very liberal test and lacks control over the experimentwise error rate. *Bonferroni's* and *Tukey's* tests both control the type I error rate very well but are conservative tests (they lack statistical power). Of the two, Bonferroni has more power when the number of comparisons is small, whereas Tukey is more powerful when testing large numbers of means. Tukey generally has greater power than *Dunn* and *Scheffé*. The Ryan, Einot, Gabriel and Welsch Q procedure (*REGWQ*) has good power and tight control of the type I error rate. In fact, when you want to test all pairs of means this procedure is probably the best. However, when group sizes are different this procedure should not be used.

7.1.5.2. Violations of Test Assumptions

Most research on *post hoc* tests has concerned whether the test performs well when the group sizes are different (an unbalanced design), when the population variances are very different, and when data are not normally distributed. The good news is that most multiple comparison procedures perform relatively well under small deviations from normality. The bad news is that they perform badly when group sizes are unequal and when population variances are different.

Hochberg's GT2 and *Gabriel's* pairwise test procedure were designed to cope with situations in which sample sizes are different. Gabriel's procedure is generally more powerful but can become too liberal when the sample sizes are very different. Also, Hochberg GT2 is very unreliable when the population variances are different and so should be used only when you are sure that this is not the case. There are several multiple comparison procedures that have been specially designed for situations in which population variances differ. SPSS provides four options for this situation: *Tamhane's T2, Dunnett's T3, Games-Howell,* and *Dunnett's C.* Tamhane's T2 is conservative and Dunnett's T3 and C keep very tight type I error control. The Games-Howell procedure is the most powerful but can be liberal when sample sizes are small. However, Games-Howell is also accurate when sample sizes are unequal.

7.1.5.3. Summary

The choice of comparison procedure will depend on the exact situation you have and whether it is more important for you to keep strict control over the familywise error rate or to have greater statistical power. However, some general guidelines can be drawn (see Toothaker, 1993). When you have equal sample sizes and you are confident that your population variances are similar then use REGWQ or Tukey as both have good power and tight control over the type I error rate. Bonferroni is generally conservative, but if you want guaranteed control over the type I error rate then this is the test to use. If sample sizes are slightly different then use Gabriel's procedure because it has greater power, but if sample sizes are very different use Hochberg's GT2. If there is any doubt that the population variances are equal then use the Games-Howell procedure because this generally seems to offer the best performance. I recommend running the Games-Howell procedure in addition to any other tests you might select because of the uncertainty of knowing whether the population variances are equivalent.

Although these general guidelines provide a convention to follow, be aware of the other procedures available and when they might be useful to use (for example, Dunnett's test is the only multiple comparison that allows you to test means against a control mean).

7.2.   Running One-Way ANOVA on SPSS

Hopefully you should all have some appreciation for the theory behind ANOVA, so let's put that theory into practice by conducting an ANOVA on the Viagra data. As with the independent *t*-test we need to enter the data into the data editor using a coding variable to specify to which of the three groups the data belong. So, the data must be entered in two columns (one called **dose** which specifies how much Viagra the subject was given and one called **libido** which indicates the person's libido over the following week). The data are in the file **Viagra.sav** but I recommend entering them by hand to gain practice in data entry. I have coded the grouping variable so that 1 = placebo, 2 = low dose and 3 = high dose (see section 1.2.3.1).

To conduct one-way ANOVA we have to first access the main dialog box using the **Analyze⇒Compare Means⇒One-way ANOVA** menu path (Figure 7.7). This dialog box has a space in which you can list one or more dependent variables and a second space to specify a grouping variable, or *factor*. Factor is another term for independent variable and should not be confused with the factors that we will come across when we learn about factor analysis. One thing that I dislike about SPSS is that in various procedures, such as one-way ANOVA, the program encourages the user to carry out multiple tests, which as we have seen is not a good thing. For example, in this procedure you are allowed to specify several dependent variables on which to conduct several ANOVAs. In reality, if you had measured several dependent variables (say you had measured not just libido but physiological arousal and anxiety too) it would preferable to analyze these data using MANOVA rather than treating each dependent measure separately (see Chapter 10). For the Viagra data we need select only **libido** from the variables list and transfer it to the box labelled *Dependent List* by clicking on ▣. Then select the grouping variable **dose** and transfer it to the box labelled *Factor* by clicking on ▣.

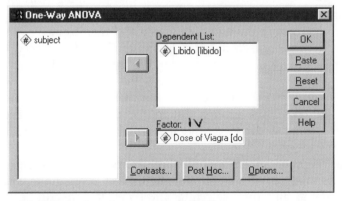

Figure 7.7: Main dialog box for one-way ANOVA

7.2.1.   *Planned Comparisons Using SPSS*

If you click on ⌐Contrasts...⌐ you access the dialog box that allows you to conduct the planned comparisons described in section 7.1.4.

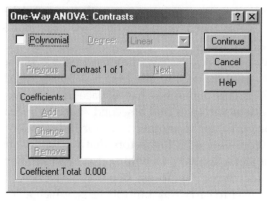

Figure 7.8: Dialog box for conducting planned comparisons

The dialog box is shown in Figure 7.8 and has two sections. The first section is for specifying trend analyses. If you want to test for trends in the data then tick the box labelled *Polynomial*. Once this box is ticked, you can select the degree of polynomial you would like. The Viagra data have only three groups and so the highest degree of trend there can be is

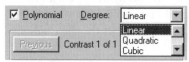

a quadratic trend (see section 7.1.4.3). Now, it is important from the point of view of trend analysis that we have coded the grouping variable in a meaningful order. Now, we expect libido to be smallest in the placebo group, to increase in the low dose group and then to increase again in the high dose group. To detect a meaningful trend, we need to have coded these groups in ascending order. We have done this by coding the placebo group with the lowest value 1, the low dose group with the middle value 2, and the high dose group with the highest coding value of 3. If we coded the groups differently, this would influence both whether a trend is detected, and if a trend is detected whether it is statistically meaningful.

For the Viagra data there are only three groups and so we should select the polynomial option ⌐ᵛ Polynomial⌐, and then select a quadratic degree by clicking on ⌐▼⌐ and then selecting *Quadratic*. If a quadratic trend is selected SPSS will test for both linear and quadratic trends.

The lower part of the dialog box in Figure 7.8 is for specifying any planned comparisons. To conduct planned comparisons we need to tell SPSS what weights to assign to each group. The first step is to decide which comparisons you want to do and then what weights must be assigned to each group for each of the contrasts. We have already gone through this process in section 7.1.4.2, and so we know that the weights for contrast 1 were –2 (placebo group), +1 (low dose group) and +1 (high dose group). We will specify this contrast first. It is important to make sure that you enter the correct weight for each group, so you should remember that the first weight that you enter should be the weight for the *first* group (that is, the group coded with the lowest value in the data editor). For the Viagra data, the group coded with the lowest value was the placebo group (which had a code of 1) and so we should enter the weighting for this group first. Click in the box labelled *Coefficients* with the mouse and then type '–2' in this box and click on ⌊_Add_⌋. Next, we need to input the weight for the second group, which for the Viagra data is the low dose group (because this group was coded in the data editor with the second highest value). Click in the box labelled *Coefficients* with the mouse and then type '1' in this box and click on ⌊_Add_⌋. Finally, we need to input the weight for the last group, which for the Viagra data is the high dose group (because this group was coded with the highest value in the data editor). Click in the box labelled *Coefficients* with the mouse and then type '1' in this box and click on ⌊_Add_⌋. The box should now look like Figure 7.9.

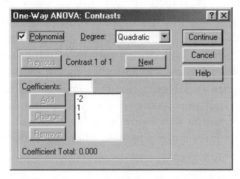

Figure 7.9: *Contrasts* dialog box completed for the first contrast of the Viagra data

Once you have inputted the weights you can change or remove any one of them by using the mouse to select the weight that you want to change. The weight will then appear in the box labelled *Coefficients* where you can type in a new weight and then click on ⌊_Change_⌋. Alternatively, you can click on any of the weights and remove it completely by clicking ⌊_Remove_⌋. Underneath the weights SPSS calculates the coefficient total which, as we saw in section 7.1.4.2, should equal zero. If the coefficient number is anything other than zero you should go back and check that the contrasts you have planned make sense and that you have followed the appropriate rules for assigning weights.

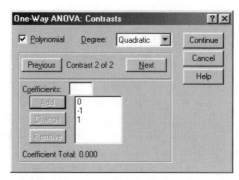

Figure 7.10: *Contrasts* dialog box completed for the second contrast of the Viagra data

Once you have specified the first contrast, click on Next. The weights that you have just entered will disappear and the dialog box will now read *Contrast 2 of 2*. We know from section 7.1.4.2 that the weights for contrast 2 were: 0 (placebo group), +1 (low dose group) and −1 (high dose group). We can specify this contrast as before. Remembering that the first weight we enter will be for the placebo group, we must enter the value zero as the first weight. Click in the box labelled *Coefficients* with the mouse and then type '0' and click on Add. Next, we need to input the weight for the low dose group by clicking in the box labelled *Coefficients* and then typing '1' and clicking on Add. Finally, we need to input the weight for the high dose group by clicking in the box labelled *Coefficients* and then typing '-1' and clicking on Add. The box should now look like Figure 7.10. Notice that the weights add up to zero as they did for contrast 1. It is imperative that you remember to input zero weights for any groups that are not in the contrast. When all of the planned contrasts have been specified click on Continue to return to the main dialog box.

7.2.2.   *Post Hoc Tests in SPSS*

Having told SPSS which planned comparisons to do, we can choose to do *post hoc* tests. In theory, if we have done planned comparisons we shouldn't need to do *post hoc* tests (because we have already tested the hypotheses of interest). Likewise, if we choose to conduct *post hoc* tests then we should not need to do planned contrasts (because we have no hypotheses to test). However, for the sake of space we will conduct some *post hoc* tests on the Viagra data. Click on Post Hoc... in the main dialog box to access the *post hoc* tests dialog box (Figure 7.11).

In section 7.1.5.3, I recommended various *post hoc* procedures for various situations. For the Viagra data there are equal sample sizes and so we need not use Gabriel's test. We should use Tukey's test and

REGWQ and check the findings with the Games-Howell procedure. We have a specific hypothesis that both the high and low dose groups should differ from the placebo group  and so we could use Dunnett's test to examine these hypotheses. Once you have selected Dunnett's test, you can change the control category (the default is to use the last category) to specify that the first category be used as the control category (because the placebo group was coded with the lowest value). You can also choose whether to conduct a two-tailed test (￼) or a one-tailed test. If you choose a one-tailed test then you must predict whether you believe that the mean of the control group will be less than the experimental groups (￼) or greater than the experimental groups (￼). These are all of the *post hoc* tests that need to be specified and when the completed dialog box looks like Figure 7.11 click on ￼ to return to the main dialog box.

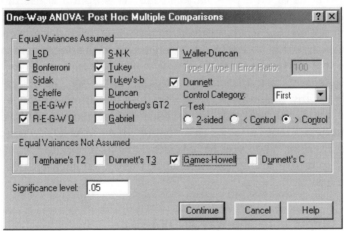

Figure 7.11: Dialog box for specifying *post hoc* tests

7.2.3.   Options

The options for one-way ANOVA are fairly straightforward. First you can ask for some descriptive statistics which will produce a table of the means, standard deviations, standard errors, ranges and confidence intervals for the means of each group. This option is useful to select because it assists in interpreting the final results. A vital option to select is the homogeneity of variance tests. As with the *t*-test, there is an assumption that the variances of the groups are equal and selecting this option tests this assumption. SPSS uses Levene's test, which tests the hypothesis that the variances of each group are equal. There is also an option to have a *Means plot* and if this option is selected then a line graph of the group means will be produced in the output.

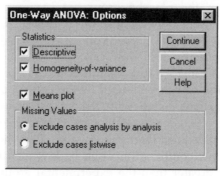

Figure 7.12: Options for one-way ANOVA

Finally, the options let us specify whether we want to exclude cases on a listwise basis or on a per-analysis basis. This option is useful only if you are conducting several ANOVAs on different dependent variables. The first option (*Exclude cases analysis by analysis*) excludes any case that has a missing value for either the independent or the dependent variable used in that particular analysis. *Exclude cases listwise* will exclude from *all analyses* any case that has a missing value for the independent variable or any of the dependent variables specified. As such, if you stick to good practice and don't conduct hundreds of ANOVAs on different dependent variables (see Chapter 10 on MANOVA) the default settings are fine. When you have selected the appropriate options, click on Continue to return to the main dialog box and then click on OK to run the analysis.

7.3.   Output from One-Way ANOVA

7.3.1.   Output for the Main Analysis

If you load up the Viagra data (or enter it in by hand) and select all of the options I have suggested, you should find that the output looks the same as what follows. If your output is different we should panic because one of us has done it wrong—hopefully not me or a lot of trees have died for nothing. Figure 7.13 shows an error bar chart of the Viagra data with a line superimposed to show the general trend of the means across groups. This graph is not automatically produced by SPSS; however, a line graph will be produced if the *Means plot* option is selected (this graph will look like Figure 7.13 but without the error bars). I have chosen to display an error bar graph because it is slightly more interesting than the line graph alone. It's clear from this chart that all of the error bars overlap, indicating that, on face value, there are no between-group differences (although this measure is only approximate). The line that joins the means seems to indicate a linear trend in that as the dose of Viagra increases so does the mean level of libido.

SPSS Output 7.3 shows the table of descriptive statistics from the one-way procedure for the Viagra data. The first thing to notice is that the means and standard deviations correspond to those shown in Table 7.1. In addition we are told the standard error. You should remember that the standard error is the standard deviation of the sampling distribution of these data (so, for the placebo group, if you took lots of samples from the population from which these data come, the means of these samples would have a standard deviation of 0.5831). We are also given confidence intervals for the mean. By now, you should be familiar with what a confidence interval tells us, and that is that if we took 100 samples from the population from which the placebo group came, then 95 of these samples would have a mean between 0.5811 and 3.8189. Although these diagnostics are not immediately important, we will refer back to them throughout the analysis.

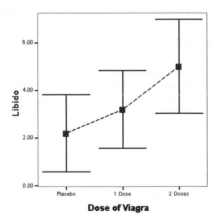

Figure 7.13: Error bar chart of the Viagra data

Descriptives

			N	Mean	Std. Deviation	Std. Error	95% Confidence Interval for Mean		Minimum	Maximum
							Lower Bound	Upper Bound		
Libido	Dose of Viagra	Placebo	5	2.2000	1.3038	.5831	.5811	3.8189	1.00	4.00
		Low Dose	5	3.2000	1.3038	.5831	1.5811	4.8189	2.00	5.00
		High Dose	5	5.0000	1.5811	.7071	3.0368	6.9632	3.00	7.00
		Total	15	3.4667	1.7674	.4563	2.4879	4.4454	1.00	7.00

SPSS Output 7.3

The next part of the output is a summary table of Levene's test. This test is designed to test the null hypothesis that the variances of the groups are the same. It is an ANOVA conducted on the absolute differences between the observed data and the mean from which the data came.[3] In this case, Levene's test is, therefore, testing whether the variances of the three groups are significantly different. If Levene's test is significant (i.e. the value of *Sig.* is less than 0.05) then we can say that the variances are significantly different. This would mean that we had violated one of the assumptions of ANOVA and we would have to take steps to rectify this matter. The most common way to rectify differences between group variances is to transform all of the data. If the variances are unequal, they can sometimes be stabilized by taking the square root of every value of the dependent variable and then reanalysing these transformed values (see Howell, 1997, pp. 323-329). However, transformations often don't help at all and in these circumstances you are sometimes left with only the option of reporting an inaccurate *F* value. In these circumstances you are well advised to report Levene's test so that people can assess the accuracy of your results for themselves (you'd be amazed how many people don't report this important statistic!). Luckily, for these data the variances are very similar (hence the high probability value); in fact, if you look at SPSS Output 7.3 you'll see that the variances of the placebo and low dose groups are identical.

Test of Homogeneity of Variances

	Levene Statistic	df1	df2	Sig.
Libido	.092	2	12	.913

SPSS Output 7.4

SPSS Output 7.5 shows the main ANOVA summary table. The table is divided into between-group effects (effects due to the model—the experimental effect) and within-group effects (this is the unsystematic variation in the data). The between-group effect is further broken down into a linear and quadratic component and these components are the trend analyses described in section 7.1.4.3). The between-group effect labelled *Combined* is the overall experimental effect. In this row we are told the sums of squares for the model ($SS_M = 20.13$) and this value corresponds to the value calculated in section 7.1.3.3. The degrees of

---

[3] The interested reader might like to try this out. Simply create a new variable called **diff** (short for difference), which is each score subtracted from the mean of the group to which that score belongs. Then remove all of the minus signs (so, take the absolute value of **diff**) and conduct a one-way ANOVA with **dose** as the independent variable and **diff** as the dependent variable. You'll find that the *F*-ratio for this analysis is 0.092, which is significant at $p = 0.913$!

freedom are equal to 2 and the mean squares for the model corresponds to the value calculated in section 7.1.3.5 (10.067). The sum of squares and mean squares represent the experimental effect. This overall effect is then broken down because we asked SPSS to conduct trend analyses of these data (we will return to these trends in due course). Had we not specified this in section 7.2.1, then these two rows of the summary table would not be produced. The row labelled *Within groups* gives details of the unsystematic variation within the data (the variation due to natural individual differences in libido and different reactions to Viagra). The table tells us how much unsystematic variation exists (the residual sum of squares, SS_R) and this value (23.60) corresponds to the value calculated in section 7.1.3.4. The table then gives the average amount of unsystematic variation, the mean squares (MS_R), which corresponds to the value (1.967) calculated in section 7.1.3.5. The test of whether the group means are the same is represented by the *F*-ratio for the combined between-group effect. The value of this ratio is 5.12, which is the same as was calculated in section 7.1.3.6. Finally SPSS tells us whether this value is likely to have happened by chance. The final column labelled *Sig.* indicates the likelihood of an *F*-ratio the size of the one obtained occurring by chance. In this case, there is a probability of 0.025 that an *F*-ratio of this size would occur by chance (that's only a 2.5% chance!). We have seen in previous chapters that social scientists use a cut-off point of 0.05 as their criterion for statistical significance. Hence, because the observed significance value is less than 0.05 we can say that there was a significant effect of Viagra. However, at this stage we still do not know exactly what the effect of Viagra was (we don't know which groups differed). One thing that is interesting here is that we obtained a significant experimental effect yet our error bar plot indicated that no difference would be found. This contradiction illustrates how the error bar chart can act only as a rough guide to the data.

ANOVA

			Sum of Squares	df	Mean Square	F	Sig.
Libido	Between Groups	(Combined)	20.133	2	10.067	5.119	.025
		Linear Term Contrast	19.600	1	19.600	9.966	.008
		Deviation	.533	1	.533	.271	.612
		Quadratic Term Contrast	.533	1	.533	.271	.612
	Within Groups		23.600	12	1.967		
	Total		43.733	14			

SPSS Output 7.5

Knowing that the overall effect of Viagra was significant, we can now look at the trend analysis. The trend analysis breaks down the experimental effect to see whether it can explained by either a linear or a quadratic relationship in the data. First, let's look at the linear component. This comparison tests whether the means increase across groups in a linear way. Again the sum of squares and mean squares are given, but the most important things to note are the value of the F-ratio and the corresponding significance value. For the linear trend the F-ratio is 9.97 and this value is significant at a 0.008 level. Therefore, we can say that as the dose of Viagra increased from nothing to a low dose to a high dose, libido increased proportionately. Moving onto the quadratic trend, this comparison is testing whether the pattern of means is curvilinear (i.e. is represented by a curve that has one bend). The error bar graph of the data strongly suggests that the means cannot be represented by a curve and the results for the quadratic trend bear this out. The F-ratio for the quadratic trend is non-significant (in fact, the value of F is less than 1 which immediately indicates that this contrast will not be significant).

7.3.2.   Reporting Results

Before moving on to the planned and *post hoc* comparisons, I'd briefly like to say something about how these results would be reported. When we report an ANOVA, we have to give details of the F-ratio and the degrees of freedom from which it was calculated. For the experimental effect in these data the F-ratio was derived from dividing the mean squares for the effect by the mean squares for the residual. Therefore, the degrees of freedom used to assess the F-ratio are the degrees of freedom for the effect of the model ($df_M = 2$) and the degrees of freedom for the residuals of the model ($df_R = 12$). Therefore, the correct way to report the main finding would be: there was a significant effect of Viagra on levels of libido ($F(2, 12) = 5.12, p < 0.05$).

   Notice that the value of the F-ratio is preceded by the values of the degrees of freedom for that effect. Also, we rarely state the exact significance value of the F-ratio: instead we report that the significance value, p, was less than the criterion value of 0.05. The linear contrast can be reported in much the same way: there was a significant linear trend ($F(1, 12) = 9.97, p < 0.01$) indicating that as the dose of Viagra increased, libido increased proportionately. Notice that the degrees of freedom have changed to reflect how the F-ratio was calculated. Also, we have now reported that the F-value was significant at a value less than the criterion value of 0.01. In the social sciences we have several *standard* levels of statistical significance. Primarily, the most important criterion is that the significance value is less than 0.05; however, if the exact significance value is much lower then we can be much more confident about the strength of the experimental effect. In these circumstances we like to make a big song and dance about the fact that our result isn't just significant at 0.05, but is significant at a much lower level as well (hooray!). The values we use are 0.05, 0.01, 0.001 and 0.0001. You are rarely ever going to be in the fortunate position of being able to report an effect that is significant at a level less than 0.0001!

7.3.3.   Output for Planned Comparisons

In section 7.2.1 we told SPSS to conduct two planned comparisons: one to test whether the control group was different to the two groups who received Viagra, and one to see whether the two doses of Viagra made a difference to libido. SPSS Output 7.6 shows the results of the planned comparisons that we requested for the Viagra data. The first table displays the contrast coefficients; these values are the ones that we entered in section 7.2.1 and it is well worth looking at this table to double-check that the contrasts are comparing what they are supposed to! As a quick rule of thumb, remember that when we do planned comparisons we arrange the weights such that we compare any group with a positive weight against any group with a negative weight. Therefore, the table of weights shows that contrast 1 compares the placebo group against the two experimental groups, and contrast 2 compares the low dose group with the high dose group. It is useful to check this table to make sure that the weights that we entered into SPSS correspond to the weights we intended to enter into SPSS!

Contrast Coefficients

		Dose of Viagra	
Contrast	Placebo	Low Dose	High Dose
1	-2	1	1
2	0	-1	1

Contrast Tests

		Contrast	Value of Contrast	Std. Error	t	df	Sig. (2-tailed)
Libido	Assume equal variances	1	3.8000	1.5362	2.474	12	.029
		2	1.8000	.8869	2.029	12	.065
	Does not assume equal variances	1	3.8000	1.4832	2.562	8.740	.031
		2	1.8000	.9165	1.964	7.720	.086

SPSS Output 7.6

The second table gives the statistics for each contrast. The first thing to notice is that statistics are produced for situations in which the group variances are equal, and when they are unequal. If Levene's test was significant then you should read the part of the table labelled *Does not assume equal variances*. However, for these data Levene's test was not significant and we can, therefore, use the part of the table labelled *Assume equal variances*. The table tells us the value of the contrast itself, which is the weighted sum of the group means. This value is obtained by taking each group mean, multiplying it by the weight for the contrast of interest, and then adding these values together.[4] The table also gives the standard error of each contrast and a t-statistic. The t-statistic is derived by dividing the contrast value by the standard error (t = 3.8/1.5362 = 1.47) and is compared against critical values of the t-distribution. The significance value of the contrast is given in the final column and this value is two-tailed. Using the first contrast as an example, if we had used this contrast to test the general hypothesis that the experimental groups would differ from the placebo group, then we should use this two-tailed value. However, in reality we tested the hypothesis that the experimental groups would increase libido above the levels seen in the placebo group: this hypothesis is one-tailed. Provided the means for the groups bear out the hypothesis we can divide the significance values by two to obtain the one-tailed probability. Hence, for contrast 1, we can say that taking Viagra significantly increased libido compared to the control group (p = 0.0145). For contrast 2 we also had a one-tailed hypothesis (that a high dose of Viagra would increase libido significantly more than a low dose) and the means bear this hypothesis out. The significance of contrast 2 tells us that a high dose of Viagra increased libido significantly more than a low dose (p (one-tailed) = 0.065/2 = 0.0325). Notice that had we not had a specific hypothesis regarding which group would have the highest mean then we would have had to conclude that the dose of Viagra had no significant effect on libido. For this reason it can be important as scientists that we generate hypotheses before collecting any data because this method of scientific discovery is more powerful.

In summary, there is an overall effect of Viagra on libido. Furthermore, the planned contrasts revealed that having Viagra significantly increased libido compared to a control group ($t(12)$ = 2.47, $p < 0.05$) and having a high dose significantly increased libido compared to a low dose ($t(12)$ = 2.03, $p < 0.05$).

7.3.4.   Output for Post Hoc Tests

If we had no specific hypotheses about the effect that Viagra might have on libido then we could carry out *post hoc* tests to compare all groups of subjects with each other. In fact, we asked SPSS to do this (see section 7.2.2) and the results of this analysis are shown in SPSS Output 7.7. This

---

[4] For the first contrast this value is:

$$\sum(\overline{X}W) = [(2.2 \times -2) + (3.2 \times 1) + (5.0 \times 1)] = 3.8.$$

table shows the results of Tukey's test (known as Tukey's HSD[5]), the Games-Howell procedure and Dunnett's test, which were all specified earlier on. If we look at Tukey's test first (because we have no reason to doubt that the population variances are unequal) it is clear from the table that each group of subjects is compared to all of the remaining groups. For each pair of groups the difference between group means is displayed, the standard error of that difference, the significance level of that difference and a 95% confidence interval. First of all, the placebo group is compared to the low dose group and reveals a non-significant difference (*Sig.* is greater than 0.05), but when compared to the high dose group there is a significant difference (*Sig.* is less than 0.05). This finding is interesting because our planned comparison showed that any dose of Viagra produced a significant increase in libido, yet these comparisons indicate that a low dose does not. Why is there this contradiction (have a think about this question before you read on)?

In section 7.1.4.2 I explained that the first planned comparison would compare the experimental groups with the placebo group. Specifically, it would compare the average of the two group means of the experimental groups $((3.2 + 5.0)/2 = 4.1)$ with the mean of the placebo group (2.2). So, it was assessing whether the difference between these values $(4.1 - 2.2 = 1.9)$ was significant. In the *post hoc* tests, when the low dose is compared to the placebo, the contrast is testing whether the difference between the means of these two groups is significant. The difference in this case is only 1, compared to a difference of 1.9 for the planned comparison. This explanation illustrates how it is possible to have apparently contradictory results from planned contrasts and *post hoc* comparisons. More important, it illustrates how careful we must be in interpreting planned contrasts.

The low dose group is then compared to both the placebo group and the high dose group. The first thing to note is that the contrast involving the low dose and placebo group is identical to the one just described. The only new information is the comparison between the two experimental conditions. The group means differ by 2.8 which is not significant. This result also contradicts the planned comparisons (remember that contrast 2 compared these groups and found a significant difference). Think why this contradiction might exist. For one thing, *post hoc* tests by their very nature are two-tailed (you use them when you have made no specific hypotheses and you cannot predict the direction of hypotheses that don't exist!) and contrast 2 was significant only when considered as a one-tailed hypothesis. However, even at the two-tailed level the planned comparison was closer to significance than

---

[5] The HSD stands for 'honestly significant difference', which has a slightly dodgy ring to it if you ask me!

the *post hoc* test and this fact illustrates that *post hoc* procedures are more conservative (i.e. have less power to detect true effects) than planned comparisons.

The rest of the table describes the Games-Howell tests and a quick inspection reveals the same pattern of results: the only groups that differed significantly were the high dose and placebo groups. These results give us confidence in our conclusions from Tukey's test because even if the populations variances are not equal (which seems unlikely given that the sample variances are very similar), then the profile of results still holds true. Finally, Dunnett's test is described and you'll hopefully remember that we asked the computer to compare both experimental groups against the control using a one-tailed hypothesis that the mean of the control group would be smaller than both experimental groups. Even as a one-tailed hypothesis, levels of libido in the low dose group are equivalent to the placebo group. However, the high dose group has a significantly higher libido than the placebo group.

Multiple Comparisons

Dependent Variable: Libido

	(I) Dose of Viagra	(J) Dose of Viagra	Mean Difference (I-J)	Std. Error	Sig.	95% Confidence Interval Lower Bound	95% Confidence Interval Upper Bound
Tukey HSD	Placebo	Low Dose	-1.0000	.887	.516	-3.3663	1.3663
		High Dose	-2.8000*	.887	.021	-5.1663	-.4337
	Low Dose	Placebo	1.0000	.887	.516	-1.3663	3.3663
		High Dose	-1.8000	.887	.147	-4.1663	.5663
	High Dose	Placebo	2.8000*	.887	.021	.4337	5.1663
		Low Dose	1.8000	.887	.147	-.5663	4.1663
Games-Howell	Placebo	Low Dose	-1.0000	.887	.479	-3.3563	1.3563
		High Dose	-2.8000*	.887	.039	-5.4390	-.1610
	Low Dose	Placebo	1.0000	.887	.479	-1.3563	3.3563
		High Dose	-1.8000	.887	.185	-4.4390	.8390
	High Dose	Placebo	2.8000*	.887	.039	.1610	5.4390
		Low Dose	1.8000	.887	.185	-.8390	4.4390
Dunnett t(>control)[a]	Low Dose	Placebo	1.0000*	.887	.945		2.8698
	High Dose	Placebo	2.8000*	.887	.999		4.6698

*. The mean difference is significant at the .05 level.

a. Dunnett t-tests treat one group as a control, and compare all other groups against it.

SPSS Output 7.7

The table in SPSS Output 7.8 shows the results of Tukey's test and the REGWQ test. These tests display subsets of groups that have the same means. Therefore, the Tukey test creates two subsets of groups with statistically similar means. The first subset contains the placebo and low dose groups (indicating that these two groups have the similar means) whereas the second subset contains the high and low dose groups.

These results demonstrate that the placebo group has a similar mean to the low dose group but not the high dose group, and that the low dose group has a similar mean to both the placebo and high dose groups. In other words, the only groups that have significantly different means are the high dose and placebo groups. The tests provide a significance value for each subset and it's clear from these significance values that the groups in subsets have non-significant means (as indicated by values of *Sig.* that are greater than 0.05).

These calculations use the harmonic mean sample size. The harmonic mean is a weighted version of the mean that takes account of the relationship between variance and sample size (see Howell, 1997, p. 222). Although you don't need to know the intricacies of the harmonic mean, it is useful that the harmonic sample size is used because it eliminates any bias that might be introduced through having unequal sample sizes. As such, one-way ANOVA provides reliable results even in unbalanced designs.

Libido

	Dose of Viagra	N	Subset for alpha = .05	
			1	2
Tukey HSD[a]	Placebo	5	2.2000	
	Low Dose	5	3.2000	3.2000
	High Dose	5		5.0000
	Sig.		.516	.147
Ryan-Einot-Gabriel-Welsch Range	Placebo	5	2.2000	
	Low Dose	5	3.2000	3.2000
	High Dose	5		5.0000
	Sig.		.282	.065

Means for groups in homogeneous subsets are displayed.

a. Uses Harmonic Mean Sample Size = 5.000

SPSS Output 7.8

7.3.5. A Second Example

Hopefully you should all now understand what the output from SPSS tells us about the groups in which we are interested. It is important to understand these principles and so I have designed a second example that you can work through alone. Imagine that I was interested in how different teaching methods affected students' knowledge. I noticed that some lecturers were aloof and arrogant in their teaching style and humiliated anyone who asked them a question, while others were encouraging and supporting of questions and comments. I took three statistics courses where I taught the same material. For one group of students I wandered around with a large cane and beat anyone who asked daft questions or got questions wrong (*punish*). In the second group I used my normal teaching style which is to encourage students to discuss things that they find difficult and to give anyone working hard a nice sweet (*reward*). The final group I remained indifferent to and neither punished nor rewarded their efforts (*indifferent*). As the dependent measure I took the students' exam marks (percentage). Based on theories of operant conditioning, we expect punishment to be a very unsuccessful way of reinforcing learning, but we expect reward to be very successful. Therefore, one prediction is that reward will produce the best learning. A second hypothesis is that punishment should actually retard learning such that it is worse than an indifferent approach to learning. The data are in Table 7.7. Enter the data and then carry out a one-way ANOVA and use planned comparisons to test the hypotheses that (1) reward results in better exam results than either punishment or indifference; and (2) indifference will lead to significantly better exam results than punishment.

Table 7.7: Data for the teaching example

Punish	Indifferent	Reward
50	63	71
45	55	67
48	54	68
47	49	62
45	65	65
49	46	58
50	53	63
54	67	69
57	58	70
55	50	61

7.4.   Further Reading

Howell, D. C. (1997). *Statistical methods for psychology* (4th edition). Belmont, CA: Duxbury. Chapters 11 and 12 provide very detailed coverage of ANOVA and Chapter 16 covers the GLM approach.

Iversen, G. R. & Norpoth, H. (1987). *ANOVA* (2nd edition). Sage university paper series on quantitative applications in the social sciences, 07-001. Newbury Park, CA: Sage. Quite high level, but a good read for those with a mathematical brain.

Klockars, A. J. & Sax, G. (1986). *Multiple comparisons*. Sage university paper series on quantitative applications in the social sciences, 07-061. Newbury Park, CA: Sage. High level but thorough coverage of multiple comparisons—in my view this book is better than Toothaker for planned comparisons.

Rosenthal, R. & Rosnow, R. L. (1985). *Contrast analysis: focused comparisons in the analysis of variance.* Cambridge: Cambridge University Press. Great for planned comparisons.

Toothaker, L. E. (1993). *Multiple comparison procedures.* Sage university paper series on quantitative applications in the social sciences, 07-089. Newbury Park, CA: Sage. Also high level, but gives an excellent précis of *post hoc* procedures.

Wright, D. B. (1997). *Understanding statistics: an introduction for the social sciences.* London: Sage. Chapter 6 gives a very readable overview of ANOVA and the GLM.

8 Complex ANOVA (GLM 2)

8.1. Analysis of Covariance (ANCOVA)

In Chapter 7, we saw how one-way ANOVA could be characterized in terms of a multiple regression equation that used dummy variables to code group membership. In addition, in Chapter 4 we saw how multiple regression could incorporate several continuous predictor variables. It should, therefore, be no surprise that the regression equation for ANOVA can be extended to include one or more continuous variables that predict the outcome (or dependent variable). Continuous variables such as these, that are not part of the main experimental manipulation but have an influence on the dependent variable, are known as *covariates* and they can be included in an ANOVA analysis. For example, in the Viagra example from Chapter 7, we might expect there to be things that influence a person's libido other than Viagra. Some possible influences on libido might be the libido of the subject's sexual partner (after all 'it takes two to tango'!), other medication that suppresses libido (such as antidepressants) and fatigue. If these variables are measured, then it is possible to control for the influence they have on the dependent variable by including them in the regression model. From what we know of hierarchical regression (see Chapter 4) it should be clear that if we enter the covariate into the regression model first, and then enter the dummy variables representing the experimental manipulation, we can see what effect an independent variable has *after* the effect of the covariate. As such, we control for (or *partial out*) the effect of the covariate. The purpose of including covariates in ANOVA is two fold:

- **To reduce within-group error variance**: In the discussion of ANOVA and *t*-tests we got used to the idea that we assess the effect of an experiment by comparing the amount of variability in the data that the experiment can explain, against the variability that it cannot explain. If we can explain some of this 'unexplained' variance (SS_R) in terms of other variables (covariates), then we reduce the error variance, allowing us to more accurately assess the effect of the independent variable (SS_M).

- **Elimination of confounds**: In any experiment, there may be unmeasured variables that confound the results (i.e. variables that vary systematically with the experimental manipulation). If any variables are known to influence the dependent variable being measured, then ANCOVA is ideally suited to remove the bias of these variables. Once a possible confounding variable has been identified, it can be measured and entered into the analysis as a covariate.

There are other reasons for including covariates in ANOVA but because I do not intend to describe the computation of ANCOVA I recommend that the interested reader consult Wildt and Ahtola (1978) or Stevens (1992, Chapter 9).

Imagine that the researcher who conducted the Viagra study in Chapter 7 suddenly realized that the libido of the subjects' sexual partners would affect the subjects' own libido (especially because the measure of libido was behavioural). Therefore, the researcher repeated the study on a different set of subjects, but this time took a measure of the partner's libido. The partner's libido was measured in terms of how often they tried to initiate sexual contact. In Chapter 7, we saw that this experimental scenario could be characterized in terms of equation (7.2). It should be clear that this equation can be extended to include this covariate (see equation (8.1)).

$$\text{Libido} = \beta_0 + \beta_3 \text{Covariate}_i + \beta_2 \text{High}_i + \beta_1 \text{Low}_i + \varepsilon_i$$
$$\text{Libido} = \beta_0 + \beta_3 \text{Partner's Libido}_i + \beta_2 \text{High}_i + \beta_1 \text{Low}_i + \beta_i$$

$$(8.1)$$

The data for this example are in Table 8.1 and can be found in the file **ViagraCov.sav**. Table 8.1 shows the subject's libido, their partner's libido, and the means (and standard deviations in brackets) of the subjects' libido scores. I recommend putting these data into the data editor by hand. This can be done in much the same way as the Viagra data from Chapter 7 except that an extra variable must be created in which to place the values of the covariate.

In essence, the data should be laid out in the data editor as they are in Table 8.1. So, create a coding variable called **dose** and use the *Labels* option to define value labels (as in Chapter 7 I recommend 1 = placebo, 2 = low dose, 3 = high dose). There were five subjects in each condition, so you need to enter 5 values of 1 into this column (so that the first 5 rows contain the value 1), followed by five values of 2, and followed by five values of 3. At this point, you should have one column with 15 rows of data entered. Next, create a second variable called **libido** and enter the 15 scores that correspond to the subject's libido. Finally, create a third variable called **partner** and use the *Labels* option to give this variable a more descriptive title of 'partner's libido'. Then, enter the 15 scores that correspond to the partner's libido. The mean values of **libido** for the subjects in the experiment are shown (with standard deviations in brackets) in the final column; this column is not required by SPSS.

Table 8.1: Data from **ViagraCov.sav**

Dose	Subjects Libido	Partner's Libido	Mean (Subjects)
Placebo	5	3	5.00 (1.22)
	5	5	
	6	6	
	6	7	
	3	1	
Low Dose	5	2	5.80 (1.48)
	4	2	
	6	4	
	8	6	
	6	5	
High Dose	5	6	5.80 (0.45)
	6	5	
	6	6	
	6	5	
	6	6	

8.1.1.   ANCOVA Using SPSS: Main Analysis

Most of the factorial ANOVA procedures include the facility to include one or more covariates. However, for simpler designs (most designs that don't involve repeated measures) it is probably best to conduct ANCOVA via the general factorial procedure. To access the main dialog box follow the menu path **Analyze⇒General Linear Model⇒Univariate...** (see Figure 8.1)[1]. The main dialog box is similar to that for one-way ANOVA, except that there is a space to specify covariates. Select **libido** and place this in the box labelled *Dependent Variable* by clicking ▶. Select **dose** and transfer it to the box labelled *Fixed Factor(s)* and then select **partner** and transfer it to the box labelled *Covariate(s)*.

---

[1] **Statistics⇒General Linear Model⇒GLM—General Factorial ...** in version 8.0 and earlier.

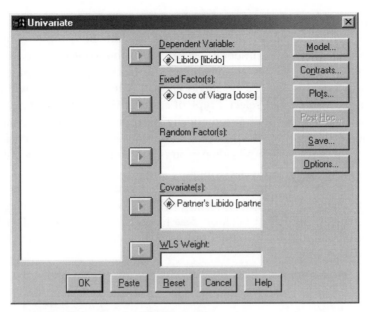

Figure 8.1: Main dialog box for GLM univariate

8.1.2. Contrasts and Other Options

There are various dialog boxes that can be accessed from the main dialog box. The first thing to notice is that if a covariate is selected, the *post hoc* tests are disabled (you cannot access this dialog box). *Post hoc* tests are not designed for situations in which a covariate is specified; however, some comparisons can still be done using contrasts.

Figure 8.2: Options for standard contrasts in GLM univariate

Click on Contrasts... to access the *contrasts* dialog box. This dialog box is different to the one we met in Chapter 7 in that you cannot enter codes to specify particular contrasts. Instead, you can specify one of several standard contrasts. These standard contrasts were listed in Table 7.6. In this example, there was a placebo control condition (coded as the first group), so a sensible set of contrasts would be simple contrasts comparing each experimental group with the control. The default contrast in SPSS is a deviation contrast and to change this we must first click on ⊠ next to the box labelled *Contrast*. A list of contrasts will drop down and you should select a type of contrast (in this case *Simple*) from this list and the list will automatically disappear. For simple contrasts you have the option of specifying a reference category (which is the category against which all other groups are compared). By default the reference category is the last category: because in this case the control group was the first category (assuming that you coded placebo as 1) we need to change this option by selecting ⊙ First . When you have selected a new contrast, you must click on Change to register this change. The final dialog box should look like Figure 8.2. Click on Continue to return to the main dialog box.

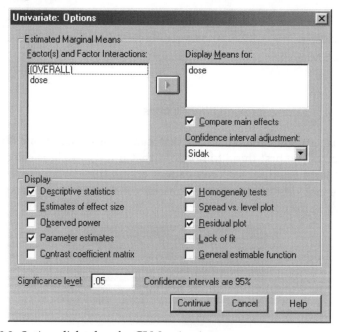

Figure 8.3: *Options dialog box for GLM univariate*

Another way to get *post hoc* tests is by clicking on Options... to access the *options* dialog box (see Figure 8.3). To specify *post hoc* tests, select the independent variable (in this case **dose**) from the box labelled *Estimated Marginal Means: Factor(s) and Factor Interactions* and transfer it to the box labelled *Display Means for* by clicking on ▣. Once a variable has been transferred, the box labelled *Compare main effects* becomes active and you should select this option (☑ Compare main effects). If this option is selected, the box labelled *Confidence interval adjustment* becomes active and you can click on ▪ to see a choice of three adjustment levels. The default is to have no adjustment and simply perform a Tukey LSD *post hoc* test (this option is not recommended); the second is to ask for a Bonferroni correction (recommended); the final option is to have a Sidak correction. The Sidak correction is similar to the Bonferroni correction but is less conservative and so should be selected if you are concerned about the loss of power associated with Bonferroni corrected values. For this example use the Sidak correction (we will use Bonferroni later in the chapter). As well as producing *post hoc* tests for the **dose** variable, placing **dose** in the *Display Means for* box will result in a table of estimated marginal means for this variable. These means provide an estimate of the *adjusted* group means (i.e. the means after the covariate has been accounted for).

The remaining options in this dialog box are as follows:

- **Descriptive statistics**: This option produces a table of means and standard deviations for each group.
- **Estimates of effect size**: This option produces the value of eta-squared (η^2), which is a measure of the size of experimental effect. In fact, eta-squared is the regression coefficient (R^2) for a non-linear regression line (i.e. a curve) assumed to pass though all group means. In a population this assumption is true, but in samples it is not: therefore, eta-squared is usually biased (see Howell, 1997, Chapter 11.11). For this reason there is little to recommend this option, and the effect size may be estimated more productively using past research or a more interpretable measure such as Cohen's F (Cohen, 1988, 1992).
- **Observed power**: This option provides an estimate of the probability that the statistical test could detect the difference between the observed group means. Again, this measure is of little use because if the *F*-test is significant then the probability that the effect was detected will, of course, be high. Likewise, if group differences were small, the observed power will be low. Observed power is of little use and I would advise that power calculations (with regard to sample size) are made before the experiment is conducted (see Cohen, 1988, 1992 and Howell, 1997 for ideas on how to do this by hand, and Field, 1998b for ideas on doing it using a computer).
- **Parameter estimates**: Produces a table of regression coefficients and their tests of significance for the variables in the regression model (see section 8.1.3.3).
- **Contrast coefficient matrix**: Produces matrices of the coding values used for any contrasts in the analysis. This option is useful only for checking which groups are being compared in which contrast.

- **H**omogeneity tests: Produces Levene's test of the homogeneity of variance assumption (see section 7.3.1).
- **Spread vs. level plot**: This option produces a chart that plots the mean of each group of a factor (*X*-axis) against the standard deviation of that group (*Y*-axis). This is a useful plot to check that there is no relationship between the mean and standard deviation. If a relationship exists then the data may need to be stabilized using a logarithmic transformation (see Howell, 1997, Chapter 11.9).
- **R**esidual plot: This option produces plots of observed-by-predicted-by-standardized residual values. These plots can be used to assess the assumption of equality of variance.

When you have selected the options required, click on Continue to return to the main dialog box. There are other options available from the main dialog box. For example, if you have several independent variables you can plot them against each other (which is useful for interpreting interaction effects—see section 8.2.4). For this analysis, there is only one independent variable and so we can click on OK to run the analysis.

8.1.3. Output from ANCOVA

8.1.3.1. Main Analysis

SPSS Output 8.1 shows (for illustrative purposes) the ANOVA table for these data when the covariate is not included. It is clear from the significance value that there are no differences in libido between the three groups; therefore Viagra seems to have no significant effect on libido. It should also be noted that the total amount of variation to be explained (SS_T) was 17.73, of which the experimental manipulation accounted for 2.13 units (SS_M), whilst 15.60 were unexplained (SS_R).

ANOVA

Libido

	Sum of Squares	df	Mean Square	F	Sig.
Dose of Viagra	2.133	2	1.067	.821	.463
Residual	15.600	12	1.300		
Total	17.733	14			

SPSS Output 8.1

SPSS Output 8.2 shows the results of Levene's test and the ANOVA table when partner's libido is included in the model as a covariate. Levene's test is non-significant, indicating that the group variances are roughly equal (hence the assumption of homogeneity of variance has been met). The format of the ANOVA table is largely the same as without the covariate, except that there is an additional row of information about the covariate (**partner**). Looking first at the significance values, it is clear that the covariate significantly predicts the dependent variable, so the subject's libido is influenced by their partner's libido. What's more interesting is that when the effect of partner's libido is removed, the effect of Viagra becomes significant (p is 0.041 which is less than 0.05). The amount of variation accounted for by the model (SS_M) has increased to 13.32 units (corrected model) of which Viagra accounts for 3.46 units. Most important, the large amount of variation in libido that is accounted for by the covariate has meant that the unexplained variance (SS_R) has been reduced to 4.41 units. Notice that SS_T has not changed; all that has changed is how that total variation is explained.

How do I interpret ANCOVA?

Levene's Test of Equality of Error Variances[a]

Dependent Variable: Libido

F	df1	df2	Sig.
.220	2	12	.806

Tests the null hypothesis that the error variance of the dependent variable is equal across groups.

a. Design: Intercept+PARTNER+DOSE

Tests of Between-Subjects Effects

Dependent Variable: Libido

Source	Type III Sum of Squares	df	Mean Square	F	Sig.
Corrected Model	13.320[a]	3	4.440	11.068	.001
Intercept	14.264	1	14.264	35.556	.000
PARTNER	11.187	1	11.187	27.886	.000
DOSE	3.464	2	1.732	4.318	.041
Error	4.413	11	.401		
Total	477.000	15			
Corrected Total	17.733	14			

a. R Squared = .751 (Adjusted R Squared = .683)

SPSS Output 8.2

This example illustrates how ANCOVA can help us to exert stricter experimental control by taking account of confounding variables to give us a 'purer' measure of effect of the experimental manipulation. Without taking account of the libido of the subjects' partners we would have concluded that Viagra had no effect on libido, yet clearly it does. However, the effect of the partner's libido seems stronger than that of Viagra. Looking back at the group means from Table 8.1 it seems pretty clear that the significant ANOVA reflects a difference between the placebo group and the two experimental groups (because the low and high dose groups have identical means whereas the placebo group has a lower mean). However, we need to check the contrasts to verify this conclusion.

SPSS Output 8.3 shows the parameter estimates selected in the *options* dialog box. These estimates are calculated using a regression analysis with **dose** split into two dummy coding variables (see section 7.1.2 and section 8.1.3.3). SPSS codes the two dummy variables such that the last category (the category coded with the highest value in the data editor—in this case the high dose group) is the reference category. This reference category (labelled dose=3 in the output) is coded with a zero for both dummy variables (see section 7.1.2 for a reminder of how dummy coding works). Dose=2, therefore, represents the difference between the group coded as 2 (low dose) and the reference category (high dose), and dose=1 represents the difference between the group coded as 1 (placebo) and the reference category (high dose). The β values literally represent the differences between the means of these groups and so the significances of the *t*-tests tell us whether the group means differ significantly. Therefore, from these estimates we could conclude that the high dose and placebo groups have similar means whereas the high and low dose groups have significantly different means. These conclusions contradict what we initially concluded from the ANOVA—can you think why? (All will be revealed in due course!) The final thing to notice is the value of β for the covariate (0.548). This value tells us that, other things being equal, if a partner's libido increases by one unit, then the subject's libido should increase by just under half a unit (although there is nothing to suggest a causal link between the two).

Parameter Estimates

Dependent Variable: Libido

Parameter	B	Std. Error	t	Sig.	95% Confidence Interval	
					Lower Bound	Upper Bound
Intercept	2.729	.647	4.219	.001	1.305	4.153
PARTNER	.548	.104	5.281	.000	.320	.777
[DOSE=1.00]	-.142	.420	-.338	.741	-1.065	.781
[DOSE=2.00]	.987	.442	2.233	.047	1.415E-02	1.960
[DOSE=3.00]	0^a	.	.	.	.	.

a. This parameter is set to zero because it is redundant.

SPSS Output 8.3

8.1.3.2. *Contrasts*

SPSS Output 8.4 shows the result of the contrast analysis specified in Figure 8.2 and compares level 2 (low dose) against level 1 (placebo) as a first comparison, and level 3 (high dose) against level 1 (placebo) as a second comparison. These contrasts are consistent with what was specified: all groups are compared to the first group. The group differences are displayed: a difference value, standard error, significance value and 95% confidence interval. These results show that the low dose group had a significantly higher libido than the placebo group (contrast 1), but that the high dose group did not differ significantly from the placebo group ($p = 0.741$). These results are consistent with the regression parameter estimates (in fact, note that contrast 2 is identical to the regression parameters for dose=1 in the previous section).

Contrast Results (K Matrix)

Dose of Viagra Simple Contrast[a]			Dependent Variable Libido
Level 2 vs. Level 1	Contrast Estimate		1.129
	Hypothesized Value		0
	Difference (Estimate - Hypothesized)		1.129
	Std. Error		.405
	Sig.		**.018**
	95% Confidence Interval for Difference	Lower Bound	.237
		Upper Bound	2.021
Level 3 vs. Level 1	Contrast Estimate		.142
	Hypothesized Value		0
	Difference (Estimate - Hypothesized)		.142
	Std. Error		.420
	Sig.		**.741**
	95% Confidence Interval for Difference	Lower Bound	-.781
		Upper Bound	1.065

a. Reference category = 1

SPSS Output 8.4

At face value, the significant effect of libido would seem to reflect a difference between the placebo group and the two Viagra groups (which have identical means), yet the contrasts so far contradict these conclusions. The reason for this inconsistency is that the initial conclusion was based on group means that had not been adjusted for the effect of the covariate. These values tell us nothing about the group differences reflected by the significant ANCOVA. SPSS Output 8.5 gives the adjusted values of the group means and it is these values that should be used for interpretation (this is the main reason for selecting the *Display Means for* option). The adjusted means show a very different pattern of responses: it looks as though the significant ANCOVA reflects a difference between the placebo and the low dose group. The high dose and placebo groups appear to have fairly similar adjusted means indicating that too much Viagra seems to lower libido back down to normal levels. These conclusions support what we know from the contrasts and regression parameters but ideally should be verified with the *post hoc* tests specified in the options menu.

Estimates

Dependent Variable: Libido

Dose of Viagra	Mean	Std. Error	95% Confidence Interval	
			Lower Bound	Upper Bound
Placebo	5.110[a]	.284	4.485	5.735
Low Dose	6.239[a]	.295	5.589	6.888
High Dose	5.252[a]	.302	4.588	5.916

a. Evaluated at covariates appeared in the model: Partner's Libido = 4.6000.

SPSS Output 8.5

SPSS Output 8.6 shows the results of the Sidak corrected *post hoc* comparisons that were requested as part of the *options* dialog box. Interestingly, the significant differences shown by the contrasts and regression parameters have gone (although the difference between the low dose and placebo group is approaching the critical value). This contradiction might result from a loss of power in the *post hoc* tests (remember that planned comparisons have greater power to detect effects than *post hoc* procedures). However, there could be other reasons why these comparisons are non-significant and we should be very cautious in our interpretation of the significant ANCOVA and subsequent comparisons.

Pairwise Comparisons

Dependent Variable: Libido

(I) Dose of Viagra	(J) Dose of Viagra	Mean Difference (I-J)	Std. Error	Sig.[a]	95% Confidence Interval for Difference[a]	
					Lower Bound	Upper Bound
Placebo	Low Dose	-1.129	.405	.052	-2.268	1.036E-02
	High Dose	-.142	.420	.983	-1.321	1.037
Low Dose	Placebo	1.129	.405	.052	-1.036E-02	2.268
	High Dose	.987	.442	.135	-.255	2.229
High Dose	Placebo	.142	.420	.983	-1.037	1.321
	Low Dose	-.987	.442	.135	-2.229	.255

Based on estimated marginal means

a. Adjustment for multiple comparisons: Sidak.

SPSS Output 8.6

8.1.3.3. Output from ANCOVA Run as a Multiple Regression

Although the ANCOVA is essentially done, it may be of interest to rerun the analysis as a hierarchical multiple regression. The output that follows comes from a regression analysis in which **partner** was entered in the first block and the two dummy variables representing the doses of Viagra were entered in a second block. As an exercise, enter these data and run the analysis yourself by adding the variable **partner** to the file **dummy.sav** used in Chapter 7. The summary of the regression model (SPSS Output 8.7) shows us the goodness-of-fit of the model first when only the covariate is used in the model, and second when both the covariate and the dummy variables are used. Therefore, the difference between the values of R^2 (0.751–0.556 = 0.195) represents the individual contribution of the dose of Viagra. Therefore, we can say that the dose of Viagra accounted for 19.5% of the variation in libido, whereas partner's libido accounted for 55.6%. This additional information provides some insight into the substantive importance of Viagra.

Can I run ANCOVA using the regression procedure?

Model Summary

Model	R	R Square	Adjusted R Square	Std. Error of the Estimate
1	.746[a]	.556	.522	.7784
2	.867[b]	.751	.683	.6334

a. Predictors: (Constant), Partner's Libido

b. Predictors: (Constant), Partner's Libido, Dummy 2, Dummy 1

ANOVA[c]

Model		Sum of Squares	df	Mean Square	F	Sig.
1	Regression	9.856	1	9.856	16.266	.001[a]
	Residual	7.877	13	.606		
	Total	17.733	14			
2	Regression	13.320	3	4.440	11.068	.001[b]
	Residual	4.413	11	.401		
	Total	17.733	14			

a. Predictors: (Constant), Partner's Libido

b. Predictors: (Constant), Partner's Libido, Dummy 2, Dummy 1

c. Dependent Variable: Libido

SPSS Output 8.7

SPSS Output 8.8 shows the remainder of the regression analysis. The table is again divided into two sections. The top half represents the effect of the covariate alone, whereas the bottom half represents the whole model (i.e. covariate and dose of Viagra included). The bottom half, therefore, contains the same values as the 'corrected model' row of the ANCOVA summary table (SPSS Output 8.2). The table of regression coefficients is more interesting. Again, this table is split into two and so the bottom of the table looks at the whole model. When the dose of Viagra is considered with the covariate, the value of β for the covariate is 0.548, which corresponds to the value in the ANCOVA parameter estimates (SPSS Output 8.3). The β values for the dummy variables represent the difference between the means of the low dose group and the placebo group (**dummy1**) and the high dose group and the placebo group (**dummy2**)—see section 7.1.2 for an explanation of why. The clever reader might notice that the means of the high and low dose groups were the same, and so the values of β should also be the same, yet they are different. This apparent anomaly is because the β values represent the differences between the *adjusted* means. The adjusted values were given in SPSS Output 8.5 and from this table we can see that:

$$\beta_{Dummy1} = \overline{X}_{Low\ (adjusted)} - \overline{X}_{Placebo\ (adjusted)} = 6.239 - 5.110 = 1.129$$

$$\beta_{Dummy2} = \overline{X}_{High\ (adjusted)} - \overline{X}_{Placebo\ (adjusted)} = 5.252 - 5.110 = 0.142$$

(8.2)

The *t*-tests conducted on these values show that the significant ANCOVA did indeed reflect a significant difference between the low dose and placebo groups. There was no significant difference between the high dose and placebo groups. To find out whether there was a difference between the low dose and high dose groups we would need to use different dummy coding (perhaps comparing the high and low to the placebo and then comparing high to low like we used for the planned comparisons in Chapter 7).

Coefficients[a]

Model		Unstandardized Coefficients		Standardized Coefficients		
		B	Std. Error	Beta	t	Sig.
1	(Constant)	3.395	.567		5.986	.000
	Partner's Libido	.465	.115	.746	4.033	.001
2	(Constant)	2.587	.538		4.812	.001
	Partner's Libido	.548	.104	.879	5.281	.000
	Dummy 1	.142	.420	.062	.338	.741
	Dummy 2	1.129	.405	.489	2.785	.018

a. Dependent Variable: Libido

SPSS Output 8.8

8.1.4.   *Additional Assumptions in ANCOVA*

When an ANCOVA is conducted we look at the overall relationship between the dependent variable and the covariate: we fit a regression line to the entire data set, ignoring to which group a subject belongs. In fitting this overall model we, therefore, assume that this overall relationship is true for all groups of subjects. If, however, the relationship between the dependent variable and covariate is different in one of the groups then this overall regression model is inaccurate (it does not represent all of the groups). This assumption is very important and is called the assumption of homogeneity of regression slopes. The best way to think of this assumption is to imagine plotting a scatterplot for each experimental condition with the covariate on one axis and the dependent variable on the other. If you then calculated, and drew, the regression line for each of these scatterplots you should find that the regression lines look more or less the same (i.e. the value of β in each group should be equal).

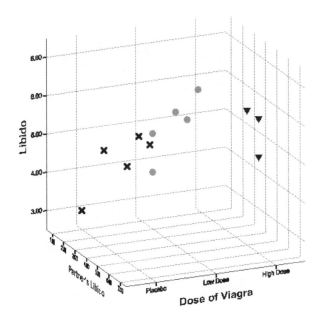

Figure 8.4: Scatterplot of libido against partner's libido for each of the experimental conditions (crosses represent the placebo group, circles the low dose group and triangles the high dose group)

Figure 8.4 shows a 3-D scatterplot that displays the relationship between partner's libido (the covariate) and the dependent variable (subject's libido) for each of the three experimental conditions. In the placebo and low dose conditions, the five points represent each subject's data; for the high dose group there are only three points because two subjects had identical data to two other subjects from that group. The regression lines are not plotted in Figure 8.4, but you should be able to imagine the line of best fit for each cluster of symbols. It should be clear that there is a positive relationship (the regression line would slope upwards from left to right) between partner's libido and subject's libido in the placebo condition (the crosses); a very similar relationship is seen in the low dose condition (the circles). However, in the high dose condition there is a negative relationship (the regression line would slope downwards from left to right). This observation gives us cause to doubt whether there is homogeneity of regression slopes.

To test the assumption of homogeneity of regression slopes we need to rerun the ANCOVA but this time use a customized model. Access the main dialog box as before and place the variables in the same boxes as before (so, the finished box should look like Figure 8.1). To customize the model we need to access the *model* dialog box (Figure 8.5) by clicking on Model… .

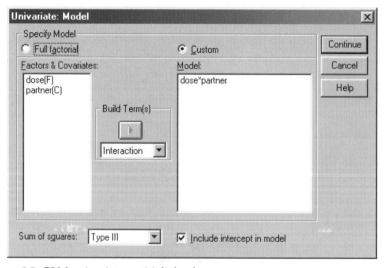

Figure 8.5: GLM univariate *model* dialog box

To customize your model, click on the circle labelled *Custom* to activate the dialog box (Figure 8.5). The variables specified in the main dialog box are listed on the left-hand side and are followed by a letter indicating the variable type (F = fixed factor, C = covariate). To test the assumption of homogeneity of regression slopes, we need to specify a model that includes only the interaction between the covariate and dependent variable. Hence, you should select both **dose** and **partner** simultaneously and then click on [▶] to move them to the box labelled *Model*. By default, the options are set up to enter interactions, so these variables will be entered as an interaction term. However, you can find out more about specifying effects in section 8.2.3. This interaction is all that we are interested in and so we can click on [Continue] to return to the main dialog box and then click on [OK] to run the analysis.

SPSS Output 8.9 shows the main summary table for the ANCOVA using only the interaction term. Look at the significance value of the covariate by dependent variable interaction (**dose*partner**), if this effect is significant then the assumption of homogeneity of regression slopes has been broken. The effect here is highly significant ($p < 0.001$); therefore the assumption is not tenable. Although this finding is not surprising given the pattern of relationships shown in Figure 8.4 it does raise concern about the main analysis, especially in the light of the marginal significance of the dependent variable and the contradictory findings of the multiple comparisons. This example illustrates why it is important to test assumptions and not to just blindly accept the results of an analysis.

Tests of Between-Subjects Effects

Dependent Variable: Libido

Source	Type III Sum of Squares	df	Mean Square	F	Sig.
Corrected Model	14.142[a]	3	4.714	14.440	.000
Intercept	15.887	1	15.887	48.665	.000
DOSE * PARTNER	14.142	3	4.714	14.440	.000
Error	3.591	11	.326		
Total	477.000	15			
Corrected Total	17.733	14			

a. R Squared = .797 (Adjusted R Squared = .742)

SPSS Output 8.9

8.2. Factorial ANOVA (Between-Groups) Using SPSS

As the name suggests, factorial ANOVA is used when you have two or more independent variables (hence it is called *factorial*). There are several types of factorial design:

- **Unrelated factorial design**: This type of experiment is where there are several independent variables and each has been measured using different subjects (between groups).

- **Related factorial design**: An experiment in which several independent variables have been measured, but the same subjects have been used in all conditions (repeated measures).
- **Mixed design**: A design in which several independent variables have been measured; some have been measured with different subjects whereas others used the same subjects.

This section extends the one-way ANOVA model to the factorial case and Chapter 9 looks at simple repeated measures designs, factorial repeated measures designs, and finally mixed designs.

8.2.1.   Two Independent Variables

An anthropologist was interested in the effects of alcohol on mate selection at night-clubs. Her rationale was that after alcohol had been consumed, subjective perceptions of physical attractiveness would become more inaccurate (the well-known 'beer-goggles effect'). She was also interested in whether this effect was different for men and women. She picked 48 students: 24 male and 24 female. She then took groups of 8 subjects to a night-club and gave them either no alcohol (subjects received placebo drinks of alcohol-free lager), 2 pints of strong lager, or 4 pints of strong lager. At the end of the evening she took a photograph of the person that the subject was chatting up. She then got a pool of independent judges to assess the attractiveness of the person in each photograph (out of 100). The data are in Table 8.2 and **goggles.sav**.

Table 8.2

Alcohol	None		2 Pints		4 Pints	
Gender	Female	Male	Female	Male	Female	Male
	65	50	70	45	55	30
	70	55	65	60	65	30
	60	80	60	85	70	30
	60	65	70	65	55	55
	60	70	65	70	55	35
	55	75	60	70	60	20
	60	75	60	80	50	45
	55	65	50	60	50	40

8.2.2.   Entering the Data and Accessing the Main Dialog Box

To enter these data into the SPSS data editor, remember this golden rule: *levels of a between-group variable go in a single column*. Applying this rule to these data, we need to create two different coding variables in the data editor. These columns will represent gender and alcohol consumption. So, create a variable called **gender** on the data editor and activate the *labels* dialog box. You should define value labels to represent the two genders. We have had a lot of experience with coding values, so you should be fairly happy about assigning numerical codes to different groups. I recommend using the code male = 0 and female = 1. Once you have done this, you can enter a code of 0 or 1 in this column indicating to which group the subject belonged. Create a second variable called **alcohol** and assign group codes by using the *labels* dialog box. I suggest that you code this variable with three values: placebo (no Alcohol) = 1, 2 pints = 2, and 4 pints = 3. You can now enter 1, 2 or 3 into this column to represent the amount of alcohol consumed by the subject. Remember that if you turn the value labels option on you will see text in the data editor rather than the numerical codes. Now, the way this coding works is as follows:

Gender	Alcohol	Subject was
0	1	Male who consumed no alcohol
0	2	Male who consumed 2 pints
0	3	Male who consumed 4 pints
1	1	Female who consumed no alcohol
1	2	Female who consumed 2 pints
1	3	Female who consumed 4 pints

Once you have created the two coding variables, you can create a third variable in which to place the values of the dependent variable. Call this variable **attract** and use the *labels* option to give it the fuller name of 'attractiveness of date'. In this example, there are two independent variables and different subjects were used in each condition: hence, we can use the general factorial ANOVA procedure in SPSS. This procedure is designed for analysing between-group factorial designs.

To access the main dialog box for a general factorial ANOVA use the file path **Analyze⇒General Linear Model⇒Univariate...**. The resulting dialog box is shown in Figure 8.6. First, select the dependent variable **attract** from the variables list on the left-hand side of the dialog box and transfer it to the space labelled *Dependent Variable* by clicking on ▣. In the space labelled *Fixed Factor(s)* we need to place any independent variables relevant to the analysis. Select **alcohol** and **gender** in the variables list (these variables can be selected simultaneously by clicking on one, holding the mouse button down and dragging the on-screen pointer over the second variable) and transfer them to the *Fixed Factor(s)* box by clicking on ▣. There are various other spaces that are available for conducting more complex analyses such as random factors ANOVA and factorial ANCOVA. Random factors ANOVA is beyond the scope of this book (interested readers should consult Jackson and Brashers, 1994) and factorial ANCOVA simply extends the principles described at the beginning of this chapter.

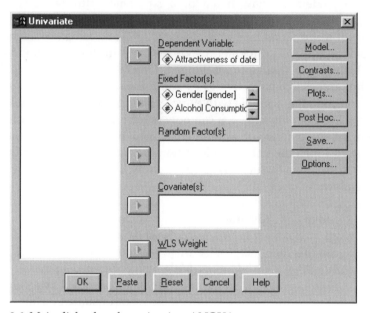

Figure 8.6: Main dialog box for univariate ANOVA

8.2.3.   Custom Models

By default SPSS conducts a full factorial analysis (i.e. it includes all of the main effects and interactions of all independent variables specified in the main dialog box). However, there may be times when you want to customize the model that you use to test for certain things. To access the *model* dialog box, click on ⎡Model...⎤ in the main dialog box (see Figure 8.7). You will notice that by default, the full factorial model is selected. Even with this selected, there is an option at the bottom to change the type of sums of squares that are used in the analysis. Although we have learnt about sums of squares and what they represent, I haven't talked about different ways of calculating sums of squares. It isn't necessary to understand the computation of the different forms of sums of squares, but it is important that you know the uses of some of the different types. By default, SPSS uses type III sums 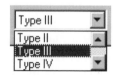 of squares, which have the advantage that they are invariant to the cell frequencies. As such, they can be used with both balanced and unbalanced (i.e. different numbers of subjects in different groups) designs, which is why they are the default option. Type IV sums of squares are like type III except that they can be used with data in which there are missing values. So, if you have any missing data in your design, you should change the sums of squares to type IV.

To customize a model, click on the circle labelled *Custom* to activate the

dialog box. The variables specified in the main dialog box will be listed on the left-hand side and will be followed, in brackets, by a letter indicating the type of variable it is (F = fixed factor, R = random factor, C = covariate). You can select one, or several, variables from this list and transfer them to the box labelled *Model* as either main effects or interactions. By default, SPSS transfers variables as interaction terms, but there are several options that allow you to enter main effects, or all two-way, three-way or four-way interactions. These options save you the trouble of having to select lots of combinations of variables (because, for example, you can select three variables, transfer them as all two-way interactions and it will create all three combinations of variables for you). Although model selection has important uses (see section 8.1.4), it is likely that you'd want to run the full factorial analysis on most occasions.

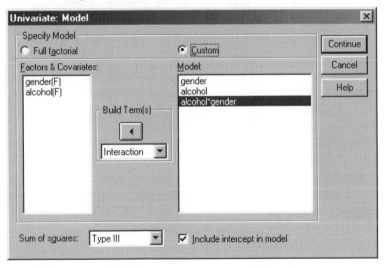

Figure 8.7: Custom models in ANOVA

8.2.4.   Graphing Interactions

Once the relevant variables have been selected, you should click on Plots... to access the dialog box in Figure 8.8. The *plots* dialog box allows you to select line graphs of your data and these graphs are very useful for interpreting interaction effects. We have only two independent variables, and so there is only one plot worth looking at (the plot that displays levels of one independent variable against the other). Select **alcohol** from the variables list on the left-hand side of the dialog box and transfer it to the space labelled *Horizontal Axis* by clicking on ▶. In the space labelled *Separate Lines* we need to place the remaining independent variable: **gender**. It doesn't actually matter which way round the variables are plotted; you should use your discretion as to which way produces the most sensible graph. When you have moved the two independent variables to the appropriate box, click on <u>Add</u> and this plot will be added to the list at the bottom of the box. It should be clear that you can plot a whole variety of graphs, and if you had a third independent variable, you have the option of plotting different graphs for each level of that third variable. The plot that has been selected will help us to interpret any interaction between gender and alcohol consumption. When you have finished specifying graphs, click on Continue to return to the main dialog box.

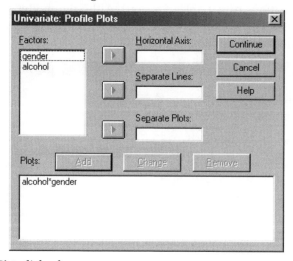

Figure 8.8: *Plots* dialog box

8.2.5.   Post Hoc Tests

Once we have specified the main analysis and plots, we can conduct either contrasts or *post hoc* tests. Contrasts can be defined in the same way as shown in section 8.1.2, whereas *post hoc* tests are obtained by clicking on Post Hoc... in the main dialog box to access the *post hoc* tests dialog box (Figure 8.9). The variable **gender** has only two levels and so we don't need to select *post hoc* tests for that variable (because any significant effects can only reflect differences between males and females). However, there were three levels of the **alcohol** variable (no alcohol, 2 pints and 4 pints): hence it is necessary to conduct *post hoc* tests. First, you should select the variable **alcohol** from the box labelled *Factors* and transfer it to the box labelled *Post Hoc Tests for*. My recommendations for which *post hoc* procedures to use are in section 7.1.5 (and I don't want to repeat myself). Suffice to say you should select the ones in Figure 8.9! Click on [Continue] to return to the main dialog box.

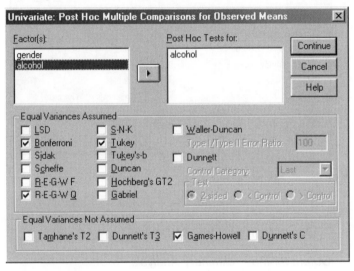

Figure 8.9: Dialog box for *post hoc* tests

8.2.6.   Options

Click on [Options...] to activate the dialog box in Figure 8.10. The options for factorial ANOVA are fairly straightforward. First you can ask for some descriptive statistics, which will display a table of the means, standard deviations, standard errors, ranges and confidence intervals for the means of each group. This is a useful option to select because it assists in interpreting the final results. A vital option to select is the homogeneity of variance tests. As with the *t*-test, there is an assumption that the variances of the groups are equal and selecting this option tests that this assumption has been met. SPSS uses Levene's test, which tests the hypothesis that the variances of each group are equal. Once these options have been selected click on [Continue] to return to the main dialog box, then click on [OK] run the analysis.

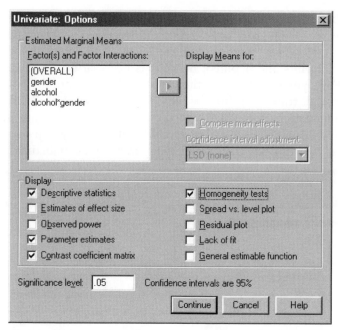

Figure 8.10: Dialog box for *options*

8.2.7.   Output from Factorial ANOVA

8.2.7.1. Output for the Preliminary Analysis

SPSS Output 8.10 shows the initial output from factorial ANOVA. This table of descriptive statistics is produced because we asked for descriptives in the *options* dialog box (see Figure 8.10) and it displays the means, standard deviations and number of subjects in all conditions of the experiment. So, for example, we can see that in the placebo condition, males typically chatted up a female that was rated at about 67% on the attractiveness scale, whereas females selected a mate that was rated as 61% on that scale. These means will be useful in interpreting the direction of any effects that emerge in the analysis.

Descriptive Statistics

	Alcohol Consumption	Gender	Mean	Std. Deviation	N
Attractiveness of Date	Placebo	Male	66.8750	10.3294	8
		Female	60.6250	4.9552	8
		Total	63.7500	8.4656	16
	2 Pints	Male	66.8750	12.5178	8
		Female	62.5000	6.5465	8
		Total	64.6875	9.9111	16
	4 Pints	Male	35.6250	10.8356	8
		Female	57.5000	7.0711	8
		Total	46.5625	14.3433	16
	Total	Male	56.4583	18.5026	24
		Female	60.2083	6.3381	24
		Total	58.3333	13.8123	48

SPSS Output 8.10

8.2.7.2. Levene's Test

SPSS Output 8.11 shows the results of Levene's test. We came across Levene's test in Chapters 6 and 7. In short, Levene's test is used to assess the tenability of the assumption of equal variances ('homogeneity of variance'). Levene's test looks at whether there are any significant differences between group variances and so a non-significant result (as found here) is indicative of the assumption being met. If Levene's test is significant then steps must be taken to equalize the variances through data transformation (taking the square root of all values of the dependent variable can sometimes achieve this goal—see Howell, 1997, pp. 323-329).

Levene's Test of Equality of Error Variances

	F	df1	df2	Sig.
Attractiveness of Date	1.527	5	42	.202

Tests the null hypothesis that the error variance of the dependent variable is equal across groups.

a. Design: Intercept+ALCOHOL+GENDER+ALCOHOL * GENDER

SPSS Output 8.11

8.2.7.3. The Main ANOVA Table

SPSS Output 8.12 is the most important part of the output because it tells us whether any of the independent variables have had an effect on the dependent variable. The important things to look at in the table are the significance values of the independent variables. The first thing to notice is that there is a significant effect of alcohol (because the significance value is less than 0.05). The *F*-ratio is highly significant, indicating that the amount of alcohol consumed significantly affected who the participant would try to chat up. We could report this effect as follows: 'There was a significant main effect of the amount of alcohol consumed at the night-club, on the attractiveness of the mate they selected (F (2, 14) = 20.07, $p < 0.001$).' What this means is that overall, when we ignore whether the subject was male or female, the amount of alcohol influenced their mate selection. The best way to see what this means is to look at a bar chart of the average mark for each level of alcohol (ignore gender completely). This graph can be plotted by using the means in SPSS Output 8.10 (see, I told you that those values would come in useful!) and the <u>Bar</u>... option of the <u>Graphs</u> menu.

Tests of Between-Subjects Effects

Dependent Variable: Attractiveness of Date

Source	Type III Sum of Squares	df	Mean Square	F	Sig.
Corrected Model	5479.167[a]	5	1095.833	13.197	.000
Intercept	163333.333	1	163333.333	1967.025	.000
ALCOHOL	3332.292	2	1666.146	**20.065**	**.000**
GENDER	168.750	1	168.750	**2.032**	**.161**
GENDER * ALCOHOL	1978.125	2	989.062	**11.911**	**.000**
Error	3487.500	42	83.036		
Total	172300.000	48			
Corrected Total	8966.667	47			

a. R Squared = .611 (Adjusted R Squared = .565)

SPSS Output 8.12

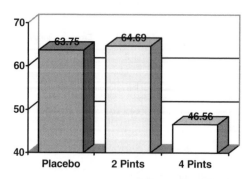

Figure 8.11: Graph showing the main effect of alcohol

Figure 8.11 clearly shows that when you ignore gender the overall attractiveness of the selected mate is very similar when no alcohol has been drunk, and when 2 pints have been drunk (the means of these groups are approximately equal). Hence, this significant main effect is *likely* to reflect the drop in the attractiveness of the selected mates when 4 pints have been drunk. This finding seems to indicate that a person is willing to accept a less attractive mate after 4 pints.

The next part of SPSS Output 8.12 tells us about the main effect of gender. This time the *F*-ratio is not significant ($p = 0.161$, which is larger than 0.05). This finding could be reported as follows: 'There was a non-significant main effect of gender on the attractiveness of selected mates ($F (1, 42) = 2.03, p = 0.161$).' What this effect means is that overall, when we ignore how much alcohol had been drunk, the gender of the subject did not influence the attractiveness of the partner that the subject selected. In other words, other things being equal, males and females selected equally attractive mates. Drawing a bar chart of the average attractiveness of mates for men and women (ignoring how much alcohol had been consumed) reveals the meaning of this main effect. Figure 8.12 shows that the average attractiveness of the partners of male and female subjects was fairly similar (the means are different by only 4%). Therefore, this non-significant effect reflects the fact that the mean attractiveness was similar. We can conclude from this that, *ceteris paribus*, men and women chose equally attractive partners.

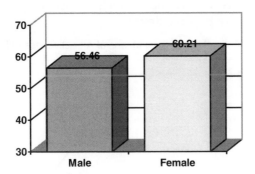

Figure 8.12: Graph to show the effect of gender on mate selection

Finally, SPSS Output 8.12 tells us about the interaction between the effect of gender and the effect of alcohol. The *F* value is highly significant (because the *p* value is less than 0.05). This effect could be reported as follows: 'There was a significant interaction effect between the amount of alcohol consumed and the gender of the person selecting a mate, on the attractiveness of the partner selected ($F (2, 42) = 11.91, p < 0.0001$).' What this actually means is that the effect of alcohol on mate selection was different for male subjects than it was for females. The SPSS output includes a plot that we asked for (see Figure 8.8) which tells us something about the nature of this interaction effect (see Figure 8.13).

Figure 8.13 clearly shows that for women, alcohol has very little effect: the attractiveness of their selected partners is quite stable across the three conditions (as shown by the near-horizontal line). However, for the men, the attractiveness of their partners is stable when only a small amount has been drunk, but rapidly declines when more is drunk. Non-parallel lines usually indicate a significant interaction effect. In this particular graph the lines actually cross, which indicates a fairly large interaction between independent variables. The interaction tells us that alcohol has little effect on mate selection until 4 pints have been drunk and that the effect of alcohol is prevalent only in male subjects. In short, the results show that women maintain high standards in their mate selection regardless of alcohol, whereas men have a few beers and then try to get off with anything on legs! One interesting point that these data demonstrate is that we earlier concluded that alcohol significantly affected how attractive a mate was selected (the **alcohol** main effect); however, the interaction effect tells us that this is true only in males (females are clearly unaffected). This shows how misleading main effects can be: it is usually the interactions between variables that are most interesting in a factorial design.

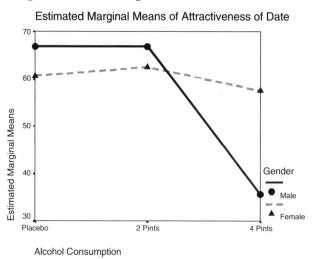

Figure 8.13: Graph of the interaction of gender and alcohol consumption in mate selection

8.2.7.4. Post Hoc Analysis

The *post hoc* tests (SPSS Output 8.13) break down the main effect of alcohol and can be interpreted as if a one-way ANOVA had been conducted on the **alcohol** variable (i.e. the reported effects for alcohol are collapsed with regard to gender). The Bonferroni and Games-Howell tests show the same pattern of results: when subjects had drunk no alcohol or 2 pints of alcohol, they selected equally attractive mates. However, after 4 pints had been consumed, participants selected significantly less attractive mates than after both 2 pints ($p < 0.001$) and no alcohol ($p < 0.001$). It is interesting to note that the mean attractiveness of partners after no alcohol and 2 pints were so similar that the probability of the obtained difference between those means is 1 (i.e. completely probable!). The Tukey test and REGWQ test confirm that the means of the placebo and 2 pint conditions were equal whereas the mean of the 4 pint group was different. It should be noted that these *post hoc* tests ignore the interactive effect of gender and alcohol.

In summary, we should conclude that alcohol has an effect on the attractiveness of selected mates. Overall, after a relatively small dose of alcohol (2 pints) humans are still in control of their judgements and the attractiveness levels of chosen partners are consistent with a control group (no alcohol consumed). However, after a greater dose of alcohol, the attractiveness of chosen mates decreases significantly. This effect is what is referred to as the 'beer-goggles effect'! More interestingly, the interaction shows a gender difference in the beer-goggles effect. Specifically, it looks as though men are significantly more likely to pick less attractive mates when drunk. Women, in comparison, manage to maintain their standards despite being drunk. What we still don't know is whether women will become susceptible to the beer-goggles effect at higher doses of alcohol.

Multiple Comparisons

Dependent Variable: Attractiveness of Date

	(I) Alcohol Consumption	(J) Alcohol Consumption	Mean Difference (I-J)	Std. Error	Sig.	95% Confidence Interval Lower Bound	95% Confidence Interval Upper Bound
Bonferroni	Placebo	2 Pints	-.9375	3.222	1.000	-8.9714	7.0964
		4 Pints	17.1875*	3.222	.000	9.1536	25.2214
	2 Pints	Placebo	.9375	3.222	1.000	-7.0964	8.9714
		4 Pints	18.1250*	3.222	.000	10.0911	26.1589
	4 Pints	Placebo	-17.1875*	3.222	.000	-25.2214	-9.1536
		2 Pints	-18.1250*	3.222	.000	-26.1589	-10.0911
Games-Howell	Placebo	2 Pints	-.9375	3.222	.955	-8.9810	7.1060
		4 Pints	17.1875*	3.222	.001	6.7981	27.5769
	2 Pints	Placebo	.9375	3.222	.955	-7.1060	8.9810
		4 Pints	18.1250*	3.222	.001	7.3104	28.9396
	4 Pints	Placebo	-17.1875*	3.222	.001	-27.5769	-6.7981
		2 Pints	-18.1250*	3.222	.001	-28.9396	-7.3104

Based on observed means.

*. The mean difference is significant at the .05 level.

Attractiveness of Date

	Alcohol Consumption	N	Subset 1	Subset 2
Tukey HSD[a,b]	4 Pints	16	46.5625	
	Placebo	16		63.7500
	2 Pints	16		64.6875
	Sig.		1.000	.954
Ryan-Einot-Gabriel-Welsch Range[b]	4 Pints	16	46.5625	
	Placebo	16		63.7500
	2 Pints	16		64.6875
	Sig.		1.000	.772

Means for groups in homogeneous subsets are displayed.
Based on Type III Sum of Squares
The error term is Mean Square(Error) = 83.036.

a. Uses Harmonic Mean Sample Size = 16.000.

b. Alpha = .05.

SPSS Output 8.13

8.3.   Further Reading

Howell, D. C. (1997). *Statistical methods for psychology* (4th edition). Belmont, CA: Duxbury. Chapters 13 and 16.

Roberts, M. J. & Russo, R. (1999). *A student's guide to analysis of variance.* London: Routledge. Chapters 8, 9 and 10 are good introductions to factorial designs.

Wildt, A. R. & Ahtola, O. (1978). *Analysis of covariance.* Sage university paper series on quantitative applications in the social sciences, 07-012. Newbury Park, CA: Sage. This text is pretty high level but very comprehensive.

9 Repeated Measures Designs (GLM 3)

9.1. One Independent Variable

'Repeated measure' is a term used when the same subjects participate in all conditions of an experiment. For example, you might test the effects of alcohol on enjoyment of a party. Some people can drink a lot of alcohol without really feeling the consequences, whereas others, like myself, only have to sniff a pint of lager and they fall to the floor and pretend to be a fish. Therefore, it is important to control for individual differences in tolerance to alcohol. To control these individual differences we can test the same people in all conditions of the experiment: we would test each person after they had consumed one pint, two pints, three pints and four pints of lager. After each drink the subject could be given a questionnaire assessing their enjoyment of the party. As such, every subject provides a score representing their enjoyment before the experimental manipulation (no alcohol consumed), after one pint, after two pints and so on. This design is said to use a repeated measure.

  This type of design has several advantages. Most important, it reduces the unsystematic variability in the design (see Chapter 6) and so provides greater power to detect effects. Repeated measures are also more economical because fewer subjects are required. However, there is a disadvantage too. In between-groups ANOVA the accuracy of the F-test depends upon the assumption that scores in different conditions are independent (Scariano and Davenport, 1987, have documented some of the consequences of violating this assumption). When repeated measures are used this assumption is violated: scores taken under different experimental conditions are likely to be related because they come from the same subjects. As such, the conventional F-test will lack accuracy. The relationship between scores in different treatment conditions means that an additional assumption has to be made and, put simplistically, we assume that the relationship between pairs of experimental conditions is similar (i.e. the level of dependence between experimental conditions is roughly equal). This assumption is called the assumption of *sphericity*.

9.1.1.   *What is Sphericity?*

Most of us are taught that it is crucial to have homogeneity of variance between conditions when analysing data from *different* subjects, but often we are left to assume that this problem 'goes away' in repeated measures designs. This is not so, and the assumption of sphericity can be likened to the assumption of homogeneity of variance in between-group ANOVA. Sphericity (denoted by ε and sometimes referred to as *circularity*) is a more general condition of *compound symmetry*. Compound symmetry holds true when both the variances across conditions are equal (this is the same as the homogeneity of variance assumption in between-group designs) and the covariances between pairs of conditions are equal. So, we assume that the variation within experimental conditions is fairly similar and that no two conditions are any more dependent than any other two. Although compound symmetry has been shown to be a sufficient condition for ANOVA using repeated measure data, it is not a necessary condition. Sphericity is a less restrictive form of compound symmetry (in fact much of the early research into repeated measures ANOVA confused compound symmetry with sphericity). Sphericity refers to the equality of variances of the *differences* between treatment levels. So, if you were to take each pair of treatment levels, and calculate the differences between each pair of scores, then it is necessary that these differences have equal variances.

9.1.2.   *How is Sphericity Measured?*

The simplest way to see whether the assumption of sphericity has been met is to calculate the differences between pairs of scores in all combinations of the treatment levels. Once this has been done, you can calculate the variance of these differences. Table 9.1 shows data from an experiment with three conditions. The differences between pairs of scores are computed for each subject and the variance for each set of differences is calculated. We saw above that sphericity is met when these variances are roughly equal. For these data, sphericity will hold when:

$$\text{variance}_{A-B} \approx \text{variance}_{A-C} \approx \text{variance}_{B-C}$$

In these data there is some deviation from sphericity because the variance of the differences between conditions A and B (15.7) is greater than the variance of the differences between A and C and between B and C (10.3). However, these data have *local circularity* (or local sphericity) because two of the variances of differences are identical. Therefore, the sphericity assumption has been met for any multiple comparisons involving these conditions (for a discussion of local circularity see

Rouanet and Lépine, 1970). The deviation from sphericity in the data in Table 9.1 does not seem too severe (all variances are *roughly* equal), but can we assess whether a deviation is severe enough to warrant action?

Table 9.1: Hypothetical data to illustrate the calculation of the variance of the differences between conditions

Group A	Group B	Group C	A–B	A–C	B–C
10	12	8	–2	2	5
15	15	12	0	3	3
25	30	20	–5	5	10
35	30	28	5	7	2
30	27	20	3	10	7
		Variance:	15.7	10.3	10.3

9.1.3.   *Assessing the Severity of Departures from Sphericity*

SPSS produces a test known as Mauchly's test, which tests the hypothesis that the variances of the differences between conditions are equal. Therefore, if Mauchly's test statistic is significant (i.e. has a probability value less than 0.05) we should conclude that there are significant differences between the variances of differences, *ergo* the condition of sphericity is not met. If, however, Mauchly's test statistic is non-significant (i.e. $p > 0.05$) then it is reasonable to conclude that the variances of differences are not significantly different (i.e. they are roughly equal). So, in short, if Mauchly's test is significant then we must be wary of the F-ratios produced by the computer.

9.1.4.   *What is the Effect of Violating the Assumption of Sphericity?*

Rouanet and Lépine (1970) provided a detailed account of the validity of the F-ratio under violations of the sphericity assumption. They argued that there are two different F-ratios that can be used to assess treatment comparisons, labelled F' and F'' respectively. F' refers to an F-ratio derived from the mean squares of the comparison in question and the specific error term for the comparison of interest—this is the F-ratio normally used. F'' is derived not from the specific error mean square but from the total error mean squares for *all* repeated measures comparisons. Rouanet and Lépine (1970) argued that F' is less powerful than F'' and so it may be the case that this test statistic misses genuine effects. In addition, they showed that for F' to be valid sphericity must hold for the *specific comparison in question* (see also Mendoza et al., 1976). F'' requires only *overall* circularity (i.e. the whole data set must be circular) but because of the non-reciprocal nature of circularity and compound symmetry, F'' does not require compound symmetry whilst F' does. So, given that F' is the statistic generally used, the effect of violating sphericity is a loss of power (compared to when F'' is used) and a test statistic (F-ratio) which simply cannot be compared to tabulated values of the F-distribution (for more details see Field, 1998a).

9.2.   Repeated Measures ANOVA Using SPSS

9.2.1.   The Main Analysis

The best way to illustrate some of the problems of repeated measure designs, and how to overcome them, is through an example. There is often concern among students as to the consistency of marking between lecturers. It is common that lecturers obtain reputations for being 'hard' or 'light' markers but there is often little to substantiate these reputations. A group of students investigated the consistency of marking by submitting the same essays to four different lecturers. The mark given by each lecturer was recorded for each of the eight essays. It was important that the same essays were used for all lecturers because this eliminated any individual differences in the standard of work that each lecturer marked. This design is repeated measures because every lecturer marked every essay. The independent variable was the lecturer who marked the report and the dependent variable was the percentage mark given.

Table 9.2: Data for essay marks example

Essay	Tutor 1 (Dr. Field)	Tutor 2 (Dr. Smith)	Tutor 3 (Dr. Scrote)	Tutor 4 (Dr. Death)
1	62	58	63	64
2	63	60	68	65
3	65	61	72	65
4	68	64	58	61
5	69	65	54	59
6	71	67	65	50
7	78	66	67	50
8	75	73	75	45

In Chapter 1 we came across the golden rule of the data editor: *each row represents data from one subject while each column represents a level of a variable.* Therefore, separate columns represent levels of a repeated measure variable. As such, there is no need for a coding variable (as with between-subject designs). The data are in Table 9.2 and can be entered into the SPSS data editor in the same format as this table (you don't need to include the column labelled *Essay*, it is included only to clarify that the tutors marked the same pieces of work). To begin with, create a variable called **tutor1** and use the *labels* dialog box to give this variable a full title of 'Dr. Field'. In the next column, create a variable called **tutor2**, and give this variable a full title of 'Dr. Smith'. The principle should now be clear: so, apply it to create the remaining variables called **tutor3** and **tutor4**.

To conduct an ANOVA using a repeated measures design, select the *define factors* dialog box by following the menu path **Analyze**⇒**General Linear Model**⇒**Repeated Measures** .... In the *define factors* dialog box (Figure 9.1), you are asked to supply a name for the within-subject (repeated measures) variable. In this case the repeated measures variable was the lecturer who marked the report, so replace the word *factor1* with the word *tutor*. The name you give to the repeated measure variable is restricted to eight characters. When you have given the repeated measure factor a name, you have to tell the computer how many levels there were to that variable (i.e. how many experimental conditions there were). In this case, there were four tutors, so we have to enter the number 4 into the box labelled *Number of Levels*. Click on ⌐Add⌐ to add this variable to the list of repeated measures variables. This variable will now appear in the white box at the bottom of the dialog box and appears as *tutor(4)*. If your design has several within-subject variables then you can add more factors to the list. When you have entered all of the within-subject factors that were measured click on ⌐Define⌐ to go to the main dialog box.

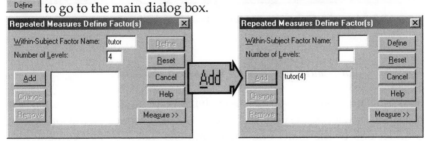

Figure 9.1: *Define factors* dialog box for repeated measures ANOVA

The main dialog box (Figure 9.2) has a space labelled Within-Subjects *Variables* that contains a list of four question marks followed by a number. These question marks are for the variables representing the four levels of the independent variable. The variables corresponding to these levels should be selected and placed in the appropriate space. We have only four variables in the data editor, so it is possible to select all four variables at once (by clicking on the variable at the top, holding the mouse button down and dragging down over the other variables). The selected variables can then be transferred by clicking on ▸. When all four variables have been transferred, you can select various options for the analysis. There are a number of options that can be accessed with the buttons at the bottom of the main dialog box. These options are similar to the ones we have already encountered.

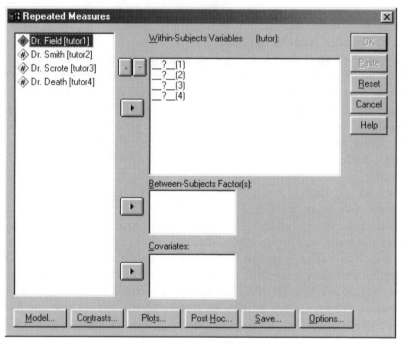

Figure 9.2: Main dialog box for repeated measures ANOVA

9.2.2.   *Defining Contrasts for Repeated Measures*

It is not possible to specify user-defined planned comparisons for repeated measures designs in SPSS. However, there is the option to conduct one of the many standard contrasts that we have come across previously (see section 8.1.2 for details of changing contrasts). If you click on ⎡Contrasts…⎤ in the main dialog box you can access the *contrasts* dialog box (Figure 9.3). The default contrast is a polynomial contrast, but to change this default select a variable in the box labelled *Factors*, click on ⎡▾⎤ next to the box labelled *Contrast*, select a contrast from the list and then click on ⎡Change⎤. If you choose to conduct a simple contrast then you can specify whether you would like to compare groups against the first or last category. The first category would be the one entered as (1) in the main dialog box and, for these data, the last category would be the one entered as (4). Therefore, the order in which you enter variables in the main dialog box is important for the contrasts you choose.

There is no particularly good contrast for the data we have (the simple contrast is not very useful because we have no control category) so I suggest using the *repeated* contrast, which will compare each tutor against the previous tutor. This contrast can be useful in repeated measure designs in which the levels of the independent variable have a meaningful order. An example is if you have measured the dependent variable at successive points in time, or administered increasing doses of a drug. When you have selected this contrast, click on Continue to return to the main dialog box.

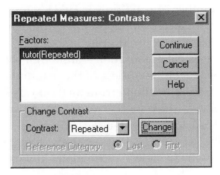

Figure 9.3: Repeated measures contrasts

9.2.3. *Post Hoc Tests and Additional Options*

There are important considerations when thinking about which *post hoc* tests to use. The violation of sphericity has implications for multiple comparisons. Boik (1981) provided an estimable account of the effects of non-sphericity on *post hoc* tests in repeated measures designs, and concluded that even very small departures from sphericity produce large biases in the *F*-test. He recommends against using these tests for repeated measure contrasts. When experimental error terms are small, the power to detect relatively strong effects can be as low as 0.05 (when sphericity = 0.80). Boik argues that the situation for *multiple* comparisons cannot be improved and concludes by recommending a multivariate analogue. Mitzel and Games (1981) found that when sphericity does not hold ($\varepsilon <$ 1) the pooled error term conventionally employed in pairwise comparisons resulted in non-significant differences between two means declared significant (i.e. a lenient type 1 error rate) or undetected differences (a conservative type 1 error rate). Mitzel and Games, therefore, recommended the use of separate error terms for each comparison. Maxwell (1980) systematically tested the power and alpha levels for five *post hoc* tests under repeated measures conditions. The tests assessed were Tukey's wholly significant difference (WSD) test which uses a pooled error term; Tukey's procedure but with a separate error term with either $(n–1)$ *df* (labelled SEP1) or $(n–1)(k–1)$ *df* (labelled SEP2); Bonferroni's procedure (BON); and a multivariate approach—the Roy-Bose simultaneous confidence interval (SCI). Maxwell tested these *a priori* procedures varying the sample size, number of levels of the repeated factor and departure from sphericity. He found that the multivariate approach was always 'too conservative for practical use' (p. 277) and this was most extreme when *n* (the number of subjects) is small relative to *k* (the number of conditions). Tukey's test inflated the alpha rate unacceptably with increasing departures from sphericity even when a separate error term was used (SEP1 and SEP2). The Bonferroni method, however, was extremely robust (although *slightly* conservative) and controlled alpha levels regardless of the manipulation. Therefore, in terms of type I error rates the Bonferroni method was best.

In terms of test power (the type II error rate) for a small sample ($n = 8$) Maxwell found WSD to be most powerful under conditions of non-sphericity, but this advantage was severely reduced when $n = 15$. Keselman and Keselman (1988) extended Maxwell's work within unbalanced designs. They too used Tukey's WSD, a modified WSD (with non-pooled error variance), Bonferroni *t*-statistics, and a multivariate approach, and found that when unweighted means were used (with unbalanced designs) none of the four tests could control the type 1 error rate. When weighted means were used only the multivariate tests could limit alpha rates although Bonferroni *t*-statistics were considerably better than the two Tukey methods. In terms of power they concluded that 'as the number of repeated treatment levels increases, BON is substantially more powerful than SCI' (p. 223).

In summary, when sphericity is violated the Bonferroni method seems to be generally the most robust of the univariate techniques, especially in terms of power and control of the type I error rate. When sphericity is definitely not violated, Tukey's test can be used. In either case, the Games-Howell procedure, which uses a pooled error term, is preferable to Tukey's test.

For readers using versions of SPSS before version 7.0, this discussion is academic, because as those readers will discover there is no facility for producing *post hoc* tests for repeated measures designs in these earlier versions! So, why have I included this discussion of which techniques are best? Well, for one thing it is possible to rerun the analysis as a between-group design and make use of the *post hoc* procedures. However, as noted above, most procedures perform very badly with related data (especially if sphericity has been violated) and so I strongly recommend against this approach. However, there are syntax files available for conducting repeated measures *post hoc* tests (available at http://www.spss.com/tech/macros/). Of these macros the Dunn-Sidak method is probably best because it is less conservative than Bonferroni corrected comparisons. To those readers who do not have access to the internet, or find the syntax window puzzling, you can apply Bonferroni comparisons by using the paired *t*-test procedure. Conduct *t*-tests on all pairs of levels of the independent variable, then apply a Bonferroni correction to the probability at which you accept any of these tests. This correction is achieved by dividing the probability value (0.05) by the number of *t*-tests conducted. The resulting probability value should be used as the criterion for statistical significance. So, for example, if we compared all levels of the independent variable of the essay data, we would make six comparisons in all and so the appropriate significance level would be $0.05/6 = 0.0083$. Therefore, we would accept *t*-tests that had a significance value less than 0.0083. One way to salvage what power you can from this procedure is to compare only groups between which you expect differences to arise (rather than comparing all pairs of treatment levels). The fewer tests you perform, the less you have to correct the significance level, and the more power you retain.

The good news for people using SPSS versions 7.5 and beyond is that some *post hoc* procedures are available for repeated measures. However, they are not accessed through the usual *post hoc* test dialog box. Instead, they can be found as part of the additional options. These options can be accessed by clicking 🔲Options... in the main dialog box to open the *GLM repeated measures: options* dialog box (see Figure 9.4). To specify *post hoc* tests, select the repeated measures variable (in this case **tutor**) from the box labelled *Estimated Marginal Means: Factor(s) and Factor Interactions* and transfer it to the box labelled *Display Means for* by clicking on 🔲. Once a variable has been transferred, the box labelled *Compare main effects* becomes active and you should select this option (☑ Compare main effects). If this option is selected, the box labelled *Confidence interval adjustment* becomes active and you can click on 🔽 to see a choice of three adjustment levels. The default is to have no adjustment and simply perform a Tukey LSD *post hoc* test (this is not recommended). The second option is a Bonferroni correction (recommended for the reasons mentioned above), and the final option is a Sidak correction, which should be selected if you are concerned about the loss of power associated with Bonferroni corrected values.

The *options* dialog box (Figure 9.4) has other useful options too. You can ask for descriptive statistics, which will provide the means, standard deviations and number of subjects for each level of the independent variable. You can also ask for a transformation matrix, which provides the coding values for any contrast selected in the *contrasts* dialog box (Figure 9.3) and is very useful for interpreting the contrasts in more complex designs. SPSS can also be asked to print out the hypothesis, error, and residual sum of squares and cross-product matrices (SSCPs) and we shall learn about the importance of these matrices in Chapter 10. The option for homogeneity of variance tests will be active only when there is a between-group factor as well (mixed designs). You can also change the level of significance at which to test any *post hoc* tests; generally, the 0.05 level is acceptable. When you have selected the options of interest, click on ⎣Continue⎦ to return to the main dialog box, and then click on ⎣ OK ⎦ to run the analysis.

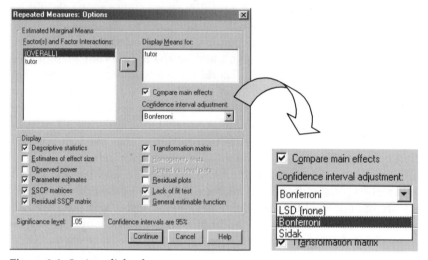

Figure 9.4: *Options* dialog box

9.2.4.   *Output for Repeated Measures ANOVA*

9.2.4.1.   *Descriptives and other Diagnostics*

SPSS Output 9.1 shows the initial diagnostics statistics. First, we are told the variables that represent each level of the independent variable. This box is useful to check that the variables were entered in the correct order. The next table provides basic descriptive statistics for the four levels of the independent variable. From this table we can see that, on average, Dr. Field gave the highest marks to the essays (that's because I'm so nice you see … or it could be because I'm stupid and so have low academic standards!). Dr. Death, on the other hand, gave very low grades. These mean values are useful for interpreting any effects that may emerge from the main analysis.

Within-Subjects Factors

Measure: MEASURE_1

TUTOR	Dependent Variable
1	TUTOR1
2	TUTOR2
3	TUTOR3
4	TUTOR4

Descriptive Statistics

	Mean	Std. Deviation	N
Dr. Field	68.8750	5.6426	8
Dr. Smith	64.2500	4.7132	8
Dr. Scrote	65.2500	6.9230	8
Dr. Death	57.3750	7.9091	8

SPSS Output 9.1

9.2.4.2. *Assessing and Correcting for Sphericity*

In section 9.1.3 you were told that SPSS produces a test of whether the data violate the assumption of sphericity. The next part of the output contains information about this test. Mauchly's test should be non-significant if we are to assume that the condition of sphericity has been met. SPSS Output 9.2 shows Mauchly's test for the tutor data, and the important column is the one containing the significance value. The significance value (0.043) is less than the critical value of 0.05, so we accept that the variances of the differences between levels are significantly different. In other words the assumption of sphericity has been violated. Knowing that we have violated this assumption a pertinent question is: how should we proceed?

Mauchly's Test of Sphericity[a]

Measure: MEASURE_1

Within Subjects Effect	Mauchly's W	Approx. Chi-Square	df	Sig.	Epsilon[b] Greenhouse-Geisser	Huynh-Feldt	Lower-bound
TUTOR	.131	11.628	5	.043	.558	.712	.333

Tests the null hypothesis that the error covariance matrix of the orthonormalized transformed dependent variables is proportional to an identity matrix.

a. Design: Intercept Within Subjects Design: TUTOR

b. May be used to adjust the degrees of freedom for the averaged tests of significance. Corrected tests are displayed in the layers (by default) of the Tests of Within Subjects Effects table.

SPSS Output 9.2

If data violate the sphericity assumption there are a number of corrections that can be applied to produce a valid *F*-ratio. SPSS produces three corrections based upon the estimates of sphericity advocated by Greenhouse and Geisser (1959) and Huynh and Feldt (1976). Both of these estimates give rise to a correction factor that is applied to the degrees of freedom used to assess the observed *F*-ratio. The calculation of these estimates is beyond the scope of this book (interested readers should consult Girden, 1992); we need know only that the three estimates differ. The Greenhouse-Geisser estimate (usually denoted as $\hat{\varepsilon}$) varies between $1/k-1$ (where *k* is the number of repeated measures conditions) and 1. The closer that $\hat{\varepsilon}$ is to 1.00, the more homogeneous the variances of differences, and hence the closer the data are to being spherical. In a situation in which there are four conditions (as with our data) the lower limit of $\hat{\varepsilon}$ will be 1/(4–1), or 0.33 (known as the lower-bound estimate of sphericity). SPSS Output 9.2 shows that the calculated value of $\hat{\varepsilon}$ is 0.558. This is closer to the lower limit of 0.33 than it is to the upper limit of 1 and it therefore represents a substantial deviation from sphericity.

Huynh and Feldt (1976) reported that when the Greenhouse-Geisser estimate is greater than 0.75 too many false null hypotheses fail to be rejected (i.e. the correction is too conservative) and Collier et al. (1967) showed that this was also true with the sphericity estimate as high as 0.90. Huynh and Feldt, therefore, proposed their own less conservative correction (usually denoted as $\tilde{\varepsilon}$). However, Maxwell and Delaney (1990) report that $\tilde{\varepsilon}$ overestimates sphericity. Stevens (1992) therefore recommends taking an average of the two and adjusting the *df* by this averaged value. Girden (1992) recommends that when estimates of sphericity are greater than 0.75 then the Huynh-Feldt correction should be used, but when sphericity estimates are less than 0.75 or nothing is known about sphericity at all, then the Greenhouse-Geisser correction should be used instead. We shall see how these values are used in the next section.

9.2.4.3. The Main ANOVA

SPSS Output 9.3 shows the results of the ANOVA for the within-subjects variable. This table can be read much the same as for one-way between-group ANOVA (see Chapter 7). There is a sum of squares for the within-subject effect of **tutor**, which tells us how much of the total variability is explained by the experimental effect. There is also an error term, which is the amount of unexplained variation across the conditions of the within-subject variable. These sums of squares are converted into mean squares by dividing by the degrees of freedom. The *df* for the effect of **tutor** is simply $k-1$, where k is the number of levels of the independent variable. The error *df* is $(n-1)(k-1)$, where n is the number of subjects (or in this case, the number of essays) and k is as before. The F-ratio is obtained by dividing the mean squares for the experimental effect (184.708) by the error mean squares (49.923). As with between-group ANOVA, this test statistic represents the ratio of systematic variance to unsystematic variance. The value of F (184.71/49.92 = 3.70) is then compared against a critical value for 3 and 21 degrees of freedom. SPSS displays the exact significance level for the *F*-ratio. The significance of *F* is 0.028, which is significant because it is less than the criterion value of 0.05. We can, therefore, conclude that there was a significant difference between the marks awarded by the four lecturers. However, this main test does not tell us which lecturers differed from each other in their marking.

Tests of Within-Subjects Effects

Measure: MEASURE_1

Source		Type III Sum of Squares	df	Mean Square	F	Sig.
TUTOR	Sphericity Assumed	554.125	3	184.708	3.700	.028
	Greenhouse-Geisser	554.125	1.673	331.245	3.700	.063
	Huynh-Feldt	554.125	2.137	259.329	3.700	.047
	Lower-bound	554.125	1.000	554.125	3.700	.096
Error(TUTOR)	Sphericity Assumed	1048.375	21	49.923		
	Greenhouse-Geisser	1048.375	11.710	89.528		
	Huynh-Feldt	1048.375	14.957	70.091		
	Lower-bound	1048.375	7.000	149.768		

a. Computed using alpha = .05

Tests of Within-Subjects Effects

Measure: MEASURE_1

Sphericity Assumed

Source	Type III Sum of Squares	df	Mean Square	F	Sig.
TUTOR	554.125	3	184.708	3.700	.028
Error(TUTOR)	1048.375	21	49.923		

a. Computed using alpha = .05

SPSS Output 9.3: Repeated measures ANOVA for versions 8.0 and 9.0 (top) and versions 7.0 and 7.5 (bottom)

Although this result seems very plausible, we have learnt that the violation of the sphericity assumption makes the *F*-test inaccurate. We know from SPSS Output 9.2 that these data were non-spherical and so we need to make allowances for this violation. The table in SPSS Output 9.3 shows the *F*-ratio and associated degrees of freedom when sphericity is assumed and the significant *F*-statistic indicated some difference(s) between the mean marks given by the four lecturers. In versions 8.0 and 9.0 of SPSS, this table also contains several additional rows giving the corrected values of *F* for the three different types of adjustment (Greenhouse-Geisser, Huynh-Feldt and lower-bound). In versions 7.0 and 7.5 you have to adjust the ANOVA table to see these corrected values. First, use the mouse and double-click on the main ANOVA table. This process opens up the table for editing and a new set of menu labels should appear at the top of the window. One of these menus is labelled

<u>Pivot</u>. Click on this menu and then select the option labelled *Move Layers to Rows*. The corrected *F* values should now be displayed.

Tests of Within-Subjects Effects

Measure		Source	Type III Sum of Squares	df	Mean Square	F	Sig.
MEASURE_1	Sphericity Assumed	TUTOR	554.125	3	184.708	3.700	.028
		Error(TUTOR)	1048.375	21	49.923		
	Greenhouse-Geisser	TUTOR	554.125	1.673	331.245	3.700	.063
		Error(TUTOR)	1048.375	11.710	89.528		
	Huynh-Feldt	TUTOR	554.125	2.137	259.329	3.700	.047
		Error(TUTOR)	1048.375	14.957	70.091		
	Lower-bound	TUTOR	554.125	1.000	554.125	3.700	.096
		Error(TUTOR)	1048.375	7.000	149.768		

a. Computed using alpha = .05

SPSS Output 9.4

SPSS Output 9.4 shows the expanded ANOVA table with the corrected values for each of the three estimates of sphericity. Notice that in all cases the *F*-ratios remain the same; it is the degrees of freedom that change (and hence the critical value against which the obtained *F*-statistic is compared). The degrees of freedom have been adjusted using the estimates of sphericity calculated in SPSS Output 9.2. The adjustment is made by multiplying the degrees of freedom by the estimate of sphericity (see Field, 1998a).[1] The new degrees of freedom are then used to ascertain the significance of *F*. For these data the corrections result in the observed *F* being non-significant when using the Greenhouse-Geisser correction (because $p > 0.05$). However, it was noted earlier that this correction is quite conservative, and so can miss effects that genuinely exist. It is, therefore, useful to consult the Huynh-Feldt corrected *F*-statistic. Using this correction, the *F* value is still significant because the probability value of 0.047 is just below the criterion value of 0.05. So, by this correction we would accept the hypothesis that the lecturers differed in their marking. However, it was also noted earlier that this correction is quite liberal and so tends to accept values as significant when, in reality, they are not significant. This leaves us with the puzzling dilemma of whether or not to accept this *F*-statistic as significant. I mentioned earlier that Stevens (1992) recommends taking an average of the two estimates, and certainly when

---

[1] For example, the Greenhouse-Geisser estimate of sphericity was 0.558. The original degrees of freedom for the model were 3; this value is corrected by multiplying by the estimate of sphericity ($3 \times 0.558 = 1.674$). Likewise the error *df* was 21; this value is corrected in the same way ($21 \times 0.558 = 11.718$). The *F*-ratio is then tested against a critical value with these new degrees of freedom (1.674, 11.718). The other corrections are applied in the same way.

the two corrections give different results (as is the case here) this is wise advice. If the two corrections give rise to the same conclusion it makes little difference which you choose to report (although if you accept the *F*-statistic as significant it is best to report the conservative Greenhouse-Geisser estimate to avoid criticism!). Although it is easy to calculate the average of the two correction factors and to correct the degrees of freedom accordingly, it is not so easy to then calculate an exact probability for those degrees of freedom. Therefore, should you ever be faced with this perplexing situation I recommend taking an average of the two significance values to give you a rough idea of which correction is giving the most accurate answer. In this case, the average of the two *p* values is $(0.063+0.047)/2 = 0.055$. Therefore, we should probably go with the Greenhouse-Geisser correction and conclude that the *F*-ratio is non-significant.

These data illustrate how important it is to use a valid critical value of *F*: it can mean the difference between a statistically significant result and a non-significant result. More importantly, it can mean the difference between making a type I error and not. Had we not used the corrections for sphericity we would have concluded erroneously that the markers gave significantly different marks.

A final option, when you have data that violate sphericity, is to use multivariate test statistics (MANOVA), because they are not dependent upon the assumption of sphericity (see O'Brien and Kaiser, 1985). MANOVA avoids the assumption of sphericity (and all the corresponding considerations about appropriate *F*-ratios and corrections) by using a specific error term for contrasts with 1 *df*, and hence each contrast is only ever associated with its specific error term (rather than the pooled error terms used in ANOVA). MANOVA is covered in depth in Chapter 10, but the repeated measure procedure in SPSS automatically produces multivariate test statistics. There is a trade-off in test power between univariate and multivariate approaches (although some authors argue that this can be overcome with suitable mastery of the techniques—O'Brien and Kaisser, 1985). Davidson (1972) compared the power of adjusted univariate techniques with those of Hotelling's T^2 (a MANOVA test statistic) and found that the univariate technique was relatively powerless to detect small reliable changes between highly correlated conditions when other less correlated conditions were also present. Mendoza et al. (1974) conducted a Monte Carlo study comparing univariate and multivariate techniques under violations of compound symmetry and normality and found that 'as the degree of violation of compound symmetry increased, the empirical power for the multivariate tests also increased. In contrast, the power for the univariate tests generally decreased' (p. 174). Maxwell and Delaney

(1990) noted that the univariate test is relatively more powerful than the multivariate test as n decreases and proposed that 'the multivariate approach should probably not be used if n is less than $a + 10$ (a is the number of levels for repeated measures)' (p. 602). As a rule it seems that when you have a large violation of sphericity ($\varepsilon < 0.7$) and your sample size is greater than ($a + 10$) then multivariate procedures are more powerful, whilst with small sample sizes or when sphericity holds ($\varepsilon > 0.7$) the univariate approach is preferred (Stevens, 1992). It is also worth noting that the power of MANOVA increases and decreases as a function of the correlations between dependent variables (Cole et al., 1994) and so the relationship between treatment conditions must be considered also.

SPSS Output 9.5 shows the multivariate test statistics for this example (details of these test statistics can be found in section 10.2.4). The column displaying the significance values clearly shows that the multivariate tests are non-significant (because p is 0.063, which is greater than the criterion value of 0.05). Bearing in mind the loss of power in these tests this result supports the decision to accept the null hypothesis and conclude that there are no significant differences between the marks given by different lecturers. The interpretation of these results should stop now because the main effect is non-significant. However, we will look at the output for contrasts to illustrate how these tests are displayed in the SPSS viewer.

Multivariate Tests[a]

Effect		Value	F	Hypothesis df	Error df	Sig.
TUTOR	Pillai's Trace	.741	4.760[c]	3.000	5.000	.063
	Wilks' Lambda	.259	4.760[c]	3.000	5.000	.063
	Hotelling's Trace	2.856	4.760[c]	3.000	5.000	.063
	Roy's Largest Root	2.856	4.760[c]	3.000	5.000	.063

a.
   Design: Intercept
   Within Subjects Design: TUTOR

b. Computed using alpha = .05

c. Exact statistic

SPSS Output 9.5

9.2.4.4. Contrasts

The transformation matrix requested in the options is shown in SPSS Output 9.6 and we have to draw on our knowledge of contrast coding (see Chapter 7) to interpret this table. The first thing to remember is that a code of 0 means that the group is not included in a contrast. Therefore, contrast 1 (labelled TUTOR_1 in the table) ignores Dr. Scrote and Dr.

Death. The next thing to remember is that groups with a negative weight are compared to groups with a positive weight. In this case this means that the first contrast compares Dr. Field against Dr. Smith. Using the same logic, contrast 2 (labelled TUTOR_2) ignores Dr. Field and Dr. Death and compares Dr. Smith and Dr. Scrote. Finally, contrast three (TUTOR_3) compares Dr. Death with Dr. Scrote. This pattern of contrasts is consistent with what we expect to get from a repeated contrast (i.e. all groups except the first are compared to the preceding category). The transformation matrix, which appears at the bottom of the output, is used primarily to confirm what each contrast represents.

TUTOR[a]

Measure: MEASURE_1

Dependent Variable	Transformed Variable		
	TUTOR_1	TUTOR_2	TUTOR_3
Dr. Field	1	0	0
Dr. Smith	-1	1	0
Dr. Scrote	0	-1	1
Dr. Death	0	0	-1

a. The contrasts for the within subjects factors are: TUTOR: Repeated contrast

SPSS Output 9.6

Tests of Within-Subjects Contrasts

Measure: MEASURE_1

Source	Transformed Variable	Type III Sum of Squares	df	Mean Square	F	Sig.
TUTOR	TUTOR_1	171.125	1	171.125	18.184	.004
	TUTOR_2	8.000	1	8.000	.152	.708
	TUTOR_3	496.125	1	496.125	3.436	.106
Error(TUTOR)	TUTOR_1	65.875	7	9.411		
	TUTOR_2	368.000	7	52.571		
	TUTOR_3	1010.875	7	144.411		

a. Computed using alpha = .05

SPSS Output 9.7

Above the transformation matrix, we should find a summary table of the contrasts (SPSS Output 9.7). Each contrast is listed in turn, and as with between-group contrasts, a *t*-test is performed that compares the two chunks of variation. So, looking at the significance values from the table, we could say that Dr. Field marked significantly more highly than Dr. Smith (TUTOR_1), but that Dr. Smith's marks were roughly equal to Dr. Scrote's (TUTOR_2) and Dr. Scrote's marks were roughly equal to Dr. Death's (TUTOR_3). However, the significant contrast should be ignored because of the non-significant main effect (remember that the data did not obey sphericity). The important point to note is that the sphericity in our data has led to some important issues being raised about correction factors, and about applying discretion to your data (believe it or not, statistics is an interactive process—the computer does not have all of the answers). In this example we would have to conclude that no significant differences existed between the marks given by different lecturers. However, the ambiguity of our data might make us consider running a similar study with a greater number of essays being marked.

9.2.4.5. Post Hoc Tests

If you selected *post hoc* tests for the repeated measures variable in the *options* dialog box (see section 9.2.3), then the table in SPSS Output 9.8 will be produced in the output viewer window.

Pairwise Comparisons

Measure: MEASURE_1

(I) TUTOR	(J) TUTOR	Mean Difference (I-J)	Std. Error	Sig.[a]	95% Confidence Interval for Difference[a] Lower Bound	Upper Bound
1	2	4.625*	1.085	.022	.682	8.568
	3	3.625	2.841	1.000	-6.703	13.953
	4	11.500	4.675	.261	-5.498	28.498
2	1	-4.625*	1.085	.022	-8.568	-.682
	3	-1.000	2.563	1.000	-10.320	8.320
	4	6.875	4.377	.961	-9.039	22.789
3	1	-3.625	2.841	1.000	-13.953	6.703
	2	1.000	2.563	1.000	-8.320	10.320
	4	7.875	4.249	.637	-7.572	23.322
4	1	-11.500	4.675	.261	-28.498	5.498
	2	-6.875	4.377	.961	-22.789	9.039
	3	-7.875	4.249	.637	-23.322	7.572

Based on estimated marginal means

*. The mean difference is significant at the .05 level.

a. Adjustment for multiple comparisons: Bonferroni.

SPSS Output 9.8

The arrangement of the table in SPSS Output 9.8 is similar to the table produced for between-group *post hoc* tests: the difference between group means is displayed, the standard error, the significance value and a confidence interval for the difference between means. By looking at the significance values we can see that the only difference between group means is between Dr. Field and Dr. Smith. Looking at the means of these groups (SPSS Output 9.1) we can see that I give significantly higher marks than Dr. Smith. However, there is a rather anomalous result in that there is no significant difference between the marks given by Dr.

Death and myself even though the mean difference between our marks is higher (11.5) than the mean difference between myself and Dr. Smith (4.6). The reason for this result is the sphericity in the data. The interested reader might like to run some correlations between the four tutors' grades. You will find that there is a very high positive correlation between the marks given by Dr. Smith and myself (indicating a low level of variability in our data). However, there is a very low correlation between the marks given by Dr. Death and myself (indicating a high level of variability between our marks). It is this large variability between Dr. Death and myself that has produced the non-significant result despite the average marks being very different (this observation is also evident from the standard errors).

9.3. Repeated Measures with Several Independent Variables

We have seen already that simple between-group designs can be extended to incorporate a second (or third) independent variable. It is equally easy to incorporate a second, third or even fourth independent variable into a repeated measure analysis. As an example, some social scientists were asked to research whether imagery could influence public attitudes towards alcohol. There is evidence that attitudes towards stimuli can be changed using positive and negative imagery (e.g. Stuart et al., 1987; but see Field and Davey, 1999) and these researchers were interested in answering two questions. On the one hand, the government had funded them to look at whether negative imagery in advertising could be used to change attitudes towards alcohol. Conversely, an alcohol company had provided funding to see whether positive imagery could be used to improve attitudes towards alcohol. The scientists designed a study to address both issues. Table 9.3 illustrates the experimental design and contains the data for this example (each row represents a single subject).

Participants viewed a total of nine mock adverts over three sessions. In one session, they saw three adverts: (1) a brand of beer (Jungle Juice) presented with a negative image (a dead body with the slogan 'drinking Jungle Juice makes your liver explode'); (2) a brand of wine (Dangleberry) presented in the context of a positive image (a sexy naked man or woman—depending on the subject's gender—and the slogan 'drinking Dangleberry wine makes you a horny stud muffin'); and (3) a brand of water (Puritan) presented alongside a neutral image (a person watching television accompanied by the slogan 'drinking Puritan water makes you behave completely normally'). In a second session (a week later), the subjects saw the same three brands, but this time Jungle Juice was accompanied by the positive imagery, Dangleberry by the neutral image, and Puritan by the negative. In a third session, the subjects saw

Jungle Juice accompanied by the neutral image, Dangleberry by the negative image, and Puritan by the positive. After each advert subjects were asked to rate the drinks on a scale ranging from −100 (dislike very much) through 0 (neutral) to 100 (like very much). The order of adverts was randomized, as was the order in which people participated in the three sessions. This design is quite complex. There are two independent variables: the type of drink (beer, wine or water) and the type of imagery used (positive, negative or neutral). These two variables completely cross over, producing nine experimental conditions.

Table 9.3: Data from **Attitude.sav**

Drink	Beer			Wine			Water		
Image	+ve	−ve	Neut	+ve	−ve	Neut	+ve	−ve	Neut
Male	1	6	5	38	−5	4	10	−14	−2
	43	30	8	20	−12	4	9	−10	−13
	15	15	12	20	−15	6	6	−16	1
	40	30	19	28	−4	0	20	−10	2
	8	12	8	11	−2	6	27	5	−5
	17	17	15	17	−6	6	9	−6	−13
	30	21	21	15	−2	16	19	−20	3
	34	23	28	27	−7	7	12	−12	2
	34	20	26	24	−10	12	12	−9	4
	26	27	27	23	−15	14	21	−6	0
Female	1	−19	−10	28	−13	13	33	−2	9
	7	−18	6	26	−16	19	23	−17	5
	22	−8	4	34	−23	14	21	−19	0
	30	−6	3	32	−22	21	17	−11	4
	40	−6	0	24	−9	19	15	−10	2
	15	−9	4	29	−18	7	13	−17	8
	20	−17	9	30	−17	12	16	−4	10
	9	−12	−5	24	−15	18	17	−4	8
	14	−11	7	34	−14	20	19	−1	12
	15	−6	13	23	−15	15	29	−1	10

9.3.1. The Main Analysis

To enter these data into SPSS we need to again recap the golden rule of the data editor, which states that each row represents a single subject's data. If a subject participates in all experimental conditions (in this case (s)he sees all types of stimuli presented with all types of imagery) then each experimental condition must be represented by a column in the data editor. In this experiment there are nine experimental conditions and so the data need to be entered in nine columns (so, the format is identical to Table 9.3). You should create the following nine variables in the data editor with the names as given. For each one, you should also enter a full variable name (see section 1.2.3) for clarity in the output.

beerpos	Beer	+	Sexy Person
beerneg	Beer	+	Corpse
beerneut	Beer	+	Person in Armchair
winepos	Wine	+	Sexy Person
wineneg	Wine	+	Corpse
wineneut	Wine	+	Person in Armchair
waterpos	Water	+	Sexy Person
waterneg	Water	+	Corpse
waterneu	Water	+	Person in Armchair

Once these variables have been created, enter the data as in Table 9.3. If you have problems entering the data then use the file **Attitude.sav**. To access the *define factors* dialog box use the menu path **Analyze⇒General Linear Model⇒Repeated Measures** .... In the *define factors* dialog box you are asked to supply a name for the within-subject (repeated measures) variable. In this case there are two within-subject factors: **drink** (beer, wine or water) and **imagery** (positive, negative and neutral). Replace the word *factor1* with the word *drink*. When you have given this repeated measures factor a name, you have to tell the computer how many levels there were to that variable. In this case, there were three types of drink, so we have to enter the number 3 into the box labelled *Number of Levels*. Click on ▢Add▢ to add this variable to the list of repeated measures variables. This variable will now appear in the white box at the bottom of the dialog box and appears as *drink(3)*. We now have to repeat this process for the second independent variable. Enter the word *imagery* into the space labelled *Within-Subject Factor Name* and then, because there were three levels of this variable, enter the number 3 into the space labelled *Number of Levels*. Click on ▢Add▢ to include this variable in the list of factors; it will appear as *imagery(3)*. The finished dialog box is shown in Figure 9.5. When you have entered both of the within-subject factors click on ▢Define▢ to go to the main dialog box.

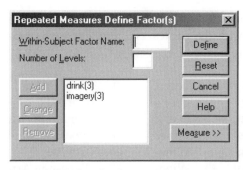

Figure 9.5: *Define factors* dialog box for factorial repeated measures ANOVA

The main dialog box is essentially the same as when there is only one independent variable except that there are now nine question marks (Figure 9.6). At the top of the <u>Within-Subjects Variables</u> box, SPSS states that there are two factors: **drink** and **imagery**. In the box below there is a series of question marks followed by bracketed numbers. The numbers in brackets represent the levels of the factors (independent variables).

_?_(1,1)	variable representing 1st level of drink and 1st level of imagery
_?_(1,2)	variable representing 1st level of drink and 2nd level of imagery
_?_(1,3)	variable representing 1st level of drink and 3rd level of imagery
_?_(2,1)	variable representing 2nd level of drink and 1st level of imagery
_?_(2,2)	variable representing 2nd level of drink and 2nd level of imagery
_?_(2,3)	variable representing 2nd level of drink and 3rd level of imagery
_?_(3,1)	variable representing 3rd level of drink and 1st level of imagery
_?_(3,2)	variable representing 3rd level of drink and 2nd level of imagery
_?_(3,3)	variable representing 3rd level of drink and 3rd level of imagery

In this example, there are two independent variables and so there are two numbers in the brackets. The first number refers to levels of the first factor listed above the box (in this case **drink**). The second number in the bracket refers to levels of the second factor listed above the box (in this case **imagery**). As with one-way repeated measures ANOVA, you are required to replace these question marks with variables from the list on the left-hand side of the dialog box. With between-group designs, in which coding variables are used, the levels of a particular factor are specified by the codes assigned to them in the data editor. However, in repeated measures designs, no such coding scheme is used and so we determine which condition to assign to a level at this stage. For example, if we entered **beerpos** into the list first, then SPSS will treat beer as the first level of **drink**, and positive imagery as the first level of the **imagery** variable. However, if we entered **wineneg** into the list first, SPSS would consider wine as the first level of **drink**, and negative imagery as the first level of **imagery**. For this reason, it is imperative that we think about the type of contrasts that we might want to do *before* entering variables into this dialog box. In this design, if we look at the first variable, **drink**, there were three conditions, two of which involved alcoholic drinks. In a sense, the water condition acts as a control to whether the effects of imagery are specific to alcohol. Therefore, for this variable we might want to compare the beer and wine condition with the water condition. This comparison could be done by either specifying a simple contrast (see Table 7.6) in which the beer and wine conditions are compared to the water, or using a difference contrast in which both alcohol conditions are compared to the water condition before being compared to each other. In either case it is essential that the water condition be entered as either the first or last level of the independent variable **drink** (because you can't specify the middle level as the reference category in a simple contrast). Now, let's think about the second factor. The imagery factor also has a control category that was not expected to change attitudes (neutral imagery). As before, we might be interested in using this category as a reference category in a simple contrast[2] and so it is important that this neutral category is entered as either the first or last level.

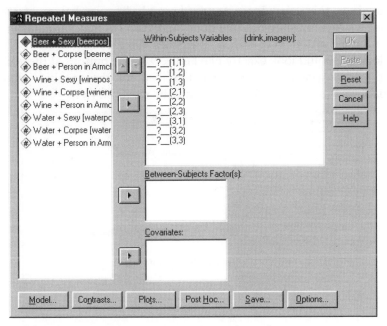

Figure 9.6

---

[2] We expect positive imagery to improve attitudes, whereas negative imagery should make attitudes more negative. Therefore, it does not make sense to do a Helmert or difference contrast for this factor because the effects of the two experimental conditions will cancel each other out.

Based on what has been discussed about using contrasts, it makes sense to have water as level 3 of the **drink** factor and neutral as the third level of the imagery factor. The remaining levels can be decided arbitrarily. I have chosen beer as level 1 and wine as level 2 of the **drink** factor. For the **imagery** variable I chose positive as level 1 and negative as level 2. These decisions mean that the variables should be entered as follows:

beerpos	▶	_?_(1,1)
beerneg	▶	_?_(1,2)
beerneut	▶	_?_(1,3)
winepos	▶	_?_(2,1)
wineneg	▶	_?_(2,2)
wineneut	▶	_?_(2,3)
waterpos	▶	_?_(3,1)
waterneg	▶	_?_(3,2)
waterneut	▶	_?_(3,3)

Coincidentally, this order is the order in which variables are listed in the data editor, this coincidence occurred simply because I thought ahead about what contrasts would be done, and then entered variables in the appropriate order! When these variables have been transferred, the dialog box should look exactly like Figure 9.7. The buttons at the bottom of the screen have already been described for the one independent variable case and so I will describe only the most relevant.

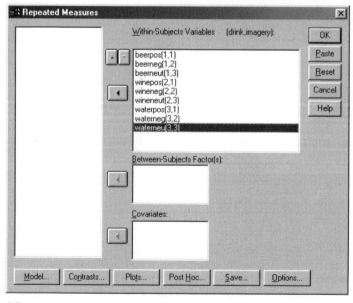

Figure 9.7

9.3.2. Contrasts

Following the main analysis it is interesting to compare levels of the independent variables to see whether they differ. With versions of SPSS before version 7.5 there is no facility for comparing all groups in repeated measures designs, and so we have to rely on the standard contrasts available (see Table 7.6). Figure 9.8 shows the dialog box for conducting contrasts and is obtained by clicking on [Contrasts...] in the main dialog box. In the previous section I described why it might be interesting to use the water and neutral conditions as base categories for the drink and imagery factors respectively. We have used the *contrasts* dialog box before in sections 8.1.2 and 9.2.2 and so all I shall say is that you should select a simple contrast for each independent variable. For both independent variables, we entered the variables such that the control category was the last one; therefore, we need not change the reference category for the simple contrast. Once the contrasts have been selected, click on [Continue] to return to the main dialog box.

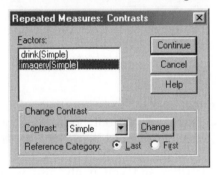

Figure 9.8

9.3.3. Graphing Interactions

When we had only one independent variable, we ignored the *plots* dialog box; however, if there are two or more factors, the *plots* dialog box is a convenient way to plot the means for each level of the factors. To access this dialog box click on [Plots...]. Select **drink** from the variables list on the left-hand side of the dialog box and transfer it to the space labelled *Horizontal Axis* by clicking on [▶]. In the space labelled *Separate Lines* we need to place the remaining independent variable: **imagery**. As before, it is down to your discretion which way round the graph is plotted. When you have moved the two independent variables to the appropriate box, click on [Add] and this interaction graph will be added to the list at the bottom of the box (see Figure 9.9). When you have finished specifying graphs, click on [Continue] to return to the main dialog box.

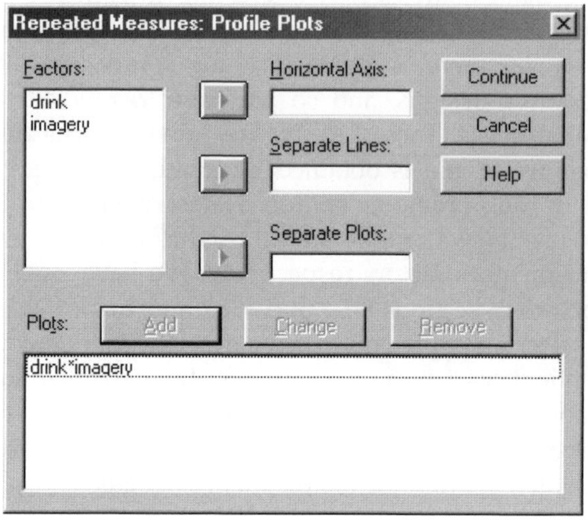

Figure 9.9

9.3.4.   *Other Options*

You should notice that *post hoc* tests are disabled for solely repeated measures designs. Therefore, the only remaining options are in the *options* dialog box, which is accessed by clicking on [Options...]. The options here are the same as for the one-way ANOVA. I recommend selecting some descriptive statistics and you might also want to select some multiple comparisons by selecting all factors in the box labelled *Factor(s) and Factor Interactions* and transferring them to the box labelled *Display Means for* by clicking on [▶] (see Figure 9.10). Having selected these variables, you should tick the box labelled *Compare main effects* ([✔ Compare main effects]) and select an appropriate correction (I chose Bonferroni). The only remaining option of particular interest is to select the *Transformation matrix* option. This option produces a lot of extra output but is important for interpreting the output from the contrasts.

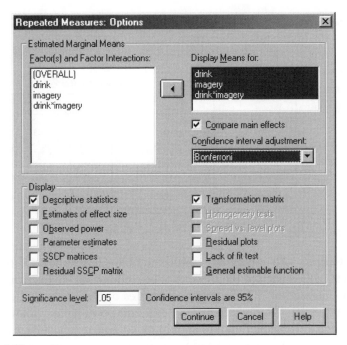

Figure 9.10

9.3.5. Output for Factorial Repeated Measures ANOVA

9.3.5.1. Descriptives and Main Analysis

SPSS Output 9.9 shows the initial output from this ANOVA. The first table merely lists the variables that have been included from the data editor and the level of each independent variable that they represent. This table is more important than it might seem, because it enables you to verify that you entered the variables in the correct order for the comparisons that you want to do. The second table is a table of descriptives and provides the mean and standard deviation for each of the nine conditions. The names in this table are the names I gave the variables in the data editor (therefore, if you didn't give these variables full names, this table will look slightly different).

The descriptives are interesting in that they tell us that the variability among scores was greatest when beer was used as a product (compare the standard deviations of the beer variables against the others). Also, when a corpse image was used, the ratings given to the products were negative (as expected) for wine and water but not for beer (so, for some reason negative imagery didn't seem to work when beer was used as a stimulus). The values in this table will help us later to interpret the main effects of the analysis.

Within-Subjects Factors

Measure: MEASURE_1

DRINK	IMAGERY	Dependent Variable
1	1	BEERPOS
	2	BEERNEG
	3	BEERNEUT
2	1	WINEPOS
	2	WINENEG
	3	WINENEUT
3	1	WATERPOS
	2	WATERNEG
	3	WATERNEU

Descriptive Statistics

	Mean	Std. Deviation	N
Beer + Sexy	21.0500	13.0080	20
Beer + Corpse	4.4500	17.3037	20
Beer + Person in Armchair	10.0000	10.2956	20
Wine + Sexy	25.3500	6.7378	20
Wine + Corpse	-12.0000	6.1815	20
Wine + Person in Armchair	11.6500	6.2431	20
Water + Sexy	17.4000	7.0740	20
Water + Corpse	-9.2000	6.8025	20
Water + Person in Armchair	2.3500	6.8386	20

SPSS Output 9.9

SPSS Output 9.10 shows the results of Mauchly's sphericity test (see section 9.1.3) for each of the three effects in the model (two main effects and one interaction). The significance values of these tests indicate that both the main effects of **drink** and **imagery** have violated this assumption and so the F-values should be corrected (see section 9.2.4.2). For the interaction the assumption of sphericity is met (because $p > 0.05$) and se we need not correct the F-ratio for this effect.

Mauchly's Test of Sphericity[b]

Measure: MEASURE_1

Within Subjects Effect	Mauchly's W	Approx. Chi-Square	df	Sig.	Epsilon[a] Greenhouse-Geisser	Huynh-Feldt	Lower-bound
DRINK	.267	23.753	2	.000	.577	.591	.500
IMAGERY	.662	7.422	2	.024	.747	.797	.500
DRINK * IMAGERY	.595	9.041	9	.436	.798	.979	.250

Tests the null hypothesis that the error covariance matrix of the orthonormalized transformed dependent variables is proportional to an identity matrix.

a. May be used to adjust the degrees of freedom for the averaged tests of significance. Corrected tests are displayed in the layers (by default) of the Tests of Within Subjects Effects table.

b. Design: Intercept - Within Subjects Design: DRINK+IMAGERY+DRINK*IMAGERY

SPSS Output 9.10

SPSS Output 9.11 shows the results of the ANOVA (with corrected F values—those of you using version 7.5 or earlier should expand the table produced using the method described in section 9.2.4.3). The output is split into sections that refer to each of the effects in the model and the error terms associated with these effects. By looking at the significance values it is clear that there is a significant effect of the type of drink used as a stimulus, a significant main effect of the type of imagery used, and a significant interaction between these two variables. I will examine each of these effects in turn.

Tests of Within-Subjects Effects

Measure: MEASURE_1

Source		Type III Sum of Squares	df	Mean Square	F	Sig.
DRINK	Sphericity Assumed	2092.344	2	1046.172	5.106	.011
	Greenhouse-Geisser	2092.344	**1.154**	1812.764	**5.106**	**.030**
	Huynh-Feldt	2092.344	1.181	1770.939	5.106	.029
	Lower-bound	2092.344	1.000	2092.344	5.106	.036
Error(DRINK)	Sphericity Assumed	7785.878	38	204.892		
	Greenhouse-Geisser	7785.878	**21.930**	355.028		
	Huynh-Feldt	7785.878	22.448	346.836		
	Lower-bound	7785.878	19.000	409.783		
IMAGERY	Sphericity Assumed	21628.678	2	10814.339	122.565	.000
	Greenhouse-Geisser	21628.678	**1.495**	14468.490	**122.565**	**.000**
	Huynh-Feldt	21628.678	1.594	13571.496	122.565	.000
	Lower-bound	21628.678	1.000	21628.678	122.565	.000
Error(IMAGERY)	Sphericity Assumed	3352.878	38	88.234		
	Greenhouse-Geisser	3352.878	**28.403**	118.048		
	Huynh-Feldt	3352.878	30.280	110.729		
	Lower-bound	3352.878	19.000	176.467		
DRINK * IMAGERY	Sphericity Assumed	2624.422	**4**	656.106	**17.155**	**.000**
	Greenhouse-Geisser	2624.422	3.194	821.778	17.155	.000
	Huynh-Feldt	2624.422	3.914	670.462	17.155	.000
	Lower-bound	2624.422	1.000	2624.422	17.155	.001
Error(DRINK*IMAGERY)	Sphericity Assumed	2906.689	**76**	38.246		
	Greenhouse-Geisser	2906.689	60.678	47.903		
	Huynh-Feldt	2906.689	74.373	39.083		
	Lower-bound	2906.689	19.000	152.984		

SPSS Output 9.11

9.3.5.2. The Effect of Drink

The first part of SPSS Output 9.11 tells us the effect of the type of drink used in the advert. For this effect we must look at one of the corrected significance values because sphericity was violated (see above). All of the corrected values are significant and so we should report the conservative Greenhouse-Geisser corrected values of the degrees of freedom. Therefore, we should report that there was a significant main effect of drink ($F(1.154, 21.930) = 5.11$, $p < 0.05$). This effect tells us that if we ignore the type of imagery that was used, subjects still rated some types of drink significantly differently.

In section 9.3.4 we requested that SPSS display means for all of the effects in the model (before conducting *post hoc* tests) and if you scan through your output you should find the table in SPSS Output 9.12 in a section headed *Estimated Marginal Means*.[3] SPSS Output 9.12 is a table of

---

[3] These means are obtained by taking the average of the means in SPSS Output 9.9 for a given condition. For example, the mean for the beer condition (ignoring imagery) is

means for the main effect of drink with the associated standard errors. The levels of this variable are labelled 1, 2 and 3 and so we must think back to how we entered the variable to see which row of the table relates to which condition. We entered this variable with the beer condition first and the water condition last. Figure 9.11 uses this information to display the means for each condition. It is clear from this graph that beer and wine are naturally rated higher than water (with beer being rated most highly). To see the nature of this effect we can look at the *post hoc* tests (see below) and the contrasts (see section 9.3.6).

Estimates

Measure: MEASURE_1

DRINK	Mean	Std. Error	95% Confidence Interval	
			Lower Bound	Upper Bound
1	11.833	2.621	6.348	17.319
2	8.333	.574	7.131	9.535
3	3.517	1.147	1.116	5.918

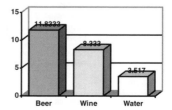

SPSS Output 9.12   **Figure 9.11**

SPSS Output 9.13 shows the pairwise comparisons for the main effect of drink corrected using a Bonferroni adjustment. This table indicates that the significant main effect reflects a significant difference ($p < 0.01$) between levels 2 and 3 (wine and water). Curiously, the difference between the beer and water conditions is larger than that for wine and water yet this effect is non-significant ($p > 0.05$). This inconsistency can be explained by looking at the standard error in the beer condition compared to the wine condition. The standard error for the wine condition is incredibly small and so the difference between means is relatively large (see Chapter 6). Try rerunning these *post hoc* tests but select the uncorrected values (LSD) in the *options* dialog box (see section 9.3.4). You should find that the difference between beer and water is now significant ($p = 0.02$). This finding highlights the importance of controlling the error rate by using a Bonferroni correction. Had we not used this correction we could have concluded erroneously that beer was rated significantly more highly than water.

$$\overline{X}_{beer} = \left(\overline{X}_{beer + sexy} + \overline{X}_{beer + corpse} + \overline{X}_{beer + neutral}\right)/3$$
$$= (21.05 + 4.45 + 10.00)/3 = 11.83.$$

Pairwise Comparisons

Measure: MEASURE_1

(I) DRINK	(J) DRINK	Mean Difference (I-J)	Std. Error	Sig.[a]	95% Confidence Interval for Difference[a]	
					Lower Bound	Upper Bound
1	2	3.500	2.849	.703	-3.980	10.980
	3	8.317	3.335	.066	-.438	17.072
2	1	-3.500	2.849	.703	-10.980	3.980
	3	4.817*	1.116	.001	1.886	7.747
3	1	-8.317	3.335	.066	-17.072	.438
	2	-4.817*	1.116	.001	-7.747	-1.886

Based on estimated marginal means

*. The mean difference is significant at the .05 level.

a. Adjustment for multiple comparisons: Bonferroni.

SPSS Output 9.13

9.3.5.3. The Effect of Imagery

SPSS Output 9.11 also indicates that the effect of the type of imagery used in the advert had a significant influence on subjects' ratings of the stimuli. Again, we must look at one of the corrected significance values because sphericity was violated (see above). All of the corrected values are highly significant and so we can again report the Greenhouse-Geisser corrected values of the degrees of freedom. Therefore, we should report that there was a significant main effect of imagery ($F(1.495, 28.403) = 122.57, p < 0.001$). This effect tells us that if we ignore the type of drink that was used, subjects' ratings of those drinks were different according to the type of imagery that was used. In section 9.3.4 we requested means for all of the effects in the model and if you scan through your output you should find the table in SPSS Output 9.14 (after the pairwise comparisons for the main effect of drink). SPSS Output 9.14 is a table of means for the main effect of imagery with the associated standard errors. The levels of this variable are labelled 1, 2 and 3 and so we must think back to how we entered the variable to see which row of the table relates to which condition. We entered this variable with the positive condition first and the neutral condition last. Figure 9.12 uses this information to illustrate the means for each condition. It is clear from this graph that positive imagery resulted in very positive ratings (compared to the neutral imagery) and negative imagery resulted in negative ratings (especially compared to the effect of neutral imagery). To see the nature of this effect we can look at the *post hoc* tests (see below) and the contrasts (see section 9.3.6).

Estimates

Measure: MEASURE_1

IMAGERY	Mean	Std. Error	95% Confidence Interval	
			Lower Bound	Upper Bound
1	21.267	.977	19.222	23.312
2	-5.583	1.653	-9.043	-2.124
3	8.000	.969	5.972	10.028

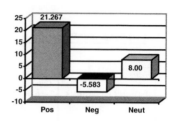

SPSS Output 9.14   **Figure 9.12**

SPSS Output 9.15 shows the pairwise comparisons for the main effect of imagery corrected using a Bonferroni adjustment. This table indicates that the significant main effect reflects significant differences (all $p <$ 0.01) between levels 1 and 2 (positive and negative), between levels 1 and 3 (positive and neutral), and between levels 2 and 3 (negative and neutral).

Pairwise Comparisons

Measure: MEASURE_1

(I) IMAGERY	(J) IMAGERY	Mean Difference (I-J)	Std. Error	Sig.[a]	95% Confidence Interval for Difference[a]	
					Lower Bound	Upper Bound
1	2	26.850*	1.915	.000	21.824	31.876
	3	13.267*	1.113	.000	10.346	16.187
2	1	-26.850*	1.915	.000	-31.876	-21.824
	3	-13.583*	1.980	.000	-18.781	-8.386
3	1	-13.267*	1.113	.000	-16.187	-10.346
	2	13.583*	1.980	.000	8.386	18.781

Based on estimated marginal means

*. The mean difference is significant at the .05 level.

a. Adjustment for multiple comparisons: Bonferroni.

SPSS Output 9.15

9.3.5.4.   The Interaction Effect (Drink × Imagery)

SPSS Output 9.11 indicated that imagery interacted in some way with the type of drink used as a stimulus. From that table we should report that there was a significant interaction between the type of drink used and imagery associated with it ($F(4, 76) = 17.16$, $p < 0.001$). This effect tells us that the type of imagery used had a different effect depending on which type of drink it was presented alongside. As before, we can use the means that we requested in section 9.3.4 to determine the nature of this interaction (this table should be below the pairwise comparisons for imagery and is shown in SPSS Output 9.16). The table of means in SPSS Output 9.16 is essentially the same as the initial descriptive statistics in SPSS Output 9.9 except that the standard errors are displayed rather than the standard deviations.

Estimates

Measure: MEASURE_1

DRINK	IMAGERY	Mean	Std. Error	95% Confidence Interval	
				Lower Bound	Upper Bound
1	1	21.050	2.909	14.962	27.138
	2	4.450	3.869	-3.648	12.548
	3	10.000	2.302	5.181	14.819
2	1	25.350	1.507	22.197	28.503
	2	-12.000	1.382	-14.893	-9.107
	3	11.650	1.396	8.728	14.572
3	1	17.400	1.582	14.089	20.711
	2	-9.200	1.521	-12.384	-6.016
	3	2.350	1.529	-.851	5.551

SPSS Output 9.16

The means in SPSS Output 9.16 are used to create the plot that we requested in section 9.3.3 and this graph is essential for interpreting the interaction. Figure 9.13 shows the interaction graph (slightly modified to make it look prettier!) and we are looking for non-parallel lines. The graph shows that the pattern of responding across drinks was similar when positive and neutral imagery was used. That is, ratings were positive for beer, they were slightly higher for wine and then they went down slightly for water. The fact that the line representing positive imagery is higher than the neutral line indicates that positive imagery gave rise to higher ratings than neutral imagery across all drinks. The bottom line (representing negative imagery) shows a different effect: ratings were lower for wine and water but not for beer. Therefore, negative imagery had the desired effect on attitudes towards wine and water, but for some reason attitudes towards beer remained fairly neutral. Therefore, the interaction is likely to reflect the fact that negative imagery has a different effect to both positive and neutral imagery (because it decreases ratings rather than increasing them). This interaction is completely in line with the experimental predictions. To verify the interpretation of the interaction effect, we need to look at the contrasts that we requested in section 9.3.2.

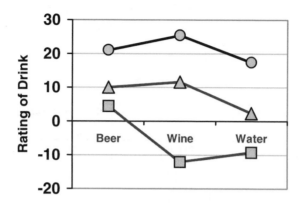

Figure 9.13: Interaction graph for **Attitude.sav**. The type of imagery is represented by the three lines: positive imagery (circles), negative imagery (squares) and neutral imagery (triangles)

9.3.6.   Contrasts for Repeated Measures Variables

In section 9.3.2 we requested simple contrasts for the **drink** variable (for which water was used as the control category) and for the **imagery** category (for which neutral imagery was used as the control category). SPSS Output 9.17 shows the summary results for these contrasts. The table is split up into main effects and interactions, and each effect is split up into components of the contrast. So, for the main effect of drink, the first contrast compares level 1 (beer) against the base category (in this case, the last category: water). If you are confused as to which level is which you are reminded that SPSS Output 9.9 lists them for you. This result is significant ($F(1, 12) = 6.22, p < 0.05$), which contradicts what was found using *post hoc* tests (see SPSS Output 9.13)—why do you think this is? The next contrast compares level 2 (wine) with the base category (water) and confirms the significant difference found with the *post hoc* tests ($F(1, 12) = 18.61, p < 0.001$). For the imagery main effect, the first contrast compares level 1 (positive) to the base category (the last category: neutral) and verifies the significant difference found with the *post hoc* tests ($F(1, 12) = 142.19, p < 0.001$). The second contrast confirms the significant difference in ratings found in the negative imagery condition compared to the neutral ($F(1, 12) = 47.07, p < 0.001$). These contrast are all very well, but they tell us only what we already knew (although note the increased statistical power with these tests shown by the higher significance values). The contrasts become much more interesting when we look at the interaction term.

Tests of Within-Subjects Contrasts

Measure: MEASURE_1

Source	DRINK	IMAGERY	Type III Sum of Squares	df	Mean Square	F	Sig.
DRINK	Level 1 vs. Level 3		1383.339	1	1383.339	6.218	.022
	Level 2 vs. Level 3		464.006	1	464.006	18.613	.000
Error(DRINK)	Level 1 vs. Level 3		4226.772	19	222.462		
	Level 2 vs. Level 3		473.661	19	24.930		
IMAGERY		Level 1 vs. Level 3	3520.089	1	3520.089	142.194	.000
		Level 2 vs. Level 3	3690.139	1	3690.139	47.070	.000
Error(IMAGERY)		Level 1 vs. Level 3	470.356	19	24.756		
		Level 2 vs. Level 3	1489.528	19	78.396		
DRINK * IMAGERY	Level 1 vs. Level 3	Level 1 vs. Level 3	320.000	1	320.000	1.576	**.225**
		Level 2 vs. Level 3	720.000	1	720.000	6.752	**.018**
	Level 2 vs. Level 3	Level 1 vs. Level 3	36.450	1	36.450	.235	**.633**
		Level 2 vs. Level 3	2928.200	1	2928.200	26.906	**.000**
Error(DRINK*IMAGERY)	Level 1 vs. Level 3	Level 1 vs. Level 3	3858.000	19	203.053		
		Level 2 vs. Level 3	2026.000	19	106.632		
	Level 2 vs. Level 3	Level 1 vs. Level 3	2946.550	19	155.082		
		Level 2 vs. Level 3	2067.800	19	108.832		

SPSS Output 9.17

9.3.6.1. *Beer vs. Water, Positive vs. Neutral Imagery*

The first interaction term looks at level 1 of drink (beer) compared to level 3 (water), when positive imagery (level 1) is used compared to neutral (level 3). This contrast is non-significant. This result tells us that the increased liking found when positive imagery is used (compared to neutral imagery) is the same for both beer and water. In terms of the interaction graph (Figure 9.13) it means that the distance between the circle and the triangle in the beer condition is the same as the distance between the circle and the triangle in the water condition. We could conclude that the improvement of ratings due to positive imagery compared to neutral is not affected by whether people are evaluating beer or water.

9.3.6.2. *Beer vs. Water, Negative vs. Neutral Imagery*

The second interaction term looks at level 1 of drink (beer) compared to level 3 (water), when negative imagery (level 2) is used compared to neutral (level 3). This contrast is significant ($F(1, 19) = 6.75$, $p < 0.05$). This result tells us that the decreased liking found when negative imagery is used (compared to neutral imagery) is different when beer is used compared to when water is used. In terms of the interaction graph (Figure 9.13) it means that the distance between the square and the triangle in the beer condition (a small difference) is significantly smaller than the distance between the square and the triangle in the water condition (a larger difference). We could conclude that the decrease in ratings due to negative imagery (compared to neutral) found when water is used in the advert is not present when beer is used.

9.3.6.3.   Wine vs. Water, Positive vs. Neutral Imagery

The third interaction term looks at level 2 of drink (wine) compared to level 3 (water), when positive imagery (level 1) is used compared to neutral (level 3). This contrast is non-significant, indicating that the increased liking found when positive imagery is used (compared to neutral imagery) is the same for both wine and water. In terms of the interaction graph (Figure 9.13) it means that the distance between the circle and the triangle in the wine condition is the same as the distance between the circle and the triangle in the water condition. We could conclude that the improvement of ratings due to positive imagery compared to neutral is not affected by whether people are evaluating wine or water.

9.3.6.4.   Wine vs. Water, Negative vs. Neutral Imagery

The final interaction term looks at level 2 of drink (wine) compared to level 3 (water), when negative imagery (level 2) is used compared to neutral (level 3). This contrast is significant ($F(1, 19) = 26.91$, $p < 0.001$). This result tells us that the decreased liking found when negative imagery is used (compared to neutral imagery) is different when wine is used compared to when water is used. In terms of the interaction graph (Figure 9.13) it means that the distance between the square and the triangle in the wine condition (a big difference) is significantly larger than the distance between the square and the triangle in the water condition (a smaller difference). We could conclude that the decrease in ratings due to negative imagery (compared to neutral) is significantly greater when wine is advertised than when water is advertised.

These contrasts, by their nature, tell us nothing about the differences between the beer and wine conditions (or the positive and negative conditions) and different contrasts would have to be run to find out more. However, what is clear so far is that relative to the neutral condition, positive images increased liking for the products more or less regardless of the product; however, negative imagery had a greater effect on wine and a lesser effect on beer. These differences were not predicted. Although it may seem tiresome to spend so long interpreting an analysis so thoroughly, you are well advised to take such a systematic approach if you want to truly understand the effects that you obtain. Interpreting interaction terms is complex, and I can think of a few well-respected researchers who still struggle with them, so don't feel disheartened if you find them hard. Try to be thorough, and break each effect down as much as possible using contrasts and hopefully you will find enlightenment.

9.4.   Mixed Design ANOVA

The final design that I need to talk about is one in which you have a mixture of between-group and repeated measures variables. It should be obvious that you need at least two independent variables for this type of design to be possible, but you can have more complex scenarios too (e.g. two between-group and one repeated measures, one between-group and two repeated measures, or even two of each). SPSS allows you to test almost any design you might want to, and of virtually any degree of complexity. However, interaction terms are difficult enough to interpret with only two variables so imagine how difficult they are if you include four! To keep the example simple, I am going to continue with the previous example (advertising and different imagery) by adding a between-group variable into the design.[4] Imagine that in the previous experiment I had taken a note of each subject's gender. Subsequent to the previous analysis it occurred to me that men and women might respond differently to the products (because, in keeping with stereotypes, men might mostly drink lager whereas women might drink wine). Therefore, I wanted to reanalyze the data taking this additional variable into account. Now, gender is a between-group variable because a participant can be only male or female: they cannot participate as a male and then change into a female and participate again! The data are the same as Table 9.3 except that we now need to tell SPSS which participants were males and which were females by adding a coding variable. You should be pretty familiar with how to define coding variables by now, so add the variable called **gender** to the data editor, and define labels as 1 = male, 2 = female. If you have problems adding this variable, then the completed data editor can be found in the file **MixedAttitude.sav**.

To carry out the analysis on SPSS follow the same instructions that we did before, so first of all access the *define factors* dialog box (Figure 9.5) by using the file path **Analyze⇒General Linear Model⇒Repeated Measures** .... We are using the same repeated measures variables as before, so complete this dialog box exactly as in the last example, then click on ⬚Define⬚ to access the main dialog box (see Figure 9.14). This box should be completed exactly as before except that we must specify

---

[4] Previously the example contained two repeated measures variables (drink type and imagery type), now it will include three variables (two repeated measures and one between-group).

gender as a between-group variable by selecting it in the variables list and clicking 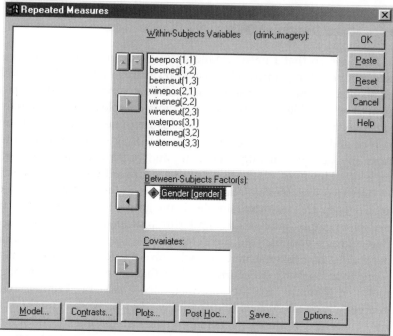 to transfer it to the box labelled *Between-Subjects Factors*.

Figure 9.14: Completed dialog box for mixed design ANOVA

Gender has only two levels (male or female) so there is no need to specify contrasts for this variable; however, you should select simple contrasts for both **drink** and **imagery** (see section 9.3.2). The addition of a between-group factor means that we can select *post hoc* tests for this variable by clicking on ⌐Post Hoc...⌐. This action brings up the *post hoc* test dialog box (see section 9.2.3), which can be used as previously explained. However, we need not specify any *post hoc* tests here because the between-group factor has only two levels. The addition of an extra variable makes it necessary to choose a different graph to the one in the previous example. Click on ⌐Plots...⌐ to access the dialog box in Figure 9.15. Place **drink** and **imagery** in the same slots as for the previous example but also place **gender** in the slot labelled *Separate Plots*. When all three variables have been specified, don't forget to click on ⌐Add⌐ to add this combination to the list of plots. By asking SPSS to plot the drink × imagery × gender interaction, we should get the same interaction graph as before, except that a separate version of this graph will be produced for male and female subjects.

As far as other options are concerned, you should select the same ones that were chosen for the previous example (see section 9.3.4). It is worth selecting estimated marginal means for all effects (because these values will help you to understand any significant effects), but to save space I did not ask for confidence intervals for these effects because we have considered this part of the output in some detail already. When all of the appropriate options have been selected, run the analysis.

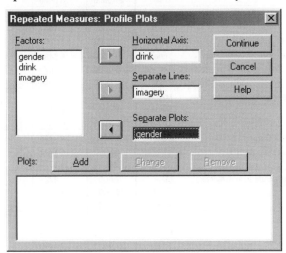

Figure 9.15: *Plots* dialog box for a three-way mixed ANOVA

9.4.1. Output for Mixed Factorial ANOVA: Main Analysis

The initial output is the same as the two-way ANOVA example: there is a table listing the repeated measures variables from the data editor and the level of each independent variable that they represent. The second table contains descriptive statistics (mean and standard deviation) for each of the nine conditions split according to whether subjects were male or female (see SPSS Output 9.18). The names in this table are the names I gave the variables in the data editor (therefore, your output may differ slightly). These descriptive statistics are interesting because they show us the pattern of means across all experimental conditions (so, we use these means to produce the graphs of the three-way interaction). We can see that the variability among scores was greatest when beer was used as a product, and that when a corpse image was used the ratings given to the products were negative (as expected) for all conditions except the men in the beer condition. Likewise, ratings of products were very positive when a sexy person was used as the imagery irrespective of the gender of the participant, or the product being advertised.

Descriptive Statistics

	Gender	Mean	Std. Deviation	N
Beer + Sexy	Male	24.8000	14.0063	10
	Female	17.3000	11.3925	10
	Total	21.0500	13.0080	20
Beer + Corpse	Male	20.1000	7.8379	10
	Female	-11.2000	5.1381	10
	Total	4.4500	17.3037	20
Beer + Person in Armchair	Male	16.9000	8.5434	10
	Female	3.1000	6.7074	10
	Total	10.0000	10.2956	20
Wine + Sexy	Male	22.3000	7.6311	10
	Female	28.4000	4.1150	10
	Total	25.3500	6.7378	20
Wine + Corpse	Male	-7.8000	4.9396	10
	Female	-16.2000	4.1312	10
	Total	-12.0000	6.1815	20
Wine + Person in Armchair	Male	7.5000	4.9721	10
	Female	15.8000	4.3919	10
	Total	11.6500	6.2431	20
Water + Sexy	Male	14.5000	6.7864	10
	Female	20.3000	6.3953	10
	Total	17.4000	7.0740	20
Water + Corpse	Male	-9.8000	6.7791	10
	Female	-8.6000	7.1368	10
	Total	-9.2000	6.8025	20
Water + Person in Armchair	Male	-2.1000	6.2973	10
	Female	6.8000	3.8816	10
	Total	2.3500	6.8386	20

SPSS Output 9.18

SPSS Output 9.19 shows the results of Mauchly's sphericity test for each of the three repeated measures effects in the model. The values of these tests are different to the previous example, because the between-group factor is now being accounted for by the test. The main effect of drink still significantly violates the sphericity assumption ($W = 0.572$, $p < 0.01$) but the main effect of imagery no longer does. Therefore, the F value for the main effect of drink (and its interaction with the between-group variable **gender**) needs to be corrected for this violation.

Mauchly's Test of Sphericity[b]

Measure: MEASURE_1

Within Subjects Effect	Mauchly's W	Approx. Chi-Square	df	Sig.	Epsilon[a]		
					Greenhouse-Geisser	Huynh-Feldt	Lower-bound
DRINK	.572	9.486	2	.009	.700	.784	.500
IMAGERY	.965	.612	2	.736	.966	1.000	.500
DRINK * IMAGERY	.609	8.153	9	.521	.813	1.000	.250

Tests the null hypothesis that the error covariance matrix of the orthonormalized transformed dependent variables is proportional to an identity matrix.

a. May be used to adjust the degrees of freedom for the averaged tests of significance. Corrected tests are displayed in the layers (by default) of the Tests of Within Subjects Effects table.

b. Design: Intercept+GENDER - Within Subjects Design: DRINK+IMAGERY+DRINK*IMAGERY

SPSS Output 9.19

SPSS Output 9.20 shows the summary table of the repeated measures effects in the ANOVA with corrected F values (those of you using version 7.5 or before will need to expand the table using the method described in section 9.2.4.3). The output is split into sections for each of the effects in the model and their associated error terms. The table format is the same as for the previous example, except that the interactions between gender and the repeated measures effects are included also. We would expect to still find the affects that were previously present (in a balanced design, the inclusion of an extra variable should not effect these effects). By looking at the significance values it is clear that this prediction is true: there are still significant effects of the type of drink used, the type of imagery used, and the interaction of these two variables.

In addition to the effects already described we find that gender interacts significantly with the type of drink used (so, men and women respond differently to beer, wine and water regardless of the context of the advert). There is also a significant interaction of gender and imagery (so, men and women respond differently to positive, negative and neutral imagery regardless of the drink being advertised). Finally, the three-way interaction between gender, imagery and drink is significant, indicating that the way in which imagery affects responses to different types of drinks depends on whether the subject is male or female. The effects of the repeated measures variables have been outlined in section 9.3.5 and the pattern of these responses will not have changed, so rather than repeat myself, I will concentrate on the new effects and the forgetful reader should look back at the previous example! If you want to check that these effects are the same, look at the tables for the estimated marginal means: they should be identical to those in SPSS Output 9.12 and SPSS Output 9.14.

Tests of Within-Subjects Effects

Measure: MEASURE_1

Source		Type III Sum of Squares	df	Mean Square	F	Sig.
DRINK	Sphericity Assumed	2092.344	2	1046.172	11.708	.000
	Greenhouse-Geisser	2092.344	1.401	1493.568	11.708	.001
	Huynh-Feldt	2092.344	1.567	1334.881	11.708	.000
	Lower-bound	2092.344	1.000	2092.344	11.708	.003
DRINK * GENDER	Sphericity Assumed	4569.011	2	2284.506	25.566	.000
	Greenhouse-Geisser	4569.011	1.401	3261.475	25.566	.000
	Huynh-Feldt	4569.011	1.567	2914.954	25.566	.000
	Lower-bound	4569.011	1.000	4569.011	25.566	.000
Error(DRINK)	Sphericity Assumed	3216.867	36	89.357		
	Greenhouse-Geisser	3216.867	25.216	127.571		
	Huynh-Feldt	3216.867	28.214	114.017		
	Lower-bound	3216.867	18.000	178.715		
IMAGERY	Sphericity Assumed	21628.678	2	10814.339	287.417	.000
	Greenhouse-Geisser	21628.678	1.932	11196.937	287.417	.000
	Huynh-Feldt	21628.678	2.000	10814.339	287.417	.000
	Lower-bound	21628.678	1.000	21628.678	287.417	.000
IMAGERY * GENDER	Sphericity Assumed	1998.344	2	999.172	26.555	.000
	Greenhouse-Geisser	1998.344	1.932	1034.522	26.555	.000
	Huynh-Feldt	1998.344	2.000	999.172	26.555	.000
	Lower-bound	1998.344	1.000	1998.344	26.555	.000
Error(IMAGERY)	Sphericity Assumed	1354.533	36	37.626		
	Greenhouse-Geisser	1354.533	34.770	38.957		
	Huynh-Feldt	1354.533	36.000	37.626		
	Lower-bound	1354.533	18.000	75.252		
DRINK * IMAGERY	Sphericity Assumed	2624.422	4	656.106	19.593	.000
	Greenhouse-Geisser	2624.422	3.251	807.186	19.593	.000
	Huynh-Feldt	2624.422	4.000	656.106	19.593	.000
	Lower-bound	2624.422	1.000	2624.422	19.593	.000
DRINK * IMAGERY * GENDER	Sphericity Assumed	495.689	4	123.922	3.701	.009
	Greenhouse-Geisser	495.689	3.251	152.458	3.701	.014
	Huynh-Feldt	495.689	4.000	123.922	3.701	.009
	Lower-bound	495.689	1.000	495.689	3.701	.070
Error(DRINK*IMAGERY)	Sphericity Assumed	2411.000	72	33.486		
	Greenhouse-Geisser	2411.000	58.524	41.197		
	Huynh-Feldt	2411.000	72.000	33.486		
	Lower-bound	2411.000	18.000	133.944		

SPSS Output 9.20

9.4.1.1. The Effect of Gender

The main effect of gender is listed separately from the repeated measure effects in a table labelled *Tests of Between-Subjects Effects*. Before looking at this table it is important to check the assumption of homogeneity of variance using Levene's test (see Chapter 6). SPSS produces a table listing Levene's test for each of the repeated measures variables in the data editor, and we need to look for any variable that has a significant value. SPSS Output 9.21 shows both tables. The table showing Levene's test indicates that variances are homogeneous for all levels of the repeated measures variables (because all significance values are greater than 0.05). If any values were significant, then this would compromise the accuracy of the F-test for gender, and we would have to consider transforming all of our data to stabilize the variances between groups (one popular transformation is to take the square root of all values). Fortunately, in this example a transformation is unnecessary. The second table shows the ANOVA summary table for the main effect of gender, and this reveals a significant effect (because the significance of 0.018 is less than the standard cut-off point of 0.05).

Levene's Test of Equality of Error Variances

	F	df1	df2	Sig.
Beer + Sexy	1.009	1	18	.328
Beer + Corpse	1.305	1	18	.268
Beer + Person in Armchair	1.813	1	18	.195
Wine + Sexy	2.017	1	18	.173
Wine + Corpse	1.048	1	18	.320
Wine + Person in Armchair	.071	1	18	.793
Water + Sexy	.317	1	18	.580
Water + Corpse	.804	1	18	.382
Water + Person in Armchair	1.813	1	18	.195

Tests the null hypothesis that the error variance of the dependent variable is equal across groups.

a. Design: Intercept+GENDER - Within Subjects Design: DRINK+IMAGERY+DRINK*IMAGERY

Tests of Between-Subjects Effects

Measure: MEASURE_1
Transformed Variable: Average

Source	Type III Sum of Squares	df	Mean Square	F	Sig.
Intercept	1246.445	1	1246.445	144.593	.000
GENDER	58.178	1	58.178	6.749	.018
Error	155.167	18	8.620		

SPSS Output 9.21

We can report that there was a significant main effect of gender ($F(1, 18) = 6.75$, $p < 0.05$). This effect tells us that if we ignore all other variables, male subjects' ratings were significantly different to females. If you requested that SPSS display means for the gender effect you should scan through your output and find the table in a section headed *Estimated Marginal Means*. SPSS Output 9.22 is a table of means for the main effect of gender with the associated standard errors. This information is plotted in Figure 9.16. It is clear from this graph that men's ratings were generally significantly more positive than females. Therefore, men gave more positive ratings than women regardless of the drink being advertised and the type of imagery used in the advert.

Estimates

Measure: MEASURE_1

Gender	Mean	Std. Error	95% Confidence Interval	
			Lower Bound	Upper Bound
Male	9.600	.928	7.649	11.551
Female	6.189	.928	4.238	8.140

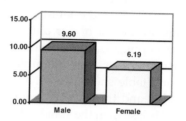

SPSS Output 9.22

Figure 9.16

9.4.1.2. The Interaction between Gender and Drink

SPSS Output 9.20 indicated that gender interacted in some way with the type of drink used as a stimulus. Remembering that the effect of drink violated sphericity, we must report Greenhouse-Geisser corrected values for this interaction with the between-group factor. From the summary table we should report that there was a significant interaction between the type of drink used and the gender of the subject ($F(1.40, 25.27) = 25.57$, $p < 0.001$). This effect tells us that the type of drink being advertised had a different effect on men and women. We can use the estimated marginal means to determine the nature of this interaction (or we could have asked SPSS for a plot of gender × drink using the dialog box in Figure 9.15). The means and interaction graph (Figure 9.17 and SPSS Output 9.23) show the meaning of this result. The graph shows the average male ratings of each drink ignoring the type of imagery with which it was presented (circles). The women's scores are shown as squares. The graph clearly shows that male and female ratings are very similar for wine and water, but men seem to rate beer more highly than women—regardless of the type of imagery used. We could interpret this interaction as meaning that the type of drink being advertised influenced ratings differently in men and women. Specifically, ratings were similar for wine and water but males rated beer higher than women. This interaction can be clarified using the contrasts specified before the analysis (see section 9.4.2).

2. Gender * DRINK

Measure: MEASURE_1

Gender	DRINK	Mean	Std. Error	95% Confidence Interval	
				Lower Bound	Upper Bound
Male	1	20.600	2.441	15.471	25.729
	2	7.333	.765	5.726	8.940
	3	.867	1.414	-2.103	3.836
Female	1	3.067	2.441	-2.062	8.196
	2	9.333	.765	7.726	10.940
	3	6.167	1.414	3.197	9.136

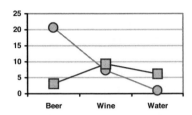

SPSS Output 9.23　　　　　　　　　　　**Figure 9.17**

9.4.1.3. The Interaction between Gender and Imagery

SPSS Output 9.20 indicated that gender interacted in some way with the type of imagery used as a stimulus. The effect of imagery did not violate sphericity, so we can report the uncorrected F value. From the summary table we should report that there was a significant interaction between the type of imagery used and the gender of the subject ($F(2, 36) = 26.55$, $p < 0.001$). This effect tells us that the type of imagery used in the advert had a different effect on men and women. We can use the estimated marginal means to determine the nature of this interaction (or we could have asked SPSS for a plot of imagery × gender using the dialog box in Figure 9.15). The means and interaction graph (Figure 9.18 and SPSS Output 9.24) show the meaning of this result. The graph shows the average male in each imagery condition ignoring the type of drink that was rated (circles). The women's scores are shown as squares. The graph clearly shows that male and female ratings are very similar for positive and neutral imagery, but men seem to be less affected by negative imagery than women—regardless of the drink in the advert. To interpret this finding more fully, we should consult the contrasts for this interaction (see section 9.4.2).

3. Gender * IMAGERY

Measure: MEASURE_1

Gender	IMAGERY	Mean	Std. Error	95% Confidence Interval	
				Lower Bound	Upper Bound
Male	1	20.533	1.399	17.595	23.471
	2	.833	1.092	-1.460	3.127
	3	7.433	1.395	4.502	10.365
Female	1	22.000	1.399	19.062	24.938
	2	-12.000	1.092	-14.293	-9.707
	3	8.567	1.395	5.635	11.498

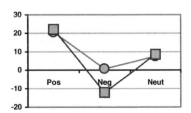

SPSS Output 9.24　　　　　　　　　　　**Figure 9.18**

9.4.1.4.   The Interaction between Drink and Imagery

The interpretation of this interaction is the same as for the two-way ANOVA (see section 9.4.1.4). You may remember that the interaction reflected the fact that negative imagery has a different effect to both positive and neutral imagery (because it decreased ratings rather than increasing them).

9.4.1.5.   The Interaction between Gender, Drink and Imagery

The three-way interaction tells us whether the drink by imagery interaction is the same for men and women (i.e. whether the combined effect of the type of drink and the imagery used is the same for male subjects as for female subjects). We can conclude that there is a significant three-way drink × imagery × gender interaction ($F(4, 72) = 3.70$, $p < 0.01$). The nature of this interaction is shown up in Figure 9.19, which shows the imagery by drink interaction for men and women separately. The male graph shows that when positive imagery is used, men generally rated all three drinks positively (the line with circles is higher than the other lines for all drinks). This pattern is true of women also (the line representing positive imagery is above the other two lines). When neutral imagery is used, men rate beer very highly, but rate wine and water fairly neutrally. Women, on the other hand rate beer and water neutrally, but rate wine more positively (in fact, the pattern of the positive and neutral imagery lines show that women generally rate wine slightly more positively than water and beer). So, for neutral imagery men still rate beer positively, and women still rate wine positively. For the negative imagery, the men still rate beer very highly, but give low ratings to the other two types of drink. So, regardless of the type of imagery used, men rate beer very positively (if you look at the graph you'll note that ratings for beer are virtually identical for the three types of imagery). Women, however, rate all three drinks very negatively when negative imagery is used. The three-way interaction is, therefore, likely to reflect these sex differences in the interaction between drink and imagery. Specifically, men seem fairly immune to the effects of imagery when beer is being used as a stimulus, whereas women are not. The contrasts will show up exactly what this interaction represents.

4. Gender * DRINK * IMAGERY

Measure: MEASURE_1

Gender	DRINK	IMAGERY	Mean	Std. Error	95% Confidence Interval	
					Lower Bound	Upper Bound
Male	1	1	24.800	4.037	16.318	33.282
		2	20.100	2.096	15.697	24.503
		3	16.900	2.429	11.797	22.003
	2	1	22.300	1.939	18.227	26.373
		2	-7.800	1.440	-10.825	-4.775
		3	7.500	1.483	4.383	10.617
	3	1	14.500	2.085	10.119	18.881
		2	-9.800	2.201	-14.424	-5.176
		3	-2.100	1.654	-5.575	1.375
Female	1	1	17.300	4.037	8.818	25.782
		2	-11.200	2.096	-15.603	-6.797
		3	3.100	2.429	-2.003	8.203
	2	1	28.400	1.939	24.327	32.473
		2	-16.200	1.440	-19.225	-13.175
		3	15.800	1.483	12.683	18.917
	3	1	20.300	2.085	15.919	24.681
		2	-8.600	2.201	-13.224	-3.976
		3	6.800	1.654	3.325	10.275

SPSS Output 9.25

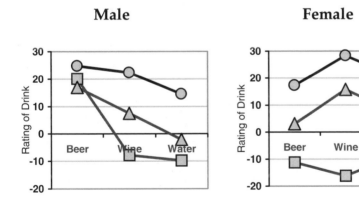

Figure 9.19: Graphs showing the drink by imagery interaction for men and women. Lines represent positive imagery (circles), negative imagery (squares) and neutral imagery (triangles)

9.4.2.   Contrasts for Repeated Measures Variables

In section 9.3.2 we requested simple contrasts for the **drink** variable (for which water was used as the control category) and for the **imagery** category (for which neutral imagery was used as the control category). SPSS Output 9.17 shows the summary results for these contrasts. The table is the same as for the previous example except that the added effects of **gender** and its interaction with other variables are now included. So, for the main effect of drink, the first contrast compares level 1 (beer) against the base category (in this case, the last category: water). This result is significant ($F(1, 18) = 15.37$, $p < 0.01$), and the next contrast compares level 2 (wine) with the base category (water) and confirms the significant difference found when gender was not included as a variable in the analysis ($F(1, 18) = 19.92$, $p < 0.001$). For the imagery main effect, the first contrast compares level 1 (positive) to the base category (neutral) and verifies the significant effect found by the *post hoc* tests ($F(1, 18) = 134.87$, $p < 0.001$). The second contrast confirms the significant difference found for the negative imagery condition compared to the neutral ($F(1, 18) = 129.18$, $p < 0.001$). No contrast was specified for gender.

Tests of Within-Subjects Contrasts

Measure: MEASURE_1

Source	DRINK	IMAGERY	Type III Sum of Squares	df	Mean Square	F	Sig.
DRINK	Level 1 vs. Level 3		1383.339	1	1383.339	15.371	.001
	Level 2 vs. Level 3		464.006	1	464.006	19.923	.000
DRINK * GENDER	Level 1 vs. Level 3		2606.806	1	2606.806	28.965	.000
	Level 2 vs. Level 3		54.450	1	54.450	2.338	.144
Error(DRINK)	Level 1 vs. Level 3		1619.967	18	89.998		
	Level 2 vs. Level 3		419.211	18	23.290		
IMAGERY		Level 1 vs. Level 3	3520.089	1	3520.089	134.869	.000
		Level 2 vs. Level 3	3690.139	1	3690.139	129.179	.000
IMAGERY * GENDER		Level 1 vs. Level 3	.556	1	.556	.021	.886
		Level 2 vs. Level 3	975.339	1	975.339	34.143	.000
Error(IMAGERY)		Level 1 vs. Level 3	469.800	18	26.100		
		Level 2 vs. Level 3	514.189	18	28.566		
DRINK * IMAGERY	Level 1 vs. Level 3	Level 1 vs. Level 3	320.000	1	320.000	1.686	.211
		Level 2 vs. Level 3	720.000	1	720.000	8.384	.010
	Level 2 vs. Level 3	Level 1 vs. Level 3	36.450	1	36.450	.223	.642
		Level 2 vs. Level 3	2928.200	1	2928.200	31.698	.000
DRINK * IMAGERY * GENDER	Level 1 vs. Level 3	Level 1 vs. Level 3	441.800	1	441.800	2.328	.144
		Level 2 vs. Level 3	480.200	1	480.200	5.592	.029
	Level 2 vs. Level 3	Level 1 vs. Level 3	4.050	1	4.050	.025	.877
		Level 2 vs. Level 3	405.000	1	405.000	4.384	.051
Error(DRINK*IMAGERY)	Level 1 vs. Level 3	Level 1 vs. Level 3	3416.200	18	189.789		
		Level 2 vs. Level 3	3416.200	18	189.789		
	Level 2 vs. Level 3	Level 1 vs. Level 3	1545.800	18	85.878		
		Level 2 vs. Level 3	1662.800	18	92.378		

SPSS Output 9.26

9.4.2.1. Drink × Gender Interaction 1: Beer vs. Water, Male vs. Female

The first interaction term looks at level 1 of drink (beer) compared to level 3 (water), comparing male and female scores. This contrast is highly significant ($F(1, 18) = 28.97$, $p < 0.001$). This result tells us that the increased ratings of beer compared to water found for men is not found for women. So, in Figure 9.17 the squares representing female ratings of beer and water are roughly level; however, the circle representing male ratings of beer is much higher than the circle representing water. The positive contrast represents this difference and so we can conclude that male ratings of beer (compared to water) were significantly greater than women's ratings of beer (compared to water).

9.4.2.2. Drink × Gender Interaction 2: Wine vs. Water, Male vs. Female

The second interaction term compares level 2 of drink (wine) to level 3 (water), contrasting male and female scores. There is no significant difference for this contrast ($F(1, 18) = 2.34$, $p = 0.14$), which tells us that the difference between ratings of wine compared to water in males is roughly the same as in females. Therefore, overall, the drink × gender interaction has shown up a difference between males and females in how they rate beer (regardless of the type of imagery used).

9.4.2.3. Imagery × Gender Interaction 1: Positive vs. Neutral, Male vs. Female

The first interaction term looks at level 1 of imagery (positive) compared to level 3 (neutral), comparing male and female scores. This contrast is not significant ($F < 1$). This result tells us that ratings of drinks presented with positive imagery (relative to those presented with neutral imagery) were equivalent for males and females. This finding represents the fact that in Figure 9.18 the squares and circles for both the positive and neutral conditions overlap (therefore male and female responses were the same.

9.4.2.4. Imagery × Gender Interaction 2: Negative vs. Neutral, Male vs. Female

The second interaction term looks at level 2 of imagery (negative) compared to level 3 (neutral), comparing male and female scores. This contrast is highly significant ($F(1, 18) = 34.13$, $p < 0.001$). This result tells us that the difference between ratings of drinks paired with negative imagery compared to neutral was different for men and women. Looking at Figure 9.18 this finding represents the fact that for men, ratings of drinks paired with negative imagery were relatively similar to ratings of drinks paired with neutral imagery (the circles have a fairly similar vertical position). However, if you look at the female ratings, then drinks were rated much less favourably when presented with negative imagery than when presented with neutral imagery (the square in the negative condition is much lower than the neutral condition).

Therefore, overall, the imagery × gender interaction has shown up a difference between males and females in terms of their ratings to drinks presented with negative imagery compared to neutral; specifically, men seem less affected by negative imagery.

9.4.2.5. Drink × Imagery × Gender Interaction 1: Beer vs. Water, Positive vs. Neutral Imagery, Male vs. Female

The first interaction term compares level 1 of drink (beer) to level 3 (water), when positive imagery (level 1) is used compared to neutral (level 3) in males compared to females ($F(1, 18) = 2.33$, $p = 0.144$). The non-significance of this contrast tells us that the difference in ratings when positive imagery is used compared to neutral imagery is roughly equal when beer is used as a stimulus as when water is used, and these differences are equivalent in male and female subjects. In terms of the interaction graph (Figure 9.19) it means that the distance between the circle and the triangle in the beer condition is the same as the distance between the circle and the triangle in the water condition and that these distances are equivalent in men and women.

9.4.2.6. Drink × Imagery × Gender Interaction 2: Beer vs. Water, Negative vs. Neutral Imagery, Male vs. Female

The second interaction term looks at level 1 of drink (beer) compared to level 3 (water), when negative imagery (level 2) is used compared to neutral (level 3). This contrast is significant ($F(1, 18) = 5.59$, $p < 0.05$). This result tells us that the difference in ratings between beer and water when negative imagery is used (compared to neutral imagery) is different between men and women. If we plot ratings of beer and water across the negative and neutral conditions, for males (circles) and females (squares) separately, we see that ratings after negative imagery are always lower than ratings for neutral imagery except for men's ratings of beer, which are actually higher after negative imagery. As such, this contrast tells us that the interaction effect reflects a difference in the way in which males rate beer compared to females when negative imagery is

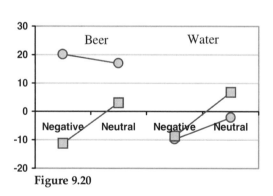

Figure 9.20

used compared to neutral. Males and females are similar in their pattern of ratings for water but different in the way in which they rate beer.

9.4.2.7. Drink × Imagery × Gender Interaction 3: Wine vs. Water, Positive vs. Neutral Imagery, Male vs. Female.

The third interaction term looks at level 2 of drink (wine) compared to level 3 (water), when positive imagery (level 1) is used compared to neutral (level 3) in males compared to females. This contrast is non-significant ($F (1, 18) < 1$). This result tells us that the difference in ratings when positive imagery is used compared to neutral imagery is roughly equal when wine is used as a stimulus as when water is used, and these differences are equivalent in male and female subjects. In terms of the interaction graph (Figure 9.19) it means that the distance between the circle and the triangle in the wine condition is the same as the distance between the circle and the triangle in the water condition and that these distances are equivalent in men and women.

9.4.2.8. Drink × Imagery × Gender Interaction 4: Wine vs. Water, Negative vs. Neutral Imagery, Male vs. Female.

The final interaction term looks at level 2 of drink (wine) compared to level 3 (water), when negative imagery (level 2) is used compared to neutral (level 3). This contrast is very close to significance ($F(1, 18) = 4.38$, $p = 0.051$). This result tells us that the difference in ratings between wine and water when negative imagery is used (compared to neutral imagery) is different between men and women (although this difference has not quite reached significance).

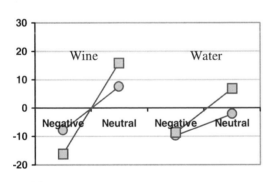

Figure 9.21

If we plot ratings of wine and water across the negative and neutral conditions, for males (circles) and females (squares), we see that ratings after negative imagery are always lower than ratings for neutral imagery, but for women rating wine the change is much more dramatic (the line is steeper). As such, this contrast tells us that the interaction effect reflects a difference in the way in which females rate wine differently to males when neutral imagery is used compared to when negative imagery is used. Males and females are similar in their pattern of ratings for water but different in the way in which they rate wine. It is noteworthy that this contrast was not significant using the usual 0.05 level; however, it is worth remembering that this cut-off point was set in a fairly arbitrary way, and so it is worth reporting these close effects and letting your reader decide whether they are meaningful or not. There is also a growing trend towards reporting effect sizes in preference to using significance levels.

9.4.2.9. Summary

These contrasts again tell us nothing about the differences between the beer and wine conditions (or the positive and negative conditions) and different contrasts would have to be run to find out more. However, what is clear so far is that differences exist between men and women in terms of their ratings towards beer and wine. It seems as though men are relatively unaffected by negative imagery when it comes to beer. Likewise, women seem more willing to rate wine positively when neutral imagery is used than men do. What should be clear from this is that complex ANOVA in which several independent variables are used results in complex interaction effects that require a great deal of concentration to interpret (imagine interpreting a four-way interaction!). Therefore, it is essential to take a systematic approach to interpretation and plotting graphs is a particularly useful way to proceed. It is also advisable to think carefully about the appropriate contrasts to use to answer the questions you have about your data. It is these contrasts that will help you to interpret interactions, so make sure you select sensible ones!

9.5.   Further Reading

Field, A. P. (1998). A bluffer's guide to sphericity. *Newsletter of the Mathematical, Statistical and Computing section of the British Psychological Society*, 6 (1), 13-22 (available from the internet at http://www.cogs.susx.ac.uk/users/andyf/research/articles/sphericity.pdf)

Howell, D. C. (1997). *Statistical methods for psychology* (4th edition). Belmont, CA: Duxbury.

Roberts, M. J. & Russo, R. (1999). *A student's guide to analysis of variance*. London: Routledge.

Wright, D. B. (1997). *Understanding statistics: an introduction for the social sciences*. London: Sage.

Reconciliation

10 MANOVA

10.1. Introduction: Similarities and Differences to ANOVA

Over the last three chapters, we have seen how the general linear model can be used to detect group differences on a single dependent variable. However, there may be circumstances in which we are interested in several dependent variables and in these cases the simple ANOVA model is inadequate. Instead, we can use the technique known as multivariate analysis of variance (or MANOVA) which can be thought of as an ANOVA for situations in which there are several dependent variables. The simple principles of ANOVA extend to MANOVA in that we can use MANOVA when there is only one independent variable or when there are several, we can look at interactions between independent variables, and we can even do contrasts to see which groups differ from each other. ANOVA can be used only in situations in which there is one dependent variable and so is known as a *univariate* test (univariate quite obviously means 'one variable'); MANOVA is designed to look at several dependent variables simultaneously and so is a *multivariate* test (multivariate means 'many variables').

If we have collected data about several dependent variables then we could simply conduct a separate ANOVA for each dependent variable (and if you read research articles you'll find that it is not unusual for researchers to do this!). Think back to Chapter 7 and you should remember that a similar question was posed regarding why ANOVA was used in preference to multiple *t*-tests. The answer to why MANOVA is used instead of multiple ANOVAs is the same: the more tests we conduct on the same data, the more we inflate the familywise error rate (see section 7.1.1). The more dependent variables that have been measured, the more ANOVAs would need to be conducted and the greater the chance of making a type I error. However, there are other reasons for preferring MANOVA to several ANOVAs. For one thing, there is important additional information that is gained from a MANOVA. If separate ANOVAs are conducted on each dependent variable, then any relationship between dependent variables is ignored. As such, we lose information about any correlations that might exist between the dependent variables. MANOVA, by including all dependent variables in the same analysis, takes account of the relationship between outcome variables. Related to this point, ANOVA can tell us only whether groups differ along a single dimension whereas MANOVA has the power to detect whether groups differ along a combination of dimensions. For example, ANOVA tells us how scores on a single dependent variable distinguish groups of subjects (so for example, we might be able to distinguish drivers, non-drivers and drunk drivers by the number of pedestrians they kill). MANOVA incorporates information about several outcome measures and, therefore, informs us of whether groups of subjects can be distinguished by a combination of scores on several dependent measures. For example, it may not be possible to distinguish drivers, non-drivers and drunk drivers only by the number of pedestrians that they kill, but they might be distinguished by *a combination* of the number of pedestrians they kill, the number of lampposts they hit, and the number of cars they crash into. So, in this sense MANOVA has greater power to detect an effect, because it can detect whether groups differ along a combination of variables whereas ANOVA can detect only if groups differ along a single variable (see Huberty and Morris, 1989 and section 10.1.2). For these reasons, MANOVA is preferable to conducting several ANOVAs.

10.1.1.   Words of Warning

From my description of MANOVA it is probably looking like a pretty groovy little test that allows you to measure hundreds of dependent variables and then just sling them into the analysis. This is not the case. As with many statistical techniques, it is not a good idea to lump all of your dependent variables together in a MANOVA unless you have good theoretical or empirical basis for doing so. Statistical procedures are just a way of number crunching and so even if you put rubbish into an analysis you will still reach conclusions that are statistically meaningful, but are unlikely to be empirically meaningful. There is a temptation to see statistics as some God-like way of determining the real truth, but statistics are merely a tool. As my statistics lecturer used to say, 'if you put garbage in, you get garbage out', and this statement is very true. In a statistical analysis there is no substitute for empirical thinking. In circumstances where there is a good theoretical basis for including some but not all your dependent variables, you should run separate analyses: one for the variables being tested on a heuristic basis and one for the theoretically meaningful variables. The point to take on board here is not to include lots of dependent variables in a MANOVA just because you have measured them.

10.1.2.   Current Controversies

Like ANOVA, MANOVA is a two-stage test in which an overall (or omnibus) test is first performed before more specific procedures are applied to tease apart group differences. Unfortunately, there are debates regarding both stages of the MANOVA procedure. For the main analysis there are four commonly used ways of assessing the overall significance of a MANOVA and debate exists about which method is best in terms of power and sample size considerations. In addition, there is substantial debate over how best to further analyze and interpret group differences when the overall MANOVA is significant. There are two main approaches to follow-up analysis: univariate ANOVAs and discriminant analysis. I will consider both.

A second controversy surrounds the power of MANOVA (i.e. the ability of MANOVA to detect an effect that genuinely exists). I mentioned in the introduction that MANOVA had greater power than ANOVA to detect effects because it could take account of the correlations between dependent variables. However, the issue of power is more complex than alluded to by my simple statement. Ramsey (1982) found that as the correlation between dependent variables increased, the power of MANOVA decreased. This led Tabachnick and Fidell (1996) to conclude that it was best to select dependent variables that were uncorrelated and, therefore, measured different aspects of the influence of the independent variable(s). In contrast, Stevens's (1980) investigation of the effect of dependent variable correlations on test power revealed that 'the power with high intercorrelations is in most cases greater than that for moderate intercorrelations, and in some cases it is dramatically higher' (p. 736). These findings directly contradict each other, which leaves us with the puzzling conundrum of what, exactly, is the relationship between power and intercorrelation of the dependent variables? Luckily, Cole et al. (1994) have done a great deal to illuminate this relationship. They found that the power of MANOVA depends on a combination of the correlation between dependent variables and the size of the effect to be detected (known as the *effect size*). In short, if you are expecting to find a large effect, then MANOVA will have greater power if the measures are somewhat different (even negatively correlated) and if the group differences are in the same direction for each measure. If you have two dependent variables, one of which exhibits a large group difference, and one of which exhibits a small, or no, group difference then power will be increased if these variables are highly correlated. The take-home message from Cole et al.'s work is that if you are interested in how powerful the MANOVA is likely to be you should consider not just the intercorrelation of dependent variables but also the size and pattern of group differences that you expect to get. However, it should be noted that Cole et al.'s work is limited to the case of where two groups are being compared and power considerations are more complex in multiple-group situations.

10.2. Theory of MANOVA

 The theory of MANOVA is very complex to understand without knowing matrix algebra, and frankly, matrix algebra is way beyond the scope of this book (those with maths brains can consult Namboodiri, 1984; or Stevens, 1992). However, I intend to give a flavour of the conceptual basis of MANOVA, using matrices, without requiring you to understand exactly how those matrices are used. Those interested in the exact underlying theory of MANOVA should read Bray and Maxwell's (1985) superb monograph on the subject.

10.2.1. Introduction to Matrices

First, I should explain what a matrix is: a matrix is simply a collection of numbers arranged in columns and rows. In fact, throughout this book you have been using a matrix without even realizing it: the SPSS data editor. In the SPSS data editor we have numbers arranged in columns and rows and this is exactly what a matrix is. A matrix can have many columns and many rows and we usually specify the dimensions of the matrix using numbers. So, a 2×3 matrix is a matrix with 2 rows and 3 columns, and a 5×4 matrix is one with 5 rows and 4 columns (examples below).

$$\begin{pmatrix} 2 & 5 & 6 \\ 3 & 5 & 8 \end{pmatrix}$$

$$\begin{pmatrix} 2 & 4 & 6 & 8 \\ 3 & 4 & 6 & 7 \\ 4 & 3 & 5 & 8 \\ 2 & 5 & 7 & 9 \\ 4 & 6 & 6 & 9 \end{pmatrix}$$

2×3 matrix　　　　　　5×4 matrix

You can think of these matrices in terms of each row representing the data from a single subject and each column as representing data relating to a particular variable. So, for the 5×4 matrix we can imagine a situation where 5 subjects were tested on 4 variables: so, the first subject scored 2 on the first variable and 8 on the fourth variable. The values within a matrix are typically referred to as *components* or *elements*.

A square matrix is one in which there are an equal number of columns and rows. In this type of matrix it is sometimes useful to distinguish between the diagonal components (i.e. the values that lie on the diagonal line from the top left component to the bottom right component) and the off-diagonal components (the values that do not lie on the diagonal). In the matrix below, the diagonal components are 5, 12, 2 and 6 because they lie along the diagonal line. The off-diagonal components are all of the other values. A square matrix in which the diagonal elements are equal to 1 and the off-diagonal elements are equal to 0 is known as an *identity matrix*.

$$
\begin{pmatrix}
5 & 3 & 6 & 10 \\
3 & 12 & 4 & 6 \\
6 & 4 & 2 & 7 \\
10 & 6 & 7 & 6
\end{pmatrix}
\qquad
\begin{pmatrix}
1 & 0 & 0 \\
0 & 1 & 0 \\
0 & 0 & 1
\end{pmatrix}
$$

square matrix   identity matrix

Hopefully, the concept of a matrix should now be slightly less scary than it was previously: it is not some magical mathematical entity, merely a way of representing a data set—just like a spreadsheet.

Now, there is a special case of a matrix where there are data from only one subject, and this is known as a *row vector*. Likewise, if there is only one column in a matrix this is known as a *column vector*. In the examples below, the row vector can be thought of as a single subject's score on four different variables, whereas the column vector can be thought of as five subjects' scores on one variable.

$$
\begin{pmatrix} 2 & 6 & 4 & 8 \end{pmatrix}
\qquad
\begin{pmatrix} 8 \\ 6 \\ 10 \\ 15 \\ 6 \end{pmatrix}
$$

row vector   column vector

Armed with this knowledge of what vectors are, we can have a brief look at how they are used to conduct a MANOVA.

10.2.2.   Some Important Matrices and their Functions

As with ANOVA, we are primarily interested in how much variance can be explained by the experimental manipulation (which in real terms means how much variance is explained by the fact that certain scores appear in certain groups). Therefore, we need to know the sum of squares due to the grouping variable (the systematic variation, SS_M), the sum of squares due to natural differences between subjects (the residual variation, SS_R) and of course the total amount of variation that needs to be explained (SS_T): for more details about these sources of variation re-read Chapters 4 and 7. However, I mentioned that MANOVA also takes into account several dependent variables simultaneously and it does this by using a matrix that contains information about the variance accounted for by each dependent variable. For the univariate *F*-test (e.g. ANOVA) we calculated the ratio of systematic variance to unsystematic variance for a single dependent variable.

In MANOVA the test statistic is derived by comparing the ratio of systematic to unsystematic variance for several dependent variables. This comparison is made by using the ratio of a matrix representing the systematic variance of all dependent variables to a matrix representing the unsystematic variance of all dependent variables. The matrix that represents the systematic variance (or the model sum of squares for all variables) is denoted by the letter *H* and is called the *hypothesis sum of squares and cross-products matrix* (or hypothesis SSCP). The matrix that represents the unsystematic variance (the residual sums of squares for all variables) is denoted by the letter *E* and is called the *error sum of squares and cross-products matrix* (or error SSCP). Finally, there is a matrix that represents the total amount of variance present for each dependent variable (the total sums of squares for each dependent variable) and this is denoted by *T* and is called the *total error sum of squares and cross-products matrix* (or total SSCP).

Later, I will show how these matrices are used in exactly the same way as the simple sums of squares (SS_M, SS_R and SS_T) in ANOVA to derive a test statistic representing the ratio of systematic to unsystematic variance in the model. The observant amongst you may have noticed that the matrices I have described are all called *sum of squares and cross-products* matrices. It should be obvious why these matrices are referred to as sum of squares matrices, but why is there a reference to cross-products in their name? We came across cross-product deviations in Chapter 3 and saw that they represented a total value for the combined error between two variables (so, in some sense they represented an unstandardized estimate of the total correlation between two variables). As such, whereas the sum of squares of a variable is the total squared difference between the observed values and the mean value, the cross-product is the total combined error between two variables. I mentioned earlier that MANOVA had the power to account for any correlation between dependent variables and it does this by using these cross-products.

10.2.3.   Calculating MANOVA by Hand: A Worked Example

Imagine that we were interested in the effects of cognitive behaviour therapy on obsessive compulsive disorder (OCD). Now, we could compare a group of OCD sufferers after cognitive behaviour therapy (CBT) and after behaviour therapy (BT) with a group of OCD sufferers who are still awaiting treatment (a no-treatment condition, NT). Now, most psychopathologies have both behavioural and cognitive elements to them. For example, in OCD if someone had an obsession with germs and contamination, this disorder might manifest itself in obsessive hand-washing and would influence not just how many times they actually wash their hands (behaviour) but also the number of times they think about washing their hands (cognitions). Similarly, someone with an obsession about bags won't just think about bags a lot, but they might carry out bag-related behaviours (such as saying 'bag' repeatedly, or buying lots of bags). If we are interested in seeing how successful a therapy is, it is not enough to look only at behavioural outcomes (such as whether obsessive behaviours are reduced); it is important to establish whether cognitions are being changed also. Hence, in this example two dependent measures were taken: the occurrence of obsession-related behaviours (**actions**) and the occurrence of obsession-related cognitions (**thoughts**). These dependent variables were measured on a single day and so represent the number of obsession-related behaviours/thoughts in a normal day.

Table 10.1: Data from **OCD.sav**

Group:	DV 1: Actions			DV 2: Thoughts		
	CBT (1)	BT (2)	NT (3)	CBT (1)	BT (2)	NT (3)
	5	4	4	14	14	13
	5	4	5	11	15	15
	4	1	5	16	13	14
	4	1	4	13	14	14
	5	4	6	12	15	13
	3	6	4	14	19	20
	7	5	7	12	13	13
	6	5	4	15	18	16
	6	2	6	16	14	14
	4	5	5	11	17	18
$\overline{X}$	4.90	3.70	5.00	13.40	15.20	15.00
s	1.20	1.77	1.05	1.90	2.10	2.36
s^2	1.43	3.12	1.11	3.60	4.40	5.56
	$\overline{X}_{grand(Actions)} = 4.53$			$\overline{X}_{grand(Thoughts)} = 14.53$		
	$s^2_{grand(Actions)} = 2.1195$			$s^2_{grand(Thoughts)} = 4.8780$		

The data are in Table 10.1 and can be found in the file **OCD.sav**. Subjects belonged to either group 1 (CBT), group 2 (BT) or group 3 (NT) and within these groups, all subjects had both actions and thoughts measured.

To begin with let's carry out univariate ANOVAs on each of the two dependent variables. A description of the ANOVA model can be found in Chapter 7 and I will draw heavily on the assumption that you have read this chapter; if you are hazy on the details of Chapter 7 then now would be a good time to (re-)read sections 7.1.3.1 to 7.1.3.6.

10.2.3.1. Univariate ANOVA for DV 1 (Actions)

There are three sums of squares that need to be calculated. First we need to assess how much variability there is to be explained within the data (SS_T), next we need to see how much of this variability can be explained by the model (SS_M), and finally we have to assess how much error there is in the model (SS_R). From Chapter 7 we can calculate each of these values:

- **$SS_{T(Actions)}$**: The total sum of squares is obtained by calculating the difference between each of the 20 scores and the mean of those scores, then squaring these differences and adding these squared values up. Alternatively, you can get SPSS to calculate the variance for the action data (regardless of which group the score falls into) and then multiplying this value by the number of scores minus 1.

$$SS_T = s_{grand}^2(n-1)$$
$$= 2.1195(30-1)$$
$$= 2.1195 \times 29$$
$$= 61.47$$

- **$SS_{M(Actions)}$**: This value is calculated by taking the difference between each group mean and the grand mean and the squaring them. Multiply these values by the number of scores in the group and then add them together.

$$SS_M = 10(4.90 - 4.53)^2 + 10(3.70 - 4.53)^2 + 10(5.00 - 4.53)^2$$
$$= 10(0.37)^2 + 10(-0.83)^2 + 10(0.47)^2$$
$$= 1.37 + 6.89 + 2.21$$
$$= 10.47$$

- **$SS_{R(Actions)}$**: This value is calculated by taking the difference between each score and the mean of the group from which it came. These

differences are then squared and then added together. Alternatively
we can get SPSS to calculate the variance within each group, multiply
each group variance by the number of scores minus and then add
them together.

$$\begin{aligned}
SS_R &= s_{CBT}^2(n_{CBT} - 1) + s_{BT}^2(n_{BT} - 1) + s_{NT}^2(n_{NT} - 1) \\
&= (1.433)(10-1) + (3.122)(10-1) + (1.111)(10-1) \\
&= (1.433 \times 9) + (3.122 \times 9) + (1.111 \times 9) \\
&= 12.9 + 28.1 + 10.0 \\
&= 51.00
\end{aligned}$$

The next step is to calculate the average sums of squares (the mean
square) of each by dividing by the degrees of freedom (see section
7.1.3.5).

SS	df	MS
$SS_{M(Actions)} = 10.47$	2	5.235
$SS_{R(Actions)} = 51.00$	27	1.889

The final stage is calculate F by dividing the mean squares for the model
by the mean squares for the error in the model.

$$F = \frac{MS_M}{MS_R} = \frac{5.235}{1.889} = 2.771$$

This value can then be evaluated against critical values of F. The point to
take home here is the calculation of the various sums of squares and
what each one relates to.

10.2.3.2. Univariate ANOVA for DV 2 (Thoughts)

As with the data for dependent variable 1 there are three sums of
squares that need to be calculated as before.

$SS_{T(Thoughts)}$:

$$\begin{aligned}
SS_T &= s_{grand}^2(n-1) \\
&= 4.878(30-1) \\
&= 4.878 \times 29 \\
&= 141.46
\end{aligned}$$

$SS_{M(Thoughts)}$:

$$SS_M = 10(13.40 - 14.53)^2 + 10(15.2 - 14.53)^2 + 10(15.0 - 14.53)^2$$
$$= 10(-1.13)^2 + 10(0.67)^2 + 10(0.47)^2$$
$$= 12.77 + 4.49 + 2.21$$
$$= 19.47$$

$SS_{R(Thoughts)}$:

$$SS_R = s_{CBT}^2(n_{CBT} - 1) + s_{BT}^2(n_{BT} - 1) + s_{NT}^2(n_{NT} - 1)$$
$$= (3.6)(10 - 1) + (4.4)(10 - 1) + (5.56)(10 - 1)$$
$$= (3.6 \times 9) + (4.4 \times 9) + (5.56 \times 9)$$
$$= 32.4 + 39.6 + 50.0$$
$$= 122$$

The next step is to calculate the average sums of squares (the mean square) of each by dividing by the degrees of freedom (see section 7.1.3.5).

SS	df	MS
$SS_{M(Thoughts)} = 19.47$	2	9.735
$SS_{R(Thoughts)} = 122.00$	27	4.519

The final stage is calculate F by dividing the mean squares for the model by the mean squares for the error in the model.

$$F = \frac{MS_M}{MS_R} = \frac{9.735}{4.519} = 2.154$$

This value can then be evaluated against critical values of F. Again, the point to take home here is the calculation of the various sums of squares and what each one relates to.

10.2.3.3. The Relationship between DVs: Cross-Products

We know already that MANOVA uses the same sums of squares as an ANOVA, and in the next section we shall see exactly how it uses these values. However, I have also mentioned that MANOVA takes account of the relationship between dependent variables and that it does this by using the cross-products. To be precise, there are three different cross-products that are of interest and these three cross-products relate to the three sums of squares that we calculated for the univariate ANOVAs: that is, there is a total cross-product, a cross-product due to the model, and a residual cross-product. Let's look at the total cross-product (CP_T) first.

Table 10.2: Calculation of the total cross-product

Group	Actions	Thoughts	Actions $-\overline{X}_{grand(Actions)}$ (D_1)	Thoughts $-\overline{X}_{grand(Thoughts)}$ (D_2)	$D_1 \times D_2$
CBT	5	14	0.47	−0.53	−0.25
	5	11	0.47	−3.53	−1.66
	4	16	−0.53	1.47	−0.78
	4	13	−0.53	−1.53	0.81
	5	12	0.47	−2.53	−1.19
	3	14	−1.53	−0.53	0.81
	7	12	2.47	−2.53	−6.25
	6	15	1.47	0.47	0.69
	6	16	1.47	1.47	2.16
	4	11	−0.53	−3.53	1.87
BT	4	14	−0.53	−0.53	0.28
	4	15	−0.53	0.47	−0.25
	1	13	−3.53	−1.53	5.40
	1	14	−3.53	−0.53	1.87
	4	15	−0.53	0.47	−0.25
	6	19	1.47	4.47	6.57
	5	13	0.47	−1.53	−0.72
	5	18	0.47	3.47	1.63
	2	14	−2.53	−0.53	1.34
	5	17	0.47	2.47	1.16
NT	4	13	−0.53	−1.53	0.81
	5	15	0.47	0.47	0.22
	5	14	0.47	−0.53	−0.25
	4	14	−0.53	−0.53	0.28
	6	13	1.47	−1.53	−2.25
	4	20	−0.53	5.47	−2.90
	7	13	2.47	−1.53	−3.78
	4	16	−0.53	1.47	−0.78
	6	14	1.47	−0.53	−0.78
	5	18	0.47	3.47	1.63
$\overline{X}_{grand}$	4.53	14.53		$CP_T = \sum(D_1 \times D_2) = 5.47$	

I mentioned in Chapter 3 that the cross-product was the difference between the scores and the mean in one group multiplied by the difference between the scores and the mean in the other group. In the case of the total cross-product, the mean of interest is the grand mean for each dependent variable (see Table 10.2). Hence, we can adapt the cross-product equation described in Chapter 3 using the two dependent variables. The resulting equation for the total cross-product is described as in equation (10.1). Therefore, for each dependent variable you take each score and subtract from it the grand mean for that variable. This leaves you with two values per subject (one for each dependent variable) which should be multiplied together to get the cross-product for each subject. The total can then be found by adding the cross-products of all subjects. Table 10.2 illustrates this process.

$$CP_T = \sum \left(x_{i(\text{Actions})} - \overline{X}_{\text{grand(Actions)}} \right)\left(x_{i(\text{Thoughts})} - \overline{X}_{\text{grand(Thoughts)}} \right) \qquad (10.1)$$

The total cross-product is a gauge of the overall relationship between the two variables. However, we are also interested in how the relationship between the dependent variables is influenced by our experimental manipulation and this relationship is measured by the model cross-product (CP_M). The CP_M is calculated in a similar way to the model sum of squares. First, the difference between each group mean and the grand mean is calculated for each dependent variable. The cross-product is calculated by multiplying the differences found for each group. Each product is then multiplied by the number of scores within the group (as was done with the sum of squares). This principle is illustrated in equation (10.2) and Table 10.3.

$$CP_M = \sum n\left[\left(\overline{x}_{\text{group(Actions)}} - \overline{X}_{\text{grand(Actions)}} \right)\left(\overline{x}_{\text{group(Thoughts)}} - \overline{X}_{\text{grand(Thoughts)}} \right) \right] \qquad (10.2)$$

Table 10.3: Calculating the model cross-product

	$\overline{X}_{\text{group}}$ Actions	$\overline{X}_{\text{group}} - \overline{X}_{\text{grand}}$ (D_1)	$\overline{X}_{\text{group}}$ Thoughts	$\overline{X}_{\text{group}} - \overline{X}_{\text{grand}}$ (D_2)	$D_1 \times D_2$	$N(D_1 \times D_2)$
CBT	4.9	0.37	13.4	−1.13	−0.418	−4.18
BT	3.7	−0.83	15.2	0.67	−0.556	−5.56
NT	5.0	0.47	15.0	0.47	0.221	2.21
$\overline{X}_{\text{grand}}$	4.53		14.53		$CP_M = \sum N(D_1 \times D_2) = -7.53$	

Finally, we also need to know how the relationship between the two dependent variables is influenced by individual differences in subjects' performances. The residual cross-product (CP_R) tells us about how the relationship between the dependent variables is affected by individual differences, or error in the model. The CP_R is calculated in a similar way to the total cross-product except that the group means are used rather than the grand mean (see equation (10.3)). So, to calculate each of the difference scores, we take each score and subtract from it the mean of the group to which it belongs (see Table 10.4).

$$CP_R = \sum \left(x_{i(\text{Actions})} - \overline{X}_{\text{group(Actions)}} \right)\left(x_{i(\text{Thoughts})} - \overline{X}_{\text{group(Thoughts)}} \right) \qquad (10.3)$$

Table 10.4: Calculation of CP_R

Group	Actions	Actions $- \overline{X}_{group(Actions)}$ (D₁)	Thoughts	Thoughts $- \overline{X}_{group(Thoughts)}$ (D₂)	$D_1 \times D_2$
	5	0.10	14	0.60	0.06
	5	0.10	11	−2.40	−0.24
	4	−0.90	16	2.60	−2.34
	4	−0.90	13	−0.40	0.36
CBT	5	0.10	12	−1.40	−0.14
	3	−1.90	14	0.60	−1.14
	7	2.10	12	−1.40	−2.94
	6	1.10	15	1.60	1.76
	6	1.10	16	2.60	2.86
	4	−0.90	11	−2.40	2.16
$\overline{X}_{CBT}$	4.9		13.4		Σ= 0.40
	4	0.30	14	−1.20	−0.36
	4	0.30	15	−0.20	−0.06
	1	−2.70	13	−2.20	5.94
	1	−2.70	14	−1.20	3.24
BT	4	0.30	15	−0.20	−0.06
	6	2.30	19	3.80	8.74
	5	1.30	13	−2.20	−2.86
	5	1.30	18	2.80	3.64
	2	−1.70	14	−1.20	2.04
	5	1.30	17	1.80	2.34
$\overline{X}_{BT}$	3.7		15.2		Σ= 22.60
	4	−1.00	13	−2.00	2.00
	5	0.00	15	0	0.00
	5	0.00	14	−1.00	0.00
	4	−1.00	14	−1.00	1.00
NT	6	1.00	13	−2.00	−2.00
	4	−1.00	20	5.00	−5.00
	7	2.00	13	−2.00	−4.00
	4	−1.00	16	1.00	−1.00
	6	1.00	14	−1.00	−1.00
	5	0.00	18	3.00	0.00
$\overline{X}_{NT}$	5		15		Σ= −10.00
				$CP_R = \sum(D_1 \times D_2) = 13$	

The observant among you may notice that the residual cross-product can also be calculated by subtracting the model cross-product from the total cross-product:

$$CP_R = CP_T - CP_M$$
$$= 5.47 - (-7.53) = 13$$

However, it is useful to calculate the residual cross-product manually in case of mistakes in the calculation of the other two cross-products. The fact that the residual and model cross-products should sum to the value of the total cross-product can be used as a useful double-check.

Each of the different cross-products tells us something important about the relationship between the two dependent variables. Although I have used a simple scenario to keep the maths relatively simple, these principles can be easily extended to more complex scenarios. For example, if we had measured three dependent variables then the cross-products between pairs of dependent variables are calculated (as they were in this example) and entered into the appropriate SSCP matrix (see next section). As the complexity of the situation increases, so does the amount of calculation that needs to be done. At times such as these the benefit of software like SPSS becomes ever more apparent!

10.2.3.4. The Total SSCP Matrix (T)

In this example we have only two dependent variables and so all of the SSCP matrices will be 2×2 matrices. If there had been three dependent variables then the resulting matrices would all be 3×3 matrices. The total sum of squares and cross-product matrix, T, contains the total sums of squares for each dependent variable and the total cross-product between the two dependent variables. You can think of the first column and first row as representing one dependent variable and the second column and row as representing the second dependent variable:

	Column 1 Actions	Column 2 Thoughts
Row 1 Actions	$SS_{T(Actions)}$	CP_T
Row 1 Thoughts	CP_T	$SS_{T(Thoughts)}$

We calculated these values in the previous sections and so we can simply place the appropriate values in the appropriate cell of the matrix:

$$T = \begin{pmatrix} 61.47 & 5.47 \\ 5.47 & 141.47 \end{pmatrix}$$

From the values in the matrix (and what they represent) it should be clear that the total SSCP represents both the total amount of variation that exists within the data and the total co-dependence that exists between the dependent variables. You should also note that the off-diagonal components are the same (they are both the total cross-product) because this value is equally important for both of the dependent variables.

10.2.3.5. The Residual SSCP Matrix (E)

The residual (or error) sum of squares and cross-product matrix, E, contains the residual sums of squares for each dependent variable and the residual cross-product between the two dependent variables. This SSCP matrix is similar to the total SSCP except that the information relates to the error in the model.

	Column 1 Actions	Column 2 Thoughts
Row 1 Actions	$SS_{R(Actions)}$	CP_R
Row 1 Thoughts	CP_R	$SS_{R(Thoughts)}$

We calculated these values in the previous sections and so we can simply place the appropriate values in the appropriate cell of the matrix:

$$E = \begin{pmatrix} 51 & 13 \\ 13 & 122 \end{pmatrix}$$

From the values in the matrix (and what they represent) it should be clear that the residual SSCP represents both the unsystematic variation that exists for each dependent variable and the co-dependence between the dependent variables that is due to chance factors alone. As before the off-diagonal elements are the same (they are both the residual cross-product).

10.2.3.6. The Model SSCP Matrix (H)

The model (or hypothesis) sum of squares and cross-product matrix, H, contains the model sums of squares for each dependent variable and the model cross-product between the two dependent variables.

	Column 1 Actions	Column 2 Thoughts
Row 1 Actions	$SS_{M(Actions)}$	CP_M
Row 1 Thoughts	CP_M	$SS_{M(Thoughts)}$

These values were calculated in the previous sections and so we can simply place the appropriate values in the appropriate cell of the matrix (see below). From the values in the matrix (and what they represent) it should be clear that the model SSCP represents both the systematic variation that exists for each dependent variable and the co-dependence between the dependent variables that is due to the model (i.e. is due to the experimental manipulation). As before the off-diagonal components are the same (they are both the model cross-product).

$$H = \begin{pmatrix} 10.47 & -7.53 \\ -7.53 & 19.47 \end{pmatrix}$$

Matrices are additive which means that you can add (or subtract) two matrices together by adding (or subtracting) corresponding components. Now, when we calculated univariate ANOVA we saw that the total sum of squares was the sum of the model sum of squares and the residual sum of squares (i.e. $SS_T = SS_M + SS_R$). The same is true in MANOVA except that we are adding matrices rather than single values.

$$T = H + E$$

$$T = \begin{pmatrix} 10.47 & -7.53 \\ -7.53 & 19.47 \end{pmatrix} + \begin{pmatrix} 51 & 13 \\ 13 & 122 \end{pmatrix}$$

$$= \begin{pmatrix} 10.47 + 51 & -7.53 + 13 \\ -7.53 + 13 & 19.47 + 122 \end{pmatrix}$$

$$= \begin{pmatrix} 61.47 & 5.47 \\ 5.47 & 141.47 \end{pmatrix}$$

The demonstration that these matrices add up should (hopefully) help you to understand that the MANOVA calculations are conceptually the same as for univariate ANOVA—the difference being that matrices are used rather than single values.

10.2.4. Principle of the MANOVA Test Statistic

In univariate ANOVA we calculate the ratio of the systematic variance to the unsystematic variance (i.e. we divide SS_M by SS_R).[1] The conceptual equivalent would therefore be to divide the matrix H by the matrix E. There is, however, a problem in that matrices are not divisible by other matrices! However, there is a matrix equivalent to division which is to multiply by what's known as the inverse of a matrix. So, if we want to

---

[1] In reality we use the mean squares but these values are merely the sums of squares corrected for the degrees of freedom.

divide *H* by *E* we have to multiply *H* by the inverse of *E* (denoted as E^{-1}). So, therefore, the test statistic is based upon the matrix that results from multiplying the model SSCP with the inverse of the residual SSCP. This matrix is called HE^{-1}.

Calculating the inverse of a matrix is incredibly difficult and there is no need for you to understand how it is done because SPSS will do it for you. However, the interested reader should consult either Stevens (1992) or Namboodiri (1984)—these texts provide very accessible accounts of how to derive an inverse matrix. For the interested reader who does consult these sources, the calculations for this example are included in appendix 12.7 (you might like to check my maths!). For the uninterested reader, you'll have to trust me on the following:

$$E^{-1} = \begin{pmatrix} 0.0202 & -0.0021 \\ -0.0021 & 0.0084 \end{pmatrix}$$

$$HE^{-1} = \begin{pmatrix} 0.2273 & -0.0852 \\ -0.1930 & 0.1794 \end{pmatrix}$$

Remember that HE^{-1} represents the ratio of systematic variance in the model to the unsystematic variance in the model and so the resulting matrix is conceptually the same as the *F*-ratio in univariate ANOVA. There is another problem, though. In ANOVA, when we divide the systematic variance by the unsystematic variance we get a single figure: the *F*-ratio. In MANOVA, when we divide the systematic variance by the unsystematic variance we get a matrix containing several values. In this example, the matrix contains four values, but had there been three dependent variables the matrix would have had nine values. In fact, the resulting matrix will always contain p^2 values, where *p* is the number of dependent variables. The problem is how to convert these matrix values into a meaningful single value. This is the point at which we have to abandon any hope of understanding the maths behind the test and talk conceptually instead.

10.2.4.1. Discriminant Function Variates

The problem of having several values with which to assess statistical significance can be simplified considerably by converting the dependent variables into underlying dimensions or factors (this process will be discussed in more detail in Chapter 11). In Chapter 4, we saw how multiple regression worked on the principle of fitting a linear model to a set of data to predict an outcome variable (the dependent variable in ANOVA terminology). This linear model was made up of a combination of predictor variables (or independent variables) each of which had a unique contribution to this linear model. We can do a similar thing here, except that we are interested in the opposite problem (namely predicting an independent variable from a set of dependent variables). So, it is possible to calculate underlying linear dimensions of the dependent variables. These linear combinations of the dependent variables are known as *variates* (or sometimes called *latent variables* or *factors*). In this context we wish to use these linear variates to predict which group a subject belongs to (i.e. whether they were given CBT, BT or no treatment), so we are using them to discriminate groups of people. Therefore, these variates are called *discriminant functions* or *discriminant function variates*. Although I have drawn a parallel between these discriminant functions and the model in multiple regression, there is a difference in that we can extract several discriminant functions from a set of dependent variables, whereas in multiple regression all independent variables are included in a single model.

That's the theory in simplistic terms, but how do we discover these discriminant functions? Well, without going into too much detail, we use a mathematical procedure of maximization, such that the first discriminant function (V_1) is the linear combination of dependent variables that maximizes the differences between groups.

It follows from this that the ratio of systematic to unsystematic variance (SS_M/SS_R) will be maximized for this first variate, but subsequent variates will have smaller values of this ratio. Remember that this ratio is an analogue of what the *F*-ratio represents in univariate ANOVA, and so in effect we obtain the maximum possible value of the *F*-ratio when we look at the first discriminant function. This variate can be described in terms of a linear regression equation (because it is a linear combination of the dependent variables).

$$Y = \beta_0 + \beta_1 X_1 + \beta_2 X_2$$
$$V_1 = \beta_0 + \beta_1 DV_1 + \beta_2 DV_2 \qquad (10.4)$$
$$V_1 = \beta_0 + \beta_1 \text{Actions} + \beta_2 \text{Thoughts}$$

Equation (10.4) shows the multiple regression equation for two predictors and then extends this to show how a comparable form of this equation can describe discriminant functions. The β values in the equation are weights (just as in regression) that tell us something about the contribution of each dependent variable to the variate in question. In regression, the values of β are obtained by the method of least squares; in discriminant function analysis the β values are obtained from the *eigenvectors* of the matrix HE^{-1}.

In a situation in which there are only two dependent variables and two groups for the independent variable, there will be only one variate. This makes the scenario very simple: by looking at the discriminant function of the dependent variables, rather than looking at the dependent variables themselves, we can obtain a single value of SS_M/SS_R for the discriminant function, and then assses this value for significance. However, in more complex cases where there are more than two dependent variables or more than three levels of the independent variable (as is the case in our example), there will be more than one variate. The number of variates obtained will be the smaller of p (the number of dependent variables) or $k-1$ (where k is the number of levels of the independent variable). In our example, both p and $k-1$ are two, so we should be able to find two variates. I mentioned earlier that the β values that describe the variates are obtained by calculating the eigenvectors of the matrix HE^{-1} and in fact, there will be two eigenvectors derived from this matrix: one with the β values for the first variate, and one with the β of the second variate. Conceptually speaking, eigenvectors are the vectors associated with a given matrix that are unchanged by transformation of that matrix to a diagonal matrix. A diagonal matrix is simply a matrix in which the off-diagonal elements are zero and by changing HE^{-1} to a diagonal matrix we eliminate all of the off-diagonal elements (thus reducing the number of values that we must consider for significance testing). Therefore, by calculating the eigenvectors and eigenvalues, we still end up with values that represent the ratio of systematic to unsystematic variance (because they are unchanged by the transformation), but there are considerably less of them. The calculation of eigenvectors is extremely complex (insane students can consider reading Strang, 1980 or Namboodiri, 1984), so you can trust me that for the matrix HE^{-1} the eigenvectors obtained are:

$$\text{eigenvector}_1 = \begin{pmatrix} 0.603 \\ -0.335 \end{pmatrix}$$

$$\text{eigenvector}_2 = \begin{pmatrix} 0.425 \\ 0.339 \end{pmatrix}$$

Replacing these values into the two equations for the variates we obtain the models described in equation (10.5).

$$V_1 = \beta_0 + 0.603\text{Actions} - 0.335\text{Thoughts}$$
$$V_2 = \beta_0 + 0.425\text{Actions} + 0.339\text{Thoughts}$$

(10.5)

If we ignore the constants (β_0) for the time being it is possible to use the equations for each variate to calculate a score for each subject on the variate. For example, the first subject in the CBT group carried out 5 obsessive actions, and had 14 obsessive thoughts. Therefore, his score on variate 1 would be -1.675:

$$V_1 = (0.603 \times 5) - (0.335 \times 14) = -1.675$$

The score for variate 2 would be 6.87:

$$V_2 = (0.425 \times 5) + (0.339 \times 14) = 6.871$$

If we calculated these variate scores for each subject and then calculated the SSCP matrices (e.g. H, E, T, and HE^{-1}) that we used previously, we would find that all of them have cross-products of zero. The reason for this is because the variates extracted from the data are orthogonal, which means that they are uncorrelated. In short, the variates extracted are independent dimensions constructed from a linear combination of the dependent variables that were measured.

This data reduction has a very useful property in that if we look at the matrix HE^{-1} calculated from the variate scores (rather than the dependent variables) we find that all of the off-diagonal elements (the cross-products) are zero. The diagonal elements of this matrix represent the ratio of the systematic variance to the unsystematic variance (i.e. SS_M/SS_R) for each of the underlying variates. So, for the data in this example, this means that instead of having four values representing the ratio of systematic to unsystematic variance, we now have only two. This reduction may not seem a lot. However, in general if we have p dependent variables, then ordinarily we would end up with p^2 values representing the ratio of systematic to unsystematic variance; by looking at discriminant functions, we reduce this number to p. If there were four dependent variables we would end up with four values rather than sixteen (which highlights the benefit of this process).

For the data in our example, the matrix HE^{-1} calculated from the variate scores is:

$$HE^{-1}_{\text{variates}} = \begin{pmatrix} 0.335 & 0.000 \\ 0.000 & 0.073 \end{pmatrix}$$

It is clear from this matrix that we have two values to consider when assessing the significance of the group differences. It probably seems like a complex procedure to reduce the data down in this way: however, it transpired that the values along the diagonal of the matrix for the variates (namely 0.335 and 0.073) are the *eigenvalues* of the original HE^{-1} matrix. Therefore, these values can be calculated directly from the data collected without first forming the eigenvectors. The calculation of these eigenvalues is included in the appendices but it is not necessary that you understand how they are derived. These eigenvalues are conceptually equivalent to the F-ratio in ANOVA and so the final step is to assess how large these values are compared to what we would expect by chance alone. There are four ways in which the values are assessed.

10.2.4.2. Pillai-Bartlett Trace (V)

Pillai's trace is given by equation (10.6) in which λ represents the eigenvalues for each of the discriminant variates, and s represents the number of variates. Pillai's trace is the sum of the proportion of explained variance on the discriminant functions. As such, it is similar to the ratio of SS_M/SS_T.

$$V = \sum_{i=1}^{s} \frac{\lambda_i}{1+\lambda_i} \tag{10.6}$$

For our data, Pillai's trace turns out to be 0.319, which can be transformed to a value that has an approximate F-distribution.

$$V = \frac{0.335}{1+0.335} + \frac{0.073}{1+0.073} = 0.319$$

10.2.4.3. Hotelling's T^2

The Hotelling-Lawley trace is simply the sum of the eigenvalues for each variate (see equation (10.7)) and so for these data its value is 0.408 (0.335 + 0.073). This test statistic is the sum of SS_M/SS_R for each of the variates and so it compares directly to the F-ratio in ANOVA.

$$T = \sum_{i=1}^{s} \lambda_i \tag{10.7}$$

10.2.4.4. Wilks's Lambda (Λ)

Wilks's lambda is the product of the *unexplained* variance on each of the variates (see equation (10.8)— the $\prod$ symbol is similar to the summation symbol (Σ) that we have encountered already except that it means *multiply* rather than add up). So, Wilks's lambda represents the ratio of error variance to total variance (SS_R/SS_T) for each variate.

$$\Lambda = \prod_{i=1}^{s} \frac{1}{1+\lambda_i} \tag{10.8}$$

For the data in this example the value is 0.698, and it should be clear that large eigenvalues (which in themselves represent a large experimental effect) lead to small values of Wilks's lambda: hence statistical significance is found when Wilks's lambda is small.

$$\Lambda = \left(\frac{1}{1+0.335}\right)\left(\frac{1}{1+0.073}\right) = 0.698$$

10.2.4.5. Roy's Largest Root

Roy's largest root, as the name suggests, is simply the eigenvalue for the first variate. So, in a sense it is the same as the Hotelling-Lawley trace but for the first variate only (see equation (10.9)).

$$\text{largest root} = \lambda_{\text{largest}} \qquad\qquad (10.9)$$

As such, Roy's largest root represents the proportion of explained variance to unexplained variance (SS_M/SS_R) for the first discriminant function.[2] For the data in this example, the value of Roy's largest root is simply 0.335 (the eigenvalue for the first variate). So, this value is conceptually the same as the *F*-ratio in univariate ANOVA. It should be apparent, from what we have learnt about the maximizing properties of these discriminant variates, that Roy's root represents the maximum possible between-group difference given the data collected. Therefore, this statistic should in many cases be the most powerful.

10.3. Assumptions of MANOVA

MANOVA has similar assumptions to ANOVA but extended to the multivariate case:

- **Independence**: Observations should be statistically independent.
- **Random sampling**: Data should be randomly sampled from the population of interest and measured at an interval level.
- **Multivariate normality**: In ANOVA, we assume that our dependent variable is normally distributed within each group. In the case of MANOVA, we assume that the dependent variables (collectively) have multivariate normality with groups.
- **Homogeneity of covariance matrices**: In ANOVA, it is assumed that the variances in each group are roughly equal (homogeneity of variance). In MANOVA we must assume that this is true for each dependent variable, but also that the correlation between any two dependent variables is the same in all groups. This assumption is

---

[2] This statistic is sometimes characterised as $\lambda_{\text{largest}}/(1 + \lambda_{\text{largest}})$ but this is not the statistic reported by SPSS.

examined by testing whether the population variance-covariance matrices are equal. [3]

10.3.1.   *Checking Assumptions*

Most of the assumptions can be checked in the same way as for univariate tests (see Chapter 7); the additional assumptions of multivariate normality and equality of covariance matrices require different procedures. The assumption of multivariate normality cannot be tested on SPSS and so the only practical solution is to check the assumption of univariate normality for each dependent variable in turn (see Chapter 2). This solution is practical (because it is easy to implement) and useful (because univariate normality is a necessary condition for multivariate normality), but it does not *guarantee* multivariate normality. So, although this approach is the best we can do, I urge readers to consult Stevens (1992, Chapter 6) who provides some alternative solutions.

The assumption of equality of covariance matrices is more easily checked. First, for this assumption to be true the univariate tests of equality of variances between groups should be met. This assumption is easily checked using Levene's test (see Chapter 7). As a preliminary check, Levene's test should not be significant for any of the dependent variables. However, Levene's test does not take account of the covariances and so the variance-covariance matrices should be compared between groups using Box's test. This test should be non-significant if the matrices are the same. However, Box's test is very susceptible to deviations from multivariate normality and so can be non-significant not because the matrices are similar, but because the assumption of multivariate normality is not tenable. Hence, it is vital to have some idea of whether the data meet the multivariate normality assumption before interpreting the result of Box's test.

10.3.2.   *Choosing a Test Statistic*

Only when there is one underlying variate will the four test statistics necessarily be the same. Therefore, it is important to know which test statistic is best in terms of test power and robustness. Both Olson (1974; 1976; 1979) and Stevens (1979) have done extensive work on the power of the four MANOVA test statistics. Olson (1974) observed that for small

---

[3] For those of you who read about SSCP matrices, if you think about the relationship between sums of squares and variance, and cross-products and correlations, it should be clear that a variance-covariance matrix is basically a standardized form of an SSCP matrix.

and moderate sample sizes the four statistics differ little in terms of power. If group differences are concentrated on the first variate (as will often be the case in social science research) Roy's statistic should prove most powerful (because it takes account of only that first variate), followed by Hotelling's trace, Wilks's lambda and Pillai's trace. However, when groups differ along more than one variate, the power ordering is the reverse (i.e. Pillai's trace is most powerful and Roy's root is least). One final issue pertinent to test power is that of sample size and the number of dependent variables. Stevens (1980) recommends using fairly small numbers of dependent variables (less than 10) unless sample sizes are large.

In terms of robustness, all four test statistics are relatively robust to violations of multivariate normality (although Roy's root is affected by platykurtic distributions—see Olson, 1976). Roy's root is also not robust when the homogeneity of covariance matrix assumption is untenable (Stevens, 1979). The work of Olson and Stevens led Bray and Maxwell (1985) to conclude that when sample sizes are equal the Pillai-Bartlett trace is the most robust to violations of assumptions. However, when sample sizes are unequal this statistic is affected by violations of the assumption of equal covariance matrices. As a rule, with unequal group sizes, check the assumption of homogeneity of covariance matrices using Box's test; if this test is non-significant, *and if the assumption of multivariate normality is tenable* (which allows us to assume that Box's test is accurate), then assume that Pillai's trace is accurate.

10.3.3.   Follow-Up Analysis

In section 10.1.2 I mentioned that there was some controversy over how best to follow up the main MANOVA. The traditional approach is to follow a significant MANOVA with separate ANOVAs on each of the dependent variables. If this approach is taken, you might well wonder why we bother with the MANOVA in the first place (earlier on I said that multiple ANOVAs were a bad thing to do). Well, the ANOVAs that follow a significant MANOVA are said to be 'protected' by the initial MANOVA (Bock, 1975). The idea is that the overall multivariate test protects against inflated type I error rates because if that initial test is non-significant (i.e. the null hypothesis is true) then any subsequent tests are ignored (any significance must be a type I error because the null hypothesis is true). However, the notion of protection is somewhat fallacious because a significant MANOVA, more often than not, reflects a significant difference for one, but not all, of the dependent variables.

Subsequent ANOVAs are then carried out on all of the dependent variables, but the MANOVA protects only the dependent variable for which group differences genuinely exist (see Bray and Maxwell, 1985, pp. 40-41). Therefore, you might want to consider applying a Bonferroni correction to the subsequent ANOVAs (Harris, 1975).

The ANOVA approach to following up a MANOVA implicitly assumes that the significant MANOVA is not due to the dependent variables representing a set of underlying dimensions that differentiate the groups. Therefore, some researchers advocate the use of discriminant analysis, which finds the linear combination(s) of the dependent variables that best *separates* (or discriminates) the groups. This procedure is more in keeping with the ethos of MANOVA because it embraces the relationships that exist between dependent variables and it is certainly useful for illuminating the relationship between the dependent variables and group membership. The major advantage of this approach over multiple ANOVAs is that it reduces and explains the dependent variables in terms of a set of underlying dimensions thought to reflect substantive theoretical or psychological dimensions. By default the standard GLM procedure in SPSS provides univariate ANOVAs, but not the discriminant analysis.[4] However, the discriminant analysis can be accessed via different menus and in the remainder of this chapter we will use the OCD data to illustrate how these analyses are done (those of you who skipped the theory section should refer to Table 10.1).

10.4.   MANOVA on SPSS

10.4.1.   The Main Analysis

Either load the data in the file **OCD.sav**, or enter the data manually. If you enter the data manually you need three columns: one column must be a coding variable for the **group** variable (I used the codes CBT = 1, BT = 2, NT = 3), and in the remaining two columns enter the scores for each dependent variable respectively. Once the data have been entered, access the main MANOVA dialog box by using the **Analyze⇒General Linear Model⇒Multivariate...** menu path (see Figure 10.1).

The ANOVAs (and various multiple comparisons) carried out after the main MANOVA are identical to running separate ANOVA procedures in SPSS for each of the dependent variables. Hence, the main dialog box and options for MANOVA are very similar to the factorial ANOVA procedure we met in Chapter 8. The main difference to the main dialog

---

[4] Users of versions before 7.5 should note that the discriminant analysis can be accessed using the **Statistics⇒General Linear Models** (or **ANOVA Models** as it was known in Version 6) **⇒Multivariate...** menu.

box is that the space labelled *Dependent Variables* has room for several variables. Select the two dependent variables from the variables list (that is **actions** and **thoughts**) and transfer them to the *Dependent Variables* box by clicking on [▶]. Select **group** from the variables list and transfer it to the *Fixed Factor(s)* box by clicking on [▶]. There is also a box in which you can place covariates. For this analysis there are no covariates; however you can apply the principles of ANCOVA to the multivariate case and conduct multivariate analysis of covariance (MANCOVA). Once you have specified the variables in the analysis, you can select any of the other dialog boxes by clicking the buttons on the right-hand side.

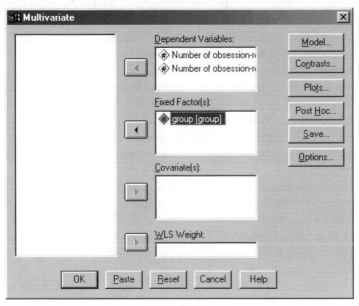

Figure 10.1: Main dialog box for MANOVA

Model...	This button opens a dialog box for customizing your analysis and selecting the type of sums of squares used (see section 8.2.3).
Plots...	This button opens a dialog box for selecting interaction graphs. This option is useful only when more than two independent variables have been measured (see section 8.2.4).

This button opens a dialog box for saving residuals of the GLM (i.e. regression diagnostics). These options are useful for checking how well the model fits the data (see Chapter 4).

10.4.2.   Multiple Comparisons in MANOVA

The default way to follow up a MANOVA is to look at individual univariate ANOVAs for each dependent variable. For these tests, SPSS has the same options as in the univariate ANOVA procedure (see Chapter 7). The Contrasts... button opens a dialog box for specifying one of several standard contrasts for the independent variable(s) in the analysis. Table 7.6 describes what each of these tests compares, but for this example it makes sense to use a *simple* contrast that compares each of the experimental groups to the no-treatment control group. The no-treatment control group was coded as the last category (it had the highest code in the data editor), so we need to select the group variable and change the contrast to a simple contrast using the last category as the reference category (see Figure 10.2). For more details about contrasts see section 7.1.4.

Instead of running a contrast, we could carry out *post hoc* tests on the independent variable to compare each group to all other groups. To access the *post hoc* tests dialog box click on Post Hoc... . The dialog box is the same as that for factorial ANOVA (see Figure 8.9) and the choice of test should be based on the same criteria as outlined in section 7.1.5. For the purposes of this example, I suggest selecting two of my usual recommendations: REGWQ and Games-Howell. Once you have selected *post hoc* tests return to the main dialog box.

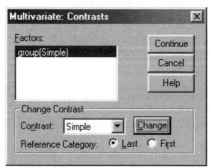

Figure 10.2: Contrasts for independent variable(s) in MANOVA

10.4.3.   Additional Options

To access the *options* dialog box, click on [Options...] in the main dialog box (see Figure 10.3). The resulting dialog box is fairly similar to that of factorial ANOVA (see section 8.2.6); however, there are a few additional options that are worth mentioning.

- **SSCP Matrices**: If this option is selected, SPSS will produce the model SSCP matrix, the error SSCP matrix and the total SSCP matrix. This option can be useful for understanding the computation of the MANOVA. However, if you didn't read the theory section you might be happy to not select this option and not worry about these matrices!
- **Residual SSCP Matrix**: If this option is selected, SPSS produces the error SSCP matrix, the error variance-covariance matrix and the error correlation matrix. The error variance-covariance matrix is the matrix upon which Bartlett's test of sphericity is based. Bartlett's test examines whether this matrix is proportional to an identity matrix (i.e. that the covariances are zero and the variances—the values along the diagonal— are roughly equal).

Figure 10.3: Additional options in MANOVA

The remaining options are the same as for factorial ANOVA and so have been described in Chapter 8); I recommend rereading that chapter before deciding which options are useful.

10.5.   Output from MANOVA

10.5.1.   Preliminary Analysis and Testing Assumptions

SPSS Output 10.1 shows an initial table of descriptive statistics that is produced by clicking on the descriptive statistics option in the *options* dialog box (Figure 10.3). This table contains the overall and group means and standard deviations for each dependent variable in turn. These values correspond to those calculated by hand in
Table 10.1 and by looking at that table it should be clear what this part of the output tells us. It is clear from the means that subjects had many more obsession-related thoughts than behaviours.

Descriptive Statistics

	group	Mean	Std. Deviation	N
Number of obsession-related thoughts	CBT	13.40	1.90	10
	BT	15.20	2.10	10
	No Treatment Control	15.00	2.36	10
	Total	14.53	2.21	30
Number of obsession-related behaviours	CBT	4.90	1.20	10
	BT	3.70	1.77	10
	No Treatment Control	5.00	1.05	10
	Total	4.53	1.46	30

SPSS Output 10.1

  SPSS Output 10.2 shows Box's test of the assumption of equality of covariance matrices (see section 10.3.1). This statistic tests the null hypothesis that the variance-covariance matrices are the same in all three groups. Therefore, if the matrices are equal (and therefore the assumption of homogeneity is met) this statistic should be *non-significant*. For these data $p = 0.18$ (which is greater than 0.05): hence, the covariance matrices are roughly equal and the assumption is tenable.

Box's Test of Equality of Covariance Matrices[a]

Box's M	9.959
F	1.482
df1	6
df2	18169
Sig.	.180

a. Design: Intercept+GROUP

Bartlett's Test of Sphericity[a]

Likelihood Ratio	.042
Approx. Chi-Square	5.511
df	2
Sig.	.064

a. Design: Intercept+GROUP

SPSS Output 10.2

If the value of Box's test was significant ($p < 0.05$) then the covariance matrices are significantly different and so the homogeneity assumption would have been violated. The effect of violating this assumption is unclear. Hakstian et al. (1979) report that Hotelling's T^2 is robust in the two-group situation when sample sizes are equal. As a general rule of thumb, if sample sizes are equal then disregard Box's test, because it is highly unstable, and assume Hotelling's and Pillai's statistics to be robust (see section 10.3.2). However, if group sizes are different, then robustness cannot be assumed (especially if Box's test is significant at $p < 0.001$). The more dependent variables you have measured, and the greater the differences in sample sizes, the more distorted the probability values produced by SPSS become. Tabachnick and Fidell (1996), therefore, suggest that if the larger samples produce greater variances and covariances then the probability values will be conservative (and so significant findings can be trusted). However, if it is the smaller samples that produce the larger variances and covariances then the probability values will be liberal and so significant differences should be treated with caution (although non-significant effects can be trusted). As such, Box's test need only really be examined when sample sizes differ: it should not be trusted when multivariate normality cannot be assumed (or is in question), and the variance-covariance matrices for samples should be inspected to assess whether the printed probabilities are likely to be conservative or liberal. In the event that you cannot trust the printed probabilities, there is little you can do except equalize the samples by randomly deleting cases in the larger groups (although with this loss of information comes a loss of power).

Bartlett's test of sphericity tests whether the assumption of sphericity has been met and is useful only in univariate repeated measures designs because MANOVA does not require this assumption.

10.5.2.   MANOVA Test Statistics

SPSS Output 10.3 shows the main table of results. Test statistics are quoted for the intercept of the model (even MANOVA can be characterized as a regression model although how this is done is beyond the scope of this text) and for the group variable. For our purposes, the group effects are of interest because they tell us whether or not the therapies had an effect on the OCD clients. You'll see that SPSS lists the four multivariate test statistics and their values correspond to those calculated in sections 10.2.4.2 to 10.2.4.5. In the next column these values are transformed into an F-ratio with two degrees of freedom. The column of real interest, however, is the one containing the significance values of these F-ratios. For these data, Pillai's trace ($p = 0.049$), Wilks's lambda ($p = 0.050$) and Roy's largest root ($p = 0.020$) all reach the criterion for significance of 0.05. However, Hotelling's trace ($p = 0.051$) is non-significant by this criterion. This scenario is interesting, because the test statistic we choose determines whether or not we reject the null hypothesis that there are no between-group differences. However, given what we know about the robustness of Pillai's trace when sample sizes are equal, we might be well advised to trust the result of that test statistic, which indicates a significant difference. Interestingly, this example highlights the additional power associated with Roy's root (you should note how this statistic is considerably more significant than all others) when the test assumptions have been met.

From this result we should probably conclude that the type of therapy employed had a significant effect on OCD. The nature of this effect is not clear from the multivariate test statistic. First, it tells us nothing about which groups differed from which, and second it tells us nothing about whether the effect of therapy was on the obsession-related thoughts, the obsession-related behaviours, or a combination of both. To determine the nature of the effect, SPSS provides us with univariate tests.

Multivariate Tests[a]

Effect		Value	F	Hypothesis df	Error df	Sig.
Intercept	Pillai's Trace	.983	745.230[c]	2.000	26.000	.000
	Wilks' Lambda	.017	745.230[c]	2.000	26.000	.000
	Hotelling's Trace	57.325	745.230[c]	2.000	26.000	.000
	Roy's Largest Root	57.325	745.230[c]	2.000	26.000	.000
GROUP	Pillai's Trace	.318	2.557	4.000	54.000	.049
	Wilks' Lambda	.699	2.555[c]	4.000	52.000	.050
	Hotelling's Trace	.407	2.546	4.000	50.000	.051
	Roy's Largest Root	.335	4.520	2.000	27.000	.020

a. Design: Intercept+GROUP

b. Computed using alpha = .05

c. Exact statistic

SPSS Output 10.3

10.5.3. Univariate Test Statistics

SPSS Output 10.4 initially shows a summary table of Levene's test of equality of variances for each of the dependent variables. These tests are the same as would be found if a one-way ANOVA had been conducted on each dependent variable in turn (see section 8.2.7.2). Levene's test should be non-significant for all dependent variables if the assumption of homogeneity of variance has been met. The results for these data clearly show that the assumption has been met. This finding not only gives us confidence in the reliability of the univariate tests to follow, but also strengthens the case for assuming that the multivariate test statistics are robust.

The next part of the output contains the ANOVA summary table for the dependent variables. The row of interest is that labelled *GROUP* (you'll notice that the values in this row are the same as for the row labelled *Corrected Model*: this is because the model fitted to the data contains only one independent variable: **group**). The row labelled *GROUP* contains an ANOVA summary table for each of the dependent variables, and values are given for the sums of squares for both actions and thoughts (these values correspond to the values of SS_M calculated in sections 10.2.3.1 and 10.2.3.2 respectively). The row labelled *Error* contains information about the residual sums of squares and mean squares for each of the dependent variables: these values of SS_R were calculated in sections 10.2.3.1 and 10.2.3.2 and I urge the reader to look back to these sections to consolidate what these values mean. The row labelled *Corrected Total* contains the values of the total sums of squares for each dependent variable (again, these values of SS_T were calculated in section 10.2.3.1 and 10.2.3.2). The important parts of this table are the columns labelled *F* and *Sig.* in which the *F*-ratios for each univariate ANOVA and their significance values are listed. What should be clear from SPSS Output 10.4 and the calculations made in sections 10.2.3.1 and 10.2.3.2 is that the values associated with the univariate ANOVAs conducted after the MANOVA are *identical* to those obtained if one-way ANOVA was conducted on each dependent variable. This fact illustrates that MANOVA offers only hypothetical protection of inflated type I error rates: there is no real-life adjustment made to the values obtained.

The values of p in SPSS Output 10.4 indicate that there was a non-significant difference between therapy groups in terms of both obsession-related thoughts ($p = 0.136$) and obsession-related behaviours ($p = 0.080$). These two results should lead us to conclude that the type of therapy has had no significant effect on the levels of OCD experienced by clients. Those of you that are still awake may have noticed something odd about this example: the multivariate test statistics led us to conclude that therapy had had a significant impact on OCD, yet the univariate results indicate that therapy has not been successful. Before reading any further, have a think about why this anomaly has occurred.

The reason for the anomaly in these data is simple: the multivariate test takes account of the correlation between dependent variables and so for these data it has more power to detect group differences. With this knowledge in mind, the univariate tests are not particularly useful for interpretation, because the groups differ along a combination of the dependent variables. To see how the dependent variables interact we need to carry out a discriminant function analysis, which will be described in section 10.6.

Levene's Test of Equality of Error Variances[a]

	F	df1	df2	Sig.
Number of obsession-related thoughts	.076	2	27	.927
Number of obsession-related behaviours	1.828	2	27	.180

Tests the null hypothesis that the error variance of the dependent variable is equal across groups.

a. Design: Intercept+GROUP

Tests of Between-Subjects Effects

Source	Dependent Variable	Type III Sum of Squares	df	Mean Square	F	Sig.
Corrected Model	Number of obsession-related thoughts	19.467[b]	2	9.733	2.154	.136
	Number of obsession-related behaviours	10.467[c]	2	5.233	2.771	.080
Intercept	Number of obsession-related thoughts	6336.533	1	6336.533	1402.348	.000
	Number of obsession-related behaviours	616.533	1	616.533	326.400	.000
GROUP	Number of obsession-related thoughts	19.467	2	9.733	2.154	.136
	Number of obsession-related behaviours	10.467	2	5.233	2.771	.080
Error	Number of obsession-related thoughts	122.000	27	4.519		
	Number of obsession-related behaviours	51.000	27	1.889		
Total	Number of obsession-related thoughts	6478.000	30			
	Number of obsession-related behaviours	678.000	30			
Corrected Total	Number of obsession-related thoughts	141.467	29			
	Number of obsession-related behaviours	61.467	29			

a. Computed using alpha = .05

b. R Squared = .138 (Adjusted R Squared = .074)

c. R Squared = .170 (Adjusted R Squared = .109)

SPSS Output 10.4

10.5.4.   SSCP Matrices

If you selected the two options to display SSCP matrices (section 10.4.3), then SPSS will produce the tables in SPSS Output 10.5 and SPSS Output 10.6. The first table (SPSS Output 10.5) displays the model SSCP (*H*), which is labelled *Hypothesis GROUP* (I have shaded this matrix light grey) and the error SSCP (*E*) which is labelled *Error* (I have shaded this matrix dark grey). The matrix for the intercept is displayed also, but this matrix is not important for our purposes. It should be pretty clear that the values in the model and error matrices displayed in SPSS Output 10.5 correspond to the values we calculated in sections 10.2.3.6 and 10.2.3.5 respectively. These matrices are useful, therefore, for gaining insight into the pattern of the data, and especially in looking at the values of the cross-products to indicate the relationship between dependent variables. In this example, the sums of squares for the error SSCP matrix are substantially bigger than in the model (or group) SSCP matrix, whereas the absolute value of the cross-products is fairly similar. This pattern suggests that if the MANOVA is significant then it might be the relationship between dependent variables that is important rather than the individual dependent variables themselves.

Between-Subjects SSCP Matrix

			Number of obsession-related behaviours	Number of obsession-related thoughts
Hypothesis	Intercept	Number of obsession-related behaviours	616.533	1976.533
		Number of obsession-related thoughts	1976.533	6336.533
	GROUP	Number of obsession-related behaviours	10.467	-7.533
		Number of obsession-related thoughts	-7.533	19.467
Error		Number of obsession-related behaviours	51.000	13.000
		Number of obsession-related thoughts	13.000	122.000

Based on Type III Sum of Squares

SPSS Output 10.5

SPSS Output 10.6 shows the residual SSCP matrix again, but this time it includes the variance-covariance matrix and the correlation matrix. These matrices are all related. If you look back to Chapter 3, you should remember that the covariance is calculated by dividing the cross-product by the number of observations (i.e. the covariance is the average cross-product). Likewise, the variance is calculated by dividing the sums of squares by the degrees of freedom (and so similarly represents the average sum of squares). Hence, the variance-covariance matrix represents the average form of the SSCP matrix. Finally, we saw in Chapter 3 that the correlation was a standardized version of the covariance (where the standard deviation is also taken into account) and so the correlation matrix represents the standardized form of the variance-covariance matrix. As with the SSCP matrix, these other matrices are useful for assessing the extent of the error in the model. The variance-covariance matrix is especially useful because Bartlett's test of sphericity is based on this matrix. Bartlett's test examines whether this matrix is proportional to an identity matrix. In section 10.2.1 we saw that an identity matrix was one in which the diagonal elements were 1, and the off-diagonal elements were 0. Therefore, Bartlett's test effectively tests whether the diagonal elements of the variance-covariance matrix are equal (i.e. group variances are the same), and that the off-diagonal elements are approximately zero (i.e. the dependent variables are not correlated). In this case, the variances are quite different (1.89 compared to 4.52) and the covariances slightly different from zero (0.48) and so Bartlett's test has come out as nearly significant (see SPSS Output 10.2). Although this discussion is irrelevant to the multivariate tests, I hope that by expanding upon them here you can relate these ideas back to the issues of sphericity raised in Chapter 9, and see more clearly how this assumption is tested.

Residual SSCP Matrix

		Number of obsession-related behaviours	Number of obsession-related thoughts
Sum-of-Squares and Cross-Products	Number of obsession-related behaviours	51.000	13.000
	Number of obsession-related thoughts	13.000	122.000
Covariance	Number of obsession-related behaviours	1.889	.481
	Number of obsession-related thoughts	.481	4.519
Correlation	Number of obsession-related behaviours	1.000	.165
	Number of obsession-related thoughts	.165	1.000

Based on Type III Sum of Squares

SPSS Output 10.6

10.5.5.   Contrasts

In section 10.4.2 I suggested carrying out a *simple* contrast that compares each of the therapy groups to the no-treatment control group. SPSS Output 10.7 shows the results of these contrasts. The table is divided into two sections conveniently labelled *1st vs. 3rd* and *2nd vs. 3rd* where the numbers correspond to the coding of the group variable (i.e. 1 represents the lowest code used in the data editor and 3 the highest). If you coded the group variable using the same codes as I did, then these contrasts represent CBT vs. NT and BT vs. NT respectively. Each contrast is performed on both dependent variables separately and so they are identical to the contrasts that would be obtained from a univariate ANOVA. The table provides values for the contrast estimate, and the hypothesized value (which will always be zero because we are testing the null hypothesis that the difference between groups is zero). The observed estimated difference is then tested to see whether it is significantly different from zero based on the standard error (it might help to reread Chapter 6 for some theory on this kind of hypothesis testing). A 95% confidence interval is produced for the estimated difference.

The first thing that you might notice is that SPSS does not produce an exact significance value for the contrast: so how can we tell whether the group differences are significant? The simple answer is to look at the confidence interval. We have seen before (Chapters 4, 5 and 6 all talk about confidence intervals) that a 95% confidence interval tells us the values of the difference between groups between which 95% of samples will fall. If these boundaries cross zero (i.e. the lower is a minus number and the upper a positive value), then this tells us that within our 95% of samples, a good proportion of samples will have group differences of zero (i.e. there will be no difference between the groups). Therefore, we cannot be confident that the observed group difference is meaningful because a different sample would have given us no group difference. If, however, the confidence interval does not cross zero (i.e. both values are positive or negative), then we can be confident that we would find a difference between the groups in 95% of samples taken from the same population. As such, we can be confident that genuine group differences exist. The take-home message here is that if the confidence interval includes zero then the contrast is non-significant; if the confidence interval does not include zero then we can say that the contrast is significant at $p < 0.05$. For these data all confidence intervals include zero (the lower bounds are negative whereas the upper bounds are positive) and so no contrasts are significant. This was expected because the univariate ANOVAs were both non-significant and so we would not expect there to be group differences.

Contrast Results (K Matrix)

			Dependent Variable	
			Number of obsession-related thoughts	Number of obsession-related behaviours
group Simple Contrast [a]				
1st vs. 3rd	Contrast Estimate		-1.600	-1.000E-01
	Hypothesized Value		0	0
	Difference (Estimate - Hypothesized)		-1.600	-1.000E-01
	Std. Error		.951	.615
	95% Confidence Interval for Difference	Lower Bound	-4.144	-1.745
		Upper Bound	.944	1.545
2nd vs. 3rd	Contrast Estimate		.200	-1.300
	Hypothesized Value		0	0
	Difference (Estimate - Hypothesized)		.200	-1.300
	Std. Error		.951	.615
	95% Confidence Interval for Difference	Lower Bound	-2.344	-2.945
		Upper Bound	2.744	.345

a. Reference category = 3

SPSS Output 10.7

10.6. Following Up MANOVA with Discriminant Analysis

I mentioned earlier on that a significant MANOVA could be followed up using either univariate ANOVA or discriminant analysis. In the example in this chapter, the univariate ANOVAs were not a useful way of looking at what the multivariate tests showed because the relationship between dependent variables is obviously having an effect. However, these data were designed especially to illustrate how the univariate ANOVAs should be treated cautiously and in real life a significant MANOVA is likely to be accompanied by at least one significant ANOVA. However, this does not mean that the relationship between dependent variables is not important, and it is still extremely important to investigate the nature of this relationship. Discriminant analysis is the best way to achieve this, and I strongly recommend that you follow up a MANOVA with both univariate tests and discriminant analysis if you want to fully understand your data.

Discriminant analysis is quite straightforward in SPSS: to access the main dialog box simply follow the menu path **Analyze⇒Classify⇒Discriminant...**(see Figure 10.4).

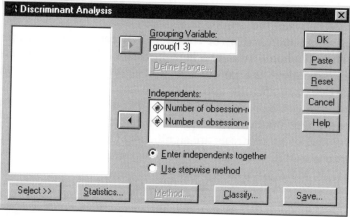

Figure 10.4: Main dialog box for discriminant analysis

The main dialog box will list the variables in the data editor on the left-hand side and provides two spaces on the right: one for the group variable and one for the predictors. In discriminant analysis we look to see how we can best separate (or discriminate) a set of groups using several predictors (so it is a little like logistic regression but where there are several groups rather than two).[5] It might be confusing to think of

---

[5] In fact, I could have just as easily described discriminant analysis rather than logistic regression in Chapter 5 because they are different ways of achieving the same end result. However, logistic regression has far fewer restrictive

actions and thoughts as independent variables (after all, they were dependent variables in the MANOVA!) which is why I refer to them as predictors—this is another example of why it is useful not to refer to variables as independent variables and dependent variables in correlational analysis.

To run the analysis, select the variable **group** and transfer it to the box labelled *Grouping Variable* by clicking on ▶. Once this variable has been transferred, the `Define Range...` button will become active and you should click this button to activate a dialog box in which you can specify the value of the highest and lowest coding values. Once you have specified the codings used for the grouping variable, you should select the variables **actions** and **thoughts** and transfer them to the box labelled *Independents* by clicking on ▶. There are two options available to determine how the predictors are entered into the model. The default is that both predictors are entered together and this is the option we require (because in MANOVA the dependent variables are analysed simultaneously). It is possible to enter the dependent variables in a stepwise manor and if this option is selected the `Method...` button becomes active, which opens a dialog box for specifying the criteria upon which predictors are entered.

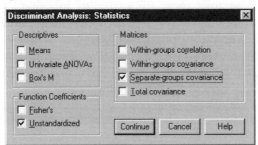

Figure 10.5: Statistics options for discriminant analysis

For the purpose of following up MANOVA, we need only be concerned with the remaining options. Click on `Statistics...` to activate the dialog box in Figure 10.5. This dialog box allows us to request group means, univariate ANOVAs and Box's test of equality of covariance matrices, all of which have already been provided in the MANOVA output (so we need not ask for them again). Furthermore, we can ask for the within-group correlation and covariance matrices, which are the same as the residual correlation and covariance matrices seen in SPSS Output 10.6. There is also an option to display a separate-groups covariance matrix, which can be useful for gaining insight into the relationships between dependent variables for each group (this matrix is

assumptions and is generally more robust, which is why I have restricted the coverage of discriminant analysis to this chapter.

something that the MANOVA procedure doesn't display and I recommend selecting it). Finally, we can ask for a total covariance matrix, which displays covariances and variances of the dependent variables overall. Another useful option is to select *Unstandardized* function coefficients. This option will produce the unstandardized βs for each variate (see equation (10.5)).When you have finished with this dialog box, click on [Continue] to return to the main dialog box.

If you click on [Classify...] you will access the dialog box in Figure 10.6. In this dialog box there are several options available. First, you can select how prior probabilities are determined: if your group sizes are equal then you should leave the default setting as it is; however, if you have an unbalanced design then it is beneficial to base prior probabilities on the observed group sizes. The default option for basing the analysis on the within-group covariance matrix is fine (because this is the matrix upon which the MANOVA is based). You should also request a combined-groups plot, which will plot the variate scores for each subject grouped according to the therapy they were given. The separate-groups plots show the same thing but using different graphs for each of the groups; when the number of groups is small it is better to select a combined plot because they are easier to interpret. The remaining options are of little interest when using discriminant analysis to follow up MANOVA. The only option that is useful is the summary table, which provides an overall gauge of how well the discriminant variates classify the actual subjects. When you have finished with the options click on [Continue] to return to the main dialog box.

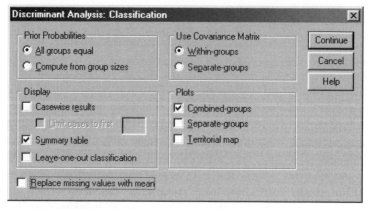

Figure 10.6: Discriminant analysis classification options

The final options are accessed by clicking on [Save...] to access the dialog box in Figure 10.7. There are three options available, two of which relate to the predicted group memberships and probabilities of group memberships from the model. These values are comparable to those obtained from a logistic regression analysis (see Chapter 5). The final option is to provide the discriminant scores. These are the scores for each subject, on each variate, obtained from equation (10.5). These scores can be useful because the variates that the analysis identifies may represent underlying social or psychological constructs. If these constructs are identifiable, then it is useful for interpretation to know what a subject scores on each dimension.

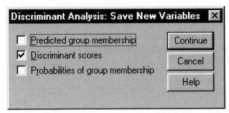

Figure 10.7: *Save new variables* dialog box in discriminant analysis

10.7.   Output from the Discriminant Analysis

SPSS Output 10.8 shows the covariance matrices for separate groups (selected in Figure 10.5). These matrices are made up of the variances of each dependent variable for each group (in fact these values are shown in Table 10.1). The covariances are obtained by taking the cross-products between the dependent variables for each group (shown in Table 10.4 as 0.40, 22.6 and −10) and dividing each by 9—the degrees of freedom, $N–1$ (where N is the number of observations). The values in this table are useful because they give us some idea of how the relationship between dependent variables changes from group to group. For example, in the CBT group behaviours and thoughts have virtually no relationship because the covariance is almost zero. In the BT group thoughts and actions are positively related, so as the number of behaviours decrease, so does the number of thoughts. In the NT condition there is a negative relationship, so if the number of thoughts increases then the number of behaviours decrease. It is important to note that these matrices don't tell us about the substantive importance of the relationships because they are unstandardized (see Chapter 3), they merely give a basic indication.

Covariance Matrices

group		Number of obsession-related behaviours	Number of obsession-related thoughts
CBT	Number of obsession-related behaviours	1.433	4.444E-02
	Number of obsession-related thoughts	4.444E-02	3.600
BT	Number of obsession-related behaviours	3.122	2.511
	Number of obsession-related thoughts	2.511	4.400
No Treatment Control	Number of obsession-related behaviours	1.111	-1.111
	Number of obsession-related thoughts	-1.111	5.556

SPSS Output 10.8

SPSS Output 10.9 shows the initial statistics from the discriminant analysis. At first we are told the eigenvalues for each variate and you should note that the values correspond to the values of the diagonal elements of the matrix HE^{-1} (calculated in appendix 12.7). These eigenvalues are converted into percentage of variance accounted for, and the first variate accounts for 82.2% of variance compared to the second variate, which accounts for only 17.8%. The next part of the output shows Wilks's lambda which has the same value (0.699), degrees of freedom (4) and significance value (0.05) as in the MANOVA (see SPSS Output 10.3). The important point to note from this table is that only one of the variates is significant (the second variate is non-significant, $p = 0.173$). Therefore, the group differences shown by the MANOVA can be explained in terms of *one* underlying dimension.

Eigenvalues

Function	Eigenvalue	% of Variance	Cumulative %	Canonical Correlation
1	.335[a]	82.2	82.2	.501
2	.073[a]	17.8	100.0	.260

a. First 2 canonical discriminant functions were used in the analysis.

Wilks's Lambda

Test of Function(s)	Wilks's Lambda	Chi-square	df	Sig.
1 through 2	.699	9.508	4	.050
2	.932	1.856	1	.173

SPSS Output 10.9

The tables in SPSS Output 10.10 are the most important for interpretation. The first table shows the standardized discriminant function coefficients for the two variates. These values are standardized versions of the values in the eigenvectors calculated in section 10.2.4.1. If you recall that the variates can be expressed in terms of a linear regression equation (see equation (10.4)), the standardized discriminant function coefficients are equivalent to the standardized betas in regression. Hence, these coefficients tell us the relative contribution of each variable to the variates. It is clear from the size of the values for these data that the number of obsessive behaviours has a greater contribution to the first variate than the number of thoughts, but that the opposite is true for variate 2. Also, remembering that standardized beta coefficients vary within ±1, it is noteworthy that both variables have a large contribution to the first variate (i.e. they are both important) because their values are quite close to 1 and −1 respectively. Bearing in mind that only the first variate is important, we can conclude that it is necessary to retain both dependent variables in the set of discriminators (because their standardized weights are of a similar magnitude). The fact that one dependent variable has a negative weight and one a positive weight indicates that group differences are explained by the difference between dependent variables.

Standardized Canonical Discriminant Function Coefficients

	Function	
	1	2
Number of obsession-related behaviours	.829	.584
Number of obsession-related thoughts	-.713	.721

Structure Matrix

	Function	
	1	2
Number of obsession-related behaviours	.711*	.703
Number of obsession-related thoughts	-.576	.817*

Pooled within-groups correlations between discriminating variables and standardized canonical discriminant functions
Variables ordered by absolute size of correlation within function.

*. Largest absolute correlation between each variable and any discriminant function

SPSS Output 10.10

Another way of looking at the relationship between dependent variables and discriminant variates is to look at the structure matrix, which gives the canonical variate correlation coefficients. These values are comparable to factor loadings (see Chapter 11) and indicate the substantive nature of the variates. Bargman (1970) argues that when some dependent variables have high canonical variate correlations while others have low ones then the ones with high correlations contribute most to group separation. As such they represent the relative contribution of each dependent variable to group separation (see Bray and Maxwell, 1985, pp. 42–45). We are again interested only in the first variate (because the second was non-significant) and looking at the structure matrix we can conclude that the number of behaviours was slightly more important in differentiating the three groups (because 0.711 is greater than 0.576). However, the number of thoughts is still very important because the value of the correlation is quite large. As with the standardized weights, the fact that one dependent variable has a positive correlation, whereas the other has a negative one, indicates that group separation is determined by the difference between the dependent variables.

Canonical Discriminant Function Coefficients

	Function	
	1	2
Number of obsession-related behaviours	.603	.425
Number of obsession-related thoughts	-.335	.339
(Constant)	2.139	-6.857

Unstandardized coefficients

Functions at Group Centroids

	Function	
group	1	2
CBT	.601	-.229
BT	-.726	-.128
No Treatment Control	.125	.357

Unstandardized canonical discriminant functions evaluated at group means

SPSS Output 10.11

The next part of the output (SPSS Output 10.11) tells us first the canonical discriminant function coefficients, which are the unstandardized versions of the standardized coefficients described above. As such, these values are the values of β in equation (10.4) and you'll notice that these values correspond to the values in the eigenvectors derived in section 10.2.4.1 and used in equation (10.5). These values are less useful than the standardized versions, but do demonstrate from where the standardized versions come. The next table gives the values of the variate centroids for each group. The centroids are simply the mean variate scores for each group. For interpretation we should look at the sign of the centroid (positive or negative), and from these data it looks as if variate 1 discriminates the BT group from the other two (notably the CBT group because the difference between centroids is greatest for these groups). The second variate (which was non-significant) seems to discriminate the NT group from the two experimental groups (but not significantly so).

The relationship between the variates and the groups is best illuminated using a combined-groups plot (selected using the dialog box in Figure 10.6). This graph plots the variate scores for each subject, grouped according to the experimental condition to which that subject belonged. In addition, the group centroids are indicated which are the average variate scores for each group.

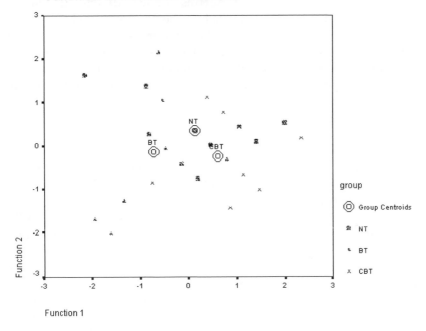

Figure 10.8: Combined-groups plot

Figure 10.8 shows this plot for the OCD data, and what is clear from the position of the centroids (the big circles labelled with the group initials) is that variate 1 discriminates the BT group from the CBT (look at the horizontal distance between these centroids). The second variate does not differentiate any groups: we know this already because it was non-significant, but the plot shows that the vertical distances between group centroids is very small which indicates no group separation on this variate.

10.8.   Conclusions

10.8.1.   The Final Interpretation

So far we have gathered an awful lot of information about our data, but how can we bring all of it together to answer our research question: can therapy improve OCD and if so which therapy is best? Well, the MANOVA tells us that therapy can have a significant effect on OCD symptoms, but the non-significant univariate ANOVAs suggested that this improvement is not simply in terms of either thoughts or behaviours. The discriminant analysis suggests that the group separation can be best explained in terms of one underlying dimension. In this context the dimension is likely to be OCD itself (which we can realistically presume is made up of both thoughts and behaviours). So, therapy doesn't necessarily change behaviours or thoughts *per se*, but it does influence the underlying dimension of OCD. So, the answer to the first question seems to be: yes, therapy can influence OCD, but the nature of this influence is unclear.

The next question is more complex: which therapy is best? Figure 10.9 shows graphs of the relationships between the dependent variables and the group means of the original data. The graph of the means shows that for actions, BT reduces the number of obsessive behaviours whereas CBT and NT do not. For thoughts, CBT reduces the number of obsessive thoughts, whereas BT and NT do not (check the pattern of the bars). Looking now at the relationships between thoughts and actions, in the BT group there is a near-linear positive relationship between thoughts and actions, so the more obsessive thoughts a person has, the more obsessive behaviours they carry out. In the CBT group there is no relationship at all (thoughts and actions vary quite independently). In the no-treatment group there is a small (and non-significant incidentally) negative relationship between thoughts and actions. What we have discovered from the discriminant analysis is that behaviours are more important in terms of OCD (as a construct) than thoughts (we know this from the canonical variate correlations). Therefore, behaviour therapy seems to be best because it addresses behaviours rather than thoughts (and so compared to CBT is preferable—hence the distance between their group centroids in Figure 10.8). However, the significance of the discriminant function does not necessarily tell us that the BT group was significantly lower than the NT group (so therapy isn't necessarily better than no therapy). So, in short BT has the most influence on OCD as a construct, because of the relative importance of behaviours in that construct compared to cognitions.

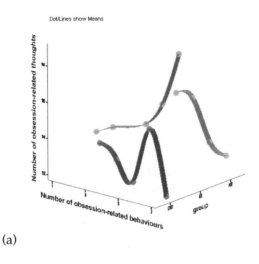

(a)

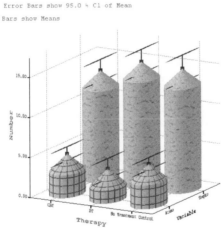

(b)

Figure 10.9: Graphs showing (a) the relationships and (b) the means between the dependent variables in each therapy group

10.8.2.   Univariate ANOVA or Discriminant Analysis?

This example should have made clear that univariate ANOVA and discriminant analysis are ways of answering different questions arising from a significant MANOVA. If univariate ANOVAs are chosen, Bonferroni corrections should be applied to the level at which you accept significance. The truth is that you should run both analyses to get a full picture of what is happening in your data. The advantage of discriminant analysis is that it tells you something about the underlying dimensions within your data (which is especially useful if you have employed several dependent measures in an attempt to capture some social or psychological construct). Even if univariate ANOVAs are significant, the discriminant analysis provides useful insight into your data and should be used. I hope that this chapter will convince you of this recommendation!

10.9. Further Reading

Bray, J. H. & Maxwell, S. E. (1985). *Multivariate analysis of variance.* Sage university paper series on quantitative applications in the social sciences, 07-054. Newbury Park, CA: Sage. This monograph on MANOVA is superb: I cannot recommend anything better.

11 Exploratory Factor Analysis

11.1.   What Is a Factor?

If we measure several variables, or ask someone several questions about themselves, the correlation between each pair of variables (or questions) can be arranged in what's known as an *R-matrix*. An R-matrix is just a table of correlation coefficients between variables (in fact, we saw small versions of these matrices in Chapter 3). The diagonal elements of an R-matrix are all 1 because each variable will correlate perfectly with itself. The off-diagonal elements are the correlation coefficients between pairs of variables, or questions.[1] The existence of clusters of large correlation coefficients between subsets of variables suggests that those variables could be measuring aspects of the same underlying dimension. These underlying dimensions are known as *factors* (or *latent variables*). By reducing a data set from a group of interrelated variables into a smaller set of *uncorrelated* factors, factor analysis achieves parsimony by explaining the maximum amount of common variance in a correlation matrix using the smallest number of explanatory concepts.

There are numerous examples of the use of factor analysis in the social sciences. The trait theorists in psychology used factor analysis endlessly to measure personality traits. Most readers will be familiar with the extraversion–introversion and neuroticism traits measured by Eysenck (1953). Most other personality questionnaires are based on factor analysis (notably Cattell's, 1966a, 16 personality factors questionnaire) and these inventories are frequently used for recruiting purposes in industry and even by some religious groups. However, although factor analysis is probably most famous for being adopted by psychologists, its use is by no means restricted to measuring dimensions of personality. Economists, for example, might use factor analysis to see whether productivity, profits and workforce can be reduced down to an underlying dimension of company growth.

Let's put some of these ideas into practice by imagining that we wanted to measure different aspects of what might make a person popular. We could administer a number of measures that we believe tap different aspects of popularity. So, we might measure a person's social skills (Social Skills), their selfishness (Selfish), how interesting others

---

[1] This matrix is called an *R-matrix*, or *R*, because it contains correlation coefficients and *R* usually denotes Pearson's correlation (see Chapter 3).

find them (Interest), the proportion of time they spend talking about the other person during a conversation (Talk1), the proportion of time they spend talking about themselves (Talk2), and their propensity to lie to people (the Liar scale). We can then calculate the correlation coefficients for each pair of variables and create an *R*-matrix. Table 11.1 shows this matrix. Any significant correlation coefficients are shown in bold type. It is clear that there are two clusters of variables that interrelate. Therefore, these variables might be measuring some common underlying dimension. The amount that someone talks about the other person during a conversation seems to correlate highly with both the level of social skills and how interesting the other finds that person. Also, social skills correlates well with how interesting others perceive a person to be. These relationships indicate that the better your social skills the more interesting and talkative you are likely to be. However, there is a second cluster of variables. The amount that people talk about themselves within a conversation correlates with how selfish they are and how much they lie. Being selfish also correlates with the degree to which a person tells lies. In short, selfish people are likely to lie and talk about themselves. In factor analysis we strive to reduce this *R*-matrix down into its component dimensions by looking at which variables seem to cluster together in a meaningful way. This data reduction is achieved by looking for variables that correlate highly with a group of other variables, but correlate very badly with variables outside of that group. In this example, there appear to be two clusters that fit the bill. The first factor seems to relate to general Sociability, whereas the second factor seems to relate to the way in which a person treats others socially (Consideration). It might, therefore, be assumed that popularity depends not only on your ability to socialize, but also on whether you are genuine towards others.

Table 11.1: An *R*-matrix

	Talk 1	Social Skills	Interest	Talk 2	Selfish	Liar
Talk 1	*Factor 1*					
Social Skills	0.772	1.000				
Interest	0.646	0.879	1.000	*Factor 2*		
Talk 2	0.074	−0.120	0.054	1.000		
Selfish	−0.131	0.031	−0.101	0.441	1.000	
Liar	0.068	0.012	0.110	0.361	0.277	1.000

11.1.1.   *Graphical Representation of Factors*

Factors (not to be confused with independent variables in factorial ANOVA) are statistical entities that can be visualized as classification axes along which measurement variables can be plotted. In plain

English, this statement means that if you imagine factors as being the axis of a graph, then we can plot variables along these axes. The co-ordinates of variables along each axis represent the correlation between that variable and each factor. Figure 11.1 shows such a plot for the popularity data (in which there were only two factors). The first thing to notice is that for both factors, the axis line ranges from −1 to 1, which are the outer limits of a correlation coefficient. Therefore, the position of a given variable depends on its correlation to the two factors. The dots represent the three variables that correlate highly with factor 1 (sociability: vertical axis) but have a low correlation with factor 2 (consideration to others: horizontal axis). Conversely, the triangles represent variables that correlate highly with consideration to others but have a low correlation to sociability. From this plot, we can tell that selfishness, the amount a person talks about themselves and their propensity to lie all contribute to a factor which could be called consideration of others. Conversely, how much a person takes an interest in other people, how interesting they are and their level of social skills contribute to a second factor, sociability. This diagram therefore supports the structure that was apparent in the R-matrix. Of course, if a third factor existed within these data it could be represented by a third axis (creating a 3-D graph). It should also be apparent that if more than three factors exist in a data set, then they cannot all be represented by a two-dimensional drawing.

If each axis on the graph represents a factor, then the variables that go to make up a factor can be plotted according to the extent to which they relate to a given factor. The co-ordinates of a variable, therefore, represent its relationship to the factors. In an ideal world a variable should have a large co-ordinate for one of the axes, and low co-ordinates for any other factors. This scenario would indicate that this particular variable related to only one factor. Variables that have large co-ordinates on the same axis are assumed to measure different aspects of some common underlying dimension. The co-ordinate of a variable along a classification axis is known as a *factor loading*. The factor loading is, therefore, the Pearson correlation between a factor and a variable. From what we know about interpreting correlation coefficients (see section 3.2.3.3) it should be clear that if we square the factor loading we obtain a measure of the substantive importance of a particular variable to a factor.

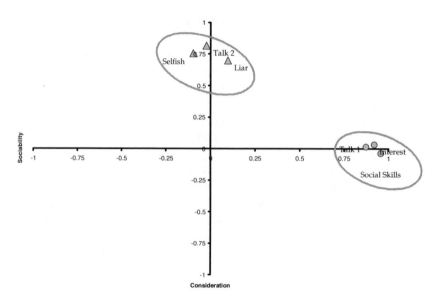

Figure 11.1: Example of a factor plot.

11.1.2.   *Mathematical Representation of Factors*

The axes drawn in Figure 11.1 are straight lines and so can be described mathematically by the equation of a straight line. Therefore, factors can also be described in terms of this equation. We have used the equation of a straight line numerous times throughout this text and so it should be familiar to you. Equation (11.1) reminds us of the equation describing a linear model and then applies this to the scenario of describing a factor. You'll notice that there is no intercept in the equation, the reason being that the lines intersect at zero (hence the intercept is also zero). The βs in the equation represent the factor loadings.

$$Y = \beta_1 X_1 + \beta_2 X_2 + \ldots + \beta_n X_n$$
$$\text{Factor}_1 = \beta_1 \text{Variable}_1 + \beta_2 \text{Variable}_2 + \ldots + \beta_n \text{Variable}_n$$

(11.1)

Sticking with our example of popularity, we found that there were two factors underlying this construct: general sociability and consideration. We can, therefore, construct an equation that describes each factor in terms of the variables that have been measured. The equations are shown in equation (11.2).

$$Y = \beta_1 X_1 + \beta_2 X_2 + \ldots + \beta_n X_n$$
$$\text{Sociability} = \beta_1 \text{Talk1} + \beta_2 \text{Social Skills} + \beta_3 \text{Interest}$$
$$+ \beta_4 \text{Talk2} + \beta_5 \text{Selfish} + \beta_6 \text{Liar} \tag{11.2}$$
$$\text{Consideration} = \beta_1 \text{Talk1} + \beta_2 \text{Social Skills} + \beta_3 \text{Interest}$$
$$+ \beta_4 \text{Talk2} + \beta_5 \text{Selfish} + \beta_6 \text{Liar}$$

First, notice that the equations are identical in form: they both include all of the variables that were measures. However, the values of β in the two equations will be different (depending on the relative importance of each variable to the particular factor). In fact, we can replace each value of β with the co-ordinate of that variable on the graph in Figure 11.1 (i.e. replace the values of β with the factor loading). The resulting equations are shown in equation (11.3).

$$Y = \beta_1 X_1 + \beta_2 X_2 + \ldots + \beta_n X_n$$
$$\text{Sociability} = 0.87 \text{Talk1} + 0.96 \text{Social Skills} + 0.92 \text{Interest}$$
$$+ 0.00 \text{Talk2} - 0.10 \text{Selfish} + 0.09 \text{Liar} \tag{11.3}$$
$$\text{Consideration} = 0.01 \text{Talk1} - 0.03 \text{Social Skills} + 0.04 \text{Interest}$$
$$+ 0.82 \text{Talk2} + 0.75 \text{Selfish} + 0.70 \text{Liar}$$

Notice that, for the Sociability factor, the values of β are high for Talk1, Social Skills and Interest. For the remaining variables (Talk2, Selfish and Liar) the values of β are very low (close to zero). This tells us that three of the variables are very important for that factor (the ones with high values of β) and three are very unimportant (the ones with low values of β). We saw that this point is true because of the way that three variables clustered highly on the factor plot. The point to take on board here is that the factor plot and these equations represent the same thing: the factor loadings in the plot are simply the β values in these equations. For the second factor, inconsideration to others, the opposite pattern can be seen in that Talk2, Selfish and Liar all have high values of β whereas the remaining three variables have β values close to zero. In an ideal world, variables would have very high β values for one factor and very low β values for all other factors.

These factor loadings can be placed in a matrix in which the columns represent each factor and the rows represent the loadings of each variable onto each factor. For the popularity data this matrix would have two columns (one for each factor) and six rows (one for each variable). This matrix, usually denoted A, can be seen below. To understand what the matrix means try relating the elements to the loadings in equation (11.3). For example, the top row represents the first variable, Talk1, which had a loading of 0.87 for the first factor *ad measured through statistical analysis*

(Sociability) and a loading of 0.01 for the second factor (Consideration). This matrix is called the *factor pattern matrix* or *component pattern matrix*.

$$A = \begin{pmatrix} 0.87 & 0.01 \\ 0.96 & -0.03 \\ 0.92 & 0.04 \\ 0.00 & 0.82 \\ -0.10 & 0.75 \\ 0.09 & 0.70 \end{pmatrix}$$

The major assumption in factor analysis is that these algebraic factors represent real-world dimensions, the nature of which must be *guessed at* by inspecting which variables have high loads on the same factor. So, psychologists believe that factors represent dimensions of the psyche, education researchers believe they represent abilities, and sociologists might believe they represent races, or social classes. However, it is an extremely contentious point whether this assumption is tenable and some believe that the dimensions derived from factor analysis are real only in the statistical sense—and are real-world fictions.

11.1.3.   Factor Scores

A factor can be described in terms of the variables measured and the relative importance of them for that factor (represented by the value of β). Therefore, having discovered which factors exist, and the equation that describes them, it should be possible to calculate a person's score on a factor, based on their scores for the constituent variables. For example, if we wanted to derive a score of sociability for a particular person, we could place their scores on the various measures into equation (11.3). This method is known as a *weighted average*. In fact, this method is overly simplistic and rarely used, but it is probably the easiest way to explain the principle. For example, imagine the six scales all range from 1 to 10 and that someone scored the following: Talk1 (4), Social Skills (9), Interest (8), Talk2 (6), Selfish (8), and Liar (6). We could replace these values into equation (11.3) to get a score for this person's sociability and their consideration to others (see equation (11.4)). The resulting scores of 19.22 and 15.21 reflect the degree to which this person is sociable and their inconsideration to others respectively. This person scores higher on sociability than inconsideration. However, the scales of measurement used will influence the resulting scores, and if different variables used different measurement scales, then factor scores for different factors cannot be compared. As such, this method of calculating factor scores is poor and more sophisticated methods are usually used.

$$\text{Sociability} = 0.87\text{Talk1} + 0.96\text{Social Skills} + 0.92\text{Interest}$$
$$+ 0.00\text{Talk2} - 0.10\text{Selfish} + 0.09\text{Liar}$$
$$\text{Sociability} = (0.87 \times 4) + (0.96 \times 9) + (0.92 \times 8) + (0.00 \times 6)$$
$$- (0.10 \times 8) + (0.09 \times 6)$$
$$= 19.22$$

$$\text{Consideration} = 0.01\text{Talk1} - 0.03\text{Social Skills} + 0.04\text{Interest}$$
$$+ 0.82\text{Talk2} + 0.75\text{Selfish} + 0.70\text{Liar}$$
$$\text{Consideration} = (0.01 \times 4) - (0.03 \times 9) + (0.04 \times 8) + (0.82 \times 6)$$
$$+ (0.75 \times 8) + (0.70 \times 6)$$
$$= 15.21$$

(11.4)

11.1.4.   The Regression Method

There are several sophisticated techniques for calculating factor scores that use factor score coefficients as weights in equation (11.1) rather than using the factor loadings. The form of the equation remains the same, but the βs in the equation are replaced with these factor score coefficients. Factor score coefficients can be calculated in several ways. The simplest way is the regression method. In this method the factor loadings are adjusted to take account of the initial correlations between variables; in doing so, differences in units of measurement and variable variances are stabilized.

To obtain the matrix of factor score coefficients (B) we multiply the matrix of factor loadings by the inverse (R^{-1}) of the original correlation or R-matrix. You might remember from the last chapter that matrices cannot be divided (see section 10.2.4.1). Therefore, if we want to divide by a matrix it cannot be done directly and instead we multiply by its inverse. Therefore, by multiplying the matrix of factor loadings by the inverse of the correlation matrix we are, conceptually speaking, dividing the factor loadings by the correlation coefficients. The resulting factor score matrix, therefore, represents the relationship between each variable and each factor taking into account the original relationships between pairs of variables. As such, this matrix represents a purer measure of the *unique* relationship between variables and factors.

The matrices for the popularity data are shown below. The resulting matrix of factor score coefficients, B, comes from SPSS. The matrices R^{-1} and A can be multiplied by hand to get the matrix B and those familiar with matrix algebra (or who have consulted Namboodiri, 1984, or Stevens, 1992) might like to verify the result (calculations are in appendix 12.8). To get the same degree of accuracy as SPSS you should work to at least 5 decimal places.

$$B = R^{-1}A$$

$$B = \begin{pmatrix} 4.76 & -7.46 & 3.91 & -2.35 & 2.42 & -0.49 \\ -7.46 & 18.49 & -12.42 & 5.45 & -5.54 & 1.22 \\ 3.91 & -12.42 & 10.07 & -3.65 & 3.79 & -0.96 \\ -2.35 & 5.45 & -3.65 & 2.97 & -2.16 & 0.02 \\ 2.42 & -5.54 & 3.79 & -2.16 & 2.98 & -0.56 \\ -0.49 & 1.22 & -0.96 & 0.02 & -0.56 & 1.27 \end{pmatrix} \begin{pmatrix} 0.87 & 0.01 \\ 0.96 & -0.03 \\ 0.92 & 0.04 \\ 0.00 & 0.82 \\ -0.10 & 0.75 \\ 0.09 & 0.70 \end{pmatrix}$$

$$B = \begin{pmatrix} 0.343 & 0.006 \\ 0.376 & -0.020 \\ 0.362 & 0.020 \\ 0.000 & 0.473 \\ -0.037 & 0.437 \\ 0.039 & 0.405 \end{pmatrix}$$

The pattern of the loadings is the same for the factor score coefficients, namely, the first three variables have high loadings for the first factor and low loadings for the second whereas the pattern is reversed for the last three variables. The difference is only in the actual value of the weightings, which are smaller because the correlations between variables are now accounted for. These factor score coefficients can be used to replace the β values in equation (11.4).

$$\text{Sociability} = 0.343\text{Talk1} + 0.376\text{Social Skills} + 0.362\text{Interest}$$
$$+ 0.000\text{Talk2} - 0.037\text{Selfish} + 0.039\text{Liar}$$
$$\text{Sociability} = (0.343 \times 4) + (0.376 \times 9) + (0.362 \times 8) + (0.000 \times 6)$$
$$- (0.037 \times 8) + (0.039 \times 6)$$
$$= 7.59$$
$$\text{Consideration} = 0.006\text{Talk1} - 0.020\text{Social Skills} + 0.020\text{Interest} \qquad (11.5)$$
$$+ 0.473\text{Talk2} + 0.437\text{Selfish} + 0.405\text{Liar}$$
$$\text{Consideration} = (0.006 \times 4) - (0.020 \times 9) + (0.020 \times 8) + (0.473 \times 6)$$
$$+ (0.437 \times 8) + (0.405 \times 6)$$
$$= 8.768$$

Equation (11.5) shows how these coefficient scores are used to produce two factor scores for each subject. In this case, the subject had the same scores on each variable as were used in equation (11.4). The resulting scores are much more similar than when the factor loadings were used as weights because the different variances among the six variables has now been controlled for. The fact that the values are very similar reflects the fact that this person not only scores highly on variables relating to sociability, but is also inconsiderate (i.e. he scores equally highly on both factors). This technique for producing factor scores ensures that the resulting scores have a mean of zero and a variance equal to the squared multiple correlation between the estimated factor scores and the true factor values. However, the downside of the regression method is that the scores can correlate not only with factors other than the one on which they are based but also with other factor scores from a different orthogonal factor.

11.1.4.1. Other Methods

To overcome the problems associated with the regression technique, two adjustments have been proposed: *the Bartlett method* and *the Anderson-Rubin method*. SPSS can produce factor scores based on any of these methods. The Bartlett method produces scores that are unbiased and that correlate only with their own factor. The mean and standard deviation of the scores is the same as for the regression method. However, factor scores can still correlate with each other. The final method is the Anderson-Rubin method, which is a modification of the Bartlett method that produces factor scores that are uncorrelated and standardized (they have a mean of 0, a standard deviation of 1). Tabachnick and Fidell (1996) conclude that the Anderson-Rubin method is best when uncorrelated scores are required but that the regression method is preferred in other circumstances simply because it is most easily understood. Although it isn't important that you understand the maths behind any of the methods, it is important that you understand what the factor scores represent: namely, a composite score for each individual on a particular factor.

11.1.4.2. Uses of Factor Scores

There are several uses of factor scores. First, if the purpose of the factor analysis is to reduce a large set of data into a smaller subset of measurement variables, then the factor scores tell us an individual's score on this subset of measures. Therefore, any further analysis can be carried out on the factor scores rather than the original data. For example, we could carry out a *t*-test to see whether females are significantly more sociable than males using the factor scores for *sociability*. A second use is in overcoming collinearity problems in regression. If, following a multiple regression analysis, we have identified sources of multicollinearity then the interpretation of the analysis is questioned (see section 4.2.5.3). In this situation, we can simply carry out a factor analysis on the predictor variables to reduce them down to a subset of uncorrelated factors. The variables causing the multicollinearity will combine to form a factor. If we then rerun the regression but using the factor scores as predictor variables then the problem of multicollinearity should vanish (because the variables are now combined into a single factor). There are ways in which we can ensure that the factors are uncorrelated (one way is to use the Anderson-Rubin method—see above). By using uncorrelated factor scores as predictors in the regression we can be confident that there will be no correlation between predictors: hence, no multicollinearity!

11.2.   Discovering Factors

By now, you should have some grasp of the concept of what a factor is, how it is represented graphically, how it is represented algebraically, and how we can calculate composite scores representing an individual's 'performance' on a single factor. I have deliberately restricted the discussion to a conceptual level, without delving into how we actually find these mythical beasts known as factors. This section will look at how we find factors. Specifically we will examine different types of method, look at the maths behind one method (principal components), investigate the criteria for determining whether factors are important, and discover how to improve the interpretation of a given solution.

11.2.1.   *Communality*

Before continuing it is important that you understand some basic things about the variance within an *R*-matrix. It is possible to calculate the variability in scores (the variance) for any given measure (or variable). You should be familiar with the idea of variance by now and comfortable with how it can be calculated (if not see Chapter 1). The total variance for a particular variable will have two components: some of it will be shared with other variables or measures (*common variance*) and some of it will be specific to that measure (*unique variance*). We tend to use the term 'unique variance' to refer to variance that can be reliably attributed to only one measure. However, there is also variance that is specific to one measure but not reliably so; this variance is called *error* or *random variance*. The proportion of common variance present in a variable is known as the *communality*. As such, a variable that has no specific variance (or random variance) would have a communality of 1; a variable that shares none of its variance with any other variable would have a communality of 0.

In factor analysis we are interested in finding common underlying dimensions within the data and so we are primarily interested only in the common variance. Therefore, when we run a factor analysis it is fundamental that we know how much of the variance present in our data is common variance. This presents us with a logical impasse: to do the factor analysis we need to know the proportion of common variance present in the data, yet the only way to find out the extent of the common variance is by carrying out a factor analysis! There are two ways to approach this problem. The first is to assume that all of the variance is common variance. As such, we assume that the communality of every variable is 1. By making this assumption we merely transpose our original data into constituent linear components (known as principal component analysis). The second approach is to estimate the amount of common variance by estimating communality values for each variable. There are various methods of estimating communalities but the most widely used (including SPSS) is to use the squared multiple correlation (SMC) of each variable with all others. So, for the popularity data, imagine you ran a multiple regression using one measure (Selfish) as the outcome and the other five measures as predictors: the resulting multiple R^2 (see section 4.2.2) would be used as an estimate of the communality for the variable Selfish. This second approach is what is done in factor analysis. These estimates allow the factor analysis to be done. Once the underlying factors have been extracted, new communalities can be calculated that represent the multiple correlation between each variable and the factors extracted. Therefore, the communality is a measure of the proportion of variance explained by the extracted factors.

11.2.2.   *Factor Analysis vs. Principal Component Analysis*

I have just explained that there are two approaches to locating underlying dimensions of a data set: factor analysis and principal component analysis. These techniques differ in the communality estimates that are used. Simplistically though, factor analysis derives a mathematical model from which factors are estimated, whereas principal component analysis merely decomposes the original data into a set of linear variates (see Dunteman, 1989, Chapter 8 for more detail on the differences between the procedures). As such, factor analysis can only estimate the underlying factors and it relies on various assumptions for these estimates to be accurate. Principal component analysis is concerned only with establishing which linear components exist within the data and how a particular variable might contribute to that component. In terms of theory, this chapter is dedicated to principal component analysis rather than factor analysis. The reasons are that principal component analysis is a psychometrically sound procedure, it is conceptually less complex than factor analysis, and it bears numerous similarities to discriminant analysis (described in the last chapter).

However, we should consider whether the techniques provide different solutions to the same problem. Based on an extensive literature review, Guadagnoli and Velicer (1988) concluded that the solutions generated from principal component analysis differ little from those derived from factor analytic techniques. In reality, there are some circumstances for which this statement is untrue. Stevens (1992) summarizes the evidence and concludes that with 30 or more variables and communalities greater than 0.7 for all variables, different solutions are unlikely; however, with less than 20 variables and any low communalities (< 0.4) differences can occur.

The flip-side of this argument is eloquently described by Cliff (1987) who observed that proponents of factor analysis 'insist that components analysis is at best a common factor analysis with some error added and at worst an unrecognizable hodgepodge of things from which nothing can be determined' (p. 349). Indeed feeling is strong on this issue with some arguing that when principal component analysis is used it should not be described as a factor analysis and that you should not impute substantive meaning to the resulting components. However, to non-statisticians the concept of a principal component is identical to that of a factor, and the differences arise largely from the calculation.[2]

11.2.3.   Theory behind Principal Component Analysis

 Principal component analysis works in a very similar way to MANOVA and discriminant function analysis (see last chapter). Although it isn't necessary to understand the mathematical principles in any detail, readers of the last chapter may benefit from some comparisons between the two techniques. Those that haven't read the last chapter, I suggest you flick through it before moving ahead!

In MANOVA, various sum of squares and cross-products matrices were calculated that contained information about the relationships between dependent variables. I mentioned before that these SSCP matrices could be easily converted to variance-covariance matrices, which represent the same information but in averaged form (i.e. taking

---

[2] For this reason I have used the terms *components* and *factors* interchangeably throughout this chapter. Although this use of terms will reduce some statisticians to tears I'm banking on these people not needing to read this book! I acknowledge the methodological differences, but I think it's easier for students if I dwell on the similarities between the techniques and not the differences.

account of the number of observations). I also said that by dividing each element by the relevant standard deviation the variance-covariance matrices becomes standardized. The result is a correlation matrix. In factor analysis we usually deal with correlation matrices (although it is possible to analyze a variance-covariance matrix too) and the point to note is that this matrix pretty much represents the same information as an SSCP matrix in MANOVA. The difference is just that the correlation matrix is an averaged version of the SSCP that has been standardized.

In MANOVA, we used several SSCP matrices that represented different components of experimental variation (the model variation and the residual variation). In principal component analysis the covariance (or correlation) matrix cannot be broken down in this way (because all data come from the same group of subjects). In MANOVA, we ended up looking at the variates or components of the SSCP matrix that represented the ratio of the model variance to the error variance. These variates were linear dimensions that separated the groups tested, and we saw that the dependent variables mapped onto these underlying components. In short, we looked at whether the groups could be separated by some linear combination of the dependent variables. These variates were found by calculating the eigenvectors of the SSCP. The number of variates obtained was the smaller of p (the number of dependent variables) or $k - 1$ (where k is the number of groups). In component analysis we do something similar (I'm simplifying things a little, but it will give you the basic idea). That is, we take a correlation matrix and calculate the variates. There are no groups of observations, and so the number of variates calculated will always equal the number of variables measured (p). The variates are described, as for MANOVA, by the eigenvectors associated with the correlation matrix. The elements of the eigenvectors are the weights of each variable on the variate (see equation (10.5)). These values are the factor loadings described earlier. The largest eigenvalue associated with each of the eigenvectors provides a single indicator of the substantive importance of each variate (or component). The basic idea is that we retain factors with relatively large eigenvalues, and ignore those with relative small eigenvalues.

In summary, component analysis works in a similar way to MANOVA. We begin with a matrix representing the relationships between variables. The linear components (also called variates, or factors) of that matrix are then calculated by determining the eigenvalues of the matrix. These eigenvalues are used to calculate eigenvectors, the elements of which provide the loading of a particular variable on a particular factor (i.e. they are the β values in equation (11.1)). The eigenvalue is also a measure of the substantive importance of the eigenvector with which it is associated.

11.2.4. *Factor Extraction: Eigenvalues and the Scree Plot?*

Not all factors are retained in an analysis, and there is debate over the criterion used to decide whether a factor is statistically important. I mentioned above that eigenvalues associated with a variate indicate the substantive importance of that factor. Therefore, it seems logical that we should retain only factors with large eigenvalues. How do we decide whether or not an eigenvalue is large enough to represent a meaningful factor? Well, one technique advocated by Cattell (1966b) is to plot a graph of each eigenvalue (Y-axis) against the factor with which it is associated (X-axis). This graph is known as a *scree plot*. I mentioned earlier that it is possible to obtain as many factors as there are variables and that each has an associated eigenvalue. By graphing the eigenvalues, the relative importance of each factor becomes apparent. Typically there will be a few factors with quite high eigenvalues, and many factors with relatively low eigenvalues, and so this graph has a very characteristic shape: there is a sharp descent in the curve followed by a tailing off (see Figure 11.2). Cattell (1966b) argued that the cut-off point for selecting factors should be at the point of inflexion of this curve. With a sample of more than 200 subjects, the scree plot provides a fairly reliable criterion for factor selection (Stevens, 1992).

How many factors should I extract?

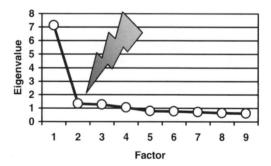

Figure 11.2: Example of a scree plot for data that have only one underlying factor. The point of inflexion is indicated by the thunderbolt!

Although scree plots are very useful, factor selection should not be based on this criterion alone. Kaiser (1960) recommended retaining all factors with eigenvalues greater than 1. This criterion is based on the idea that the eigenvalues represent the amount of variation explained by a factor and that an eigenvalue of 1 represents a substantial amount of variation. As is often the case in statistics, the two criteria often provide different solutions! To confuse matters further Jolliffe (1972, 1986) reports that Kaiser's criterion is too strict and suggests retaining all factors with eigenvalues more than 0.7. The difference between how many factors are retained using Kaiser's methods compared to Jolliffe's can be dramatic. In situations for which the three criteria provide different solutions the communalities of the factors need to be considered.

In principal component analysis we begin with communalities of 1 with all factors retained (because we assume that all variance is common variance). At this stage all we have done is to find the linear variates that exist in the data—so we have just transformed the data without discarding any information. However, to discover what common variance *really* exists between variables we must decide which factors are meaningful and discard any that are too trivial to consider. Therefore, we discard some information. The factors we retain will not explain all of the variance in the data (because we have discarded some information) and so the communalities after extraction will always be less than 1. The factors retained do not map perfectly onto the original variables—they merely reflect the common variance present in the data. If the communalities represent a loss of information then they are important statistics. The closer the communalities are to 1, the better our factors are at explaining the original data. It is logical that the more factors retained, the greater the communalities will be (because less information is discarded); therefore, the communalities are good indices of whether too few factors have been retained.

Generally speaking, research has indicated that Kaiser's guideline is accurate when the number of variables is less than 30 and the resulting communalities (after extraction) are all greater than 0.7. Kaiser's criterion is also accurate when the sample size exceeds 250 and the average communality is greater than or equal to 0.6. In any other circumstances you are best advised to use a scree plot provided the sample size is greater than 200 (see Stevens, 1992, pp. 378-380 for more detail). By default, SPSS uses Kaiser's criterion to extract factors. Therefore, if you use the scree plot to determine how many factors are retained you may have to rerun the analysis specifying that SPSS extracts the number of factors you require.

11.2.5.   Improving Interpretation

11.2.5.1. Factor Rotation

Once factors have been extracted, it is possible to calculate to what degree variables load onto these factors (i.e. calculate the loading of the variable on each factor). Generally, you will find that most variables have high loadings on the most important factor, and small loadings on all other factors. This characteristic makes interpretation difficult, and so a technique called factor rotation is used to discriminate between factors. If a factor is a classification axis along which variables can be plotted, then factor rotation effectively rotates these factor axes such that variables are loaded maximally to only one factor. Figure 11.3 demonstrates how this process works using an example in which there are only two factors. Imagine that a sociologist was interested in classifying university lecturers as a demographic group. She discovered that two underlying dimensions best describe this group: alcoholism and achievement (go to any academic conference and you'll see that academics drink heavily!). The first factor, alcoholism, has a cluster of variables associated with it (dark dots) and these could be measures such as the number of units drunk in a week, dependency, and obsessive personality. The second factor, achievement, also has a cluster of variables associated with it (light dots) and these could be measures relating to salary, job status, and number of research publications. Initially, the full lines represent the factors, and by looking at the co-ordinates it should be clear that the light dots have high loadings for factor 2 (they are a long way up this axis), and medium loadings on factor 1 (they are not very far up this axis). Conversely, the dark dots have high loadings for factor 1 and medium loadings on factor 2. By rotating the axes (dotted lines), we ensure that both clusters of variables are intersected by the factor to which they relate most. So, after rotation, the loadings of the variables are maximized onto one factor (the factor that intersects the cluster) and minimized on the remaining factor(s). If an axis passes through a cluster of variables, then these variables will have a loading of approximately zero on the opposite axis. If this idea is confusing, then look at Figure 11.3 and think about the values of the co-ordinates before and after rotation (this is best achieved by turning the book when you look at the rotated axes).

There are two types of rotation that can be done. The first is *orthogonal rotation*, and the left-hand side of Figure 11.3 represents this method. In Chapter 7 we saw that the term 'orthogonal' means unrelated, and in this context it means that we rotate factors while keeping them independent. Before rotation, all factors are independent (i.e. they do not correlate at all) and orthogonal rotation ensures that the factors remain uncorrelated. That is why in Figure 11.3 the axes are turned while remaining perpendicular.[3] The other form of rotation is *oblique rotation*. The difference with oblique rotation is that the factors are allowed to correlate (hence, the axes of the right-hand diagram of Figure 11.3 do not remain perpendicular).

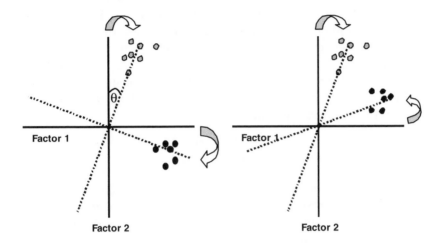

Figure 11.3: Schematic representations of factor rotation. The left graph displays orthogonal rotation whereas the right graph displays oblique rotation (see text for more details). θ is the angle through which the axes are rotated

The choice of rotation depends on whether there is a good theoretical reason to suppose that the factors should be related or independent, and also how the variables cluster on the factors before rotation. On the first point, we might not expect alcoholism to be completely independent of achievement (after all, high achievement leads to high stress, which can lead to the drinks cabinet!). Therefore, on theoretical grounds, we might choose oblique rotation. On the second point, Figure 11.3 demonstrates how the positioning of clusters is important in determining how successful the rotation would be (note the position of the black dots). Specifically, if an orthogonal rotation was carried out on the right-hand diagram it would be considerably less successful in maximizing loadings than the oblique rotation that is displayed. One approach is to run the analysis using both types of rotation. Pedhazur and Schmelkin (1991) suggest that if the oblique rotation demonstrates a negligible correlation between the extracted factors then it is reasonable to use the orthogonally rotated solution. If the oblique rotation reveals a correlated factor structure, then the orthogonally rotated solution should be

---

[3] This term means that the axes are at right angles to one another.

discarded. In any case, an oblique rotation should be used only if there are good reasons to suppose that the underlying factors *could* be related in theoretical terms.

The mathematics behind factor rotation are complex (especially oblique rotation). However, to obtain a matrix of rotated factor loadings the matrix of unrotated factor loadings, A, has to be multiplied by a matrix called the factor transformation matrix, Λ. The factor transformation matrix is a square matrix and its size depends on how many factors were extracted from the data. If two factors were extracted then it will be a 2 × 2 matrix, but if four factors were extracted then it becomes a 4 × 4 matrix. The values in the factor transformation matrix consist of sines and cosines of the angle of axis rotation (θ). For the case of two factors the matrix would be:

$$\Lambda = \begin{pmatrix} \cos\theta & -\sin\theta \\ \sin\theta & \cos\theta \end{pmatrix}$$

Therefore, you should think of this matrix as representing the angle through which the axes have been rotated, or the degree to which factors have been rotated. The angle of rotation necessary to optimize the factor solution is found in an iterative way and different methods can be used (see section 11.5.3).

11.2.5.2. Substantive Importance of Factor Loadings

Once a factor structure has been found, it is important to decide which variables make up which factors. Earlier I said that the factor loadings were a gauge of the substantive importance of a given variable to a given factor. Therefore, it makes sense that we use these values to place variables with factors. It is possible to assess the statistical significance of a factor loading (after all it is simply a correlation coefficient); however there are various reasons why this option is not as easy as it seems (see Stevens, 1992, p. 382). Typically, researchers take a loading of an absolute value of more than 0.3 to be important. However, the significance of a factor loading will depend on the sample size. Stevens (1992) produced a table of critical values against which loadings can be compared. To summarize, he recommends that for a sample size of 50 a loading of 0.722 can be considered significant, for 100 the loading should be greater than 0.512, for 200 it should be greater than 0.364, for 300 it should be greater than 0.298, for 600 it should be greater than 0.21, and for 1000 it should be greater than 0.162. These values are based on an alpha level of 0.01 (two-tailed), which allows for the fact that several loadings will need to be tested (see Stevens, 1992, pp.382-384 for further detail). Therefore, in very large samples, small loadings can be considered statistically meaningful. SPSS does not provide significance tests of factor loadings but by applying Stevens's guidelines you should gain some insight into the structure of variables and factors.

The significance of a loading gives little indication of the substantive importance of a variable to a factor. This value can be found by squaring the factor loading to give an estimate of the amount of variance in a factor accounted for by a variable (like R^2). In this respect Stevens (1992) recommends interpreting only factor loadings with an absolute value greater than 0.4 (which explain around 16% of variance).

11.3.   Research Example

Factor analysis is frequently used to develop questionnaires: after all if you want to measure an ability or trait, you need to ensure that the questions asked relate to the construct that you intend to measure. I have noticed that a lot of students become very stressed about SPSS. Therefore I wanted to design a questionnaire to measure a trait that I termed 'SPSS anxiety'. I decided to devise a questionnaire to measure various aspects of students' anxiety towards learning SPSS. I generated questions based on interviews with anxious and non-anxious students and came up with 23 possible questions to include. Each question was a statement followed by a five-point Likert scale ranging from 'strongly disagree' through 'neither agree or disagree' to 'strongly agree'. The questionnaire is printed in Figure 11.4.

The questionnaire was designed to predict how anxious a given individual would be about learning how to use SPSS. What's more, I wanted to know whether anxiety about SPSS could be broken down into specific forms of anxiety. So, in other words, are there other traits that might contribute to anxiety about SPSS? With a little help from a few lecturer friends I collected 2571 completed questionnaires (at this point it should become apparent that this example is fictitious!). The data are stored in the file **SAQ.sav**. Load the data file into the SPSS data editor and have a look at the variables and their properties. The first thing to note is that each question (variable) is represented by a different column. We know that in SPSS cases (or people's data) are stored in rows and variables are stored in columns and so this layout is consistent with past chapters. The second thing to notice is that there are 23 variables labelled **q1** to **q23** and that each has a label indicating the question. By labelling my variables I can be very clear about what each variable represents (this is the value of giving your variables full titles rather than just using restrictive column headings).

		SD	D	N	A	SA
SD = Strongly Disagree, D = Disagree, N = Neither, A = Agree, SA = Strongly Agree						
1	Statistics make me cry	⌇	⌇	⌇	⌇	⌇
2	My friends will think I'm stupid for not being able to cope with SPSS	⌇	⌇	⌇	⌇	⌇
3	Standard deviations excite me	⌇	⌇	⌇	⌇	⌇
4	I dream that Pearson is attacking me with correlation coefficients	⌇	⌇	⌇	⌇	⌇
5	I don't understand statistics	⌇	⌇	⌇	⌇	⌇
6	I have little experience of computers	⌇	⌇	⌇	⌇	⌇
7	All computers hate me	⌇	⌇	⌇	⌇	⌇
8	I have never been good at mathematics	⌇	⌇	⌇	⌇	⌇
9	My friends are better at statistics than me	⌇	⌇	⌇	⌇	⌇
10	Computers are useful only for playing games	⌇	⌇	⌇	⌇	⌇
11	I did badly at mathematics at school	⌇	⌇	⌇	⌇	⌇
12	People try to tell you that SPSS makes statistics easier to understand but it doesn't	⌇	⌇	⌇	⌇	⌇
13	I worry that I will cause irreparable damage because of my incompetence with computers	⌇	⌇	⌇	⌇	⌇
14	Computers have minds of their own and deliberately go wrong whenever I use them	⌇	⌇	⌇	⌇	⌇
15	Computers are out to get me	⌇	⌇	⌇	⌇	⌇
16	I weep openly at the mention of central tendency	⌇	⌇	⌇	⌇	⌇
17	I slip into a coma whenever I see an equation	⌇	⌇	⌇	⌇	⌇
18	SPSS always crashes when I try to use it	⌇	⌇	⌇	⌇	⌇
19	Everybody looks at me when I use SPSS	⌇	⌇	⌇	⌇	⌇
20	I can't sleep for thoughts of eigenvectors	⌇	⌇	⌇	⌇	⌇
21	I wake up under my duvet thinking that I am trapped under a normal distribution	⌇	⌇	⌇	⌇	⌇
22	My friends are better at SPSS than I am	⌇	⌇	⌇	⌇	⌇
23	If I am good at statistics people will think I am a nerd	⌇	⌇	⌇	⌇	⌇

Figure 11.4: The SPSS Anxiety Questionnaire (SAQ)

11.3.1.   Initial Considerations

11.3.1.1. Sample Size

Correlation coefficients fluctuate from sample to sample, much more so in small samples than in large. Therefore, the reliability of factor analysis is also dependent on sample size. Much has been written about the necessary sample size for factor analysis resulting in many 'rules-of-thumb'. The common rule is to suggest that a researcher has at least 10-15 subjects per variable. Although I've heard this rule bandied about on numerous occasions its empirical basis is unclear (although Nunnally, 1978 did recommend having 10 times as many subjects as variables). Kass and Tinsley (1979) recommended having between 5 and 10 subjects per variable up to a total of 300 (beyond which test parameters tend to be stable regardless of the subject to variable ratio). Indeed, Tabachnick and Fidell (1996) agree that 'it is comforting to have at least 300 cases for factor analysis' (p. 640) and Comrey and Lee (1992) class 300 as a good sample size, 100 as poor and 1000 as excellent.

Fortunately, recent years have seen empirical research done in the form of experiments using simulated data (Monte Carlo studies). Arrindell and van der Ende (1985) used real-life data to investigate the effect of different subject to variable ratios. They concluded that changes in this ratio made little difference to the stability of factor solutions. More recently, Guadagnoli and Velicer (1988) found that the most important factors in determining reliable factor solutions was the absolute sample size and the absolute magnitude of factor loadings. In short, they argue that if a factor has four or more loadings greater than 0.6 then it is reliable regardless of sample size. Furthermore, factors with 10 or more loadings greater than 0.40 are reliable if the sample size is greater than 150. Finally, factors with a few low loadings should not be interpreted unless the sample size is 300 or more. More recently MacCallum et al. (1999) have shown that the minimum sample size or sample to variable ratio depends on other aspects of the design of the study. In short, their study indicated that as communalities become lower the importance of sample size increases. With all communalities above 0.6, relatively small samples (less than 100) may be perfectly adequate. With communalities in the 0.5 range, samples between 100 and 200 can be good enough provided there are relatively few factors each with only a small number of indicator variables. In the worst scenario of low communalities (well below 0.5) and a larger number of underlying factors they recommend samples above 500.

What's clear from this work is that a sample of 300 or more will probably provide a stable factor solution but that a wise researcher will measure enough variables to adequately measure all of the factors that theoretically they would expect to find.

11.3.1.2. Data Screening

At various places in this book I have used the expression 'if you put garbage in, you get garbage out'. This saying applies particularly to factor analysis because SPSS will nearly always find a factor solution to a set of variables. However, the solution is unlikely to have any real meaning if the variables analysed are not sensible. The first thing to do when conducting a factor analysis is to look at the inter-correlation between variables. If our test questions measure the same underlying dimension (or dimensions) then we would expect them to correlate with each other (because they are measuring the same thing). Even if questions measure different aspects of the same things (for example we could measure overall anxiety in terms of sub-components such as worry, intrusive thoughts and physiological arousal), there should still be high inter-correlations between the variables relating to these sub-traits. If we find any variables that do not correlate with any other variables (or very few) then you should consider excluding these variables before the factor analysis is run. One extreme of this problem is when the R-matrix resembles an identity matrix (see section 10.2.2). In this case, variables correlate only with themselves and all other correlation coefficients are close to zero. SPSS tests this using Bartlett's test of sphericity (see next section). The correlations between variables can be checked using the *correlate* procedure (see Chapter 3) to create a correlation matrix of all variables. This matrix can also be created as part of the main factor analysis.

The opposite problem is when variables correlate too highly. Although mild multicollinearity is not a problem for factor analysis it is important to avoid extreme multicollinearity (i.e. variables that are very highly correlated) and *singularity* (variables that are perfectly correlated). As with regression, singularity causes problems in factor analysis because it becomes impossible to determine the unique contribution to a factor of the variables that are highly correlated (as was the case for multiple regression). Therefore, at this early stage we look to eliminate any variables that don't correlate with any other variables or that correlate very highly with other variables ($R < 0.9$). Multicollinearity can be detected by looking at the determinant of the R-matrix (see next section).

As well as looking for interrelations, you should ensure that variables have roughly normal distributions and are measured at an interval level (which Likert scales are, perhaps wrongly, assumed to be!). The assumption of normality is important only if you wish to generalize the results of your analysis beyond the sample collected.

11.4. Running the Analysis

Access the main dialog box (Figure 11.5) by using the **Analyze⇒Data Reduction⇒Factor ...** menu path. Simply select the variables you want to include in the analysis (remember to exclude any variables that were identified as problematic during the data screening) and transfer them to the box labelled *Variables* by clicking on ▸.

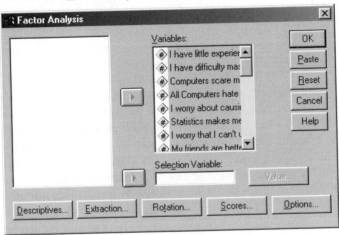

Figure 11.5: Main dialog box for factor analysis

There are several options available, the first of which can be accessed by clicking on Descriptives... to access the dialog box in Figure 11.6. The *Univariate decriptives* option provides means and standard deviations for each variable. Most of the other options relate the correlation matrix of variables (the *R*-matrix described earlier). The *Coefficients* option produces the *R*-matrix, and the *Significance levels* option will produce a matrix indicating the significance value of each correlation in the *R*-matrix. You can also ask for the *Determinant* of this matrix and this option is vital for testing for multicollinearity or singularity. The determinant of the *R*-matrix should be greater than 0.00001; if it is less than this value then look through the correlation matrix for variables that correlate very highly ($R > 0.8$) and consider eliminating one of the variables (or more depending on the extent of the problem) before proceeding. As mentioned in section 5.4.2.1, the choice of which of the two variables to eliminate will be fairly arbitrary and finding multicollinearity in the data should raise questions about the choice of items within your questionnaire.

KMO and Bartlett's test of sphericity produces the Kaiser-Meyer-Olkin measure of sampling adequacy and Bartlett's test (see Chapter 10). With a sample of 2571 we shouldn't have cause to worry about the sample size (see section 11.3.1.1). The value of KMO should be greater than 0.5 if the sample is adequate. As you should know by now, Bartlett's test examines whether the population correlation matrix resembles an identity matrix (i.e. it tests whether the off-diagonal components are zero). If the population correlation matrix resembles an identity matrix then it means that every variable correlates very badly with all other variables (i.e. all correlation coefficients are close to zero). If it *were* an identity matrix then it would mean that all variables are perfectly independent from one another (all correlation coefficients are zero). Given that we are looking for clusters of variables that measure similar things, it should be obvious why this scenario is problematic: if no variables correlate then there are no clusters to find.

The *Reproduced* option produces a correlation matrix based on the model (rather than the real data). Differences between the matrix based on the model and the matrix based on the observed data indicate the residuals of the model (i.e. differences). SPSS produces these residuals in the lower table of the reproduced matrix and we want relatively few of these values to be greater than 0.05. Luckily, to save us scanning this matrix, SPSS produces a summary of how many residuals lie above 0.05. The *Reproduced* option should be selected to obtain this summary. The *Anti-image* option produces an anti-image matrix of covariances and correlations. These matrices contain measures of sampling adequacy for each variable along the diagonal and the negatives of the partial correlation/covariances on the off-diagonals. The diagonal elements, like the KMO measure, should all be greater than 0.5 if the sample is adequate for a given pair of variables. If any pair of variables has a value less than this, consider dropping one of them from the analysis. The off-diagonal elements should all be very small (close to zero) in a good model. When you have finished with this dialog box click on Continue to return to the main dialog box.

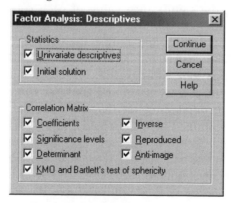

Figure 11.6: Descriptives in factor analysis

11.4.1. *Factor Extraction on SPSS*

To access the *extraction* dialog box (Figure 11.7), click on ▢Extraction... in the main dialog box. There are a number of ways of conducting a factor analysis and when and where you use the various methods depend on numerous things. For our purposes we will use *principal component* analysis which strictly speaking isn't factor analysis; however, the two procedures usually yield identical results (see section 11.2.2). The method chosen will depend on what you hope to do with the analysis. Tinsley and Tinsley (1987) give an excellent account of the different methods available. There are two things to consider: whether you want to generalize the findings from your sample to a population and whether you are exploring your data or testing a specific hypothesis. This chapter describes techniques for exploring data using factor analysis. Hypothesis testing requires considerable complexity and can be done with computer programs such as LISREL (which some of you might find hidden away in your SPSS options). Those interested in hypothesis testing techniques (known as confirmatory factor analysis) are advised to read Pedhazur and Schmelkin (1991, Chapter 23) for an introduction. Assuming we want to explore our data we then need to consider whether we want to apply our findings to the sample collected (descriptive method) or to generalize our findings to a population (inferential methods). When factor analysis was originally developed it was assumed that it would be used to explore data to generate future hypotheses. As such, it was assumed that the technique would be applied to the entire population of interest. Therefore, certain techniques assume that the sample used is the population, and so results cannot be extrapolated beyond that particular sample. Principal component analysis is an example of one of these techniques, as is principal factors analysis (*principal axis factoring*) and image covariance analysis (*image factoring*). Principal component analysis and principal factors analysis are the preferred methods and usually result in similar solutions (see section 11.2.2). When these methods are used conclusions are restricted to the sample collected and generalization of the results can be achieved only if analysis using different samples reveals the same factor structure.

Another approach has been to assume that subjects are randomly selected and that the variables measured constitute the population of interest. By assuming this, it is possible to develop techniques from which the results can be generalized from the sample subjects to a larger population. However, a constraint is that any findings hold true only for the set of variables measured. Techniques in this category include the maximum likelihood method (see Harman, 1976) and Kaiser's alpha factoring. The choice of method depends largely on what generalizations, if any, you want to make from your data.

In the *Analyze* box there are two options: to analyze the *Correlation matrix* or to analyze the *Covariance matrix*. You should be happy with the idea that these two matrices are actually different versions of the same thing: the correlation matrix is the standardized version of the covariance matrix. Analysing the correlation matrix is a useful default method because it takes the standardized form of the matrix; therefore, if variables have been measured using different scales this will not affect the analysis. In this example, all variables have been measured using the same measurement scale (a five-point Likert scale), but often you will want to analyze variables that use different measurement scales. Analysing the correlation matrix ensures that differences in measurement scales are accounted for. In addition, even variables measured using the same scale can have very different variances and this too creates problems for principal component analysis. Using the correlation matrix eliminates this problem also. There are statistical reasons for preferring to analyze the covariance matrix[4] and generally the results will differ from analysis on the correlation matrix. However, the covariance matrix should be analysed only when your variables are commensurable.

The *Display* box has two options within it: to display the *Unrotated factor solution* and a *Scree plot*. The scree plot was described earlier and is a useful way of establishing how many factors should be retained in an analysis. The unrotated factor solution is useful in assessing the improvement of interpretation due to rotation. If the rotated solution is little better than the unrotated solution then it is possible that an inappropriate (or less optimal) rotation method has been used.

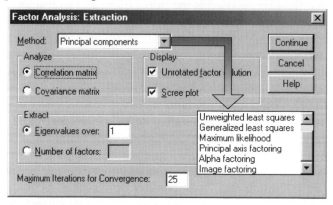

Figure 11.7: Dialog box for factor extraction

---

[4] The reason being that correlation coefficients are insensitive to variations in the dispersion of data whereas covariance is and so produces better-defined factor structures (see Tinsley and Tinsley, 1987).

The *Extract* box provides options pertaining to the retention of factors. You have the choice of either selecting factors with eigenvalues greater than a user-specified value or retaining a fixed number of factors. For the *Eigenvalues over* option the default is Kaiser's recommendation of eigenvalues over 1, but you could change this to Jolliffe's recommendation of 0.7 or any other value you want. It is probably best to run a primary analysis with the *Eigenvalues over* 1 option selected, select a scree plot, and compare the results. If looking at the scree plot and the eigenvalues over 1 lead you to retain the same number of factors then continue with the analysis and be happy. If the two criteria give different results then examine the communalities and decide for yourself which of the two criteria to believe. If you decide to use the scree plot then you may want to redo the analysis specifying the number of factors to extract. The number of factors to be extracted can be specified by selecting *Number of factors* and then typing the appropriate number in the space provided (e.g. 4).

11.4.2.   Rotation

We have already seen that the interpretability of factors can be improved through rotation. Rotation maximizes the loading of each variable on one of the extracted factors whilst minimizing the loading on all other factors. This process makes it much clearer which variables relate to which factors. Rotation works through changing the absolute values of the variables whilst keeping their differential values constant. Click on [Rotation...] to access the dialog box in Figure 11.8.

Varimax, quartimax and equamax are all orthogonal rotations whilst direct oblimin and promax are oblique rotations. Quartimax rotation attempts to maximize the spread of factor loadings for a variable across all factors. Therefore, interpreting variables becomes easier. However, this often results in lots of variables loading highly onto a single factor. Varimax is the opposite in that it attempts to maximize the dispersion of loadings within factors. Therefore, it tries to load a smaller number of variables highly onto each factor resulting in more interpretable clusters of factors. Equamax is a hybrid of the other two approaches and is reported to behave fairly erratically (see Tabachnick and Fidell, 1996). For a first analysis, you should probably select *Varimax* because it is a good general approach that simplifies the interpretation of factors.

The case with oblique rotations is more complex because correlation between factors is permitted. In the case of direct oblimin, the degree to which factors are allowed to correlate is determined by the value of delta. The default value is zero and this ensures that high correlation between factors is not allowed (this is known as direct quartimin rotation). If you choose to set delta greater than zero (up to 0.8), then you can expect highly correlated factors; if you set delta less than zero (down to –0.8) you can expect less correlated factors. The default setting of zero is sensible for most analyses and I don't recommend changing it unless you know what you are doing (see Pedhazur and Schmelkin, 1991, p. 620). Promax is a faster procedure designed for very large data sets.

The exact choice of rotation will depend largely on whether or not you think that the underlying factors should be related. If you expect the factors to be independent then you should choose one of the orthogonal rotations (I recommend varimax). If, however, there are theoretical grounds for supposing that your factors might correlate then direct oblimin should be selected.

The dialog box also has options for displaying the *Rotated solution* and a *Loading plot*. The rotated solution is displayed by default and is essential for interpreting the final rotated analysis. The loading plot will provide a graphical display of each variable plotted against the extracted factors up to a maximum of three factors (unfortunately SPSS cannot produce four- or five-dimensional graphs!). This plot is basically similar to Figure 11.1 and it uses the factor loading of each variable for each factor. With two factors these plots are fairly interpretable, and you should hope to see one group of variables clustered close to the X-axis and a different group of variables clustered around the Y-axis. If all variables are clustered between the axes, then the rotation has been relatively unsuccessful in maximizing the loading of a variable onto a single factor. With three factors these plots can become quite messy and certainly put considerable strain on the visual system! However, they can still be a useful way to determine the underlying structures within the data.

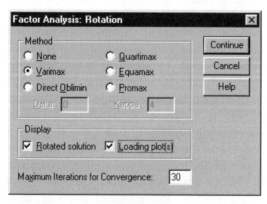

Figure 11.8: Factor analysis: *rotation* dialog box

A final option is to set the *Maximum Iterations for Convergence*, which specifies the number of times that the computer will search for an optimal solution. In most circumstances the default of 25 is more than adequate for SPSS to find a solution for a given data set. However, if you have a large data set (like we have here) then the computer might have difficulty finding a solution (especially for oblique rotation). To allow for the large data set we are using change the value to 30.

11.4.3.   Scores

The *factor scores* dialog box can be accessed by clicking [Scores] in the main dialog box. This option allows you to save factor scores (see section 11.1.3) for each subject in the data editor. SPSS creates a new column for each factor extracted and then places the factor score for each subject within that column. These scores can then be used for further analysis, or simply to identify groups of subjects who score highly on particular factors. There are three methods of obtaining these scores, all of which were described in sections 11.1.4 and 11.1.4.1. If you want to ensure that factor scores are uncorrelated then select the *Anderson-Rubin* method; if correlations between factor scores are acceptable then choose the *Regression* method.

As a final option, you can ask SPSS to produce the factor score coefficient matrix. This matrix was the matrix *B* described in section 11.1.4. This matrix can be useful if, for whatever reason, you wish to construct factor equations such as those in equation (11.5), because it provides you with the values of β for each of the variables.

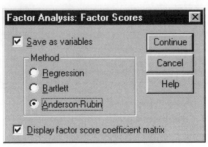

Figure 11.9: Factor analysis: *factor scores* dialog box

11.4.4.   Options

This set of options can be obtained by clicking on [Options] in the main dialog box. Missing data are a problem for factor analysis just like most other procedures and SPSS provides a choice of excluding cases or estimating a value for a case. Tabachnick and Fidell (1996) have an excellent chapter on data screening (Chapter 4). Based on their advice, you should consider the distribution of missing data. If the missing data are non-normally distributed or the sample size after exclusion is too small then estimation is necessary. SPSS uses the mean as an estimate (*Replace with mean*). These procedures lower the standard deviation of variables and so can lead to significant results that would otherwise be non-significant. Therefore, if missing data are random, you might consider excluding cases. SPSS allows you to either *Exclude cases listwise* in which case any subject with missing data for any variable is excluded, or to *Exclude cases pairwise* in which case a subject's data are excluded only from calculations for which a datum is missing.

The final two options relate to how coefficients are displayed. By default SPSS will list variables in the order in which they are entered into the data editor. Usually, this format is most convenient. However, when interpreting factors it is sometimes useful to list variables by size. By selecting *Sorted by size*, SPSS will order the variables by their factor loadings. In fact, it does this sorting fairly intelligently so that all of the variables that load highly onto the same factor are displayed together. The second option is to *Suppress absolute values less than* a specified value (by default 0.1). This option ensures that factor loadings within ±0.1 are not displayed in the output. Again, this option is useful for assisting in interpretation. The default value is not that useful and I recommend changing it either to 0.4 (for interpretation purposes) or to a value reflecting the expected value of a significant factor loading given the sample size (see section 11.2.5.2). For this example set the value at 0.4.

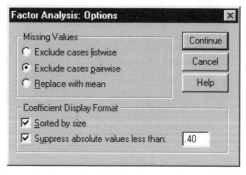

Figure 11.10: Factor analysis: *options* dialog box

11.5.   Interpreting Output from SPSS

Select the same options as I have in the screen diagrams and run a factor analysis with orthogonal rotation. Having done this, select the *Direct Oblimin* option in Figure 11.8 and repeat the analysis. You should obtain two outputs identical in all respects except that one used an orthogonal rotation and the other an oblique.

For the purposes of saving space in this section I set the default SPSS options such that each variable is referred to only by its label on the data editor (e.g. Q12). On the output *you* obtain, you should find that the SPSS uses the value label (the question itself) in all of the output. When using the output in this chapter just remember that Q1 represents question 1, Q2 represents question 2 and Q17 represents question 17. By referring back to Figure 11.4 and matching the question number to the variable name you can identify each question.

11.5.1.   Preliminary Analysis

The first body of output concerns data screening, assumption testing and sampling adequacy. You'll find several large tables (or matrices) that tell us interesting things about our data. If you selected the *Univariate descriptives* option in Figure 11.6 then the first table will contain descriptive statistics for each variable (the mean, standard deviation and number of cases). This table is not included here, but you should have enough experience to be able to interpret this table. The table also includes the number of missing cases; this summary is a useful way to determine the extent of missing data.

SPSS Output 11.1 shows the *R*-matrix (or correlation matrix)[5] produced using the *Coefficients* and *Significance levels* options in Figure 11.6. The top half of this table contains the Pearson correlation coefficient between all pairs of questions whereas the bottom half contains the one-tailed significance of these coefficients. You should be comfortable with the idea that to do a factor analysis we need to have variables that correlate fairly well, but not perfectly. Also, any variables that correlate with no others should be eliminated. Therefore, we can use this correlation matrix to check the pattern of relationships. The easiest way to do this is by scanning the significance values and looking for any variable for which the majority of values are greater than 0.05. Then scan the correlation coefficients themselves and look for any greater than 0.9. If any are found then you should be aware that a problem could arise because of singularity in the data: check the determinant of the correlation matrix and, if necessary, eliminate one of the two variables causing the problem. The determinant is listed at the bottom of the matrix (blink and you'll miss it). For these data its value is 5.271E–04 (which is 0.0005271) which is greater than the necessary value of 0.00001 (see section 11.4). Therefore, we can be confident that multicollinearity is

---

[5] To save space I have edited out several columns of data from the large tables: only data for the first and last five questions in the questionnaire are included.

not a problem for these data. In summary, all questions in the SAQ correlate fairly well with all others (this is partly because of the large sample) and none of the correlation coefficients are particularly large; therefore, there is no need to consider eliminating any questions at this stage.

Correlation Matrix[a]

		Q01	Q02	Q03	Q04	Q05	Q19	Q20	Q21	Q22	Q23
Correlation	Q01	1.000	-.099	-.337	.436	.402	-.189	.214	.329	-.104	-.004
	Q02	-.099	1.000	.318	-.112	-.119	.203	-.202	-.205	.231	.100
	Q03	-.337	.318	1.000	-.380	-.310	.342	-.325	-.417	.204	.150
	Q04	.436	-.112	-.380	1.000	.401	-.186	.243	.410	-.098	-.034
	Q05	.402	-.119	-.310	.401	1.000	-.165	.200	.335	-.133	-.042
	Q06	.217	-.074	-.227	.278	.257	-.167	.101	.272	-.165	-.069
	Q07	.305	-.159	-.382	.409	.339	-.269	.221	.483	-.168	-.070
	Q08	.331	-.050	-.259	.349	.269	-.159	.175	.296	-.079	-.050
	Q09	-.092	.315	.300	-.125	-.096	.249	-.159	-.136	.257	.171
	Q10	.214	-.084	-.193	.216	.258	-.127	.084	.193	-.131	-.062
	Q11	.357	-.144	-.351	.369	.298	-.200	.255	.346	-.162	-.086
	Q12	.345	-.195	-.410	.442	.347	-.267	.298	.441	-.167	-.046
	Q13	.355	-.143	-.318	.344	.302	-.227	.204	.374	-.195	-.053
	Q14	.338	-.165	-.371	.351	.315	-.254	.226	.399	-.170	-.048
	Q15	.246	-.165	-.312	.334	.261	-.210	.206	.300	-.168	-.062
	Q16	.499	-.168	-.419	.416	.395	-.267	.265	.421	-.156	-.082
	Q17	.371	-.087	-.327	.383	.310	-.163	.205	.363	-.126	-.092
	Q18	.347	-.164	-.375	.382	.322	-.257	.235	.430	-.160	-.080
	Q19	-.189	.203	.342	-.186	-.165	1.000	-.249	-.275	.234	.122
	Q20	.214	-.202	-.325	.243	.200	-.249	1.000	.468	-.100	-.035
	Q21	.329	-.205	-.417	.410	.335	-.275	.468	1.000	-.129	-.068
	Q22	-.104	.231	.204	-.098	-.133	.234	-.100	-.129	1.000	.230
	Q23	-.004	.100	.150	-.034	-.042	.122	-.035	-.068	.230	1.000
Sig. (1-tailed)	Q01		.000	.000	.000	.000	.000	.000	.000	.000	.410
	Q02	.000		.000	.000	.000	.000	.000	.000	.000	.000
	Q03	.000	.000		.000	.000	.000	.000	.000	.000	.000
	Q04	.000	.000	.000		.000	.000	.000	.000	.000	.043
	Q05	.000	.000	.000	.000		.000	.000	.000	.000	.017
	Q06	.000	.000	.000	.000	.000	.000	.000	.000	.000	.000
	Q07	.000	.000	.000	.000	.000	.000	.000	.000	.000	.000
	Q08	.000	.006	.000	.000	.000	.000	.000	.000	.000	.005
	Q09	.000	.000	.000	.000	.000	.000	.000	.000	.000	.000
	Q10	.000	.000	.000	.000	.000	.000	.000	.000	.000	.001
	Q11	.000	.000	.000	.000	.000	.000	.000	.000	.000	.000
	Q12	.000	.000	.000	.000	.000	.000	.000	.000	.000	.009
	Q13	.000	.000	.000	.000	.000	.000	.000	.000	.000	.004
	Q14	.000	.000	.000	.000	.000	.000	.000	.000	.000	.007
	Q15	.000	.000	.000	.000	.000	.000	.000	.000	.000	.001
	Q16	.000	.000	.000	.000	.000	.000	.000	.000	.000	.000
	Q17	.000	.000	.000	.000	.000	.000	.000	.000	.000	.000
	Q18	.000	.000	.000	.000	.000	.000	.000	.000	.000	.000
	Q19	.000	.000	.000	.000	.000		.000	.000	.000	.000
	Q20	.000	.000	.000	.000	.000	.000		.000	.000	.039
	Q21	.000	.000	.000	.000	.000	.000	.000		.000	.000
	Q22	.000	.000	.000	.000	.000	.000	.000	.000		.000
	Q23	.410	.000	.000	.043	.017	.000	.039	.000	.000	

a. Determinant = 5.271E-04

SPSS Output 11.1

SPSS Output 11.2 shows the inverse of the correlation matrix (R^{-1}), which is used in various calculations (including factor scores—see section 11.1.4). This matrix is produced using the *Inverse* option in Figure 11.6 but in all honesty is useful only if you want some insight into the calculations that go on in a factor analysis. Most of us have more interesting things to do than gain insight into the workings of factor analysis and the practical use of this matrix is minimal—so ignore it!

SPSS Output 11.3 shows several very important parts of the output: the Kaiser-Meyer-Olkin measure of sampling adequacy, Bartlett's test of sphericity and the anti-image correlation and covariance matrices (note that these matrices have been edited down to contain only the first and last five variables). The anti-image correlation and covariance matrices provide similar information (remember the relationship between covariance and correlation) and so only the anti-image correlation matrix need be studied in detail as it is the most informative. These tables are obtained using the *KMO and Bartlett's test of sphericity* and the *Anti-image* options in Figure 11.6.

Inverse of Correlation Matrix

	Q01	Q02	Q03	Q04	Q05	Q19	Q20	Q21	Q22	Q23
Q01	1.595	-.028	.087	-.268	-.233	.017	-.024	.011	.002	-.078
Q02	-.028	1.232	-.224	-.057	.013	-.037	.076	.062	-.148	-.003
Q03	.087	-.224	1.661	.138	.057	-.175	.118	.122	-.009	-.103
Q04	-.268	-.057	.138	1.626	-.203	-.049	-.006	-.149	-.045	-.023
Q05	-.233	.013	.057	-.203	1.410	-.024	-.016	-.074	.045	-.006
Q06	.034	-.078	-.072	-.011	-.055	-.023	.080	.069	.058	.025
Q07	.039	.025	.127	-.152	-.072	.105	.077	-.386	.019	-.012
Q08	-.087	-.051	-.013	-.134	-.045	.074	.034	-.039	-.035	.003
Q09	-.023	-.242	-.208	.043	-.027	-.141	.050	-.047	-.156	-.110
Q10	-.017	-.015	-.023	.009	-.124	-.012	.056	.026	.023	.017
Q11	-.075	.061	.121	-.041	.000	-.010	-.140	-.009	.055	.015
Q12	-.011	.046	.147	-.259	-.091	.060	-.100	-.141	.026	-.038
Q13	-.145	-.011	-.055	.040	.007	.014	.028	-.061	.077	-.042
Q14	-.064	.033	.115	-.007	-.040	.063	.002	-.110	.041	-.034
Q15	.138	.050	.013	-.098	.021	.013	-.054	.058	.034	-.030
Q16	-.454	-.017	.142	-.063	-.155	.071	-.008	-.158	-.005	.033
Q17	-.084	-.045	.063	-.064	-.030	-.074	.025	-.077	.015	.080
Q18	-.041	.028	.070	-.044	.004	.047	-.004	-.136	-.037	.033
Q19	.017	-.037	-.175	-.049	-.024	1.264	.120	.048	-.141	-.045
Q20	-.024	.076	.118	-.006	-.016	.120	1.370	-.511	-.014	-.034
Q21	.011	.062	.122	-.149	-.074	.048	-.511	1.830	-.036	.018
Q22	.002	-.148	-.009	-.045	.045	-.141	-.014	-.036	1.200	-.202
Q23	-.078	-.003	-.103	-.023	-.006	-.045	-.034	.018	-.202	1.094

SPSS Output 11.2

The KMO statistic (see Kaiser, 1970) can be calculated for individual and multiple variables and represents the ratio of the squared correlation between variables to the squared partial correlation between variables. In this instance, the statistic is calculated for all 23 variables simultaneously. The KMO statistic varies between 0 and 1. A value of 0 indicates that the sum of partial correlations is large relative to the sum of correlations, indicating diffusion in the pattern of correlations (hence, factor analysis is likely to be inappropriate). A value close to 1 indicates that patterns of correlations are relatively compact and so factor analysis should yield distinct and reliable factors. Kaiser (1974) recommends accepting values greater than 0.5 as acceptable (values below this should lead you to either collect more data or rethink which variables to include). Furthermore, values between 0.5 and 0.7 are mediocre, values between 0.7 and 0.8 are good, values between 0.8 and 0.9 are great and values above 0.9 are superb (see Hutcheson and Sofroniou, 1999, pp.224-225 for more detail). For these data the value is 0.93 which falls into the range of being superb: so, we should be confident that factor analysis is appropriate for these data.

KMO and Bartlett's Test

Kaiser-Meyer-Olkin Measure of Sampling Adequacy.		.930
Bartlett's Test of Sphericity	Approx. Chi-Square	19334.492
	df	253
	Sig.	.000

Anti-image Matrices

Anti-image Correlation

	Q01	Q02	Q03	Q04	Q05	Q19	Q20	Q21	Q22	Q23
Q01	**.930**	-2.00E-02	5.320E-02	-.167	-.156	1.231E-02	-1.61E-02	6.436E-03	1.459E-03	-5.92E-02
Q02	-2.00E-02	**.875**	-.157	-4.05E-02	1.019E-02	-2.93E-02	5.877E-02	4.139E-02	-.121	-2.39E-03
Q03	5.320E-02	-.157	**.951**	8.381E-02	3.725E-02	-.121	7.790E-02	6.983E-02	-6.57E-03	-7.63E-02
Q04	-.167	-4.05E-02	8.381E-02	**.955**	-.134	-3.42E-02	-4.07E-02	-8.64E-02	-3.25E-02	-1.71E-02
Q05	-.156	1.019E-02	3.725E-02	-.134	**.960**	-1.77E-02	-1.14E-02	-4.59E-02	3.455E-02	-4.75E-03
Q06	2.016E-02	-5.33E-02	-4.23E-02	-6.77E-03	-3.52E-02	-1.53E-02	5.144E-02	3.867E-02	3.984E-02	1.846E-02
Q07	2.264E-02	1.648E-02	7.159E-02	-8.66E-02	-4.43E-02	6.802E-02	4.796E-02	-.208	1.278E-02	-8.07E-03
Q08	-4.91E-02	-3.28E-02	-7.21E-03	-7.49E-02	-2.72E-02	4.696E-02	2.094E-02	-2.05E-02	-2.28E-02	2.202E-02
Q09	-1.64E-02	-.193	-.142	2.960E-02	-1.98E-02	-.111	3.803E-02	-3.06E-02	-.126	-9.25E-02
Q10	-1.22E-02	-1.21E-02	-1.62E-02	6.031E-03	-9.32E-02	-9.16E-03	4.272E-02	1.699E-02	1.867E-02	1.462E-02
Q11	-4.07E-02	3.757E-02	6.429E-02	-2.22E-02	-3.27E-05	-5.81E-03	-8.18E-02	-4.58E-03	3.425E-02	9.600E-03
Q12	-6.62E-03	3.129E-02	8.667E-02	-.154	-5.83E-02	4.030E-02	-6.47E-02	-7.93E-02	1.802E-02	-2.79E-02
Q13	-8.51E-02	-7.60E-03	-3.16E-02	2.303E-02	4.238E-03	8.994E-03	1.785E-02	-3.33E-02	5.233E-02	-2.99E-02
Q14	-3.98E-02	2.313E-02	6.946E-02	-4.26E-03	-2.63E-02	4.399E-02	1.124E-02	-6.32E-02	2.896E-02	-2.56E-02
Q15	8.860E-02	3.680E-02	8.159E-02	-6.21E-02	1.413E-02	9.384E-03	-3.74E-02	3.483E-02	2.485E-02	-2.28E-02
Q16	-.264	-1.14E-02	8.057E-02	-3.62E-02	-9.57E-02	4.659E-02	-5.30E-02	-8.54E-02	-3.26E-03	2.298E-02
Q17	-4.74E-02	-2.87E-02	3.467E-02	-3.55E-02	-1.80E-02	-4.68E-02	1.547E-02	-4.06E-02	1.004E-02	5.457E-02
Q18	-2.31E-02	1.825E-02	3.880E-02	-2.45E-02	2.489E-03	2.980E-02	-2.54E-03	-7.17E-02	-2.40E-02	2.257E-02
Q19	1.231E-02	-2.93E-02	-.121	-3.42E-02	-1.77E-02	**.941**	9.081E-02	3.145E-02	-.115	-3.84E-02
Q20	-1.61E-02	5.877E-02	7.790E-02	-4.07E-02	-1.14E-02	9.081E-02	**.889**	-.323	-1.12E-02	-2.81E-02
Q21	6.436E-03	4.139E-02	6.983E-02	-8.64E-02	-4.59E-02	3.145E-02	-.323	**.929**	-2.41E-02	1.275E-02
Q22	1.459E-03	-.121	-6.57E-03	-3.25E-02	3.455E-02	-.115	-1.12E-02	-2.41E-02	**.878**	-.176
Q23	-5.92E-02	-2.39E-03	-7.63E-02	-1.71E-02	-4.75E-03	-3.84E-02	-2.81E-02	1.275E-02	-.176	**.766**

SPSS Output 11.3

I mentioned that KMO can be calculated for multiple and individual variables. The KMO values for individual variables are produced on the diagonal of the anti-image correlation matrix (I have highlighted the values in bold). These values make the anti-image correlation matrix an extremely important part of the output (although the anti-image covariance matrix can be ignored). As well as checking the overall KMO statistic, it is important to examine the diagonal elements of the anti-image correlation matrix: the value should be above 0.5 for all variables. For these data all values are well above .5 which is good news! If you find any variables with values below 0.5 then you should consider excluding them from the analysis (or run the analysis with and without that variable and note the difference). Removal of a variable affects the KMO statistics, so if you do remove a variable be sure to re-examine the new anti-image correlation matrix. As for the rest of the anti-image correlation matrix, the off-diagonal elements represent the partial correlations between variables. For a good factor analysis we want these correlations to be very small (the smaller the better). So, as a final check you can just look through to see that the off-diagonal elements are small (they should be for these data).

Bartlett's measure tests the null hypothesis that the original correlation matrix is an identity matrix. For factor analysis to work we need some relationships between variables and if the R-matrix were an identity matrix then all correlation coefficients would be zero. Therefore, we want this test to be *significant* (i.e. have a significance value less than 0.05). A significant test tells us that the R-matrix is not an identity matrix; therefore, there are some relationships between the variables we hope to include in the analysis. For these data, Bartlett's test is highly significant ($p < 0.001$), and therefore factor analysis is appropriate.

11.5.2. Factor Extraction

The first part of the factor extraction process is to determine the linear components within the data set (the eigenvectors) by calculating the eigenvalues of the R-matrix (see section 11.2.3). We know that there are as many components (eigenvectors) in the R-matrix as there are variables, but most will be unimportant. To determine the importance of a particular vector we look at the magnitude of the associated eigenvalue. We can then apply criteria to determine which factors to retain and which to discard. By default SPSS uses Kaiser's criterion of retaining factors with eigenvalues greater than 1 (see Figure 11.7).

SPSS Output 11.4 lists the eigenvalues associated with each linear component (factor) before extraction, after extraction and after rotation. Before extraction, SPSS has identified 23 linear components within the data set (we know that there should be as many eigenvectors as there are variables and so there will be as many factors as variables—see section 11.2.3). The eigenvalues associated with each factor represent the variance explained by that particular linear component and SPSS also displays the eigenvalue in terms of the percentage of variance explained (so, factor 1 explains 31.696% of total variance). It should be clear that the first few factors explain relatively large amounts of variance (especially factor 1) whereas subsequent factors explain only small amounts of variance. SPSS then extracts all factors with eigenvalues greater than 1, which leaves us with four factors. The eigenvalues associated with these factors are again displayed (and the percentage of variance explained) in the columns labelled *Extraction Sums of Squared Loadings*. The values in this part of the table are the same as the values before extraction, except that the values for the discarded factors are ignored (hence, the table is blank after the fourth factor). In the final part of the table (labelled *Rotation Sums of Squared Loadings*), the eigenvalues of the factors after rotation are displayed. Rotation has the effect of optimizing the factor structure and one consequence for these data is that the relative importance of the four factors is equalized. Before rotation, factor 1 accounted for considerably more variance than the remaining three (31.696% compared to 7.560, 5.725, and 5.336%), however after extraction it accounts for only 16.219% of variance (compared to 14.523, 11.099 and 8.475% respectively).

Total Variance Explained

Component	Initial Eigenvalues			Extraction Sums of Squared Loadings			Rotation Sums of Squared Loadings		
	Total	% of Variance	Cumulative %	Total	% of Variance	Cumulative %	Total	% of Variance	Cumulative %
1	7.290	31.696	31.696	7.290	31.696	31.696	3.730	16.219	16.219
2	1.739	7.560	39.256	1.739	7.560	39.256	3.340	14.523	30.742
3	1.317	5.725	44.981	1.317	5.725	44.981	2.553	11.099	41.842
4	1.227	5.336	50.317	1.227	5.336	50.317	1.949	8.475	50.317
5	.988	4.295	54.612						
6	.895	3.893	58.504						
7	.806	3.502	62.007						
8	.783	3.404	65.410						
9	.751	3.265	68.676						
10	.717	3.117	71.793						
11	.684	2.972	74.765						
12	.670	2.911	77.676						
13	.612	2.661	80.337						
14	.578	2.512	82.849						
15	.549	2.388	85.236						
16	.523	2.275	87.511						
17	.508	2.210	89.721						
18	.456	1.982	91.704						
19	.424	1.843	93.546						
20	.408	1.773	95.319						
21	.379	1.650	96.969						
22	.364	1.583	98.552						
23	.333	1.448	100.000						

Extraction Method: Principal Component Analysis.

SPSS Output 11.4

SPSS Output 11.5 shows the table of communalities before and after extraction. Remember that the communality is the proportion of common variance within a variable (see section 11.2.1). Principal component analysis works on the initial assumption that all variance is common; therefore, before extraction the communalities are all 1 (see column labelled *Initial*). In effect, all of the variance associated with a variable is assumed to be common variance. Once factors have been extracted, we have a better idea of how much variance is, in reality, common. The communalities in the column labelled *Extraction* reflect this common variance. So, for example, we can say that 43.5% of the variance associated with question 1 is common, or shared, variance. Another way to look at these communalities is in terms of the proportion of variance explained by the underlying factors. Before extraction, there are as many factors as there are variables, so all variance is explained by the factors and communalities are all 1. However, after extraction some of the factors are discarded and so some information is lost. The retained factors cannot explain all of the variance present in the data, but they can explain some. The amount of variance in each variable that can be explained by the retained factors is represented by the communalities after extraction.

Communalities

	Initial	Extraction
Q01	1.000	.435
Q02	1.000	.414
Q03	1.000	.530
Q04	1.000	.469
Q05	1.000	.343
Q06	1.000	.654
Q07	1.000	.545
Q08	1.000	.739
Q09	1.000	.484
Q10	1.000	.335
Q11	1.000	.690
Q12	1.000	.513
Q13	1.000	.536
Q14	1.000	.488
Q15	1.000	.378
Q16	1.000	.487
Q17	1.000	.683
Q18	1.000	.597
Q19	1.000	.343
Q20	1.000	.484
Q21	1.000	.550
Q22	1.000	.464
Q23	1.000	.412

Extraction Method: Principal Component

Component Matrix[a]

	Component			
	1	2	3	4
Q18	.701			
Q07	.685			
Q16	.679			
Q13	.673			
Q12	.669			
Q21	.658			
Q14	.656			
Q11	.652			-.400
Q17	.643			
Q04	.634			
Q03	-.629			
Q15	.593			
Q01	.586			
Q05	.556			
Q08	.549	.401		-.417
Q10	.437			
Q20	.436		-.404	
Q19	-.427			
Q09		.627		
Q02		.548		
Q22		.465		
Q06	.562		.571	
Q23				.507

Extraction Method: Principal Component Analysis.
a. 4 components extracted.

SPSS Output 11.5

SPSS Output 11.5 also shows the component matrix before rotation. This matrix contains the loadings of each variable onto each factor. By default SPSS displays all loadings; however, we requested that all loadings less than 0.4 be suppressed in the output (see Figure 11.10) and so there are blank spaces for many of the loadings. This matrix is not particularly important for interpretation, but it is interesting to note that before rotation most variables load highly onto the first factor (that is why this factor accounts for most of the variance in SPSS Output 11.4).

At this stage SPSS has extracted four factors. Factor analysis is an exploratory tool and so it should be used to guide the researcher to make various decisions: you shouldn't leave the computer to make them. One important decision is the number of factors to extract. In section 11.2.4 we saw various criteria for assessing the importance of factors. By Kaiser's criterion we should extract four factors and this is what SPSS has done. However, this criterion is accurate when there are less than 30 variables and communalities after extraction are greater than 0.7 or when the sample size exceeds 250 and the average communality is greater than 0.6. The communalities are shown in SPSS Output 11.5, and none exceed 0.7. The average of the communalities can be found by adding them up and dividing by the number of communalities (11.573/23 = 0.503). So, on both grounds Kaiser's rule may not be accurate. However, you should consider the huge sample that we have, because the research into Kaiser's criterion gives recommendations for much smaller samples. By Jolliffe's criterion (retain factors with eigenvalues greater than 0.7) we should retain 10 factors (see SPSS Output 11.4), but there is little to recommend this criterion over Kaiser's. As a final guide we can use the scree plot which we asked SPSS to produce by using the option in Figure 11.7. The scree plot is shown in SPSS Output 11.6 with a thunderbolt indicating the point of inflexion on the curve. This curve is difficult to interpret because the curve begins to tail off after three factors, but there is another drop after four factors before a stable plateau is reached. Therefore, we could probably justify retaining either two or four factors. Given the large sample, it is probably safe to assume Kaiser's criterion; however, you might like to rerun the analysis specifying that SPSS extract only two factors (see Figure 11.7) and compare the results.

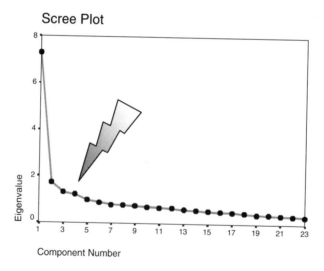

SPSS Output 11.6

SPSS Output 11.7 shows an edited version of the reproduced correlation matrix that was requested using the option in Figure 11.6. The top half of this matrix (labelled *Reproduced Correlation*) contains the correlation coefficients between all of the questions based on the factor model. The diagonal of this matrix contains the communalities after extraction for each variable (I've changed these values to bold type, you can check the values against SPSS Output 11.5).

Reproduced Correlations

		Q01	Q02	Q03	Q04	Q05	Q19	Q20	Q21	Q22	Q23
Reproduced Correlation	Q01	.435[b]	-.112	-.372	.447	.376	-.204	.342	.449	-2.54E-02	4.463E-02
	Q02	-.112	.414[b]	.380	-.134	-.122	.357	-.301	-.254	.333	.246
	Q03	-.372	.380	.530[b]	-.399	-.345	.403	-.440	-.488	.275	.158
	Q04	.447	-.134	-.399	.469[b]	.399	-.231	.353	.480	-4.97E-02	4.179E-02
	Q05	.376	-.122	-.345	.399	.343[b]	-.207	.292	.412	-6.03E-02	2.794E-02
	Q06	.218	-3.34E-02	-.200	.278	.273	-.147	-2.06E-02	.244	-.209	-8.17E-02
	Q07	.366	-.148	-.373	.419	.380	-.254	.219	.430	-9.89E-02	-3.72E-02
	Q08	.412	2.192E-03	-.270	.390	.312	-.104	.164	.282	.417	-.136
	Q09	-4.25E-02	.430	.352	-7.31E-02	-7.97E-02	.363	-.218	-.191	-.197	.323
	Q10	.172	-6.12E-02	-.181	.212	.205	-.137	5.763E-03	.188	-.209	-.202
	Q11	.423	-9.74E-02	-.357	.419	.348	-.198	.200	.342	-.136	1.064E-02
	Q12	.402	-.219	-.440	.448	.397	-.302	.354	.503	-.203	-7.88E-02
	Q13	.347	-.122	-.342	.395	.360	-.231	.163	.384	-.159	-2.16E-02
	Q14	.362	-.155	-.373	.411	.370	-.254	.241	.431	-.230	-.141
	Q15	.311	-.158	-.337	.343	.306	-.236	.175	.336	-.152	-4.93E-02
	Q16	.440	-.217	-.458	.466	.400	-.299	.373	.494	-.145	-.140
	Q17	.439	-4.80E-02	-.331	.434	.359	-.162	.196	.347	-.183	-3.16E-02
	Q18	.368	-.149	-.376	.424	.388	-.259	.215	.439	.294	.196
	Q19	-.204	.357	.403	-.231	-.207	.343[b]	-.308	-.324	-6.78E-02	2.125E-02
	Q20	.342	-.301	-.440	.353	.292	-.308	.484[b]	.457	-9.59E-02	3.196E-02
	Q21	.449	-.254	-.488	.480	.412	-.324	.457	.550[b]	.464	.408
	Q22	-2.54E-02	.333	.275	-4.97E-02	-6.03E-02	-6.78E-02	-9.59E-02	.464	.464[b]	.408
	Q23	4.463E-02	.246	.158	4.179E-02	2.794E-02	2.125E-02	3.196E-02	.408	.408	.412[b]
Residual[a]	Q01		1.291E-02	3.503E-02	-1.13E-02	2.694E-02	1.500E-02	-.128	-.120	-7.90E-02	-4.91E-02
	Q02	1.291E-02		-6.15E-02	2.169E-02	2.930E-03	-.153	9.905E-02	4.922E-02	-.102	-.147
	Q03	3.503E-02	-6.15E-02		1.893E-02	3.485E-02	-6.11E-02	.115	7.125E-02	-7.09E-02	-8.01E-03
	Q04	-1.13E-02	2.169E-02	1.893E-02		1.785E-03	4.510E-02	-.110	-6.98E-02	-4.87E-02	-7.56E-02
	Q05	2.694E-02	2.930E-03	3.485E-02	1.785E-03		4.136E-02	-9.24E-02	-7.76E-02	-7.22E-02	-6.96E-02
	Q06	-8.72E-04	-4.08E-02	-2.66E-02	1.197E-04	-1.55E-02	-2.01E-02	.122	2.875E-02	4.344E-02	1.304E-02
	Q07	-6.11E-02	-1.12E-02	-9.13E-03	-1.00E-02	-4.07E-02	-1.46E-02	1.628E-03	5.261E-02	1.040E-02	-3.31E-02
	Q08	-8.11E-02	-5.18E-02	1.106E-02	-4.07E-02	-4.36E-02	-5.59E-02	1.145E-02	1.407E-02	1.976E-02	8.616E-02
	Q09	-4.99E-02	-.115	-5.19E-02	-5.15E-02	-1.60E-02	-.114	5.965E-02	5.467E-02	-.161	-.152
	Q10	4.194E-02	-2.28E-02	-1.29E-02	3.359E-03	5.299E-02	9.852E-03	7.830E-02	4.732E-03	6.599E-02	4.844E-02
	Q11	-6.60E-02	-4.64E-02	6.094E-03	-5.05E-02	-5.01E-02	-2.07E-03	5.579E-02	4.747E-03	4.741E-02	.116
	Q12	-5.67E-02	2.375E-02	3.036E-02	-6.06E-03	-5.01E-02	3.574E-02	-5.63E-02	-6.21E-02	-3.10E-02	-5.71E-02
	Q13	7.634E-03	-2.12E-02	2.367E-02	-5.11E-02	-5.81E-02	4.134E-03	4.082E-02	-9.81E-03	7.402E-03	2.583E-02
	Q14	-2.39E-02	-9.23E-03	1.909E-03	-5.97E-02	-5.51E-02	-2.55E-04	-1.52E-02	-3.16E-02	-1.08E-02	-2.69E-02
	Q15	-6.49E-02	-7.26E-03	2.494E-02	-8.76E-03	-4.49E-02	2.658E-02	3.088E-02	-3.59E-02	6.223E-02	7.911E-02
	Q16	5.880E-02	4.966E-02	3.929E-02	-4.99E-02	-5.04E-02	3.159E-02	-.108	-7.36E-02	-3.59E-03	-3.22E-02
	Q17	-6.86E-02	-3.90E-02	3.147E-02	-5.16E-02	-4.89E-02	-1.23E-03	9.384E-03	1.601E-02	1.900E-02	4.880E-02
	Q18	-2.04E-02	-1.49E-02	9.980E-04	-4.24E-02	-6.59E-02	2.821E-03	1.985E-02	-8.65E-03	2.343E-02	-4.88E-02
	Q19	1.500E-02	-.153	-6.11E-02	4.510E-02	4.136E-02		5.985E-02	4.882E-02	-6.01E-02	-7.31E-02
	Q20	-.128	9.905E-02	.115	-.110	-9.24E-02	5.985E-02		1.034E-02	-3.19E-02	-5.59E-02
	Q21	-.120	4.922E-02	7.125E-02	-6.98E-02	-7.76E-02	4.882E-02	1.034E-02		-3.31E-02	-9.96E-02
	Q22	-7.90E-02	-.102	-7.09E-02	-4.87E-02	-7.22E-02	-6.01E-02	-3.19E-02	-3.31E-02		-.177
	Q23	-4.91E-02	-.147	-8.01E-03	-7.56E-02	-6.96E-02	-7.31E-02	-5.59E-02	-9.96E-02	-.177	

Extraction Method: Principal Component Analysis.

a. Residuals are computed between observed and reproduced correlations. There are 91 (35.0%) nonredundant residuals with absolute values > 0.05.

b. Reproduced communalities

SPSS Output 11.7

The correlations in the reproduced matrix differ from those in the *R*-matrix because they stem from the model rather than the observed data. If the model were a perfect fit of the data then we would expect the reproduced correlation coefficients to be the same as the original correlation coefficients. Therefore, to assess the fit of the model we can look at the differences between the observed correlations and the correlations based on the model. For example, if we take the correlation between questions 1 and 2, the correlation based on the observed data is –0.099 (taken from SPSS Output 11.1). The correlation based on the model is –0.112, which is slightly higher. We can calculate the difference as follows:

$$\text{residual} = r_{\text{observed}} - r_{\text{from model}}$$
$$\text{residual}_{Q_1 Q_2} = (-0.099) - (-0.112)$$
$$= 0.013 \; or \; 1.3E\text{-}02$$

You should notice that this difference is the value quoted in the lower half of the reproduced matrix (labelled *Residual*) for the questions 1 and 2. Therefore, the lower half of the reproduced matrix contains the differences between the observed correlation coefficients and the ones predicted from the model. For a good model these values will all be small. In fact, we want most values to be less than 0.05. Rather than scan this huge matrix, SPSS provides a footnote summary, which states how many residuals have an absolute value greater than 0.05. For these data there are 91 residuals (35%) that are greater than 0.05. There are no hard and fast rules about what proportion of residuals should be below 0.05; however, if more than 50% are greater than 0.05 you probably have grounds for concern.

11.5.3.   Factor Rotation

The first analysis I asked you to run was using an orthogonal rotation. However, you were asked to rerun the analysis using oblique rotation too. In this section the results of both analyses will be reported so as to highlight the differences between the outputs. This comparison will also be a useful way to show the circumstances in which one type of rotation might be preferable to another.

11.5.3.1. Orthogonal Rotation (Varimax)

SPSS Output 11.8 shows the rotated component matrix (also called the rotated factor matrix in factor analysis) which is a matrix of the factor loadings for each variable onto each factor. This matrix contains the same information as the component matrix in SPSS Output 11.5 except that it is calculated *after* rotation. There are several things to consider about the format of this matrix. First, factor loadings less than 0.4 have not been displayed because we asked for these loadings to be suppressed using the option in Figure 11.10. If you didn't select this option, or didn't adjust the criterion value to 0.4, then your output will differ. Second, the variables are listed in the order of size of their factor loadings. By default, SPSS orders the variables as they are in the data editor; however, we asked for the output to be *Sorted by size* using the option in Figure 11.10. If this option was not selected your output will look different. Finally, for all other parts of the output I suppressed the variable labels (for reasons of space) but for this matrix I have allowed the variable labels to be printed to aid interpretation.

The original logic behind suppressing loadings less than 0.4 was based on Stevens's (1992) suggestion that this cut-off point was appropriate for interpretative purposes (i.e. loadings greater than 0.4 represent substantive values). However, this means that we have suppressed several loadings that are undoubtedly significant (see section 11.2.5.2). However, significance itself is not important.

Compare this matrix with the unrotated solution (SPSS Output 11.5). Before rotation, most variables loaded highly onto the first factor and the remaining factors didn't really get a look in. However, the rotation of the factor structure has clarified things considerably: there are four factors and variables load very highly onto only one factor (with the exception of one question). The suppression of loadings less than 0.4 and ordering variables by loading size also makes interpretation considerably easier (because you don't have to scan the matrix to identify substantive loadings).

The next step is to look at the content of questions that load onto the same factor to try to identify common themes. If the mathematical factor produced by the analysis represents some real-world construct then common themes among highly loading questions can help us identify what the construct might be. The questions that load highly on factor 1 seem to all relate to using computers or SPSS. Therefore we might label this factor *fear of computers*. The questions that load highly on factor 2 all seem to relate to different aspects of statistics; therefore, we might label this factor *fear of statistics*. The three questions that load highly on factor 3 all seem to relate to mathematics; therefore, we might label this factor *fear of mathematics*. Finally, the questions that load highly on factor 4 all contain some component of social evaluation from friends; therefore, we might label this factor *peer evaluation*. This analysis seems to reveal that the initial questionnaire, in reality, is composed of four sub-scales: fear of computers, fear of statistics, fear of maths, and fear of negative peer evaluation. There are two possibilities here. The first is that the SAQ failed to measure what it set out to (namely SPSS anxiety) but does measure some related constructs. The second is that these four constructs are sub-components of SPSS anxiety; however, the factor analysis does not indicate which of these possibilities is true.

The final part of the output is the factor transformation matrix (see section 11.2.5.1). This matrix provides information about the degree to which the factors were rotated to obtain a solution. If no rotation were necessary, this matrix would be an identity matrix. If orthogonal rotation were completely appropriate then we would expect a symmetrical matrix (same values above and below the diagonal). However, in reality the matrix is not easy to interpret although very unsymmetrical matrices might be taken as a reason to try oblique rotation. For the inexperienced factor analyst you are probably best advised to ignore the factor transformation matrix.

Rotated Component Matrix

	Component			
	1	2	3	4
I have little experience of computers	.800			
SPSS always crashes when I try to use it	.684			
I worry that I will cause irreparable damage because of my incompetenece with computers	.647			
All computers hate me	.638			
Computers have minds of their own and deliberately go wrong whenever I use them	.579			
Computers are useful only for playing games	.550			
Computers are out to get me	.459			
I can't sleep for thoughts of eigen vectors		.677		
I wake up under my duvet thinking that I am trapped under a normal distribtion		.661		
Standard deviations excite me		-.567		
People try to tell you that SPSS makes statistics easier to understand but it doesn't	.473	.523		
I dream that Pearson is attacking me with correlation coefficients		.516		
I weep openly at the mention of central tendency		.514		
Statiscs makes me cry		.496		
I don't understand statistics		.429		
I have never been good at mathematics			.833	
I slip into a coma whenever I see an equation			.747	
I did badly at mathematics at school			.747	
My friends are better at statistics than me				.648
My friends are better at SPSS than I am				.645
If I'm good at statistics my friends will think I'm a nerd				.586
My friends will think I'm stupid for not being able to cope with SPSS				.543
Everybody looks at me when I use SPSS				.427

Extraction Method: Principal Component Analysis.
Rotation Method: Varimax with Kaiser Normalization.

   a. Rotation converged in 9 iterations.

Component Transformation Matrix

Component	1	2	3	4
1	.635	.585	.443	-.242
2	.137	-.168	.488	.846
3	.758	-.513	-.403	.008
4	.067	.605	-.635	.476

Extraction Method: Principal Component Analysis.
Rotation Method: Varimax with Kaiser Normalization.

SPSS Output 11.8

11.5.3.2. Oblique Rotation

When an oblique rotation is conducted the factor matrix is split into two matrices: the *pattern matrix* and the *structure matrix*. For orthogonal rotation these matrices are the same. The pattern matrix contains the factor loadings and is comparable to the factor matrix that we interpreted for the orthogonal rotation. The structure matrix takes into account the relationship between factors (in fact it is a product of the pattern matrix and the matrix containing the correlation coefficients between factors). Most researchers interpret the pattern matrix, because it is usually simpler; however, there are situations in which values in the pattern matrix are suppressed because of relationships between the factors. Therefore, the structure matrix is a useful double-check.

Pattern Matrix[a]

	Component			
	1	2	3	4
I can't sleep for thoughts of eigen vectors	.706			
I wake up under my duvet thinking that I am trapped under a normal distribtion	.591			
Standard deviations excite me	-.511			
I dream that Pearson is attacking me with correlation coefficients	.405			
I weep openly at the mention of central tendency	.400			
Statiscs makes me cry				
I don't understand statistics				
My friends are better at SPSS than I am		.643		
My friends are better at statistics than me		.621		
If I'm good at statistics my friends will think I'm a nerd		.615		
My friends will think I'm stupid for not being able to cope with SPSS		.507		
Everybody looks at me when I use SPSS				
I have little experience of computers			.885	
SPSS always crashes when I try to use it			.713	
All computers hate me			.653	
I worry that I will cause irreparable damage because of my incompetenece with computers			.650	
Computers have minds of their own and deliberately go wrong whenever I use them			.588	
Computers are useful only for playing games			.585	
People try to tell you that SPSS makes statistics easier to understand but it doesn't	.412		.462	
Computers are out to get me			.411	
I have never been good at mathematics				-.902
I slip into a coma whenever I see an equation				-.774
I did badly at mathematics at school				-.774

Extraction Method: Principal Component Analysis.
Rotation Method: Oblimin with Kaiser Normalization.

a. Rotation converged in 29 iterations.

SPSS Output 11.9

For the pattern matrix for these data (SPSS Output 11.8) the same four factors seem to have emerged (although for some variables the factor loadings are too small to be displayed). Factor 1 seems to represent fear of statistics, factor 2 represents fear of peer evaluation, factor 3 represents fear of computers and factor 4 represents fear of mathematics. The structure matrix (SPSS Output 11.9) differs in that shared variance is not ignored. The picture becomes more complicated because with the exception of factor 2, several variables load highly onto more than one factor. This has occurred because of the relationship between factors 1 and 3 and factors 3 and 4. This example should highlight why the pattern matrix is preferable for interpretative reasons: because it contains information about the *unique* contribution of a variable to a factor.

Structure Matrix

	Component			
	1	2	3	4
I wake up under my duvet thinking that I am trapped under a normal distribtion	.695		.477	
I can't sleep for thoughts of eigen vectors	.685			
Standard deviations excite me	-.632		-.407	
I weep openly at the mention of central tendency	.567		.516	-.491
I dream that Pearson is attacking me with correlation coefficients	.548		.487	-.485
Statiscs makes me cry	.520		.413	-.501
I don't understand statistics	.462		.453	
My friends are better at SPSS than I am		.660		
My friends are better at statistics than me		.653		
If I'm good at statistics my friends will think I'm a nerd		.588		
My friends will think I'm stupid for not being able to cope with SPSS		.546		
Everybody looks at me when I use SPSS	-.435	.446		
I have little experience of computers			.777	
SPSS always crashes when I try to use it	.404		.761	
All computers hate me	.401		.723	
I worry that I will cause irreparable damage because of my incompetenece with computers			.723	-.429
Computers have minds of their own and deliberately go wrong whenever I use them	.426		.671	
People try to tell you that SPSS makes statistics easier to understand but it doesn't	.576		.606	
Computers are out to get me			.561	-.441
Computers are useful only for playing games			.556	
I have never been good at mathematics				-.855
I slip into a coma whenever I see an equation			.453	-.822
I did badly at mathematics at school			.451	-.818

Extraction Method: Principal Component Analysis.
Rotation Method: Oblimin with Kaiser Normalization.

SPSS Output 11.10

The final part of the output is a correlation matrix between the factors (SPSS Output 11.11). This matrix contains the correlation coefficients between factors. As predicted from the structure matrix, factor 2 has little or no relationship with any other factors (correlation coefficients are low), but all other factors are interrelated to some degree (notably factors 1 and 3, and factors 3 and 4). The fact that these correlations exist tell us that the constructs measured can be interrelated. If the constructs were independent then we would expect oblique rotation to provide an identical solution to an orthogonal rotation and the component correlation matrix should be an identity matrix (i.e. all factors have correlation coefficients of 0). Therefore, this final matrix gives us a guide to whether it is reasonable to assume independence between factors: for these data it appears that we cannot assume independence. Therefore, the results of the orthogonal rotation should not be trusted: the obliquely rotated solution is probably more meaningful.

On a theoretical level the dependence between our factors does not cause concern; we might expect a fairly strong relationship between fear of maths, fear of statistics and fear of computers. Generally, the less mathematically and technically minded people struggle with statistics. However, we would not expect these constructs to correlate with fear of peer evaluation (because this construct is more socially based). In fact, this factor is the one that correlates fairly badly with all others—so on a theoretical level, things have turned out rather well!

Component Correlation Matrix

Component	1	2	3	4
1	1.000	-.154	.364	-.279
2	-.154	1.000	-.185	8.155E-02
3	.364	-.185	1.000	-.464
4	-.279	8.155E-02	-.464	1.000

Extraction Method: Principal Component Analysis.
Rotation Method: Oblimin with Kaiser Normalization.

SPSS Output 11.11

11.5.4.   *Factor Scores*

Having reached a suitable solution and rotated that solution we can look at the factor scores. SPSS Output 11.12 shows the component score matrix B (see section 11.1.4) from which the factor scores are calculated and the covariance matrix of factor scores. The component score matrix is not particularly useful in itself. It can be useful in understanding how the factor scores have been computed, but with large data sets like this one you are unlikely to want to delve into the mathematics behind the factor scores. However the covariance matrix of scores is useful. This matrix in effect tells us the relationship between factor scores (it is an unstandardized correlation matrix). If factor scores are uncorrelated then this matrix should be an identity matrix (i.e. diagonal elements will be 1 but all other elements are 0). For these data the covariances are all zero (remembering that 4.37E–16 is actually 0.000000000000000437) indicating that the resulting scores are uncorrelated.

Component Score Coefficient Matrix

	Component 1	Component 2	Component 3	Component 4
Q01	-.053	.173	.089	.110
Q02	.102	-.129	.086	.281
Q03	.087	-.195	.013	.137
Q04	-.011	.170	.045	.107
Q05	.021	.131	.014	.083
Q06	.383	-.211	-.088	.014
Q07	.213	.004	-.078	.038
Q08	-.129	-.074	.460	.013
Q09	.025	-.029	.108	.354
Q10	.244	-.161	-.021	-.036
Q11	-.066	-.087	.379	-.059
Q12	.097	.161	-.116	.051
Q13	.224	-.065	-.019	.013
Q14	.180	.040	-.084	.043
Q15	.114	-.055	.061	-.058
Q16	-.015	.146	.046	.014
Q17	-.057	-.067	.372	.005
Q18	.242	-.001	-.104	.043
Q19	.048	-.115	.061	.199
Q20	-.195	.359	-.061	-.002
Q21	-.039	.270	-.064	.059
Q22	-.036	.162	-.048	.382
Q23	.032	.211	-.162	.379

Extraction Method: Principal Component Analysis.
Rotation Method: Varimax with Kaiser Normalization.

Component Score Covariance Matrix

Component	1	2	3	4
1	1.000	1.093E-16	.000	.000
2	1.093E-16	1.000	4.373E-16	.000
3	.000	4.373E-16	1.000	.000
4	.000	.000	.000	1.000

Extraction Method: Principal Component Analysis.
Rotation Method: Varimax with Kaiser Normalization.

SPSS Output 11.12

In the original analysis we asked for scores to be calculated based on the Anderson-Rubin method (hence why they are uncorrelated). You will find these scores in the data editor. There should be four new columns of data (one for each factor) labelled *FAC1_1*, *FAC2_1*, *FAC3_1* and *FAC4_1* respectively. If you asked for factor scores in the oblique rotation then these scores will appear in the data editor in four other columns labelled *FAC2_1* and so on. These factor scores can be listed in the output viewer using the **Analyze⇒Reports⇒Case Summaries...**

command path (see section 4.4.1.6). Given that there are over 1500 cases you might like to restrict the output to the first 10 or 20. SPSS Output 11.13 shows the factor scores for the first 10 subjects. It should be pretty clear that subject 9 scored highly on all four factors and so this person is very anxious about statistics, computing and maths, but less so about peer evaluation (factor 4). Factor scores can be used in this way to assess the relative fear of one person compared to another, or we could add the scores up to obtain a single score for each subject (that we might assume represents SPSS anxiety as a whole). We can also use factor scores in regression when groups of predictors correlate so highly that there is multicollinearity.

Case Summaries[a]

	Case Number	FAC1_1	FAC2_1	FAC3_1	FAC4_1
1	1	.10584	-.92797	-1.82768	-.45958
2	2	-.58279	-.18934	-.04137	.29330
3	3	-.54761	.02968	.19913	-.97142
4	4	.74664	.72272	-.68650	-.18533
5	5	.25167	-.51497	-.63353	.68296
6	6	1.91613	-.27351	-.68205	-.52710
7	7	-.26055	-1.40960	-.00435	.90986
8	8	-.28574	-.91775	-.08948	1.03732
9	9	1.71753	1.15063	3.15671	.81083
10	10	-.69153	-.73340	.18379	1.49529

a. Limited to first 10 cases.

SPSS Output 11.13

11.6. Summary

To sum up, the analyses revealed four underlying scales in our questionnaire that may, or may not, relate to genuine sub-components of SPSS anxiety. It also seems as though an obliquely rotated solution was preferred due to the interrelationships between factors. The use of factor analysis is purely exploratory; it should be used only to guide future hypotheses, or to inform researchers about patterns within data sets. A great many decisions are left to the researcher using factor analysis and I urge you to make informed decisions, rather than basing decisions on the outcomes you would like to get. For this reason this chapter has been as thorough as possible.

11.7.   Further Reading

Dunteman, G. E. (1989). *Principal components analysis*. Sage university paper series on quantitative applications in the social sciences, 07-069. Newbury Park, CA: Sage. This monograph is quite high level but comprehensive.

Pedhazur, E. and Schmelkin, L. (1991). *Measurement, design and analysis*. Hillsdale, NJ: Erlbaum. Chapter 22 is an excellent introduction to the theory of factor analysis.

Tabachnick, B. G. and Fidell, L. S. (1996). *Using multivariate statistics* (3rd edition). New York: Harper and Row. Chapter 13 is a technical but wonderful overview of factor analysis.

12 Appendix

12.1. Table of the Standard Normal Distribution

From Howell, D. C. (1997). *Statistical methods for psychology* (4th edition). Belmont, CA: Duxbury. Reprinted with permission of Brooks/Cole Publishing, a division of Thomson Learning. Fax 800 730-2215.

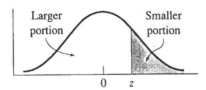

z	Larger Portion	Smaller Portion	y	z	Larger Portion	Smaller Portion	y
.00	.5000	.5000	.3989	.23	.5910	.4090	.3885
.01	.5040	.4960	.3989	.24	.5948	.4052	.3876
.02	.5080	.4920	.3989	.25	.5987	.4013	.3867
.03	.5120	.4880	.3988	.26	.6026	.3974	.3857
.04	.5160	.4840	.3986	.27	.6064	.3936	.3847
.05	.5199	.4801	.3984	.28	.6103	.3897	.3836
.06	.5239	.4761	.3982	.29	.6141	.3859	.3825
.07	.5279	.4721	.3980	.30	.6179	.3821	.3814
.08	**.5319**	**.4681**	**.3977**	.31	.6217	.3783	.3802
.09	.5359	.4641	.3973	.32	.6255	.3745	.3790
.10	.5398	.4602	.3970	.33	.6293	.3707	.3778
.11	.5438	.4562	.3965	.34	.6331	.3669	.3765
.12	.5478	.4522	.3961	.35	.6368	.3632	.3752
.13	.5517	.4483	.3956	.36	.6406	.3594	.3739
.14	.5557	.4443	.3951	.37	.6443	.3557	.3725
.15	.5596	.4404	.3945	.38	.6480	.3520	.3712
.16	.5636	.4364	.3939	.39	.6517	.3483	.3697
.17	.5675	.4325	.3932	.40	.6554	.3446	.3683
.18	.5714	.4286	.3925	.41	.6591	.3409	.3668
.19	.5753	.4247	.3918	.42	.6628	.3372	.3653
.20	.5793	.4207	.3910	.43	.6664	.3336	.3637
.21	.5832	.4168	.3902	.44	.6700	.3300	.3621
.22	.5871	.4129	.3894	.45	.6736	.3264	.3605

z	Larger Portion	Smaller Portion	y	z	Larger Portion	Smaller Portion	y
.46	.6772	.3228	.3589	.90	.8159	.1841	.2661
.47	.6808	.3192	.3572	.91	.8186	.1814	.2637
.48	.6844	.3156	.3555	.92	.8212	.1788	.2613
.49	.6879	.3121	.3538	.93	.8238	.1762	.2589
.50	.6915	.3085	.3521	.94	.8264	.1736	.2565
.51	.6950	.3050	.3503	.95	.8289	.1711	.2541
.52	.6985	.3015	.3485	.96	.8315	.1685	.2516
.53	.7019	.2981	.3467	.97	.8340	.1660	.2492
.54	.7054	.2946	.3448	.98	.8365	.1635	.2468
.55	.7088	.2912	.3429	.99	.8389	.1611	.2444
.56	.7123	.2877	.3410	1.00	.8413	.1587	.2420
.57	.7157	.2843	.3391	1.01	.8438	.1562	.2396
.58	.7190	.2810	.3372	1.02	.8461	.1539	.2371
.59	.7224	.2776	.3352	1.03	.8485	.1515	.2347
.60	.7257	.2743	.3332	1.04	.8508	.1492	.2323
.61	.7291	.2709	.3312	1.05	.8531	.1469	.2299
.62	.7324	.2676	.3292	1.06	.8554	.1446	.2275
.63	.7357	.2643	.3271	1.07	.8577	.1423	.2251
.64	.7389	.2611	.3251	1.08	.8599	.1401	.2227
.65	.7422	.2578	.3230	1.09	.8621	.1379	.2203
.66	.7454	.2546	.3209	1.10	.8643	.1357	.2179
.67	.7486	.2514	.3187	1.11	.8665	.1335	.2155
.68	.7517	.2483	.3166	1.12	.8686	.1314	.2131
.69	.7549	.2451	.3144	1.13	.8708	.1292	.2107
.70	.7580	.2420	.3123	1.14	.8729	.1271	.2083
.71	.7611	.2389	.3101	1.15	.8749	.1251	.2059
.72	.7642	.2358	.3079	1.16	.8770	.1230	.2036
.73	.7673	.2327	.3056	1.17	.8790	.1210	.2012
.74	.7704	.2296	.3034	1.18	.8810	.1190	.1989
.75	.7734	.2266	.3011	1.19	.8830	.1170	.1965
.76	.7764	.2236	.2989	1.20	.8849	.1151	.1942
.77	.7794	.2206	.2966	1.21	.8869	.1131	.1919
.78	.7823	.2177	.2943	1.22	.8888	.1112	.1895
.79	.7852	.2148	.2920	1.23	.8907	.1093	.1872
.80	.7881	.2119	.2897	1.24	.8925	.1075	.1849
.81	.7910	.2090	.2874	1.25	.8944	.1056	.1826
.82	.7939	.2061	.2850	1.26	.8962	.1038	.1804
.83	.7967	.2033	.2827	1.27	.8980	.1020	.1781
.84	.7995	.2005	.2803	1.28	.8997	.1003	.1758
.85	.8023	.1977	.2780	1.29	.9015	.0985	.1736
.86	.8051	.1949	.2756	1.30	.9032	.0968	.1714
.87	.8078	.1922	.2732	1.31	.9049	.0951	.1691
.88	.8106	.1894	.2709	1.32	.9066	.0934	.1669
.89	.8133	.1867	2685	1.33	.9082	.0918	.1647

z	Larger Portion	Smaller Portion	y	z	Larger Portion	Smaller Portion	y
1.34	.9099	.0901	.1626	1.78	.9625	.0375	.0818
1.35	.9115	.0885	.1604	1.79	.9633	.0367	.0804
1.36	.9131	.0869	.1582	1.80	.9641	.0359	.0790
1.37	.9147	.0853	.1561	1.81	.9649	.0351	.0775
1.38	.9162	.0838	.1539	1.82	.9656	.0344	.0761
1.39	.9177	.0823	.1518	1.83	.9664	.0336	.0748
1.40	.9192	.0808	.1497	1.84	.9671	.0329	.0734
1.41	.9207	.0793	.1476	1.85	.9678	.0322	.0721
1.42	.9222	.0778	.1456	1.86	.9686	.0314	.0707
1.43	.9236	.0764	.1435	1.87	.9693	.0307	.0694
1.44	.9251	.0749	.1415	1.88	.9699	.0301	.0681
1.45	.9265	.0735	.1394	1.89	.9706	.0294	.0669
1.46	.9279	.0721	.1374	1.90	.9713	.0287	.0656
1.47	.9292	.0708	.1354	1.91	.9719	.0281	.0644
1.48	.9306	.0694	.1334	1.92	.9726	.0274	.0632
1.49	.9319	.0681	.1315	1.93	.9732	.0268	.0620
1.50	.9332	.0668	.1295	1.94	.9738	.0262	.0608
1.51	.9345	.0655	.1276	1.95	.9744	.0256	.0596
1.52	.9357	.0643	.1257	1.96	.9750	.0250	.0584
1.53	.9370	.0630	.1238	1.97	.9756	.0244	.0573
1.54	.9382	.0618	.1219	1.98	.9761	.0239	.0562
1.55	.9394	.0606	.1200	1.99	.9767	.0233	.0551
1.56	.9406	.0594	.1182	2.00	.9772	.0228	.0540
1.57	.9418	.0582	.1163	2.01	.9778	.0222	.0529
1.58	.9429	.0571	.1145	2.02	.9783	.0217	.0519
1.59	.9441	.0559	.1127	2.03	.9788	.0212	.0508
1.60	.9452	.0548	.1109	2.04	.9793	.0207	.0498
1.61	.9463	.0537	.1092	2.05	.9798	.0202	.0488
1.62	.9474	.0526	.1074	2.06	.9803	.0197	.0478
1.63	.9484	.0516	.1057	2.07	.9808	.0192	.0468
1.64	.9495	.0505	.1040	2.08	.9812	.0188	.0459
1.65	.9505	.0495	.1023	2.09	.9817	.0183	.0449
1.66	.9515	.0485	.1006	2.10	.9821	.0179	.0440
1.67	.9525	.0475	.0989	2.11	.9826	.0174	.0431
1.68	.9535	.0465	.0973	2.12	.9830	.0170	.0422
1.69	.9545	.0455	.0957	2.13	.9834	.0166	.0413
1.70	.9554	.0446	.0940	2.14	.9838	.0162	.0404
1.71	.9564	.0436	.0925	2.15	.9842	.0158	.0396
1.72	.9573	.0427	.0909	2.16	.9846	.0154	.0387
1.73	.9582	.0418	.0893	2.17	.9850	.0150	.0379
1.74	.9591	.0409	.0878	2.18	.9854	.0146	.0371
1.75	.9599	.0401	.0863	2.19	.9857	.0143	.0363
1.76	.9608	.0392	.0848	2.20	.9861	.0139	.0355
1.77	.9616	.0384	.0833	2.21	.9864	.0136	.0347

z	Larger Portion	Smaller Portion	y	z	Larger Portion	Smaller Portion	y
2.22	.9868	.0132	.0339	2.66	.9961	.0039	.0116
2.23	.9871	.0129	.0332	2.67	.9962	.0038	.0113
2.24	.9875	.0125	0325	2.68	.9963	.0037	.0110
2.25	.9878	.0122	.0317	2.69	.9964	.0036	.0107
2.26	.9881	.0119	.0310	2.70	9965	.0035	.0104
2.27	.9884	.0116	.0303	2.71	.9966	.0034	.0101
2.28	.9887	.0113	.0297	2.72	.9967	.0033	.0099
2.29	.9890	.0110	.0290	2.73	.9968	.0032	.0096
2.30	.9893	.0107	.0283	2.74	.9969	.0031	.0093
2.31	.9896	.0104	.0277	2.75	.9970	.0030	.0091
2.32	.9898	.0102	.0270	2.76	.9971	.0029	.0088
2.33	.9901	.0099	.0264	2.77	.9972	.0028	.0086
2.34	.9904	.0096	.0258	2.78	.9973	.0027	.0084
2.35	.9906	.0094	.0252	2.79	.9974	.0026	.0081
2.36	.9909	.0091	.0246	2.80	.9974	.0026	.0079
2.37	.9911	.0089	.0241	2.81	.9975	.0025	.0077
2.38	.9913	.0087	.0235	2.82	.9976	.0024	.0075
2.39	.9916	.0084	.0229	2.83	.9977	.0023	.0073
2.40	.9918	.0082	.0224	2.84	.9977	.0023	.0071
2.41	.9920	.0080	.0219	2.85	.9978	.0022	.0069
2.42	.9922	.0078	.0213	2.86	.9970	.0021	.0067
2.43	.9925	.0075	.0208	2.87	.9979	.0021	.0065
2.44	.9927	.0073	.0203	2.88	.9980	.0020	.0063
2.45	.9929	.0071	.0198	2.89	.9981	.0019	.0061
2.46	.9931	.0069	.0194	2.90	.9981	.0019	.0060
2.47	.9932	.0068	.0189	2.91	.9982	.0018	.0058
2.48	.9934	.0066	.0184	2.92	.9982	.0018	.0056
2.49	.9936	.0064	.0180	2.93	.9983	.0017	.0055
2.50	.9938	.0062	.0175	2.94	.9984	.0016	.0053
2.51	.9940	.0060	.0171	2.95	.9984	.0016	.0051
2.52	.9941	.0059	.0167	2.96	.9985	.0015	.0050
2.53	.9943	.0057	.0163	2.97	.9985	.0015	.0048
2.54	.9945	.0055	.0158	2.98	.9986	.0014	.0047
2.55	.9946	.0054	.0154	2.99	.9986	.0014	.0046
2.56	.9948	.0052	.0151	3.00	.9987	.0013	.0044
2.57	.9949	.0051	.0147	...	...	...	...
2.58	.9951	.0049	.0143	3.25	.9994	.0006	.0020
2.59	.9952	.0048	.0139	...	...	...	...
2.60	.9953	.0047	.0136	3.50	.9998	.0002	.0009
2.61	.9955	.0045	.0132	...	...	...	...
2.62	.9956	.0044	.0129	3.75	.9999	.0001	.0004
2.63	.9957	.0043	.0126	...	...	...	...
2.64	.9959	.0041	.0122	4.00	1.0000	.0000	.0001
2.65	.9960	.0040	.0119				

12.2. Chapter 2

SPSSExam.sav

EXAM	COMP.	LECT.	NUM.	UNI
68	50	85.0	2	0
33	40	98.0	4	0
89	56	78.0	4	0
65	52	97.5	7	0
60	43	37.0	5	0
75	44	68.5	5	0
28	44	8.0	3	0
78	57	88.5	3	0
40	58	69.5	6	0
38	38	57.5	1	0
59	42	70.5	3	0
59	41	40.0	1	0
30	47	8.5	1	0
80	54	84.0	2	0
62	59	71.5	2	0
53	54	91.5	2	0
64	27	81.5	5	0
25	56	62.5	3	0
29	57	72.5	2	0
92	50	34.0	2	0
40	53	44.5	2	0
34	48	52.0	4	0
22	67	48.0	3	0
63	45	43.5	4	0
36	55	38.0	4	0
38	42	55.5	3	0
36	49	70.0	3	0
30	37	67.0	6	0
75	54	75.0	3	0
60	49	67.0	4	0
37	66	48.5	4	0
68	55	62.0	4	0
50	42	62.5	6	0
53	62	90.5	6	0
69	53	54.0	3	0
47	52	57.5	2	0
72	56	47.5	2	0
47	55	31.5	2	0
72	54	59.5	2	0
71	50	97.5	2	0
80	54	72.5	4	0
99	54	57.0	3	0
69	57	46.0	2	0
43	56	30.5	2	0
31	42	85.5	4	0
48	48	62.0	3	0
45	43	48.5	4	0
47	62	10.5	3	0
81	45	12.5	1	0
32	46	49.0	1	0
31	62	100.0	6	1
77	39	42.0	7	1
60	48	46.5	6	1
87	56	70.5	6	1
58	49	66.0	8	1
74	46	36.5	8	1
80	52	66.0	8	1
77	44	42.0	6	1
18	54	75.0	7	1
15	48	76.5	8	1
73	51	64.0	7	1
76	48	51.0	8	1
65	54	55.0	8	1
28	61	80.5	7	1
42	46	60.0	5	1
65	73	27.0	14	1
86	55	68.5	10	1
75	39	82.5	8	1
80	51	86.0	5	1
97	35	84.5	5	1
86	54	48.5	5	1
34	58	21.0	5	1
66	41	45.0	2	1
56	30	84.5	7	1
95	55	37.5	4	1
81	57	69.5	10	1
71	41	43.0	8	1
33	48	14.0	9	1
54	54	54.0	4	1
82	50	70.5	4	1
43	56	66.5	4	1
57	52	34.5	2	1
72	50	79.0	12	1
69	59	52.5	7	1
88	65	73.0	5	1
74	40	74.5	3	1
81	67	59.0	10	1
40	49	18.5	7	1

22	51	61.0	4	1	58	47	78.0	3	1
83	57	80.5	5	1	26	35	72.5	5	1
66	58	56.0	7	1	77	54	65.5	9	1
39	49	76.0	3	1	94	57	100.0	13	1
72	54	58.5	5	1	34	37	61.5	8	1
36	67	21.5	4	1	35	48	71.0	5	1

12.3. Chapter 3

ExamAnx.sav

NUM.	REV.	EXAM	ANX.	GEN.					
1	4	40	86.29	1	36	9	10	79.04	2
2	11	65	88.71	2	37	72	85	37.13	1
3	27	80	70.17	1	38	10	7	81.46	1
4	53	80	61.31	1	39	12	5	83.07	2
5	4	40	89.52	1	40	30	85	50.83	1
6	22	70	60.50	2	41	15	20	82.26	1
7	16	20	81.46	2	42	8	45	78.23	2
8	21	55	75.82	2	43	34	60	72.59	1
9	25	50	69.37	2	44	22	70	74.20	2
10	18	40	82.26	2	45	21	50	75.82	2
11	18	45	79.04	1	46	27	25	70.98	1
12	16	85	80.65	1	47	6	50	97.58	1
13	13	70	70.17	1	48	18	40	67.76	1
14	18	50	75.01	2	49	8	80	75.01	1
15	98	95	34.71	1	50	19	50	73.40	2
16	1	70	95.16	1	51	0	35	93.55	2
17	14	95	75.82	1	52	52	80	58.89	2
18	29	95	79.04	2	53	38	50	53.25	2
19	4	50	91.13	2	54	19	49	84.68	1
20	23	60	64.53	1	55	23	75	89.52	2
21	14	80	80.65	1	56	11	25	71.79	2
22	12	75	77.43	1	57	27	65	82.26	1
23	22	85	65.34	2	58	17	80	69.37	1
24	84	90	0.056	2	59	13	50	62.11	1
25	23	30	71.79	2	60	42	70	68.56	2
26	26	60	81.46	2	61	4	40	93.55	1
27	24	75	63.73	1	62	8	80	84.68	2
28	72	75	27.46	2	63	6	10	82.26	1
29	37	27	73.40	2	64	11	20	81.46	2
30	10	20	89.52	1	65	7	40	82.26	1
31	3	75	89.52	2	66	15	40	91.13	1
32	36	90	75.01	2	67	4	70	91.94	2
33	43	60	43.58	1	68	28	52	86.29	2
34	19	30	82.26	1	69	22	50	72.59	1
35	12	80	79.04	1	70	29	60	63.73	2

71	2	80	63.73	1		88	13	85	62.11	2
72	16	60	71.79	2		89	1	30	84.68	1
73	59	65	57.28	1		90	3	5	92.74	1
74	10	15	84.68	2		91	5	10	84.68	2
75	13	85	84.68	1		92	12	90	83.07	2
76	8	20	77.43	2		93	19	70	73.40	1
77	5	80	82.26	2		94	2	20	87.91	2
78	2	100	10.00	1		95	19	85	71.79	1
79	38	100	50.83	2		96	11	35	86.29	1
80	4	80	87.91	1		97	15	30	84.68	2
81	10	10	83.88	1		98	23	70	75.82	1
82	6	70	84.68	2		99	13	55	70.98	2
83	68	100	20.20	2		100	14	75	78.23	2
84	8	70	87.10	1		101	1	2	82.26	1
85	1	70	83.88	2		102	9	40	79.04	1
86	14	65	67.76	1		103	20	50	91.13	2
87	42	75	95.97	2						

grades.sav

STATS	GCSE						
1	1		3	3		5	5
1	1		3	3		5	6
1	3		3	4		6	4
2	3		3	4		6	5
2	3		4	2		6	4
2	4		4	2		6	4
2	5		4	2		6	4
3	1		5	3			
3	2		5	3			

pbcorr.sav

TIME	GEN.	RECO.							
41	1	0		51	0	1		35	0	1
40	0	1		50	1	0		32	0	1
40	1	0		53	1	0		40	0	1
38	1	0		53	1	0		40	1	0
34	1	0		45	0	1		52	1	0
46	0	1		46	1	0		47	1	0
42	1	0		36	1	0		52	0	1
42	1	0		34	0	1		52	0	1
47	1	0		31	0	1		52	0	1
42	0	1		50	1	0		51	1	0
45	1	0		51	0	1		51	1	0
46	1	0		54	0	1		45	1	0
44	1	0		52	0	1		43	1	0
54	0	1		54	0	1		48	1	0
57	1	0		54	1	0		32	0	1
51	1	0		52	1	0		33	0	1

32	0	1	33	0	1	35	0	1
33	0	1	34	0	1	34	0	1
33	0	1	35	0	1	34	0	1
34	0	1	35	0	1	40	0	1

12.4. Chapter 4

Record2.sav

ADVERTS	SALES	AIR.	ATTR.				
10.25	330	43	10	669.81	190	34	8
985.68	120	28	7	612.23	150	21	6
1445.56	360	35	7	922.01	230	34	7
1188.19	270	33	7	50.00	310	63	7
574.51	220	44	5	2000.00	340	31	7
568.95	170	19	5	1054.02	240	25	7
471.81	70	20	1	385.04	180	42	7
537.35	210	22	9	1507.97	220	37	7
514.06	200	21	7	102.56	40	25	8
174.09	300	40	7	204.56	190	26	7
1720.80	290	32	7	1170.91	290	39	7
611.47	70	20	2	689.54	340	46	7
251.19	150	24	8	784.22	250	36	6
97.97	190	38	6	405.91	190	12	4
406.81	240	24	7	179.77	120	2	8
265.39	100	25	5	607.25	230	29	8
1323.28	250	35	5	1542.32	190	33	8
196.65	210	36	8	1112.47	210	28	7
1326.59	280	27	8	856.98	170	10	6
1380.68	230	33	8	836.33	310	38	7
792.34	210	33	7	236.90	90	19	4
957.16	230	28	6	1077.85	140	13	6
1789.65	320	30	9	579.32	300	30	7
656.13	210	34	7	1500.00	340	38	8
613.69	230	49	7	731.36	170	22	8
313.36	250	40	8	25.68	100	23	6
336.51	60	20	4	391.74	200	22	9
1544.89	330	42	7	233.99	80	20	7
68.95	150	35	8	275.70	100	18	6
785.69	150	8	6	56.89	70	37	7
125.62	180	49	7	255.11	50	16	8
377.92	80	19	8	566.50	240	32	8
217.99	180	42	6	102.56	160	26	5
759.86	130	6	7	250.56	290	53	9
1163.44	320	36	6	68.59	140	28	7
842.95	280	32	7	642.78	210	32	7
125.17	200	28	6	1500.00	300	24	7
236.59	130	25	8	102.56	230	37	6

756.98	280	30	8	70.92	10	4	6
51.22	160	19	7	1567.54	240	29	6
644.15	200	47	6	263.59	270	43	7
15.31	110	22	5	1423.56	290	26	7
243.23	110	10	8	715.67	220	28	7
256.89	70	1	4	777.23	230	37	8
22.46	100	1	6	509.43	220	32	5
45.68	190	39	6	964.11	240	34	7
724.93	70	8	5	583.62	260	30	7
1126.46	360	38	7	923.37	170	15	7
1985.11	360	35	5	344.39	130	23	7
1837.51	300	40	5	1095.57	270	31	8
135.98	120	22	7	100.02	140	21	5
237.70	150	27	8	30.42	60	28	1
976.64	220	31	6	1080.34	210	18	7
1452.68	280	19	7	799.89	210	28	7
1600.00	300	24	9	1071.75	240	37	8
268.59	140	1	7	893.35	210	26	6
900.88	290	38	8	283.16	200	30	8
982.06	180	26	6	917.01	140	10	7
201.35	140	11	6	234.56	90	21	7
746.02	210	34	6	456.89	120	18	9
1132.87	250	55	7	206.97	100	14	7
1000.00	250	5	7	1294.09	360	38	7
75.89	120	34	6	826.85	180	36	6
1351.25	290	37	9	564.15	150	32	7
202.70	60	13	8	192.60	110	9	5
365.98	140	23	6	10.65	90	39	5
305.26	290	54	6	45.68	160	24	7
263.26	160	18	7	42.56	230	45	7
513.69	100	2	7	20.45	40	13	8
152.60	160	11	6	635.19	60	17	6
35.98	150	30	8	1002.27	230	32	7
102.56	140	22	7	1177.04	230	23	6
215.36	230	36	6	507.63	120	0	6
426.78	230	37	8	215.68	150	35	5
507.77	30	9	3	526.48	120	26	6
233.29	80	2	7	26.89	60	19	6
1035.43	190	12	8	883.87	280	26	7
102.64	90	5	9	9.10	120	53	8
526.14	120	14	7	103.56	230	29	8
624.53	150	20	5	169.58	230	28	7
912.34	230	57	6	429.50	40	17	6
215.99	150	19	8	223.63	140	26	8
561.96	210	35	7	145.58	360	42	8
474.76	180	22	5	985.96	210	17	6
231.52	140	16	7	500.92	260	36	8
678.59	360	53	7	226.65	250	45	7

1051.16	200	20	7
68.09	150	15	7
1547.15	250	28	8
393.77	100	27	6
804.28	260	17	8
801.57	210	32	8
450.56	290	46	9
26.59	220	47	8
179.06	70	19	1
345.68	110	22	8
295.84	250	55	9
2271.86	320	31	5
1134.57	300	39	8
601.43	180	21	6

45.29	180	36	6
759.51	200	21	7
832.86	320	44	7
56.89	140	27	7
709.39	100	16	6
56.89	120	33	6
767.13	230	33	8
503.17	150	21	7
700.92	250	35	9
910.85	190	26	7
888.56	240	14	6
800.61	250	34	6
1500.00	230	11	8
785.69	110	20	9

Record1.sav contains the first two columns of **Record2.sav** (adverts and sales).

dfbeta.sav

CASE	X	Y
1	30	1
2	29	2
3	28	3
4	27	4
5	26	5
6	25	6
7	24	7
8	23	8
9	22	9
10	21	10
11	20	11

12	19	12
13	18	13
14	17	14
15	16	15
16	15	16
17	14	17
18	13	18
19	12	19
20	11	20
21	10	21
22	9	22

23	8	23
24	7	24
25	6	25
26	5	26
27	4	27
28	3	28
29	2	29
30	1	15

12.5.   Chapter 5

display.sav

AGE	FB	DISPLAY
24	0	0
26	0	0
30	0	0
31	0	0
36	0	0
29	0	1
28	0	0
36	0	0
34	0	1
31	0	0
32	0	0

AGE	FB	DISPLAY
30	1	1
26	0	0
35	1	0
36	0	0
36	0	0
25	0	1
24	0	0
24	1	1
26	0	0
29	0	0
34	1	1

AGE	FB	DISPLAY
31	1	1
40	1	0
45	0	0
30	0	0
30	0	0
36	0	0
45	1	1
40	0	0
41	0	1
32	0	0
48	1	1

AGE	FB	DISPLAY
43	1	1
46	1	1
40	1	1
41	1	0
43	1	1
44	0	1
39	1	0
49	1	1
52	1	1
56	1	1
58	1	1

53	1	1	64	1	1	64	1	1	79	1	1
52	1	0	65	1	1	63	0	1	76	1	1
51	1	1	69	1	1	73	1	1	74	1	0
59	0	0	68	1	1	74	1	1	83	1	1
60	0	0	70	1	1	78	1	1	82	1	1
60	1	0	71	1	0	79	1	1			
63	1	1	67	1	1	82	1	1			

penalty.sav

PSWQ	ANX.	PREV.	SCORE		PSWQ	ANX.	PREV.	SCORE
18	21	56	1		4	20	53	1
17	32	35	1		1	23	47	1
16	34	35	1		20	26	45	0
14	40	15	1		25	29	35	0
5	24	47	1		16	21	55	0
1	15	67	1		18	34	24	0
4	10	75	1		17	38	15	0
12	19	53	1		29	39	15	0
11	29	35	1		24	46	4	0
15	14	65	1		25	49	0	0
23	5	85	1		22	47	0	0
11	6	86	1		26	42	5	0
14	34	23	1		23	41	16	0
22	27	46	1		25	40	18	0
12	26	46	1		28	35	24	0
5	16	67	1		18	36	23	0
6	14	67	1		17	31	34	0
4	5	84	1		14	35	24	0
7	10	74	1		15	42	16	0
8	13	64	1		11	20	56	0
12	19	55	1		10	24	42	0
14	26	46	1		15	19	56	0
13	27	43	1		14	18	56	0
1	29	35	1		16	34	24	0
7	30	35	1		17	35	24	0
10	31	33	1		25	36	26	0
15	26	45	1		24	32	33	0
16	28	35	1		17	35	24	0
18	10	74	1		27	39	16	0
17	8	76	1		28	38	15	0
14	12	75	1		27	41	14	0
20	24	44	1		25	42	14	0
18	23	47	1		26	45	8	0
2	16	65	1		22	48	0	0
6	14	66	1		28	49	0	0
4	19	55	1		28	46	4	0
4	18	56	1		24	26	45	0
2	17	64	1					

12.6.   Chapter 7

dummy.sav

DOSE	LIB	DUM1	DUM2								
1	3	0	0	2	5	0	1	3	7	1	0
1	2	0	0	2	2	0	1	3	4	1	0
1	1	0	0	2	4	0	1	3	5	1	0
1	1	0	0	2	2	0	1	3	3	1	0
1	4	0	0	2	3	0	1	3	6	1	0

Contrast.sav

DOSE	LIB	DUM1	DUM2								
1	3	-2	0	2	5	1	-1	3	7	1	1
1	2	-2	0	2	2	1	-1	3	4	1	1
1	1	-2	0	2	4	1	-1	3	5	1	1
1	1	-2	0	2	2	1	-1	3	3	1	1
1	4	-2	0	2	3	1	-1	3	6	1	1

12.7.   Chapter 10

12.7.1.   Calculation of E^{-1}

$$E = \begin{pmatrix} 51 & 13 \\ 13 & 122 \end{pmatrix}$$

determinant of E, $|E| = (51 \times 122) - (13 \times 13) = 6053$

$$\text{matrix of minors for } E = \begin{pmatrix} 122 & 13 \\ 13 & 51 \end{pmatrix}$$

$$\text{pattern of signs for } 2 \times 2 \text{ matrix} = \begin{pmatrix} + & - \\ - & + \end{pmatrix}$$

$$\text{matrix of cofactors} = \begin{pmatrix} 122 & -13 \\ -13 & 51 \end{pmatrix}$$

The inverse of a matrix is obtained by dividing the matrix of cofactors for E by $|E|$, the determinant of E.

$$E^{-1} = \begin{pmatrix} \frac{122}{6053} & \frac{-13}{6053} \\ \frac{-13}{6053} & \frac{51}{6053} \end{pmatrix} = \begin{pmatrix} 0.0202 & -0.0021 \\ -0.0021 & 0.0084 \end{pmatrix}$$

12.7.2. Calculation of HE^{-1}

$$HE^{-1} = \begin{pmatrix} 10.47 & -7.53 \\ -7.53 & 19.47 \end{pmatrix} \begin{pmatrix} 0.0202 & -0.0021 \\ -0.0021 & 0.0084 \end{pmatrix}$$

$$= \begin{pmatrix} [(10.47 \times 0.0202) + (-7.53 \times -0.0021)] & [(10.47 \times -0.0021) + (-7.53 \times 0.0084)] \\ [(-7.53 \times 0.0202) + (19.47 \times -0.0021)] & [(-7.53 \times -0.0021) + (19.47 \times 0.0084)] \end{pmatrix}$$

$$= \begin{pmatrix} 0.2273 & -0.0852 \\ -0.1930 & 0.1794 \end{pmatrix}$$

12.7.3. Calculation of Eigenvalues

The eigenvalues or roots of any square matrix are the solutions to the determinantal equation $|A - \lambda I| = 0$, in which A is the square matrix in question and I is an identity matrix of the same size as A. The number of eigenvalues will equal the number of rows (or columns) of the square matrix. In this case the square matrix of interest is HE^{-1}.

$$|HE^{-1} - \lambda I| = \left| \begin{pmatrix} 0.2273 & -0.0852 \\ -0.1930 & 0.1794 \end{pmatrix} - \begin{pmatrix} \lambda & 0 \\ 0 & \lambda \end{pmatrix} \right|$$

$$= \left| \begin{pmatrix} (0.2273 - \lambda) & -0.0852 \\ -0.1930 & (0.1794 - \lambda) \end{pmatrix} \right|$$

$$= [(0.2273 - \lambda)(0.1794 - \lambda) - (-0.1930 \times -0.0852)]$$

$$= \lambda^2 - 0.2273\lambda - 0.1794\lambda + 0.0407 - 0.0164$$

$$= \lambda^2 - 0.4067\lambda + 0.0243$$

Therefore the equation $|HE^{-1} - \lambda I| = 0$ can be expressed as:

$$\lambda^2 - 0.4067\lambda + 0.0243 = 0$$

To solve the roots of any quadratic equation of the general form $a\lambda^2 + b\lambda + c = 0$ we can apply the following formula:

$$\lambda_i = \frac{-b \pm \sqrt{(b^2 - 4ac)}}{2a}$$

For the quadratic equation obtained, $a = 1$, $b = -0.4067$, $c = 0.0243$. If we replace these values into the formula for discovering roots, we get

$$\lambda_i = \frac{-b \pm \sqrt{\left(b^2 - 4ac\right)}}{2a}$$

$$= \frac{0.4067 \pm \sqrt{\left[\left(-0.4067\right)^2 - 0.0972\right]}}{2}$$

$$= \frac{0.4067 \pm 0.2612}{2}$$

$$= \frac{0.6679}{2} \text{ or } \frac{0.1455}{2}$$

$$= 0.334 \text{ or } 0.073$$

Hence, the eigenvalues are 0.334 and 0.073.

12.8. Chapter 11

12.8.1.   *Calculation of Factor Score Coefficients*

$B = R^{-1} A$

$$B = \begin{pmatrix} 4.76 & -7.46 & 3.91 & -2.35 & 2.42 & -0.49 \\ -7.46 & 18.49 & -12.42 & 5.45 & -5.54 & 1.22 \\ 3.91 & -12.42 & 10.07 & -3.65 & 3.79 & -0.96 \\ -2.35 & 5.45 & -3.65 & 2.97 & -2.16 & 0.02 \\ 2.42 & -5.54 & 3.79 & -2.16 & 2.98 & -0.56 \\ -0.49 & 1.22 & -0.96 & 0.02 & -0.56 & 1.27 \end{pmatrix} \begin{pmatrix} 0.87 & 0.01 \\ 0.96 & -0.03 \\ 0.92 & 0.04 \\ 0.00 & 0.82 \\ -0.10 & 0.75 \\ 0.09 & 0.70 \end{pmatrix}$$

12.8.1.1. Column 1 of matrix B

To get the first element of the first column of matrix B, you need to multiply each element in the *first column* of matrix A with the correspondingly placed element in the *first row* of matrix R^{-1}. Add these six products together to get the final value of the first element. To get the second element of the first column of matrix B, you need to multiply each element in the *first column* of matrix A with the correspondingly placed element in the *second row* of matrix R^{-1}. Add these six products together to get the final value ... and so on.

$$B_{11} = (4.75924 \times 0.87407) + (-7.46190 \times 0.95768) + (3.90949 \times 0.92138)$$
$$+ (-2.35093 \times -0.00237) + (2.42104 \times -0.09575) + (-0.48607 \times 0.096)$$
$$= 0.343$$

$$B_{12} = (-7.4619 \times 0.87407) + (18.48556 \times 0.95768) + (-12.41679 \times 0.92138)$$
$$+ (5.445 \times -0.00237) + (-5.54427 \times -0.09575) + (1.22155 \times 0.096)$$
$$= 0.376$$

$$B_{13} = (3.90949 \times 0.87407) + (-12.41679 \times 0.95768) + (10.07382 \times 0.92138)$$
$$+ (-3.64853 \times -0.00237) + (3.78869 \times -0.09575) + (-0.95731 \times 0.096)$$
$$= 0.362$$

$$B_{14} = (-2.35093 \times 0.87407) + (5.445 \times 0.95768) + (-3.64853 \times 0.92138)$$
$$+ (2.96922 \times -0.00237) + (-2.16094 \times -0.09575) + (0.02255 \times 0.096)$$
$$= 0.000$$

$$B_{15} = (2.42104 \times 0.87407) + (-5.54427 \times 0.95768) + (3.78869 \times 0.92138)$$
$$+ (-2.16094 \times -0.00237) + (2.97983 \times -0.09575) + (-0.56017 \times 0.096)$$
$$= -0.037$$

$$B_{16} = (-0.48607 \times 0.87407) + (1.22155 \times 0.95768) + (-0.95731 \times 0.92138)$$
$$+ (0.02255 \times -0.00237) + (-0.56017 \times -0.09575) + (1.27072 \times 0.096)$$
$$= 0.039$$

12.8.1.2. Column 2 of matrix B

To get the first element of the second column of matrix B, you need to multiply each element in the *second column* of matrix A with the correspondingly placed element in the *first row* of matrix R^{-1}. Add these six products together to get the final value. To get the second element of the second column of matrix B, you need to multiply each element in the *second column* of matrix A with the correspondingly placed element in the *second row* of matrix R^{-1}. Add these six products together to get the final value … and so on.

$$B_{11} = (4.75924 \times 0.00842) + (-7.46190 \times -0.03653) + (3.90949 \times 0.03178)$$
$$+ (-2.35093 \times 0.81556) + (2.42104 \times 0.75435) + (-0.48607 \times 0.69936)$$
$$= 0.006$$

$$B_{12} = (-7.4619 \times 0.00842) + (18.48556 \times -0.03653) + (-12.41679 \times 0.03178)$$
$$+ (5.445 \times 0.81556) + (-5.54427 \times 0.75435) + (1.22155 \times 0.69936)$$
$$= -0.020$$

$$B_{13} = (3.90949 \times 0.00842) + (-12.41679 \times -0.03653) + (10.07382 \times 0.03178)$$
$$+ (-3.64853 \times 0.81556) + (3.78869 \times 0.75435) + (-0.95731 \times 0.69936)$$
$$= 0.020$$

$$B_{14} = (-2.35093 \times 0.00842) + (5.445 \times -0.03653) + (-3.64853 \times 0.03178)$$
$$+ (2.96922 \times 0.81556) + (-2.16094 \times 0.75435) + (0.02255 \times 0.69936)$$
$$= 0.473$$

$$B_{15} = (2.42104 \times 0.00842) + (-5.54427 \times -0.03653) + (3.78869 \times 0.03178)$$
$$+ (-2.16094 \times 0.81556) + (2.97983 \times 0.75435) + (-0.56017 \times 0.69936)$$
$$= 0.437$$

$$B_{16} = (-0.48607 \times 0.00842) + (1.22155 \times -0.03653) + (-0.95731 \times 0.03178)$$
$$+ (0.02255 \times 0.81556) + (-0.56017 \times 0.75435) + (1.27072 \times 0.69936)$$
$$= 0.405$$

References

Agresti, A. & Finlay, B. (1986). *Statistical methods for the social sciences* (2nd edition). San Francisco: Dellen.

Arrindell, W. A. & van der Ende, J. (1985). An empirical test of the utility of the observer-to-variables ratio in factor and components analysis. *Applied Psychological Measurement*, 9, 165–178.

Bargman, R. E. (1970). Interpretation and use of a generalized discriminant function. In R. C. Bose et al. (eds.), *Essays in probability and statistics*. Chapel Hill: University of North Carolina Press.

Barnett, V. & Lewis, T. (1978). *Outliers in statistical data*. New York: Wiley.

Belsey, D. A., Kuh, E. & Welsch, R. (1980). *Regression diagnostics: identifying influential data and sources of collinearity*. New York: Wiley.

Berry, W. D. (1993). *Understanding regression assumptions*. Sage university paper series on quantitative applications in the social sciences, 07–092. Newbury Park, CA: Sage.

Berry, W. D. & Feldman, S. (1985). *Multiple regression in practice*. Sage university paper series on quantitative applications in the social sciences, 07–050. Beverly Hills, CA: Sage.

Bock, R. D. (1975). *Multivariate statistical methods in behavioural research*. New York: McGraw-Hill.

Boik, R. J. (1981). A priori tests in repeated measures designs: effects of nonsphericity. *Psychometrika*, 46 (3), 241–255.

Bowerman, B. L. & O'Connell, R. T. (1990). *Linear statistical models: an applied approach* (2nd edition). Belmont, CA: Duxbury.

Bray, J. H. & Maxwell, S. E. (1985). *Multivariate analysis of variance*. Sage university paper series on quantitative applications in the social sciences, 07–054. Newbury Park, CA: Sage.

Cattell, R. B. (1966a). *The scientific analysis of personality*. Chicago: Aldine.

Cattell, R. B. (1966b). The scree test for the number of factors. *Multivariate Behavioral Research*, 1, 245–276.

Cliff, N. (1987). *Analyzing multivariate data*. New York: Harcourt, Brace Jovanovich.

Cohen, J. (1968). Multiple regression as a general data-analytic system. *Psychological Bulletin*, 70 (6), 426–443.

Cohen, J. (1988). *Statistical power analysis for the behavioural sciences* (2nd edition). New York: Academic Press.

Cohen, J. (1992). A power primer. *Psychological Bulletin*, 112 (1), 155–159.

Cole, D. A., Maxwell, S. E., Arvey, R. & Salas, E. (1994). How the power of MANOVA can both increase and decrease as a function of the intercorrelations among the dependent variables. *Psychological Bulletin*, 115 (3), 465–474.

Collier, R. O., Baker, F. B., Mandeville, G. K. & Hayes, T. F. (1967). Estimates of test size for several test procedures based on conventional variance ratios in the repeated measures design. *Psychometrika*, 32 (2), 339–352.

Comrey, A. L. & Lee, H. B. (1992). *A first course in factor analysis* (2nd edition). Hillsdale, NJ: Erlbaum.

Cook, R. D. & Weisberg, S. (1982). *Residuals and influence in regression*. New York: Chapman & Hall.

Cronbach, L. J. (1957). The two disciplines of scientific psychology. *The American Psychologist*, 12, 671–684.

Davidson, M. L. (1972). Univariate versus multivariate tests in repeated-measures experiments. *Psychological Bulletin*, 77, 446–452.

Dunteman, G. E. (1989). *Principal components analysis*. Sage university paper series on quantitative applications in the social sciences, 07–069. Newbury Park, CA: Sage.

Durbin, J. & Watson, G. S. (1951). Testing for serial correlation in least squares regression, II. *Biometrika*, 30, 159–178.

Einspruch, E. L. (1998). *An introductory guide to SPSS for Windows*. Thousand Oaks, CA: Sage.

Erlebacher, A. (1977). Design and analysis of experiments contrasting the within- and between-subjects manipulations of the independent variable. *Psychological Bulletin*, 84, 212–219.

Eysenck, H. J. (1953). *The structure of human personality*. New York: Wiley.

Field, A. P. (1998a). A bluffer's guide to sphericity. *Newsletter of the Mathematical, Statistical and Computing Section of the British Psychological Society*, 6 (1), 13–22 (available from the internet at http://www.cogs.susx.ac.uk/users/andyf/research/articles/sphericity.pdf).

Field, A. P. (1998b). Review of nQuery Adviser Release 2.0. *British Journal of Mathematical and Statistical Psychology*, 52 (2), 368-369.

Field, A. P. & Davey, G. C. L. (1999). Reevaluating evaluative conditioning: a nonassociative explanation of conditioning effects in the visual evaluative conditioning paradigm. *Journal of Experimental Psychology: Animal Processes*, 25 (2), 211–224.

Foster, J. J. (1998). *Data analysis using SPSS for Windows: a beginner's guide*. London: Sage.

Girden, E. R. (1992). *ANOVA: repeated measures*. Sage university paper series on quantitative applications in the social sciences, 07–084. Newbury Park, CA: Sage.

Greenhouse, S. W. & Geisser, S. (1959). On methods in the analysis of profile data. *Psychometrika*, 24, 95–112.

Guadagnoli, E. & Velicer, W. (1988). Relation of sample size to the stability of component patterns. *Psychological Bulletin*, 103, 265–275.

Hakstian, A. R., Roed, J. C. & Lind, J. C. (1979). Two-sample T^2 procedure and the assumption of homogeneous covariance matrices. *Psychological Bulletin*, 86, 1255–1263.

Harman, B. H. (1976). *Modern factor analysis* (3rd edition, revised). Chicago: University of Chicago Press.

Harris, R. J. (1975). *A primer of multivariate statistics*. New York: Academic.

Hoaglin, D. & Welsch, R. (1978). The hat matrix in regression and ANOVA. *American Statistician*, 32, 17–22.

Hoddle, G., Batty, D., & Ince, P. (1998). How not to take penalties in important soccer matches. *Journal of Cretinous Behaviour*, 1, 1–2.

Hosmer, D. W. & Lemeshow, S. (1989). *Applied logistic regression*. New York: Wiley.

Howell, D. C. (1997). *Statistical methods for psychology* (4th edition). Belmont, CA: Duxbury.

Huberty, C. J. & Morris, J. D. (1989). Multivariate analysis versus multiple univariate analysis. *Psychological Bulletin*, 105, 302–308.

Hutcheson, G. & Sofroniou, N. (1999). *The multivariate social scientist*. London: Sage.

Huynh, H. and Feldt, L. S. (1976). Estimation of the Box correction for degrees of freedom from sample data in randomised block and split-plot designs. *Journal of Educational Statistics*, 1 (1), 69–82.

Iversen, G. R. & Norpoth, H. (1987). *ANOVA* (2nd edition). Sage university paper series on quantitative applications in the social sciences, 07-001. Newbury Park, CA: Sage.

Jackson, S. & Brashers, D. E. (1994). *Random factors in ANOVA*. Sage university paper series on quantitative applications in the social sciences, 07–098. Thousand Oaks, CA: Sage.

Jolliffe, I. T. (1972). Discarding variables in a principal component analysis, I: artificial data. *Applied Statistics*, 21, 160–173.

Jolliffe, I. T. (1986). *Principal component analysis*. New York: Springer-Verlag.

Kaiser, H. F. (1960). The application of electronic computers to factor analysis. *Educational and Psychological Measurement*, 20, 141–151.

Kaiser, H. F. (1970). A second-generation little jiffy. *Psychometrika*, 35, 401–415.

Kaiser, H. F. (1974). An index of factorial simplicity. *Psychometrika*, 39, 31–36.

Kass, R. A. & Tinsley, H. E. A. (1979). Factor analysis. *Journal of Leisure Research*, 11, 120–138.

Keselman, H. J. & Keselman, J. C. (1988). Repeated measures multiple comparison procedures: effects of violating multisample sphericity in unbalanced designs. *Journal of Educational Statistics*, 13 (3), 215–226.

Kinnear, P. R. & Gray, C. D. (1997). *SPSS for Windows made simple* (2nd edition). Hove: Psychology Press.

Klockars, A. J. & Sax, G. (1986). *Multiple comparisons*. Sage university paper series on quantitative applications in the social sciences, 07–061. Newbury Park, CA: Sage.

Loftus, G. R. & Masson, M. E. J. (1994). Using confidence intervals in within-subject designs. *Psychonomic Bulletin and Review*, 1 (4), 476–490.

Lunney, G. H. (1970). Using analysis of variance with a dichotomous dependent variable: an empirical study. *Journal of Educational Measurement*, 7 (4), 263–269.

MacCallum, R. C., Widaman, K. F., Zhang, S. & Hong, S. (1999). Sample size in factor analysis. *Psychological Methods*, 4 (1), 84–99.

Maxwell, S. E. (1980). Pairwise multiple comparisons in repeated measures designs. *Journal of Educational Statistics*, 5 (3), 269–287.

Maxwell, S. E. & Delaney, H. D. (1990). *Designing experiments and analyzing data*. Belmont, CA: Wadsworth.

Menard, S. (1995). *Applied logistic regression analysis*. Sage university paper series on quantitative applications in the social sciences, 07–106. Thousand Oaks, CA: Sage.

Mendoza, J. L., Toothaker, L. E. & Crain, B. R. (1976). Necessary and sufficient conditions for F ratios in the $L \times J \times K$ factorial design with two repeated factors. *Journal of the American Statistical Association*, 71, 992–993.

Mendoza, J. L., Toothaker, L. E. & Nicewander, W. A. (1974). A Monte Carlo comparison of the univariate and multivariate methods for the groups by trials repeated measures design. *Multivariate Behavioural Research*, 9, 165–177.

Mitzel, H. C. & Games, P. A. (1981). Circularity and multiple comparisons in repeated measures designs. *British Journal of Mathematical and Statistical Psychology*, 34, 253–259.

Myers, R. (1990). *Classical and modern regression with applications* (2nd edition). Boston, MA: Duxbury.

Namboodiri, K. (1984). *Matrix algebra: an introduction.* Sage university paper series on quantitative applications in the social sciences, 07–38. Beverly Hills, CA: Sage.

Norušis, M. J. (1997). *SPSS® for Windows™ Base system user's guide, release 7.5.* SPSS Inc.

Nunnally, J. C. (1978). *Psychometric theory.* New York: McGraw-Hill.

O'Brien, M. G. & Kaiser, M. K. (1985). MANOVA method for analyzing repeated measures designs: an extensive primer. *Psychological Bulletin,* 97 (2), 316–333.

Olson, C. L. (1974). Comparative robustness of six tests in multivariate analysis of variance. *Journal of the American Statistical Association,* 69, 894–908.

Olson, C. L. (1976). On choosing a test statistic in multivariate analysis of variance. *Psychological Bulletin,* 83, 579–586.

Olson, C. L. (1979). Practical considerations in choosing a MANOVA test statistic: a rejoinder to Stevens. *Psychological Bulletin,* 86, 1350–1352.

Pedhazur, E. & Schmelkin, L. (1991). *Measurement, design and analysis.* Hillsdale, NJ: Erlbaum.

Ramsey, P. H. (1982). Empirical power of procedures for comparing two groups on *p* variables. *Journal of Educational Statistics,* 7, 139–156.

Roberts, M. J. & Russo, R. (1999). *A student's guide to analysis of variance,* London: Routledge.

Rosenthal, R. & Rosnow, R. L. (1985). *Contrast analysis: focused comparisons in the analysis of variance.* Cambridge: Cambridge University Press.

Rouanet, H. & Lépine, D. (1970). Comparison between treatments in a repeated-measurement design: ANOVA and multivariate methods. *The British Journal of Mathematical and Statistical Psychology,* 23, 147–163.

Rowntree, D. (1981). *Statistics without tears: a primer for non-mathematicians.* London: Penguin.

Scariano, S. M. & Davenport, J. M. (1987). The effects of violations of independence in the one-way ANOVA. *The American Statistician,* 41 (2), 123–129.

Siegel, S. & Castellan, N. J. (1988). *Nonparametric statistics for the behavioral sciences* (2nd edition). New York: McGraw-Hill.

SPSS Inc. (1997). *SPSS® Base 7.5 syntax reference guide.* SPSS Inc.

Stevens, J. P. (1979). Comment on Olson: choosing a test statistic in multivariate analysis of variance. *Psychological Bulletin,* 86, 355–360.

Stevens, J. P. (1980). Power of the multivariate analysis of variance tests. *Psychological Bulletin,* 88, 728–737.

Stevens, J. P. (1992). *Applied multivariate statistics for the social sciences* (2nd edition). Hillsdale, NJ: Erlbaum.

Strang, G. (1980). *Linear algebra and its applications* (2nd edition). New York: Academic Press.

Stuart, E. W., Shimp, T. A. & Engle, R. W. (1987). Classical conditioning of consumer attitudes: four experiments in an advertising context. *Journal of Consumer Research,* **14**, 334–349.

Studenmund, A. H. & Cassidy, H. J. (1987). *Using econometrics: a practical guide.* Boston: Little, Brown.

Tabachnick, B. G. & Fidell, L. S. (1996). *Using multivariate statistics* (3rd edition). New York: Harper & Row.

Tinsley, H. E. A. & Tinsley, D. J. (1987). Uses of factor analysis in counseling psychology research. *Journal of Counseling Psychology,* 34, 414–424.

Toothaker, L. E. (1993). *Multiple comparison procedures.* Sage university paper series on quantitative applications in the social sciences, 07–089. Newbury Park, CA: Sage.

Wildt, A. R. & Ahtola, O. (1978). *Analysis of covariance.* Sage university paper series on quantitative applications in the social sciences, 07–012. Newbury Park, CA: Sage.

Wright, D. B. (1997). *Understanding statistics: an introduction for the social sciences.* London: Sage.

Index